"By a generous meas___ ___est American presidential autobiography—no other book tells us as vividly or fully what it is like to be president of the United States. . . . And he can write."
—Larry McMurtry,
The New York Times Book Review

"*My Life* is, without question, the best written U.S. presidential tome of all time."
—Douglas Brinkley, *Financial Times*

"A hell of a good story."
—Frank McCourt, *Entertainment Weekly*

"Consistently fascinating."   —*The Seattle Times*

"[A] saga worthy of Cecil B. DeMille, a rags-to-riches tale full of the stuff of human frailty, with a cast of hundreds, complete with low-life villains and high-minded heroes and, as such stories require, an upbeat ending. . . . The 1990s come to life once again as a time of uncommon tumult and riveting personalities. . . . The personalities on parade are as vivid as the events."   —*The Star-Ledger* (Newark)

"It's an almost voluptuous pleasure to read Clinton when he's recounting and analyzing a political race or a legislative battle, whether it's one of his own or somebody else's."   —*The New Yorker*

"Might just be the perfect representation of the man himself." —*The Plain Dealer*

"Clinton talks with disarming frankness [and] writes with grace and fluidity. . . . He is also a born storyteller." —*The New Republic*

"He manages to create the distinct impression that he is sitting in the living room talking to the reader. . . . Anyone who is genuinely interested in American politics will find his insights and anecdotes fascinating. . . . The book helps to elucidate the question of 'how he did it.'" —*Deseret Morning News*

"Tremendously interesting and entertaining. . . . Clinton's is a truly American story to which the average person can relate. . . . Future politicians will find it a must-read, and average Americans will identify with the highs and lows we all experience as we make our way through life." —*Chattanooga Times Free Press*

"Takes readers through a strong account of the achievements and failures of his administration. . . . No other presidential memoir is likely to be so lively. . . . Bill Clinton is hard to dismiss, and so is an account of his extraordinary life." —*The Tennessean*

"A reading of *My Life* is a necessity for lovers of good autobiography. It reads like a down-home history of a life and, thus, anchors Clinton as a superb storyteller. . . . Candid. . . . Honest. . . . Stimulating." —*The Huntsville Times*

My Life

THE PRESIDENTIAL YEARS

Bill Clinton

My Life

THE PRESIDENTIAL YEARS

VINTAGE BOOKS
A Division of Random House, Inc.
New York

FIRST VINTAGE BOOKS EDITION, JUNE 2005

Vintage ISBN: 1-4000-9673-1

Book design by Christopher M. Zucker

www.vintagebooks.com
www.clintonfoundation.org

Printed in the United States of America
10 9 8 7 6 5 4 3 2 1

PHOTOGRAPH CREDITS

Photo insert researched, edited, and designed by Vincent Virga,
with the assistance of Carolyn Huber (adjusted for this format by
Christopher Zucker). Every effort has been made to identify copyright
holders; in case of oversight, and upon notification of the publisher,
corrections will be made in subsequent printings.

Unless otherwise noted, all photos are from the Clinton Presidential
Materials Project, Little Rock, Arkansas.
AP/Wide World Photos: page 10, bottom right; page 15, top left.
The Architect of the Capitol: page 1, top left.
Author's collection: page 5, top right; page 15, middle right.
Diana Walker/*Time*: page 2, top left; page 13, bottom; page 16, top left.

My Life

THE PRESIDENTIAL YEARS

PROLOGUE

WHEN I WAS A YOUNG MAN just out of law school and eager to get on with my life, on a whim I briefly put aside my reading preference for fiction and history and bought one of those how-to books: *How to Get Control of Your Time and Your Life,* by Alan Lakein. The book's main point was the necessity of listing short-, medium-, and long-term life goals, then categorizing them in order of their importance, with the A group being the most important, the B group next, and the C the last, then listing under each goal specific activities designed to achieve them. I still have that paperback book, now almost thirty years old. And I'm sure I have that old list somewhere buried in my papers, though I can't find it. However, I do remember the A list. I wanted to be a good man, have a good marriage and children, have good friends, make a successful political life, and write a great book.

Whether I'm a good man is, of course, for God to judge. I know that I am not as good as my strongest supporters believe or as I hope to become, nor as bad as my harshest critics assert. I have been graced beyond measure by my family life with Hillary and Chelsea. Like all families' lives, ours is not perfect, but it has been wonderful. Its flaws, as all the world knows, are mostly mine, and its continuing promise is grounded in their love. No person I know ever had more or better friends. Indeed, a strong case can be made that I rose to the presidency on the shoulders of my personal friends, the now legendary FOBs.

My life in politics was a joy. I loved campaigns and I loved governing. I always tried to keep things moving in the right direction, to give more people a chance to live their dreams, to lift people's spirits, and to bring them together. That's the way I kept score.

As for the great book, who knows? It sure is a good story.

ONE

ON SUNDAY, January 17, 1993, Al and Tipper Gore, Hillary, and I began inaugural week with a tour of Monticello, followed by a discussion of Thomas Jefferson's importance to America with young people.

After the event, we boarded our bus for the 120-mile trip to Washington. The bus symbolized our commitment to giving the federal government back to the people. Besides, we cherished the fond memories it held, and we wanted one last ride. We stopped for a brief church service in the pretty Shenandoah Valley town of Culpeper, then made our way to Washington. Just as in the campaign, there were well-wishers, and a few critics, along the way.

By the time we got to the capital, the public events of our inaugural, entitled "An American Reunion: New Beginnings, Renewed Hope," were already under way. My good friend Harry Thomason, advisor Rahm Emanuel, and Mel French, a friend from Arkansas who would become chief of protocol in my second term, had organized an extraordinary series of events, with as many as possible free of charge or within the price range of the working people who had elected me. On Sunday and Monday, the Mall between the Capitol Building and the Washington Monument was filled by an outdoor festival featuring food, music, and crafts. That night we had a "Call for Reunion" concert on the steps of the Lincoln Memorial, with a star-studded lineup including Diana Ross and Bob Dylan, who thrilled the crowd of 200,000 that filled the space from the stage all the way back to the Washington Monument. Standing beneath Lincoln's statue, I gave a short speech appealing for national unity, saying that Lincoln "gave new life to Jefferson's dream that we are all created free and equal."

After the concert, the Gores and my family led a procession of thousands of people carrying flashlights across the

Potomac River on Memorial Bridge to the Lady Bird Johnson Circle just outside Arlington National Cemetery. At 6 p.m., we rang a replica of the Liberty Bell, to start "Bells of Hope" ringing all across America and even aboard the space shuttle *Endeavour*. Then there was a fireworks display followed by several receptions. By the time we got back to Blair House, the official guest residence just across the street from the White House, we were tired but exhilarated, and before falling asleep I took some time to review the latest draft of my inaugural address.

I still wasn't satisfied with it. Compared with my campaign speeches, it seemed stilted. I knew it had to be more dignified, but I didn't want it to drag. I did like one passage, built around the idea that our new beginning had "forced the spring" to come to America on this cold winter day. It was the brainchild of my friend Father Tim Healy, former president of Georgetown University. Tim had died suddenly of a heart attack while walking through Newark airport a few weeks after the election. When friends went to his apartment, they found in his typewriter the beginning of a letter to me that included suggested language for the inaugural speech. His phrase "force the spring" struck all of us, and I wanted to use it in his memory.

Monday, January 18, was the holiday celebrating Martin Luther King Jr.'s birthday. In the morning I held a reception for the diplomatic representatives of other nations in the inner quadrangle at Georgetown, addressing them from the steps of Old North Building. It was the same spot on which George Washington stood in 1797 and the great French general and Revolutionary War hero Lafayette spoke in 1824. I told the ambassadors that my foreign policy would be built on three pillars—economic security at home, restructuring the armed forces to meet the new challenges of the post–Cold War world, and support for democratic values across the globe. The day before, President Bush had ordered an air strike on a suspected weapons-production site in Iraq, and on this day, U.S. planes hit Saddam Hussein's air-defense positions. I supported the effort to bring Saddam into full compliance with UN resolutions and asked the diplomats to emphasize that to their governments. After the diplomatic event, I spoke to Georgetown students and alumni, including many of my old classmates, urging them to support my national service initiative.

From Georgetown, we drove to Howard University for a ceremony honoring Dr. King, then to a luncheon at the beautiful Folger Library for more than fifty people Al, Tipper, Hillary, and I met during the campaign who had made a strong impression on us. We called them "Faces of Hope," because of their courage in the face of adversity or their innovative ways of dealing with contemporary challenges. We wanted to thank these people for inspiring us, and to remind everyone, amidst the glamour of the inaugural week, that a lot of Americans were still having a hard time.

The Faces of Hope included two former members of rival gangs in Los Angeles who joined forces after the riots to give kids a better future; two of the Vietnam veterans who had sent me their medals; a school principal who had created a violence-free magnet school in Chicago's highest-crime neighborhood, with students who regularly scored above state and national learning levels; a Texas judge who had created an innovative program for troubled kids; a young Arizona boy who had made me more aware of the family pressures caused by the extra hours his father had to work; a Native American doctor from Montana who worked to improve mental-health services to her people; men who had lost their jobs to low-wage foreign competition; people struggling with costly health problems the government didn't help with; a young entrepreneur scrapping for venture capital; people who ran community centers for broken families; a policeman's widow whose husband was killed by a mental patient who bought a handgun without a background check; an eighteen-year-old financial wizard who was already working on Wall Street; a woman who had started a large recycling program at her plant; and many others. Michael Morrison, the young man who drove his wheelchair down an icy New Hampshire highway to work for me, was there. So was Dimitrios Theofanis, the Greek immigrant from New York who had asked me to make his boy free.

All of the Faces of Hope had taught me something about the pain and promise of America in 1992, but none more than Louise and Clifford Ray, whose three sons were hemophiliacs who had contracted the HIV virus through transfusions of tainted blood. They also had a daughter who was not infected. Frightened people in their small Florida community pushed to have the Ray boys removed from school, fearing that their children could be infected if one of them started bleeding and the blood got on them. The Rays filed a lawsuit to keep the kids in class and settled it out of court, then decided to move to Sarasota, a larger city where the school officials welcomed them. The oldest son, Ricky, was obviously very ill and fighting to hang on to his life. After the election, I called Ricky in the hospital to encourage him and invite him to the inauguration. He was looking forward to coming, but he didn't make it; at fifteen, he lost his fight, just five weeks before I became President. I was so glad that the Rays came to the luncheon anyway. When I took office, they championed the cause of hemophiliacs with AIDS, and successfully lobbied Congress for the passage of the Ricky Ray Hemophilia Relief Fund. But it took eight long years, and their grief still wasn't over. In October 2000, three months before the end of my presidency, the Rays' second son, Robert, died of AIDS at twenty-two. If only anti-retroviral therapy had been available a few years earlier. Now that it is, I spend a lot of time trying to get the medicine to many of the Ricky Rays across the world. I want them to be Faces of Hope, too.

On Tuesday morning, Hillary and I started the day with a visit to the graves of John and Robert Kennedy at Arlington National Cemetery. Accompanied by John Kennedy Jr., Ethel Kennedy, several of her children, and Senator Ted Kennedy, I knelt at the eternal flame and said a short prayer, thanking God for their lives and service and asking for wisdom and strength in the great adventures just ahead. At noon, I hosted a lunch for my fellow governors at the Library of Congress, thanking them for all I had learned from them in the past twelve years. After an afternoon event at the

Kennedy Center highlighting America's children, we drove out to the Capitol Centre in Landover, Maryland, for the Gala Concert, where Barbra Streisand, Wynton Marsalis, k.d. lang, rock legends Chuck Berry and Little Richard, Michael Jackson, Aretha Franklin, Jack Nicholson, Bill Cosby, the Alvin Ailey Dance Theater, and other artists kept us entertained for hours. Fleetwood Mac brought the crowd to its feet with our campaign theme song, "Don't Stop Thinkin' About Tomorrow."

After the concert, there was a late-night prayer service at the First Baptist Church, and it was after midnight when I got back to Blair House. Though it was getting better, I still wasn't satisfied with the inaugural address. My speechwriters, Michael Waldman and David Kusnet, must have been tearing their hair out, because as we practiced between one and four in the morning on inauguration day, I was still changing it. Bruce Lindsey, Paul Begala, Bruce Reed, George Stephanopoulos, Michael Sheehan, and my wordsmith friends Tommy Caplan and Taylor Branch stayed up with me. So did Al Gore. The terrific staff at Blair House was used to taking care of foreign heads of state who kept all kinds of hours, so they were ready with gallons of coffee to keep us awake and snacks to keep us in a reasonably good humor. By the time I went to bed for a couple of hours' sleep, I was feeling better about the speech.

Wednesday morning dawned cold and clear. I began the day with an early-morning security briefing, then I received instructions on how my military aide would handle the launching of our nuclear weapons. The President has five military aides, one outstanding young officer from each service branch; one of them is near him at all times.

Though a nuclear exchange seemed unthinkable with the Cold War over, assuming the control of our arsenal was a sober reminder of the responsibilities just a few hours away. There's a difference between knowing about the presidency and actually being President. It's hard to describe in words, but I left Blair House with my eagerness tempered by humility.

The last activity before the inauguration was a prayer

service at the Metropolitan African Methodist Episcopal Church. It was important to me. With input from Hillary and Al Gore, I had picked the participating clergy, the singers, and the music. Hillary's family and mine were there. Mother was beaming. Roger was grinning, and enjoying the music. Both our pastors from home participated in the service, as did Al and Tipper's ministers, and George Stephanopoulos's father, the Greek Orthodox dean of the Holy Trinity Cathedral in New York. Father Otto Hentz, who, almost thirty years earlier, had asked me to consider becoming a Jesuit, said a prayer. Rabbi Gene Levy from Little Rock and Imam Wallace D. Mohammad spoke. Several black clergymen who were friends of mine participated, with Dr. Gardner Taylor, one of America's greatest preachers of any race or denomination, giving the principal address. My Pentecostal friends from Arkansas and Louisiana sang, along with Phil Driscoll, a fabulous singer and trumpeter Al knew from Tennessee, and Carolyn Staley sang "Be Not Afraid," one of my favorite hymns and a good lesson for the day. Tears welled up in my eyes several times during the service, and I left it uplifted and ready for the hours ahead.

We went back to Blair House to look at the speech for the last time. It had gotten a lot better since 4 a.m. At ten, Hillary, Chelsea, and I walked across the street to the White House, where we were met on the front steps by President and Mrs. Bush, who took us inside for coffee with the Gores and the Quayles. Ron and Alma Brown were also there. I wanted Ron to share a moment he had done so much to make possible. I was struck by how well President and Mrs. Bush dealt with a painful situation and a sad parting—it was obvious that they had become close to several members of the staff and would miss and be missed by them. At about 10:45, we all got into limousines. Following tradition, President Bush and I rode together, with Speaker Foley and Wendell Ford, the gravelly-voiced senator from Kentucky who was co-chairman of the Joint Congressional Committee on Inaugural Ceremonies and who had worked hard for the narrow victory that Al and I had won in his state.

Fortunately, the ongoing Capitol restoration project had

required the last three inaugurations to be held on the building's west front. Before that, they had taken place on the other side, facing the Supreme Court and the Library of Congress. Most of the people who came could not have seen the ceremonies from that viewpoint. The crowd, which filled the large grounds of the Capitol and spilled back over onto the Mall and up Constitution and Pennsylvania avenues, was estimated by the National Park Service to be between 280,000 and 300,000 people. Whatever the number, the throng was big, and full of all kinds of people, old and young, of all races and faiths, from all walks of life. I was happy that so many people who had made this day possible were there to share in it.

Many of the FOBs who came illustrated the extent to which I was indebted to my personal friends: Marsha Scott and Martha Whetstone, who organized my campaigns in northern California, were old friends from Arkansas; Sheila Bronfman, leader of the Arkansas Travelers, had lived around the corner from Hillary and me when I was attorney general; Dave Matter, my leader in western Pennsylvania, had succeeded me as class president at Georgetown; Bob Raymar and Tom Schneider, two of my most important fund-raisers, were friends from law school and Renaissance Weekend. There were so many people like them who had made this day possible.

The ceremony started at 11:30. All the principals walked out onto the platform according to protocol order with their congressional escorts. President Bush went just before me, with the Marine Band, under Colonel John Bourgeois, playing "Hail to the Chief" for both of us. I gazed out onto the vast crowd.

Then Al Gore took the oath of office, administered by Supreme Court Justice Byron White. The oath was originally going to be administered by retired Supreme Court Justice Thurgood Marshall, a great civil rights lawyer whom President Johnson had made the first black on the high court, but he had fallen ill. It would have been unusual for a retired justice to do the honors, but Marshall's son, Thurgood Jr., was on Gore's staff. Another son, John, was a

Virginia state trooper who had led our inaugural motorcade from Monticello to Washington. Marshall died four days after the inauguration. He was mourned, missed, and deeply appreciated by the legions of Americans who remembered what America was like before he set out to change it.

After the oath, the great mezzo-soprano Marilyn Horne, whom I had first met when she performed in Little Rock a few years earlier, sang a medley of classic American songs. Then it was my turn. Hillary stood to my left, holding our family Bible. With Chelsea on my right, I put my left hand on the Bible, raised my right hand, and repeated the oath of office after Chief Justice Rehnquist, solemnly swearing to "faithfully execute" the office of the President, and "to the best of my ability, preserve, protect, and defend the Constitution of the United States, so help me God."

I shook hands with the chief justice and President Bush, then hugged Hillary and Chelsea and told them I loved them. Then Senator Wendell Ford called me to the podium as "the President of the United States." I began by placing the present moment in the stream of American history:

> Today we celebrate the mystery of American renewal. This ceremony is held in the depth of winter. But, by the words we speak and the faces we show the world, we force the spring. A spring reborn in the world's oldest democracy, that brings forth the vision and courage to reinvent America. When our founders boldly declared America's independence to the world and our purposes to the Almighty, they knew that America, to endure, would have to change. . . . Each generation of Americans must define what it means to be an American.

After a salute to President Bush, I described the current situation:

> Today, a generation raised in the shadows of the Cold War assumes new responsibilities in a world warmed by the sunshine of freedom but threatened

still by ancient hatreds and new plagues. Raised in
unrivaled prosperity, we inherit an economy that is
still the world's strongest, but is weakened. . . .
Profound and powerful forces are shaking and
remaking our world, and the urgent question of
our time is whether we can make change our friend
and not our enemy. . . . There is nothing wrong
with America that cannot be cured by what is right
with America.

Still, I warned, "It will not be easy; it will require sacrifice. . . . We must provide for our nation the way a family
provides for its children." I asked my fellow citizens to
think of posterity, "the world to come—the world for
whom we hold our ideals, from whom we have borrowed
our planet, and to whom we bear sacred responsibility. We
must do what America does best: offer more opportunity to
all and demand responsibility from all."

I said that, in our time,

there is no longer a clear division between what is
foreign and what is domestic. The world economy,
the world environment, the world AIDS crisis, the
world arms race—they affect us all. . . . America
must continue to lead the world we did so much to
make.

I closed the speech with a challenge to the American
people, telling them that, by their votes, they had "forced
the spring," but that government alone could not create the
nation they wanted: "You, too, must play your part in our
renewal. I challenge a new generation of young Americans
to a season of service. . . . There is so much to be done. . . .
From this joyful mountaintop of celebration, we hear a call
to service in the valley. We have heard the trumpets. We
have changed the guard. And now, each in our way, and
with God's help, we must answer the call."

Although several commentators panned the speech, saying it was devoid of both ringing phrases and compelling
specifics, I felt good about it. It had flashes of eloquence, it

was clear, it said we were going to reduce the deficit while increasing critical investments in our future, and it challenged the American people to do more to help those in need and to heal our divisions. And it was short, the third-shortest inaugural address in history, after Lincoln's second inaugural, the greatest of them all, and Washington's second speech, which lasted less than two minutes. Essentially, Washington just said, Thanks, I'm going back to work, and if I don't do a good job, reprimand me. By contrast, William Henry Harrison gave the longest address in history, in 1841, speaking without a coat on a cold day for well over an hour and catching a bad case of pneumonia, which cost him his life thirty-three days later. At least I was mercifully and uncharacteristically brief, and the people knew how I saw the world and what I intended to do.

By far the most beautiful words of the day were spoken by Maya Angelou, a tall woman with a deep strong voice whom I had asked to write a poem for the occasion, the first poet to do so since Robert Frost spoke at President Kennedy's inauguration in 1961. I had followed Maya's career since I'd read her memoir, *I Know Why the Caged Bird Sings*, which recounts her early years as a traumatized mute girl in a poor black community in Stamps, Arkansas.

Maya's poem, "On the Pulse of Morning," riveted the crowd. Built on powerful images of a rock to stand on, a river to rest by, and a tree with roots in all the cultures and kinds that make up the American mosaic, the poem issued a passionate plea in the form of a neighborly invitation:

> Lift up your faces, you have a piercing need
> For this bright morning dawning for you.
> History, despite its wrenching pain,
> Cannot be unlived, and if faced
> With courage, need not be lived again.
> Lift up your eyes upon
> The day breaking for you.
> Give birth again
> To the dream.
> . . . .

Here on the pulse of this new day
You may have the grace to look up and out
And into your sister's eyes, and into
Your brother's face, your country
And say simply
Very simply
With hope
Good morning.

Billy Graham ended our good morning with a brief benediction, and Hillary and I left the stage to accompany the Bushes down the back steps of the Capitol, where the presidential helicopter, Marine One, was waiting to take them on the first leg of their journey home. We went back inside for lunch with the Congressional Committee, then drove up Pennsylvania Avenue toward the viewing stand in front of the White House for the inaugural parade. With Chelsea, we got out of the car and walked the last few blocks of the route so that we could wave to the crowds packed several deep along the way.

After the parade, we went into our new home for the first time, with only about two hours to greet the staff, rest, and get ready for the evening. Miraculously, the movers had gotten all our belongings in during the inaugural ceremonies and the parade.

At seven, we started our evening marathon with a dinner, followed by visits to all eleven inaugural balls. My brother sang for me at the MTV Youth Ball, and at another I played a tenor saxophone duet on "Night Train" with Clarence Clemons. However, at most of the balls Hillary and I would first say a few words of thanks, then dance to a few bars of one of our favorite songs, "It Had to Be You," showing off her beautiful purple gown. Meanwhile, Chelsea was off with friends from Arkansas at the Youth Ball, and Al and Tipper kept their own schedule. At the Tennessee ball, Paul Simon regaled them with his hit "You Can Call Me Al." At the Arkansas Ball, I introduced Mother to Barbra Streisand and told them both I thought they'd get along. They did more than that. They became fast friends, and Barbra called my mother every week until she died. I still have a picture of them walking hand in hand on that inaugural evening.

When we got back to the White House, it was after 2 a.m. We had to be up the next morning for a public reception, but I was too excited to go right to bed. We had a full house: Hillary's parents, Mother and her husband Dick, our siblings, Chelsea's friends from home, and our friends Jim and Diane Blair and Harry and Linda Thomason. Only our parents had retired.

I wanted to look around. We had been in the second-floor living quarters before, but this was different. It was beginning to sink in that we actually lived there and would have to make it a home. Most of the rooms had high ceilings and beautiful but comfortable furniture. The presidential bedroom and living room face the south, with a small room off the bedroom that would become Hillary's sitting room. Chelsea had a bedroom and study across the hall, just beyond the formal dining room and the small kitchen. At the other end of the hall were the main guest bedrooms, one of which had been Lincoln's office and has one of his handwritten copies of the Gettysburg Address.

Next to the Lincoln Bedroom is the Treaty Room, so named because the treaty ending the Spanish-American War was signed there in 1898. For several years it had been the private office of the President, usually configured with multiple televisions so the Chief Executive could watch all the news programs at once. I believe President Bush had four TVs there. I decided I wanted it to be a quiet place where I could read, reflect, listen to music, and hold small meetings. The White House carpenters made me floor-to-ceiling bookshelves, and the staff brought up the table on which the Spanish-American War treaty had been signed. In 1869, it had been Ulysses Grant's cabinet table, with space for the President and his seven department heads to sit around it. Since 1898 it had been used for the signing of all treaties, including the temporary nuclear test ban under President Kennedy and the Camp David Accords under President Carter. Before the year was out, I would be using it too.

I filled out the room with a late-eighteenth-century

Chippendale sofa, the oldest piece of furniture in the White House collection, and an antique table bought by Mary Todd Lincoln, on which we put the silver commemorative cup from the 1898 treaty. When I got my books and CDs in, and hung some of my old pictures, including an 1860 photo of Abraham Lincoln and Yousuf Karsh's famous photograph of Churchill, the place had a comfortable, peaceful atmosphere in which I would spend countless hours in the years ahead.

On my first day as President, I started out by taking Mother down to the Rose Garden, to show her exactly where I had stood when I shook hands with President Kennedy almost thirty years ago. Then, in a departure from traditional practice, we opened the White House to the public, providing tickets to two thousand people who had been selected in a postcard lottery. Al, Tipper, Hillary, and I stood in line shaking hands with the ticket holders, then with others who waited in the cold rain for their time to walk through the lower south entrance into the Diplomatic Reception Room to say hello. One determined young man without a ticket had hitchhiked overnight to the White House with his sleeping bag. After six hours, we had to stop, so I went outside to speak to the rest of the crowd gathered on the South Lawn. That night, Hillary and I stood in line for another few hours, to greet our friends from Arkansas and classmates from Georgetown, Wellesley, and Yale.

A few months after the inauguration, a book was published filled with beautiful photographs that capture the excitement and meaning of the inaugural week, with an explanatory text written by Rebecca Buffum Taylor. In her epilogue to the book, Taylor writes:

> A shift in political values takes time. Even if successful, its clarity must wait until months or years have passed, until the lens has been extended and recedes again, until far and middle distance merge with what can be seen today.

The words were penetrating, and probably correct. But I couldn't wait years, months, or even days to see if the campaign and the inauguration had effected a shift in values, deepening the roots and broadening the reach of the American community. I had too much to do, and once again the work quickly turned from poetry to prose, not all of it pretty.

TWO

THE NEXT YEAR involved an amazing combination of major legislative achievements, frustrations and successes in foreign policy, unforeseen events, personal tragedy, honest errors, and clumsy violations of the Washington culture, which, when combined with compulsive leaking by a few staffers, ensured press coverage that often resembled what I'd experienced during the New York primary.

On January 22, we announced that Zoë Baird had withdrawn her name from consideration for attorney general. Since we had learned about her employment of illegal immigrant workers and her failure to pay Social Security taxes for them during the vetting process, I had to say that we had failed to evaluate the matter properly, and that I, not she, was responsible for the situation. Zoë had not misled us in any way. When the household workers were hired, she had just gotten a new job, and her husband had the summer off from teaching. Apparently, each assumed the other had handled the tax matter. I believed her and kept working for her nomination for three weeks after she first offered to withdraw it. Later, I appointed Zoë to the Foreign Intelligence Advisory Board, where she made a real contribution to the work Admiral Bill Crowe's group did.

On the same day, the press became infuriated with the new White House when we denied them the privilege, which they'd had for years, of walking from the press room, located between the West Wing and the residence, up to the press secretary's office on the first floor near the Cabinet Room. This strolling allowed them to hang out in the halls and pepper whoever came by with questions. Apparently, a couple of people high up in the Bush administration had mentioned to their new counterparts that this arrangement impeded efficiency and increased leaks, and the decision was made to change it. I don't recall being consulted about it, but perhaps

I was. The press raised the roof, but we stuck with the decision, figuring they'd get over it. There's no question that the new policy contributed to freer movement and conversation among the staff, but it's hard to say it was worth the animosity it engendered. And since, in the first few months, the White House leaked worse than a tar-paper shack with holes in the roof and gaps in the walls, it's impossible to say that confining the press to quarters did much good.

That afternoon, the anniversary of *Roe* v. *Wade*, I issued executive orders ending the Reagan-Bush ban on fetal-tissue research; abolishing the so-called Mexico City rule, which prohibited federal aid to international planning agencies that were in any way involved in abortions; and reversing the Bush "gag rule" barring abortion counseling at family planning clinics that receive federal funds. I had pledged to take these actions in the campaign, and I believed in them. Fetal-tissue research was essential to finding better treatments for Parkinson's disease, diabetes, and other conditions. The Mexico City rule arguably led to more abortions, by reducing the availability of information on alternative family planning measures. And the gag rule used federal funds to prevent family planning clinics from telling pregnant women—often frightened, young, and alone—about an option the Supreme Court had declared a constitutional right. Federal funds still could not be used to fund abortions, at home or abroad.

On January 25, Chelsea's first day at her new school, I announced that Hillary would head a task force to come up with a comprehensive health-care plan, working with Ira Magaziner as the lead staff person, domestic policy advisor Carol Rasco, and Judy Feder, who had led our health-care transition team. I was pleased that Ira had agreed to work on health care. We had been friends since 1969, when he had come to Oxford as a Rhodes scholar a year after I did. Now a successful businessman, he had worked on the campaign economic team. Ira believed delivering universal health coverage was both morally and economically imperative. I knew he would give Hillary the kind of support she needed for the grueling task ahead of us.

Heading up the effort to reform health care was an unprecedented thing for a First Lady to do, as was my decision to give Hillary and her staff offices in the West Wing, where the policy action is, as opposed to the traditional office space in the East Wing, where the social affairs of the White House are run. Both decisions were controversial; when it came to the First Lady's role, it seemed Washington was more conservative than Arkansas. I decided Hillary should lead the health-care effort because she cared and knew a lot about the issue, she had time to do the job right, and I thought she would be able to be an honest broker among all the competing interests in the health-care industry, government agencies, and consumer groups. I knew the whole enterprise was risky; Harry Truman's attempt to provide universal health coverage had nearly destroyed his presidency, and Nixon and Carter never even got their bills out of committee. With the most Democratic Congress in decades, Lyndon Johnson got Medicare for the elderly and Medicaid for the poor, but didn't even try to insure the rest of those without coverage. Nevertheless, I thought we should try for universal coverage, which every other wealthy nation had long enjoyed, for both health and economic reasons. Almost 40 million people had no health insurance, yet we were spending 14 percent of our gross national product on health care, 4 percent more than Canada, the country with the next-highest rate.

On the night of the twenty-fifth, at their urgent request, I met with the Joint Chiefs of Staff to discuss the gays-in-the-military issue. Earlier in the day, the *New York Times* had reported that, because of strong military opposition to the change, I would delay issuing formal regulations lifting the ban for six months, while the views of senior officers, as well as practical problems, were considered. It was a reasonable thing to do. When Harry Truman ordered the racial integration of the military, he had given the Pentagon even more time to figure out how to carry it out in a way that was consistent with its primary mission of maintaining a well-prepared, cohesive fighting force with high morale. In the meantime, Defense Secretary Les Aspin would tell the military to stop asking recruits about their sexual orientation and to stop discharging homosexual men and women who had not been discovered to have committed a homosexual act, which was a violation of the Uniform Code of Military Justice.

The Joint Chiefs' early request for a meeting created a problem. I was more than willing to hear them out, but I didn't want the issue to get any more publicity than it already was receiving, not because I was trying to hide my position, but because I didn't want the public to think I was paying more attention to it than to the economy. That's exactly what the congressional Republicans wanted the American people to think. Senator Dole was already talking about passing a resolution removing my authority to lift the ban; he clearly wanted this to be the defining issue of my first weeks in office.

In the meeting, the chiefs acknowledged that there were thousands of gay men and women serving with distinction in the 1.8 million–member military, but they maintained that letting them serve openly would be, in General Powell's words, "prejudicial to good order and discipline." The rest of the Joint Chiefs were with the chairman. When I raised the fact that it apparently had cost the military $500 million to kick 17,000 homosexuals out of the service in the previous decade, despite a government report saying there was no reason to believe they could not serve effectively, the chiefs replied that it was worth it to preserve unit cohesion and morale.

The chief of naval operations, Admiral Frank Kelso, said the navy had the greatest practical problems, given the close and isolated living arrangements on ships. The army chief, General Gordon Sullivan, and U.S. Air Force General Merrill McPeak were opposed, too. But the most adamant opponent was the commandant of the Marine Corps, General Carl Mundy. He was concerned about more than appearances and practicalities. He believed that homosexuality was immoral, and that if gays were permitted to serve openly, the military would be condoning immoral behavior and could no longer attract the finest young Americans. I disagreed with Mundy, but I liked him. In fact, I liked and

respected them all. They had given me their honest opinions, yet had made it clear that if I ordered them to take
action they'd do the best job they could, although if called
to testify before Congress they would have to state their
views frankly.

A couple of days later, I had another night meeting on
the issue, with members of the Senate Armed Services Committee, including Senators Sam Nunn, James Exon, Carl
Levin, Robert Byrd, Edward Kennedy, Bob Graham, Jeff
Bingaman, John Glenn, Richard Shelby, Joe Lieberman, and
Chuck Robb. Nunn, while opposed to my position, had
agreed to the six-month delay. Some of my staffers were
upset with him for his early and forceful opposition, but I
wasn't; after all, he was personally conservative, and as
chairman of the committee, he honored the military culture
and saw it as his duty to protect it. He was not alone. Charlie Moskos, the Northwestern University sociologist who
had worked with Nunn and me on the DLC national-service
proposal and who said he had known a gay officer during
the Korean War, was also against lifting the ban, saying that
it preserved the "expectation of privacy" to which soldiers
living in close quarters were entitled. Moskos said we
should stick with what the great majority of military people
wanted, because the main thing we needed in the military
was the ability and willingness to fight. The problem I saw
with his argument, and Sam Nunn's, is that they could have
been used with equal force against Truman's order on integration or against current efforts to open more positions to
women in the military.

Senator Byrd took a harder line than Nunn, echoing
what I had heard from General Mundy. He believed homosexuality was a sin; said he would never let his grandson,
whom he adored, join a military that admitted gays; and
asserted that one reason the Roman Empire fell was the
acceptance of pervasive homosexual conduct in the Roman
legions from Julius Caesar on down. In contrast to Byrd and
Nunn, Chuck Robb, who was conservative on many issues
and had survived heated combat in Vietnam, supported my

position, based on his wartime contact with men who were both gay and brave. He wasn't the only Vietnam combat veteran in Congress who felt that way.

The cultural divide was partly, but not completely, partisan and generational. Some younger Democrats opposed lifting the ban, while some older Republicans were for lifting it, including Lawrence Korb and Barry Goldwater. Korb, who had enforced the ban as an assistant secretary of defense under Reagan, said it was not necessary for maintaining the quality and strength of our forces. Goldwater, a former chairman of the Senate Armed Services Committee, a veteran, and the founder of the Arizona National Guard, was an old-fashioned conservative with libertarian instincts. In a statement published in the *Washington Post*, he said that allowing gays to serve was not a call for cultural license but a reaffirmation of the American value of extending opportunity to responsible citizens and limiting the reach of government into people's private lives. In his typically blunt way, he said he didn't care whether a soldier *was* straight, but whether he could *shoot* straight.

As things turned out, Goldwater's support and all my arguments were academic. The House passed a resolution opposing my position by more than three to one. The Senate opposition was not as great but was still substantial. That meant that if I persisted, the Congress would overturn my position with an amendment to the defense appropriations bill that I couldn't easily veto, and even if I did, the veto would be overridden in both houses.

While all this was going on, I saw a poll showing that by 48 to 45 percent the public disagreed with my position. The numbers didn't look too bad for such a controversial issue, but they were, and they showed why Congress thought it was a dead-bang loser for them. Only 16 percent of the electorate strongly approved of lifting the ban, while 33 percent very strongly disapproved. Those were the people whose votes could be influenced by a congressman's position. It's hard to get politicians in swing districts to take a 17 percent deficit on any issue into an election. Interestingly, the biggest divisions were these: self-identified born-again Christians opposed my position 70 to 22 percent, while people who said they knew homosexuals personally approved of it 66 to 33 percent.

With congressional defeat inevitable, Les Aspin worked with Colin Powell and the Joint Chiefs on a compromise. Almost exactly six months later, on July 19, I went to the National Defense University at Fort McNair to announce it to the officers in attendance. "Don't ask, don't tell" basically said that if you say you're gay, it's presumed that you intend to violate the Uniform Code of Military Justice and you can be removed, unless you can convince your commander you're celibate and therefore not in violation of the code. But if you don't say you're gay, the following things will not lead to your removal: marching in a gay-rights parade in civilian clothes; hanging out in gay bars or with known homosexuals; being on homosexual mailing lists; and living with a person of the same sex who is the beneficiary of your life insurance policy. On paper, the military had moved a long way, to "live and let live," while holding on to the idea that it couldn't acknowledge gays without approving of homosexuality and compromising morale and cohesion. In practice it often didn't work out that way. Many anti-gay officers simply ignored the new policy and worked even harder to root out homosexuals, costing the military millions of dollars that would have been far better spent making America more secure.

In the short run, I got the worst of both worlds—I lost the fight, and the gay community was highly critical of me for the compromise, simply refusing to acknowledge the consequences of having so little support in Congress, and giving me little credit for lifting another ban on gays, the ban against serving in critical national security positions, or for the substantial number of gays and lesbians who were working throughout the administration. By contrast, Senator Dole won big. By raising the issue early, and repeatedly, he guaranteed it so much publicity that it appeared I was working on little else, which caused a lot of Americans who had elected me to fix the economy to wonder what on earth I was doing and whether they'd made a mistake.

I was finding it a challenge to keep another campaign commitment: cutting the White House staff by 25 percent. It was a nightmare for chief of staff Mack McLarty, especially since we had a more ambitious agenda than the previous administration's and were getting more than twice as much mail. On February 9, just a week before I was slated to announce my economic program, I proposed the 25 percent reduction, cutting the staff by 350 people, down to 1,044 employees. Everybody took a hit; even Hillary's office would be smaller than Barbara Bush's, though she would take on greater responsibilities. The reduction I regretted most was the elimination of twenty career positions in the correspondence section. I would have preferred to reduce their numbers by attrition, but Mack said there was no other way to meet the goal. Besides, we had to have some money to modernize the White House. The staff couldn't even send and receive e-mail, and the phone system hadn't been changed since the Carter years. We couldn't do conference calls, but anyone could press one of the big lighted extension buttons and listen in on someone else's conversation, including mine. Soon we had a better system installed.

We also beefed up one part of the White House staff: the casework operation that was designed to help individual citizens who had personal problems with the federal government, often involving an effort to obtain disability, veterans, or other benefits. Usually citizens call on their U.S. senators or representatives for help in such matters, but because I had run a highly personalized campaign, many Americans felt they could call on me. I got an especially memorable request on February 20, when Peter Jennings, the ABC news anchor, moderated a televised "Children's Town Meeting" in the White House, in which young people between the ages of eight and fifteen asked me questions. The kids asked if I helped Chelsea with her homework, why no women had been elected President, what I would do to help Los Angeles after the riots, how health care would be paid for, and whether I could do anything to stop violence in schools. A lot of them were interested in the environment.

But one of the children wanted help. Anastasia Somoza was a beautiful girl from New York City who was confined to a wheelchair because of cerebral palsy. She explained that she had a twin sister, Alba, who also had cerebral palsy but who, unlike her, couldn't speak. "So because she can't speak, they put her in a special education class. But she uses computers to speak. And I would like her to be in a regular education class just like me." Anastasia said she and her parents were convinced that Alba could do regular school-work if given a chance. Federal law required children with disabilities to be educated in the "least restrictive" environ-ment, but the critical decision about what is least restrictive is made at the child's school. It took about a year, but even-tually Alba got into a regular class.

Hillary and I kept in touch with the Somoza family, and in 2002, I spoke at the girls' high school graduation. They both went on to college, because Anastasia and her parents were determined to give Alba all the opportunities she deserved, and weren't shy about asking others, including me, to help. Every month, the agency liaison who headed the casework operation sent me a report on the people we'd helped, along with a few of the moving thank-you letters they sent.

In addition to the staff cuts, I announced an executive order to cut administrative expenses 3 percent throughout the government, and a reduction in the salaries of top appointees and in their perks, like limousine service and pri-vate dining rooms. In a move that would prove to be a tremendous morale booster, I changed the rules of the White House Mess to allow more junior staff to use what had been the private preserve of high-level White House officials.

Our young staffers were working long hours and week-ends, and it seemed foolish to me to require them all to leave for lunch, order in, or bring a paper bag with food from home. Besides, access to the White House Mess implied that they, too, were important. The mess was a wood-paneled room with good food prepared by navy personnel. I ordered lunch from it almost every day and enjoyed going down to visit with the young people who worked in the kitchen. Once a week they served Mexican dishes I especially liked. After I left office, the mess was again closed to all but senior staff. I believe our policy was good for morale and productivity.

With all the extra work and fewer people to do it, we would have to rely more than ever not only on those junior staffers, but also on the thousand-plus volunteers who put in long hours, some of them virtually full-time. The volunteers opened the mail, sent form replies when appropriate, filled requests for information, and did countless other tasks, without which the White House would have been far less responsive to the American people. All the volunteers got in return for their efforts, apart from the satisfaction of serving, was an annual thank-you reception Hillary and I hosted for them on the South Lawn. The White House couldn't function without them.

Besides the specific cuts I had already decided on, I was convinced that with a longer-term systematic approach, we could save a lot more money and improve government services. In Arkansas, I had initiated a Total Quality Management program that had achieved positive results. On March 3, I announced that Al Gore would lead a six-month review of all federal operations. Al took to the job like a duck to water, bringing in outside experts and consulting widely with government employees. He kept at it for eight years, helping us to eliminate hundreds of programs and 16,000 pages of regulations, to reduce the federal workforce by 300,000, making this the smallest federal government since 1960, and to save $136 million in tax money.

While we were getting organized and dealing with the controversies in the press, most of my time in January and February was devoted to filling in the details of the economic plan. On Sunday, January 24, Lloyd Bentsen appeared on *Meet the Press*. He was supposed to give nonspecific answers to all questions regarding the details of the plan, but he went a little further than that, announcing that we would propose a consumption tax of some kind and that a broad-based energy tax was under consideration. The next day, interest rates on the government's thirty-year bond fell from 7.29 to 7.19 percent, the lowest rate in six years.

Meanwhile, we were struggling with the budget details. All the spending cuts and taxes that raised real money were controversial. For example, when I met with Senate and House leaders on the budget, Leon Panetta suggested that we have a one-time three-month delay in increasing the Social Security cost-of-living allowance. Most experts agreed that the COLA was too high, given the low rate of inflation, and the delay would save $15 billion over five years. Senator Mitchell said that the suggested delay was regressive and unfair, and that he couldn't support it. Neither would the other senators. We'd have to find that $15 billion elsewhere.

Over the weekend of January 30–31, I brought the cabinet and senior White House staff to Camp David, the presidential retreat in Maryland's Catoctin Mountains. Camp David is a beautiful wooded site, with comfortable cabins and recreational facilities, staffed by men and women from the navy and the Marine Corps. It was the perfect setting for us to get to know one another better and talk about the year ahead. I also invited my campaign advisors Stan Greenberg, Paul Begala, and Mandy Grunwald. They felt that they had been shut out of the transition, and that an obsession with the deficit had overtaken every other objective I had advanced in the campaign. They thought Al and I were courting disaster by disregarding the deeper concerns and interests of the people who had elected us. I sympathized with them. For one thing, they hadn't been in on the hours of discussions that led most of us to the conclusion that if we didn't deal with the deficit, we couldn't achieve sustained strong growth and that my other campaign commitments, at least those that cost money, would die in the stagnant backwater of a sluggish economy.

I let Mandy and Stan start the discussion. Mandy outlined the anxiety of the middle class about jobs, retirement, health care, and education. Stan said that voters' most important concerns were, in order, jobs, health-care reform, welfare reform, and then deficit reduction, and that if deficit reduction was going to require the middle class to pay more taxes, I had darn sure better do something else for them. Hillary then described how we'd failed in Arkansas in my first term by doing too many things at once, without a clear story line and an effort to prepare people for a long, sustained struggle. Then she told them about the success we'd had the second time around, by focusing on one or two issues every two years, and laying out long-term goals, along with short-term benchmarks of progress against which we could be judged. That kind of approach, she said, enabled me to develop a story line people could understand and support. In response, someone pointed out that we couldn't develop a story line as long as we were awash in leaks, all of which concerned the most controversial proposals. After the weekend, the consultants tried to come up with a communications strategy that would take us beyond the daily leaks and controversies.

The rest of the retreat was devoted to more informal, personal conversations. On Saturday night there was a session, run by a facilitator who was a friend of Al Gore's, in which we were supposed to bond by sitting in a group, taking turns telling something about ourselves the others didn't know. Though the exercise got mixed reviews, I actually enjoyed it, and managed to confess that, as a child, I was overweight and often ridiculed. Lloyd Bentsen thought the whole exercise was silly and went back to his cabin; if there was something about him the rest of us didn't know, it was intentional. Bob Rubin stayed, but said he didn't have anything to say—apparently such group unburdening wasn't the key to his success at Goldman Sachs. Warren Christopher did participate, probably because he was the most disciplined man on the planet and thought this baby-boomer version of Chinese water torture would somehow strengthen his already considerable character. All in all, the weekend was helpful, but the real bonding would come in the fires of the struggles, victories, and defeats that lay ahead.

On Sunday night, we were back in the White House to host the annual National Governors Association dinner. It was Hillary's first formal event as First Lady, and she was nervous, but it went well. The governors were concerned about the economy, which diminished state revenues, forcing them to cut services, raise taxes, or both. They understood the necessity of reducing the deficit, but didn't want it to come at their expense, in the form of responsibilities shifting from the federal government to the states without funds being provided to pay for them.

On February 5, I signed my first bill into law, keeping another campaign commitment. With the Family and Medical Leave Act, the United States at last joined more than 150 other countries in guaranteeing workers some time off when a baby is born or a family member is sick. The bill's principal sponsor, my longtime friend Senator Chris Dodd of Connecticut, had worked for years to enact it. President Bush had vetoed it twice, saying it would prove too burdensome for business. While the legislation had some strong Republican supporters, most Republicans had voted against it for the same reason. I believed that family leave would be good for the economy. With most parents in the workforce, by choice or necessity, it is imperative that Americans be able to do well both on the job and at home. People who are worried about their infants or their sick parents are less productive than those who go to work knowing they've done right by their families. During my time as President, more than thirty-five million people would take advantage of the Family and Medical Leave law.

In the next eight years, and even after I left office, more people would mention it to me than any other bill I signed. Many of their stories were powerful. Early one Sunday morning, when I came in from my jog, I ran into a family touring the White House. One of the children, a teenage girl, was in a wheelchair and obviously very ill. I greeted them and said that if they'd wait for me to shower and get dressed for church, I'd take them into the Oval Office for a picture. They waited and we had a good visit. I especially enjoyed my talk with the brave young girl. As I walked away, her father grabbed my arm and turned me around, saying, "My little girl is probably not going to make it. The last three weeks I've spent with her have been the most important of my life. I couldn't have done it without the family leave law."

In early 2001, when I took my first shuttle flight from New York to Washington as a private citizen, one of the flight attendants told me that both her parents had been desperately ill at the same time, one with cancer, the other with Alzheimer's. She said there was no one to care for them in their last days except her and her sister, and they wouldn't have been able to do it without the family leave law. "You know, the Republicans are always talking about family values," she said, "but I think how your parents die is an important part of family values."

On February 11, as we worked to finish the economic plan, I finally got an attorney general, having decided, after a false start or two, on Janet Reno, the prosecuting attorney of Dade County, Florida. I had known about and admired Janet's work for years, especially her innovative "drug courts," which gave first-time offenders the chance to avoid going to jail if they agreed to undergo drug treatment and check in regularly with the court. My brother-in-law Hugh Rodham had worked in the Miami drug court as an attorney with the public defender's office. At his invitation, I had attended two sessions of the court myself in the 1980s, and was struck by the unusual but effective way the prosecutor, defense lawyer, and judge worked together to convince the defendants that this was their last opportunity to stay out of prison. The program was very successful, with a much lower recidivism rate than the prison system, at far less cost to the taxpayers. In the campaign, I had pledged to support federal funding to establish drug courts based on the Miami model all across the country.

Senator Bob Graham gave Reno a glowing endorsement when I called him. So did my friend Diane Blair, who had gone to Cornell with her thirty years earlier. So did Vince Foster, who was a very good judge of people. After he interviewed Janet, he called me and said in his droll way, "I think

we've got a live one." Reno also was immensely popular
with her constituents, based on her reputation as a no-
nonsense, tough but fair prosecutor. She was a native
Floridian, about six feet tall, and had never married. Public
service was her life, and she had performed it well. I thought
she could strengthen the often-frayed relationships between
federal law enforcement and its state and local counterparts. It concerned me a little that, like me, she was a
stranger to Washington's ways, but in Miami she had had
extensive experience working with federal authorities on
immigration and narcotics cases, and I thought she would
learn enough to get along.

Over the weekend, we worked hard to finish the economic plan. Paul Begala had come to work in the White
House a couple of weeks earlier, in large measure to help me
explain what I was about to do in a way that was consistent
with my campaign message of restoring opportunity for
the middle class, something he believed most members of the
economic team didn't care enough about. Begala felt that the
entire team should stress three points: that deficit reduction
is not an end in itself, but the means to achieve the real objectives—economic growth, more jobs, and higher incomes;
that our plan represented a fundamental change in the way
government had been working, ending the irresponsibility
and unfairness of the past by asking the wealthy big corporations, and other special interests that had benefited dispro-
portionately from the tax cuts and deficits of the 1980s, to
pay their fair share of cleaning up the mess; and that we
should not say we were asking people to "sacrifice" but to
"contribute" to America's renewal, a more patriotic and
positive formulation. Begala wrote a memo containing his
arguments and suggesting a new theme: "It's NOT the
deficit, stupid." Gene Sperling, Bob Reich, and George
Stephanopoulos agreed with Paul, and were glad to have
some inside help in arguing the message.

While all this was going on in public, we were struggling
hard with some big questions. By far the largest was
whether to include health-care reform along with the economic plan in the omnibus Budget Reconciliation Act.

There was a compelling argument for doing so: first, the budget, unlike all other legislation, isn't subject to the filibuster rule, the Senate practice that allows just forty-one senators to kill any bill by debating it to death, blocking a vote until the Senate has to move on to other business. Since the Senate had forty-four Republicans, the probability that they would at least try to filibuster health care was high.

Hillary and Ira Magaziner badly wanted health care in the budget, the congressional leaders were open to it, and Dick Gephardt had urged Hillary to do it, because he was sure the Republican senators would try to filibuster health care if it were proposed by itself. George Mitchell was sympathetic for another reason: If health-care reform were introduced as a separate bill, it would be referred to the Senate Finance Committee, whose chairman, Senator Pat Moynihan of New York, was, to put it mildly, skeptical that we could come up with a workable health-care plan so quickly. Moynihan recommended that we first do welfare reform, and spend the next two years developing a health-care proposal.

The economic team was adamantly opposed to including health care in the budget, and they had good reasons, too. Ira Magaziner and many health-care economists believed, correctly as it turned out, that greater competition in the health-care marketplace, which our plan would promote, would produce significant savings without price controls. But the Congressional Budget Office would not give credit for these savings in any budget we presented. Thus, to provide universal coverage, we had either to include a provision for backup price controls in the plan, raise taxes and cut other spending even further, or reduce the deficit target, which might adversely affect our strategy to lower interest rates.

I decided to delay the decision until after I put the details of the economic plan before the people and the Congress. Not long afterward, the decision was made for me. On March 11, Senator Robert Byrd, the senior Senate Democrat and ultimate authority on the body's rules, told us he would not make an exception for health care to the "Byrd rule," which prohibited the inclusion of nongeneric items in the budget-reconciliation bill. We had enlisted everyone we could think of to make the case to Byrd, but he was adamant that health-care reform could not be construed as part of the basic budget process. Now, if the Republicans could sustain a filibuster, our health-care plan would be dead on arrival.

In the second week of February, we decided to kick the health-care can down the road and complete the rest of the economic plan. I had become deeply immersed in the details of budgeting, determined to understand the human impact of our decisions. Most of the team wanted to cut farm supports and other rural programs, which they thought were unjustifiable. Alice Rivlin pushed hard for the cuts, suggesting I could then say I had ended welfare for farmers "as we know it." It was a takeoff on one of my best campaign lines, a pledge to "end welfare as we know it." I reminded my mostly urban budgeteers that farmers were good people who had chosen hard work in an uncertain environment, and though we had to make some cuts in their programs, "we don't have to enjoy it." Since we couldn't restructure the whole farm program, reduce the subsidies in other nations' budgets, or eliminate all the foreign barriers to our food exports, we ended up reducing the existing farm benefits modestly. But I didn't enjoy it.

Another thing we had to consider in proposing cuts, of course, was whether they had a chance to pass. For example, someone said we could save a lot of money by eliminating all the so-called highway-demonstration projects, which were specific spending items members of Congress obtained for their districts or states. When the suggestion came up, my new congressional liaison, Howard Paster, shook his head in disbelief. Paster had worked in both the House and Senate and for both Democratic and Republican lobbying firms. A New Yorker with a brusque, candid manner, Howard snapped, "How many votes does the bond market have?" Of course, he knew we had to convince the bond market that our deficit-reduction plan was credible, but he wanted us to remember that it first had to pass, and inflicting personal pain on members of Congress was unlikely to prove a successful strategy.

Some of the proposals we considered were so absurd they were comical. When someone suggested we impose fees for Coast Guard services, I asked how they would work. It was explained that the Coast Guard was quite often called upon to bring in boats that were in distress, often due to the negligence of the operators. I laughed and said, "So when we pull up alongside, or throw down a rope from a helicopter, before we do the rescue, we're going to ask, 'Visa? MasterCard?' " We let that one go, but eventually we did come up with more than 150 budget cuts.

Deciding on the tax increases was no easier than choosing the budget cuts. The toughest issue for me was the BTU tax. It was bad enough that I was going back on my commitment to cut middle-class taxes; now I was told we had to raise them, both to reach the $140 billion deficit reduction target in the fifth year and to turn the psychology of the bond market. The middle class had been shafted in the eighties, and Bush had been crippled by signing a gas-tax increase. In one fell swoop, if I proposed the BTU tax I would make the Republicans the anti-tax party again, largely to satisfy the hunger of the prosperous interest-rate setters for a little middle-class pain, in this case about $9 a month in direct costs, rising to $17 when indirect costs, in the form of higher prices for consumer products, were included. Lloyd Bentsen said that he had never had any fallout from voting for energy taxes, and that Bush was hurt by signing the 1990 gas-tax increase because of his "read my lips" pledge and the fact that the most militant anti-taxers were hard-core Republicans. Gore again pushed for the BTU tax, saying it would promote energy conservation and independence.

Finally, I gave in, but made some other changes in Treasury's tax proposals that I hoped would reduce the tax burden on average Americans. I insisted that we include in the budget the full $26.8 billion cost of my campaign proposal to more than double the tax cut for millions of working families with incomes of $30,000 or less, called the Earned Income Tax Credit (EITC), and for the first time offer a more modest EITC to more than 4 million working poor Americans without dependents. This proposal would ensure that, even with the energy tax, working families with incomes of $30,000 or less would still receive a meaningful tax cut. On the campaign trail, I had said at virtually every stop, "No one with children who works full-time should live in poverty." In 1993, there were a lot of people in that situation. After we doubled the EITC, more than 4 million of them moved out of poverty into the middle class during my presidency.

As we were trying to close the deal, Laura Tyson said she felt she had to point out that there was no significant economic difference between a fifth-year reduction of $140 billion and one of $120 or $125 billion. Congress would probably pare back whatever I proposed anyway. She argued that, if it eased our political problems or was simply better policy, we would save ourselves some headaches by reducing the figure to $135 billion or even a little less. Reich, Sperling, Blinder, Begala, and Stephanopoulos all agreed with her. The others held out for the high number. Bentsen said we could save $3 billion by dropping the estimated cost of welfare reform from the budget. I agreed. After all, we hadn't developed our proposal yet, and the number was just a guess. We knew we'd have to spend more on training, child care, and transportation to help poor people move from welfare to work, but if we moved enough people off the rolls, the net cost might go down, not up. Moreover, I believed we could pass welfare reform separately with bipartisan support.

Later, Lloyd Bentsen added a final piece to the plan, removing the $135,000 earnings cap on the 1.45 percent payroll tax that funded Medicare. This was necessary to make sure that our numbers on extending Medicare's solvency added up, but it did ask for more from the wealthiest Americans, whose top rate we were already proposing to raise to 39.6 percent, and who would almost certainly never cost the Medicare program as much as they would now pay into it. When I asked Bentsen about it, he just smiled and said he knew what he was doing. He was confident that he and other high-income Americans who would pay the extra tax would more than make it back in the stock market boom that our economic program would spark.

On Monday, February 15, I gave my first televised address from the Oval Office, a ten-minute outline of the economic program I would unveil two days later to a joint session of Congress. Even though the economy was in a statistical recovery, it was a jobless one, burdened by the quadrupling of the debt in the last twelve years. Since all the deficits were the result of the tax cuts for the wealthy, soaring health costs, and increases in defense spending, we were investing less in "the things that make us stronger and smarter, richer and safer," like education, children, transportation, and local law enforcement. At the rate we were going, our living standards, which usually doubled every twenty-five years, wouldn't do so again for another one hundred years. Reversing the trend would require a dramatic change in our national priorities, with a combination of tax increases and spending cuts to reduce the deficit and invest more in our future. I said that I had hoped to pursue this course without asking more of middle-class Americans, because they had borne hardships and had been treated unfairly in the previous twelve years, but the deficit had grown far beyond the earlier estimates on which I had built my budget proposals in the campaign. Now "more Americans must contribute today so that all Americans can do better tomorrow." However, unlike what had happened in the 1980s, most of the new taxes would be paid by wealthier Americans; "for the first time in more than a decade, we're all in this together." In addition to deficit reduction, my economic plan would provide incentives to businesses to create new jobs; a short-term stimulus to add 500,000 jobs right away; investments in education and training, with special programs to help displaced defense workers; welfare reform and the big increase in the EITC; Head Start opportunities and vaccinations for all children who need them; and the national service initiative to allow young people to earn money for college in return for serving in their communities. I acknowledged that these proposals would not be easily or quickly implemented, but when they were, we could "restore the vitality of the American dream."

On Wednesday night, in the address to Congress, I explained the strategy behind the plan and outlined the specifics. Its guiding principles were four: to shift more public and private spending from consumption to investment in order to create more jobs; to honor work and family; to produce a budget with conservative estimates, not the unrealistic "rosy scenario" figures that had been used in the past; and to pay for the changes with real cuts in spending and fair taxes.

To create more jobs, I proposed a permanent investment tax credit for small businesses, which employed 40 percent of the workforce but were creating most of our new jobs, and the establishment of community development banks and empowerment zones, two of my campaign commitments, which were designed to bring new loans and investments into poor areas. I also asked for more money for roads, bridges, mass transit, high-tech information systems, and environmental cleanups to increase productivity and employment.

On education, I recommended increased investments in and higher standards for public schools, and incentives to encourage more students to go to college, including my national service initiative. I complimented Congress on passing the family leave law, and asked them to follow up with tougher child-support enforcement. On crime, I asked for passage of the Brady bill, military-style boot camps for first-time nonviolent offenders, and my proposal to put 100,000 new police on the streets.

I then asked Congress to help me change the way government worked, by enacting campaign finance reform and registration requirements for lobbyists, and eliminating the tax deduction for lobbyists' expenses. I committed to reduce the size of the federal workforce by 100,000, and to cut administrative expenses, saving $9 billion. I asked Congress to help me slow spiraling health-care costs, and said that we could continue modest defense downsizing but that our responsibilities as the world's only superpower required us to spend enough to keep our military the best trained and equipped in the world.

I saved taxes for last, recommending that we increase the top income tax rate from 31 to 36 percent on incomes over $180,000, with a 10 percent surcharge on incomes over $250,000; raise the corporate income tax rate from 34 to 36 percent on incomes over $10 million; end the tax subsidy that made it more profitable for a company to shut down its American operations and move overseas than to reinvest at home; subject more of the income of the best-off Social Security recipients to taxation; and enact the BTU tax. The income tax rates would increase on only the top 1.2 percent of earners; the Social Security increase would apply to 13 percent of recipients; and the energy tax would cost about $17 per month for people with incomes of $40,000 or more a year. For families with incomes of $30,000 or less, the EITC would more than offset the cost of the BTU tax. The taxes and budget would enable us to reduce the deficit by about $500 billion over five years at present economic estimates.

At the end of the speech, I did my best to bring home the magnitude of the deficit problem, pointing out that if present trends continued, within a decade the annual deficit would increase to at least $635 billion a year from this year's $290 billion, and that interest payments on our accumulated debt would become America's largest budget item, taking more than twenty cents of every tax dollar. To show I was serious about deficit reduction, I invited Alan Greenspan to sit with Hillary in the First Lady's box in the House gallery. To show he was serious about it, Greenspan came, overcoming his understandable reluctance to make what could be seen as a political appearance.

After the speech, which was generally well received, all the commentators noted that I had abandoned the middle-class tax cut. So I had, but a lot of my other promises were fulfilled in the economic plan. Over the next few days, Al

Gore, the cabinet members, and I fanned out across the country to sell it. Alan Greenspan praised it. So did Paul Tsongas, who said the Clinton who spoke to Congress was not the Clinton he ran against, which, of course, is what my political advisors and some congressional Democrats were worried about.

There were enough important and controversial proposals in the speech to keep Congress busy for the rest of the year, not to mention the other legislation that already was, or soon would be, on their calendar. I knew that there would be a lot of ups and downs before the economic program passed, and that I wouldn't be able to spend all of my time pushing it. Foreign problems and domestic developments wouldn't permit it.

On the home front, February ended in violence. On the twenty-sixth, a bomb exploded at Manhattan's World Trade Center, killing six people and injuring more than one thousand. The investigation quickly revealed it to be the work of terrorists from the Middle East, who hadn't covered their tracks very well. The first arrests were made March 4; eventually, six of the conspirators were convicted in federal court in New York and each sentenced to 240 years in prison. I was pleased with the effectiveness of our law-enforcement work, but troubled by the evident vulnerability of our open society to terror. My national security team began to devote more attention to terror networks and what we could do to protect ourselves and free societies around the world against them.

On February 28, four agents from the Bureau of Alcohol, Tobacco, and Firearms were killed and sixteen others wounded at the onset of a confrontation with a religious cult, the Branch Davidians, at their compound outside Waco, Texas. The Davidians were suspected of illegal firearms violations. The sect's messianic leader, David Koresh, believed he was Christ reincarnate, the only person who knew the secret of the seven seals referred to in the book of Revelation. Koresh had almost hypnotic mind control over the men, women, and children who followed him; a large arsenal of weapons, which he was obviously prepared to use; and enough food to hold out for a long time. The standoff between the Davidians and the FBI dragged out for almost two months. During that time, several adults and children left, but most of them stayed, with Koresh promising to surrender but always finding an excuse to delay doing so.

On Sunday night, April 18, Janet Reno came to the White House to tell me that the FBI wanted to storm the compound, apprehend Koresh and any of his followers who had taken part in killing the agents or some other crime, and free the rest of them. Janet said she was concerned by FBI reports that Koresh was sexually abusing children, most of them preteens, and that he might be planning a mass suicide. The FBI had also told her that it couldn't keep so many of its resources tied down in one place forever. They wanted to raid the compound the next day, using armored vehicles to break holes in the buildings, then blast tear gas into them, a maneuver they estimated would force all the members to surrender within two hours. Reno had to approve the assault and wanted my okay first.

Several years earlier, I had faced a similar situation as governor. A right-wing extremist group had established a compound in the mountains of north Arkansas. Among the men, women, and children who lived there were two suspects wanted for murder. The people lived in several cabins, each of which had a trapdoor that led to a dugout from which they could fire on approaching authorities. And they had a lot of weapons to fire. The FBI wanted to storm them, too. At a meeting I convened with the FBI, our state police, and cooperating law-enforcement people from Missouri and Oklahoma, I listened to the FBI's case, then said that before I could approve the action, I wanted someone who'd fought in the jungles of Vietnam to fly over the place in a helicopter and make an assessment. The battlewise veteran who made the inspection for me returned to say, "If those

people can shoot at all, you'll lose fifty men in the assault."
I called off the raid, put a blockade around the camp, cut off
food stamp aid to the several families who had been receiving it, and prevented anyone who left the premises to get
supplies from going back. Eventually the holdouts gave in,
and the suspects were apprehended with no loss of life.

When Janet made her case to me, I thought we should try
what had worked in Arkansas before we approved the FBI
raid. She countered that the FBI was tired of waiting; that
the standoff was costing the government a million dollars a
week and tying up law-enforcement resources needed elsewhere; that the Branch Davidians could hold out longer than
the Arkansas people had; and that the possibilities of child
sexual abuse and mass suicide were real, because Koresh
was crazy and so were many of his followers. Finally, I told
her that if she thought it was the right thing to do, she could
go ahead.

The next day, as I watched CNN on a television just outside the Oval Office, I saw Koresh's compound in flames.
The raid had gone terribly wrong. After the FBI fired the
tear gas into the buildings where the people were holed up,
the Davidians started a fire. It got worse when they opened
the windows to let the tear gas out and also let in a hard
wind off the Texas plains, which stoked the flames. When it
ended, more than eighty people had died, including twenty-
five children; only nine survived. I knew I needed to speak to
the press and take responsibility for the fiasco. So did Dee
Dee Myers and Bruce Lindsey. But several times during the
day, when I wanted to go ahead, George Stephanopoulos
urged me to wait, saying we didn't know whether anyone
was still alive or whether, if Koresh heard my words, he
might snap and kill them, too. Janet Reno did appear before the cameras, explained what happened, and took full
responsibility for the raid. As the first woman to hold the
attorney general's post, she thought it was important not to
pass the buck. By the time I finally talked to the press about
Waco, Reno was being praised and I was being criticized for
letting her take the fall.

For the second time in less than twenty-four hours, I had

accepted advice that ran counter to my instincts. I didn't blame George. He was young and cautious and had given me his honest, albeit mistaken, opinion. But I was furious at myself, first for agreeing to the raid against my better judgment, then for delaying a public acknowledgment of responsibility for it. One of the most important decisions a President has to make is when to take the advice of the people who work for him and when to reject it. Nobody can be right all the time, but it's a lot easier to live with bad decisions that you believed in when you made them than with those your advisors say are right but your gut says are wrong. After Waco, I resolved to go with my gut.

Perhaps one reason I didn't trust my instincts enough is that the administration was being hammered hard in Washington and I was being second-guessed at every turn. After a great initial appearance on Capitol Hill, Hillary was being criticized for the closed meetings of her health-care task force. Since they were consulting with hundreds of people, nothing they did was secret; they were simply trying to move with dispatch over many immensely complicated matters to reach my overly ambitious goal of presenting a health-care plan to Congress within one hundred days. The task force heard testimony from over 1,100 groups, had more than 200 meetings with members of Congress, and held public meetings all around the country. Its reputation for being secretive was exaggerated. In the end, the task force operation proved too unwieldy and was allowed to expire, and we couldn't make the hundred-day deadline anyway.

As if all this weren't enough, I also suffered the defeat of my short-term stimulus package, which was designed to create 500,000 jobs by getting money out quickly to cities and states for infrastructure projects. The economy was still growing slowly, it needed the boost, and the modest nonrecurring expenditures wouldn't have made our deficit problem worse. The House passed the bill handily and the Senate was for it, too, but Bob Dole had more than forty Republican senators who were willing to filibuster it. After the first filibuster vote, we should have tried to negotiate a smaller package with Dole, or accepted a less ambitious compromise proposal offered by Senators John Breaux and David Boren, two conservative Democrats. Senator Robert Byrd, who was handling the proposal, was adamant that if we didn't bend, we could break the filibuster. But we couldn't, and finally admitted defeat on April 21, two days after Waco.

In my first term, the Republicans resorted to the filibuster to an unprecedented extent, thwarting the will of the congressional majority, out of either conviction or a desire to prove that I couldn't lead. Senator George Mitchell had to have twelve votes to break filibusters just in my first hundred days.

On March 19, we suffered a personal blow that put politics in perspective when Hillary's dad had a massive stroke. Hillary rushed to his bedside at St. Vincent's Hospital in Little Rock, with Chelsea and my brother-in-law Tony. Dr. Drew Kumpuris, Hugh's doctor and our friend, told Hillary that her father had suffered severe brain damage and was in a deep coma from which, in all probability, he would never emerge. I got there two days later. Hillary, Chelsea, Dorothy, and his sons, Hugh and Tony, had been taking turns talking, even singing, to Hugh, who looked as if he was just sleeping peacefully. We didn't know how long he would last, and I could stay only a day. I left Hillary in the good company of her family, the Thomasons, Carolyn Huber, who had known Hugh ever since her days as the administrator of the Governor's Mansion, and Lisa Caputo, Hillary's press secretary and a favorite of Hugh's because like him she came from eastern Pennsylvania, near his hometown of Scranton.

The next Sunday, I flew home again for a couple of days. I wanted to be with my family, even though there was nothing to do but wait. The doctor told us that Hugh was essentially brain dead. Over the weekend, the family decided to take him off the machine that was breathing for him, and we all said prayers and good-byes, but Hugh didn't go for it. His strong old heart just kept beating. Though I had been able to attend to most of my duties in Arkansas, I had to return to

Washington on Tuesday. I hated to leave, knowing it was the last time I'd ever see my father-in-law. I loved Hugh Rodham, with his no-nonsense gruffness and fierce family loyalty. I was grateful that he had accepted me into the fold twenty years earlier, when I was scruffy, penniless, and, worst of all, a Democrat. I would miss our pinochle games and political arguments, and just knowing he was around.

On April 4, with Hugh still hanging on, Hillary had to return to Washington, too, to get Chelsea back to school after spring break, and to get back to work. She had promised to give a speech on April 6 at the University of Texas at Austin for Liz Carpenter, who had been Lady Bird Johnson's press secretary. Liz pressed her not to cancel, and she decided to go. At a time when she was grief-stricken, she reached deep inside herself to say that, as we moved into the new millennium, "We need a new politics of meaning. We need a new ethos of individual responsibility and caring. We need a new definition of civil society which answers the unanswerable questions posed by both the market forces and the governmental ones, as to how we can have a society that fills us up again and makes us feel that we are part of something bigger than ourselves." Hillary had been moved to make this argument by reading an article written by Lee Atwater shortly before he died at forty of cancer. Atwater had become famous and feared for his ruthless attacks on Democrats while working for Presidents Reagan and Bush. As he faced death, he found that a life devoted only to getting power, wealth, and prestige left a lot to be desired, and he hoped that in a parting shot, he could push us to a higher purpose. In Austin, on April 6, bearing her own sorrow, Hillary tried to define that purpose. I loved what she said and was proud of her for saying it.

The next day, Hugh Rodham died. We had a memorial service for him in Little Rock, then took him home to Scranton for the funeral at the Court Street Methodist Church. I eulogized the man who had put aside his Republican convictions to work for me in 1974, and who, through a lifetime of learning from personal experience, had let go of all the bigotries he had grown up with. He lost his racism when he worked with a black man in Chicago. He lost his homophobia when he was befriended and looked after by his gay neighbors, a doctor and a nurse, in Little Rock. He had grown up in football-fanatical eastern Pennsylvania, where the Catholic stars went to Notre Dame and the Protestant ones like him played for Penn State. The divide revealed a prejudice against Catholics that was also part of Hugh's upbringing. He gave that up, too. We all thought it fitting that his last days were spent in St. Vincent's Hospital, where the Catholic nuns took loving care of him.

THREE

THOUGH MOST OF the headlines of my early months in office concerned the effort to define, defend, and pass my economic plan; gays in the military; and Hillary's health-care work, foreign policy was always there, an ever-present part of my daily routine and concern. The general impression among Washington observers was that I wasn't too interested in foreign affairs and wanted to spend as little time as possible on them. It's true that the overwhelming focus of the campaign had been on domestic issues; our economic troubles demanded that. But, as I had said over and over, increasing global interdependence was erasing the divide between foreign and domestic policy. And the "new world order" President Bush had proclaimed after the fall of the Berlin Wall was rife with chaos and big, unresolved questions.

Early on, my national security advisor, Tony Lake, had declared that success in foreign affairs is often defined by preventing or defusing problems before they develop into headaches and headline grabbers. "If we do a really good job," he said, "the public may never know it, because the dogs won't bark." When I took office, we had a whole kennel full of barking hounds, with Bosnia and Russia howling the loudest, and several others, including Somalia, Haiti, North Korea, and Japan's trade policy, growling in the background.

The breakup of the Soviet Union and the collapse of communism in the Warsaw Pact nations raised the prospect that Europe might become democratic, peaceful, and united for the first time in history. Whether it would happen turned on four great questions: Would East and West Germany be reunited; would Russia become a truly democratic, stable, nonimperial nation; what would happen to Yugoslavia, a cauldron of diverse ethnic provinces, which had been held together by the iron will of Marshal Tito; and would Russia and the former Communist countries be integrated into the

European Union and the transatlantic NATO alliance with the United States and Canada?

By the time I became President, Germany had been reunited under the visionary leadership of Chancellor Helmut Kohl, with the strong support of President Bush and despite reservations in Europe about the political and economic power of a resurgent Germany. The other three questions were still open, and I knew that one of my most important responsibilities as President was to see that they were answered correctly.

During the election campaign, both President Bush and I had supported aid to Russia. At first I was more assertive than he was, but after prodding by former president Nixon, Bush announced that the G-7, the seven largest industrial nations—the United States, Germany, France, Italy, the United Kingdom, Canada, and Japan—would provide $24 billion to support democracy and economic reform in Russia. By the time Yeltsin came to Washington in June 1992 as Russia's president, he was grateful and openly supporting Bush's reelection. As I mentioned earlier, Yeltsin did agree to a courtesy meeting with me at Blair House on June 18, thanks to the friendship between Foreign Minister Andrei Kozyrev and Toby Gati, one of my foreign policy advisors. It didn't bother me that Yeltsin was supporting Bush; I just wanted him to know that if I won, I would support him.

In November, a couple of days after the election, Yeltsin called to congratulate me and to urge me to come to Moscow as soon as possible to reaffirm America's support for his reforms in the face of mounting opposition at home. Yeltsin had a hard row to hoe. He had been elected president of Russia in June 1991, when Russia was still part of the crumbling Soviet Union. In August, Soviet president Mikhail Gorbachev was put under house arrest at his summer retreat on the Black Sea by conspirators intent on staging a coup d'état. Russian citizens took to the Moscow streets in protest. The defining moment of the drama came when Yeltsin, in office for just two months, climbed on a tank in front of the Russian White House, the parliamentary building under siege by the coup plotters. He urged the

Russian people to defend their hard-won democracy. In effect, he was telling the reactionaries, "You may steal our freedom, but you'll have to do it over my dead body." Yeltsin's heroic clarion call galvanized domestic and international support, and the coup failed. By December, the Soviet Union had dissolved into a collection of independent states, and Russia had taken the Soviet seat on the United Nations Security Council.

But Yeltsin's problems were not over. Reactionary elements, smarting from their loss of power, opposed his determination to withdraw Soviet troops from the Baltic nations of Estonia, Lithuania, and Latvia. Economic disaster loomed, as the rotting remains of the Soviet economy were exposed to free-market reforms, which brought inflation and the sale of state-owned assets at low prices to a new class of ultra-rich businessmen called "oligarchs," who made America's robber barons of the late nineteenth century look like Puritan preachers. Organized-crime networks also moved into the vacuum created by the collapse of the Soviet state and spread their tentacles across the globe. Yeltsin had destroyed the old system, but had not yet been able to build a new one. He also had not developed a good working relationship with the Duma, Russia's parliament, partly because he was by nature averse to compromise, partly because the Duma was full of people who longed for the old order or an equally oppressive new one rooted in ultra-nationalism.

Yeltsin was up to his ears in alligators, and I wanted to help him. I was encouraged to do so by Bob Strauss, whom President Bush had sent to Moscow as our ambassador even though he was an ardent Democrat and a former chairman of the Democratic National Committee. Strauss said I could work with Yeltsin and give him good political advice, and he urged me to do both.

I was inclined to accept Yeltsin's invitation to go to Russia, but Tony Lake said Moscow shouldn't be my first foreign stop, and the rest of my team said it would divert attention from our domestic agenda. They made strong arguments, but the United States had a big stake in Russia's success, and we sure didn't want hard-liners, either Communists or ultra-nationalists, in control there. Boris made it easier when he suggested a meeting in a mutually acceptable third country.

About this time, I persuaded my old friend and Oxford housemate Strobe Talbott to leave *Time* magazine and come to work in the State Department to help us with policy on the former Soviet Union. By then, Strobe and I had been discussing Russian history and politics for almost twenty-five years. Ever since he translated and edited Khrushchev's memoirs, Strobe had known and cared more about Russia and the Russian people than anyone else I knew. He had a fine analytical mind and a fertile imagination behind his proper professorial façade, and I trusted both his judgment and his willingness to tell me the unvarnished truth. There was no position in the State Department hierarchy that described what I wanted Strobe to do, so he set out to create one, with the blessing of Warren Christopher and the help of Dick Holbrooke, an investment banker and veteran foreign policy hand who had provided advice during the campaign and who would become one of the most important figures in my administration.

Eventually, Strobe's new job had a title: ambassador-at-large and special advisor to the secretary of state on the new independent states of the former Soviet Union. He later became deputy secretary of state. I don't think five people could repeat Strobe's title, but everybody knew what he did: he was our "go to" man on Russia. For eight years, he was by my side in all my meetings with Presidents Yeltsin and Vladimir Putin, eighteen with Yeltsin alone. Since Strobe spoke fluent Russian and took copious notes, his participation with me and his own interactions with the Russians guaranteed a precision and accuracy in our work that would prove invaluable. Strobe chronicles our eight-year odyssey in his book *The Russia Hand*, which is remarkable not only for its insights but for the verbatim accounts of the colorful conversations I had with Yeltsin. Unlike what happens in most books of the genre, the quotes are not reconstructions; they are, for good or ill, what we actually said.

Strobe's main point is that I became my own "Russia hand" because, while not an expert on Russia, I knew "one big thing: on the twin issues that had constituted the casus belli of the cold war—democracy versus dictatorship at home and cooperation versus competition abroad"—Yeltsin and I were, "in principle, on the same side."

During the transition period, I had talked to Strobe a lot about the deteriorating situation in Russia and the imperative of averting disaster. At Renaissance Weekend, Strobe and his wife, Brooke, who had campaigned full-time with Hillary and was about to become head of the White House Fellows program, were jogging with me on Hilton Head beach. We wanted to talk about Russia, but the leader of our group, the great Olympic hurdler Edwin Moses, set such a brisk pace that I couldn't keep up and talk at the same time. We came upon Hillary taking her morning walk, so the three of us had an excuse to slow down and visit. President Bush was in Moscow signing the START II treaty with Yeltsin. It was good news, though like everything progressive Yeltsin did, it was facing strong opposition in the Duma. I told Strobe that things were changing so much in Russia that we couldn't have a completely defensive strategy; we had to help solidify and accelerate positive developments, especially those that would improve the Russian economy.

In February, I went over to Strobe's house one night to see his family and talk about Russia. Strobe told me about a recent meeting he'd had with Richard Nixon, in which the former President had urged us to support Yeltsin heavily. The $24 billion assistance package President Bush had announced the previous spring hadn't done that, because the international financial institutions wouldn't release the money until Russia had restructured its economy. We needed to do something now.

In early March, Yeltsin and I agreed to meet on April 3 and 4 in Vancouver, Canada. On March 8, Richard Nixon called on me at the White House to urge me personally to support Yeltsin. After a brief visit with Hillary and Chelsea, in which he reminded them that he was raised a Quaker and that his daughters, like Chelsea, had gone to Sidwell Friends School, he got down to business, saying I would be remembered as President more for what I did with Russia than for my economic policy. Later that night, I called Strobe to report on the Nixon conversation and to stress again how important it was that we do something at Vancouver to help Russia, with a high-impact follow-up at the annual G-7 summit in Tokyo in July. All through March, as I got updates from our foreign policy team and Larry Summers and his assistant David Lipton at Treasury, I pushed them to think bigger and do more.

Meanwhile, in Moscow, the Duma was reducing Yeltsin's power and endorsing the fruitless inflationary policies of the Russian Central Bank. On March 20, Yeltsin struck back with a speech announcing a public referendum for April 25 to determine whether he or the Duma ran the country; until then, he said, his presidential decrees would remain in effect, no matter what the Duma did. I watched the speech on one of two television sets in my private dining room off the Oval Office. The other TV was showing the NCAA tournament basketball game between the Arkansas Razorbacks and St. John's University. I had a dog in both hunts.

My entire foreign policy team and I had a vigorous debate about how I should respond to Yeltsin's speech. They all cautioned restraint, because Yeltsin was stretching the limits of his constitutional authority, and because he might lose. I disagreed. Yeltsin was in the fight of his life against the old Communists and other reactionaries. He was going to the people with a referendum. And I didn't care about the risk of losing—I reminded our team that I had lost plenty of times myself. I had no interest in hedging my bets, and instructed Tony Lake to draft a statement of strong support. When he presented it to me, I made it even stronger and gave it to the press. In this case, I went with my gut instincts and placed a bet that Russia would stick with Yeltsin, and stay on the right side of history. My optimism was bolstered by Arkansas' come-from-behind victory in the ball game.

Finally, in March, I got an assistance program I could support: $1.6 billion in direct aid to help Russia stabilize its economy, including money to provide housing for decommissioned military officers, positive work programs for now underemployed and frequently unpaid nuclear scientists, and more assistance in dismantling nuclear weapons under the recently enacted Nunn-Lugar program; food and medicine for those suffering from shortages; aid to support small business, independent media outlets, nongovernmental organizations, political parties, and labor unions; and an exchange program to bring tens of thousands of students and young professionals to the United States. The aid package was four times what the previous administration had allocated and three times what I had originally recommended.

Although a public poll said that 75 percent of the American people were opposed to giving Russia more money, and we were already in a hard fight for the economic plan, I felt we had no choice but to press ahead. America had spent trillions of dollars on defense to win the Cold War; we couldn't risk reversal over less than $2 billion and a bad poll. To the surprise of my staff, the congressional leaders, including the Republicans, agreed with me. At a meeting I convened to push the plan, Senator Joe Biden, the chairman of the Foreign Relations Committee, strongly endorsed the aid package. Bob Dole came around on the argument that we didn't want to foul up the post–Cold War era the way the victors in World War I had done. Their shortsightedness contributed mightily to World War II, in which Dole had served so heroically. Newt Gingrich was passionately in favor of helping Russia, saying it was a "great defining moment" for America and we had to do the right thing. As I told Strobe, Newt was trying to "out-Russia" me, which I was only too happy to have him do.

When Yeltsin and I got together on April 3, the meeting began a little awkwardly, with Yeltsin explaining that he had to walk a fine line between receiving U.S. assistance to help Russia's transition to democracy and looking as if he was under America's thumb. When we got to the details of our aid package, he said he liked it but needed more for housing for the military people he was bringing home from the Baltic states, many of whom were actually living in tents. After we resolved that issue, Yeltsin abruptly went on the offensive, demanding that I repeal the Jackson-Vanik amendment, a 1974 law tying U.S. trade to free immigration from Russia, and end the observance of Captive Nations Week, which highlighted Soviet domination of countries like Poland and Hungary that were now free. Both these laws were largely symbolic, without real impact on our relations, and I couldn't expend the political capital to change them and at the same time succeed in getting real help to Russia.

After the first session, my people worried that I'd let Yeltsin harangue me the way Khrushchev had hectored Kennedy in their famous meeting in Vienna in 1961. They didn't want me to look weak. I wasn't worried about that, because the historical analogy was flawed. Yeltsin wasn't trying to make me look bad as Khrushchev had done to Kennedy; he was trying to make himself look good against enemies at home who were trying to do him in. In the week before our summit, they had tried to impeach him in the Duma. They had failed, but the motion got a lot of votes. I could take a little bombastic posturing if it helped to keep Russia on the right road.

In the afternoon, we agreed on a way to institutionalize our cooperation, with a commission headed by Vice President Gore and Russian prime minister Viktor Chernomyrdin. The idea was developed by Strobe and Georgi Mamedov, the Russian deputy foreign minister, and it worked better than any of us could have imagined, thanks largely to the consistent and concentrated efforts made over the years by Al Gore and his Russian counterparts in working through a host of difficult, contentious problems.

On Sunday, April 4, we met in a more formal setting to discuss security issues, with Yeltsin and his advisors sitting across the table from me and mine. As before, Yeltsin began aggressively, demanding that we change our arms control positions and open American markets to Russian products like satellite rocket launchers without requiring export controls that would prohibit Russian sales of military technology to America's adversaries like Iran and Iraq. With the help of our hard-nosed expert, Lynn Davis, I hung tough on export controls and rebuffed the arms control demands by referring them to our staffs for further study.

The atmosphere brightened when we moved on to economics. I described the economic package as "cooperation," not "assistance," then asked Lloyd Bentsen to outline the proposals we would make to the G-7 in Tokyo. Yeltsin became alarmed when he realized that we couldn't get him any money before the April 25 referendum. Though I couldn't give Boris the $500 million check he wanted, at the press conference following our final session I made it plain that a lot of money was coming, because the United States supported Russia's democracy, its reforms, and its leader.

I left Vancouver with more confidence in Yeltsin and a better understanding of the magnitude of his challenges and his visceral determination to overcome them. And I liked him. He was a big bear of a man, full of apparent contradictions. He had grown up in primitive conditions that made my childhood look like a Rockefeller's, and he could be crude, but he had a fine mind capable of grasping the subtleties of a situation. He would attack one minute and embrace the next. He seemed by turns coldly calculating and genuinely emotional, petty and generous, mad at the world and full of fun. Once when we were walking through my hotel together, a Russian journalist asked him if he was happy with our meeting. He responded quickly, "Happy? One cannot be happy outside the presence of a beautiful woman. But I am satisfied." As everyone knows, Yeltsin had a fondness for vodka, but, by and large, in all our dealings he was alert, well prepared, and effective in representing his country. Compared with the realistic alternatives, Russia was lucky to have him at the helm. He loved his country, loathed communism, and wanted Russia to be both great and good. Whenever anyone made a snide remark about Yeltsin's drinking, I was reminded of what Lincoln allegedly said when Washington snobs made the same criticism of General Grant, by far his most aggressive and successful commander in the Civil War: "Find out what he drinks, and give it to the other generals."

When I got back to Washington, I increased the aid

package again, proposing $2.5 billion for all the former Soviet states, with two-thirds going to Russia. On April 25, a large majority of Russian voters supported Yeltsin, his policies, and his desire for a new Duma. After a little more than one hundred days in office, we had made great strides in bolstering Yeltsin and Russian democracy. Unfortunately, the same could not be said about our efforts to end the slaughter and ethnic cleansing in Bosnia.

In 1989, as the Soviet Union crumbled and communism's demise in Europe accelerated, the question of what political philosophy would replace it was being answered in different ways in different countries. The westernmost part of the former Soviet empire plainly preferred democracy, a cause championed for decades by immigrants to the United States from Poland, Hungary, Czechoslovakia, and the Baltic states. In Russia, Yeltsin and other democrats were fighting a rear-guard action against Communists and ultra-nationalists. In Yugoslavia, as the nation struggled to reconcile the competing claims of its ethnic and religious constituencies, Serbian nationalism prevailed over democracy under the leadership of the country's dominant political figure, Slobodan Milosevic.

By 1991, Yugoslavia's westernmost provinces, Slovenia and Croatia, both predominantly Catholic, had declared independence from Yugoslavia. Fighting then broke out between Serbia and Croatia, and spilled over into Bosnia, the most ethnically diverse province of Yugoslavia, where Muslims constituted about 45 percent of the population, Serbs were just over 30 percent, and Croatians about 17 percent. The so-called ethnic differences in Bosnia were really political and religious. Bosnia had been the meeting place of three imperial expansions: the Catholic Holy Roman Empire from the west, the Orthodox Christian movement from the east, and the Muslim Ottoman Empire from the south. In 1991, the Bosnians were governed by a coalition of national unity headed by the leading Muslim politician, Alija Izetbegovic, and including the militant Serbian nationalist leader Radovan Karadzic, a Sarajevo psychiatrist.

At first Izetbegovic wanted Bosnia to be an autonomous multi-ethnic, multi-religious province of Yugoslavia. When Slovenia and Croatia were recognized by the international community as independent nations, Izetbegovic decided that the only way Bosnia could escape Serbian dominance was to seek independence, too. Karadzic and his allies, who were tied closely to Milosevic, had a very different agenda. They were supportive of Milosevic's desire to turn as much of Yugoslavia as he could hold on to, including Bosnia, into a Greater Serbia. On March 1, 1992, a referendum was held on whether Bosnia should become an independent nation in which all citizens and groups would be treated equally. The result was an almost unanimous approval of independence, but only two-thirds of the electorate voted. Karadzic had ordered the Serbs to stay away from the polls and most of them did. By then, Serb paramilitary forces had begun killing unarmed Muslims, driving them from their homes in Serb-dominated areas in the hope of carving up Bosnia into ethnic enclaves, or "cantons," by force. This cruel policy came to be known by a curiously antiseptic name: ethnic cleansing.

The European Community envoy, Lord Carrington, tried to get the parties to agree to peacefully divide the country into ethnic regions but failed, because there was no way to do it without leaving large numbers of one group on land controlled by another, and because many Bosnians wanted to keep their country together, with the different groups living together in peace, as they had done successfully for most of the previous five hundred years.

In April 1992, the European Community recognized Bosnia as an independent state for the first time since the fifteenth century. Meanwhile, Serbian paramilitary forces continued to terrorize Muslim communities and kill civilians, all the while using the media to convince local Serbs that it was they who were under attack from the Muslims and who had to defend themselves. On April 27, Milosevic announced a new state of Yugoslavia comprising Serbia and Montenegro. He then made a show of withdrawing his army from Bosnia, while leaving armaments, supplies, and Bosnian Serb soldiers under the leadership of his handpicked commander,

Ratko Mladic. The fighting and killing raged throughout 1992, with European Community leaders struggling to contain it and the Bush administration, uncertain of what to do and unwilling to take on another problem in an election year, content to leave the matter in Europe's hands.

To its credit, the Bush administration did urge the United Nations to impose economic sanctions on Serbia, a measure initially opposed by Secretary-General Boutros Boutros-Ghali, the French, and the British, who said they wanted to give Milosevic a chance to stop the very violence he had incited. Finally, sanctions were imposed in late May, but with little effect, as supplies continued to reach the Serbs from friendly neighbors. The United Nations also continued to maintain the arms embargo against the Bosnian government that originally had been imposed against all Yugoslavia in late 1991. The problem with the embargo was that the Serbs had enough weapons and ammunition on hand to fight for years; therefore, the only consequence of maintaining the embargo was to make it virtually impossible for the Bosnians to defend themselves. Somehow they managed to hold out throughout 1992, acquiring some arms by capturing them from Serb forces, or in small shipments from Croatia that managed to evade the NATO blockade of the Croatian coast.

In the summer of 1992, as television and print media finally brought the horror of a Serb-run detention camp in northern Bosnia home to Europeans and Americans, I spoke out in favor of NATO air strikes with U.S. involvement. Later, when it became clear that the Serbs were engaging in the systematic slaughter of Bosnian Muslims, especially targeting local leaders for extermination, I suggested lifting the arms embargo. Instead, the Europeans focused on ending the violence. British prime minister John Major attempted to get the Serbs to lift the siege of Bosnian towns and put their heavy weapons under UN supervision. At the same time, many private and government humanitarian missions were launched to provide food and medicine, and the United Nations sent in eight thousand troops to protect the aid convoys.

In late October, just before our election, Lord David

Owen, the new European negotiator, and the UN negotiator, former U.S. secretary of state Cyrus Vance, put forward a proposal to turn Bosnia into a number of autonomous provinces that would be responsible for all government functions except defense and foreign affairs, which would be handled by a weak central government. The cantons were sufficiently numerous, with the dominant ethnic groups geographically divided in a way that Vance and Owen thought would make it impossible for the Serb-controlled areas to merge with Milosevic's Yugoslavia to form a Greater Serbia. There were several problems with their plan, the two largest of which were that the sweeping powers of the canton governments made it clear that Muslims couldn't safely return to their homes in Serb-controlled areas, and that the vagueness of the canton boundaries invited continued Serb aggression intended to expand their areas, as well as the ongoing, though less severe, conflict between Croats and Muslims.

By the time I became President, the arms embargo and European support for the Vance-Owen plan had weakened Muslim resistance to the Serbs, even as evidence of their slaughter of Muslim civilians and violations of human rights in detention camps continued to surface. In early February, I decided not to endorse the Vance-Owen plan. On the fifth, I met with Prime Minister Brian Mulroney of Canada and was pleased to hear him say he didn't like it either. A few days later, we completed a Bosnian policy review, with Warren Christopher announcing that the United States would like to negotiate a new agreement and would be willing to help enforce it.

On February 23, UN Secretary-General Boutros-Ghali agreed with me on an emergency plan to airdrop humanitarian supplies to the Bosnians. The next day, in my first meeting with John Major, he too supported the airdrops. The airdrops would help a lot of people stay alive, but would do nothing to address the causes of the crisis.

By March, we seemed to be making some progress. Economic sanctions had been strengthened and seemed to be hurting the Serbs, who were also concerned about the possibility of military action by NATO. But we were a long way from a unified policy. On the ninth, in my first meeting with French president François Mitterrand, he made clear to me that, although he had sent five thousand French troops to Bosnia as part of a UN humanitarian force to deliver aid and contain the violence, he was more sympathetic to the Serbs than I was, and less willing to see a Muslim-led unified Bosnia.

On the twenty-sixth, I met with Helmut Kohl, who deplored what was happening and who, like me, had favored lifting the arms embargo. But we couldn't budge the British and French, who felt lifting the embargo would only prolong the war and endanger the UN forces on the ground that included their troops but not ours. Izetbegovic was also in the White House on the twenty-sixth to meet with Al Gore, whose national security aide, Leon Fuerth, was responsible for our success in making the embargo more effective. Both Kohl and I told Izetbegovic we were doing our best to get the Europeans to take a stronger stand to support him. Five days later, we succeeded in getting the United Nations to extend a "no fly" zone over all of Bosnia, to at least deprive the Serbs of the benefit of their monopoly on airpower. It was a good thing to do, but it didn't slow the killing much.

In April, a team of U.S. military, diplomatic, and humanitarian aid personnel returned from Bosnia urging that we intervene militarily to stop the suffering. On the sixteenth, the United Nations accepted our recommendation for declaring a "safe area" around Srebrenica, a town in eastern Bosnia where Serb killing and ethnic cleansing had been especially outrageous. On the twenty-second, at the dedication of the U.S. Holocaust Memorial Museum, Holocaust survivor Elie Wiesel publicly pleaded with me to do more to stop the violence. By the end of the month, my foreign policy team recommended that if we could not secure a Serbian cease-fire, we should lift the arms embargo against the Muslims and launch air strikes against Serb military targets. As Warren Christopher left for Europe to seek support for this policy, the Bosnian Serb leader, Radovan Karadzic, hoping to avoid the air strikes, finally signed the UN peace plan, even though his assembly had rejected it just six days earlier.

I didn't believe for a minute that his signature signaled a change in his long-term objectives.

At the end of our first one hundred days, we were nowhere near a satisfactory solution to the Bosnian crisis. The British and French rebuffed Warren Christopher's overtures and reaffirmed their right to take the lead in dealing with the situation. The problem with their position, of course, was that if the Serbs could take the economic hit of the tough sanctions, they could continue their aggressive ethnic cleansing without fear of further punishment. The Bosnian tragedy would drag on for more than two years, leaving more than 250,000 dead and 2.5 million driven from their homes, until NATO air attacks, aided by Serb military losses on the ground, led to an American diplomatic initiative that would bring the war to an end.

I had stepped into what Dick Holbrooke called "the greatest collective security failure of the West since the 1930s." In his book *To End a War*, Holbrooke ascribes the failure to five factors: (1) a misreading of Balkan history, holding that the ethnic strife was too ancient and ingrained to be prevented by outsiders; (2) the apparent loss of Yugoslavia's strategic importance after the end of the Cold War; (3) the triumph of nationalism over democracy as the dominant ideology of post-Communist Yugoslavia; (4) the reluctance of the Bush administration to undertake another military commitment so soon after the 1991 Iraq war; and (5) the decision of the United States to turn the issue over to Europe instead of NATO, and the confused and passive European response. To Holbrooke's list I would add a sixth factor: some European leaders were not eager to have a Muslim state in the heart of the Balkans, fearing it might become a base for exporting extremism, a result that their neglect made more, not less, likely.

My own options were constrained by the dug-in positions I found when I took office. For example, I was reluctant to go along with Senator Dole in unilaterally lifting the arms embargo, for fear of weakening the United Nations (though we later did so in effect, by declining to enforce it). I also didn't want to divide the NATO alliance by unilaterally bombing Serb military positions, especially since there were European, but no American, soldiers on the ground with the UN mission. And I didn't want to send American troops there, putting them in harm's way under a UN mandate I thought was bound to fail. In May 1993, we were still a long way from a solution.

At the end of the first one hundred days of a new presidency, the press always does an assessment of how well the new administration is doing in keeping its campaign promises and dealing with the other challenges that have arisen. The consensus of the reviews was that my initial performance was mixed. On the positive side of the ledger, I had created a National Economic Council in the White House and put together an ambitious economic program to reverse twelve years of trickle-down economics, and it was making progress in the Congress. I had signed the family leave law, and the "motor voter" law to make voter registration easier, and had reversed the Reagan-Bush abortion policies, including the ban on fetal-tissue research and the gag rule. I had reduced the size of the White House staff, despite its increasing workload; for example, we received more mail in the first three and a half months than had come to the White House in all of 1992. I had also ordered a reduction of 100,000 in total federal employment, and put Vice President Gore in charge of finding new savings and better ways to serve the public with a "reinventing government" initiative whose considerable results would eventually prove the skeptics wrong. I had sent legislation to Congress to create my national service program, to double the Earned Income Tax Credit and create empowerment zones in poor communities, and to dramatically cut the cost of college loans, saving billions of dollars for both students and taxpayers. I had put health-care reform on a fast track and had taken strong action to strengthen democracy and reform in Russia. And I was blessed with a hardworking and able staff and cabinet who, apart from the leaks, worked well together, without the backbiting and infighting that had characterized many previous administrations. After a slow start, I had filled more required presidential appointments in the first hundred days than President Reagan or President Bush had in the same period of time, not bad considering how cumbersome and overly intrusive the whole appointments process had become. At one point, Senator Alan Simpson, the witty Republican whip from Wyoming, joked to me that the process was so overdone that he "wouldn't even want to have dinner with someone who could be confirmed by the U.S. Senate."

On the negative side, I had temporarily dropped the middle-class tax cut in the face of the growing deficit; lost the stimulus program to a Republican filibuster; maintained the Bush policy of forcibly returning Haitian refugees, though we were taking in more Haitians by other means; lost the gays-in-the-military fight; delayed presenting the health-care plan beyond my hundred-day goal; mishandled at least the public part of the Waco raid; and failed to convince Europe to join with the United States in taking a stronger stand in Bosnia, although we had increased humanitarian aid, strengthened sanctions against Serbia, and created an enforceable no-fly zone.

One reason my scorecard was mixed was that I was trying to do so much in the face of determined Republican opposition and mixed feelings among the American people about how much government could or should do. After all, the people had been told for twelve years that government was the source of all our problems, and was so incompetent it couldn't organize a two-car parade. Clearly, I had overestimated how much I could do in a hurry. The country had been going in one direction for more than a decade, living with wedge politics, reassuring bromides about how great we were, and the illusory, though fleeting, comforts of spending more and taxing less today and ignoring the consequences for tomorrow. It was going to take more than a hundred days to turn things around.

In addition to the pace of change, I may have overestimated the amount of change I could achieve, as well as how much of it the American people could digest. In one post–hundred days analysis, a Vanderbilt University political scientist, Erwin Hargrove, observed, "I wonder whether the president isn't spreading himself too thin." He was probably right, but there was so much to do, and I didn't stop trying to do it all at once until the voters hit me between the eyes with a two-by-four in the 1994 midterm elections. I had let my sense of urgency blot out the memory of another of my laws of politics: Everyone is for change in general, but against it in particular, when they themselves have to change.

The public struggles of the first hundred days didn't occur in a vacuum; at the same time, my family was adjusting to a dramatic change in our way of life and dealing with the loss of Hillary's dad. I loved being President and Hillary was deeply committed to her health-care work. Chelsea liked her school and was making new friends. We enjoyed living in the White House, hosting the social events, and having our friends stay with us.

The White House staff was getting used to a first family that kept longer, and later, hours. Though I came to rely on them and greatly value their service, it took me a while to get used to all the help I had in the White House. As governor, I'd lived in a mansion with a fine staff, and had been driven everywhere by the state police security detail. But on weekends, Hillary and I usually cooked for ourselves, and I drove the car to church on Sundays. Now I had valets who laid my clothes out every morning, packed for my trips, and went along to unpack and steam the wrinkles out; butlers who stayed late, came early, and worked weekends, serving me food and bringing me diet drinks and coffee; navy stewards who performed those same functions when I was in the Oval Office and traveling; a kitchen staff who prepared food for us even on weekends; ushers to take me up and down in the elevator and bring me papers to sign and memos to read at all hours; round-the-clock medical care; and the Secret Service, who wouldn't even let me ride in the front seat, much less drive.

One of the things I liked best about living in the White

House was the fresh flowers that filled the residence and office spaces. The White House always had beautifully arranged flowers. It's one of the things I would miss most after I left.

When we moved in, Hillary redid the little kitchen so that we could eat dinner there at night when it was just the three of us. The upstairs dining room was beautiful, but too big and formal for our taste unless we had guests. Hillary also fixed up the solarium on the third floor, a bright room that leads out to a balcony and the White House roof. We turned it into a family room. Whenever we had relatives or friends staying with us, we always gravitated to the solarium, to talk, watch TV, and play cards or board games. I became addicted to Master Boggle and a game called UpWords; it's basically a three-dimensional Scrabble game in which you get more points not by using odd letters or landing on certain spaces, but by building words upon words. I tried to get my family and friends into UpWords, succeeding with some more than others. My brother-in-law Hugh played countless games of UpWords with me, and Roger liked it. But Hillary, Tony, and Chelsea preferred our old standby, pinochle. I continued to play hearts with my staff and we all got hooked on a new card game that Steven Spielberg and Kate Capshaw taught us when they were visiting. It had a perfect name for Washington political life: Oh Hell!

The Secret Service had been with me since the New Hampshire primary, but once I got into the White House, I presented a challenge to them with my morning jogs. I had several jogging routes. Sometimes I drove out to Haines Point, which had a three-mile route around a public golf course. It was flat, but could be tough in the winter when the winds off the Potomac were strong. From time to time I also ran at Fort McNair, which has an oval route on the grounds of the National Defense University. My favorite jog by far was just to run out the Southwest Gate of the White House to the Mall, then up to the Lincoln Memorial, back down to the Capitol, and home. I met a lot of interesting people on those runs, and never tired of running through American history. When the Secret Service finally asked me to stop because of security concerns, I did, but I missed it.

To me, these public runs were a way to keep in touch with the world beyond the White House. To them, with the memory of John Hinckley's assassination attempt on President Reagan never far from their minds and with more knowledge than I had of the hate mail I was getting, my contacts with the public were a worrisome risk to be managed.

Al Gore helped me a lot in the early days, encouraging me to keep making hard decisions and put them behind me, and giving me a continuing crash course in how Washington works. Part of our regular routine was having lunch alone in my private dining room once a week. We took turns saying grace, then proceeded to talk about everything from our families to sports, books, and movies to the latest items on his agenda or mine. We kept our lunch schedule up for eight years, except when one of us was gone for several days at a stretch. Though we had a lot in common, we were very different, and the lunches kept us closer than we otherwise would have been in the Washington pressure cooker, and eased my adjustment to my new life.

All things considered, I felt pretty good, personally and politically, about the first one hundred days. Still, I was under a lot of stress. So was Hillary. For all our excitement and commitment, we were tired going in, not having taken any real time off after the election. Then we were denied the honeymoon traditionally given new Presidents, partly because of the way the gays-in-the military issue surfaced early, perhaps because we made the press angry by restricting access to the West Wing. Hillary's father's death was a painful loss to her. I missed Hugh, too, and for a while, it was harder for both of us to operate at the top of our games. Though we very much enjoyed the work, the physical and emotional toll of the first hundred days was considerable.

FOUR

WHILE DEFICIT REDUCTION was essential to my economic strategy, it was not sufficient to build a sustained, widely shared recovery. In the early months, we filled out the agenda with initiatives to expand trade, increase investment in education and training, and promote a host of micro-economic issues aimed at particular trouble spots or targets of opportunity. For example, I offered proposals to help military and civilian personnel who had lost their jobs as a result of the post–Cold War decline in defense spending; urged our major federal research labs—Los Alamos and Sandia in New Mexico, and Livermore in California—to use the massive scientific and technological resources that had helped win the Cold War to develop new technologies with commercial applications; announced a micro-loan program to support budding entrepreneurs, including welfare recipients eager to get off the rolls, who often had good ideas but couldn't meet the credit standards of traditional lenders; increased the volume of Small Business Administration loans, especially to women and minorities; and named a National Commission to Ensure a Strong and Competitive Airline Industry, chaired by former Virginia governor Jerry Baliles. The airline manufacturers and carriers were in trouble because of the economic downturn, fewer orders for military planes, and stiff competition from the European manufacturer Airbus.

I also offered plans to help communities develop commercial uses for the military facilities that would be closed as defense was downsized. As governor, I had dealt with the closing of an air force base, and I was determined to give more aid to those facing the same challenge now. Since California was, by itself, the world's sixth-largest economy, and it had been hit especially hard by defense downsizing and other problems, we developed a special plan to promote recovery there. John Emerson had the responsibility of riding herd on the project and other matters of concern to his native state. He was so unrelenting in doing so that he became known around the White House as the "Secretary of California."

One of the most effective things we did was to reform the regulations governing financial institutions under the 1977 Community Reinvestment Act. The law required federally insured lenders to make an extra effort to give loans to low- and modest-income borrowers, but before 1993 it had never had much impact. After the changes we made, between 1993 and 2000, banks would offer more than $800 billion in home mortgage, small-business, and community development loans to borrowers covered by the law, a staggering figure that amounted to well over 90 percent of all the loans made in the twenty-three years of the Community Reinvestment Act.

May was an interesting month, and valuable for my continuing political education. On the fifth, I awarded my first Presidential Medal of Freedom to my old mentor Senator Fulbright on his eighty-eighth birthday. Al Gore's father was at the ceremony, and when he reminded Fulbright that he himself was only eighty-five, Fulbright replied, "Albert, if you behave yourself, you'll make it, too." I admired both men for what they'd done for America; I wondered if I would live as long as they had; if so, I hoped I could wear the years as well.

In the third week of the month, I went to California to emphasize the investments in the economic plan for education and inner-city development at a town hall meeting in San Diego, a community college in Van Nuys with a large Hispanic enrollment, and a sporting-goods store in South Central Los Angeles where the riots had occurred a year earlier. I especially enjoyed the last event. The athletic store, called the Playground, had a basketball court out back, which had become a gathering place for young people. Ron Brown was with me, and we took some of the kids and played each other in an impromptu basketball game, after which I talked about the potential of empowerment zones to create more successful businesses like the Playground in poor communities all across America. I'm pretty sure this was the first time a President ever played basketball with inner-city kids in their backyard, and I hoped that pictures of the game would send a message to America about the new administration's priorities, and to young people in particular that I cared about them and their futures.

Unfortunately, most Americans never heard about the basketball game because I got a haircut. I hadn't found a barber in Washington yet; I couldn't go back to Arkansas every three weeks to see Jim Miles, and my hair was too long. Hillary had had her hair done by a man in Los Angeles, Cristophe Schatteman, who was a friend of the Thomasons and whom I liked very much. I asked Cristophe if he would be willing to give me a quick trim. He agreed to do it and met me in my private quarters on Air Force One. Before we started, I asked the Secret Service not once, but twice, to make sure I wouldn't cause any delay in takeoffs or landings if I put off our departure for a few minutes. They checked with the airport personnel, who said it would be no problem. Then I asked Cristophe just to make me presentable as quickly as possible. He did, in ten minutes or so, and we took off.

The next thing I knew, there was a story out that I had kept two runways tied up for an hour, inconveniencing thousands of people, while I got a $200 haircut from a fancy hairdresser who was known only by his first name. Forget the basketball game with inner-city kids; the irresistible news was that I had shed my Arkansas roots and populist politics for an expensive indulgence. It was a great story, but it wasn't true. First of all, I didn't pay $200 for the ten-minute trim. Second, I didn't keep anybody waiting to take off or land, as the Federal Aviation Administration records showed when they were finally released a few weeks later. I was appalled that anyone would think I'd do such a thing. I might have been President, but Mother would still have given me a whipping if I'd kept a lot of people waiting an hour while I got a haircut, much less a $200 one.

The haircut story was crazy. I didn't handle it well, because I got angry, which is always a mistake. A big part of its attraction was that Cristophe was a Hollywood hairdresser. Many people in Washington's political and press establishment have a love-hate relationship with Hollywood. They like to mix with movie and television stars but tend to view the entertainment community's political interests and commitments as somehow less authentic than their own. In fact, most people in both groups are good citizens with a lot in common. Someone once said that politics is show business for ugly people.

A few weeks later, *Newsday*, a Long Island newspaper, obtained the Federal Aviation Administration records of flight activities at the Los Angeles airport that day, proving that the reported delays had never occurred. *USA Today* and a few other papers also printed a correction.

One thing that probably kept the haircut story alive and mostly uncorrected was something that had nothing to do with it. On May 19, on the advice of David Watkins, who was in charge of administrative operations at the White House, and with the concurrence of the White House counsel's office, Mack McLarty fired the seven employees of the White House Travel Office. The office makes all arrangements for the press when they travel with the President, and bills their employers for the costs. Hillary and I had both asked Mack to look into the Travel Office operations because she was told that the office allowed no competitive bidding on its charter flights, and I got a complaint from a White House reporter about bad meals and high costs. After an audit by the accounting firm KPMG Peat Marwick turned up an off-the-books ledger with $18,000 not properly accounted for and other irregularities, the employees were dismissed.

Once I mentioned the reporter's complaint to Mack, I forgot all about the Travel Office until the firings were announced. The reaction of the press corps was extremely negative. They liked the way they had been cared for, especially on foreign trips. And they had known the people in the Travel Office for years and couldn't imagine that they would do anything wrong. Many in the press felt the Travel Office staff virtually worked for them, not the White House, and felt they should have at least been notified, if not fully consulted, as the investigation proceeded. Despite the criticism, the reconstituted Travel Office provided the same services with fewer federal employees at lower costs to the press.

The Travel Office affair proved to be a particularly powerful example of the culture clash between the new White House and the established political press. The director of the Travel Office was later indicted for embezzlement based on Travel Office funds found in his personal account, and, according to press reports, he offered to plead guilty to a lesser charge and spend a few months in jail. Instead, the prosecutor insisted on going to trial on the felony charge. After several famous journalists testified for him as character witnesses, he was acquitted. Despite investigations of the Travel Office by the White House, the General Accounting Office, the FBI, and the independent counsel's office, no evidence of wrongdoing, conflicts of interest, or criminality by anyone at the White House was ever found, nor did anyone dispute the Travel Office's financial problems and mismanagement found in the Peat Marwick audit.

I couldn't believe the American people were seeing me primarily through the prism of the haircut, the Travel Office, and gays in the military. Instead of a President fighting to change America for the better, I was being portrayed as a man who had abandoned down-home for uptown, a knee-jerk liberal whose mask of moderation had been removed. I had recently done a television interview in Cleveland in which a man said he no longer supported me because I was spending all my time on gays in the military and Bosnia. I replied that I'd just done an analysis of how I'd spent my time in the first hundred days: 55 percent on the economy and health care, 25 percent on foreign policy, 20 percent on other domestic issues. When he asked how much time I'd spent on gays in the military, and I told him just a few hours, he simply replied, "I don't believe you." All he knew was what he read and saw.

The Cleveland encounter and the haircut and Travel Office fiascoes were object lessons about how little all of us outsiders knew about what mattered in Washington, and how the failure of understanding could blot out our efforts to communicate what we were doing to improve what really mattered to the rest of America. A few years later, Doug Sosnik, one of my wittiest staffers, coined a phrase that captured the buzz saw we had walked into. When we were about to leave for Oslo on a trip to promote the Middle East peace process, Sharon Farmer, my lively African-American photographer, said she wasn't looking forward to the trip to cold Norway. "That's okay, Sharon," Doug replied. "It's not a 'home game' for you. Nobody likes the 'away games.' " Midway through 1993, I was just hoping my entire term wouldn't be one long "away game."

I did some serious thinking about the trouble I was in. It seemed to me that the roots of the problem were these: the White House staff had too little experience in, and too few connections with, Washington's established power centers; we were trying to do too many things at once, creating an impression of disarray and preventing the people from hearing what we had actually accomplished; our lack of a clear message made otherwise minor issues look as if I was governing on the cultural and political left, not from the dynamic center, as I had promised; the impression was being reinforced by the one-note Republican attack that my budget plan was nothing but a big tax increase; and I had been blind to the considerable political obstacles I faced. I was elected with 43 percent of the vote; I had underestimated how hard it would be to turn Washington around after twelve years on a very different course, and how politically—even psychologically—jarring the changes would be to Washington's main players; many Republicans never considered my presidency legitimate in the first place and were acting accordingly; and the Congress, with a Democratic majority with its own way of doing things and a Republican minority determined to prove I was too liberal and couldn't govern, was not about to pass all the legislation I wanted as quickly as I wanted to pass it.

I knew I had to change, but just like everyone else, I found that was harder to do myself than to recommend to others. Still, I managed to make two changes that were particularly helpful. I persuaded David Gergen, a friend from Renaissance Weekend and veteran of three Republican administrations, to come into the White House as counselor to the President, to help us with organization and communication. In his *U.S. News & World Report* column David had given some thoughtful advice, some of it quite critical, with which I agreed; he liked and respected Mack McLarty; he was a bona fide member of the Washington establishment who thought and kept score the way they did; and for the sake of the country, he wanted us to succeed. For the next several months, David had a calming impact on the White House, immediately moving to improve relations with the press by restoring their direct access to the communications office, something we should have done long before.

Along with Gergen's appointment, we made some other staff changes: Mark Gearan, Mack McLarty's able and popular deputy chief of staff, would replace George Stephanopoulos as communications director, with Dee Dee Myers staying as press secretary and taking over the daily briefings; and George would move to a new senior advisor position, to help me coordinate policy, strategy, and day-to-day decisions. At first he was disappointed not to be doing the daily press briefings any longer, but he soon mastered a job much like the one he had done in the campaign, and he did it so well that his influence and impact within the White House increased.

The other positive change we made was to unclutter my day, providing two hours in the middle of most days for me to read, think, rest, and make phone calls. It would make a big difference.

Things were looking up by the end of the month, when the House passed my budget, 219–213. The Senate then took it up, and immediately scrapped the BTU tax in favor of a 4.3-cents-a-gallon increase in the gasoline tax and more spending cuts. The bad news was that the gas tax would promote less energy conservation than the BTU tax; the good news was that it would cost middle-class Americans less, only about $33 a year.

On May 31, my first Memorial Day as President, after the traditional ceremony in Arlington National Cemetery, I went to another ceremony at the newly opened section of the Vietnam Veterans Memorial, a long black marble wall with the names of all the members of the U.S. armed forces who had been killed or were missing in the war etched on it. Early that morning I had jogged over to the wall from the White House to look at the names of my friends from Hot Springs. I knelt at the spot where my friend Bert Jeffries's name was, touched it, and said a prayer.

I knew it would be a tough event, full of people for whom the Vietnam War continued to be the defining moment in their lives and to whom the thought of someone like me as Commander in Chief was abhorrent. But I was determined to go, to face those who still held my views on Vietnam against me, and to tell all Vietnam veterans that I honored their service and that of their fallen comrades and would work to resolve the still-open cases of prisoners of war and soldiers still listed as missing in action.

Colin Powell introduced me with conviction and class, strongly signaling the respect he thought I should receive as Commander in Chief. Nevertheless, when I got up to speak, loud protesters attempted to drown me out. I spoke to them directly:

> To all of you who are shouting, I have heard you. I ask you now to hear me. . . . Some have suggested that it is wrong for me to be here with you today because I did not agree a quarter of a century ago with the decision made to send the young men and women to battle in Vietnam. Well, so much the better. . . . Just as war is freedom's cost, disagreement is freedom's privilege, and we honor it here today. . . . The message of this memorial is quite simple: these men and women fought for freedom, brought honor to their communities, loved their country, and died for it. . . . There's not a person in this crowd today who did not know someone on this wall. Four of my high school classmates are

there. . . . Let us continue to disagree, if we must, about the war. But let us not let it divide us as a people any longer.

The event started roughly, but ended well. Robert McNamara's prediction that my election had ended the Vietnam War wasn't quite accurate, but maybe we were getting there.

June began with a disappointment that was both personal and political, as I withdrew my nomination of Lani Guinier, a University of Pennsylvania professor, a longtime lawyer for the NAACP Legal Defense Fund, and my law school classmate, to be the first career civil rights lawyer to head the Civil Rights Division. After I named her in April, the conservatives went after Guinier with a vengeance, attacking her as a "quota queen" and accusing her of advocating the abandonment of the constitutional principle of "one man, one vote" because she had supported a system of cumulative voting, under which each voter would get as many votes as there are contested seats on a legislative body, and could cast all the votes for a single candidate. In theory, cumulative voting would dramatically increase the odds of minority candidates being elected.

At first, I didn't pay too much attention to the rantings of the right, thinking that what they really disliked about Guinier was her long record of successful civil rights fights, and that, as she made the rounds of the Senate, she would win enough votes to be confirmed easily.

I was wrong. My friend Senator David Pryor came to see me and urged me to withdraw Lani's nomination, saying that her interviews with the senators were going poorly, and reminding me that we also had an economic program to pass and not a vote to spare. Majority Leader George Mitchell, who had been a federal judge before he came to the Senate, strongly agreed with David; he said Lani couldn't be confirmed and we needed to end it as soon as possible. I was informed that Senators Ted Kennedy and Carol Moseley Braun, the Senate's only African-American member, felt the same way.

I decided I had better read Lani's articles. They made a persuasive case for her position, but were in conflict with my support for affirmative action and opposition to quotas, and seemed to abandon one man, one vote in favor of one man, many votes: spread them out however you like.

I asked her to come see me so that we could talk it through. As we discussed the problem in the Oval Office, Lani was understandably offended by the battering she had taken, amazed that anyone would see the academic musings in her articles as a serious obstacle to her confirmation, and dismissive of the difficulties her nomination presented to the senators whose votes she needed, perhaps through several filibusters. My staff had told her we didn't have the votes to confirm her, but she declined to withdraw, feeling she had a right to be voted on. Finally, I told her that I felt I had to withdraw her nomination, that I hated to do it, but we were going to lose, and though it was cold comfort, her withdrawal would make her a heroine in the civil rights community.

In the aftermath, I was heavily criticized for abandoning a friend in the face of political pressure, mostly by people who didn't know what was going on in the background. Eventually, I nominated Deval Patrick, another brilliant African-American lawyer with a strong civil rights background, to lead the Civil Rights Division, and he did a fine job. I still admire Lani Guinier, and regret that I lost her friendship.

I spent much of the first two weeks of June picking a Supreme Court justice. A few weeks earlier, Byron "Whizzer" White had announced his retirement after thirty-one years on the High Court. As I said earlier, I first wanted to appoint Governor Mario Cuomo, but he wasn't interested. After reviewing more than forty candidates, I settled on three: my Interior Secretary Bruce Babbitt, who had been attorney general of Arizona before becoming governor; Judge Stephen Breyer, chief judge of the First Circuit Court of Appeals in Boston, who had compiled an impressive record on the bench; and Judge Ruth Bader Ginsburg of the United States Court of

Appeals for the District of Columbia circuit, a brilliant woman with a compelling life story whose record was interesting, independent, and progressive. I met with Babbitt and Breyer and was convinced they both would be good justices, but I hated to lose Babbitt at Interior, as did large numbers of environmentalists who called the White House to urge that I keep him there, and Breyer had a minor "nanny" problem, though Senator Kennedy, who was pushing him hard, assured me that he would be confirmed.

Like everything else that happened in the White House in the early months, my interviews with both men leaked, so I decided to see Ginsburg in my private office in the residence of the White House on a Sunday night. I was tremendously impressed with her. I thought that she had the potential to become a great justice, and that, at the least, she could do the three things I felt a new justice needed to do on the Rehnquist Court, which was closely divided between moderates and conservatives: decide cases on the merits, not on ideology or the identities of the parties; work with the conservative Republican justices to reach consensus when possible; and stand up to them when necessary. In one of her articles, Ginsburg had written: "The greatest figures of the American judiciary have been independent thinking individuals with open but not empty minds; individuals willing to listen and to learn. They have exhibited a readiness to reexamine their own premises, liberal or conservative, as thoroughly as those of others."

When we announced her appointment, it hadn't leaked. The press had written that I intended to appoint Breyer, based on a tip from a leaker who didn't know what he was talking about. After Judge Ginsburg made her brief but moving statement, one of the reporters said her appointment gave the impression that my decision to appoint her, rather than Breyer, reflected a certain "zig-zag quality" to the process of decision making in the White House. He then asked whether I could refute that impression. I didn't know whether to laugh or cry. I replied, "I have long since given up the thought that I could disabuse some of you of turning any

substantive decision into anything but political process."
Apparently, when it came to appointments, the name of the
game wasn't supposed to be "follow the leader" but "follow
the leaker." I have to confess that I was almost as happy
about surprising the press as I was with the choice I had
made.

In the last week of June, the Senate finally passed my budget
by only 50–49, with one Democrat and one Republican not
voting, and Al Gore breaking the tie. No Republican voted
for it, and we lost six conservative Democrats. Senator
David Boren of Oklahoma, whom I had known since 1974,
when he first ran for governor and I ran for Congress, gave
us a vote to stave off defeat, but indicated that he would
oppose the final bill unless it contained more spending cuts
and fewer taxes.

    Now that the Senate and House had approved the
budget plans, they would have to reconcile their differences
and then we'd have to fight for passage in both houses all
over again. Since we had won by such small margins in both
places, any concession made by one chamber to the other
could lose a vote or two, all it would take to defeat the
whole package. Roger Altman came over from Treasury
with his chief of staff, Josh Steiner, to set up a "war room"
to organize the campaign for final passage. We needed to
know where every vote was, and what we could argue or
offer to wavering members to get a majority. After all the
blood we'd spilled over minor issues, this was a fight worth
making. For the next six and a half weeks, the economic
future of the country, not to mention the future of my presidency, hung in the balance.

On the day after the Senate passed the budget, I ordered the
military into action for the first time, firing twenty-three
Tomahawk missiles into Iraq's intelligence headquarters, in
retaliation for a plot to assassinate President George H. W.
Bush during a trip he had made to Kuwait. More than a
dozen people involved in the plot had been arrested in

Kuwait on April 13, one day before the former President had been scheduled to arrive. The materials in their possession were conclusively traced to Iraqi intelligence, and on May 19 one of the arrested Iraqis confirmed to the FBI that the Iraqi intelligence service was behind the plot. I asked the Pentagon to recommend a course of action, and General Powell came to me with the missile attack on the intelligence headquarters as both a proportionate response and an effective deterrent. I felt we would have been justified in hitting Iraq harder, but Powell made a persuasive case that the attack would deter further Iraqi terrorism, and that dropping bombs on more targets, including presidential palaces, would have been unlikely to kill Saddam Hussein and almost certain to kill more innocent people. Most of the Tomahawks hit the target, but four of them overshot, three landing in an upscale Baghdad neighborhood and killing eight civilians. It was a stark reminder that no matter how careful the planning and how accurate the weapons, when that kind of firepower is unleashed, there are usually unintended consequences.

On July 6, I was in Tokyo for my first international meeting, the sixteenth annual G-7 summit. Historically, these meetings had been talkfests, with few meaningful policy commitments and little follow-up coming out of them. We didn't have the luxury of another meeting where nothing happened. The world economy was dragging, with growth in Europe the slowest in more than a decade, and in Japan the slowest in nearly two decades. We were making some headway on the economic front; in the last five months, over 950,000 more Americans had found work, about as many new jobs as the economy had produced in the previous three years.

I went to Japan with an agenda: to get the agreement of European and Japanese leaders to coordinate their internal economic policies with ours, in order to raise the level of global growth; convince Europe and Japan to drop tariffs on manufacturing goods, which would create jobs in all our countries and increase the chances of finishing the seven-year-old Uruguay Round of world trade talks by the December 15 deadline; and send a clear, unified signal of financial and political support for Yeltsin and Russian democracy.

The odds of success on any of these items, much less all three, were not great, in part because none of the leaders were particularly strong coming into the meeting. Between the tough medicine in my economic plan and the bad press over problems, both real and imagined, my public approval had dropped steeply since the inauguration. John Major was hanging on in England, but was hurt by constant unfavorable comparison to his predecessor, Margaret Thatcher, something the Iron Lady did nothing to discourage. François Mitterrand was a fascinating, brilliant man, a Socialist in his second seven-year term, who was limited in what he could deliver by the fact that the French prime minister and his governing coalition, who controlled economic policy, were from opposing political parties. Carlo Ciampi, the Italian prime minister, was a former governor of the Italian Central Bank and a modest man who was known for riding his bicycle to work. Despite his intelligence and appeal, he was hampered by the fractured and inherently unstable Italian political environment. Kim Campbell, Canada's first female prime minister, was an impressive, clearly dedicated person who had just taken office after the resignation of Brian Mulroney. She was essentially finishing Mulroney's long run at the helm, with the polls showing a rising tide of support for the opposition leader, Jean Chrétien. Our host, Kiichi Miyazawa, was widely regarded as a lame duck in a Japanese political system in which the long monopoly of the Liberal Democratic Party was coming to an end. Miyazawa may have been a lame duck, but he was an impressive one, with a sophisticated understanding of the world. He spoke colloquial English about as well as I did. And he was also a patriot who wanted the G-7 meeting to reflect well on his country.

The conventional wisdom held that Helmut Kohl, the long-serving German chancellor, was also in trouble, because his poll numbers were down and his Christian

Democratic Party had suffered some recent losses in local elections, but I thought Kohl still had plenty of life in his leadership. He was a huge man, about my height and weighing well over three hundred pounds. He spoke with great conviction in a direct, often brusque manner, and he was a world-class storyteller with a good sense of humor. And in more than size he was the largest figure on the European continent in decades. He had reunified Germany, funneling massive sums of money from West to East Germany to lift the incomes of those who had made far less under communism. Kohl's Germany had become the largest financial supporter of Russian democracy. He was also the leading force behind the emerging European Union, and he was in favor of admitting Poland, Hungary, and the Czech Republic into both the EU and the NATO alliance. Finally, Kohl was deeply troubled by Europe's passivity in Bosnia and thought, as I did, that the United Nations should lift the arms embargo because it was unfair to the Bosnian Muslims. On all the great questions facing Europe, he was on the right side, and pushing hard for his point of view. He felt if he got the big things right, the polls would follow. I liked Helmut Kohl a lot. Over the next several years, through many meals, visits, and phone calls, we would forge a political and personal bond that would bear great fruit for Europeans and Americans alike.

I was optimistic about the prospects for the G-7 because I was bringing a strong agenda to the meeting and because I believed all the other leaders were smart enough to know that the best way to get out of trouble at home was to do something meaningful in Tokyo. Just as the conference opened, we crossed one threshold, when our trade ministers agreed that all of us would lower tariffs to zero on ten different manufacturing sectors, opening markets for hundreds of billions of dollars' worth of trade. It was Mickey Kantor's first victory as our trade ambassador. He had proved to be a tough, effective negotiator, with skills that eventually would produce more than two hundred agreements, sparking an expansion of trade that would account for almost 30 percent of our economic growth over the next eight years.

After we agreed on a generous aid package, the G-7 meeting also left no doubt that the rich nations were all committed to helping Russia. On the matter of coordinating our economic policies, the results were more ambiguous. I was working to bring the deficit down, and Germany's central bank had just lowered interest rates, but Japan's willingness to stimulate its economy and open its borders to more foreign trade and competition remained unclear. That was progress I'd have to achieve in our bilateral talks with the Japanese, which began right after the G-7 meeting.

In 1993, because Japan was dealing with economic stagnation and political uncertainty, I knew it would be hard to get changes in trade policy, but I had to try. Clearly our large trade deficit with Japan was due in part to protectionism. For example, they wouldn't buy our skis, saying they weren't the right width. I had to find a way to push open Japanese markets without damaging our important security partnership, which was essential to building a stable future for Asia. While I was making these points in a speech to Japanese students at Waseda University, Hillary went on her own charm offensive in Japan, finding an especially warm reception among the increasingly large number of young, well-educated working women.

Prime Minister Miyazawa agreed in principle to my suggestion that we achieve a framework agreement committing ourselves to specific measurable steps to improve our trade relationship. So did the Japanese Foreign Ministry, whose senior civil servant, the father of Japan's new crown princess, was determined to reach an agreement. The big obstacle was the Ministry of International Trade and Industry (MITI), whose leaders felt that their policies had made Japan a great power and saw no reason to change. Late one night, after we finished our talks, representatives of the two ministries were literally screaming their arguments at each other in the lobby of the Hotel Okura. Our staffs got as close as they could to an agreement, with Mickey Kantor's deputy, Charlene Barshefsky, driving such a hard bargain the Japanese called her "Stonewall." Then Miyazawa and I got together over a traditional Japanese meal at the Hotel Okura to see if we could resolve the remaining differences. We did, in what was later called the "Sushi Summit," though Miyazawa always joked that the sake we drank contributed more than the sushi to the final outcome.

The framework agreement committed America to reduce its budget deficit and Japan to take steps over the next year to open its markets in automobile and auto parts, computers, telecommunications, satellites, medical equipment, financial services, and insurance, with objective standards for measuring success on specific timetables. I was convinced that the agreement would be economically beneficial to both the United States and Japan and that it would help Japanese reformers succeed in leading their remarkable nation to its next era of greatness. Like most such agreements, it didn't produce all one could hope for in either country, but it was still a very good thing.

As I left Japan for Korea, the press reports back home said that my first G-7 meeting was a triumph for my personal diplomacy with the other leaders and my outreach to the Japanese people. It was nice to get some positive press coverage, and even better to have met the objectives we set for the G-7 and the Japanese negotiations. I had enjoyed getting to know and work with the other leaders. And after the G-7, I felt more confident in my ability to advance America's interests in the world and understood why so many Presidents preferred foreign policy to the frustrations they faced on the home front.

In South Korea, I visited our troops along the DMZ, which had divided North and South Korea since the armistice ending the Korean War was signed. I walked out onto the Bridge of No Return, stopping about ten feet from the stripe of white paint dividing the two countries and staring at the young North Korean soldier guarding his side in the last lonely outpost of the Cold War. In Seoul, Hillary and I were the guests of President Kim Young-Sam in the official guest residence, which had an indoor swimming pool. When I went for a dip, music suddenly filled the air. I found myself swimming to many of my favorite tunes, from Elvis to jazz, a nice example of Korea's famous hospitality. After a meeting with the president and a speech to the parliament, I left South Korea grateful for our long alliance and determined to maintain it.

FIVE

I RETURNED TO the rigors of Washington. In the third week of July, on the recommendation of Janet Reno, I dismissed the director of the FBI, William Sessions, after he refused to resign despite numerous problems within the agency. We had to find a replacement. White House counsel Bernie Nussbaum urged me to choose Louis Freeh, a former FBI agent whom President Bush had appointed to the federal bench in New York after a stellar career as a federal prosecutor. When I met with Freeh, I asked him what he thought about the FBI's assertion at Waco that they had proceeded with the raid because it was wrong to keep so many of their resources tied down in one place for so long. Without knowing what I thought, he said forthrightly that he disagreed: "They get paid to wait." That impressed me. I knew Freeh was a Republican, but Nussbaum assured me that he was a professional and a stand-up guy who would not use the FBI for political purposes. We scheduled the announcement for the twentieth. The day before, when word got out about the appointment, a retired FBI agent who was a friend of mine called Nancy Hernreich, who ran the Oval Office operations, to tell me not to do it. He said Freeh was too political and self-serving for the current climate. It gave me pause, but I sent word back that it was too late; the offer had been extended and accepted. I would just have to trust Bernie Nussbaum's judgment.

When we announced Freeh's appointment in a morning ceremony in the Rose Garden, I noticed Vince Foster standing at the back, near one of the grand old magnolia trees planted by Andrew Jackson. Vince had a smile on his face, and I remember thinking he must be relieved that he and the counsel's office were working on things like Supreme Court and FBI appointments, instead of answering endless questions about the Travel Office. The whole ceremony seemed perfect, almost too good to be true. It was, in more ways than one.

That night I appeared on Larry King's show from the
library on the ground floor of the White House to talk about
my battle for the budget and whatever else was on his and
his callers' minds. Like everyone else, I liked Larry King. He
has a good sense of humor and a human touch, even when
he's asking tough questions. About forty-five minutes into
the program, things were going so well that Larry asked me
if I'd do an extra thirty minutes, so that we could take more
questions from viewers. I agreed immediately and was looking forward to it, but at the next break Mack McLarty
showed up and said we had to end the interview after an
hour. At first I was irritated, thinking my staff was worried
that I might make a mistake if I kept going, but the look in
Mack's eyes told me something else was going on.

After Larry and I wrapped up the interview and I shook
hands with his crew, Mack walked me upstairs to the residence. Holding back tears, he told me Vince Foster was dead.
Vince had left the Rose Garden after the ceremony for Louis
Freeh, driven out to Fort Marcy Park, and shot himself with
an old revolver that was a family heirloom. We had been
friends virtually all our lives. Our backyards had touched
when I lived with my grandparents in Hope. We had played
together even before Mack and I started kindergarten. I
knew Vince had been upset by the Travel Office controversy
and held himself responsible for the criticism directed at the
counsel's office. He had also been wounded by questions
raised about his competence and integrity in several *Wall
Street Journal* editorials.

Just the night before, I had called Vince to invite him to
watch a movie with me. I was hoping to give him some
encouragement, but he had already gone home for the night
and said he needed to spend some time with his wife, Lisa. I
did my best in our phone conversation to persuade him to
shrug off the *Journal* editorials. The *Journal* was a fine
paper, but not that many people read its editorials; most of
those who did were, like the editorial writers, conservatives
who were lost to us anyway. Vince listened, but I could tell I
hadn't convinced him. He had never been subject to public
criticism before and, like so many people when they're

pounded in the press for the first time, he seemed to think that everyone had read the negative things said about him and believed them.

After Mack told me what had happened, Hillary called me from Little Rock. She already knew and was crying. Vince had been her closest friend at the Rose firm. She was frantically searching for an answer we would never completely find—why this had happened. I did my best to convince her there was nothing she could have done, all the while wondering what *I* could have done. Then Mack and I went over to Vince's house to be with the family. Webb and Suzy Hubbell were there, as were several of Vince's friends from Arkansas and the White House. I tried to console everyone, but I was hurting too, and feeling, as I had when my Oxford classmate Frank Aller killed himself, angry at Vince for doing it and angry at myself for not seeing it coming and doing something, anything, to try to stop it. I was also sad for all my friends from Arkansas who had come to Washington wanting nothing more than to serve and do good, only to find their every move second-guessed. Now Vince, the tall, handsome, strong, and self-assured person they felt was the most stable of them all, was gone.

For whatever reason, Vince came to the end of his rope. In his briefcase, Bernie Nussbaum found a note that had been torn into little pieces. When put back together, it said, "I was not meant for the job in the spotlight of public life in Washington. Here ruining people is considered sport. . . . The public will never believe the innocence of the Clintons and their loyal staff." Vince was overwhelmed, exhausted, and vulnerable to attacks by people who didn't play by the same rules he did. He was rooted in the values of honor and respect, and uprooted by those who valued power and personal assault more. And his untreated depression stripped him of the defenses that allowed the rest of us to survive.

The next day I spoke to the staff, telling them that there are things in life we can't control and mysteries we can't understand; that I wanted them to take more care with themselves, their friends, and their families; and that we couldn't "deaden our sensitivities by working too hard."

That last bit of advice had always been easier for me to give than to take.

We all went to Little Rock for Vince's funeral at St. Andrew's Catholic Cathedral, then drove home to Hope, to lay Vince to rest in the cemetery where my grandparents and father were buried. Many people with whom we'd gone to kindergarten and grade school were there. By then, I had given up trying to understand Vince's depression and suicide in favor of accepting them and being grateful for his life. In my eulogy at the funeral, I tried to capture all of Vince's wonderful qualities, what he meant to all of us, how much good he'd done at the White House, and how profoundly honorable he was. I quoted from Leon Russell's moving "A Song for You": "I love you in a place where there's no space or time. I love you for in my life you are a friend of mine."

It was summertime, and the watermelon crop had begun to come in. Before I left town, I stopped at Carter Russell's place and sampled both the red- and yellow-meated ones. Then I discussed the finer points of Hope's main product with the traveling press, who knew I needed a respite from the pain and were uncommonly kind to me that day. I flew back to Washington thinking Vince was home, where he belonged, and thanking God that so many people cared about him.

The next day, July 24, I welcomed the current class of American Legion Boys Nation senators to the White House, on the thirtieth anniversary of my coming to the Rose Garden to meet President Kennedy. A number of my fellow delegates were also there for the reunion. Al Gore was lobbying hard for our economic plan, but he broke away for a couple of minutes to tell the boys, "I have only one word of advice. If you can manage somehow to get a picture of you shaking hands with President Clinton, it might come in handy later on." I shook hands and posed for pictures with all of them, as I would do in six of my eight years in the White House, for both Boys and Girls Nation. I hope some of those photos turn up in campaign ads one day.

I spent the rest of the month and the early days of August lobbying individual representatives and senators on the economic plan. Roger Altman's war room was working the public side, having me do telephone press conferences in states whose members of Congress could go either way. Al Gore and the cabinet were making literally hundreds of calls and visits. The outcome was uncertain, and tilting away from us, for two reasons. The first was Senator David Boren's proposal to scrap any energy tax; keep most, but not all, of the taxes on the high-income Americans, and make up the difference by eliminating much of the Earned Income Tax Credit; reduce the cost-of-living adjustments for Social Security and military and civilian pensions; and cap expenditures for Medicare and Medicaid below the projected requirements for new recipients and cost increases. Boren couldn't pass his proposal out of committee, but he gave Democrats from conservative states a place to go. It was also endorsed by Democratic senator Bennett Johnston of Louisiana and Republican senators John Danforth of Missouri and Bill Cohen of Maine.

When the budget had first passed, 50–49, with Al Gore breaking the tie, Bennett Johnston had voted against it, along with Sam Nunn, Dennis DeConcini of Arizona, Richard Shelby of Alabama, Richard Bryan of Nevada, and Frank Lautenberg of New Jersey. Shelby was already drifting toward the Republican Party in an increasingly Republican state; Sam Nunn was a hard no; DeConcini, Bryan, and Lautenberg were worried about the anti-tax mood in their states. As I've said, I had made it the first time without them because two senators, one Republican and one Democrat, didn't vote. The next time, they would all show up. With all the Republicans against us, if Boren voted no and none of the others changed, I would lose 51–49. Besides those six, Senator Bob Kerrey was also saying he might vote against the program. Our relationship had been strained by the presidential campaign, and Nebraska was a heavily Republican state. Still, I was optimistic about Kerrey because he was genuinely committed to reducing the deficit, and he was very close to the Senate Finance Committee chairman, Pat Moynihan, who was strongly supporting my plan.

In the House of Representatives, I had a different

problem. Every Democrat knew he or she had maximum leverage, and many were bargaining with me over details of the plan or for help on specific issues. Many of the Democrats who came from anti-tax districts were especially afraid of voting for another increase in the gas tax only three years after Congress had last raised it. Besides the Speaker and his leadership team, my strongest supporter was the powerful chairman of the House Ways and Means Committee, Illinois congressman Dan Rostenkowski. Rostenkowski was a superb legislator who combined a fine mind with Chicago street skills, but he was being investigated for converting public funds to political uses, and the assumption was that the investigation would reduce his influence over other members. Every time I met with members of Congress, the press would ask me about Rostenkowski. To his everlasting credit, Rosty bulled right ahead, rounding up votes and telling his colleagues they had to do the right thing. He was still effective, and he had to be. The slightest misstep could lose a vote or two, plunging us off the razor's edge into defeat.

In early August, as the budget drama moved to its climax, Warren Christopher finally secured the agreement of the British and the French to conduct NATO air strikes in Bosnia, but the strikes could occur only if both NATO and the UN approved them, the so-called dual key approach. I was afraid we could never turn both keys, because Russia had a veto on the Security Council and was closely tied to the Serbs. The dual key would prove to be a frustrating impediment to protecting the Bosnians, but it marked another step in the long, tortuous process of moving Europe and the UN to a more aggressive posture.

By August 3, we had settled on a final budget plan, with $255 billion in budget cuts and $241 billion in tax increases. Some Democrats were still worried that any gas-tax increase would kill us with those middle-class voters who were angry anyway about not getting a tax cut. Conservative Democrats said it didn't do enough to reduce the deficit through cutting spending on the entitlements of Medicare, Medicaid, and Social Security. More than 20 percent of our savings already came from reducing future payments to doctors and hospitals under Medicare, plus another big chunk from subjecting more of the Social Security income of better-off retirees to taxation. That's all I could do without losing more votes in the House than we could gain.

That night, in a televised address from the Oval Office, I made one last pitch for public support for the plan, saying it would create eight million jobs in the next four years, and announcing that I would sign an executive order the following day to establish a deficit-reduction trust fund, assuring that all the new taxes and spending cuts would be used for that purpose only. The trust fund was especially important to Senator Dennis DeConcini of Arizona, and I credited him for the idea in the TV address. Of the six senators who had voted against the plan the first time, DeConcini was my only hope. I had had the others to dinner, met with and called them, and had their closest friends in the administration lobby them, to no avail. If DeConcini didn't change, we were beat.

The next day, he did, saying he would vote yes because of the trust fund. Now, if Bob Kerrey stayed with us we would get fifty votes in the Senate, and Al Gore could break the tie again. But before we got there, the budget first had to pass the House. We had one more day to find a majority of 218 votes, and we still weren't there. More than thirty Democrats were wavering. They were afraid of the taxes, though we had done printouts for each of the members showing how many people in their districts would get a tax cut under the EITC, as compared with those who would get an income tax increase. In many cases, the ratio was ten to one or better, and in barely more than a dozen were their constituents so well off that the district would see more tax increases than decreases. Still, they were all worried about the gas tax. I could have passed the plan easily had I dropped the gas tax and offset the loss by abandoning the EITC tax cut. It would have been far less politically damaging. Poor working people had no lobbyists in Washington; they would never have known. But I would have. Besides, if we were going to soak the rich, the bond market wanted us to spray the middle class with a little bit of pain.

That afternoon, Leon Panetta and House majority

leader Dick Gephardt, who was working tirelessly for the budget, had struck a deal with Congressman Tim Penny of Minnesota, the leader of a group of conservative Democrats who wanted more spending cuts, promising the budget cutters another vote during the fall appropriations process to cut spending even more. Penny was satisfied, and his approval brought us seven or eight more votes.

We lost two of our earlier yes votes when Billy Tauzin of Louisiana, who later became a Republican, and Charlie Stenholm of Texas, who represented a district where most of the voters were Republican, said they would vote no. They hated the gas tax and said the unified Republican opposition to the plan had convinced their constituents that it was nothing but a tax increase.

Less than an hour before the vote, I spoke with Congressman Bill Sarpalius from Amarillo, Texas, who had voted against the plan in May. In our fourth phone conversation of the day, Bill said he had decided to vote for the plan, because so many more of his constituents would get tax cuts than tax increases, and because Energy Secretary Hazel O'Leary had pledged to shift more government work to the Pantex plant in his district. We made many commitments like that. Someone once said that the two things people should never watch being made are sausages and laws. It was ugly, and uncertain.

When the voting began, I still didn't know whether we were going to win or lose. After David Minge, who represented a rural district in Minnesota, said he would vote no, it all came down to three people: Pat Williams of Montana, Ray Thornton of Arkansas, and Marjorie Margolies-Mezvinsky of Pennsylvania. I really didn't want Margolies-Mezvinsky to have to vote with us. She was one of the very few Democrats who represented a district with more constituents who'd get tax hikes than tax cuts, and in her campaign she had promised not to vote for any tax increases. It was a tough vote for Pat Williams, too. Far more of his constituents would get tax cuts than tax increases, but Montana was a huge, sparsely populated state where people had to drive long distances, so the gas tax would hit them harder than most Americans. But Pat Williams was a good politician and a tough populist who deplored what trickle-down economics had done to his people. There was at least a chance that he could survive the vote.

Compared with Williams and Margolies-Mezvinsky, Thornton had an easy vote. He represented central Arkansas, where there were far more people who would get a tax cut than a tax increase. He was popular and could not have been blown out of his seat with a stick of dynamite. He was my congressman, and my presidency was on the line. And he had lots of cover: both Arkansas senators, David Pryor and Dale Bumpers, were strong supporters of the plan. But in the end Thornton said no. He had never voted for a gas tax before and he wouldn't start now, not to get the deficit down, not to revive the economy, not to save my presidency or the career of Marjorie Margolies-Mezvinsky.

Finally, Pat Williams and Margolies-Mezvinsky came down the aisle and voted yes, giving us a one-vote victory. The Democrats cheered their courage and the Republicans jeered. They were especially cruel to Margolies-Mezvinsky, waving and singing, "Good-bye, Margie." She had earned an honored place in history, with a vote she shouldn't have had to cast. Dan Rostenkowski was so happy he had tears in his eyes. Back in the White House, I let out a whoop of joy, and relief.

The next day, the drama moved to the Senate. Thanks to George Mitchell and his leadership team, and our lobbying, we had held all the senators from the first vote except David Boren. Dennis DeConcini had bravely stepped into his place, but the outcome was still in doubt, because Bob Kerrey remained uncommitted. On Friday he met with me for ninety minutes; then, about an hour and a half before the vote, he spoke on the Senate floor, saying directly to me, "I could not and should not cast a vote that brings down your presidency." While he would vote yes, he said I would have to do more to control entitlement spending. I agreed to work with him on this. He was pleased with that, as well as with my acceptance of Tim Penny's proposal for an October vote on more cuts.

Kerrey's vote made it a 50–50 tie. Then, just as he had in the first vote on June 25, Al Gore, as president of the Senate, cast the tie-breaking vote. In a statement after the vote, I thanked George Mitchell and all the senators who "voted for change," and Al Gore for "his unwavering contribution in the landslide." Al loved to joke that whenever he voted, we always won.

I signed the legislation on August 10. It reversed twelve years in which the national debt had quadrupled with deficits built on overly optimistic revenue numbers and an almost theological belief that low taxes and high levels of spending would somehow bring enough growth to balance the budget. At the ceremony I specifically acknowledged those senators and representatives whose support never wavered from beginning to end, and who therefore were never mentioned in the news stories. Every yes voter in both houses of the Congress could rightfully say that, but for him or her, we would not be here today.

We had come a long way since those heated debates around the dining-room table in Little Rock the previous December. All by themselves, the Democrats had replaced a wrongheaded but deeply embedded economic theory with a sensible one. Our new economic idea had become reality.

Unfortunately, the Republicans, whose policies had created the problem in the first place, had done a good job portraying the plan as nothing but a tax increase. It was true that most of the spending cuts kicked in later than the tax increases, but that was also true of the alternative budget offered by Senator Dole. In fact, Dole's plan had an even higher percentage of its cuts in the last two years of the five-year budget than mine did. It simply takes time to reduce defense and health spending; you can't slash it all at once. Moreover, our "future" investments in education, training, research, technology, and the environment were already at unacceptably low levels, having been held down in the eighties as tax cuts, defense appropriations, and health costs soared. My budget began to reverse that trend.

Predictably, the Republicans said my economic plan would cause the sky to fall in, calling it a "job killer" and a "one-way ticket to recession." They were wrong. Our bond market gambit would work beyond our wildest dreams, bringing lower interest rates, a soaring stock market, and a booming economy. Just as Lloyd Bentsen had predicted, the wealthiest Americans would get their tax money back, and more, in investment income. The middle class would get their gas-tax money back many times over, in lower home mortgage rates and lower interest costs for car payments, student loans, and credit card purchases. Working families with modest incomes benefited from the Earned Income Tax Credit right away.

In later years I was often asked what great new idea my economic team and I brought to economic policy making. Rather than give a complicated explanation of the bond market/deficit reduction strategy, I always gave a one-word answer: "arithmetic." The American people had been told for more than a decade that their government was a gluttonous leviathan swallowing their hard-earned tax dollars to no good end. Then the same politicians who told them that, and served up tax cuts to starve the evil beast, would turn right around and spend themselves to reelection, leaving the false impression that the voters could have programs they didn't pay for, and that the only reason we had big deficits was wasteful spending on foreign aid, welfare, and other programs for poor people, a tiny fraction of the budget. Spending on "them" was bad; spending and tax cuts for "us" were good. As my fiscally conservative friend Senator Dale Bumpers used to say: "You let me write $200 billion a year in hot checks and I'll show you a good time, too."

We had brought arithmetic back to the budget, and broken America of a bad habit. Unfortunately, though the benefits began to accrue right away, the people wouldn't feel them for some time. In the meantime, my fellow Democrats and I bore the brunt of the public's withdrawal pains. I couldn't expect gratitude. Even with an abscessed tooth, nobody likes to go to the dentist.

SIX

AFTER THE BUDGET PASSED, Congress went on its August recess and I was eager to take my family on vacation for two much-needed weeks on Martha's Vineyard. Vernon and Ann Jordan had arranged for us to stay on the edge of Oyster Pond in a cottage that belonged to Robert McNamara.

But before I could leave, there was a busy week of work. On the eleventh I nominated Army General John Shalikashvili to succeed Colin Powell as chairman of the Joint Chiefs of Staff when Colin's term ended in late September. Shali, as everyone called him, had entered the army as a draftee and risen through the ranks to his current position as the commander of NATO and U.S. forces in Europe. He was born in Poland, to a family from Georgia in the former Soviet Union. Before the Russian Revolution, his grandfather had been a general in the czar's army and his father had been an officer, too. When Shali was sixteen, his family moved to Peoria, Illinois, where he taught himself English by watching John Wayne movies. I thought he was the right man to lead our forces in the post–Cold War world, especially given all the problems in Bosnia.

In mid-month, Hillary and I flew to St. Louis, where I signed the Mississippi River flood relief legislation, after an enormous flood had caused the upper Mississippi River to overrun its banks all the way from Minnesota and the Dakotas down to Missouri. The bill-signing ceremony marked my third visit to the flooded areas. Farms and businesses had been destroyed, and some small towns within the hundred-year flood plain had been completely wiped out. On every trip, I marveled at the number of citizens from all over America who just showed up to help.

Then we flew on to Denver, where we welcomed Pope John Paul II to the United States. I had a productive meeting with His Holiness, who supported our mission in Somalia and my desire to do more in Bosnia. After we finished, he graciously received all the Catholics on the White House staff and on my Secret Service detail who had been able to come to Denver with me. The next day I signed the Colorado Wilderness Act, my first major environmental legislation, protecting more than 600,000 acres of national forests and public lands in the National Wilderness Preservation System.

Then I went on to Tulsa, Oklahoma, to speak to my old colleagues at the National Governors Association about health care. Though the ink was barely dry on the budget plan, I wanted to get started on health care and thought the governors might help, because the rising costs of Medicaid, state employees' health insurance, and health care for the uninsured were a big burden on state budgets.

On the nineteenth, my forty-seventh birthday, I announced that Bill Daley of Chicago would become the chair of our task force on the North American Free Trade Agreement. Six days earlier, with Canada and Mexico, we had completed the side deals to NAFTA on labor and environmental rights, which I had promised in the campaign, as well as one protecting our markets from import "surges." Now that they were in place, I was ready to go all out to pass NAFTA in the Congress. I thought Bill Daley was the ideal person to head the campaign for it. He was a Democratic lawyer from Chicago's most famous political family; his brother was the city's mayor, as his father had been before him, and he had good relationships with several labor leaders. NAFTA would be a very different fight from the budget. A lot of Republicans would support it, and we had to find enough Democrats to go along over the objections of the AFL-CIO.

After the Daley announcement we finally flew off to Martha's Vineyard. That night the Jordans hosted a birthday party for me, with old friends and some new ones. Jackie Kennedy Onassis and her companion, Maurice Tempelsman, came, along with Bill and Rose Styron, and Katharine

Graham, the publisher of the *Washington Post* and one of the people I most admired in Washington. The next day we went sailing and swimming with Jackie and Maurice, Ann and Vernon, Ted and Vicki Kennedy, and Ed and Caroline Kennedy Schlossberg. Caroline and Chelsea climbed up on a high platform of Maurice's yacht and jumped into the water. They dared Hillary to follow suit, and Ted and I urged her on. Only Jackie encouraged her to take a safer route to the water. With her usual good judgment, Hillary listened to Jackie.

I spent the next ten days hanging around Oyster Pond, catching crabs with Hillary and Chelsea, walking on the beach that bordered the pond and the Atlantic Ocean, getting to know some of the people who lived in the area year-round, and reading.

The vacation ended all too quickly, and we returned to Washington to the start of Chelsea's first year in high school, Hillary's campaign for health-care reform, Al Gore's first recommendations for savings through his National Performance Review, and a newly redecorated Oval Office. I loved working there. It was always light and open, even on cloudy days, because of the tall windows and glass door toward the south and east. At night the indirect lighting reflected off the curved ceiling, which added light and made it comfortable to work at home. The room was elegant yet inviting, and I always felt comfortable there, alone or in large groups. Kaki Hockersmith, a decorator friend from Arkansas, helped us with a new, brighter look: gold curtains in blue trim, gold high-back chairs, couches upholstered in gold-and-red stripes, and a beautiful deep blue rug with the presidential seal in the center, mirroring the one on the ceiling overhead. Now I liked it even better.

September was also the biggest foreign policy month of my presidency. On September 8, President Izetbegovic of Bosnia came to the White House. The threat of NATO air strikes had succeeded in restraining the Serbs and getting peace talks going again. Izetbegovic assured me that he was committed to a peaceful settlement as long as it was fair to the Bosnian Muslims. If one was reached, he wanted my commitment to send NATO forces, including U.S. troops, to Bosnia to enforce it. I reaffirmed my intention to do so.

On September 9, Yitzhak Rabin called to tell me that Israel and the PLO had reached a peace agreement. It was achieved in secret talks the parties held in Oslo, which we were informed of shortly before I took office. On a couple of occasions, when the talks were in danger of being derailed, Warren Christopher had done a good job of keeping them on track. The talks were kept confidential, which enabled the negotiators to deal candidly with the most sensitive issues and agree on a set of principles that both sides could accept. Most of our work lay in the future, in helping with the immensely difficult task of resolving the tough issues, hammering out the terms of implementation, and raising the money to finance the costs of the agreement, from increased security for Israel to economic development and refugee relocation and compensation for the Palestinians. I had already gotten encouraging signs of financial support from other countries, including Saudi Arabia, where King Fahd, though still angry about Yasser Arafat's support for Iraq in the Gulf War, was supportive of the peace process.

We were still a long way from a comprehensive solution, but the Declaration of Principles was a huge step forward. On September 10, I announced that the Israeli and Palestinian leaders would sign the agreement on the South Lawn of the White House on Monday, the thirteenth, and that because the PLO had renounced violence and recognized Israel's right to exist, the United States would resume its dialogue with them. A couple of days before the signing, the press asked me if Arafat would be welcome at the White House. I said that it was up to the parties directly involved to decide who would represent them in the ceremony. In fact, I badly wanted Rabin and Arafat to attend and urged them to do so; if they didn't, no one in the region would believe they were fully committed to implementing the principles, and, if they did, a billion people across the globe would see them on television and they would leave the

White House even more committed to peace than when they arrived. When Arafat said he would be there, I again asked Rabin to come. He accepted, though he was still a bit on edge about it.

In retrospect, the leaders' decision to come may look easy. At the time, it was a gamble for both Rabin and Arafat, who couldn't be sure how their people would react. Even if a majority of their constituents supported them, extremists on both sides were bound to be inflamed by the compromises on fundamental issues inherent in the Declaration of Principles. Rabin and Arafat showed both vision and guts in consenting to come and speak. The agreement would be signed by Foreign Minister Shimon Peres and Mahmoud Abbas, better known as Abu Mazen, both of whom had been intimately involved in the Oslo negotiations. Secretary Christopher and Russian foreign minister Andrei Kozyrev would witness the accord.

On the morning of the thirteenth, the atmosphere around the White House was alive with excitement as well as tension. We had invited more than 2,500 people to the event, which George Stephanopoulos and Rahm Emanuel had labored over. I was especially happy Rahm was working on this because he had served in the Israeli army. President Carter, who had negotiated the Camp David Accords between Egypt and Israel, would be there. So would President Bush, who, with Gorbachev, had co-sponsored talks in Madrid in 1991 involving Israel, the Palestinians, and the Arab states. President Ford was invited but couldn't get to Washington before the celebration dinner in the evening. All former secretaries of state and national security advisors who had worked for peace over the past twenty years were also invited. Chelsea was taking the morning off from school, as were the Gore children. This was something they didn't want to miss.

The night before, I had gone to bed at ten, early for me, and awakened at three in the morning. Unable to go back to sleep, I got my Bible and read the entire book of Joshua. It inspired me to rewrite some of my remarks, and to wear a blue tie with golden horns, which reminded me of those

Joshua had used to blow down the walls of Jericho. Now the horns would herald the coming of a peace that would return Jericho to the Palestinians.

We had two minor flaps early in the morning. When I was told that Arafat intended to appear in his trademark garb, a kaffiyeh and an olive green uniform, and that he might want to dress it up with the revolver he often wore on his hip, I balked and sent word that he couldn't bring the gun. He was here to make peace; the pistol would send the wrong message, and he certainly would be safe without it. He agreed to come unarmed. When the Palestinians saw that they were identified in the agreement as the "Palestinian delegation," not the PLO, they balked. Israel agreed to the preferred designation.

Then there was the question of whether Rabin and Arafat would shake hands. I knew Arafat wanted to do it. Before arriving in Washington, Rabin had said he would do the handshake "if it will be needed," but I could tell he didn't want to. When he arrived at the White House, I raised the subject. He avoided making a commitment, telling me how many young Israelis he had buried because of Arafat. I told Yitzhak that if he was really committed to peace, he'd have to shake Arafat's hand to prove it. "The whole world will be watching, and the handshake is what they will be looking for." Rabin sighed, and in his deep, world-weary voice, said, "I suppose one does not make peace with one's friends." "Then you'll do it?" I asked. He almost snapped at me, "All right. All right. But no kissing." The traditional Arab greeting was a kiss on the cheek, and he wanted no part of that.

I knew Arafat was a great showman and might try to kiss Rabin after the handshake. We had decided that I would shake hands with each of them first, then sort of motion them together. I was sure that if Arafat didn't kiss me, he wouldn't try kissing Rabin. As I stood in the Oval Office discussing it with Hillary, George Stephanopoulos, Tony Lake, and Martin Indyk, Tony said he knew a way I could shake hands with Arafat while avoiding a kiss. He described the procedure and we practiced it. I played Arafat and he played me, showing me what to do. When I shook his hand and moved in for the kiss, he put his left hand on my right arm where it was bent at the elbow, and squeezed; it stopped me cold. Then we reversed roles and I did it to him. We practiced it a couple of more times until I felt sure Rabin's cheek would remain untouched. We all laughed about it, but I knew avoiding the kiss was deadly serious for Rabin.

Just before the ceremony, all three delegations gathered in the large oval Blue Room on the main floor of the White House. The Israelis and the Palestinians still weren't talking to each other in public, so the Americans went back and forth between the two groups as they moved around the rim of the room. We looked like a bunch of awkward kids riding a slow-moving carousel.

Mercifully, it was over before long, and we walked downstairs to start the ceremony. Everyone else walked out on cue, leaving Arafat, Rabin, and me alone for a moment. Arafat said hello to Rabin and held out his hand. Yitzhak's hands were firmly grasped behind his back. He said tersely, "Outside." Arafat just smiled and nodded his understanding. Then Rabin said, "You know, we are going to have to work very hard to make this work." Arafat replied, "I know, and I am prepared to do my part."

We walked out into the bright sunshine of a late-summer day. I opened the ceremony with a brief welcome and words of thanks, support, and encouragement for the leaders and their determination to achieve a "peace of the brave." Peres and Abbas followed me with brief speeches, then sat down to sign the agreement. Warren Christopher and Andrei Kozyrev witnessed it while Rabin, Arafat, and I stood behind and to the right. When the signing was completed, all eyes shifted to the leaders; Arafat stood on my left and Rabin to my right. I shook hands with Arafat, with the blocking maneuver I had practiced. I then turned and shook hands with Rabin, after which I stepped back out of the space between them and spread my arms to bring them together. Arafat lifted his hand toward a still reluctant Rabin. When Rabin extended his hand, the crowd let out an audible gasp, followed by thunderous applause, as they completed the kissless handshake. All the world was cheering, except for diehard protesters in the Middle East who were inciting violence, and demonstrators in front of the White House claiming we were endangering Israel's security.

After the handshake, Christopher and Kozyrev made brief remarks, then Rabin moved to the microphone. Sounding like an Old Testament prophet, he spoke in English, and directly to the Palestinians: "We are destined to live together, on the same soil in the same land. We, the soldiers who have returned from battles stained with blood . . . , say to you today, in a loud and clear voice: Enough of blood and tears. Enough! . . . We, like you, are people—people who want to build a home, to plant a tree, to love, to live side by side with you in dignity, in affinity as human beings, as free men." Then, quoting the book of Koheleth, which Christians call Ecclesiastes, Rabin said, "To everything there is a season and a time to every purpose under heaven. A time to be born and a time to die, a time to kill and a time to heal, . . . a time of war and a time of peace. The time for peace has come." It was a magnificent speech. He had used it to reach out to his adversaries.

When Arafat's time came, he took a different tack. He had already reached out to the Israelis with smiles, friendly gestures, and his eager handshake. Now, in a rhythmic, singsong voice, he spoke to his people in Arabic, recounting their hopes for the peace process and reaffirming the legitimacy of their aspirations. Like Rabin, he promoted peace, but with an edge: "Our people do not consider that exercising the right to self-determination could violate the rights of their neighbors or infringe on their security. Rather, putting an end to their feelings of being wronged and of having suffered an historic injustice is the strongest guarantee to achieve coexistence and openness between our two peoples and future generations."

Arafat had chosen generous gestures to speak to the Israelis and tough words to reassure the doubters back home. Rabin had done the reverse. He had been heartfelt and genuine toward the Palestinians in his speech; now he used body language to reassure his doubters back in Israel. All the while Arafat was speaking, he looked uncomfortable and skeptical, so ill at ease that he gave the impression of someone who was dying to excuse himself. Their different tactics, side by side, made for a fascinating and revealing juxtaposition. I made a mental note to take it into account in future negotiations with them. But I shouldn't have worried. Before long, Rabin and Arafat would develop a remarkable working relationship, a tribute to Arafat's regard for Rabin and the Israeli leader's uncanny ability to understand how Arafat's mind worked.

I closed the ceremony by bidding the descendants of Isaac and Ishmael, both children of Abraham, "Shalom, salaam, peace," and urging them to "go as peacemakers." After the event I had a brief meeting with Arafat and a private lunch with Rabin. Yitzhak was drained from the long flight and the emotion of the occasion. It was an amazing turn in his eventful life, much of which had been spent in uniform, fighting the enemies of Israel, including Arafat. I asked him why he had decided to support the Oslo talks and the agreement they produced. He explained to me that he had come to realize that the territory Israel had occupied since the 1967 war was no longer necessary to its security and, in fact, was a source of insecurity. He said that the intifada that had broken out some years before had shown that occupying territory full of angry people did not make Israel more secure, but made it more vulnerable to attacks from within. Then, in the Gulf War, when Iraq fired Scud missiles into Israel, he realized that the land did not provide a security buffer against attacks with modern weapons from the outside. Finally, he said, if Israel were to hold on to the West Bank permanently, it would have to decide whether to let the Arabs there vote in Israeli elections, as those who lived within the pre-1967 borders did. If the Palestinians got the right to vote, given their higher birthrate, within a few decades Israel would no longer be a Jewish state. If they were denied the right to vote, Israel would no longer be a democracy but an apartheid state. Therefore, he concluded, Israel should give up the territory, but only if doing so brought real peace and normal relations with its neighbors, including Syria. Rabin thought he could make a deal with Syrian president Hafez al-Assad before or soon after the Palestinian process was completed. Based on my conversations with Assad, so did I.

Over time, Rabin's analysis of the meaning of the West Bank to Israel would become widely accepted among pro-peace Israelis, but in 1993 it was novel, insightful, and courageous. I had admired Rabin even before meeting him in 1992, but that day, watching him speak at the ceremony and listening to his argument for peace, I had seen the greatness of his leadership and his spirit. I had never met anyone quite like him, and I was determined to help him achieve his dream of peace.

After the lunch, Rabin and the Israelis flew home for the High Holy Days and the task of selling the agreement to the Knesset, the Israeli parliament, stopping on the way in Morocco to brief King Hassan, who had long taken a moderate position toward Israel, on the agreement.

That night Hillary and I hosted a celebratory dinner for about twenty-five couples, including President and Mrs. Carter, President and Mrs. Ford, and President Bush, six of the nine living secretaries of state, and Democratic and Republican congressional leaders. The Presidents had agreed to come, not only to celebrate the peace breakthrough, but also to participate in the public kickoff of the campaign for NAFTA the next day. During the evening I took all of them up to my office on the residence floor, where we took a picture to commemorate a rare occasion in American history when four Presidents dined together at the White House. After the dinner the Carters and Bush accepted our invitation to spend the night. The Fords declined, for a very good reason: they had booked the Washington hotel suite in which they had spent their first night as a married couple.

The next day we kept the momentum for peace going, as Israeli and Jordanian diplomats signed an agreement that moved them closer to a final peace, and several hundred

Jewish and Arab-American businesspeople gathered at the State Department to commit themselves to a joint effort to invest in the Palestinian areas when conditions were peaceful enough to permit a stable economy to develop.

Meanwhile, the other Presidents joined me at a signing ceremony for the NAFTA side agreements in the East Room of the White House. I made the case that NAFTA would be good for the economies of the United States, Canada, and Mexico, creating a giant market of nearly 400 million people; that it would strengthen U.S. leadership in our hemisphere and in the world; and that the failure to pass it would make the loss of jobs to low-wage competition in Mexico more, not less, likely. Mexico's tariffs were two and a half times as high as ours, and even so, next to Canada, it was the largest purchaser of U.S. products. The mutual phaseout of tariffs had to be a net plus to us.

Then Presidents Ford, Carter, and Bush spoke up for NAFTA. They were all good, but Bush was especially effective, and wittily generous to me. He complimented my speech by saying, "Now I understand why he's inside looking out and I'm outside looking in." The Presidents gave bipartisan gravitas to the campaign, and we needed all the help we could get. NAFTA faced intense opposition from an unusual coalition of liberal Democrats and conservative Republicans, who shared a fear that a more open relationship with Mexico would cost America good jobs without helping ordinary Mexicans, who they believed would continue to be underpaid and overworked no matter how much money their employers made out of trading with the United States. I knew they might be right about the second part, but I believed NAFTA was essential, not just to our relationships with Mexico and Latin America but also to our commitment to building a more integrated, cooperative world.

Though it was becoming clear that a vote on health-care reform would not come until the following year, we still had to get our bill up to Capitol Hill so that the legislative process could begin. At first, we considered just sending an outline of the proposal to the committees of jurisdiction and letting them write the bill, but Dick Gephardt and others insisted that our chances of success would be better if we started off with specific legislation. After a meeting with congressional leaders in the Cabinet Room, I suggested to Bob Dole that we work together on legislation. I did it because Dole and his chief of staff, an impressive former nurse named Sheila Burke, genuinely cared about health care, and, in any case, if I produced a bill he didn't like, he could filibuster it to death. Dole declined to work on drafting a joint proposal, saying I should just present my own bill and we'd work out a compromise later. When he said that, he may have meant it, but it didn't turn out that way.

I was scheduled to present the health-care plan to a joint session of Congress on September 22. I was feeling upbeat. That morning I had signed the bill creating AmeriCorps, the national service program; it was one of my most important personal priorities. I also nominated Eli Segal, who had shepherded the bill through Congress, to be the first chief executive of the Corporation for National Service. Attendees at the signing ceremony on the back lawn of the White House included young people who had answered my call to do community service that summer; two old veterans of FDR's Civilian Conservation Corps, whose projects still marked the American landscape; and Sargent Shriver, the first director of the Peace Corps. Thoughtfully, Sarge had lent me one of the pens President Kennedy had used thirty-two years earlier to sign the Peace Corps legislation, and I used it to bring AmeriCorps into being. Over the next five years, nearly 200,000 young Americans would join the ranks of AmeriCorps, a larger number than had served in the entire forty-year history of the Peace Corps.

On the evening of the twenty-second, I felt confident as I walked down the aisle of the House Chamber and looked up at Hillary sitting in the balcony with two of America's most famous doctors, the pediatrician Dr. T. Berry Brazelton, a longtime friend of hers, and Dr. C. Everett Koop, who had served as President Reagan's surgeon general, a position he used to educate the nation about AIDS and the importance of preventing its spread. Both Brazelton and Koop

were advocates of health-care reform who would lend credibility to our efforts.

My confidence slipped when I glanced at the teleprompter to begin my speech. It wasn't there. Instead, I was
looking at the beginning of the speech to Congress on the economic plan that I'd delivered in February. The budget had
been enacted more than a month earlier; Congress didn't
need to hear that speech again. I turned to Al Gore, who was
sitting in his customary seat behind me, explained the problem, and asked him to get George Stephanopoulos to fix it.
Meanwhile I started the speech. I had a written copy with me
and I knew what I wanted to say anyway, so I wasn't too worried, though it was a bit distracting to see all those irrelevant
words scrolling by on the teleprompter. At the seven-minute
mark, the right text finally came up. I don't think anyone
knew the difference at the time, but it was reassuring to get
my crutch back.

As simply and directly as I could, I explained the problem—that our system cost too much and covered too few—
and outlined the basic principles of our plan: security,
simplicity, savings, choice, quality, and responsibility. Everyone would have coverage, through private insurers, that
would not be lost when there was an illness or a job change;
there would be far less paperwork because of a uniform
minimum-benefit package; we would reap large savings
through lower administrative costs, which were then significantly higher than those of other wealthy nations, and a
crackdown on fraud and abuse. According to Dr. Koop,
that could save tens of billions of dollars.

Under our plan, Americans would be able to choose their
own health plan and keep their own doctors, choices that
were vanishing for more and more Americans whose insurance was carried by health maintenance organizations
(HMOs), which tried to hold down costs by restricting
patient choices and conducting extensive reviews before
approving expensive treatments. Quality would be assured
by the issuance of report cards on health-care plans to con-
sumers, and the provision of more information to doctors.
Responsibility would be enforced across the board against

health insurance companies that wrongfully denied care, providers who padded their bills, drug companies that over-charged, lawyers who brought bogus suits, and citizens whose irresponsible choices weakened their health and exploded costs to everyone else.

I proposed that all employers provide health insurance, as 75 percent of them were already doing, with a discount for small-business owners who otherwise couldn't afford the insurance. The subsidy would be paid for by an increase in cigarette taxes. Self-employed people would be able to deduct all the costs of their health-care premiums from their taxable incomes.

If the system I proposed had been adopted, it would have reduced inflation in health-care costs, spread the burden of paying for health care more fairly, and provided health security to millions of Americans who didn't have it. And it would have put an end to the kinds of horrible injustices I had personally encountered, like the case of a woman who had to give up a $50,000-a-year job that supported her six children because her youngest child was so ill she couldn't keep her health insurance, and the only way for the mother to get health care for the child was to go on welfare and sign up for Medicaid; or the case of a young couple with a sick child whose only health insurance came through one parent's employer, a small nonprofit corporation with twenty employees. The child's care was so costly that the employer was given the choice by its insurer of firing the employee with the sick child or raising the premiums of all the other employees by $200. I thought America could do better than that.

Hillary, Ira Magaziner, Judy Feder, and all those who helped them had crafted a plan that we could implement while reducing the deficit. And contrary to how it was later portrayed, health experts generally praised it at the time as moderate and workable. It certainly wasn't a government takeover of the health-care system, as its critics charged, but that story came later. On the night of the twenty-second, I was just glad that the teleprompter was working.

Toward the end of September, Russia dashed back into the headlines, as hard-line parliamentarians tried to depose Yeltsin. In response, he dissolved parliament and called new elections for December 12. We used the crisis to increase support for our Russian aid package, which passed the House, 321–108, on September 29 and the Senate, 87–11, on September 30.

By Sunday, October 3, the conflict between Yeltsin and his reactionary opponents in the Duma erupted into a battle on the streets of Moscow. Armed groups carrying hammer-and-sickle flags and portraits of Stalin fired rocket-propelled grenades into the building that housed a number of Russian television stations. Other reform leaders in former Communist countries, including Václav Havel, issued statements in support of Yeltsin, and I did, too, telling reporters that it was clear that Yeltsin's opponents had started the violence, that Yeltsin had "bent over backwards" to avoid using excessive force, and that the United States would support him and his effort to hold free and fair elections for parliament. The next day Russian military forces shelled the parliament building and threatened to storm it, forcing the surrender of the rebellion's leaders. Aboard Air Force One, on my way to California, I called Yeltsin with a message of support.

The battle in Moscow's streets was the top news story across the world that night, but the news in America led with a different story, which marked one of the darkest days of my presidency and made famous the phrase "Black Hawk Down."

In December 1992, President Bush, with my support, had sent U.S. troops to Somalia to help the UN after more than 350,000 Somalis had died in a bloody civil war, which brought famine and disease in its wake. At the time, Bush's national security advisor, General Brent Scowcroft, had told Sandy Berger they would be home before my inauguration. That didn't happen because Somalia had no functioning government, and without our troop presence, armed thugs would have stolen the supplies the UN had been providing and starvation would have set in again. Over the next several months, the United Nations sent in about 20,000 troops and we reduced the American force to just over 4,000, down from 25,000. After seven months, crops were growing, starvation had ended, refugees were returning, schools and hospitals were reopening, a police force had been created, and many Somalis were engaged in a process of reconciliation moving toward democracy.

Then, in June, the clan of Somali warlord Mohammed Aidid killed twenty-four Pakistani peacekeepers. Aidid, whose armed thugs controlled a good part of the capital city of Mogadishu and didn't like the reconciliation process, wanted to control Somalia. He thought he had to run the UN out to do so. After the Pakistanis were killed, Secretary-General Boutros-Ghali and his representative for Somalia, retired American admiral Jonathan Howe, became determined to get Aidid, believing the UN mission could not succeed unless he was brought to justice. Because Aidid was well protected by heavily armed forces, the United Nations was unable to apprehend him and asked the United States to help. Admiral Howe, who had been a deputy to Brent Scowcroft in the Bush White House, was convinced, especially after the Pakistani peacekeepers were killed, that arresting Aidid and putting him on trial was the only way to end the clan-based conflicts that kept Somalia mired in violence, failure, and chaos.

Just a few days before he retired as chairman of the Joint Chiefs of Staff, Colin Powell came to me with a recommendation that I approve a parallel American effort to capture Aidid, though he thought we had only a 50 percent chance of getting him, with a 25 percent chance of getting him alive. Still, he argued, we couldn't behave as if we didn't care that Aidid had murdered UN forces who were serving with us. Repeated UN failures to capture Aidid had only raised his status and tarnished the humanitarian nature of the UN mission, I agreed.

The American commander of the Rangers was Major General William Garrison. The army's Tenth Mountain Division, headquartered in Fort Drum, New York, also had troops in Somalia under the overall commander of U.S. forces

there, General Thomas Montgomery. They both reported to
Marine General Joseph Hoar, the commander of the U.S.
Central Command at MacDill Air Force Base in Tampa,
Florida. I knew Hoar and had great confidence in his judg-
ment and ability.

On October 3, acting on a tip that two of Aidid's top
aides were in Mogadishu's "Black Sea" neighborhood,
which he controlled, Major General Garrison ordered the
Army Rangers to mount an assault on the building where
the men were thought to be. They flew into Mogadishu in
Black Hawk helicopters in broad daylight. It was a much
riskier operation during the day than it would have been on
a dark night, when helicopters and troops are less visible
and their night-vision devices give them the ability to operate as well as they can in daylight. Garrison decided to take
the risk because his troops had carried out three previous
daylight operations successfully.

The Rangers stormed the building and captured Aidid's
lieutenants and some lesser figures. Then the raid went terribly wrong. Aidid's forces fought back, downing two of the
Black Hawks. The pilot of the first copter was pinned in the
wreckage. The Rangers would not abandon him: they never
leave their men on the field of battle, dead or alive. When
they went back in, the real fireworks began. Before long,
ninety U.S. soldiers were surrounding the copter, engaged in
a massive shoot-out with hundreds of Somalis. Eventually,
General Montgomery's Rapid Deployment Force entered
the action, but the Somali resistance was strong enough to
prevent the rescue operation from succeeding throughout
the night. When the battle was over, nineteen Americans
were dead, dozens were wounded, and Black Hawk pilot
Mike Durant had been captured. More than five hundred
Somalis were dead and more than a thousand wounded.
Enraged Somalis dragged the body of the slain Black Hawk
crew chief through the streets of Mogadishu.

Americans were outraged and astounded. How had our
humanitarian mission turned into an obsession with getting
Aidid? Why were American forces doing Boutros-Ghali's
and Admiral Howe's bidding? Senator Robert Byrd called

for an end to "these cops-and-robbers operations." Senator John McCain said, "Clinton's got to bring them home." Admiral Howe and General Garrison wanted to pursue Aidid; according to their sources in Mogadishu, many of his clan allies had fled the city and it wouldn't take much to finish the job.

On the sixth, our national security team convened in the White House. Tony Lake had also brought in Robert Oakley, who had been America's top civilian in Mogadishu from December through March. Oakley believed that the United Nations, including his old friend Admiral Howe, had made a mistake by isolating Aidid from the political process and by becoming so obsessed with tracking him down. By extension, he disagreed with our decision to try to apprehend Aidid for the UN.

I had a lot of sympathy for General Garrison and the men who wanted to go back and finish the job. I was sick about the loss of our troops and I wanted Aidid to pay. If getting him was worth eighteen dead and eighty-four wounded Americans, wasn't it worth finishing the job? The problem with that line of reasoning was that if we went back in and nabbed Aidid, dead or alive, then we, not the UN, would own Somalia, and there was no guarantee that we could put it together politically any better than the UN had. Subsequent events proved the validity of that view: after Aidid died of natural causes in 1996, Somalia remained divided. Moreover, there was no support in Congress for a larger military role in Somalia, as I learned in a White House meeting with several members; most of them demanded an immediate withdrawal of our forces. I strongly disagreed, and in the end we compromised on a six-month transition period. I didn't mind taking Congress on, but I had to consider the consequences of any action that could make it even harder to get congressional support for sending American troops to Bosnia and Haiti, where we had far greater interests at stake.

In the end, I agreed to dispatch Oakley on a mission to get Aidid to release Mike Durant, the captured pilot. His instructions were clear: The United States would not retaliate if Durant was released immediately and unconditionally. We would not trade the people who had just been captured. Oakley delivered the message and Durant was freed. I beefed up our forces and set a fixed date for their withdrawal, giving the UN six more months to establish control or set up an effective Somali political organization. After Durant's release, Oakley opened negotiations with Aidid and eventually secured a truce of sorts.

The battle of Mogadishu haunted me. I thought I knew how President Kennedy felt after the Bay of Pigs. I was responsible for an operation that I had approved in general but not in its particulars. Unlike the Bay of Pigs, it was not a failure in strictly military terms—Task Force Ranger had arrested Aidid's lieutenants by dropping into the middle of Mogadishu in broad daylight, executing its complex and difficult mission, and enduring unexpected losses with courage and skill. But the losses shocked America, and the battle that produced them was inconsistent with our larger humanitarian mission and the UN's.

What plagued me most was that when I approved the use of U.S. forces to apprehend Aidid, I did not envision anything like a daytime assault in a crowded, hostile neighborhood. I assumed we would try to get him when he was on the move, away from large numbers of civilians and the cover they gave his armed supporters. I thought I was approving a police action by U.S. troops who had far better capacity, equipment, and training than their UN counterparts. Apparently, that's also what Colin Powell thought he was asking me to approve; when I discussed it with him after I left the White House and he was secretary of state, Powell said he would not have approved an operation like that one unless it was conducted at night. But we hadn't discussed that, nor apparently had anyone else imposed any parameters on General Garrison's range of options. Colin Powell had retired three days before the raid and John Shalikashvili had not yet been confirmed as his replacement. The operation was not approved by General Hoar at Cent-Com or by the Pentagon. As a result, instead of authorizing an aggressive police operation, I had authorized a military assault in hostile territory.

In a handwritten letter to me the day after the fight, General Garrison took full responsibility for his decision to go forward with the raid, outlining his reasons for the decision: the intelligence was excellent; the force was experienced; the capacity of the enemy was known; the tactics were appropriate; planning for contingencies had been done; an armored reaction force would have helped, but might not have reduced U.S. casualties, because the task-force troops would not leave behind their fallen comrades, one of whom was pinned in the wreckage of his helicopter. Garrison closed his letter by saying, "The Mission was a success. Targeted individuals were captured and extracted from the target. . . . President Clinton and Secretary Aspin need to be taken off the blame line."

I respected Garrison and agreed with his letter, except for the last point. There was no way I could, or should, be taken off the "blame line." I believe the raid was a mistake, because carrying it out in the daytime underestimated the strength and determination of Aidid's forces and the attendant possibility of losing one or more of the helicopters. In wartime, the risks would have been acceptable. On a peace-keeping mission, they were not, because the value of the prize was not worth the risk of significant casualties and the certain consequences of changing the nature of our mission in the eyes of both Somalis and Americans. Arresting Aidid and his top men because the UN forces couldn't do it was supposed to be incidental to our operations there, not its main purpose. It was worth doing under the right circumstances, but when I gave my consent to General Powell's recommendation, I should also have required prior approval of the Pentagon and the White House for any operations of this magnitude. I certainly don't blame General Garrison, a fine soldier whose career was unfairly damaged. The decision he made, given his instructions, was defensible. The larger implications of it should have been determined higher up.

In the weeks ahead, I visited several of the wounded

soldiers at Walter Reed Army Hospital and had two moving
meetings with the families of the soldiers who had lost their
lives. In one, I was asked tough questions by two grieving
fathers, Larry Joyce and Jim Smith, a former Ranger who
had lost a leg in Vietnam. They wanted to know what their
sons had died for and why we had changed course. When I
gave the Medal of Honor, posthumously, to Delta snipers
Gary Gordon and Randy Shugart for their heroism in trying
to save Mike Durant and his helicopter crew, their families
were still in great pain. Shugart's father was furious at me,
and angrily told me that I wasn't fit to be Commander in
Chief. After the price he'd paid, he could say anything he
wanted as far as I was concerned. I couldn't tell if he felt the
way he did because I had not served in Vietnam, because I
had approved the policy that led to the raid, or because I
had declined to go back after Aidid after October 3. Regardless, I didn't believe the emotional, political, or strategic
benefits of catching or killing Aidid justified further loss of
life on either side, or a greater shifting of responsibility for
Somalia's future from the UN to the United States.

After Black Hawk Down, whenever I approved the
deployment of forces, I knew much more about what the
risks were, and made much clearer what operations had to
be approved in Washington. The lessons of Somalia were
not lost on the military planners who plotted our course in
Bosnia, Kosovo, Afghanistan, and other trouble spots of the
post–Cold War world, where America was often asked to
step in to stop hideous violence, and too often expected to
do it without the loss of lives to ourselves, our adversaries,
or innocent bystanders. The challenge of dealing with complicated problems like Somalia, Haiti, and Bosnia inspired
one of Tony Lake's best lines: "Sometimes I really miss the
Cold War."

SEVEN

I SPENT MUCH OF the rest of October dealing with the aftermath of Somalia and fending off efforts in Congress to limit my ability to commit American troops to Haiti and Bosnia.

On the twenty-sixth we finally celebrated a light moment, Hillary's first birthday in the White House. It was a surprise costume party. Her staff had arranged for us to dress up like James and Dolley Madison. When she got back from a long day of health-care work, she was led upstairs in a totally dark White House to find her costume. She came downstairs, looking wonderful in her hoop skirt and wig, to find me in white wig and colonial tights, and several of her staff dressed up like her in all her manifestations, with different hairdos and in different roles, from pushing health care to making tea and cookies. With my hair going white anyway, my wig looked good, but I looked ridiculous in the tights.

The next day, dressed in normal clothes, Hillary and I personally delivered our health-care legislation to Congress. Hillary had been briefing members of Congress from both parties for weeks and getting rave reviews. Many House Republicans had praised our efforts, and Senator John Chafee of Rhode Island, who represented the Senate Republicans, said that while he disagreed with parts of our plan, he thought we could work together to produce a good compromise. I was beginning to believe we might actually have an honest debate that would produce something close to universal coverage.

Our critics had a field day with the bill's length, 1,342 pages. Every year Congress passes bills more than a thousand pages long dealing with less profound and complex subjects. Moreover, our bill would have eliminated far more pages of laws and regulations than it proposed to add. Everyone in Washington knew that, but the American people didn't. The bill's length gave credibility to the effective ads the health insurance companies were already running against the plan. They featured two actors as a normal-looking couple named Harry and Louise, who talked wearily about their fears that the government was going to "force us to pick from a few health plans designed by government bureaucrats." The ads were completely misleading but clever and widely seen. In fact, the bureaucratic costs imposed by the insurance companies were a big reason Americans paid more for health care but still didn't have the universal coverage that citizens in every other prosperous nation took for granted. The insurance companies wanted to keep the profits of an inefficient and unfair system; tapping into the well-known skepticism of Americans about any major government action was the best way to do it.

In early November, *Congressional Quarterly* reported that I had enjoyed a higher success rate with Congress than any President in his first year since President Eisenhower in 1953. We had passed the economic plan, reduced the deficit, and implemented many of my campaign promises, including the EITC expansion, the empowerment zones, a capital gains tax cut for small business, the childhood immigration initiative, and student-loan reform. Congress had also approved national service, the Russian aid package, the motor voter bill, and the family leave law. Both houses of Congress had passed versions of my crime bill, which would begin funding the 100,000 community police officers I had promised during the campaign. The economy had already produced more private-sector jobs than had been produced in the previous four years. Interest rates were still low, and investment was up.

Al Gore's campaign mantra was coming true. Now everything that should be up was up and everything that should be down was down, with one big exception. Despite the successes, my approval ratings were still low. On November 7, in a special *Meet the Press* interview I did with Tim Russert and Tom Brokaw on the show's forty-sixth anniversary, Russert asked me why my ratings were down. I told him I didn't know, though I had a few ideas.

A few days earlier I had read a list of our accomplishments to a group from Arkansas who were visiting the White House. When I finished, one of my home staters said, "Then there must be a conspiracy to keep this a secret; we don't hear about any of this." Part of the fault was mine. As soon as I finished a task, I moved on to the next one, without doing a lot of follow-up communications. In politics, if you don't toot your own horn, it usually stays untooted. Part of the problem was the constant intrusion of crises like Haiti and Somalia. Part of it was the nature of the press coverage. The haircut, the Travel Office, and stories about the White House staff and our decision-making process were, I believed, either wrongly or overly reported.

A few months earlier, a national survey had shown that I had received an unusually high amount of negative press coverage. I had brought some of it on myself in mishandling press relations early. And maybe the press, which was so often called liberal, was in fact more conservative than I was, at least when it came to changing how things were supposed to work in Washington. Certainly they had different notions of what was important. Also, most of the people covering me were young, trying to build their careers in a system of twenty-four-hour news coverage where every story was expected to have a political edge and there were no kudos from colleagues for positive stories. This was almost inevitable in an environment where the print and network news media faced more competition from cable channels and where the lines between traditional press, tabloids, partisan publications, and political talk shows on TV and radio were being blurred.

The Republicans also deserved a lot of credit for the fact that my poll ratings were worse than my performance: they had been effective in their constant attacks and negative characterizations of the health-care and economic plans, and they had made the most of my mistakes. Since I had been elected, Republicans had won special U.S. Senate elections in Texas and Georgia, governors' races in Virginia and New Jersey, and the mayoral races in New York and Los Angeles. In each case, the outcome was determined by decisive local factors, but I sure didn't have much positive influence. People didn't yet feel the economy getting better, and the old anti-tax, anti-government rhetoric still had a lot of juice. Finally, some of the things we were doing that would help millions of Americans were either too complex for easy consumption, like the Earned Income Tax Credit, or too controversial to avoid being politically damaging, even when they were good policy.

November offered two examples of sound policy and questionable politics. After Al Gore plainly bested Ross Perot in a heavily watched TV debate on NAFTA, it passed the House, 234–200. Three days later the Senate followed suit, 61–38. Mark Gearan reported to the press that Al and I had called or seen two hundred members of Congress, and the cabinet had made nine hundred calls. President Carter also helped, calling members of Congress all day long for a week. We also had to make deals on a wide range of issues; the lobbying effort for NAFTA looked even more like sausage making than the budget fight had. Bill Daley and our whole team had won a great economic and political victory for America, but like the budget, it came at a high price, dividing our party in Congress and infuriating many of our strongest supporters in the labor movement.

The Brady bill also passed in November, after the Senate Republicans backed off a filibuster inspired by the National Rifle Association. I signed the bill, with Jim and Sarah Brady in attendance. Ever since John Hinckley Jr. shot Jim in Hinckley's attempt to assassinate President Reagan, Jim and Sarah had crusaded for sensible gun-safety laws. They had worked for seven years to pass a bill requiring a waiting period for all handgun purchases so that the buyers' backgrounds could be checked for criminal or mental-health problems. President Bush had vetoed an earlier version of the Brady bill because of the intense opposition of the NRA, which said it infringed on the constitutional right to keep and bear arms. The NRA believed the brief waiting period was an unacceptable burden on lawful gun buyers and declared that we could achieve the same result by increasing the penalties for illegally buying guns. Most Americans were for the Brady bill, but once it passed, it was no longer a voting issue with them. By contrast, the NRA was determined to defeat as many members of Congress who voted against them as possible. By the time I left office, the Brady background checks had kept more than 600,000 felons, fugitives, and stalkers from buying handguns. It had saved countless lives. But, like the budget, it exposed many of those brave enough to vote for it to harsh attacks, which were effective enough to drive several of them from office.

Not everything positive I did was controversial. On the sixteenth, I signed the Religious Freedom Restoration Act, which was intended to protect a reasonable range of religious expression in public areas like schools and workplaces. The bill was designed to reverse a 1990 Supreme Court decision giving states more authority to regulate religious expression in such areas. America is full of people deeply committed to their very diverse faiths. I thought the bill struck the right balance between protecting their rights and the need for public order. It was sponsored in the Senate by Ted Kennedy and Republican Orrin Hatch of Utah, and passed 97–3. The House adopted it by a voice vote. Though the Supreme Court later struck it down, I remain convinced it was a good and needed piece of legislation.

I always felt that protecting religious liberty and making the White House accessible to all religious faiths was an important part of my job. I assigned a member of the White House public liaison staff to be our bridge to the religious communities. I attended every one of the National Prayer Breakfasts that are held each year as Congress begins its work, speaking and staying for the entire event so that I could visit with the people of different faiths and political parties who came to pray for God's guidance in our work. And every year when Congress resumed after the August recess, I hosted an interfaith breakfast in the State Dining Room that allowed me to hear the concerns of religious leaders and share mine with them. I wanted to keep open the lines of communication to them, even those who disagreed with me, and work with them whenever I could on social problems at home and humanitarian problems around the world.

I believe strongly in separation of church and state, but I also believe that both make indisputable contributions to the strength of our nation, and that on occasion they can work together for the common good without violating the Constitution. Government is, by definition, imperfect and experimental, always a work in progress. Faith speaks to the inner life, to the search for truth and the spirit's capacity for profound change and growth. Government programs don't work as well in a culture that devalues family, work, and mutual respect. And it's hard to live by faith without acting on the scriptural admonitions to care for the poor and downtrodden, and to "love thy neighbor as thyself."

I was thinking about the role of faith in our national life in mid-November when I traveled to Memphis to address the convocation of the Church of God in Christ at Mason Temple Church. There had been a number of news reports about the rising tide of violence against children in African-American neighborhoods, and I wanted to discuss with the ministers and laypeople what we could do about it. There were obvious economic and social forces behind the disappearance of work in our inner cities, the breakdown of the family, the problems in schools, and the rise of welfare dependency, out-of-wedlock births, and violence. But the crushing combination of difficulties had created a culture that accepted as normal the presence of violence and the absence of work and two-parent families, and I was convinced that government alone could not change that culture. Many black churches were beginning to address these issues, and I wanted to encourage them to do more.

When I got to Memphis, I was among friends. The Church of God in Christ was the fastest-growing African-American denomination. Its founder, Charles Harrison Mason, received the inspiration for his church's name in Little Rock, on a spot where I had helped lay a plaque two years earlier. His widow was in the church that day. The presiding bishop, Louis Ford of Chicago, had played a lead-ing role in the presidential campaign.

Mason Temple is hallowed ground in the history of civil rights. Martin Luther King Jr. had preached his last sermon there, on the night before he was killed. I evoked the spirit of King and his uncanny prediction that his life might not last much longer to ask my friends to examine honestly "the great crisis of the spirit that is gripping America today."

Then I put away my notes and gave what many com-mentators later said was the best speech of my eight years as President, speaking to friends from my heart in the language of our shared heritage:

> If Martin Luther King were to reappear by my side today and give us a report card on the last twenty-five years, what would he say? You did a good job, he would say, voting and electing people who for-merly were not electable because of the color of their skin. . . . You did a good job, he would say, letting people who have the ability to do so live wherever they want to live, go wherever they want to go in this great country. . . . He would say you did a good job creating a black middle class . . . in opening opportunity.
>
> But, he would say, I did not live and die to see the American family destroyed. I did not live and die to see thirteen-year-old boys get automatic weapons and gun down nine-year-olds just for the kick of it. I did not live and die to see young people destroy their own lives with drugs and then build fortunes destroying the lives of others. That is not what I came here to do. I fought for freedom, he would say, but not for the freedom of people to kill each other with reckless abandon, not for the free-dom of children to have children and the fathers of the children walk away from them and abandon them as if they don't amount to anything. I fought for people to have the right to work but not to

have whole communities and people abandoned. This is not what I lived and died for.

I did not fight for the right of black people to murder other black people with reckless abandon. . . .

There are changes we can make from the outside in; that's the job of the President and the Congress and the governors and the mayors and the social service agencies. And then there's some changes we're going to have to make from the inside out, or the others won't matter. . . . Sometimes there are no answers from the outside in; sometimes all the answers have to come from the values and the stirrings and the voices that speak to us from within. . . .

Where there are no families, where there is no order, where there is no hope . . . who will be there to give structure, discipline, and love to these children? You must do that. And we must help you.

So in this pulpit, on this day, let me ask all of you in your heart to say: We will honor the life and the work of Martin Luther King. . . . Somehow, by God's grace, we will turn this around. We will give these children a future. We will take away their guns and give them books. We will take away their despair and give them hope. We will rebuild the families and the neighborhoods and the communities. We won't make all the work that has gone on here benefit just a few. We will do it together, by the grace of God.

The Memphis speech was a hymn of praise to a public philosophy rooted in my personal religious values. Too many things were falling apart; I was trying to put them together.

On November 19 and 20, I went back to putting things together, flying to Seattle for the first-ever leaders' meeting of the Asia-Pacific Economic Cooperation organization. Before 1993, APEC had been a forum for finance ministers to discuss economic issues. I had suggested that the leaders themselves should meet every year to discuss our common interests, and I wanted to use our first meeting, on Blake Island, just off the coast of Seattle, to pursue three objectives: a free-trade area covering the Americas and the Asian Pacific nations; an informal discussion of political and security issues; and the creation of habits of cooperation, which clearly were going to be more important than ever in the twenty-first century. The Asia-Pacific nations accounted for half the world's output and presented some of its most challenging political and security problems. In the past, the United States had never dealt with the region with the kind of comprehensive approach we followed toward Europe. I thought it was the moment to do so.

I enjoyed my time with the new Japanese prime minister, Morihiro Hosokawa, a reformer who had broken the Liberal Democratic Party's monopoly on power and who had continued to open Japan economically. I was also glad for the chance to talk at length with China's president, Jiang Zemin, in a more informal setting. We still had differences over human rights, Tibet, and economics, but we had a shared interest in building a relationship that would not isolate but integrate China into the global community. Both Jiang and Hosokawa shared my concern about the looming crisis with North Korea, which seemed determined to become a nuclear power, something I was determined to avoid and would need their help to accomplish.

Back in Washington, Hillary and I hosted our first state dinner, for South Korean president Kim Young-Sam. I always enjoyed the official state visits. They were the most ritualized events to occur at the White House, beginning with the official welcoming ceremony. Hillary and I would stand at the South Portico of the White House to greet our guests as they drove up. After greeting them, we would walk out onto the South Lawn for a brief receiving line, and the visiting dignitary and I would stand onstage, facing an impressive array of uniformed men and women from our armed services. The military band would play both nations' national anthems, after which I would escort my visitor on a review of the troops. We would then walk back to the stage to give brief remarks, often pausing on the way to wave to a crowd of schoolchildren, citizens from the visiting nation who were living in the United States, and Americans who had roots in the other country.

Before the state dinner, Hillary and I would host a small reception for the visiting delegation in the Yellow Oval Room on the residence floor. Al and Tipper, the secretary of state, the secretary of defense, and a few others would join us to visit with foreign guests. After the reception, a military honor guard of one man or woman from each service would escort us down the stairs past the portraits of my predecessors to a receiving line for the guests. During dinner, which was usually in the State Dining Room (with larger groups, dinner would be in the East Room or outside under a tent), we would be entertained by the U.S. Marine Corps Strolling Strings or their counterparts from the air force; I was always thrilled when they entered the room. After dinner, we had musical entertainment, often selected to suit the tastes of our guest. For example, Václav Havel wanted to hear Lou Reed, whose hard-driving music had inspired Havel's partisans in Czechoslovakia's Velvet Revolution. I took every opportunity I could to bring all kinds of musicians to the White House. Over the years we had Earth, Wind and Fire, Yo-Yo Ma, Placido Domingo, Jessye Norman, and many other classical, jazz, blues, Broadway, and gospel musicians as well as dancers from several disciplines. For the entertainment, we usually had room to invite more guests than could be accommodated at the dinner. Afterward, anyone who wanted to stay returned to the foyer of the White House for dancing. Usually, the honored guests were tired and soon left for Blair House, the official guest residence. Hillary and I would stay for a dance or two, then go upstairs while the revelers stayed at it for another hour or so.

In late November, I participated in the annual tradition going back to President Coolidge, of pardoning a Thanksgiving turkey, after which Hillary, Chelsea, and I left for a long Thanksgiving weekend at Camp David. I had a lot to be thankful for. My approval ratings were rising again, and American Airlines announced the settlement of its five-day-old strike. The strike could have been quite damaging to the economy; it was settled with the intense and skillful involvement of Bruce Lindsey. I was happy that my fellow citizens could fly home for the holiday.

Thanksgiving at Camp David became an annual tradition with our families and a few friends. We always had our Thanksgiving meal in Laurel, the largest cabin on the grounds, with its big dining and conference room, a large open space with a fireplace and television, and a private office for me. And we went by the dining hall to greet the navy and marine personnel and their families who kept the camp going. At night we watched movies and bowled. And at least once over the weekend, no matter how cold and rainy it was, Hillary's brothers, Roger, and I would play golf with whoever else was brave enough to go with us. Amazingly, Dick Kelley always played, though he was already almost eighty in 1993.

I loved every one of our Thanksgivings at Camp David, but the first one was special, because it was Mother's last. By late November, her cancer had spread and contaminated her bloodstream. She had to have blood transfusions every day just to stay alive. I didn't know how much longer she could last, but the transfusions made her look deceptively healthy and she was determined to live each day to the fullest. She enjoyed the football games on television, the meals, and visiting with the young servicemen and -women at the Camp David bar. The last thing she wanted to talk about was death. She was too alive to dwell on it.

On December 4, I went to California again, to hold an economic summit on the state's continuing difficulties, and spoke to a large group of people in the entertainment community, at the headquarters of Creative Artists Agency, asking them to join me in a partnership to reduce the massive amount of violence the media directed at young people, as well as the culture's assault on family and work. Over the next two weeks, I kept two of my commitments from the budget battle: I went to Marjorie Margolies-Mezvinsky's district for the conference on entitlements, and I appointed Bob Kerrey as co-chair, along with Senator John Danforth of Missouri, of a commission to study Social Security and other entitlements.

On December 15, I hailed the joint declaration of British prime minister John Major and Irish prime minister Albert Reynolds, which proposed a framework for the peaceful resolution of the Troubles in Northern Ireland. It was a wonderful Christmas present, one that I hoped would give me an opportunity to play a role in resolving a problem I had first become interested in as a student at Oxford. On the same day, I named an old friend from the McGovern days, John Holum, to head the Arms Control and Disarmament Agency and used the occasion to emphasize my nonproliferation agenda: ratification of the convention controlling chemical weapons, achieving a comprehensive nuclear test ban treaty, achieving permanent extension of the Nuclear Non-Proliferation Treaty (NPT), which expired in 1995, and fully funding the Nunn-Lugar program to secure and destroy Russian nuclear weapons and material.

On December 20, I signed a bill that was especially important to Hillary and me. The National Child Protection Act provided for a national database that any child-care provider could use to check the background of any job applicant. It was the brainchild of the writer Andrew Vachss, in response to stories of children subject to awful abuse in child-care centers. Most parents had to work, and therefore had to leave their preschool children in day care. They had a right to know their children would be safe and well cared for.

The Christmas season gave Hillary and me the chance to see Chelsea perform twice: in *The Nutcracker* with the Washington Ballet Company, where she went for class every day after school, and in a Christmas skit at the church we had chosen, Foundry United Methodist, on Sixteenth Street, not far from the White House. We liked Foundry's pastor, Phil

Wogaman, and the fact that the church included people of various races, cultures, incomes, and political affiliations, and openly welcomed gays.

The White House is special at Christmastime. Every year a large Christmas tree is brought in for the oval Blue Room on the main floor. It is decorated, as are all the public rooms, according to the year's theme. Hillary made American crafts the theme of our first Christmas. Artisans from around the country gave us Christmas ornaments and other works in glass, wood, and metal. Every Christmas, the State Dining Room has a huge gingerbread White House, which kids especially enjoy seeing. In 1993, about 150,000 people came through the White House during the holidays to see the decorations.

We also got another big tree for the Yellow Oval Room on the residence floor, and filled it with ornaments Hillary and I had been collecting since our first Christmas together. Traditionally, Chelsea and I put on most of the ornaments, following a practice we began as soon as she was old enough. Between Thanksgiving and Christmas we hosted a large number of receptions and parties for Congress, the press, the Secret Service, the residence staff, the White House staff and cabinet, other administration officials and supporters from around the country, family, and friends. Hillary and I would stand in line for hours, greeting people and taking pictures, as choirs and other musical groups from around the country performed throughout the house. It was an exhausting but happy way to thank the people who made our work possible and our lives richer.

Our first Christmas was especially important to me because I knew that, like our first Camp David Thanksgiving, it would almost certainly be our last one with Mother. We persuaded her and Dick to come spend a week with us, which she agreed to do when I promised I'd take her home in time for her to get ready to go to Las Vegas for Barbra Streisand's much-heralded New Year's Eve concert. Barbra really wanted her to come, and Mother was determined to go. She loved Barbra, and in her mind, Las Vegas was the closest thing she'd seen to heaven on earth. I didn't know what she'd do if it turned out there was no gambling or fancy entertainment in the afterlife.

While we were enjoying Christmas, Whitewater became an issue once more. For the previous several weeks, the *Washington Post* and the *New York Times* had been chasing rumors that Jim McDougal might be indicted again. In 1990, he had been tried and acquitted on charges arising out of the failure of Madison Guaranty. Apparently, the Resolution Trust Corporation was looking into whether McDougal had made illegal campaign contributions to politicians, including me. During the campaign, we had commissioned a report that proved we had lost money on the Whitewater investment. My campaign contributions were a matter of public record, and neither Hillary nor I had ever borrowed any money from Madison. I knew the whole Whitewater business was simply an attempt by my enemies to discredit me and impair my ability to serve.

Nonetheless, Hillary and I decided we should hire a lawyer. David Kendall had been at Yale Law School with us. He had represented clients in savings-and-loan cases and understood how to organize and synthesize complex and apparently unconnected material. There was a brilliant mind behind David's modest Quaker demeanor, and a willingness to fight against injustice. He had been jailed for his civil rights activity in Mississippi during Freedom Summer in 1964, and had argued death penalty cases for the NAACP Legal Defense Fund. Best of all, David Kendall was a terrific human being who would see us through the darkest moments of the years ahead with strength, judgment, and a great sense of humor.

On December 18, Kendall told us that the *American Spectator*, a right-wing monthly magazine, was about to publish an article by David Brock in which four Arkansas state troopers claimed they had procured women for me when I was governor. Only two of the troopers agreed to be interviewed on CNN. There were some allegations in the story that could be easily disproved, and the two troopers had credibility problems of their own, unrelated to their allegations against me: they had been investigated for insurance fraud involving a state vehicle they wrecked in 1990. David Brock later apologized to Hillary and me for the story. If you want to know more, read his brave memoir, *Blinded by the Right*, in which he reveals the extraordinary efforts made to discredit me by wealthy right-wingers with ties to Newt Gingrich and some adversaries of mine in Arkansas. Brock acknowledges that he allowed himself to be used in the smear by people who didn't care whether the damaging information they paid for was true or not.

The trooper story was ridiculous, but it hurt. It hit Hillary hard because she thought we'd left all that behind in the campaign. Now she knew it might never end. For the moment, there was nothing to do but carry on and hope the story would blow over. While it was raging, we went to the Kennedy Center one night for a performance of Handel's *Messiah*. When Hillary and I appeared in the President's box on the balcony, the large audience stood and cheered. We were moved by the kind and spontaneous gesture. I didn't realize how upset I had been until I felt tears of gratitude fill my eyes.

After a memorable Christmas week, Hillary, Chelsea, and I flew Mother and Dick home to Arkansas. Hillary and Chelsea stayed with Dorothy Rodham in Little Rock, and I drove with Mother and Dick to Hot Springs. We all went to dinner with some of my friends from high school at Rocky's Pizza, one of Mother's favorite haunts, just across the street from the racetrack. After dinner Mother and Dick wanted to go to bed, so I took them home, then went bowling with my friends, after which we came back to the little house on Lake Hamilton to play cards and talk until the early hours of the morning.

The next day Mother and I sat alone together over a cup of coffee for what turned out to be our last visit. She was upbeat as always, saying the only reason the trooper story came out when it did was that my poll ratings had rebounded in the last month to their highest level since my inauguration. Then she chuckled and said she knew the two troopers weren't the "brightest lights on the horizon," but she sure wished "the boys would find some other way to make a living."

For a brief moment I got her to think about the sand running out of the hourglass. She was working on her memoirs with a fine collaborator from Arkansas, James Morgan, and she had put her entire story on tape, but there were still several chapters in the drafting stage. I asked her what she wanted to happen if she didn't finish them. She smiled and said, "You're going to finish them, of course." I said, "What are my instructions?" She said I should check the facts, change anything that was wrong, and clarify anything that was confusing. "But I want this to be my story in my words. So don't change it unless you think I've been too hard on someone who's still alive." With that, she went back to discussing politics and her trip to Las Vegas.

Later that day I kissed Mother good-bye, drove to Little Rock to pick up Hillary and Chelsea, and flew to Fayetteville to see the number one–ranked Arkansas Razorbacks play basketball, then on to the Renaissance Weekend with our friends Jim and Diane Blair. After a jam-packed year, so full of highs and lows, it was good to have a few days with old friends. I walked on the beach, played touch football with the kids and golf with my friends, went to the panels, and enjoyed the company.

But my thoughts were never far from Mother. She was a marvel, still beautiful at seventy, even after a mastectomy, chemotherapy treatments that took all her hair and forced her to wear a wig, and daily blood transfusions that would have put most people in bed. She was ending her life as she had lived it, going all out, grateful for her blessings, without a shred of self-pity for her pain and illness, and eager for the adventures of every new day she could get. She was relieved that Roger's life was on track, and convinced that I was mastering my job. She would have loved to live to be one hundred, but if her time was up, so be it. She had found her peace with God. He could call her home, but He would have to catch her on the run.

EIGHT

THE YEAR 1994 was one of the hardest of my life, one in which important successes in foreign and domestic policy were overshadowed by the demise of health-care reform and an obsession with bogus scandal. It began with personal heartbreak and ended in political disaster.

On the night of January 5, Mother called me at the White House. She had just returned home from her trip to Las Vegas. I told her I had been calling her hotel room for several days and never found her in. She laughed and said she had been out day and night, having the time of her life in her favorite city, and she didn't have time to sit around waiting for the phone to ring. She had loved Barbra Streisand's concert, and was especially pleased that Barbra had introduced her and dedicated a song to her. Mother was in high spirits and seemed strong; she just wanted to check in and tell me she loved me. It wasn't much different from the countless calls we'd shared over the years, usually on Sunday nights.

About 2 a.m. the phone rang again, waking Hillary and me. Dick Kelley was on the line, crying. He said, "She's gone, Bill." After a perfect but exhausting week, Mother had just gone to sleep and died. I knew it was coming, but I wasn't ready to let her go. Now our last phone conversation seemed too routine, too full of idle chitchat; we had talked like people who think they have forever to talk to each other. I was aching to redo it, but all I could do was tell Dick that I loved him, that I was so grateful to him for making her last years happy, and that I'd get home as quickly as I could. Hillary knew what had happened from my end of the conversation. I hugged her and wept. She said something about Mother and her love of life, and I realized that the phone conversation was just the kind Mother would have chosen to be our last one. My mother was always about life, not death.

I called my brother, who I knew would be devastated. He worshipped Mother, all the more because she never gave up on him. I told him he had to hold up for her and keep building his life. Then I called my friend Patty Howe Criner, who had been part of our lives for more than forty years, and asked her to help Dick and me with the funeral arrangements. Hillary woke Chelsea and we told her. She had already lost a grandfather, and she and Mother, whom she called Ginger, had a close, tender relationship. On the wall of her study room, she had a terrific pen-and-ink portrait of Mother by Hot Springs artist Gary Simmons, entitled *Chelsea's Ginger*. It was moving to watch my daughter coming to terms with the loss of someone else she loved, trying to express her grief and keep her composure, letting go and holding on. *Chelsea's Ginger* is hanging in her room in Chappaqua today.

Later that morning we put out a release announcing Mother's death, which was all over the news immediately. By coincidence, Bob Dole and Newt Gingrich were on the morning news programs. Undeterred by the moment, interviewers asked about Whitewater; to one, Dole replied that it "cries out" for the appointment of an independent counsel. I was stunned. I would have thought that even the press and my adversaries would take a time-out on the day of my mother's death. To his credit, a few years later Dole apologized to me. By then, I better understood what had happened. Washington's narcotic of choice is power. It dulls the senses and clouds the judgment. Dole was not even close to being its worst abuser. I was touched by his apology.

That same day Al Gore went to Milwaukee to deliver a foreign-policy speech I had agreed to make, and I flew home. Dick and Mother's house was full of their friends, family, and the food Arkansas folks bring to ease common grieving. We all laughed and told stories about her. The next day Hillary and Chelsea arrived, as did some of Mother's other friends from out of state, including Barbra Streisand and Ralph Wilson, the owner of the Buffalo Bills, who had invited Mother to the Super Bowl the previous year when he learned she was a huge Bills fan.

No church was big enough to hold all Mother's friends and it was too cold to hold the funeral service at her preferred venue, the racetrack, so we scheduled it for the Convention Center. About three thousand people came, including Senator Pryor, Governor Tucker, and all my college roommates. But most of the attendees were simple working people whom Mother had met and befriended over the years. All the women from her "birthday club" were there, too. There were twelve members, each with a birthday in a different month. They celebrated them together over monthly lunches. After Mother died, as she requested, the other women picked a replacement; and they renamed their group the Virginia Clinton Kelley Birthday Club.

The Reverend John Miles presided over the service, referring to Mother as an "American original." "Virginia," he said, "was like a rubber ball; the harder life put her down, the higher she bounced." Brother John reminded the crowd of Mother's automatic response to every problem: "That's no hill for a stepper."

The service featured the hymns she loved. We all sang "Amazing Grace" and "Precious Lord, Take My Hand." Her friend Malvie Lee Giles, who once lost her voice completely, then got it back "from God" with an extra octave to spare, sang "His Eye Is on the Sparrow," and Mother's favorite, "A Closer Walk with Thee." Our Pentecostal friend Janice Sjostrand sang a powerful hymn Mother had heard at my inaugural church service, "Holy Ground." When Barbra Streisand, who was sitting behind me, heard Janice, she touched my shoulder and shook her head in amazement. When the service was over, she asked, "Who is that woman and what is that music? It's magnificent!" Barbra was so inspired by Mother's funeral music that she made her own album of hymns and inspirational songs, including one written in Mother's memory, "Leading with Your Heart."

After the funeral we drove Mother home to Hope. All along the way, people were standing by the road to show their respect. She was buried in the cemetery across the street from where her father's store had been, in the plot that had long awaited her, beside her parents and my father. It was January 8, the birthday of her favorite man outside the family, Elvis Presley.

After a reception at the Sizzlin' Steakhouse, we drove to the airport to fly back to Washington. There was no time to grieve; I had to go back to putting things together. As soon as I dropped Hillary and Chelsea off, I left for a long-planned trip to Europe to establish a process for opening NATO's door to the Central European nations in a way that wouldn't cause Yeltsin too many problems in Russia. I was determined to do everything I could to create a Europe that was united, free, democratic, and secure for the first time in history. I had to make sure NATO expansion didn't simply lead to a new division of Europe farther to the east.

In Brussels, after a speech in the city hall to a group of young Europeans, I received a special gift. Belgium was celebrating the hundredth anniversary of the death of my favorite Belgian, Adolphe Sax, inventor of the saxophone, and the mayor of Dinant, Sax's hometown, presented me with a beautiful new Selmer tenor sax made in Paris.

The next day the NATO leaders approved my Partnership for Peace proposal to increase our security cooperation with Europe's new democracies until we could achieve the expansion of NATO itself.

On January 11, I was in Prague with Václav Havel, twenty-four years to the week after my first trip there as a student. Havel, a small, soft-spoken man with dancing eyes and a biting wit, was a hero to the forces of freedom everywhere. He had been in prison for years and used the time to write eloquent and provocative books. When he was released, he led Czechoslovakia through a peaceful Velvet Revolution, then oversaw the orderly division of the country into two states. Now he was the president of the Czech Republic, eager to build a successful market economy and to claim the security of NATO membership. Havel was a good friend of our UN ambassador, Madeleine Albright, who was born in Czechoslovakia and delighted in every opportunity she had to speak with him in their native tongue.

Havel took me to one of the jazz clubs that had been

hotbeds of support for his Velvet Revolution. After the group played a couple of tunes, he brought me up to meet the band and presented me with another new saxophone, this one made in Prague by a company that, in Communist times, had produced saxophones for the military bands throughout the Warsaw Pact nations. He invited me to play it with the band. We did "Summertime" and "My Funny Valentine," with Havel enthusiastically joining in on the tambourine.

On the way to Moscow, I stopped briefly in Kiev to meet with Ukraine's president, Leonid Kravchuk, to thank him for the agreement that he, Yeltsin, and I would sign the following Friday, committing Ukraine to eliminate 176 intercontinental ballistic missiles and 1,500 nuclear warheads targeted at the United States. Ukraine was a large country of sixty million people with great potential. Like Russia, it was wrestling with the question of exactly what kind of future it wanted. Kravchuk faced considerable opposition in parliament to getting rid of his nuclear weapons, and I wanted to support him.

Hillary met me in Moscow. She brought Chelsea, too, because we didn't want her to be alone right after Mother's death. Staying together in the guest quarters of the Kremlin and seeing Moscow in the dead of winter would be a good distraction for all of us. Yeltsin knew I was hurting because he also had recently lost his mother, whom he adored.

Whenever we had a chance we took to the streets, shopping for Russian artifacts and buying bread at a small bakery. I lit a candle for Mother at Kazan Cathedral, now fully restored from the ravages of Stalinism, and visited the patriarch of the Russian Orthodox Church in the hospital. On January 14, after an impressive welcoming ceremony in the Kremlin's St. George's Hall, a massive white room with high arches and columns with the names of more than two hundred years of Russia's war heroes emblazoned in gold, Yeltsin and I signed the nuclear agreement with Ukranian president Kravchuk, and held talks about economic and security initiatives.

In the press conference afterward, Yeltsin expressed his appreciation for the American aid package and the one approved at the Tokyo G-7 meeting, for the commitment of $1 billion more in each of the next two years, and for our decision to reduce tariffs on five thousand Russian products. He gave a qualified endorsement of the Partnership for Peace, on the strength of my commitment to work out a special cooperative agreement between NATO and Russia. I was also pleased that we had agreed, as of May 30, not to target our nuclear missiles against each other or any other country, and that the United States would buy $12 billion worth of highly enriched uranium from Russia over the next twenty years, gradually removing it from any possibility of being used to make weapons.

I thought all these actions were good for both the United States and Russia, but not everyone agreed. Yeltsin was having some problems with his new parliament, especially with Vladimir Zhirinovsky, the leader of a sizable bloc of militant nationalists who wanted to return Russia to imperial glory and were convinced I was trying to reduce its power and reach. To push back a bit, I repeated my mantra that the Russian people should define their greatness in terms relevant to the future, not the past.

After the press conference, I did a town hall meeting with young people at the Ostankino television station. They asked questions about all the current issues, but they also wanted to know whether American students could learn anything from Russia, how old I was when I first thought of becoming President, what advice I could give a young Russian who wanted to go into politics, and how I wanted to be remembered. The students made me hopeful about the future of Russia. They were intelligent, idealistic, and fiercely committed to democracy.

The trip was going well, advancing important American interests in building a safer, freer world, but you would never have known it back home, where the only thing the politicians and press wanted to talk about was Whitewater. I even got questions about it on my trip from the American press accompanying me. Even before I left, the *Washington Post* and the *New York Times* had joined the Republicans in demanding that Janet Reno appoint an independent counsel. The only new development in recent months was that David Hale, a Republican who had been indicted in 1993 for defrauding the Small Business Administration, had said I had asked him to make a loan to Susan McDougal for which she was ineligible. I had not done so.

The standard for appointing an independent counsel under both the old law, which had expired, and the new one being considered by Congress was "credible evidence" of wrongdoing. In its January 5 editorial calling for an independent counsel in Whitewater, the *Washington Post* explicitly acknowledged that "there has been no credible charge in this case that either the President or Mrs. Clinton did anything wrong." Nevertheless, the *Post* said the public interest demanded an independent counsel, because Hillary and I had been partners in the Whitewater real estate deal (on which we lost money), before McDougal bought Madison Guaranty (from which we had never borrowed money). Even worse, we had apparently failed to take the full tax deduction for our losses. It was probably the first time in history when the flames of outrage against a politician were fanned because of money he lost, loans he didn't receive, and a tax deduction he didn't take. The *Post* said the Justice Department was headed by presidential appointees who couldn't be trusted to investigate me or to decide whether someone else should investigate me.

The independent counsel law was enacted in reaction to President Nixon's firing of Watergate special prosecutor Archibald Cox, who had been appointed by Nixon's attorney general and therefore was an executive branch employee subject to termination. Congress recognized both the need for independent investigations of alleged wrongdoing by the President and his major appointees and the danger of giving unlimited power to an unaccountable prosecutor with limitless resources. That's why the law required credible evidence of wrongdoing. Now the press was saying the President should agree to an independent counsel *without* such evidence, whenever anyone with whom he had ever been associated was being investigated.

In the Reagan-Bush years, more than twenty people were convicted of felonies by independent counsels. After six years of investigations and a finding by Senator John Tower's commission that President Reagan had authorized the illegal sales of arms to the Nicaraguan rebels, Iran-Contra prosecutor Lawrence Walsh indicted Caspar Weinberger and five others, but President Bush pardoned them. The only independent counsel investigation into a President's activities before he took office involved President Carter, who was investigated for a disputed loan to a peanut warehouse he and his brother, Billy, owned. The special prosecutor the President requested finished his investigation in six months, exonerating the Carters.

By the time I got to Moscow, several Democratic senators and President Carter had joined the Republicans and the press in calling for an independent counsel, though they couldn't give a reason that approached credible evidence of wrongdoing. Most of the Democrats didn't know a thing about Whitewater; they were just anxious to show they didn't object to Democratic Presidents being investigated, and they didn't want to be on the other side of the *Washington Post* and the *New York Times*. They also probably thought that Janet Reno could be trusted to appoint a professional prosecutor who would deal with the problem promptly. Regardless, it was clear that we had to do something, in Lloyd Bentsen's words, "to lance the boil."

When I arrived in Moscow, I got on a conference call with my staff, David Kendall, and Hillary, who was still in Washington, to discuss what we should do. David Gergen, Bernie Nussbaum, and Kendall were against asking for an independent counsel, because there were no grounds for one, and if we got unlucky, an unscrupulous prosecutor could pursue an endless disruptive investigation. Moreover, it wouldn't have to last long to bankrupt us; I had the lowest net worth of any President in modern history. Nussbaum, a world-class lawyer who had worked with Hillary on the congressional Watergate inquiry, was adamantly against a special prosecutor. He called it "an evil institution," because it gave unaccountable prosecutors the ability to do anything they wanted; Bernie said I owed it to the presidency, and to myself, to resist a special prosecutor with everything I had. Nussbaum also pointed out that the *Washington Post*'s disdain for the Justice Department's inquiry was unfounded, since my records were being reviewed by a career prosecutor who had been nominated for a Justice Department position by President Bush.

Gergen agreed, but argued forcefully that I should turn over all our records to the *Washington Post*. So did Mark Gearan and George Stephanopoulos. David said Len Downie, the *Post*'s executive editor, had achieved his spurs with Watergate and had convinced himself we were covering something up. The *New York Times* seemed to think so, too. Gergen thought the only way to defuse the pressure for an independent counsel was to produce the documents.

All the lawyers—Nussbaum, Kendall, and Bruce Lindsey—were against releasing the records because, while we had agreed to give the Justice Department everything we'd found, the records were incomplete and scattered, and we were still in the process of rounding them up. They said as soon as we couldn't answer a question or produce a document, the press would return to the drumbeat for an independent counsel. In the meantime, we'd get lots of bad stories full of innuendo and speculation.

The rest of my staff, including George Stephanopoulos and Harold Ickes, who had come to work as deputy chief of staff in January, thought that because the Democrats were taking the path of least resistance, the special prosecutor was inevitable, and we should just go on and ask for it, so we could get back to the people's business. I asked Hillary what she thought. She said that asking for the prosecutor would set a terrible precedent, basically changing the standard from requiring credible evidence of wrongdoing to giving in whenever a media frenzy could be stirred up, but that it had to be my decision. I could tell she was tired of fighting my staff.

I told everyone on the call that I wasn't worried about an investigation, because I hadn't done anything wrong and neither had Hillary, nor did I have any objections to releasing the records. After all, we had endured a lot of irresponsible Whitewater stories since the campaign. My instincts were to release the records and fight the prosecutor, but if the consensus was to do the reverse, I could live with it. Nussbaum was distraught, predicting that whoever was appointed would be frustrated when nothing was there, and would keep widening the investigation until he found something someone I knew had done wrong. He said if I felt I had to do more, we should just dump the records on the press and even offer to testify before the Senate Judiciary Committee. Stephanopoulos thought that was a terrible idea because of all the publicity it would generate. He said Reno would appoint an independent counsel who would satisfy the press and the whole thing would be over in a few months. Bernie disagreed, saying that if Congress passed a new independent counsel law and I signed it, which I had promised to do, the judges on the Washington, D.C., Court of Appeals would appoint a new prosecutor and start all over again. George got angry, saying Bernie was paranoid and it would never happen. Bernie knew that Chief Justice Rehnquist would name the panel and it would be dominated by conservative Republicans. He laughed nervously at George's outburst and said maybe the chances of a second prosecutor were only fifty-fifty.

After further discussion I asked to speak with just Hillary and David Kendall. I told them I thought we had to go along with the consensus of the nonlegal staff for a special prosecutor. After all, I had nothing to hide, and all the clamor was diverting the attention of Congress and the country from our larger agenda. The next day the White House asked Janet Reno to appoint a special prosecutor. Though I had said I could live with it, I almost didn't live through it.

It was the worst presidential decision I ever made, wrong on the facts, wrong on the law, wrong on the politics, wrong for the presidency and the Constitution. Perhaps I did it because I was completely exhausted and grieving over Mother; it took all the concentration I could muster just to do the job I had left her funeral to do. What I should have done is release the records, resist the prosecutor, give an extensive briefing to all the Democrats who wanted it, and ask for their support. Of course, it might not have made any difference. At the time I wasn't that worried about it, because I knew I hadn't broken any laws, and I still believed that the press wanted the truth.

Within a week Janet Reno appointed Robert Fiske, a Republican former prosecutor from New York, who would have completed his investigation in a timely way had he been left to do his job. Of course, Fiske was not allowed to finish, but I'm getting ahead of myself. For now, agreeing to the special prosecutor was like taking aspirin for a cold; it brought temporary relief. Very temporary.

On the way home from Russia, after a brief stop in Belarus, I flew to Geneva, for my first meeting with President Assad of Syria. He was a ruthless but brilliant man who had once wiped out a whole village as a lesson to his opponents, and whose support of terrorist groups in the Middle East had isolated Syria from the United States. Assad rarely left Syria, and when he did it was almost always to come to Geneva to meet with foreign leaders. On our visit, I was impressed by his intelligence and his almost total recall of detailed events going back more than twenty years. Assad was famous for long meetings—he could go on for six or seven hours without taking a break. I, on the other hand, was tired and needed to drink coffee, tea, or water to stay awake. Fortunately, the meeting ran only a few hours. Our discussion produced the two things I wanted: Assad's first explicit statement that he was willing to make peace and establish normal relations with Israel, and his commitment to withdraw all Syrian forces from Lebanon and respect its independence once a comprehensive Middle East peace was reached. I knew the success of the meeting resulted from more than personal chemistry. Assad had received a lot of economic support from the former Soviet Union; that was gone now, so he needed to reach out to the West. To do that, he had to stop supporting terrorism in the region, which would be easy to do if he made an agreement with Israel that succeeded in giving back to Syria the Golan Heights, lost in the 1967 war.

I returned to Washington to a whole series of those all-too-typical days when everything happens at once. On the seventeenth, Los Angeles was struck with the most costly earthquake in U.S. history, which caused billions of dollars of damage to homes, hospitals, schools, and businesses. I flew out on the nineteenth with James Lee Witt, director of the Federal Emergency Management Agency (FEMA), to view the damage, including a large stretch of interstate highway that had completely split open. On the twentieth, virtually the entire cabinet and I met with Mayor Dick Riordan and other state and local leaders in an airplane hangar in Burbank to plan emergency efforts. Thanks to a remarkable partnership, the recovery occurred quickly: the main freeway was rebuilt in three months; FEMA gave financial help to more than 600,000 families and businesses; and thousands of homes and businesses were rebuilt with Small Business Administration loans. The entire effort involved more than $16 billion in direct aid. I was distressed for Californians; they'd borne the brunt of the recession and the defense downsizing, suffered severe fires, and now the earthquake. One of the local officials joked to me that he was just waiting for a plague of locusts. His sense of humor reminded me of Mother Teresa's famous observation that she knew God would never give her a heavier burden than she could carry, but sometimes she wished He didn't have so much confidence in her. I returned to Washington to do an interview with Larry King on the first anniversary of the start of my presidency, telling him that I liked my job, even on the bad days. After all, I hadn't signed up to have a good time, but to change the country.

A few days later, President Assad's eldest son, whom he had groomed to succeed him, was killed in a car accident. When I called to express my condolences, Assad was obviously heartbroken, a reminder that the worst thing that can happen in life is losing a child.

That week I named the deputy secretary of defense, Bill Perry, to succeed Les Aspin, who had resigned as secretary not long after the day of Black Hawk Down. We had conducted an exhaustive search, and all the while the best candidate had been right under our noses. Perry had led several defense-related organizations, been a professor of mathematics and engineering, and done a superb job at the Pentagon, promoting Stealth technology, procurement reform, and realistic budgeting. He was a soft-spoken, modest man whose demeanor disguised a surprising toughness. He would turn out to be one of my best appointments, probably the finest secretary of defense since General George Marshall.

On the twenty-fifth, I gave my State of the Union address. It's the only time in a year when a President gets the chance to speak to the American people, unfiltered, for a whole hour, and I wanted to make the most of it. After a tribute to the late House Speaker Tip O'Neill, who had died the day before Mother, I summarized the long list of congressional achievements in 1993, saying that the economy was producing jobs; that millions of Americans had saved money by refinancing their homes at lower rates; that only 1.2 percent of the American people had had their income taxes increased; that the deficit would be 40 percent lower than previously predicted; and that we would reduce the federal payrolls by more than 250,000 instead of the 100,000 I had previously promised.

The rest of the speech was an outline of my 1994 agenda, beginning with education. I asked Congress to pass my Goals 2000 initiative to help public schools reach the national education goals the governors and the Bush administration had given the country, through reforms like school choice, charter schools, and connecting all our schools to the Internet by 2000; and to measure schools' progress toward reaching the goals the old-fashioned way, by whether our students were learning what they needed to know.

I also asked for more investments in new job-creating technologies and defense conversion projects; urged passage of the crime bill and a ban on assault weapons; and promoted three environmental laws: a Safe Drinking Water

Act, a revitalized Clean Water Act, and a reformed Superfund program. The Superfund was a public/private partnership to clean up polluted sites that had been abandoned and
had become ugly, unusable health hazards. It was important
to me and to Al Gore, and by the time we left office we had
cleaned up three times as many Superfund sites as the Reagan and Bush administrations combined.

I then asked Congress to pass both welfare reform and
health-care reform in 1994. One million people were on the
welfare rolls because it was the only way they could get
health care for their children. When people left welfare for
low-wage jobs without benefits, they were in the incredible
position of paying taxes to support the Medicaid program,
which provided health care for families that had stayed on
welfare. At some time during each year, nearly sixty million
Americans found themselves without health insurance.
More than eighty million Americans had "pre-existing conditions," health problems that meant they were paying more
for insurance, if they could get it, and often couldn't change
jobs without losing it. Three out of four Americans had policies with "lifetime limits" on how much of their health-care
costs would be covered, meaning they could lose their insurance just when they needed it most. The system hurt small
businesses, too; their premiums were 35 percent higher than
those paid by large businesses and government. To control
costs, more and more Americans were being forced into
health maintenance organizations, which restricted patients
in their choice of a doctor, and doctors in their choice of
care, and forced health-care professionals to spend more
and more time on paperwork and less on their patients. All
these problems were rooted in one fundamental fact: we had
a crazy-quilt pattern of coverage in which insurance companies called the shots.

I told the Congress I knew it was hard to change the system. Roosevelt, Truman, Nixon, and Carter had all tried
and failed. The effort virtually destroyed Truman's presidency, driving his approval ratings below 30 percent and
helping the Republicans gain control of the Congress. This
happened because, for all our problems, most Americans

had some kind of coverage, liked their doctors and hospitals, and knew we had a good system of health-care delivery. All those things were still true. Those who profited from the way health care was financed were spending huge sums to convince the Congress and the people that fixing what was wrong with the health-care system would destroy what it did right.

I thought my argument was effective except for one thing: at the end of the health-care portion of the speech, I held up a pen and said I would use it to veto any bill that didn't guarantee health insurance to all Americans. I did it because a couple of my advisors had said that people wouldn't think I had the strength of my convictions unless I demonstrated that I wouldn't compromise. It was an unnecessary red flag to my opponents in Congress. Politics is about compromise, and people expect Presidents to win, not posture for them. Health-care reform was the hardest of all hills to climb. I couldn't do it alone, without compromise. As it turned out, my error didn't matter, because Bob Dole would decide to kill any health-care reform.

In the short run, the State of the Union speech dramatically increased public support for my agenda. Newt Gingrich later said to me that after hearing the speech, he told the House Republicans that if I could persuade the congressional Democrats to deliver on my proposals, our party would be in the majority for a long time. Newt sure didn't want that, so, like Bob Dole, he would try to keep as much from happening before the midterm elections as possible.

In the last week of January, we had a heated debate with our foreign policy team over whether to grant a visa to Gerry Adams, leader of Sinn Fein, the political arm of the Irish Republican Army. America had great significance to both sides in the Irish conflict. For years, ardent American supporters of the IRA had provided funds for its violent activities. Sinn Fein had a larger number of partisans here among Irish Catholics who disowned terrorism but wanted to see an end to discrimination against their co-religionists and more political autonomy, with Catholic participation, in

Northern Ireland. The British and the Irish Protestants had their supporters, too, who deplored any dealings with Sinn Fein because of its ties to the IRA, and who believed that we had no business meddling in the affairs of the United Kingdom, our strongest ally. That argument had carried the day with all my predecessors, including those sympathetic to the legitimate grievances of Northern Ireland's Catholics. Now, with the Declaration of Principles, we had to revisit it.

In the declaration, for the first time ever, the UK pledged that the status of Northern Ireland would be determined by the wishes of its citizens, and Ireland renounced its historic claim to the six counties in the north until a majority of its people voted to change its status. The more moderate Unionist and Irish Nationalist parties were cautiously supportive of the agreement. The Reverend Ian Paisley, leader of the extreme Democratic Unionist Party, was outraged by it. Gerry Adams and Sinn Fein said they were disappointed because the principles lacked specificity as to how the peace process would operate and how Sinn Fein would be able to participate in it. Notwithstanding the ambiguous responses, the British and Irish governments clearly had created pressure on all the parties to work with them for peace.

From the time the declaration was issued, Adams's allies in America had been asking me to grant him a visa to visit the United States. They said it would increase his standing and his ability to get involved in the process and to press the IRA toward giving up violence. John Hume, leader of the moderate Social Democratic and Labour Party, who had built a career on nonviolent action, said he had changed his position on giving Adams a visa; he now thought it would advance the peace process. A number of Irish-American activists agreed, including my friend Bruce Morrison, who had organized our outreach to the Irish-American community in 1992, and our ambassador to Ireland, Jean Kennedy Smith. There was support in Congress from her brother, Senator Ted Kennedy; Senators Chris Dodd, Pat Moynihan, and John Kerry; and New York congressmen Peter King and Tom Manton. House Speaker Tom Foley, who had long been active in Irish issues, remained strongly opposed to the visa.

In early January, Irish prime minister Albert Reynolds informed us that, like John Hume, he now favored granting the visa because Adams was working for peace, and he felt the visa would give him leverage to move the IRA away from violence and into the peace process. The British government remained vehemently opposed to the visa, because of the long history of IRA terror and because Adams had neither renounced violence nor embraced the Declaration of Principles as the basis for settling the problem.

I told Albert Reynolds I would consider a visa if Adams had a formal invitation to speak in the United States. Shortly afterward, Adams, along with the leaders of Northern Ireland's other parties, was invited to participate in a peace conference in New York hosted by an American foreign policy group. This put the visa question front and center, where it became the first important issue on which my foreign policy advisors couldn't reach a consensus.

Warren Christopher and the State Department, including our ambassador to Great Britain, Ray Seitz, were strongly opposed to issuing the visa, arguing that since Adams wouldn't renounce violence, it would make us look soft on terrorism and that it could do irreparable damage to our vaunted "special relationship" with Great Britain, including our ability to secure British cooperation on Bosnia and other important matters. The Justice Department, the FBI, and the CIA agreed with State. Their unanimous opinion was entitled to great weight.

Three people were working the Irish issue at the National Security Council: Tony Lake, NSC staff director Nancy Soderberg, and our European affairs person, Army Major Jane Holl. With my support, they were taking an independent look at the visa question, while trying to reach a consensus position with the State Department, working through Undersecretary Peter Tarnoff. The NSC team became convinced that Adams favored an end to IRA violence, full participation by Sinn Fein in the peace process, and a democratic future for Northern Ireland. Their analysis made sense. The Irish were beginning to prosper economically, Europe as a whole was moving toward greater

economic and political integration, and tolerance for terrorism among the Irish had dropped. On the other hand, the
IRA was a tough nut to crack, full of hard men who had
built a life on hatred of the British and the Ulster Unionists,
and for whom the idea of peaceful coexistence and continuing to be a part of the UK was anathema. Since the population of the northern counties was about 10 percent more
Protestant than Catholic, and the Declaration of Principles
committed both Ireland and the UK to a democratic future
based on majority rule, Northern Ireland was likely to
remain a part of the UK for some time to come. Adams
understood that, but he also knew that terror wouldn't
bring victory and he seemed genuine when he said he
wanted the IRA to give it up in return for an end to discrimination against and isolation of Catholics.

Based on this analysis, the NSC determined that we
should grant the visa, because it would boost Adams's leverage within Sinn Fein and the IRA, while increasing American influence with him. That was important, because unless
the IRA renounced violence and Sinn Fein became a part of
the peace process, the Irish problem could not be resolved.

The debate raged on until a few days before the conference
was scheduled to open, with both the British government and
Adams's allies in the Congress and the Irish-American community turning up the heat. I listened carefully to both sides,
including an impassioned last-minute plea not to do it from
Warren Christopher and a message from Adams saying the
Irish people were taking risks for peace and I should take a
risk, too. Nancy Soderberg said she had come around on the
visa because she was convinced that Adams was serious about
making peace and that at present he couldn't say more about
his desire to move away from violence than he already had
without damaging his position within Sinn Fein and the IRA.
Nancy had advised me on foreign policy since the campaign,
and I had developed great respect for her judgment. I was also
impressed that Tony Lake agreed with her. As my national
security advisor, he had to deal with the British on many other
issues that could be adversely affected by the visa. He also
understood the implications of the decision in terms of our

overall efforts to combat terrorism. Vice President Gore also clearly grasped the larger context in which the decision had to be made, and he favored the visa, too. I decided to issue it, but to restrict it so that Adams couldn't do any fund-raising or travel outside New York during his three-day stay.

The British were furious. They thought Adams was just a fast-talking deceiver who had no intention of giving up the violence that had included an attempt to assassinate Margaret Thatcher and had already claimed the lives of thousands of British citizens, including innocent children, government officials, and a member of the royal family, Lord Mountbatten, who had overseen the end of British rule in India. The Unionist parties boycotted the conference because Adams was coming. For days John Major refused to take my phone calls. The British press was filled with articles and columns saying I had damaged the special relationship between our countries. One memorable headline read: "Slimy Snake Adams Spits Venom at Yanks."

Some of the press implied that I had issued the visa to appeal to the Irish vote in America and because I was still angry at Major for his attempts to help President Bush during the campaign. It wasn't true. I had never been as upset with Major as the British believed, and I admired him for sticking his neck out with the Declaration of Principles; he had a slim majority in Parliament and needed the votes of the Irish Unionists to keep it. Moreover, I despised terrorism, as did the American people; politically, there was a lot more downside than upside to the decision. I was granting the visa because I thought it was the best shot we had to bring the violence to an end. I remembered Yitzhak Rabin's adage: You do not make peace with your friends.

Gerry Adams came to the United States on January 31 and received a warm reception from Irish-Americans sympathetic to the cause. During the visit he promised to push Sinn Fein to make concrete positive decisions. Afterward the British accelerated their efforts to get political talks going with the Northern Irish parties, and the Irish government increased its pressure on Sinn Fein to cooperate. Seven months later the IRA declared a cease-fire. The visa decision had worked. It was the beginning of my deep engagement in the long, emotional, complicated search for peace in Northern Ireland.

On February 3, I began the day at my second National Prayer Breakfast. Mother Teresa was the guest speaker, and I argued that we should emulate her in bringing more humility and a spirit of reconciliation to politics. That afternoon I did a little reconciliation work myself, lifting our long trade embargo on Vietnam, based on remarkable cooperation from the Vietnamese government in resolving POW and MIA cases and in returning the remains of slain servicemen to the United States. My decision was strongly supported by Vietnam veterans in Congress, especially Senators John Kerry, Bob Kerrey, and John McCain, and Congressman Pete Peterson of Florida, who had been a prisoner of war in Vietnam for more than six years.

In the second week of February, after the brutal shelling of the Sarajevo marketplace by Bosnian Serbs had killed dozens of innocent people, NATO finally voted, with the approval of the UN secretary-general, to bomb the Serbs if they didn't move their heavy guns more than a dozen miles away from the city. It was long overdue, but still not a vote without risk for the Canadians, whose forces in Srebrenica were surrounded by the Serbs, or for the French, British, Spanish, and Dutch, who also had relatively small, and vulnerable, numbers of troops on the ground.

Soon afterward, the heavy weapons were removed or put under UN control. Senator Dole was still pushing for a unilateral lifting of the arms embargo, but for the moment I was willing to stick with it, because we had finally gotten a green light for the NATO air strikes, and because I didn't want others to use our unilateral abandonment of the Bosnian embargo as an excuse to disregard the embargoes we supported in Haiti, Libya, and Iraq.

In the middle of the month, Hillary and Chelsea left for Lillehammer, Norway, to represent America at the Winter Olympics, and I flew down to Hot Springs for a day to see Dick Kelley. It had been five weeks since Mother's funeral, and I wanted to check on him. Dick was lonely in their little house, where Mother's presence was still strong in every room, but the old navy veteran was getting his sea legs back and thinking about how to get on with his life.

I spent the next two weeks plugging health-care reform and the crime bill in different venues across the country, and dealing with foreign policy. We got a piece of good news when Saudi Arabia agreed to buy $6 billion worth of American planes, after intense efforts by Ron Brown, Mickey Kantor, and Transportation Secretary Federico Peña.

We also got a shock when the FBI arrested thirty-one-year veteran CIA agent Aldrich Ames and his wife, breaking one of the biggest espionage cases in American history. For nine years, Ames had made a fortune giving up information that led to the deaths of more than ten of our sources inside Russia, and had done severe damage to our intelligence capability. After years of trying to catch a spy they knew was there, the FBI, with CIA cooperation, finally nailed him. The Ames case called into question both the vulnerability of our intelligence apparatus and our policy toward Russia: if they were spying on us, shouldn't we cancel or suspend aid to them? In a bipartisan congressional meeting and in responses to press questions, I argued against suspending aid. Russia was engaged in an internal struggle between yesterday and tomorrow; yesterday's Russia was spying on us, but our aid was being used to support tomorrow's Russia, by strengthening democracy and economic reform, and securing and destroying its nuclear weapons. Besides, the Russians weren't the only ones with spies.

Toward the end of the month, a militant Israeli settler, outraged at the prospect of turning the West Bank back to the Palestinians, gunned down several worshippers at the Mosque of Abraham in Hebron. The murderer had struck during the Muslim holy month of Ramadan, at a site sacred to both Muslims and Jews because it is thought to be the burial site of Abraham and his wife, Sarah. It seemed clear that his intention was to spark a violent reaction that would derail the peace process. To head that off, I asked Warren Christopher to contact Rabin and Arafat and invite them to send negotiators to Washington as soon as possible and have them stay until they had settled on concrete actions to implement their agreement.

On February 28, NATO fighters shot down four Serb planes for violating the no-fly zone, the first military action in the forty-four-year history of the alliance. I hoped that the air strikes, along with our success in relieving the siege of Sarajevo, would convince the allies to take a stronger posture toward Serb aggression in and around the embattled towns of Tuzla and Srebrenica as well.

One of those allies, John Major, was in America that day to talk about Bosnia and Northern Ireland. I took him first to Pittsburgh, where his grandfather had worked in the steel mills in the nineteenth century. Major seemed to enjoy retracing his roots to the industrial heartland of America. That night he stayed at the White House, the first foreign leader to do so during my tenure. The next day we held a press conference, which was unmemorable except for the larger message it sent: that our disagreement over the Adams visa would not undermine the Anglo-American relationship or keep us from working together closely on Bosnia and other issues. I found Major to be serious, intelligent, and, as I said earlier, genuinely committed to resolving the Irish problem, despite the fact that the very effort to do so posed a threat to his already precarious situation in Parliament. I thought he was a better leader than his press coverage often suggested, and after our two days together we maintained a friendly and productive working relationship.

NINE

WHILE I WAS hard at work on foreign affairs, the new world of Whitewater was beginning to take shape at home. In March, Robert Fiske began his job in earnest by sending out subpoenas to several members of the White House staff, including Maggie Williams and Lisa Caputo, who worked for Hillary and were friends of Vince Foster's. Mack McLarty set up a Whitewater Response Team, led by Harold Ickes, to coordinate responses to questions from Fiske and from the press; to free the rest of the staff, and me, to do the public work we came to Washington to do; and to minimize conversations our staff might have about Whitewater among themselves or with Hillary or me. Any such conversations could only expose our young staffers to depositions, political attacks, and big legal bills. A lot of people had already acquired a vested interest in finding something wrong; if there was nothing illegal in our long-ago land deal, perhaps they could catch someone doing something wrong in the handling of it.

The system worked well enough for me. After all, I had learned how to lead parallel lives as a child: most of the time, I could shut out all the accusations and innuendo and go on with my work. I knew it would be harder to cope with for those who had never lived with the constant threat of arbitrary and destructive attacks, especially in an atmosphere in which there was a presumption of guilt attached to any charge. To be sure, there were some legal experts, like Sam Dash, who talked about how cooperative we were compared with the Reagan and Nixon administrations, because we didn't resist subpoenas and we turned all our records over to the Justice Department and then to Fiske. But the goalposts had been moved: unless Hillary and I could prove ourselves innocent of whatever charges any adversary could come up with, most of the questions would be asked, and the stories written, in a tone of intense suspicion; the underlying current was that we must have done something wrong.

For example, as our financial records found their way into the press, the *New York Times* reported that, starting with a $1,000 investment, Hillary had made $100,000 in the commodities market in 1979, with the help of Jim Blair. Blair was one of my closest friends; he did help Hillary and a number of his other friends in trading commodities, but she took her own risks, paid more than $18,000 in brokerage fees, and, following her own instincts, got out of the market before it dropped. Leo Melamed, the Republican former chairman of the Chicago Mercantile Exchange, on which agricultural commodities are traded, reviewed all of Hillary's trades and said there was nothing wrong with them. It didn't matter. For years, the critics would refer to Hillary's commodity profit as prima facie evidence of corruption.

The presumption of wrongdoing was reflected in a *Newsweek* story saying Hillary did not put up her own money for her "sweet deal," with an analysis that it said was based on the expert opinion of Professor Marvin Chirelstein of Columbia Law School, one of the nation's leading authorities on corporate law and contracts, who had taught me at Yale and who had been asked by our lawyer to review our tax returns for 1978–79, the period of the Whitewater investment. Chirelstein disputed the *Newsweek* story, saying, "I never said anything like that," and that he was "outraged" and "humiliated."

About the same time, *Time* magazine ran a cover photograph purporting to show George Stephanopoulos peering over my shoulder as I sat at my desk fretting over Whitewater. In fact, the photo captured an earlier routine scheduling meeting at which several people were present. At least two others were in the original picture. *Time* simply cropped them out.

In April, Hillary held a press conference to answer questions about her commodity trades and Whitewater. She did a fine job and I was proud of her. She even got a laugh from the press corps when she acknowledged that her belief in a "zone of privacy" might have made her less responsive to press questions about her past personal dealings than she should have been, but that "after resisting for a long time, I've been rezoned."

The presumption of guilt imposed on us was extended to others. For example, Roger Altman and Bernie Nussbaum were both heavily criticized for discussing criminal referrals issued against Madison Guaranty by the Resolution Trust Corporation, because the RTC was a part of the Treasury Department and Altman was overseeing it temporarily. Presumably, the critics thought Nussbaum could have been trying to influence the RTC proceedings. In fact, the discussions were a result of the need to answer press questions arising out of leaks about the Madison investigation, and they had been approved by the Treasury Department's ethics counsel.

Edwin Yoder, an old-fashioned progressive columnist, said Washington was being overtaken by "ethical cleansers." In a column on the Nussbaum-Altman meeting, he said:

> I wish someone would begin by explaining to me why it is so very wicked for White House staff to want information from elsewhere within the executive branch about charges and rumors concerning the president. . . .

Robert Fiske found the contacts between the White House and the Treasury Department to be legal, but that didn't stop the smearing of Nussbaum and Altman. Back then, all our political appointees needed to be read their Miranda warnings three times a day. Bernie Nussbaum resigned in early March; he never got over my foolish decision to ask for an independent counsel, and he didn't want to be a source of further problems. Altman would leave government service a few months later. They were both able, honest public servants.

In March, Roger Ailes, a longtime Republican operative who had become president of CNBC, accused the administration of "a cover-up with regard to Whitewater that includes . . . land fraud, illegal contributions, abuse of power . . . suicide cover-up—possible murder." So much for the "credible evidence of wrongdoing" standard.

William Safire, the *New York Times* columnist who had been a speechwriter for Nixon and Agnew, and who seemed determined to prove that all their successors were just as bad as they were, was especially avid in his unsupported assertions that Vince's death was linked to illegal conduct by Hillary and me. Of course, Vince's suicide note had said exactly the reverse, that we had done nothing wrong, but that didn't prevent Safire from speculating that Vince had improperly kept records damaging to us in his office.

We now know that a lot of the so-called information that fueled the damaging but erroneous stories was fed to the press by David Hale and the right-wingers who adopted him for their own purposes. In 1993, Hale, the Republican municipal judge in Little Rock, was charged with defrauding the Small Business Administration of $900,000 in federal funds that were supposed to have been used to make loans to minority businesses through his company, Capital Management Services (a later GAO audit indicated he had defrauded the SBA of $3.4 million). Instead, he gave the money to himself through a series of dummy corporations. Hale discussed his plight with Justice Jim Johnson, the old Arkansas racist who had run against Win Rockefeller for governor in 1966 and against Senator Fulbright in 1968. Johnson took Hale under his wing, and in August put him in contact with a conservative group called Citizens United, whose principals were Floyd Brown and David Bossie. Brown had produced the infamous Willie Horton ads against Mike Dukakis in 1988. Bossie had helped him write a book for the 1992 campaign entitled *Slick Willie: Why America Cannot Trust Bill Clinton*, in which the authors gave "special thanks" to Justice Jim Johnson.

Hale claimed that I had pressed him to lend $300,000 from Capital Management to a company owned by Susan McDougal, for the purpose of giving it out to leading Arkansas Democrats. In return, McDougal would lend Hale more than $800,000 from Madison Guaranty, enabling him to get another million dollars from the Small Business Administration. It was an absurd and untrue story, but Brown and Bossie peddled it hard. Apparently, my old Arkansas nemesis Sheffield Nelson also helped, by pushing it to his contact at the *New York Times*, Jeff Gerth.

By March 1994, the media was wringing its hands about some documents shredded by the Rose firm; one of the boxes that held the papers had Vince Foster's initials on it. The firm explained that the shredding involved material unrelated to Whitewater and was a normal procedure involving papers that were no longer needed. No one in our White House knew about the routine destruction of unneeded records unrelated to Whitewater at the Rose firm. Moreover, we had nothing to cover up, and there still wasn't a bit of evidence to indicate that we did.

It got so bad that even the highly respected journalist David Broder referred to Bernie Nussbaum as "unfortunate" for allegedly tolerating arrogance and abuse of power that led to "the all-too-familiar words—investigation, subpoena, grand jury, resignation" that had "echoed through Washington again this past week." Broder even compared the "war rooms" that managed our campaigns for the economic plan and NAFTA to Nixon's enemies list.

Nussbaum was unfortunate, all right; there would have been no investigation, subpoenas, or grand jury if I had listened to him and refused to give in to the demands for an independent counsel to "clear the air." Bernie's real offense was that he thought I should abide by the rule of law and accepted standards of propriety, rather than the constantly shifting standards of the Whitewater media, which were designed to produce the very results they professed to deplore. Nussbaum's successor, longtime Washington attorney Lloyd Cutler, had a justifiably good reputation in the Washington establishment. In the coming months, his presence and advice would help a great deal, but he couldn't turn the Whitewater tide.

Rush Limbaugh was having a field day on his show, wallowing in the Whitewater mud. He claimed that Vince had been murdered in an apartment Hillary owned, and that his body had been moved to Fort Marcy Park. I could not imagine how that made Vince's wife and kids feel. Later, Limbaugh falsely charged that "journalists and others working on or involved in Whitewatergate have been beaten and harassed in Little Rock. Some have died."

Not to be outdone by Limbaugh, former Republican congressman Bill Dannemeyer called for congressional hearings on the "frightening" number of people connected to me who had died "under other than natural circumstances." Dannemeyer's grisly list included my campaign finance co-chairman, Vic Raiser, and his son, who had died tragically in a plane crash on a trip to Alaska in 1992, and Paul Tully, the political director of the Democratic Party who had died of a heart attack while working on the campaign in Little Rock. I had delivered eulogies at both funerals, and later appointed Vic's widow, Molly, as chief of protocol.

Jerry Falwell outdid Dannemeyer by releasing *Circle of Power*, a video about "countless people who mysteriously died" in Arkansas; the film implied that I was somehow responsible. Then came Falwell's sequel, *The Clinton Chronicles*, which he promoted on his television show, *The Old Time Gospel Hour*. The video featured Dannemeyer and Justice Jim Johnson, and accused me of being involved with cocaine smuggling, having witnesses killed, and arranging the murders of a private investigator and the wife of a state trooper. A lot of the "witnesses" were paid for their testimonials, and Falwell sold a great many videos.

As Whitewater unfolded, I tried to keep some perspective, and to remember that not everyone was caught up in the hysteria. For example, *USA Today* ran a fair story on Whitewater that included interviews with Jim McDougal, who said Hillary and I didn't do anything wrong, and Chris Wade, the real estate agent in north Arkansas who supervised the Whitewater land, who also said we were telling the truth about our limited involvement with the property.

I could understand why right-wingers like Rush Limbaugh, Bill Dannemeyer, Jerry Falwell, and a paper like the *Washington Times* would say such things. The *Washington Times* was avowedly right-wing, financed by the Reverend

Sun Myung Moon, and edited by Wes Pruden Jr., whose father, the Reverend Wesley Pruden, had been chaplain of the White Citizens' Council in Arkansas and an ally of Justice Jim Johnson's in their lost crusade against civil rights for blacks. What I couldn't believe was that the *New York Times*, the *Washington Post*, and others in the media I had always respected and trusted had been sucker punched by the likes of Floyd Brown, David Bossie, David Hale, and Jim Johnson.

Around this time I hosted a dinner at the White House to observe Black History Month. Among the attendees were my old law school professor Burke Marshall and his friend Nicholas Katzenbach, who had done so much to advance civil rights in the Kennedy Justice Department. Nick came up to me and told me that he was on the board of the *Washington Post* and that he was ashamed of the paper's coverage of Whitewater and the "terrible damage" that had been done to me and the presidency over charges that didn't amount to a hill of beans: "What is this about?" he asked. "It sure isn't about the public interest."

Whatever it was about, it was working. A poll in March said that half the people thought Hillary and I were lying about Whitewater, and a third of them thought we had done something illegal. I have to confess that Whitewater, especially the attacks on Hillary, took a bigger toll on me than I thought it would. The charges were baseless and unsupported by any reliable evidence. I had other problems, but except for occasionally being hardheaded, Hillary was above reproach. It killed me to see her hurt by one false charge after another, all the more so because I had made things worse by giving in to the naïve notion that an independent counsel would clear the air. I had to work hard to keep my anger in check, and I didn't always succeed. The cabinet and staff seemed to understand and tolerate my occasional flare-ups, and Al Gore helped me get through them. Though I kept working hard and continued to love my job, my normally sunny disposition and innate optimism would be put to one severe test after another.

It helped to laugh about it. Every spring there are three

press dinners, hosted by the Gridiron Club, the White House correspondents, and the radio and television correspondents. They give the press an opportunity to poke fun at the President and other politicians, and the President gets a chance to reply. I looked forward to these occasions because they allowed all of us to let our guards down a little, and because they reminded me that the press was not a monolith and was made up mostly of good people trying to be fair. Also, as Proverbs says, "A happy heart doeth good like medicine, but a broken spirit drieth the bones."

I was in pretty good spirits on April 12 at the Radio and Television Correspondents' dinner, and I got off some good lines, like "I really am delighted to be here. If you believe that I've got some land in northwest Arkansas I'd like to show you"; "Some say my relations with the press have been marked by self-pity. I like to think of it as the outer limits of my empathy. I feel my pain"; "It's three days before April fifteenth, and most of you have to spend more time on my taxes than your own"; and "I still believe in a place called Help!"

The work of what Hillary would later call the "vast right-wing conspiracy" has been chronicled in great detail by Sidney Blumenthal in *The Clinton Wars* and by Joe Conason and Gene Lyons in *The Hunting of the President*. As far as I know, none of their factual assertions have been refuted. When those books were published, the people in the mainstream media who had been part of the Whitewater mania ignored their charges, dismissed the authors as being too sympathetic to Hillary and me, or blamed us for the way we handled the Whitewater problem and for complaining. I'm sure we could have handled it better, but so could they.

In the early days of Whitewater, one of my friends was forced to resign his government post because of something he had done wrong before he came to Washington. The Rose Law Firm filed a complaint against Webb Hubbell with the Arkansas Bar Association for allegedly overcharging his clients and padding his expenses. Webb resigned from the Justice Department, but assured Hillary there was nothing to the charges, saying that the whole problem arose because his wealthy but irascible father-in-law, Seth Ward, had refused to pay the Rose firm for the costs of a patent infringement case they had lost. It seemed plausible, but it wasn't true.

It turned out that Webb *had* overcharged his clients, and in so doing, had injured the Rose firm and reduced the income of all his partners, including Hillary. If his case had played out normally, he probably would have reached an agreement with the law firm to repay it for the cost of reimbursing its clients and would have lost his license for a year or two. The bar association might or might not have referred him to the state prosecuting attorney; if it had, Hubbell probably would have been able to avoid going to prison by reimbursing the firm. Instead, Webb was caught up in the independent counsel's net.

When the facts first came out, I was stunned. Webb and I had been friends and golfing partners for years, and I thought I knew him well. I still think he's a good man who made a bad mistake, one he had to pay too high a price for, because he refused to become a pawn in Starr's game.

While all this was going on, I stayed on the other track of my parallel lives, the one I came to Washington to pursue. In March, I devoted considerable time to pushing two bills that I thought would help workers without college degrees. Most people could no longer keep one job or even stay with one employer for their entire working lives, and the churning job market treated them in markedly different ways. Our 6.5 percent unemployment rate was misleading; it was 3.5 percent for college graduates, more than 5 percent for those with two years of college, over 7 percent for high school graduates, and more than 11 percent for high school dropouts. At events in Nashua and Keene, New Hampshire, I said I wanted to convert the program of unemployment benefits into a reemployment system with a broader range of better-designed training programs. And I wanted Congress to approve a school-to-work program, to provide one or two years of high-quality training for young people who didn't want to get a four-year college degree. By the end of the month, I was able to sign the Goals 2000 bill. Finally, we had a congressional commitment to meet the national education goals I had worked on back in 1989, to measure students' progress toward them, and to encourage local school districts to adopt the most promising reforms. It was a good day for Secretary Dick Riley.

On March 18, Presidents Alija Izetbegovic of Bosnia and Franjo Tudjman of Croatia were at the White House to sign an agreement negotiated with the help of my special envoy, Charles Redman, that established a federation in the areas of Bosnia in which their populations were in a majority, and set up a process to move toward a confederation with Croatia. The fighting between Muslims and Croatians had not been as severe as that in which both sides had engaged with the Bosnian Serbs, but the agreement was still an important step toward peace.

The last days of March marked the beginning of a serious crisis with North Korea. After agreeing in February to let inspectors from the International Atomic Energy Agency (IAEA) check their declared nuclear sites on March 15, North Korea blocked them from completing their work. The reactor they were studying operated on fuel rods. Once the rods had been exhausted for their original purpose, the spent fuel could be reprocessed into plutonium in sufficient quantities to make nuclear weapons. North Korea also was planning to build two larger reactors, which would have produced many more spent fuel rods. The rods were a dangerous asset in the hands of the most isolated country in the world, a poor one that could not even feed its own people and might feel the temptation to sell the plutonium to the wrong buyer. Within a week I had decided to send Patriot missiles to South Korea and to ask the UN to impose economic sanctions against North Korea. As Bill Perry told a group of editors and reporters on March 30, I was determined to stop North Korea from developing a nuclear arsenal, even at the risk of war. In order to make absolutely certain that the North Koreans knew we were serious, Perry continued the tough talk over the next three days, even saying that we would not rule out a preemptive military strike.

Meanwhile, Warren Christopher made sure our message had the right balance. The State Department said we preferred a peaceful solution, and our ambassador to South Korea, Jim Laney, described our position as one of "watchfulness, firmness, and patience." I believed that if North Korea really understood our position, as well as the economic and political benefits it could realize by abandoning its nuclear program in favor of cooperation with its neighbors and the United States, we could work it out. If we didn't, Whitewater would soon look like the sideshow it was.

On March 26, I was in Dallas for a happy weekend off, to serve as best man in my brother's wedding to Molly Martin, a beautiful woman he'd met when, after spending a few years in Nashville, he'd moved to Los Angeles in the hope of reviving his singing career. I was really happy for Roger.

On the day after the wedding, we all went to see the Arkansas Razorbacks defeat the University of Michigan in the NCAA Basketball Tournament quarterfinals. That week *Sports Illustrated* had me on the cover in a Razorback jogging suit; the article inside included a picture of me palming a basketball. After the kind of coverage I'd been getting, the piece was manna from heaven. A week later I was in the arena in Charlotte, North Carolina, when Arkansas won the national championship, defeating Duke 76–72.

On April 6, Justice Harry Blackmun announced his retirement from the Supreme Court. Hillary and I had become friends of Justice Blackmun and his wife, Dotty, through Renaissance Weekend. He was a fine man, an excellent justice, and a sorely needed moderate voice on the Rehnquist Court. I knew I owed the country a worthy replacement. My first choice was Senator George Mitchell, who had announced his retirement from the Senate a month earlier. He was a good majority leader, he had been loyal and extremely helpful to me, and it was far from certain that we could hold on to his seat in the November election. I didn't want him to leave the Senate but was excited by the prospect of appointing George to the Supreme Court. He had been a federal judge before coming to the Senate, and would be a big personality on the Court, someone who could move votes and whose voice would be heard, even in dissent. For the second time in five weeks, Mitchell turned me down. He said that if he were to leave the Senate at this time, whatever chance we had to pass health care would evaporate, hurting the American people, the Democrats up for reelection, and my presidency.

I quickly settled on two other prospects: Judge Stephen Breyer, who had already been vetted; and Judge Richard Arnold, chief judge of the Eighth Circuit Court of Appeals, which sits in St. Louis and includes Arkansas within its jurisdiction. Arnold was a former aide to Dale Bumpers who came from a long line of distinguished Arkansas lawyers. He was probably the most brilliant man on the federal bench. He graduated at the top of his class at Yale and at Harvard Law School, and had learned Latin and Greek, in part so that he could read early biblical texts. I probably would have appointed him, except for the fact that he had been treated for cancer and his prognosis was not clear. My Republican predecessors had filled the federal courts with young conservatives who would be around a long time, and I didn't want to risk giving them another position. In May, I made the decision to nominate Judge Breyer. He was equally qualified, and I had been impressed with him in our earlier interview after Justice White resigned. Breyer would be confirmed easily. Richard Arnold, I'm happy to say, is still serving on the Eighth Circuit and still plays an occasional round of golf with me.

Early in April, NATO bombed in Bosnia again, this time to stop the Serbs' siege of Gorazde. On the same day, mass violence raged in Rwanda. A plane crash killing the Rwandan president and the president of Burundi sparked the beginning of a horrendous slaughter inflicted by leaders of the majority Hutu on the Tutsis and their Hutu sympathizers. The Tutsis constituted only 15 percent of the population but were thought to have disproportionate economic and political power. I ordered the evacuation of all Americans and sent troops to guarantee their safety. Within one hundred days, more than 800,000 people in a country of only 8 million would be murdered, most of them with machetes. We were so preoccupied with Bosnia, with the memory of Somalia just six months old, and with opposition in Congress to military deployments in faraway places not vital to our national interests that neither I nor anyone on my foreign policy team adequately focused on sending troops to stop the slaughter. With a few thousand troops and help from our allies, even making allowances for the time it would have taken to deploy them, we could have saved lives. The failure to try to stop Rwanda's tragedies became one of the greatest regrets of my presidency.

In my second term, and after I left office, I did what I could to help the Rwandans put their country and their lives back together. Today, at the invitation of President Paul Kagame, Rwanda is one of the countries in which my foundation is working to stem the tide of AIDS.

On April 22, Richard Nixon died, one month and a day after writing a remarkable seven-page letter to me about his recent trip to Russia, Ukraine, Germany, and England. Nixon said I had earned the respect of the leaders he visited and could not let Whitewater or any other domestic issue "divert attention from our major foreign policy priority—the survival of political and economic freedom in Russia." He was worried about Yeltsin's political position and the rise of anti-Americanism in the Duma, and he urged me to keep my close relationship with Yeltsin, but also to reach out to other democrats in Russia; to improve the design and administration of our foreign aid program; and to put a leading businessman in charge of getting more private investment into Russia. Nixon said the ultra-nationalist Zhirinovsky should be exposed "for the fraud he is," rather than suppressed, and that we should seek "to keep the bad guys—Zhirinovsky, Rutskoi, and the Communists—divided, and to try to get the good guys—Chernomyrdin, Yavlinski, Shahrai, Travkin—to coalesce if possible in a united front for responsible reform."

Finally, Nixon said I should not spread directed aid dollars all over the former Soviet Union, but concentrate our resources beyond Russia on Ukraine: "It is indispensable." The letter was a tour de force, Nixon at his best in the eighth decade of his life.

All the living former Presidents came to President Nixon's funeral on the grounds of his presidential library and birthplace. I was somewhat surprised when his family asked me to speak, along with Bob Dole, Henry Kissinger, and California governor Pete Wilson, who as a young man had worked for Nixon. In my remarks, I expressed appreciation for his "wise counsel, especially with regard to Russia," and I remarked on his continuing vigorous and clearheaded interest in America and the world, mentioning his call and letter to me a month before his death. I referred to Watergate only by indirection, with a plea for reconciliation: "Today is a day for his family, his friends, and his nation to remember President Nixon's life in totality . . . may the day of judging President Nixon on anything less than his entire life and career come to an end." Some of my party's Nixon-haters didn't like what I said. Nixon had done a lot more than Watergate with which I disagreed—the enemies list, the prolongation of the Vietnam War and the expanded bombing, the Red-baiting of his opponents for the House and Senate in California. But he had also opened the door to China, signed bills establishing the Environmental Protection Agency, the Legal Services Corporation, and the Occupational Safety and Health Administration, and had supported affirmative action. Compared with the Republicans who took over the party in the 1980s and 1990s, President Nixon was a wild-eyed liberal.

On the day after the funeral, I called in to the Larry King show because he was interviewing Dick Kelley and James Morgan about Mother's book, *Leading with My Heart*, which was just coming out. I told Larry that when I got back from the foreign trip I had taken after her funeral, I found myself halfway to the phone in our kitchen before I realized I couldn't call her on Sunday night anymore. It would be months before the urge to make that call stopped coming over me.

On April 29, with virtually the entire cabinet in attendance, I hosted Native American and Native Alaskan tribal leaders on the South Lawn, apparently bringing them to the White House for the first time since the 1820s. Some of them were so wealthy from Indian gaming that they flew to Washington in their own planes. Others, who lived on isolated reservations, were so poor they had to "pass the hat" among their tribes to collect enough money for a plane ticket. I pledged to respect their rights of self-determination, tribal sovereignty, and religious freedom, and to work hard to improve the federal government's relations with them. And I signed executive orders to guarantee that our commitments would be kept. Finally, I pledged to do more to support education, health care, and economic development for the poorest tribes.

By the end of April, it was clear that we had lost the health-care communications battle. A *Wall Street Journal* article on April 29 described the $300 million misinformation campaign that had been run against us:

> The baby's scream is anguished, the mother's voice desperate. "Please," she pleads into the phone as she seeks help for her sick child.
>
> "We're sorry; the government health center is closed now," says the recording on the other end of the line. "However, if this is an emergency, you may call 1-800-GOVERNMENT." She tries it, only to be greeted by another recording: "We're sorry, all health-care representatives are busy now. Please stay on the line and our first available . . ."
>
> "Why did they let the government take over?" she asks plaintively. "I need my family doctor back."

The story goes on to say that the only problem with the radio spot, produced by a Washington-based group called Americans for Tax Reform, is that it isn't true.

Another massive campaign of direct mail, by a group called the American Council for Health Reform, maintained that under the Clinton plan people would face five years in jail if they bought extra health care. In fact, our plan explicitly stated that people were free to purchase any health-care services they wanted.

The ad campaign was false, but it was working. In fact, a *Wall Street Journal*/NBC News poll, published March 10 in an article titled "Many Don't Realize It's the Clinton Plan They Like," showed that when people were asked about our health plan, a majority opposed it. But when asked about what they wanted in a health plan, the major provisions that were actually in our plan were all supported by more than 60 percent of the people. The article said, "When the group is read a description of the Clinton bill without identifying it as the President's plan and of the four other leading proposals in Congress, the Clinton plan is the first choice of everyone in the room."

The poll authors, one Republican and one Democrat, are quoted as saying, "The White House should find this both satisfying and sobering. Satisfying because the basic ideas which they have drawn up are the right ideas in the view of many people. But sobering because they clearly have communicated very little to the public and in that respect have ceded too much to the interest groups."

Despite this, Congress was moving forward. The bill had been referred to five committees in Congress, three in the House and two in the Senate. The House Labor committee voted out a health-care bill in April that was actually more comprehensive than our bill. The other four committees were hard at work trying to forge consensus.

The first week of May was another example of everything happening at once. I answered the questions of international journalists in a global forum sponsored by President Carter's center at CNN's headquarters in Atlanta; signed the School-to-Work bill; congratulated Rabin and Arafat for their agreement on handling the handover of Gaza and Jericho; lobbied the House of Representatives to pass a ban on deadly assault weapons; cheered its passage by two votes, in the face of fierce opposition from the NRA; announced that the United States would increase its assistance to South Africa in the aftermath of its first full and fair election, and that Al and Tipper Gore, Hillary, Ron Brown, and Mike Espy would head our delegation to President Mandela's inauguration; held a White House event to highlight the special problems of women without health insurance; tightened sanctions on Haiti because of the continued killing and mutilation of Aristide supporters by Lieutenant General Raoul Cedras; appointed Bill Gray, head of the United Negro College Fund and former chairman of the House Budget Committee, to be special advisor to me and Warren Christopher on Haiti; and got sued by Paula Jones. It was just another week at the office.

Paula Jones had first appeared in public the previous February at the Conservative Political Action Committee convention in Washington, D.C., where Cliff Jackson introduced her, allegedly for the purpose of "clearing her name." In David Brock's *American Spectator* article based on the allegations of the Arkansas state troopers, one of their charges was that I had met with a woman in a Little Rock hotel suite who later told the trooper who had taken her there that she wanted to be my "regular girlfriend." Though she was identified in the article only as Paula, Jones claimed her family and friends recognized her when they read the article. She said she wanted to clear her name, but instead of suing the *Spectator* for libel, she accused me of sexually harassing her and said that, after she rebuffed my unwanted advances, she was denied the annual pay raises normally given to state employees. At the time she was a clerical employee of the Arkansas Industrial Development Commission. Initially, Jones's debut with Cliff Jackson didn't get much publicity, but on May 6, two days before the statute of limitations expired, she filed suit against me, seeking $700,000 for my alleged harassment.

Before she filed the suit, Jones's first lawyer had made contact with a man in Little Rock who got in touch with my office, telling us that the lawyer had said that her case was

weak and that if I would pay her $50,000 and help her and
her husband, Steve, who turned out to be a conservative
Clinton hater, get jobs in Hollywood, she wouldn't sue me. I
didn't pay because I hadn't sexually harassed her, and contrary to her other allegation, she had received her annual
pay increases. Now I had to hire another lawyer to defend
myself, Washington attorney Bob Bennett.

I spent most of the rest of May campaigning across the
country for the health-care and crime bills, but there were
always other things going on as well. By far the best of them
was the birth of our first nephew, Tyler Cassidy Clinton,
whom Roger and Molly brought into the world on May 12.

On the eighteenth, I signed an important Head Start
reform bill, on which Secretaries Shalala and Riley had
worked hard; it increased the number of poor children
served by the preschool program, improved its quality, and
provided services for children under three for the first time
with our new Early Head Start initiative.

The next day I welcomed Prime Minister P. V. Nara-
simha Rao of India to the White House. The Cold War and
clumsy diplomacy had kept India and the United States
apart for too long. With a population of nearly one billion,
India was the world's largest democracy. Over the previous
three decades, tensions with China had driven it closer to
the Soviet Union, and the Cold War had pushed the United
States closer to India's neighbor Pakistan. Since becoming
independent, the two nations had been involved in a bitter,
seemingly endless dispute over Kashmir, the predominantly
Muslim region in northern India. With the Cold War over, I
thought I had an opportunity, as well as an obligation, to
improve U.S.-India relations.

The main sticking point was the conflict between our
efforts to limit the spread of nuclear weapons and India's
drive to develop them, which the Indians saw as a necessary
deterrent to China's nuclear arsenal and a prerequisite to its
becoming a world power. Pakistan had developed a nuclear
program, too, creating a dangerous situation on the Indian
subcontinent. I believed that their nuclear arsenals made

both India and Pakistan less secure, but the Indians didn't see it that way and were determined not to let the United States interfere with what they saw as their legitimate prerogative to proceed with their nuclear program. Even so, the Indians wanted to improve our relations as much as I did. While we didn't resolve our differences, Prime Minister Rao and I broke the ice and began a new chapter in Indo-U.S. relations, which continued to warm throughout my two terms and afterward.

On the day I met with Prime Minister Rao, Jackie Kennedy Onassis died after a battle with cancer. She was only sixty-four. Jackie was the most private of our great public icons, to most people an indelible image of elegance, grace, and grieving. To those lucky enough to know her, she was what she seemed to be, but much more—a bright woman full of life, a fine mother and good friend. I knew how much her children, John and Caroline, and her companion, Maurice Tempelsman, would miss her. Hillary would miss her, too; she had been a source of constant encouragement, sound advice, and genuine friendship.

At the end of May, I had to decide whether to extend most-favored-nation status to China. MFN was actually a slightly misleading term for normal trade relations without any extra tariffs or other barriers. America already had a sizable trade deficit with China, one that would grow over the years as the United States purchased between 35 and 40 percent of Chinese exports annually. After the violence in Tiananmen Square and the crackdown on dissidents that followed, Americans from across the political spectrum felt the Bush administration had been too quick to reestablish normal relations with Beijing. During the election campaign I had been critical of President Bush's policy, and in 1993 I had issued an executive order requiring progress on a range of issues from emigration to human rights to forced prison labor before I would extend MFN to China. In May, Warren Christopher sent me a report saying that all the emigration cases had been resolved; that we had signed a memorandum of understanding on how to deal with the prison labor issue; and that for the first time China had said that it would adhere to the Universal Declaration of Human Rights. On the other hand, Christopher said, there were still human rights abuses in the arrest and detention of peaceful political dissidents and the repression of Tibet's religious and cultural traditions.

China was extremely sensitive to other nations "interfering" in its political affairs. The Chinese leaders also felt that they were managing all the change they could handle with their economic modernization program and attendant huge population shifts from inland provinces to booming coastal cities. Because our engagement had produced some positive results, I decided, with the unanimous support of my foreign policy and economic advisors, to extend MFN and, for the future, to delink our human rights efforts from trade. The United States had a big stake in bringing China into the global community. Greater trade and involvement would bring more prosperity to Chinese citizens; more contacts with the outside world; more cooperation on problems like North Korea, where we needed it; greater adherence to the rules of international law; and, we hoped, the advance of personal freedom and human rights.

In the first week of June, Hillary and I went to Europe to honor the fiftieth anniversary of D-day, June 6, 1944, when the United States and its allies crossed the English Channel and stormed the beaches of Normandy. It was the largest naval invasion in history and marked the beginning of the end of World War II in Europe.

The trip began in Rome, with a visit to the Vatican to see the pope and Italy's new prime minister, Silvio Berlusconi, the country's biggest media owner and a political novice, who had put together an interesting coalition that included an extreme right-wing party that evoked comparisons with fascism. Despite his incomplete recovery from a broken leg, His Holiness Pope John Paul II was vigorous in discussing world issues, ranging from whether religious liberty could be secured in China to the possibilities of cooperation with moderate Muslim countries to our differences over how best to limit population explosion and promote sustainable development in poor nations.

Berlusconi was, in some ways, Italy's first television-age politician: charismatic, strong-willed, and determined to bring his own brand of discipline and direction to Italy's notoriously unstable political life. His critics accused him of trying to impose a neo-fascist order on Italy, a charge he strongly denied. I was pleased with Berlusconi's assurances that he was committed to preserving democracy and human rights, maintaining Italy's historic partnership with the United States, and fulfilling Italy's NATO responsibilities in Bosnia.

On June 3, I spoke at the American cemetery at Nettuno, once scarred by battle, now lush with pine and cypress trees. Row after row of marble headstones display the names of the 7,862 soldiers buried there. The names of another 3,000 Americans whose bodies were never found are inscribed in the chapel nearby. All of them died too young, in the liberation of Italy. This was the battle theater in which my father had served.

The next day we were in England, at Mildenhall Air Force Base near Cambridge, where we went to another American cemetery, this one with the names of 3,812 airmen, soldiers, and sailors who had been based there, and another Wall of the Missing with more than 5,000 names on it, including two who never returned from their flights over the English Channel: Joe Kennedy Jr., the oldest of the Kennedy children, who everyone thought would become the politician in the family; and Glenn Miller, the American bandleader whose music was all the rage in the 1940s. At the event the Air Force Band played Miller's theme song, "Moonlight Serenade."

After a meeting with John Major at Chequers, the fifteenth-century country residence of the British prime minister, Hillary and I attended a mammoth dinner in Portsmouth, where I was seated next to the queen. I was taken with her grace and intelligence and the clever manner in which she discussed public issues, probing me for information and insights without venturing too far into expressing her own political views, which was taboo for the British head of state. Her Majesty impressed me as someone who, but for the circumstance of her birth, might have become a successful politician or diplomat. As it was, she had to be both, without quite seeming to be either.

After the dinner we were guests of the royal family on their yacht, the HMS *Britannia*, where we had the pleasure of spending time with the Queen Mother, who at ninety-three was still lively and lovely, with luminous, piercing eyes. The following morning, the day before D-day, we all attended the Drumhead Service, the religious ceremony for "the Forces Committed" to battle. Princess Diana, who was separated but not divorced from Prince Charles, also came. After saying hello to Hillary and me, she went out into the crowd to shake hands with her fellow countrymen, who were obviously happy to see her. During the little time I had spent with Charles and Diana, I liked them both and wished that life had dealt them a different hand.

When the service was over, we boarded the *Britannia* for lunch and sailed out into the English Channel, to begin the crossing among a huge fleet of ships. After a short sail, we said good-bye to the royal family and boarded a small boat crewed by U.S. Navy SEALs, which took us to the aircraft carrier *George Washington* for the rest of the voyage. Hillary and I enjoyed dinner with some of the six thousand sailors and marines who manned the ship, and I worked on my speeches.

On D-day, I spoke at Pointe du Hoc, Utah Beach, and the U.S. cemetery in Colleville-sur-Mer. Each site was filled with veterans from World War II.

I also took a walk on Utah Beach with three veterans, one of whom had won the Medal of Honor for heroism on that fateful day fifty years earlier. This was his first trip back. He told me we were standing almost exactly where he had landed in 1944. Then he pointed up the beach and told me his brother had landed a few hundred yards in that direction. He said, "It's funny how life works out. I won the Medal of Honor and my brother was killed." "You still miss him, don't you?" I asked. I'll never forget his reply: "Every day, for fifty years."

At the ceremony, I was introduced by Joe Dawson of Corpus Christi, Texas, who, as a young captain, was credited as being the first officer to successfully reach the top of the forbidding bluffs of Normandy under withering German fire. Almost 9,400 Americans died at Normandy, including thirty-three pairs of brothers, a father and his son, and eleven men from tiny Bedford, Virginia. I acknowledged that those who survived and had returned to the scene of their triumph "may walk with a little less spring in their step and their ranks are growing thinner. But let us never forget, when they were young, these men saved the world."

The next day I was in Paris to meet with Mayor Jacques Chirac, speak to the French National Assembly in the Palais Bourbon, and attend a dinner hosted by President François Mitterrand at the Elysée Palace. Mitterrand's dinner ended about midnight, and I was surprised when he asked me if Hillary and I would like to see the "New Louvre," the magnificent creation of Chinese-American architect I. M. Pei. Mitterrand was seventy-seven and in ill health, but he was eager to show off France's latest masterpiece. When François, U.S. ambassador Pamela Harriman, Hillary, and I arrived, we found that our tour guide was none other than Pei himself. We looked at the magnificent glass pyramid, the restored and adapted old buildings, and the excavated Roman ruins for more than an hour and a half. Mitterrand's energy never flagged as he supplemented Pei's narrative to make sure we didn't miss anything.

The final day of the trip was a personal one, a return to Oxford to receive an honorary degree. It was one of those perfect English spring days. The sun was shining, a breeze was blowing, and the trees, wisteria, and flowers were all in bloom. In brief remarks, I referred to the D-day commemoration, then said, "History does not always give us grand crusades, but it always gives us opportunities." We had plenty of them, at home and abroad: restoring economic growth, extending the reach of democracy, ending environmental destruction, building a new security in Europe, and halting "the spread of nuclear weapons and terrorism." Hillary and I had had an unforgettable week, but it was time to get back to those "opportunities."

The day after I returned, Senator Kennedy's Labor and
Human Resources Committee reported out a health-care
reform bill. It was the first time legislation providing universal coverage had ever even made it out of a full congressional committee. One Republican, Jim Jeffords of
Vermont, had voted for it. Jeffords encouraged me to keep
reaching out to Republicans. He said that with a couple of
amendments that wouldn't gut the bill we could pick up a
few more votes.

Our euphoria was short-lived. Two days later, Bob Dole,
after having told me earlier that we would work out a compromise on the issue, announced that he would block any
health-care legislation and make my program a major issue
in the November congressional elections. A few days later,
Newt Gingrich was quoted as saying the Republican strategy
was to make health-care reform unpassable by voting against
improving amendments. He was as good as his word. On
June 30, the House Ways and Means Committee voted out a
universal coverage bill without a single Republican vote.

The Republican leaders had received a memorandum
from William Kristol, former chief of staff to Vice President
Dan Quayle, urging them to kill health-care reform. Kristol
said the Republicans couldn't afford to allow anything to
pass; a success on health care would present a "serious
political threat to the Republican Party," while its demise
would be a "monumental setback for the President." At the
end of May, at a Memorial Day retreat, the Republican
congressional leaders decided to adopt Kristol's position. I
wasn't surprised that Gingrich would follow Kristol's hard
line; his goal was to win the House and push the country to
the right. Dole, on the other hand, was genuinely interested
in health care and knew we needed to reform the system.
But he was running for President. All he had to do was to
hold forty-one of his fellow Republicans for a filibuster and
we were sunk.

On June 21, I transmitted to Congress a welfare reform bill
designed by Donna Shalala, Bruce Reed, and their topflight
policy people to make welfare "a second chance, not a way

of life." The bill was the product of months of consultations with every affected interest group, from governors to people on welfare. The legislation required able-bodied people to go to work after two years on welfare, during which time the government would provide education and training for them. If there was no private-sector job available, the welfare recipient would be required to take a government-subsidized one.

Other provisions were designed to make sure recipients wouldn't be worse off economically in the workforce than they had been on welfare, including more money for child-support enforcement, and continuing health and nutritional coverage for a transition period under Medicaid and the food stamp program. These changes, plus the large EITC tax cut for low-wage workers enacted in 1993, would be more than enough to make even low-wage jobs more attractive than welfare. Of course, if we passed health-care reform, lower-income workers would have permanent, not just temporary, health coverage, and welfare reform would be even more successful.

I also proposed to end the perverse incentive in the present system under which young teen mothers received more aid if they moved out of their homes than if they continued to live with their parents and stayed in school. And I urged Congress to toughen the child-support enforcement law, to force absent parents to come up with more of the startling $34 billion worth of court-ordered, but still unpaid, child support. Secretary Shalala had already granted several states "waivers" from existing federal rules to pursue many of these reforms, and they were producing results: the welfare rolls were already dropping sharply.

June was a big month for international affairs: I tightened sanctions on Haiti; Hillary and I hosted a state dinner for the emperor and empress of Japan, both highly intelligent, gentle people who spread goodwill for their country wherever they went; and I met with King Hussein of Jordan, and the presidents of Hungary, Slovakia, and Chile. By far the biggest foreign policy issue, however, was North Korea.

As I mentioned earlier, North Korea had prevented inspections by the IAEA to make sure their spent fuel rods were not being reprocessed into plutonium for nuclear weapons. In March, when the inspections were stopped, I had pledged to seek UN sanctions against North Korea and refused to rule out military action. It got worse after that. In May, North Korea began to discharge fuel from a reactor in a way that prevented the inspectors from adequately monitoring its operation and determining what use was being made of the spent fuel.

President Carter called me on June 1 and said he would like to go to North Korea to try to resolve the problem. I sent Ambassador Bob Gallucci, who was handling the matter for us, down to Plains, Georgia, to brief Carter on the seriousness of the North Korean violations. He still wanted to go, and after consulting with Al Gore and my national security team, I decided it was worth trying. About three weeks earlier, I had received a sobering estimate of the staggering losses both sides would suffer if war broke out. I was in Europe for D-day, so Al Gore called Carter and told him that I had no objection to his going to North Korea as long as President Kim Il Sung understood that I would not agree to a suspension of the sanctions unless North Korea let the inspectors do their jobs, agreed to freeze its nuclear program, and committed to a new round of talks with the United States on building a non-nuclear future.

On June 16, President Carter called from Pyongyang and then did a live interview on CNN saying that Kim would not expel the inspectors from its nuclear complex as long as good-faith efforts were made to resolve the differences over international inspections. Carter then said that because of this "very positive step," our administration should ease its sanction efforts and start high-level negotiations with North Korea. I replied that if North Korea was prepared to freeze its nuclear program, we would return to talks, but it wasn't clear to me that North Korea had agreed to that.

Based on previous experience, I was unwilling to trust North Korea and would leave the sanctions hanging until we received official confirmation of North Korea's change in policy. Within a week we got it, when President Kim sent me a letter confirming what he had told Carter and accepting our other preconditions for talks. I thanked President Carter for his efforts and announced that North Korea had agreed to all our conditions, and that North and South Korea had agreed to discuss a possible meeting between their presidents. In return, I said that the United States was willing to start talks with North Korea in Geneva the following month, and that while they were taking place we would suspend our sanctions efforts.

At the end of June, I announced several staff changes that I hoped would better equip us to deal with our large legislative agenda and the elections just four months away. A few weeks earlier Mack McLarty had told me he thought it was time for him to change jobs. He had taken a lot of hits for the Travel Office and had endured countless press stories criticizing our decision-making process. Mack suggested that I appoint Leon Panetta chief of staff, because he had a good understanding of Congress and the press and would run a tight ship. When word got out about Mack, others also favored Leon for the job. Mack said he would like to try to build bridges to moderate Republicans and conservative Democrats in Congress, and to oversee our preparations for the Summit of the Americas, to be held in Miami in December.

I thought Mack had done a better job than he had gotten credit for, managing a much smaller White House with a much heavier workload, and playing a pivotal role in our victories on the economic plan and NAFTA. As Bob Rubin often said, Mack had established a collegial atmosphere within the White House and with the cabinet that many previous administrations never achieved. This environment had helped us to get a lot done, both in Congress and with the government agencies. It had also encouraged the kind of free and open debate that led to criticism of our decision-making process, but that, given the complexity and novelty of many of our challenges, led to better decisions.

Moreover, I doubted there was much we could do, apart from reducing the leaks, to avoid the negative press coverage. Professor Thomas Patterson, an authority on the media's role in elections, had recently published an important book, *Out of Order*, which helped me to better understand what was going on, and to take it less personally. Patterson's thesis was that press coverage of presidential campaigns had become steadily more negative over the past twenty years or so, as the press had come to see itself as the "mediator" between candidates and the public, with the responsibility to tell the voters how they should view the candidates and what was wrong with them. In 1992, Bush, Perot, and I had all received more negative than positive coverage.

In his postscript to the 1994 edition of *Out of Order*, Patterson said that, after the '92 election, the media for the first time had taken its negative bias from the campaign straight into its coverage of the administration. Now, he said, a President's news coverage "depends less on his actual performance in office than on the media's cynical bias. The press nearly always magnifies the bad and underplays the good." For example, the nonpartisan Center for Media and Public Affairs said that, on my handling of domestic policy issues, the coverage was 60 percent negative, mostly focusing on broken campaign commitments, even though, as Patterson said, I had kept "dozens" of my campaign commitments and that I was a President who "should have acquired a reputation for fulfilling his promises," in part by prevailing in Congress on 88 percent of contested votes, a mark bettered only by Eisenhower in 1953 and Johnson in 1965. Patterson concluded that the negative coverage drove down not only my approval rating but also public support for my programs, including health care, and thus "imposed extraordinary costs on the Clinton presidency and the national interest."

In the summer of 1994, Thomas Patterson's book helped me to see that there might be nothing I could do to change the press coverage. If that was true, I had to learn to handle it better. Mack McLarty had never sought the chief of staff's job, and Leon Panetta was willing to take on the challenge. He had already built a record at OMB that would be hard to improve on—our first two budgets were the first in seven-teen years to be adopted by Congress on time; the budgets guaranteed three years of deficit reduction in a row for the first time since Truman was President; and perhaps most impressive, they brought the first reduction in discretionary domestic spending in twenty-five years, while still providing increases for education, Head Start, job training, and new technologies. Perhaps as chief of staff, Leon could more clearly communicate what we had done and were trying to accomplish for America. I named him, and appointed Mack counselor to the President, with the job description he had recommended.

TEN

JUNE BROUGHT THE first real action from Robert Fiske. He had decided to conduct an independent inquiry into Vince Foster's death since so many questions had been raised about it in the media and by Republicans in Congress. I was glad Fiske was looking at it. The scandal machine was trying to get blood out of a turnip, and maybe this would shut them up and give Vince's family some relief.

Some of the charges and antics would have been funny except for the tragedy involved. One of the loudest and most sanctimonious of the "Foster was murdered" crowd was Republican congressman Dan Burton of Indiana. In an attempt to prove that Vince couldn't have killed himself, Burton went out in his backyard and shot a revolver into a watermelon. It was nutty. I never could figure out what Burton was trying to prove.

Fiske interviewed Hillary and me. It was a straightforward, professional session, and afterward I knew he would be thorough and believed he would finish his inquiry in a timely fashion. On June 30, he issued preliminary findings on Vince's death, as well as on the much-ballyhooed conversations between Bernie Nussbaum and Roger Altman. Fiske said that Vince's death was a suicide and found no evidence that it had anything to do with Whitewater. He also found that Nussbaum and Altman had not acted improperly.

From then on, Fiske was scorned by the conservative Republicans and their allies in the media. The *Wall Street Journal* had already pushed the press to be even more aggressive in writing stories critical of Hillary and me, however much they might later be "overtaken by other facts." Some conservative commentators and members of Congress began calling for Fiske's resignation. Senator Lauch Faircloth of North Carolina was especially vocal, spurred on by a new staff member, David Bossie, who had been Floyd

Brown's partner in Citizens United, a right-wing group that had already spread a lot of false stories about me.

On the same day that Fiske issued his report, I drove another nail in my own coffin by signing the new independent counsel law. The law permitted Fiske to be reappointed, but the "Special Division" of the D.C. Circuit Court of Appeals could also remove him and appoint another prosecutor, starting the process all over again. Under the statute, the judges on the Special Division would be selected by Chief Justice Rehnquist, who had been an extremely conservative Republican activist before he came to the Supreme Court.

I wanted Fiske to be grandfathered in, but my new head of legislative affairs, Pat Griffin, said some Democrats were afraid it wouldn't look good. Lloyd Cutler said there was nothing to worry about because Fiske was clearly independent and there was no way he would be replaced. He told Hillary he would "eat his hat" if it happened.

In early July, I returned to Europe for the G-7 summit in Naples. On the way, I stopped in Riga, Latvia, to meet with the leaders of the Baltic states and celebrate the withdrawal of Russian troops from Lithuania and Latvia, a move we had helped to speed up by providing a large number of housing vouchers for Russian officers who wanted to go home. There were still Russian troops in Estonia, and President Lennart Meri, a filmmaker who had always opposed Russian domination of his country, was determined to get them out as soon as possible. After the meeting there was a moving celebration in Riga's Freedom Square, where I was welcomed by about forty thousand people waving flags in gratitude for America's steadfast support of their newfound freedom.

The next stop was Warsaw, to meet with President Lech Walesa and emphasize my commitment to bringing Poland into NATO. Walesa had become a hero, and free Poland's natural choice for president, by leading the Gdansk shipyard workers' revolt against communism more than a decade earlier. He was deeply suspicious of Russia and wanted Poland in NATO as soon as possible. He also wanted more American investment in Poland, saying the country's future required more American generals, "starting with General Motors and General Electric."

That night Walesa hosted a dinner to which he invited leaders of all political views. I listened with fascination to a heated argument between Mrs. Walesa, a feisty mother of eight children, and a legislative leader who was also a potato farmer. She was railing against communism, while he argued that farmers had been better off under communism than they were today. I thought they were going to come to blows. I tried to help by reminding the legislator that even under communism the Polish farms were in private hands; all the Polish Communists had done was to purchase the food and sell it in Ukraine and Russia. He conceded the point, but said he had always had a market and a good price for his crops. I told him he had never been under a completely Communist system like Russia's, where the farms themselves were collectivized. Then I explained how the American system worked, and how all successful free-market systems also had some form of cooperative marketing and price supports. The farmer remained skeptical, and Mrs. Walesa remained adamant. If democracy is about free and unfettered debate, it had certainly taken hold in Poland.

My first day at the Naples summit was devoted to Asia. Kim Il Sung had died the previous day, just as talks with North Korea resumed in Geneva, throwing the future of our agreement with North Korea into doubt. The other G-7 member with a big interest in the issue was Japan. There had been tensions between the Japanese and the Koreans for decades, going back before World War II. If North Korea had nuclear weapons, there would be great pressure on Japan to develop a nuclear deterrent, an action that, given their own painful experience, the Japanese did not want to take. The new Japanese prime minister, Tomiichi Murayama, who had become Japan's first socialist prime minister by joining in a coalition with the Liberal Democratic Party, assured me that our solidarity on North Korea would remain intact. Out of respect for Kim Il Sung's death, the Geneva talks were suspended for a month.

The most important decisions we made in Naples were to provide an aid package to Ukraine and to include Russia in the political part of all future summits. Bringing Russia into the prestigious circle gave Yeltsin and other reformers pushing for closer ties to the West a big boost, and guaranteed that our future gatherings would be more interesting. Yeltsin was always entertaining.

Chelsea, Hillary, and I loved Naples, and after the meetings, we took a day to see Pompeii, which the Italians had done a marvelous job of recovering from the ashes of the volcano that engulfed the town in A.D. 79. We saw wall paintings with colors that had retained their rich texture, including some that were first-century versions of political posters; open-air food stands that were early precursors of today's fast-food restaurants; and the remains of several bodies remarkably preserved by the ashes, among them a man lying with his hand over the face of his obviously pregnant wife, with two other children beside them. It was a powerful reminder of the fragile and fleeting nature of life.

The European trip ended in Germany. Helmut Kohl took us to visit his hometown, Ludwigshafen, before I flew to Ramstein Air Base to see our troops, many of whom would soon be leaving the military in the post–Cold War downsizing. The servicemen and -women at Ramstein, just like their counterparts in the U.S. Navy I had met in Naples, mentioned only one domestic issue to me: health care. Most of them had children, and in the military they had taken health coverage for granted. Now they worried that because of defense downsizing they were going home to a country that would no longer provide health care for their kids.

Berlin was booming, full of construction cranes, as the city prepared to resume its role as the capital of a united Germany. Hillary and I walked with the Kohls out of the Reichstag along the line where the Berlin Wall had stood and through the magnificent Brandenburg Gate. President Kennedy and President Reagan had given memorable speeches just outside the gate on the western side of the wall. Now I was standing on a podium on the eastern side of unified Berlin, facing an enthusiastic crowd of fifty thousand Germans, many of them young people wondering about their future in a very different world from the one their parents had known.

I urged the Germans to lead Europe toward greater unity. If they did so, I pledged in German, "Amerika steht an Ihrer Seite jetzt und für immer." (America is on your side, now and forever.) The Brandenburg Gate had long been a symbol of its time, sometimes a monument to tyranny and a tower of conquest, but now it was what its builders had meant it to be, a gateway to the future.

When I returned home, the foreign policy work continued. Increased repression in Haiti had led to a new flood of boat people and the suspension of all commercial air traffic. By the end of the month, the UN Security Council had approved an invasion to dislodge the dictatorship, an action that seemed more and more inevitable.

On July 22, I announced a large increase in emergency aid to Rwandan refugees, with U.S. military forces establishing a base in Uganda to support round-the-clock shipments of relief supplies to the tremendous number of refugees in camps near the Rwandan border. I also ordered the military to establish a safe water supply and distribute as much clean water as possible to those at risk of cholera and other diseases, and announced that the United States would be delivering twenty million oral rehydration therapy packages over the next two days to help stem the cholera outbreak. Within a week we had delivered more than 1,300 tons of food, medicine, and other supplies, and were producing and distributing more than 100,000 gallons of safe water a day. The entire effort would require about 4,000 troops and cost nearly $500 million, but even after all the slaughter, it would still save many lives.

On July 25, King Hussein and Prime Minister Rabin came to town to sign the Washington declaration, formally ending the state of belligerency between Jordan and Israel and committing themselves to negotiating a full peace agreement. They had been talking secretly for some time, and Warren Christopher had worked hard to facilitate their agreement. The next day, the two leaders spoke to a joint session of Congress, and the three of us held a press conference to reaffirm our commitment to a comprehensive peace involving all the parties to the Middle East conflict.

The Israeli-Jordanian agreement stood in stark contrast to recent terrorist attacks against a Jewish center in Buenos Aires, and others in Panama and London, all of which Hezbollah was believed to be responsible for. Hezbollah was armed by Iran and aided by Syria in conducting operations against Israel from southern Lebanon. Since the peace process could not be completed without an agreement between Israel and Syria, Hezbollah's activities presented a serious potential obstacle. I had called President Assad to tell him about the Israeli-Jordanian announcement, to ask him to support it, and to assure him that Israel and the United States were still committed to successful negotiations with his country. Rabin left the door open to talks with Syria by saying that the Syrians could limit but not end Hezbollah's activities. Hussein responded that not just Syria but the entire Arab world should follow Jordan's lead and reconcile with Israel.

I closed the press conference by saying that Hussein and Rabin must have "put peace in the air all over the world." Boris Yeltsin had just informed me that he and President Meri had agreed that all Russian troops would be withdrawn from Estonia by August 31.

In August it gets hot in Washington, and Congress usually leaves town. In 1994, Congress stayed in session almost the entire month to deal with crime and health care. Both the Senate and House had passed versions of the crime bill, which provided 100,000 more community police, tougher penalties for repeat offenders, and more funds for both prison construction and prevention programs to keep young people out of trouble.

When the conference committee met to resolve the differences between the Senate and House crime bills, the Democrats folded the assault weapons ban into the compromise bill. As I've said, the ban had passed the House as a separate matter by only two votes, in the face of furious opposition by the National Rifle Association. The NRA had already lost the fight to defeat the Brady bill and was determined to prevail on this one, so that Americans would retain their right to "keep and bear" rapid-fire large-magazine weapons designed for one purpose only: to kill a great many people in a hurry. These weapons worked; crime victims shot with them were three times more likely to die than those whose assailants fired regular handguns.

The conference decided to combine the ban with the crime bill because, while we had a clear majority for the ban in the Senate, we didn't have the sixty votes necessary to break a certain filibuster by NRA supporters. The Democrats in the conference knew it would be much harder to filibuster the overall crime bill than the assault weapons ban standing alone. The problem with the strategy was that it forced the House Democrats from rural pro-gun districts to vote on the assault weapons ban all over again, risking the failure of the whole bill, and putting them at risk of losing their seats if they voted for it.

On August 11, the House defeated the new crime bill, 225–210, on a procedural vote, with 58 Democrats voting against it and only 11 Republicans voting for it. A few of the Democratic "no" votes were liberals who opposed the bill's expansion of the death penalty, but most of our defectors were voting with the NRA. A sizable group of Republicans said they wanted to support the bill, including the assault weapons ban, but thought it spent too much money overall, especially on prevention programs. We were in trouble on one of my most important campaign commitments, and I had to do something to turn it around.

The next day, before the National Association of Police Officers in Minneapolis, with Mayor Rudy Giuliani of New York and Mayor Ed Rendell of Philadelphia, I tried to frame the choice as one between the police and the people on one side and the NRA on the other. Surely we had not reached the point where the only way to keep congressional seats safe was to leave the American people and police officers in greater danger.

Three days later, at a ceremony in the Rose Garden, the issue was put in even sharper focus by Steve Sposato, a Republican businessman whose wife had been killed when a deranged man with an assault weapon went on a shooting spree in the San Francisco office building where she worked. Sposato, who had brought his young daughter, Megan, with him, made a compelling appeal for the assault weapons ban.

Late in the month, the crime bill came to a vote again. Unlike health care, we were working on crime through good-faith bipartisan negotiation. This time we won, 235–195, having picked up almost 20 Republican votes by negotiating a substantial cut in the costs of the bill. Some liberal Democrats were persuaded to change their votes on the strength of the bill's prevention programs, and a few more Democrats from pro-gun districts stuck their necks out. Four days later, Senator Joe Biden shepherded the crime bill through the Senate, 61–38, when 6 Republicans provided the votes necessary to break a filibuster. The crime legislation would have a profoundly positive impact, helping to usher in the largest sustained drop in crime on record.

Just before the House vote, Speaker Tom Foley and majority leader Dick Gephardt had made a last-ditch appeal to me to remove the assault weapons ban from the bill. They argued that many Democrats who represented closely divided districts had already cast a very difficult vote for the economic program, and had already defied the NRA once on the Brady bill vote. They said that if we made them walk the plank again on the assault weapons ban, the overall bill might not pass, and that if it did, many Democrats who voted for it would not survive the election in November. Jack Brooks, the House Judiciary Committee chairman from Texas, told me the same thing. Brooks had been in the House for more than forty years and was one of my favorite congressmen. He represented a district full of NRA members and had led the effort to defeat the assault weapons ban when it first came to a vote. Jack was convinced that if we didn't drop the ban, the NRA would beat a lot of Democrats by terrifying gun owners.

I was troubled by what Foley, Gephardt, and Brooks had said, but I was convinced that our members could win a debate with the NRA over the issue in their backyards. Dale Bumpers and David Pryor knew how to explain their votes to Arkansans. Senator Howell Heflin of Alabama, whom I had known almost twenty years, had an ingenious explanation for his support of the crime bill. He said he had never voted for gun control, but the crime bill banned only nineteen assault weapons, and he didn't know anyone who owned those weapons. On the other hand, the bill expressly prohibited restrictions on owning hundreds of other weapons, including "every weapon I am familiar with."

It was a persuasive point, but not everyone could make it the way Howell Heflin did. Foley, Gephardt, and Brooks were right and I was wrong. The price of a safer America would be heavy casualties among its defenders.

Maybe I was pushing the Congress, the country, and the administration too hard. At my press conference on August 19, a reporter asked me a very perceptive question: "I was wondering if you've thought about this, that as a President elected with 43 percent, you may be trying to do too much, too fast . . . exceeding your mandate," by pushing through so much legislation with so little Republican support. Even though we had accomplished a lot, I was wondering about that, too. I wouldn't have to wonder much longer.

While we were winning on the crime bill, we kept on losing with health care. In early August, George Mitchell introduced a compromise bill to increase the percentage of the insured population to 95 percent without an employer mandate, leaving open the possibility of imposing one in later years to get to 100 percent, if the bill's voluntary procedures didn't succeed in doing so. I announced my support for Mitchell's bill the next day, and we began to shop it to moderate Republicans, but it was no use. Dole was determined to defeat any meaningful reform; it was good politics. On the day the crime bill passed, the Senate recessed for two weeks with no further action on health care. Dole had failed in his efforts to kill the crime bill, but he had prevailed in derailing health care.

The other big news in August was in the parallel world of Whitewater. After I signed the independent counsel statute, Chief Justice Rehnquist appointed Judge David Sentelle to head the Special Division that had responsibility for naming independent counsels under the new law. Sentelle was an ultra-conservative protégé of Senator Jesse Helms, who had decried the influence of "leftist heretics" who wanted America to become a "collectivist, egalitarian, materialistic, race-conscious, hyper-secular, and socially permissive state." The three-member panel also contained another conservative judge, so Sentelle could do whatever he wanted.

On August 5, Sentelle's panel fired Robert Fiske and replaced him with Kenneth Starr, who had been a court of appeals judge and solicitor general in the Bush administration. Unlike Fiske, Starr had no prosecutorial experience, but he had something far more important: he was much more conservative and partisan than Fiske. In a terse statement Judge Sentelle said he was replacing Fiske with Starr to guarantee the "appearance of independence," a test Fiske could not meet because he was "affiliated with the incumbent administration." It was an absurd argument. Fiske was a Republican whose only affiliation with the administration was that Janet Reno had appointed him to a job he did not seek. Had the Special Division reappointed him, there would have been no more affiliation.

In his place, Judge Sentelle's panel appointed someone with not an apparent but a real and blatant conflict of interest. Starr had been an outspoken proponent of the Paula Jones lawsuit, appearing on TV and even offering to write a friend-of-the-court brief on her behalf. Five former presidents of the American Bar Association criticized the Starr appointment because of its apparent political bias. So did the *New York Times*, after it emerged that Judge Sentelle had had lunch with Fiske's biggest critic, Senator Lauch

Faircloth, and Jesse Helms just a couple of weeks before the Fiske-Starr switch. The three said they were just discussing prostate problems.

Of course, Starr had no intention of stepping aside. His bias against me was the very reason he was chosen and why he took the job. We now had a bizarre definition of an "independent" counsel: he had to be independent of me, but it was fine to be closely tied to my political enemies and legal adversaries.

The Starr appointment was unprecedented. In the past, there had been an effort to ensure that special prosecutors would be not only independent but also fair and respectful of the institution of the presidency. Leon Jaworski, the Watergate special prosecutor, was a conservative Democrat who had supported President Nixon for reelection in 1972. Lawrence Walsh, the Iran-Contra prosecutor, was an Oklahoma Republican who had supported President Reagan. I had never wanted the Whitewater inquiry to be a "home game," in Doug Sosnik's words, but I thought I was at least entitled to a neutral field. It was not to be. Since there was nothing to Whitewater, the only way to use the investigation against me was to turn it into one long "away game." Robert Fiske was too fair and too fast for that job. He had to go.

Lloyd Cutler didn't eat his hat, but less than a week after the Starr appointment he left, too, having fulfilled his commitment to serve a brief stint in the counsel's office. I replaced him with Abner Mikva, a former Illinois congressman and court of appeals judge with an impeccable reputation and a clearheaded view of the forces we were up against. I was sorry that, after such a long and distinguished career, Lloyd had to learn that people he thought he knew and could trust were playing by different rules than he was.

When Congress left town, we took off for Martha's Vineyard again. Hillary and I needed some time off. So did Al Gore. A few days earlier he had ruptured his Achilles tendon in a basketball game. It was a painful injury, requiring a prolonged recovery. Al would come back stronger than before, using his forced immobility to work out with weights. In the meantime, on crutches, he traveled to forty states and four foreign countries, including Egypt, where he brokered a compromise on the sensitive issue of population control at the Cairo Conference on Sustainable Development. He also continued overseeing the Reinventing Government Initiative. By mid-September, we had already achieved savings of $47 billion, enough to pay for the entire crime bill; begun a competitive venture with the automakers to develop a "clean car"; cut the application form for an SBA loan from a hundred pages to one; reformed FEMA so that it was no longer the least popular federal agency but the most admired one, thanks to James Lee Witt; and saved more than $1 billion through cancellations of unneeded construction projects under Roger Johnson's leadership at the General Services Administration. Al Gore was doing a lot on one good leg.

Our week on the Vineyard was interesting for several reasons. Vernon Jordan set up a golf game with Warren Buffett and Bill Gates, America's wealthiest men. I liked them both, and was particularly impressed that Buffett was a die-hard Democrat who believed in civil rights, fair taxation, and a woman's right to choose.

The most memorable evening for me was a dinner at Bill and Rose Styron's, where the guests of honor were the superb Mexican writer Carlos Fuentes and my literary hero, Gabriel García Márquez. García Márquez was friends with Fidel Castro, who, in an effort to export some of his problems to us, was in the process of unleashing a mass exodus of Cubans to the United States, reminiscent of the Mariel boat lift, which had caused me so many problems in 1980. Thousands of Cubans, at great risk to themselves, had set out in small boats and rafts for the ninety-mile voyage to Florida.

García Márquez was opposed to the U.S. embargo on Cuba and tried to talk me out of it. I told him that I would not lift the embargo, but that I supported the Cuban Democracy Act, which gave the President authority to improve relations with Cuba in return for greater movement toward freedom and democracy there. I also asked him to tell Castro that if the influx of Cubans continued, he would get a very different response from the United States than he had received in 1980 from President Carter. "Castro has already cost me one election," I said. "He can't have two." I relayed the same message through President Salinas of Mexico, who had a good working relationship with Castro. Not long afterward, the United States and Cuba reached an agreement by which Castro pledged to stem the exodus, and we promised to take twenty thousand more Cubans each year through the normal process. Castro faithfully observed the accord for the remainder of my term. Later, García Márquez would joke that he was the only man who was friends with both Fidel Castro and Bill Clinton.

After we discussed Cuba, García Márquez lavished most of his attention on Chelsea, who said she had read two of his books. He later told me that he didn't believe a fourteen-year-old girl could understand his work, so he launched into an extended discussion with her about *One Hundred Years of Solitude*. He was so impressed that he later sent her an entire set of his novels.

The only business I did on vacation involved Ireland. I granted a visa to Joe Cahill, a seventy-six-year-old hero to Irish Republicans. In 1973, Cahill had been convicted of gunrunning in Ireland, and he continued to promote violence for years afterward. I gave him a visa because he now wanted to promote peace among the IRA's American supporters, as part of an understanding under which the IRA would, at long last, announce a cease-fire. Cahill came to America on August 30, and the next day the IRA announced a total cessation of violence, opening the way for Sinn Fein's participation in the peace talks. It was a victory for Gerry Adams and for the Irish government.

When we returned from our vacation, we moved into Blair House for three weeks while the White House air-conditioning system was being repaired. A massive stone-by-stone restoration of the nearly two hundred–year-old exterior, begun during the Reagan administration, was also still going on. A portion of the White House would be covered by scaffolding all through my first term.

Our family always enjoyed the time we spent in Blair House, and this extended visit was no exception, though it caused us to miss a dramatic moment back across the street. On September 12 an inebriated man who was disappointed with his life broke into a small airplane and took off for downtown Washington and the White House. He was trying either to kill himself by crashing into the building or to stage a landing on the South Lawn, like the one executed by a young German pilot in Moscow's Red Square a few years earlier. Unfortunately, his little Cessna hit the ground too late for the landing, bounced over the hedge and under the giant magnolia tree on the west side of the entrance, then slammed into the large stone base of the White House, killing him instantly. A few years later, another troubled man with a pistol vaulted the White House fence before he was wounded and apprehended by officers of the Uniformed Division of the Secret Service. The White House was a magnet for more than ambitious politicians.

The crisis in Haiti came to a head in September. General Cedras and his thugs had intensified their reign of terror, executing orphaned children, raping young girls, killing priests, mutilating people and leaving body parts in the open to terrify others, and slashing the faces of mothers with machetes while their children watched. By this time, I had been working for a peaceful solution for two years, and I was fed up. More than a year earlier, Cedras had signed an agreement to give up power, but when the time came to leave, he simply refused to go.

It was time to throw him out, but public opinion and congressional sentiment were strongly against it. Though the Congressional Black Caucus, Senator Tom Harkin, and Senator Chris Dodd supported me, the Republicans were solidly opposed, and most Democrats, including George Mitchell, thought I was just taking them out onto another precipice without public support or congressional authorization. There was even division within the administration.

Al Gore, Warren Christopher, Bill Gray, Tony Lake, and Sandy Berger were for it. Bill Perry and the Pentagon were not, but they had been working on an invasion plan in case I ordered them to proceed.

I thought we had to go forward. Innocent people were being slaughtered in our own backyard, and we were already spending a small fortune taking care of Haitian refugees. The United Nations was unanimous in supporting the ouster of Cedras.

On September 16, in a last-minute attempt to avoid an invasion, I sent President Carter, Colin Powell, and Sam Nunn to Haiti to try to persuade General Cedras and his supporters in the military and parliament to peacefully accept Aristide's return and Cedras's departure from the country. For different reasons, they all disagreed with my determination to use force to restore Aristide. Though the Carter Center had monitored Aristide's overwhelming election victory, President Carter had developed a relationship with Cedras and was skeptical of Aristide's commitment to democracy. Nunn was opposed to Aristide's return until parliamentary elections were held, because he didn't trust Aristide to protect minority rights without an established countervailing force in parliament. Powell thought only the military and the police could govern Haiti, and that they would never work with Aristide.

As subsequent events would prove, there was some merit to their arguments. Haiti was deeply divided economically and politically and had no previous experience with democracy, no significant middle class, and little of the institutional capacity required to operate a modern state. Even if Aristide was returned without a hitch, he might not succeed. Still, he had been elected overwhelmingly, and Cedras and his crew were killing innocent people. We could at least stop that.

Despite their reservations, the distinguished trio pledged to faithfully communicate my policy. They wanted to avoid a violent American entry, which could make matters even worse. Nunn spoke to members of Haiti's parliament; Powell told the Haitian military leaders in graphic terms what would happen if the United States invaded; and Carter worked on Cedras.

The next day I went to the Pentagon to review the invasion plan with General Shalikashvili and the Joint Chiefs, and, by teleconference, with Admiral Paul David Miller, the commander of the overall operation, and Lieutenant General Hugh Shelton, commander of the Eighteenth Airborne Corps, who would lead our troops onto the island. The invasion plan called for a unified operation involving all branches of the military. Two aircraft carriers were in the waters off Haiti, one transporting Special Operations forces and the other carrying soldiers from the Tenth Mountain Division. Air force planes were set to provide necessary air support. The marines were assigned to occupy Cap Haitien, Haiti's second-largest city. Planes carrying Eighty-second Airborne Division paratroopers would fly out of North Carolina and drop them over the island at the outset of the assault. Navy SEALs would go in early and scan designated areas. They had already done a test run that morning, coming out of the water and onto land without incident. Most troops and equipment were to enter Haiti in an operation called "RoRo," for "roll on, roll off"; troops and vehicles would roll onto landing vessels for the trip to Haiti, then roll off on the Haitian shoreline. When the mission was accomplished, the process would be reversed. Besides the U.S. forces, we had support from twenty-five other countries that had joined the UN coalition.

As the deadline for our attack approached, President Carter called me pleading for more time to persuade Cedras to leave. Carter desperately wanted to avoid a forced invasion. So did I. Haiti had no military capability; it would be like shooting fish in a barrel. I agreed to give him three more hours, but made it clear that any agreement he made with the general could not include another delay in the handover to Aristide. Cedras couldn't have more time to murder children, rape young girls, and slash women's faces. We had already spent $200 million taking care of the Haitians who had left their country. I wanted them to be able to go home.

In Port-au-Prince, as the three-hour deadline ran out, an

angry mob gathered outside the building where the Americans were still talking. Every time I talked with Carter,
Cedras had proposed a different deal, but they all gave him
some wiggle room to hang around and delay Aristide's
return. I rejected them all. With the danger outside and the
deadline for invasion at hand, Carter, Powell, and Nunn
kept trying to persuade Cedras, to no avail. Carter pleaded
for more time. I agreed to another delay, until 5 p.m. The
planes with the paratroopers were scheduled to arrive just
after dark, at about six. If the three of them were still there
negotiating then, they would be in much greater danger
from the mob.

At 5:30 p.m. they were still in place and already in
greater peril, because Cedras knew the operation had
begun. He had had someone watching the airstrip in North
Carolina, when our sixty-one planes carrying the paratroopers took off. I called President Carter and told him
that he, Colin, and Sam had to leave immediately. The three
of them made one last appeal to the titular head of Haiti,
eighty-one-year-old President Emile Jonassaint, who at last
told them he would choose peace instead of war. When all
the cabinet members but one agreed with him, Cedras
finally relented, less than an hour before the skies over Port-
au-Prince would have been filled with parachutes. Instead, I
ordered the planes to turn around and come home.

The next day General Shelton led the first of the fifteen-
thousand-member multinational force into Haiti without a
shot being fired. Shelton cut a striking figure. He was about
six feet five inches tall, with chiseled features and a slow
southern drawl. Though he was a couple of years older than
I, he still did regular parachute jumps with his troops. He
looked as if he could have deposed Cedras all by himself. I
had visited General Shelton not long before at Fort Bragg,
after a plane crash at nearby Pope Air Force Base had killed
several servicemen. On Shelton's office wall were pictures of
two great Confederate Civil War generals, Robert E. Lee
and Stonewall Jackson. When I saw Shelton on television as
he stepped ashore, I remarked to one of my staff that Amer-

ica had come a long way if a man who revered Stonewall Jackson could be the liberator of Haiti.

Cedras promised to cooperate with General Shelton and to leave power by October 15, as soon as the general amnesty law required by the UN agreement was passed. Although I almost had to forcibly remove them from Haiti, Carter, Powell, and Nunn had done a courageous job under difficult and potentially dangerous circumstances. A combination of dogged diplomacy and imminent force had avoided bloodshed. Now it was up to Aristide to honor his commitment of "no to violence, no to vengeance, yes to reconciliation." As with so many such statements, this would prove to be easier said than done.

Because the restoration of democracy in Haiti occurred without incident, it didn't turn out to have the negative impact the Democrats had feared. We should have been in good shape going into the elections: the economy was producing 250,000 jobs a month, with unemployment dropping from over 7 percent to under 6 percent; the deficit was coming down; we had passed important legislation on crime, education, national service, trade, and family leave; and I was making headway on our foreign policy agenda with Russia, Europe, China, Japan, the Middle East, Northern Ireland, Bosnia, and Haiti. But despite the record and the results, we were in trouble heading into the last six weeks of the election, for a variety of reasons: many people hadn't felt the economic improvements yet; no one believed the deficit was coming down; most people were unaware of the legislative victories and didn't know or didn't care about the foreign policy progress; the Republicans and their media and interest group allies had constantly and effectively attacked me as a wild-eyed liberal who wanted to tax them into the poorhouse and take their doctors and guns away; and the general press coverage was overwhelmingly negative.

The Center for Media and Public Affairs issued a report saying that in my first sixteen months, there was an average of nearly five negative comments a night on the evening network news programs, far more than the first President Bush had received in his first two years. The center's director, Robert Lichter, said I had the "misfortune of being president at the dawning of an age that combines attack-dog journalism with tabloid news." There were some exceptions, of course. Jacob Weisberg wrote that "Bill Clinton has been more faithful to his word than any other chief executive in recent memory," but that "voters mistrust Clinton in part because the media keeps telling them not to trust him." Jonathan Alter wrote in *Newsweek*, "In less than two years, Bill Clinton had already achieved more domestically than John F. Kennedy, Gerald Ford, Jimmy Carter and George Bush combined. Although Richard Nixon and Ronald Reagan often had their way with Congress, *Congressional Quarterly* says it's Clinton who has had the most legislative success of any President since Lyndon Johnson. The standard for measuring results domestically should not be the coherence of the process but how actual lives are touched and changed. By that standard, he's doing well."

Alter may have been right, but if so, it was a well-kept secret.

ELEVEN

THINGS GREW WORSE as September drew to a close. Acting baseball commissioner Bud Selig announced that the players' strike couldn't be resolved and he was canceling the rest of the season, and the World Series, for the first time since 1904. Bruce Lindsey, who had helped to settle the airline strike, tried to resolve the standoff. I even invited the representatives of the players and owners to the White House, but we couldn't settle it. If our national pastime was being canceled, things could not be going in the right direction.

On September 26, George Mitchell formally threw in the towel on health-care reform. Senator Chafee had continued to work with him, but he couldn't bring enough Republicans along to break Senator Dole's filibuster. The $300 million that the health insurance and other lobbies had spent to stop health-care reform was well invested. I put out a brief statement saying I would try again next year.

Though I had felt for months that we were beaten, I was still disappointed, and I felt bad that Hillary and Ira Magaziner were taking the rap for the failure. It was unfair for three reasons. First, our proposals were not the big government–run nightmare that the health-insurance companies' ad campaigns had made them out to be; second, the plan was the best Hillary and Ira could do, given the charge from me: universal coverage without a tax increase; and finally, it wasn't they who had derailed health-care reform—Senator Dole's decision to kill any meaningful compromise had done that. I tried to cheer up Hillary by telling her that there were bigger mistakes in life than "getting caught red-handed" trying to provide health insurance to forty million Americans who were without it.

In spite of our defeat, all the work Hillary, Ira Magaziner, and the rest of our people had done would not be in vain. In the years ahead, many of our proposals would find their way

into law and practice. Senator Kennedy and Republican senator Nancy Kassebaum of Kansas would pass a bill guaranteeing that workers wouldn't lose their insurance when they
changed jobs. And in 1997, we would pass the Children's
Health Insurance Program (CHIP), providing health care to
millions of children in the largest expansion of health insurance since Medicaid was enacted in 1965. CHIP would help
bring about the first decline in twelve years in the number of
Americans without health insurance.

There would be many other health-care victories as well:
a bill allowing women to stay in the hospital for more than
twenty-four hours after childbirth, ending HMO-ordered
"drive-by" deliveries; increased coverage for mammograms
and prostate screenings; a diabetes self-management program called the most important advance since insulin by the
American Diabetes Association; large increases in biomedical research and in the care and treatment of HIV/AIDS at
home and abroad; childhood immunization rates above 90
percent for the first time; and the application by executive
order of a patient's "bill of rights" guaranteeing the choice
of a doctor and the right to prompt, adequate treatment
for the eighty-five million Americans covered by federally
funded plans.

But that was all in the future. For now, we had taken a
good shellacking. That's the image people would take into
the elections.

Near the end of the month, Newt Gingrich gathered more
than three hundred Republican incumbents and candidates
for a rally on the Capitol steps to sign a "Contract with
America." The details of the contract had been percolating
for some time. Newt had put them together to show that the
Republicans were more than naysayers; they had a positive
agenda. The contract was something new to American politics. Traditionally, midterm elections had been fought seat
by seat. National conditions and a President's level of popu-
larity could be a boost or a drag, but the conventional wisdom held that local factors were more important. Gingrich

was convinced that the conventional wisdom was wrong. He boldly asked the American people to give the Republicans a majority, saying, "If we break this contract, throw us out. We mean it."

The contract called for a constitutional balanced budget amendment and the line-item veto, which enables the President to delete specific items in appropriations bills without having to veto the entire piece of legislation; stiffer penalties for criminals and repeal of the prevention programs in my crime bill; welfare reform, with a two-year limit on able-bodied recipients; a $500 child tax credit, another $500 credit for the care of a parent or grandparent, and tougher child-support enforcement; repeal of the taxes on upper-income Social Security recipients that were part of the 1993 budget; a 50 percent cut in the capital gains tax, and other tax cuts; an end to unfunded federal mandates on state and local government; a large increase in defense spending; tort reform to limit punitive damages; term limits for senators and representatives; a requirement that Congress, as an employer, follow all laws it has imposed on other employers; a reduction in congressional committee staffs by a third; and a requirement that 60 percent of each house of Congress approve any future tax increase.

I agreed with many of the particulars of the contract. I was already pushing welfare reform and tougher child-support enforcement, and had long supported the line-item veto and ending unfunded mandates. I liked the family tax credits. Though several of the specifics were appealing, the contract was, at its core, a simplistic and hypocritical document. In the twelve years before I became President, the Republicans, with the support of a few Democrats in Congress, had quadrupled the national debt by cutting taxes and increasing spending; now that Democrats were reducing the deficit, they wanted the Constitution to require a balanced budget, even as they recommended large tax cuts and big increases in defense spending without saying what other spending they would cut to pay for them. Just as they had done in the 1980s and would do again in the 2000s, the

Republicans were trying to abolish arithmetic. As Yogi Berra said, it was déjà vu all over again, but in a nice new package.

Besides giving the Republicans a national platform for the 1994 campaign, Gingrich provided them with a list of words to use in defining their Democratic opponents. His political action committee, GOPAC, published a pamphlet entitled *Language: A Key Mechanism of Control*. Among the "contrasting words" Newt suggested for labeling Democrats were: betray, cheat, collapse, corruption, crisis, decay, destruction, failure, hypocrisy, incompetent, insecure, liberal, lie, pathetic, permissive, shallow, sick, traitors. Gingrich was convinced that if he could institutionalize that kind of name-calling, he could define the Democrats into a minority party for a long time.

The Democrats thought the Republicans had made a critical error in announcing the contract, and proceeded to attack it by showing the large cuts in education, health care, and environmental protection that would be necessary to fund the tax cuts, increase defense, and balance the budget. They even renamed Newt's plan the "Contract *on* America." They were absolutely right, but it didn't work. Post-election polls would show that the public knew only two things about the contract: that the Republicans had a plan, and that balancing the budget was part of it.

Beyond attacking the Republicans, the Democrats were determined to fight the election the old-fashioned way, state by state, district by district. I had already done a lot of fundraisers for them, but not a single one for a national campaign to advertise what we had accomplished, or what our future agenda would be in contrast to the Republican contract.

We capped off another productive legislative year on September 30, the last day of the fiscal year, by passing all thirteen appropriation bills on time, something that hadn't happened since 1948. The appropriations represented the first back-to-back years of deficit reduction in two decades, reducing the federal payroll by 272,000, and still increasing investments in education and other important areas. It was an impressive achievement, but nowhere near as attention-grabbing as the balanced budget amendment.

I limped into October with approval ratings of around 40 percent, but good things would happen that month to improve my standing and apparently to increase the Democrats' election prospects. The only sad development was the resignation of Agriculture Secretary Mike Espy. Janet Reno had asked for a court-appointed independent counsel to look into allegations of wrongdoing by Espy involving acceptance of gifts, such as sports tickets and trips. Judge Sentelle's panel appointed Donald Smaltz, another Republican activist, to investigate Espy. I was heartsick about it. Mike Espy had supported me through thick and thin in 1992. He had left a safe seat in Congress, where even the white voters of Mississippi supported him, to become the first black agriculture secretary, and he had done an excellent job, including raising the standards for food safety.

The October news was mostly positive. On October 4, Nelson Mandela came to the White House for a state visit. His smile always brightened even the darkest days, and I was glad to see him. We announced a joint commission to promote mutual cooperation, to be headed by Vice President Gore and Deputy President Thabo Mbeki, Mandela's likely successor. The joint commission idea was working so well with Russia that we wanted to try it in another country that was important to us, and South Africa certainly was. If Mandela's reconciliation government succeeded, it could lift all of Africa and inspire similar efforts in trouble spots around the world. I also announced assistance for housing, electricity, and health care for South Africa's poor, densely populated townships; rural economic initiatives; and an investment fund to be headed by Ron Brown.

While I was meeting with Mandela, the Senate followed the House in passing, with broad bipartisan support, the last important piece of my education agenda from the campaign, the Elementary and Secondary Education Act. The bill ended the practice of uncritically giving poor children a watered-down curriculum; too often, children from disadvantaged backgrounds were put in special education classes, not because they lacked normal learning capacity, but because they had fallen behind in poor schools and had too

little support at home. Dick Riley and I were convinced
that, with smaller classes and extra attention from teachers, they could catch up. The bill also contained incentives
to increase parental involvement; gave federal support to
allow students and parents to choose a public school other
than the one to which they were assigned; and funded public charter schools designed to promote innovation and
allowed to operate free of school district requirements that
can stifle creativity. In just two years, in addition to the
ESEA, bipartisan supporters in Congress had enacted Head
Start reform; put the National Education Association goals
into law; reformed the student-loan program; created the
national service program; passed the school-to-work program to create apprenticeships for high school graduates
who don't go on to college; and dramatically increased our
commitment to adult education and lifelong learning.

The education package was one of the most important
achievements of my first two years in office. Although it
would increase the quality of learning and economic opportunities for millions of Americans, almost no one knew
about it. Because education reforms had broad support in
both parties, the efforts to pass them generated relatively little controversy, and therefore weren't considered particularly newsworthy.

We ended the first week of the month on a high note,
when the unemployment rate fell to 5.9 percent, the lowest
since 1990 (down from over 7 percent when I took office),
with 4.6 million new jobs. Later in the month, economic
growth in the third quarter of the year was pegged at 3.4
percent, with inflation at 1.6 percent. NAFTA was making a
contribution to the growth. Overall exports to Mexico were
up 19 percent in just a year, with car and truck exports up
600 percent.

On October 7, Iraq massed a large number of troops just
two and a half miles from the Kuwait border, raising the
specter of another Gulf War. With strong international support, I rapidly deployed 36,000 troops to Kuwait, backed
up by an aircraft carrier battle group and fighter planes. I

also ordered an updated list of targets for our Tomahawk missiles. The British announced they would beef up their forces as well. On the ninth, the Kuwaitis moved most of their 18,000-man army to the border. The next day, the Iraqis, surprised by the strength and speed of our response, announced that they would pull back their forces, and within a month the Iraqi parliament recognized Kuwait's sovereignty, borders, and territorial integrity. A couple of days after the immediate Iraq crisis passed, the Protestant paramilitary groups in Northern Ireland announced that they would join the IRA in observing a complete cease-fire.

The good news spilled over into the third week of October. On the fifteenth, President Aristide returned to Haiti. Three days later I announced that after sixteen months of intense negotiations, we had reached an agreement with North Korea to end the threat of nuclear proliferation on the Korean peninsula. The agreed framework, signed in Geneva on October 21 by our negotiator, Bob Gallucci, and the North Koreans, committed North Korea to freeze all activity at existing nuclear reactors and allow them to be monitored; ship 8,000 unloaded fuel rods out of the country; dismantle its existing nuclear facilities; and ultimately account for the spent fuel it had produced in the past. In return, the United States would organize an international consortium to build light water reactors that didn't produce usable amounts of weapons-grade material; we would guarantee 500,000 tons of heavy oil per year; trade, investment, and diplomatic barriers would be reduced; and the United States would give formal assurances against the use or the threat to use nuclear weapons against North Korea.

Three successive administrations had tried to bring North Korea's nuclear program under control. The pact was a tribute to the hard work of Warren Christopher and Ambassador Bob Gallucci, and to our clear determination not to allow North Korea to become a nuclear power, or a seller of nuclear weapons and materials.

After I left office, the United States learned that in 1998 North Korea had begun to violate the spirit if not the letter of the agreement by producing highly enriched uranium in a laboratory—enough, perhaps, to make one or two bombs. Some people said this development called the validity of our 1994 agreement into question. But the plutonium program we ended was much larger than the later laboratory effort. North Korea's nuclear reactor program, had it proceeded, would have produced enough weapons-grade plutonium to make several nuclear weapons a year.

On October 17, Israel and Jordan announced that they had reached a peace agreement. Yitzhak Rabin and King Hussein invited me to witness the signing ceremony on October 26, in the Wadi Araba border crossing in the great Rift Valley. I accepted, in the hope that I could use the trip to push for progress on the other Middle East tracks. I stopped first in Cairo, where President Mubarak and I met with Yasser Arafat. We encouraged him to do more to combat terrorism, especially by Hamas, and pledged to help resolve his differences with the Israelis concerning the delayed turnover of designated areas to Palestinian control.

The next day I witnessed the ceremony and thanked the Israelis and Jordanians for their courage in leading the way to peace. It was a hot and clear day, and the breathtaking backdrop of the Rift Valley was perfect for the grandeur of the occasion, but the sun was so bright bouncing off the desert sand that it almost blinded me. I nearly passed out, and if my alert presidential aide, Andrew Friendly, hadn't come to my rescue with sunglasses, I might have fainted and spoiled the whole occasion.

After the ceremony Hillary and I drove the short distance with King Hussein and Queen Noor to their vacation home in Aqaba. It was Hillary's birthday, and they gave her a cake with trick candles Hillary couldn't blow out, prompting me to kid her that her advancing years had diminished her lung capacity. Both Hussein and Noor were intelligent, gracious, and visionary. Noor, a Princeton graduate, was the daughter of a distinguished Arab-American father and Swedish mother. Hussein was a short but powerfully built man with a winning smile, a dignified manner, and wise eyes. He had survived several assassination attempts in his long reign, and he knew well that "taking risks for peace" was far more than a fine-sounding phrase. Hussein and Noor became real friends of ours. We laughed a lot together, forgetting our duties whenever we could in favor of stories about our lives, our kids, and our shared interests, including horses and motorcycles. In the years ahead, Noor would join us in vacation sing-alongs in Wyoming; I would go to their home in Maryland for one of Hussein's birthday parties; and Hillary and Noor would talk often. They were a blessing in our lives.

Later that day I became the first American President to speak to the Jordanian parliament in Amman. The best-received lines in the speech were directed to the Arab world at large: "America refuses to accept that our civilizations must collide. We respect Islam. . . . The traditional values of Islam, devotion to faith and good work, to family and society, are in harmony with the best of American ideals. Therefore, we know our people, our faiths, our cultures can live in harmony with each other."

The next morning I flew to Damascus, the oldest continuously inhabited city in the world, to see President Assad. No American President had been there in twenty years because of Syria's support for terrorism and its domination of Lebanon. I wanted Assad to know that I was committed to a Syrian-Israeli peace based on UN Resolutions 242 and 338, and that, if an agreement were reached, I would work hard to improve relations with his country. I took some heat for going to Syria because of its support for Hezbollah and other violent anti-Israeli groups, but I knew there would never be security and stability in the region unless Syria and Israel were reconciled. My meeting with Assad produced no big breakthrough, but he did give me some encouraging hints about how we might move forward. It was clear that he wanted to make peace, but when I suggested that he ought to go to Israel, reach out to the Israeli citizens, and make his case in the Knesset as Anwar Sadat had done, I could tell that I was beating a dead horse. Assad was brilliant but literal-minded and extremely cautious. He enjoyed the security of his beautiful marble palace and his daily routine in Damascus, and he couldn't imagine taking the political risk of flying to Tel Aviv. As soon as our meeting and the obligatory press conference were over, I flew to Israel to tell Rabin what I'd learned.

In a speech to the Knesset, Israel's parliament, I thanked and praised Rabin and assured the Knesset members that as Israel took steps toward peace, the United States would move to enhance its security and economic progress. It was a timely message because Israel had recently suffered yet another deadly terrorist attack. Unlike the Palestinian agreement, which many Israelis opposed, the Jordan peace pact had the support of nearly everyone in the Knesset, including the leader of the Likud opposition, Benjamin "Bibi" Netanyahu. The Israelis admired and trusted King Hussein; they remained uncertain about Arafat.

On the twenty-eighth, after an emotional visit to Yad Vashem, Israel's magnificent Holocaust memorial, Hillary and I said good-bye to Yitzhak and Leah Rabin, and I flew to Kuwait to see the emir and to thank our troops for forcing the withdrawal of Iraqi forces from the Kuwait border through their rapid deployment to the area. After Kuwait, I flew to Saudi Arabia for a few hours to see King Fahd. I had been impressed by Fahd's call, in early 1993, asking me to stop the ethnic cleansing of the Bosnian Muslims. On this occasion, Fahd received me warmly and thanked me for America's rapid move to defuse the crisis with Iraq. It had been a successful and encouraging visit, but I had to go home to face the election music.

TWELVE

BY OCTOBER, the polls we were getting didn't look too bad, but the atmosphere on the campaign trail still didn't feel good. Before we left for the Middle East, Hillary had called our old pollster Dick Morris for his assessment. Dick took a survey for us and the results were discouraging. He said that most people didn't believe that the economy was getting better or that the deficit was declining; that they didn't know about any of the good things the Democrats and I had done; and that the attacks on Gingrich's contract weren't working.

My approval rating had risen above 50 percent for the first time in a while, and voters responded positively when told about the family leave law, the 100,000 new police in the crime bill, the education standards and school reform, and our other achievements. Dick said we could cut our losses if the Democrats would stop talking about the economy, the deficit, and the contract, and concentrate instead on their popular legislative accomplishments. And he recommended that when I returned to Washington, I should stay off the campaign trail and remain "presidential," saying and doing things that would reinforce my higher ratings. Morris believed that would do more to help the Democrats than my plunging back into the political fray. Neither recommendation was followed.

The Democrats had no mechanism to move a new message quickly into every contested state and congressional district where it would make a difference; though I had done a lot of fund-raising for individual candidates and the House and Senate campaign committees, they had wanted to spend the money in the traditional way.

I called back to the White House from the Middle East trip and said I thought that, on my return, I should stay at work and make news rather than go back to the campaign trail. When I got home I was surprised to find my schedule packed with trips to Pennsylvania, Michigan, Ohio, Rhode Island, New York, Iowa, Minnesota, California, Washington, and Delaware. Apparently, when my own poll numbers started rising, Democrats around the country asked that I campaign for them. They had been there for me; now I had to be there for them.

While campaigning, I tried to keep emphasizing our shared accomplishments: signing the California Desert Protection Act, which protected 7.5 million acres of magnificent lands in the wilderness and national park systems; highlighting the large financial benefits of the new direct student-loan program at the University of Michigan; and doing as many radio interviews about our record as I could. But I also did big rallies with boisterous crowds, where I had to speak loudly to be heard. My campaign riffs were effective for the party faithful, but not for the larger audience who saw them on television; on TV, the hot campaign rhetoric turned a statesman-like President back into the politician the voters weren't sure about. Going back on the campaign trail, while understandable and perhaps unavoidable, was a mistake.

On November 8, we got the living daylights beat out of us, losing eight Senate seats and fifty-four House seats, the largest defeat for our party since 1946, when the Democrats were routed after President Truman tried to get health insurance for all Americans. The Republicans were rewarded for two years of constant attacks on me and for their solidarity on the contract. The Democrats were punished for too much good government and too little good politics. I had contributed to the demise by allowing my first weeks to be defined by gays in the military; by failing to concentrate on the campaign until it was too late; and by trying to do too much too fast in a news climate in which my victories were minimized, my losses were magnified, and the overall impression was created that I was just another pro-tax, big-government liberal, not the New Democrat who had won the presidency. Moreover, the public mood was still anxious; people didn't feel their lives were improving and they were sick of all the fighting in Washington. Apparently they thought divided government would force us to work together.

Ironically, I had hurt the Democrats by both my victories and my defeats. The loss of health care and the passage of NAFTA demoralized many of our base voters and depressed our turnout. The victories on the economic plan with its tax increases on high-income Americans, the Brady bill, and the assault weapons ban inflamed the Republican base voters and increased their turnout. The turnout differential alone probably accounted for half of our losses, and contributed to a Republican gain of eleven governorships. Mario Cuomo lost in New York with a miserable Democratic turnout. In the South, thanks largely to an extraordinary effort by the Christian Coalition, Republicans routinely ran five or six points ahead of their positions in the preelection polls. In Texas, George W. Bush defeated Governor Ann Richards, despite the fact that she had a 60 percent job approval rating.

The NRA had a great night. They beat both Speaker Tom Foley and Jack Brooks, two of the ablest members of Congress, who had warned me this would happen. Foley was the first Speaker to be defeated in more than a century. Jack Brooks had supported the NRA for years and had led the fight against the assault weapons ban in the House, but as chairman of the Judiciary Committee he had voted for the overall crime bill even after the ban was put into it. The NRA was an unforgiving master: one strike and you're out. The gun lobby claimed to have defeated nineteen of the twenty-four members on its hit list. They did at least that much damage and could rightly claim to have made Gingrich the House Speaker. In Oklahoma, Congressman Dave McCurdy, a DLC leader, lost his Senate race because of, in his words, "God, gays, and guns."

On October 29, a man named Francisco Duran, who had driven all the way from Colorado, protested the crime bill by opening fire on the White House with an assault weapon. He got off twenty to thirty rounds before he was subdued. Luckily, no one was hurt. Duran may have been

an aberration, but he reflected the almost pathological
hatred I had engendered among paranoid gun owners with
the Brady bill and the assault weapons ban. After the election I had to face the fact that the law-enforcement groups
and other supporters of responsible gun legislation, though
they represented the majority of Americans, simply could
not protect their friends in Congress from the NRA. The
gun lobby outspent, outorganized, outfought, and outdema-
gogued them.

The election had a few bright spots. Ted Kennedy and
Senator Dianne Feinstein prevailed in tough campaigns.
So did my friend Senator Chuck Robb of Virginia, who
defeated conservative talk-show host Oliver North of Iran-
Contra fame, with the help of an endorsement from his
Republican colleague Senator John Warner, who liked Robb
and couldn't stand the thought of North in the Senate.

In the Upper Peninsula of Michigan, Congressman Bart
Stupak, a former police officer, survived a tough challenge
in his conservative district by going on the offensive to
defend himself against the charge that his vote for the economic plan hurt his constituents. Stupak ran ads comparing
the exact number of those who got tax cuts with those who
had gotten tax increases. The ratio was about ten to one.

Senator Kent Conrad and Congressman Earl Pomeroy
were reelected in North Dakota, a conservative Republican
state, because they, like Stupak, aggressively defended their
votes and made sure the voters knew the good things that
had been accomplished. Perhaps it was easier to counter the
blizzard of negative TV ads in a small state or a rural district. Regardless, if more of our members had done what
Stupak, Conrad, and Pomeroy did, we would have won
more seats.

The two heroes of the budget battle in the House met
different fates. Marjorie Margolies-Mezvinsky lost her
wealthy suburban Pennsylvania district, but Pat Williams
survived in rural Montana.

I was profoundly distressed by the election, far more
than I ever let on in public. We probably would not have
lost either the House or the Senate if I had not included the

gas tax and the tax on upper-income Social Security recipients in the economic plan, and if I had listened to Tom Foley, Jack Brooks, and Dick Gephardt about the assault weapons ban. Of course, if I had made those decisions, I would have had to drop the EITC tax cut for lower-income working families, or accept less deficit reduction, with the attendant risk of an unfavorable response from the bond market; and I would have left more police officers and children at the mercy of assault weapons. I remained convinced that those hard decisions were good for America. Still, too many Democrats had paid a big price at the hands of voters who nevertheless would later reap the benefits of their courage in greater prosperity and safer streets.

We might not have lost either house if, as soon as it became clear that Senator Dole would filibuster any meaningful health reform, I had announced a delay in health care until we reached a bipartisan consensus, and had taken up and passed welfare reform instead. That would have been popular with alienated middle-class Americans who voted in droves for Republicans, and, unlike different decisions on the economic plan and the assault weapons ban, this course of action would have helped the Democrats without hurting the American people.

Gingrich had proved to be a better politician than I was. He understood that he could nationalize a midterm election with the contract, with incessant attacks on the Democrats, and with the argument that all the conflicts and bitter partisanship in Washington the Republicans had generated must be the Democrats' fault since we controlled both Congress and the White House. Because I had been preoccupied with the work of the presidency, I hadn't organized, financed, and forced the Democrats to adopt an effective national counter-message. The nationalization of midterm elections was Newt Gingrich's major contribution to modern electioneering. From 1994 on, if one party did it and the other didn't, the side without a national message would sustain unnecessary losses. It happened again in 1998 and 2002.

Though far more Americans had received tax cuts than income tax increases, and we had reduced the government to a much smaller size than it had been under Reagan and Bush, the Republicans also won on their same old promises of lower taxes and smaller government. They were even rewarded for problems they had created; they had killed health care, campaign finance reform, and lobbying reform with Senate filibusters. In that sense, Dole deserves a lot of credit for the Republican landslide, too; most people couldn't believe that a minority of forty-one senators could defeat any measure except the budget. All the voters knew was that they didn't yet feel more prosperous or more secure; there was too much fighting in Washington and we were in charge; and the Democrats were for big government.

I felt much as I did when I was defeated for reelection as governor in 1980: I had done a lot of good, but no one knew it. The electorate may be operationally progressive, but philosophically it is moderately conservative and deeply skeptical of government. Even if I had enjoyed more balanced press coverage, the voters probably would have had a hard time sorting out what I had accomplished in all the flurry of activity. Somehow I had forgotten the searing lesson of my 1980 loss: You can have good policy without good politics, but you can't give the people good government without both. I would not forget it again, but I never got over all those good people who lost their seats because they helped me dig America out of the deficit hole of Reaganomics, made our streets safer, and tried to provide health insurance to all Americans.

On the day after the election, I tried to make the best of a bad situation, promising to work with the Republicans and asking them "to join me in the center of the public debate where the best ideas for the next generation of American progress must come." I suggested we work together on welfare reform and the line-item veto, which I supported. For the time being, there was nothing more I could do.

Many of the pundits already were predicting my demise in 1996, but I was more hopeful. The Republicans had convinced many Americans that the Democrats and I were too liberal and too tied to big government, but time was on my side for three reasons: because of our economic plan, the deficit would keep coming down and the economy would continue to improve; the new Congress, especially the House, was well to the right of the American people; and, despite their campaign promises, the Republicans would soon be proposing cuts in education, health care, and aid to the environment to pay for their tax cuts and defense increases. It would happen because that's what ultra-conservatives wanted to do, and because I was determined to hold them to the laws of arithmetic.

THIRTEEN

WITHIN A WEEK of the election, I was hard at work again, as were the Republicans. On November 10, I named Patsy Fleming as national AIDS policy director, in recognition of her outstanding work in developing our AIDS policy, which included a 30 percent increase in overall AIDS funding, and I outlined a series of new initiatives to combat AIDS. The announcement was dedicated to the guiding light of the AIDS fight, Elizabeth Glaser, who was desperately ill with AIDS and would die in three weeks.

The same day, I announced that the United States would no longer enforce the arms embargo in Bosnia. The move had strong support in Congress and was necessary because the Serbs had resumed their aggression, with an assault on the town of Bihac; by late November, NATO was bombing Serb missile sites in the area. On the twelfth, I was en route to Indonesia for the annual APEC leaders' meeting, where the eighteen Asian Pacific nations committed themselves to creating an Asian free market by 2020, with the wealthier nations doing so by 2010.

On the home front, Newt Gingrich, basking in the after-glow of his big victory, kept up the withering personal attacks that had proved so successful in the campaign. Just before the election, he had taken a page from his pamphlet of smear words, calling me "the enemy of normal Americans." On the day after the election, he called Hillary and me "counterculture McGovernicks," his ultimate condemnation.

The epithet Gingrich hurled at us was correct in some respects. We had supported McGovern, and we weren't part of the culture that Gingrich wanted to dominate America: the self-righteous, condemning, Absolute Truth–claiming dark side of white southern conservatism. I was a white Southern Baptist who was proud of my roots and confirmed in my faith. But I knew the dark side all too well. Since I was a boy, I had watched people assert their piety and moral superiority as justifications for claiming an entitlement to political power, and for demonizing those who begged to differ with them, usually over civil rights. I thought America was about building a more perfect union, widening the circle of freedom and opportunity, and strengthening the bonds of community across the lines that divide us.

Even though I was intrigued by Gingrich and impressed by his political skills, I didn't think much of his claim that his politics represented America's best values. I had been raised not to look down on anyone and not to blame others for my own problems or shortcomings. That's exactly what the "New Right" message did. But it had enormous political appeal because it offered both psychological certainty and escape from responsibility: "they" were always right, "we" were always wrong; "we" were responsible for all the problems, even though "they" had controlled the presidency for all but six of the last twenty-six years. All of us are vulnerable to arguments that let us off the hook, and in the 1994 election, in an America where hardworking middle-class families felt economic anxiety and were upset by the pervasiveness of crime, drugs, and family dysfunction, there was an audience for the Gingrich message, especially when we didn't offer a competing one.

Gingrich and the Republican right had brought us back to the 1960s again; Newt said that America had been a great country until the sixties, when the Democrats took over and replaced absolute notions of right and wrong with more relativistic values. He pledged to take us back to the morality of the 1950s, in order to "renew American civilization."

Of course there were political and personal excesses in the 1960s, but the decade and the movements it spawned also produced advances in civil rights, women's rights, a clean environment, workplace safety, and opportunities for the poor. The Democrats believed in and worked for those things. So did a lot of traditional Republicans, including many of the governors I'd served with in the late 1970s and 1980s. In focusing only on the excesses of the 1960s, the New Right reminded me a lot of the carping that white southerners did against Reconstruction for a century after the Civil War. When I was growing up, we were still being taught how mean the Northern forces were to us during Reconstruction, and how noble the South was, even in defeat. There was something to it, but the loudest complaints always overlooked the good done by Lincoln and the national Republicans in ending slavery and preserving the Union. On the big issues, slavery and the Union, the South was wrong.

Now it was happening again, as the right wing used the excesses of the sixties to obscure the good done in civil rights and other areas. Their blanket condemnation reminded me of a story Senator David Pryor used to tell about a conversation he'd had with an eighty-five-year-old man who told him he had lived through two world wars, the Depression, Vietnam, the civil rights movement, and all the other upheavals of the twentieth century. Pryor said, "You sure have seen a lot of changes." "Yeah," the old man replied, "and I was against every one of them!"

Still, I didn't want to demonize Gingrich and his crowd as they had done to us. He had some interesting ideas, especially in the areas of science, technology, and entrepreneurialism, and he was a committed internationalist in foreign policy. Also, I had thought for years that the Democratic Party needed to modernize its approach, to focus less on preserving the party's industrial-age achievements and more on meeting the challenges of the information age, and to clarify our commitment to middle-class values and concerns. I welcomed the chance to compare our New Democrat ideas on economic and social problems with those embodied in the "Contract with America." Politics at its best is about the competition of ideas and policy.

But Gingrich didn't stop there. The core of his argument was not just that his ideas were better than ours; he said his *values* were better than ours, because Democrats were weak on family, work, welfare, crime, and defense, and because, being crippled by the self-indulgent sixties, we couldn't draw distinctions between right and wrong.

The political power of his theory was that it forcefully

and clearly confirmed the negative stereotypes of Democrats that Republicans had been working to embed in the nation's consciousness since 1968. Nixon had done it; Reagan had done it; and George Bush had done it, too, when he turned the 1988 election into a referendum on Willie Horton and the Pledge of Allegiance. Now Newt had taken the art of "reverse plastic surgery" to a whole new level of sophistication and harshness.

The problem with his theory was that it didn't fit the facts. Most Democrats were tough on crime, supported welfare reform and a strong national defense, and had been much more fiscally responsible than the New Right Republicans. Most were also hardworking, law-abiding Americans who loved their country, worked in their communities, and tried to raise their children well. Never mind the facts; Gingrich had his story line down pat, and he applied it every chance he got.

Soon he would charge, without a shred of evidence, that 25 percent of my White House aides were recent drug users. Then he said that Democratic values were responsible for the large number of out-of-wedlock births to teen mothers, whose babies should be taken away from them and put into orphanages. When Hillary questioned whether infants separated from their mothers would really be better off, he said she should watch the 1938 movie *Boys Town*, in which poor boys are raised in a Catholic orphanage, well before the dreaded 1960s ruined us all.

Gingrich even blamed the Democrats and their "permissive" values for creating a moral climate that encouraged a troubled South Carolina woman, Susan Smith, to drown her two young sons in October 1994. When it came out that Smith might have been unbalanced because she had been sexually abused as a child by her ultra-conservative stepfather, who was on the board of his local chapter of the Christian Coalition, Gingrich was unfazed. All sins, even those committed by conservatives, were caused by the moral relativism the Democrats had imposed on America since the 1960s.

I kept waiting for Gingrich to explain how the Democrats' moral bankruptcy had corrupted the Nixon and

Reagan administrations and led to the crimes of Watergate and Iran-Contra. I'm sure he could have found a way. When he was on a roll, Newt was hard to stop.

As we headed into December, a little sanity crept back into political life when the House and the Senate passed the Global Agreement on Tariffs and Trade, GATT, with large bipartisan majorities. The agreement reduced tariffs worldwide by a whopping $740 billion, opening previously closed markets to American products and services, giving poor countries a chance to sell products to consumers beyond their borders, and providing for the establishment of the World Trade Organization to create uniform trade rules and adjudicate disputes. Ralph Nader and Ross Perot campaigned hard against the pact, claiming it would have horrible consequences, from a loss of American sovereignty to an increase in abusive child labor. Their vocal opposition had little effect; the labor movement was less intensely opposed to GATT than it had been to NAFTA, and Mickey Kantor had done a good job in making the case for GATT to Congress.

Almost unnoticed in the comprehensive legislation that included GATT was the Retirement Protection Act of 1994. The problem of underfunded pensions was first brought to my attention by a citizen at the Richmond debate during the campaign. The bill required corporations with large underfunded plans to increase their contributions, and it stabilized the national pension insurance system and provided better protection to forty million Americans. The Retirement Protection Act and GATT were the last in a long line of major legislative achievements in my first two years, and, given the election results, bittersweet ones.

In early December, Lloyd Bentsen resigned as secretary of Treasury, and I appointed Bob Rubin to succeed him. Bentsen had done a remarkable job, and I didn't want him to leave, but he and his wife, B.A., wanted to return to private life. The choice of a successor was easy: Bob Rubin had built the National Economic Council into the most important innovation in White House decision making in decades, was respected on Wall Street, and wanted the economy to work for all Americans. Soon afterward, I named Laura Tyson to succeed Bob at the National Economic Council.

After hosting a state dinner for the new president of Ukraine, Leonid Kuchma, I flew to Budapest, Hungary, for only eight hours, to attend the meeting of the Conference on Security and Cooperation in Europe and sign a series of denuclearization agreements with President Yeltsin, Prime Minister Major, and the presidents of Ukraine, Kazakhstan, and Belarus. It should have produced good news coverage about our shared determination to reduce our arsenals by several thousand warheads and to prevent the spread of nuclear weapons to other nations. Instead, the story coming out of Budapest was Yeltsin's speech criticizing me for trading in the Cold War for a "cold peace" by rushing NATO enlargement to include the Central European nations. In fact, I had done the reverse, by establishing the Partnership for Peace as an interim step to include a much larger number of countries; by setting up a deliberate process for adding new NATO members; and by working hard to establish a NATO-Russian partnership.

Since I had no advance warning about Yeltsin's speech, and he spoke after I did, I was stunned and angry, because I didn't know what had set him off and because I had no opportunity to respond. Apparently, Yeltsin's advisors had convinced him that NATO would admit Poland, Hungary, and the Czech Republic in 1996, just when he would be running for reelection against the ultra-nationalists, who hated NATO expansion, and I would be running against the Republicans, who supported it.

Budapest was embarrassing, a rare moment when people on both sides dropped the ball, but I knew it would pass. A few days later, Al Gore went to see Yeltsin when he was in Moscow for the fourth meeting of the Gore-Chernomyrdin Commission for Economic, Scientific and Technical Cooperation. Boris told him that he and I were still partners, and Al assured Yeltsin that our NATO policy hadn't changed. I wasn't about to jam him for domestic political reasons, any more than I would let him keep NATO's doors closed indefinitely.

On December 9, I was in Miami to open the Summit of

the Americas, the first meeting of all the hemisphere's leaders since 1967. The thirty-three democratically elected leaders of Canada, Central and South America, and the Caribbean were there, including forty-one-year-old President Aristide of Haiti and his neighbor, President Joaquín Balaguer of the Dominican Republic, who was eighty-eight years old, blind, and infirm, but mentally still sharp as a tack.

I had initiated the summit to promote a free trade area in all the Americas, from the Arctic Circle to Tierra del Fuego; to strengthen democracy and effective government throughout the region; and to show that America was determined to be a good neighbor. The gathering was a big success. We committed ourselves to establishing a free trade area of the Americas by 2005, and left feeling that we were going into the future together, a future where, in the words of the great Chilean poet Pablo Neruda, "There is no such thing as a lone struggle, no such thing as a lone hope."

On December 15, I gave a televised address to outline my proposals for middle-class tax cuts in the coming budgets. The move was opposed by some people in the administration and criticized by some in the media as an attempt to copy the Republicans, or as a belated attempt to return to a 1992 campaign promise the voters had punished me for not keeping. For both policy and political reasons, I was trying to get back in the tax-cut hunt with the Republicans before the new Congress convened. The GOP contract contained tax proposals that I thought were unaffordable and too heavily tilted to upper-income Americans. On the other hand, the United States was still suffering from two decades of middle-class income stagnation, the main reason people hadn't felt the economy improving. We had made a dent in the problem by doubling the Earned Income Tax Credit. Now the right kind of tax cuts could raise middle-class incomes without derailing deficit reduction or our ability to invest in the future, and would fulfill my 1992 campaign commitment.

In the speech, I proposed a Middle-Class Bill of Rights, including a $500 child tax credit for families with incomes of $75,000 or less; tax deductibility for college tuition; expanded Individual Retirement Accounts (IRAs); and the conversion of the funds the government was spending on dozens of job-training programs into cash vouchers that would go directly to workers so they could choose their own training program. I told the American people that we could finance the tax package through further cost savings from Al Gore's Reinventing Government initiative and still keep reducing the deficit.

Just before Christmas, Al Gore and I announced the designation of the first cities and rural communities as "empowerment zones," making them eligible, under the 1993 economic plan, for tax incentives and federal funds to spur job development in places that had been left behind in previous recoveries.

December 22 was Dee Dee Myers's last day as press secretary. She had done a good job under difficult circumstances. Dee Dee had been with me in the snows of New Hampshire. Since then we had weathered a lot of storms and played countless games of hearts together. I knew she would do well when she left, and she did.

After our annual New Year's trip to Renaissance Weekend, Hillary and I took a couple of extra days off to go home, so that we could see her mother and Dick Kelley, and I could go duck hunting with friends in eastern Arkansas. Every year, when the ducks fly south from Canada for the winter, one of the two main flyways is down the Mississippi River. Many of them land in the rice paddies and ponds of the Arkansas Delta, and over the last few years several farmers had established duck hunting camps on their land, both for their own enjoyment and to supplement their incomes.

It's wonderful seeing the ducks fly at morning light. We also saw large geese high overhead, flying in perfect V formation. Only two ducks came down within shooting range that cloudy morning, and the guys who were with me let me shoot them both. They had more days to hunt than I did. I pointed out to the reporters who were along that all our guns were protected by the crime bill and that we didn't need assault weapons to bag the ducks, including one I got with a lucky shot from about seventy yards.

The next day Hillary and I attended the dedication of William Jefferson Clinton Elementary Magnet School in Sherwood, just outside North Little Rock. It was a beautiful facility, with a multi-purpose room named for my mother and a library named for Hillary. I confess that I liked having my name on a new school; no one owed more to his teachers than I did.

I needed that trip home. I had worked like a dog for two years. I had gotten so much done, but often "couldn't see the forest for the trees." The coming year was going to present a new set of challenges. To meet them, I needed more chances to recharge my batteries and water my roots.

As I returned to Washington, I was looking forward to watching the Republicans try to keep their campaign promises, and to the battle to preserve and fully implement all the legislation enacted the previous two years. When Congress passes a new law, the work of the executive branch has just begun. For example, the crime bill provided funding for 100,000 new police in our communities. We had to set up an office in the Justice Department to distribute the funds, establish criteria for eligibility for them, create and administer an application process, and monitor how the money was spent, so that we could make progress reports to Congress and the American people.

On January 5, I had my first meeting with the new congressional leaders. Besides Bob Dole and Newt Gingrich, the Republican team included Senator Trent Lott of Mississippi, and two Texans, Congressman Dick Armey, the House majority leader, and Congressman Tom DeLay, the House majority whip. The new Democratic leaders were Senator Tom Daschle of South Dakota and Congressman Dick Gephardt, as well as the Senate Democratic whip, Wendell Ford of Kentucky, and his counterpart in the House, David Bonior of Michigan.

Though the meeting with the congressional leaders was cordial, and there were some areas of the GOP contract on which we could work together, I knew there was no way we could avoid several heated struggles over important matters about which we had honest differences. Clearly, I and my entire team would have to be very focused and disciplined, in both our actions and our communications strategy. When a reporter asked me whether our relations would be marked by "compromise or combat," I responded, "My answer to that is, Mr. Gingrich will whisper in your right ear and I will whisper in your left ear."

When the congressmen left, I went into the press room to announce that Mike McCurry would be the new press secretary. Until then, Mike had been Warren Christopher's spokesman at State. During the presidential campaign, as press secretary for Senator Bob Kerrey, he had taken some pretty hard shots at me. I didn't care about that; he was supposed to be against me in the primary season, and he had done a good job at State explaining and defending our foreign policy.

We had some more new blood on our team. Erskine Bowles had come to the White House from the Small Business Administration as deputy chief of staff, switching jobs with Phil Lader. Erskine was especially well suited to the mixture of careful compromise and guerrilla war that would characterize our relations with the new Congress, because he was a gifted entrepreneur and world-class deal maker who knew when to hold and when to fold. He would support Panetta well and provide skills that complemented those of Leon's other deputy, the hard-charging Harold Ickes.

Like so many months, January was filled with both good and bad news: Unemployment was down to 5.4 percent, with 5.6 million new jobs; Kenneth Starr showed his "independence" when, unbelievably, he said he was going to reinvestigate Vince Foster's death; Yitzhak Rabin's government was threatened when nineteen Israelis were killed by two terrorist bombs, an act that weakened support for his peace efforts; and I signed the first bill of the new Congress, one I strongly supported, requiring the nation's lawmakers to comply with all the requirements they imposed on other employers.

On January 24, I gave the State of the Union address to the first Republican Congress in forty years. It was a delicate moment; I had to be conciliatory without seeming weak, strong without looking hostile. I began by asking Congress to put aside "partisanship and pettiness and pride" and suggesting that we work together on welfare reform, not to punish the poor but to empower them. I then introduced perhaps the best example of the potential of America's welfare recipients, Lynn Woolsey, a woman who had worked her way off welfare all the way to becoming a member of the House of Representatives from California.

Then I challenged the Republicans on several fronts. If they were going to vote for a balanced budget amendment, they should say *how* they proposed to balance the budget and whether they would cut Social Security. I asked them not to abolish AmeriCorps, as they had threatened to do. If they wanted to strengthen the crime bill, I would work with them, but I would oppose repealing proven prevention programs, the plan to put 100,000 more police on the streets, or the assault weapons ban. I said I would never do anything to infringe on legitimate firearms ownership and use, "but a lot of people laid down their seats in Congress so that police officers and kids wouldn't have to lay down their lives under a hail of assault weapon attacks, and I will not let that be repealed."

I finished the speech with an outreach to the Republicans, pushing my middle-class tax cuts but saying I would work with them on the issue, admitting that on health care, "We bit off more than we could chew," but asking them to work with me step by step, and to start by making sure people didn't lose their health insurance when they changed jobs or a family member was sick; and seeking their support for a bipartisan foreign policy agenda.

The State of the Union is not only the President's chance to speak for an unfiltered hour to the American people each year; it is also one of the most important rituals in American politics. How many times the President is interrupted by applause, especially standing ovations; what provokes the Democrats or Republicans to clap, and what they seem to agree on; the reactions of important senators and representatives; and the symbolic significance of the people chosen to sit in the First Lady's box are all noted by the press and witnessed by the American people on television. For this State of the Union, I had a speech designed to last fifty minutes, allowing ten minutes for applause. Because there was so much conciliation, as well as some meaty confrontation, the applause interruptions, more than ninety of them, took the speech to eighty-one minutes.

By the time of the State of the Union, we were two weeks into one of the biggest crises of my first term. On the evening of January 10, after Bob Rubin was sworn in as secretary of Treasury in the Oval Office, he and Larry Summers stayed to meet with me and a few of my advisors about the financial crisis in Mexico. The value of the peso had been declining precipitously, undermining Mexico's ability to borrow money or to repay existing debts. The problem was exacerbated because, as Mexico's condition deteriorated, in order to raise money it had issued short-term debt instruments called *tesobonos*, which had to be repaid in dollars. As the value of the peso continued to decline, it took more and more of them to finance the dollar value of Mexico's short-term debt. Now, with only $6 billion in reserves, Mexico had $30 billion of payments due in 1995, $10 billion in the first three months of the year.

If Mexico defaulted on its obligations, the economic "meltdown," as Bob Rubin tried to avoid calling it, could accelerate, with massive unemployment, inflation, and, very likely, a steep and prolonged recession because the international financial institutions, other governments, and private investors would all be unwilling to put more money at risk there.

As Rubin and Summers explained, the economic collapse of Mexico could have severe consequences for the United States. First, Mexico was our third-largest trading partner. If it couldn't buy our products, American companies and employees would be hurt. Second, economic dislocation in Mexico could lead to a 30 percent increase in illegal immigration, or half a million more people each year. Third, an impoverished Mexico would almost certainly become more vulnerable to increased activity by illegal drug cartels, which were already sending large quantities of narcotics across the border into the United States. Finally, a default by Mexico could have a damaging impact on other countries, by shaking investors' confidence in emerging markets in the rest of Latin America, Central Europe, Russia, South Africa, and other countries we were trying to help modernize and prosper. Since about 40 percent of American exports went to developing countries, our economy could be hurt badly.

Rubin and Summers recommended that we ask the Congress to approve $25 billion in loans to allow Mexico to pay its debt on schedule and retain the confidence of creditors and investors, in return for Mexico's commitment to financial reforms and more timely reporting on its financial condition, in order to prevent this from happening again. They warned, however, that risks were attached to their recommendation. Mexico might fail anyway and we could lose whatever money we had extended. If the policy succeeded, it could create the problem economists call "moral hazard." Mexico was on the brink of collapse not only because of flawed government policies and weak institutions, but also because investors had continued to finance its operations long past the point of prudence. By giving the money to Mexico to repay wealthy investors for unwise decisions, we might create an expectation that such decisions were risk free.

The risks were compounded by the fact that most Americans didn't understand the consequences to the American economy of a Mexican default. Most congressional Democrats would think the bailout proved that NAFTA was ill advised in the first place. And many of the newly elected Republicans, especially in the House, didn't share the Speaker's enthusiasm for international affairs. A surprising number of them didn't even have passports. They wanted to restrict immigration from Mexico, not send billions of dollars there.

After I listened to the presentation, I asked a couple of questions, then said we had to go forward with the loan. I thought the decision was clear-cut, but not all my advisors agreed. Those who wanted to speed my political recovery after the crushing midterm defeat thought I was nuts, or, as we say in Arkansas, "three bricks shy of a full load." When George Stephanopoulos heard Treasury's $25 billion figure for the loan, he thought Rubin and Summers must have meant $25 *million*; he thought I was about to shoot myself in the foot. Panetta favored the loan, but warned that if Mexico didn't repay us, it could cost me the election in 1996.

The risks were considerable, but I had confidence in Mexico's new president, Ernesto Zedillo, an economist with a doctorate from Yale who had stepped into the breach when his party's original candidate for president, Luis Colosio, was assassinated. If anybody could bring Mexico back, Zedillo could.

Besides, we simply couldn't stand aside and let Mexico fail without trying to help. In addition to the economic problems it would cause both for us and for the Mexicans, we would be sending a terrible signal of selfishness and shortsightedness throughout Latin America. There was a long history of Latin American resentment of America as arrogant and insensitive to their interests and problems. Whenever America reached out in genuine friendship—with FDR's Good Neighbor Policy, JFK's Alliance for Progress, and President Carter's return of the Panama Canal—we did better. During the Cold War, when we supported the overthrow of democratically elected leaders, backed dictators, and tolerated their human rights abuses, we got the reaction we deserved.

I called the congressional leaders to the White House, explained the situation, and asked for their support. All of them pledged it, including Bob Dole and Newt Gingrich, who aptly described the Mexico problem as "the first crisis of the twenty-first century." As Rubin and Summers made the rounds on Capitol Hill, we picked up support from Senator Paul Sarbanes of Maryland, Senator Chris Dodd, and Republican senator Bob Bennett of Utah, a highly intelligent,

old-fashioned conservative who quickly grasped the consequences of inaction and would stick with us throughout the
crisis. Several governors were also supportive, including Bill
Weld of Massachusetts, who had a great interest in Mexico,
and George W. Bush of Texas, whose state, along with
California, would be hardest hit if the Mexican economy
collapsed.

Despite the merits of the case and the support of Alan
Greenspan, it became obvious by the end of the month that
we weren't doing well in Congress. Anti-NAFTA Democrats
were sure the aid package was a step too far, and the new
Republican members were in open revolt.

By the end of the month, Rubin and Summers had begun
to consider acting unilaterally, by providing the money to
Mexico out of the Exchange Stabilization Fund. The fund
was created in 1934, when America took the dollar off the
gold standard, and was used to minimize currency fluctua-
tions; it had about $35 billion and could be used by the
Treasury secretary with the President's approval. On the
twenty-eighth, the need for American action took on even
greater urgency when the Mexican finance minister called
Rubin and told him default was imminent, with more than a
billion dollars' worth of *tesobonos* coming due the following week.

The matter came to a head on Monday night, January
30. Mexico's reserves were down to $2 billion, and the
value of the peso had dropped another 10 percent during
the day. That evening, Rubin and Summers came to the
White House to see Leon Panetta and Sandy Berger, who
was handling the issue for the National Security Council. In
blunt terms, Rubin told them, "Mexico has about forty-
eight hours to live." Gingrich called to say he couldn't pass
the aid package for another two weeks, if at all. Dole had
already said the same thing. They had tried, as had Tom
Daschle and Dick Gephardt, but the opposition was too
strong.

I returned to the White House from a fund-raiser at
about 11 p.m. and went to Leon's office to hear the grim
message. Rubin and Summers briefly restated the conse-

quences of a Mexican default, then said we needed "only" $20 billion in loan guarantees, not $25 billion, because International Monetary Fund director Michel Camdessus had put together almost $18 billion in aid that the IMF would extend if the United States acted; combined with smaller contributions from other countries and the World Bank, that brought the total aid package to just under $40 billion.

Though they favored going forward, Sandy Berger and Bob Rubin again pointed out the risks. A newly published poll in the *Los Angeles Times* said the American people opposed helping Mexico by 79 percent to 18 percent. I replied, "So a year from now, when we have another million illegal immigrants, we're awash in drugs from Mexico, and lots of people on both sides of the Rio Grande are out of work, when they ask me, 'Why didn't you do something?' what will I say? That there was a poll that said 80 percent of Americans were against it? This is something we have to do." The meeting lasted about ten minutes.

The next day, January 31, we announced the aid package with money from the Exchange Stabilization Fund. The loan agreement was signed a couple of weeks later at the Treasury Building, to howls of protest in Congress and grumbles among our G-7 allies, who were upset that the IMF director had made the $18 billion commitment to Mexico, and to us, without their prior approval. The first money was released in March, after which we continued to make regular disbursements, even though things didn't really get better in Mexico for several months. By the end of the year, however, investors had entered the Mexican markets again and foreign exchange reserves had begun to build up. Ernesto Zedillo had also instituted the reforms he had promised.

Though it was tough at first, the aid package worked. In 1982, when the Mexican economy collapsed, it had taken almost a decade for growth to return. This time, after a year of severe recession, the Mexican economy started to grow again. After 1982, it had taken seven years for Mexico to regain access to the capital markets. In 1995, it took only seven months. In January 1997, Mexico repaid its loan in full, with interest, more than three years ahead of schedule. Mexico had borrowed $10.5 billion of the $20 billion we made available, and it paid a total of $1.4 billion in interest, almost $600 million more than the money would have earned had it been invested in U.S. Treasury notes, as other Exchange Stabilization Fund monies were. The loan turned out to be not only good policy but also a good investment.

New York Times columnist Tom Friedman called the Mexican loan guarantee "the least popular, least understood, but most important foreign policy decision of the Clinton Presidency." He may have been right. As for popular opposition, 75 percent of the people had also opposed the Russian aid package; my decision to restore Aristide in Haiti was unpopular; and my subsequent actions in Bosnia and Kosovo met with initial popular resistance. Polls can be helpful in telling a President what the American people think, and which arguments may be most persuasive at a particular time, but they cannot dictate a decision that requires looking down the road and around the corner. The American people hire a President to do the right thing for our country over the long run. Helping Mexico was the right thing for America. It was the only sensible economic course, and by taking it, we proved ourselves to be, once again, a good neighbor.

On February 9, Helmut Kohl came to see me. He had just been reelected, and he confidently predicted that I would be as well. He told me we were living in turbulent times, but the end would bring me out all right. At the press conference after our meeting, Kohl paid a moving tribute to Senator Fulbright, who had died shortly after midnight at the age of eighty-nine. Kohl said he came from a generation who, when they were students, "wanted nothing more than to obtain a Fulbright scholarship," and that, across the world, Fulbright's name was associated "with openness, with friendship, and with people striving together." At the time of his passing, more than 90,000 Americans and 120,000 students from other countries had been Fulbright scholars.

I had gone to Senator Fulbright's home to visit him not long before he died. He had had a stroke and his speech was somewhat impaired, but his eyes were bright, his mind was working, and we had a good last visit. Fulbright would loom large in American history—as I said at his memorial service, "Always the teacher and always the student."

On February 13, Laura Tyson and the other members of the Council of Economic Advisers, Joe Stiglitz and Martin Baily, gave me a copy of the latest *Economic Report of the President*. It highlighted our progress since 1993, as well as the persistent problems of income stagnation and inequality. I used the occasion to push the Middle-Class Bill of Rights and my proposal to increase the minimum wage by 90 cents over two years, from $4.25 to $5.15 an hour. The raise would benefit 10 million workers, adding $1,800 a year to their incomes. Half the increase was necessary just to get the minimum wage (after inflation) back to what it had been in 1991, the last time it was raised.

The minimum wage was a favorite cause of most Democrats, but most Republicans opposed minimum wage increases, claiming that they cost jobs by increasing the cost of doing business. There was little evidentiary support for their position. Indeed, some young labor economists had recently found that a moderate minimum wage increase might lead to a modest increase—not decrease—in employment. I had recently seen a television interview with a minimum wage worker in a factory in southwest Virginia. When asked about rumors that the increase might cause her employer to lay off her and other co-workers and do more work with machines, the woman smiled and told the interviewer, "Honey, I'll take my chances."

In the fourth week of February, Hillary and I paid a two-day state visit to Canada, where we stayed at the American ambassador's residence with Ambassador Jim and Janet Blanchard. Jim and I had become friends in the 1980s, when he was governor of Michigan. Canada is our largest trading partner and closest ally. We share the longest unguarded border in the world. In 1995, we were working together on

Haiti, on helping Mexico, and on NATO, NAFTA, the Summit of the Americas, and APEC. While we had occasional disputes over trade in wheat and timber and over salmon-fishing rights, our friendship was broad and deep.

We spent a lot of time with Prime Minister Jean Chrétien and his wife, Aline. Chrétien would become one of my best friends among world leaders, a strong ally, confidant, and frequent golfing partner.

I also spoke to the Canadian parliament, thanking them for our economic and security partnerships and the rich cultural contributions of Canadians to American life, including Oscar Peterson, my favorite jazz pianist; singer-songwriter Joni Mitchell, who wrote "Chelsea Morning"; and Yousuf Karsh, the great photographer who had become famous for his portrait of Churchill scowling after Karsh jerked the omnipresent cigar out of his hand, and who had photographed Hillary and me in less forbidding poses.

March got off to a good start, at least from my point of view, when the Senate failed, by only one vote, to get the two-thirds majority necessary to pass the balanced budget amendment. Though the amendment was popular, virtually every economist thought it was a bad idea because it restricted the ability of the government to run deficits under appropriate circumstances during a recession or a national emergency. Before 1981, America had not had much of a deficit problem; only after twelve years of trickle-down economics had quadrupled the national debt did politicians begin to argue that they would never make responsible economic decisions unless forced to do so by a constitutional amendment.

While the debate was going on, I urged the new Republican majority, who were pushing the amendment, to say exactly how they were going to balance the budget. I had produced a budget less than a month into my term; they had been in control of Congress for nearly two months and had still not presented one. They were finding it difficult to transform their campaign rhetoric into specific recommendations.

Soon, the Republicans offered a taste of the budget to

come by proposing a package of cuts, called rescissions, in the current year's budget. The cuts they chose proved that the Democrats had been right on target in their criticism of the contract during the campaign. The GOP rescissions included the elimination of 15,000 AmeriCorps positions, 1.2 million summer jobs for young people, and $1.7 billion in education funds, including nearly half of our drug-prevention funds, at a time when drug use among young people was still rising. Worst of all, they wanted to cut the school lunch program and WIC, the nutrition program for women, infants, and children under five, which, until then, had always had strong support from both Republicans and Democrats. The White House and the Democrats had a field day fighting those cuts.

Another GOP proposal that met stiff resistance was its move to eliminate the Department of Education, which, like the school lunch program, had always enjoyed strong bipartisan support. When Senator Dole said the department had done more harm than good, I joked that he might be right, because for most of the time since its inception, the department had been under the control of Republican secretaries of education. By contrast, Dick Riley was doing far more good than harm.

While pushing back on the Republican proposals, I was also promoting our agenda in ways that didn't require congressional approval and demonstrated that I had gotten the message from the last election. In the middle of March, I announced a regulatory reform effort developed by Al Gore's Reinventing Government project that focused on improving our environmental protection efforts through providing market incentives to the private sector, rather than imposing detailed regulations; the 25 percent reduction in paperwork requirements would save them 20 million work hours per year.

The "Rego" effort was working. We had already reduced the federal workforce by more than 100,000 and eliminated 10,000 pages of federal personnel manuals; soon we would earn almost $8 billion by auctioning slices of the broadcast spectrum for the first time; and eventually we would scrap

16,000 pages of federal regulations with no harm to the public interest. All the Rego changes were developed according to a simple credo: protect people, not bureaucracy; promote results, not rules; get action, not rhetoric. Al Gore's highly successful initiative confounded our adversaries, elated our allies, and escaped the notice of most of the public because it was neither sensational nor controversial.

By my third St. Patrick's Day as President, the occasion had grown from a celebration into an annual opportunity for the United States to advance the peace process in Northern Ireland. That year, I was giving the traditional Irish greeting, *céad míle fáilte*, "a hundred thousand welcomes," to a new Irish prime minister, John Bruton, who was continuing the peace policy of his predecessor. At noon, I met Gerry Adams for the first time at the Capitol, as Newt Gingrich hosted his first St. Patrick's Day Speaker's luncheon. I had given Adams a second visa after Sinn Fein had agreed to discuss with the British government the IRA's laying down of arms, and had invited him, along with John Hume and representatives of Northern Ireland's other main political parties, both Unionist and Republican, to the St. Patrick's Day reception at the White House that night.

When Adams showed up at the lunch, John Hume encouraged me to go over and shake hands with him, so I did. At the White House reception that night, the assembled crowd listened to a superb Irish tenor, Frank Patterson. Adams was having such a good time that he wound up singing a duet with Hume.

All this may sound routine now, but at the time it represented a sea change in American policy, one the British government and many in our own State Department still opposed. Now I was consorting not only with John Hume, the champion of peaceful change, but with Gerry Adams, whom the British still considered a terrorist. Physically, Adams was a striking contrast to the gentle, slightly rumpled, professorial Hume. He was bearded, taller, younger, and leaner, hardened by his years on the edge of destruction.

But Adams and Hume shared some important traits. Behind their glasses were eyes that revealed intelligence, conviction, and that uniquely Irish mixture of sadness and humor born of hopes often dashed but never abandoned. Against all odds, they both were trying to free their people from the shackles of the past. Before long, David Trimble, who led the largest Unionist party, would join them at the White House on St. Patrick's Day and in the quest for peace.

On March 25, Hillary began her first extended overseas trip without me, a twelve-day visit to Pakistan, India, Nepal, Bangladesh, and Sri Lanka. She took Chelsea along on what would be an important effort for the United States and a grand personal odyssey for them both. While the rest of my family was far away, I traveled closer to home, going to Haiti to visit the troops, meet with President Aristide, exhort the people of Haiti to embrace a peaceful democratic future, and participate in the handover of authority from our multinational force to the United Nations. In six months, forces from thirty nations had worked together under American leadership to remove more than 30,000 weapons and explosive devices from the streets and train a permanent police force. They had ended repressive violence; reversed the outmigration of Haitians, who were now coming home; and protected democracy in our hemisphere. Now the United Nations mission of more than 6,000 military personnel, 900 police officers, and dozens of economic, political, and legal advisors would take over for eleven months, until the election and inauguration of a new president. The United States would play a part, but our force levels and expenses would drop, as thirty-two other nations stepped forward to participate.

In 2004, after President Aristide resigned and flew into exile amidst renewed violence and strife, I thought back to what Hugh Shelton, the commander of the American forces, had told me: "The Haitians are good people and they deserve a chance." Aristide certainly made mistakes and was often his own worst enemy, but the political opposition never really cooperated with him. Also, after the Republicans took over Congress in 1995, they were unwilling to give the financial assistance that might have made a difference.

Haiti will never develop into a stable democracy without more help from the United States. Still, our intervention saved lives and gave Haitians their first taste of the democracy they had voted for. Even with Aristide's serious problems, the Haitians would have been far worse off under Cedras and his murderous coup. I remain glad that we gave Haiti a chance.

The Haitian intervention also provided strong evidence of the wisdom of multilateral responses in the world's trouble spots. Nations working together, and through the UN, spread the responsibilities and costs of such operations, reduce resentment against the United States, and build invaluable habits of cooperation. In an increasingly interdependent world, we should work this way whenever we can.

FOURTEEN

I SPENT THE first two and a half weeks of April meeting with world leaders. Prime Minister John Major, President Hosni Mubarak, and Prime Minister Benazir Bhutto of Pakistan and Prime Minister Tansu Ciller of Turkey, two intelligent, very modern women leaders of Muslim countries, came to see me.

Meanwhile, Newt Gingrich gave a speech on his first hundred days as Speaker. To hear him tell it, you would think the Republicans had revolutionized America overnight, and in the process changed our form of government to a parliamentary system under which he, as prime minister, set the course for domestic policy, while I, as President, was restricted to handling foreign affairs.

For the moment, the Republicans were dominating the news, based on the novelty of their control of Congress and their assertions that they were making big changes. Actually, they had enacted only three relatively minor parts of their contract, all of which I supported. The hard decisions were still ahead of them.

In a speech to the American Society of Newspaper Editors, I spelled out the parts of the contract I agreed with, on which I would seek compromise, and those I opposed and would veto. On April 14, four days after Senator Dole announced his candidacy for President, I quietly filed for reelection. On the eighteenth, I held a press conference and was asked more than twenty questions about a wide variety of topics, foreign and domestic. The next day they would all be forgotten and there would be only two words on the lips of every American: Oklahoma City.

In late morning I learned that a truck bomb had exploded outside the Alfred P. Murrah Federal Building in Oklahoma City, leaving the building a rubble and killing an unknown number of people. I immediately declared a state of emergency and sent an investigative team to the site. When the magnitude of the recovery effort became apparent, firefighters and other emergency workers came from all over the country to help Oklahoma City dig through the rubble in a desperate attempt to find any survivors.

America was riveted and heartbroken by the tragedy; it claimed the lives of 168 people, including nineteen children who were in the building's day-care center when the bomb exploded. Most of the dead were federal employees who worked for the several agencies that had offices in the Murrah Building. Many people assumed that Islamic militants were responsible, but I cautioned against jumping to conclusions about the perpetrators' identity.

Soon after the bombing, Oklahoma lawmen arrested Timothy McVeigh, an alienated military veteran who had come to hate the federal government. By the twenty-first, McVeigh was in FBI custody and had been arraigned. He had chosen April 19 to bomb the federal building because it was the anniversary of the FBI raid on the Branch Davidians at Waco, an event that, to right-wing extremists, represented the ultimate exercise of arbitrary, abusive government power. Anti-government paranoia had been building in America for years, as more and more people took the historical skepticism of Americans toward government to a level of outright hatred. This animus led to the rise of armed militia groups that rejected the legitimacy of federal authority and asserted the right to be a law unto themselves.

The atmosphere of hostility was intensified by right-wing radio talk-show hosts, whose venomous rhetoric pervaded the airwaves daily, and by Web sites encouraging people to rise up against the government and offering practical assistance, including easy-to-follow instructions on how to make bombs.

In the wake of Oklahoma City, I tried to comfort and encourage those who had lost their loved ones, and the country at large, and to step up our efforts to protect Americans from terrorism. In the more than two years since the World Trade Center bombing, I had increased counterterrorism resources for the FBI and CIA and instructed them to work together more closely. Our law-enforcement efforts had succeeded in returning several terrorists to the United States for trial after they fled to foreign countries and in preventing terrorist attacks on the United Nations, on the Holland and Lincoln tunnels in New York City, and on planes flying out of the Philippines to America's West Coast.

Two months before Oklahoma City, I had sent antiterrorism legislation to Congress asking, among other things, for one thousand more law-enforcement officials to fight terrorism; a new counterterrorism center under the direction of the FBI to coordinate our efforts; and approval to use military experts, normally prohibited from involvement in domestic law enforcement, to help with terrorist threats and incidents within the country involving chemical, biological, and nuclear weapons.

After Oklahoma City, I asked the congressional leaders for expedited consideration of the legislation and, on May 3, proposed amendments to strengthen it: greater law-enforcement access to financial records; authority to conduct electronic surveillance on suspected terrorists when they move from place to place, without having to go back to court for a new order to tap each specific site; increased penalties for knowingly providing firearms or explosives for terrorist acts against current or former federal employees and their families; and a requirement that markers, called taggants, be put into all explosive materials so that they could be traced. Some of these measures were bound to be controversial, but, as I said to a reporter on May 4, terrorism "is the major threat to the security of Americans." I wish I had been wrong.

On Sunday, Hillary and I flew to Oklahoma City for a memorial service at the Oklahoma State Fairgrounds. The service had been organized by Cathy Keating, the wife of Governor Frank Keating, whom I had first met more than thirty years earlier when we were students at Georgetown. Frank and Cathy were obviously still in a lot of pain, but they and the mayor of Oklahoma City, Ron Norick, had risen to the challenge of the search-and-recovery operation and of meeting Oklahomans' need for grieving. At the service, the

Reverend Billy Graham got a standing ovation when he said, "The spirit of this city and of this nation will not be defeated." In moving remarks, the governor said that if anyone thought Americans had lost the capacity for love and caring and courage, they should come to Oklahoma.

I tried to speak for the nation in saying, "You have lost too much, but you have not lost everything. And you have certainly not lost America, for we will stand with you for as many tomorrows as it takes." I shared a letter I had received from a young widow and mother of three whose husband had been killed by the terrorist downing of Pan Am 103 over Lockerbie, Scotland, in 1988. She asked those who had lost loved ones not to turn their hurt into hate, but instead to do the things their loved ones had "left undone, thus ensuring they did not die in vain." After Hillary and I met with some of the victims' families, I needed to remember those wise words too. One of the Secret Service agents killed was Al Whicher, who had served on my detail before going to Oklahoma; his wife and three children were among the families there.

So often referred to by the demeaning term "federal bureaucrats," the slain employees had been killed because they served us, helping the elderly and disabled, supporting farmers and veterans, enforcing our laws. They were family members, friends, neighbors, PTA members, and workers in their communities. Somehow they had been morphed into heartless parasites of tax dollars and abusers of power, not only in the twisted minds of Timothy McVeigh and his sympathizers but also by too many others who bashed them for power and profit. I promised myself that I would never use the thoughtless term "federal bureaucrat" again, and that I would do all I could to change the atmosphere of bitterness and bigotry out of which this madness had come.

Whitewater World didn't stop for Oklahoma City. The day before Hillary and I left for the memorial service, Ken Starr and three aides came to the White House to question us. I was accompanied to the session in the Treaty Room by Ab Mikva and Jane Sherburne of the White House counsel's office, and my private attorneys, David Kendall and his partner Nicole Seligman. The interview was uneventful, and when it concluded, I asked Jane Sherburne to show Starr and his deputies the Lincoln Bedroom, with its furniture brought to the White House by Mary Todd Lincoln and a copy of the Gettysburg Address, which Lincoln had written in his own hand after the fact so that it could be auctioned to raise money for war veterans. Hillary thought I was being too nice to them, but I was just behaving as I'd been raised to do, and I hadn't yet given up all my illusions that the inquiry would, in the end, follow a legitimate course.

During the same week my longtime friend Senator David Pryor announced that he would not seek reelection in 1996. We had known each other for nearly thirty years. David Pryor and Dale Bumpers were far more than just my home-state senators; we had served consecutively as governor, and together we had helped to keep Arkansas a progressive Democratic state as most of the South moved into the Republican fold. Pryor and Bumpers had been invaluable to my work and my peace of mind, not only because they had supported me on tough issues but because they were my friends, men who had known me a long time. They could make me listen and laugh, and reminded their colleagues that I wasn't the person they kept reading about. After David retired, I would have to get him on the golf course to obtain the advice and perspective that were near at hand as long as he was in the Senate.

At the White House correspondents' dinner on April 29, my remarks were brief, and except for a line or two, I didn't try to be funny. Instead, I thanked the assembled press for their powerful and poignant coverage of the Oklahoma City tragedy and the herculean recovery effort, assured them that "we are going to get through this, and when we do, we'll be even stronger," and closed with W. H. Auden's words:

> In the deserts of the heart
> Let the healing fountain start.

On May 5, at the Michigan State University commencement, I spoke not only to the graduates but also to the armed militia groups, many of which were active in remote areas of rural Michigan. I said that I knew that most militia members, while they dressed up on weekends in fatigues and conducted military exercises, had not broken any laws, and I expressed appreciation for those who had condemned the bombing. Then I attacked those who had gone beyond harsh words to advocating violence against law-enforcement officers and other government employees, while comparing themselves to the colonial militias, "who fought for the democracy you now rail against."

For the next few weeks, in addition to hammering away at those who condoned violence, I asked all Americans, including radio talk-show hosts, to weigh their words more carefully, to make sure that they did not encourage violence in the minds of people less stable than themselves.

Oklahoma City prompted millions of Americans to reassess their own words and attitudes toward government and toward people whose views differed from their own. In so doing, it began a slow but inexorable moving away from the kind of uncritical condemnation that had become all too prevalent in our political life. The haters and extremists didn't go away, but they were on the defensive and, for the rest of my term, would never quite regain the position they had enjoyed before Timothy McVeigh took the demonization of government beyond the limits of humanity.

In the second week of May, I boarded Air Force One to fly to Moscow to celebrate the fiftieth anniversary of the end of World War II in Europe. Even though Helmut Kohl, François Mitterrand, John Major, Jiang Zemin, and other leaders were scheduled to be there, my decision was controversial because Russia was involved in a bloody battle against separatists in the predominantly Muslim republic of Chechnya, civilian casualties were mounting, and most outside observers thought that Russia had used excessive force and insufficient diplomacy.

I made the trip because our nations were allies in World War II, which had claimed the lives of one in eight Soviet citizens: twenty-seven million of them died in battle or from disease, starvation, and freezing. Also, we were allies once again, and our partnership was essential to Russia's economic and political progress, to our cooperation in securing and destroying nuclear weapons, to the orderly expansion of NATO and the Partnership for Peace, and to our fight against terrorism and organized crime. Finally, Yeltsin and I had two thorny issues to resolve: the problem of Russia's cooperation with Iran's nuclear program and the question of how to handle NATO expansion in a way that would bring Russia into the Partnership for Peace and wouldn't cost Yeltsin the election in 1996.

On May 9, I stood with Jiang Zemin and several other leaders in Red Square as we watched a military parade featuring old veterans marching shoulder to shoulder, often holding hands and leaning against one another to steady themselves as they paraded one last time for Mother Russia. The next day, after the commemorative ceremonies, Yeltsin and I met in St. Catherine's Hall in the Kremlin. I started the meeting with Iran, telling Yeltsin that we had worked together to get all the nuclear weapons out of Ukraine, Belarus, and Kazakhstan; now we had to make sure that we didn't allow states that could harm us both, like Iran, to become nuclear powers. Yeltsin was prepared for this; he immediately said no centrifuges would be sold and suggested we refer the question of the reactors, which Iran claimed it wanted for peaceful purposes only, to the Gore-Chernomyrdin commission. I agreed, provided Yeltsin would publicly commit to Russia's not giving Iran nuclear technology that could be used for military purposes. Boris said okay and we shook hands on it. We also agreed to begin visits to Russia's biological weapons plants in August, as part of a broader effort to reduce the threat of biological and chemical weapons proliferation.

On the question of NATO enlargement, after I told Yeltsin indirectly that we wouldn't push it before his election in 1996, he finally agreed to join the Partnership for Peace. Although he didn't agree to announce his decision publicly, for fear of being seen as conceding too much, he promised that Russia would sign the documents by May 25, and that was good enough for me. The trip had been a success.

On the way home, I stopped in Ukraine for another World War II ceremony, a speech to university students, and a moving visit to Babi Yar, the hauntingly beautiful wooded ravine where, almost fifty-four years earlier, the Nazis had slaughtered more than 100,000 Jews and several thousand Ukrainian nationalists, Soviet prisoners of war, and Gypsies. Just the day before, the United Nations had voted to permanently extend the Nuclear Nonproliferation Treaty, which had been the bedrock of our efforts to contain the proliferation of nuclear weapons for more than twenty-five years. Since several nations were still trying to obtain them, the extension of NPT was one of my most important nonproliferation objectives. Babi Yar and Oklahoma City were sober reminders of the human capacity for evil and destruction; they reinforced the importance of the NPT and the agreement I had made restricting Russian nuclear sales to Iran.

By the time I got back to Washington, the Republicans had begun to move on their proposals, and I spent most of the rest of the month trying to beat them back, threatening to veto their rescission package, their attempts to weaken our clean water program, and the large cuts they had proposed in education, health care, and foreign aid.

In the third week of May, I announced that, for the first time since the beginning of the Republic, the two blocks of Pennsylvania Avenue that front the White House would be closed to vehicular traffic. I agreed to this decision reluctantly, after a panel of experts from the Secret Service, Treasury, and past Republican and Democratic administrations told me that it was necessary to secure the White House from a bomb. In the aftermath of Oklahoma City and the Japanese subway attack, I felt I had to go along with the recommendation, but I didn't like it.

By the end of the month, Bosnia was back in the news. The Serbs tightened their blockade around Sarajevo, and their snipers began firing on innocent children again. On May 25, NATO conducted air strikes on the Serb stronghold of Pale, and the Serbs, in retaliation, seized UN peacekeepers and chained them to ammunition dumps in Pale as hostages against further strikes; they also killed two UN soldiers from France in the seizure of a UN outpost.

Our airpower had been used extensively in Bosnia to conduct the longest-lasting humanitarian mission in history; to enforce the no-fly zone, which kept the Serbs from bombing Bosnian Muslims; and to maintain a fire-free zone around Sarajevo and other populated areas. Along with the UN peacekeepers and the embargo, our pilots had made a real difference: casualties had dropped from 130,000 in 1992 to under 3,000 in 1994. Nonetheless, the war was still raging, and more would have to be done to bring it to an end.

The other main foreign policy developments in June occurred around the G-7 summit hosted by Jean Chrétien in Halifax, Nova Scotia. Jacques Chirac, who had just been elected president of France, stopped by to see me on his way to Canada. Chirac had warm feelings for America. As a young man, he had spent time in our country, including a brief period working in a Howard Johnson's restaurant in Boston. He had an insatiable curiosity about a wide variety of issues. I liked him a lot, and liked the fact that his wife was also in politics, with a career of her own.

Despite the good chemistry between us, our relationship had been somewhat strained by his decision to resume testing France's nuclear weapons while I was trying to get worldwide support for a comprehensive nuclear test-ban treaty, a goal of every American President since Eisenhower. After Chirac assured me that when the tests were completed he would support the treaty, we moved on to Bosnia, where he was inclined to be tougher on the Serbs than Mitterrand had been. He and John Major were supporting the creation of a rapid reaction force to respond to attacks on UN peacekeepers, and I pledged U.S. military support to help them and the other UN forces get into and out of Bosnia if they and the regular peacekeepers had to be withdrawn. But I also told Chirac that if the force didn't work and the UN troops were forced out of Bosnia, we would have to lift the arms embargo.

At the G-7, I had three objectives: to secure greater

cooperation among the allies on terrorism, organized crime, and narco-trafficking; to identify major financial crises quickly and handle them better, with more timely and accurate information and with investments in developing nations to reduce poverty and promote environmentally responsible growth; and to resolve a serious trade dispute with Japan.

The first two were easily achieved; the third was a real problem. In two and a half years, we had made progress with Japan, completing fifteen separate trade agreements. However, in the two years since Japan had pledged to open its markets to U.S. automobiles and auto parts, the sector that accounted for more than half our total bilateral trade deficit, we had made almost no headway at all. Eighty percent of American dealerships sold Japanese cars; only 7 percent of Japanese dealerships sold cars from any other country, and rigid government regulation kept our parts out of Japan's repair market. Mickey Kantor had reached the limits of his patience and had recommended putting a 100 percent tariff on Japanese luxury cars. In a meeting with Prime Minister Murayama, I told him that because of our security relationship and the sluggish Japanese economy, the United States would continue to negotiate with Japan, but we had to have action soon. By the end of the month we had it. Japan agreed that two hundred dealerships would offer U.S. cars immediately, and a thousand would do so within five years; that the regulations keeping our parts out would be changed; and that Japanese automakers would increase their production in the United States and use more American-made parts.

During the entire month of June, I was also embroiled in the unfolding battle with the Republicans over the budget. On the first day of the month, I went to a farm in Billings, Montana, to highlight the differences between my approach to agriculture and that of the Republicans in Congress. The agricultural aid program had to be reauthorized in 1995, and therefore was part of the budget debate. I told the farm families that while I favored a modest reduction in overall agricultural spending, the Republican plan cut assistance too sharply and did too little for family farmers. For several years, Republicans had done better than Democrats in rural America because they were more culturally conservative, but when push came to shove, the Republicans cared more about large agribusiness than family farmers.

I also went horseback riding, mostly because I liked to ride and loved the broad sweep of the Montana landscape, but also because I wanted to show that I wasn't a cultural alien rural Americans couldn't support. After the farm event, my advance man, Mort Engleberg, had asked one of our hosts what he thought of me. The farmer replied, "He's all right. And he ain't anything like they make him out to be." I heard that a lot in 1995, and just hoped I wouldn't have to bring perception into line with reality one voter at a time.

Our ride got interesting when one of my Secret Service agents fell off his horse; the agent was unhurt, but the horse took off like a rocket across the open range. To the amazement of the press and the Montanans watching, my deputy chief of staff, Harold Ickes, rode off after the runaway steed at a blistering pace, chased him down, and returned him to his owner. Harold's exploit seemed totally at odds with his image as a high-strung, urban, liberal activist. As a young man, he had worked on ranches out west, and he hadn't forgotten how to ride.

On June 5, Henry Cisneros and I unveiled a "National Homeownership Strategy" of one hundred things we were going to do to increase home ownership to two-thirds of the population. The big decline in the deficit had kept mortgage rates low even as the economy picked up, and in a couple of years, we would reach Henry's goal for the first time in American history.

At the end of the first week of June, I vetoed my first bill, the $16 billion GOP rescission package, because it cut too much out of education, national service, and the environment, while leaving untouched unnecessary highway demonstration projects, courthouses, and other federal buildings that were pet projects of Republican members. They may have hated government in general, but, like most incumbents, they still wanted to spend themselves to reelection. I offered to work with the Republicans to cut even more spending, but said it would have to come out of pork-barrel projects and other nonessential spending, not investments in our children and our future. A couple of days later, I had another reason to fight for those investments, as Hillary's brother Tony and his wife, Nicole, gave us a new nephew—Zachary Boxer Rodham.

I was still trying to find the right balance between confrontation and accommodation when I went to Claremont, New Hampshire, for a town meeting with Speaker Gingrich. I had said I thought it would be good for Newt to talk to people in New Hampshire as I had in 1992, and he took me up on it. We both made positive opening comments about the need for honest debate and cooperation rather than the kind of name-calling sound bites that make the evening news. Gingrich even joked that he had followed my campaign example by stopping at a Dunkin' Donuts shop on the way to the meeting.

In the course of answering questions from citizens, we agreed to work together for campaign finance reform, even shaking hands on it; talked about other areas where we saw eye to eye; had an interesting, civilized disagreement about health care; and disagreed about the utility of the United Nations and whether Congress should fund AmeriCorps.

The discussion with Gingrich was well received in a country weary of partisan warfare. Two of my Secret Service agents, who almost never said anything to me about politics, told me how glad they were to see the two of us in a positive discussion. The next day, at the White House Conference on Small Business, several Republicans said the same thing. If we could have continued in the same vein, I believe the Speaker and I could have resolved most of our differences in a way that would have been good for America. At his best, Newt Gingrich was creative, flexible, and brimming over with new ideas. But that wasn't what had made him Speaker; his searing attacks on the Democrats had done that. It's hard to restrain the source of your power, as Newt was reminded the next day when he was criticized by Rush Limbaugh and the conservative *Manchester Union Leader* for being too pleasant to me. It was a mistake he wouldn't often repeat in the future, at least not in public.

After the meeting I went to Boston for a fund-raiser for Senator John Kerry, who was up for reelection and would likely face a tough opponent in Governor Bill Weld. I had a good relationship with Weld, perhaps the most progressive of all the Republican governors, but I didn't want to lose Kerry in the Senate. He was one of the Senate's leading authorities on the environment and high technology. He had also devoted an extraordinary amount of time to the problem of youth violence, an issue he had cared about since his days as a prosecutor. Caring about an issue in which there are no votes today but which will have a big impact on the future is a very good quality in a politician.

On June 13, in a nationally televised address from the Oval Office, I offered a plan to balance the budget in ten years. The Republicans had proposed to do it in seven, with big spending cuts in education, health care, and the environment, and large tax cuts. By contrast, my plan had no cuts in education, health services for the elderly, the family supports necessary to make welfare reform work, or essential environmental protections. It restricted tax cuts to middle-income people, with an emphasis on helping Americans pay for the rapidly rising costs of a college education. Also, by taking ten years instead of seven to get to balance, my plan's annual contractionary impact would be less, reducing the risk of slowing economic growth.

The timing and substance of the speech were opposed by many congressional Democrats and some members of my cabinet and staff, who thought it was too early to get into the budget debate with the Republicans; their public support was dropping now that they were making decisions instead of just saying no to me, and a lot of Democrats thought it was foolish to get in their way with a plan of my own before it was absolutely necessary to put one out. After the beating we'd taken during my first two years, they thought the Republicans should have to endure at least a year of their own medicine.

It was a persuasive argument. On the other hand, I was the President; I was supposed to lead, and we had already cut the deficit by a third with no Republican support. If I later had to veto Republican budget bills, I wanted to do so after demonstrating a good-faith effort to make honorable compromises. Besides, in New Hampshire, the Speaker and I had pledged to try to work together. I wanted to hold up my end of the bargain.

My budget decision was supported by Leon Panetta, Erskine Bowles, most of the economic team, the Democratic deficit hawks in Congress, and Dick Morris, who had been advising me since the '94 elections. Most of the staff didn't like Dick because he was difficult to deal with, liked to go around established White House procedures, and had worked for Republicans. He also had some off-the-wall ideas from time to time and wanted to politicize foreign policy too much, but I had worked with him long enough to know when to accept, and when to reject, his advice.

Dick's main advice was that I had to practice the politics of "triangulation," bridging the divide between Republicans and Democrats and taking the best ideas of both. To many liberals and some in the press corps, triangulation was compromise without conviction, a cynical ploy to win reelection. Actually, it was just another way of articulating what I had advocated as governor, with the DLC, and in 1992 during the campaign. I had always tried to synthesize new ideas and traditional values, and to change government policies as conditions changed. I wasn't splitting the difference between liberals and conservatives; instead, I was trying to build a new consensus. And, as the coming showdown with the Republicans over the budget would show, my approach was far from lacking in conviction. Eventually, Dick's role would become known to the public and he would become a regular part of our weekly strategy sessions, which were normally held every Wednesday night. He also brought in Mark Penn and his partner, Doug Schoen, to do polling for us. Penn and

Schoen were a good team who shared my New Democrat philosophy and would remain with me for the rest of my presidency. Soon we would also be joined by veteran media consultant Bob Squier and his partner, Bill Knapp, who understood and cared about policy as well as promotion.

On June 29, I finally reached an agreement with the Republicans on the rescission bill, once they restored more than $700 million for education, AmeriCorps, and our safe drinking water program. Senator Mark Hatfield, the chairman of the Senate Appropriations Committee and an old-fashioned progressive Republican, had worked closely with the White House to make the compromise possible.

The next day in Chicago, with police officers and citizens who had been wounded by assault weapons, I defended the assault weapons ban and asked Congress to support Senator Paul Simon's legislation to close a big loophole in the law and ban cop-killer bullets. The policeman who introduced me said he had survived severe combat in Vietnam without a mark, but had nearly been killed by a criminal who used an assault weapon to riddle his body with bullets. Current law already banned the bullets that pierced protective vests worn by police officers, but the banned ammunition was defined not by its armor-piercing capability, but by what the ammunition was made of; ingenious entrepreneurs had discovered other elements, not mentioned in the law, that could also be made into bullets that pierced vests and killed cops.

The National Rifle Association was sure to fight the bill, but they were down a little from their high-water mark in 1994. After their executive director had referred to federal law-enforcement officers as "jackbooted thugs," former President Bush had resigned from the organization in protest. A few months earlier, at an event in California, the comedian Robin Williams had lampooned the NRA's opposition to banning cop-killer bullets with a good line: "Of course we can't ban them. Hunters need them. Somewhere out there in the woods, there's a deer wearing a Kevlar vest!" As we headed into the second half of 1995, I hoped Robin's joke and President Bush's protest were harbingers of a larger trend toward common sense on the gun issue.

In July, the partisan fights abated a little. On the twelfth, at James Madison High School in Vienna, Virginia, I continued efforts to bring the American people together, this time on the subject of religious liberty.

There was a lot of controversy about how much religious expression could be allowed in public schools. Some school officials and teachers believed that the Constitution prohibited any of it. That was incorrect. Students were free to pray individually or together; religious clubs were entitled to be treated like any other extracurricular organizations; in their free time, students were free to read religious texts; they could include their religious views in their homework as long as they were relevant to the assignment; and they could wear T-shirts promoting their religion if they were allowed to wear those that promoted other causes.

I asked Secretary Riley and Attorney General Reno to prepare a detailed explanation of the range of religious expression permitted in schools and to provide copies to every school district in America before the start of the next school year. When the booklet was issued, it substantially reduced conflict and lawsuits, and in so doing won support across the religious and political spectrum.

I had long been working on the issue, having established a White House liaison to faith communities, and signed the Religious Freedom Restoration Act. Near the end of my second term, Professor Rodney Smith, an expert on the First Amendment, said my administration had done more to protect and advance religious liberty than any since James Madison's. I don't know if that's accurate, but I tried.

A week after the religious liberty event, I was faced with the biggest current challenge to building a more united American community: affirmative action. The term refers to preferences given to racial minorities or women by governmental entities in employment, contracts for products and services, access to small-business loans, and admissions to universities. The purpose of affirmative action programs is to reduce the impact of long-term systemic exclusion of people based on race or gender from opportunities open to others in our society. The policy began under Kennedy and Johnson and was expanded under the Nixon administration, with strong bipartisan support, out of recognition that the impact of past discrimination could not be overcome by simply outlawing discrimination from now on, coupled with a desire to avoid requiring strict quotas, which could lead to benefits going to unqualified people and reverse discrimination against white males.

By the early 1990s, opposition to affirmative action had built up: from conservatives who said that any race-based preferences amounted to reverse discrimination and therefore were unconstitutional; from whites who had lost out on contracts or university admissions to blacks or other minorities; and from those who believed that affirmative action programs, while well intentioned, were too often abused or had achieved their purpose and outlived their usefulness. There were also some progressives who were uncomfortable with race-based preferences and who urged that the criteria for preferential treatment be redefined in terms of economic and social disadvantage.

The debate intensified when the Republicans won control of Congress in 1994; many of them had promised to end affirmative action, and after twenty years of stagnant middle-class incomes, their position appealed to working-class whites and small-business people, as well as to white students and their parents who were disappointed when they were rejected by the college or university of their choice.

Matters came to a head in June 1995, when the Supreme Court decided the case of *Adarand Constructors, Inc.* v. *Peña,* in which a white contractor sued the secretary of transportation to invalidate a contract awarded to a minority bidder under an affirmative action program. The Court ruled that the government could continue to act against "the lingering effects of racial discrimination," but that, from now on, race-based programs would be subject to the high standard of review called "strict scrutiny," which required the government to show that it had a compelling interest in solving a problem and that the problem could not be addressed effectively by a narrower non-race-based remedy. The Supreme Court decision required us to revisit federal affirmative action programs. Civil rights leaders wanted to keep them strong and comprehensive, while many Republicans were urging that they be abandoned altogether.

On July 19, after intense consultations with both proponents and critics of the policy, I offered my response to the *Adarand* decision, and to those who wanted to abolish affirmative action altogether, in a speech at the National Archives. In preparation, I had ordered a comprehensive review of our affirmative action programs, which concluded that affirmative action for women and minorities had given us the finest, most integrated military in the world, with 260,000 new positions made available to women in the last two and a half years alone; the Small Business Administration had dramatically increased loans to women and minorities without reducing loans to white males or giving loans to unqualified applicants; large private corporations with affirmative action programs reported that increasing the diversity of their workforces had increased their productivity and competitiveness in the global marketplace; government procurement policies had helped to build women- and minority-owned firms, but had on occasion been misused and abused; and there was still a need for affirmative action because of continuing racial and gender disparities in employment, income, and business ownership.

Based on these findings, I proposed to crack down on fraud and abuse in the procurement programs and do a better job of moving firms out of them once they could compete; to comply with the *Adarand* decision by focusing set-aside programs on areas where both the problem and the need for affirmative action were provable; and to do more to help distressed communities and disadvantaged people, no matter what their race or gender. We would retain the principle of affirmative action but reform its practices to ensure that there were no quotas, no preferences for unqualified persons or companies, no reverse discrimination against whites, and no continuation of programs after their equal opportunity purpose had been achieved. In a phrase, my policy was "Mend it, but don't end it."

The speech was well received by the civil rights, corporate, and military communities, but it didn't persuade everyone. Eight days later Senator Dole and Congressman Charles Canady of Florida introduced bills to repeal all federal affirmative action laws. Newt Gingrich had a more positive response, saying he didn't want to get rid of affirmative action until he came up with something to replace it that still gave a "helping hand."

While I was searching for common ground, the Republicans spent much of July moving their budget proposals through the Congress. They proposed big cuts in education and training. The Medicare and Medicaid cuts were so large that they increased substantially the out-of-pocket costs for seniors, who, because of medical inflation, were already paying a higher percentage of their income for health care than they had before the programs were created in the 1960s. The Environmental Protection Agency cuts were so severe that they would effectively end enforcement of the Clean Air and Clean Water acts. They voted to abolish AmeriCorps and cut assistance for the nation's homeless population in half. They effectively ended the family planning program that previously had been supported by Democrats and Republicans alike as a way to help prevent unwanted pregnancies and abortions. They wanted to slash the foreign aid budget, already only 1.3 percent of total federal spending, weakening our ability to fight terrorism and the spread of nuclear weapons, open new markets for American exports, and support the forces of peace, democracy, and human rights around the world.

Unbelievably, just five years after President Bush had signed the Americans with Disabilities Act, which had passed with large bipartisan majorities, the Republicans even proposed to cut the services and supports necessary for disabled people to exercise their rights under the law. After the disability cuts were made public, I got a call one night from Tom Campbell, my roommate for four years at

Georgetown. Tom was an airline pilot who made a comfortable living but was by no means wealthy. In an agitated voice, he said he was concerned about the proposed budget cuts for the disabled. His daughter Ciara had cerebral palsy. So did her best friend, who was being raised by a single mother working at a minimum-wage job to which she traveled one hour each way every day by bus. Tom asked some questions about the budget cuts and I answered them. Then he said, "So let me get this straight. They're going to give me a tax cut and cut the aid Ciara's friend and her mother get to cover the costs of the child's wheelchair and the four or five pairs of expensive special shoes she has to have every year and the transportation assistance the mother gets to travel to and from her minimum-wage job?" "That's right," I said. He replied, "Bill, that's immoral. You've got to stop it."

Tom Campbell was a devout Catholic and an ex-marine who had been raised in a conservative Republican home. If the New Right Republicans had gone too far for Americans like him, I knew I could beat them back. On the last day of the month, Alice Rivlin announced that the improving economy had led to a lower deficit than we had expected, and that we could now balance the budget in nine years without the harsh GOP cuts. I was closing in on them.

FIFTEEN

THERE WERE THREE positive developments in foreign affairs in July: I normalized relations with Vietnam, with the strong support of most Vietnam veterans in Congress, including John McCain, Bob Kerrey, John Kerry, Chuck Robb, and Pete Peterson; Saddam Hussein released two Americans who had been held prisoner since March, after a strong plea from Congressman Bill Richardson; and South Korean President Kim Young-Sam, in Washington for the dedication of the Korean War Memorial, strongly endorsed the agreement we had made with North Korea to end its nuclear program. Because Jesse Helms and others had criticized the deal, Kim's support was helpful, especially since he had been a political prisoner and advocate for democracy when South Korea was still an authoritarian state.

Unfortunately, the good news was dwarfed by what was happening in Bosnia. After being reasonably quiet for most of 1994, things had begun to go wrong at the end of November, when Serb warplanes attacked Croatian Muslims in western Bosnia. The attack was a violation of the no-fly zone, and in retaliation NATO bombed the Serb airfield, but didn't destroy it or all the planes that had flown.

In March, when the cease-fire President Carter had announced began to unravel, Dick Holbrooke, who had left his post as ambassador to Germany to become assistant secretary of state for European and Canadian affairs, sent our special envoy to the former Yugoslavia, Bob Frasure, to see Milosevic in the futile hope of ending the Bosnian Serb aggression and securing at least limited recognition for Bosnia in return for lifting the UN sanctions on Serbia.

By July, the fighting was in full swing again, with the Bosnian government forces making some gains in the middle of the country. Instead of trying to regain the lost territory, General Mladic decided to attack three isolated

Muslim towns in eastern Bosnia, Srebrenica, Zepa, and Gorazde. The towns were filled with Muslim refugees from nearby areas, and though they had been declared UN safe areas, they were protected by only a small number of UN troops. Mladic wanted to take the three towns so that all of eastern Bosnia would be controlled by the Serbs, and he was convinced that, as long as he held UN peacekeepers hostage, the UN would not allow NATO to bomb in retaliation. He was right, and the consequences were devastating.

On July 10, the Serbs took Srebrenica. By the end of the month they had also taken Zepa, and refugees who escaped from Srebrenica had begun to tell the world of the horrifying slaughter of Muslims there by Mladic's troops. Thousands of men and boys were gathered in a soccer field and murdered en masse. Thousands more were trying to escape through the heavily wooded hills.

After Srebrenica was overrun, I pressured the UN to authorize the rapid reaction force we had discussed at the G-7 meeting in Canada a few weeks earlier. Meanwhile, Bob Dole was pushing to lift the arms embargo. I asked him to postpone the vote and he agreed. I was still trying to find a way to save Bosnia that restored the effectiveness of the UN and NATO, but by the third week of July, Bosnian Serbs had made a mockery of the UN and, by extension, of the commitments of NATO and the United States. The safe areas were far from safe, and NATO action was severely limited because of the vulnerability of European troops who couldn't defend themselves, much less the Muslims. The Bosnian Serb practice of UN hostage-taking had exposed the fundamental flaw of the UN's strategy. Its arms embargo had kept the Bosnian government from achieving military parity with the Serbs. The peacekeepers could protect the Bosnian Muslims and Croatians only as long as the Serbs believed NATO would punish their aggression. Now the hostage-taking had erased that fear and given the Serbs a free hand in eastern Bosnia. The situation was slightly better in central and western Bosnia, because the Croatians and Muslims had been able to obtain some arms despite the UN embargo.

In an almost desperate attempt to regain the initiative, the foreign and defense ministers of NATO met in London. Warren Christopher, Bill Perry, and General Shalikashvili went to the conference determined to reverse the building momentum for a withdrawal of UN forces from Bosnia and, instead, to increase NATO's commitment and authority to act against the Serbs. Both the loss of Srebrenica and Zepa and the move in Congress to lift the arms embargo had strengthened our ability to push for more aggressive action. At the meeting, the ministers eventually accepted a proposal developed by Warren Christopher and his team to "draw a line in the sand" around Gorazde and to remove the "dual key" decision making that had given the UN veto authority over NATO action. The London conference was a turning point; from then on, NATO would be much more assertive. Not long afterward, the NATO commander, General George Joulwan, and our NATO ambassador, Robert Hunter, succeeded in extending the Gorazde rules to the Sarajevo safe area.

In August, the situation took a dramatic turn. The Croatians launched an offensive to retake the Krajina, a part of Croatia that the local Serbs had proclaimed their territory. European and some American military and intelligence officials had recommended against the action in the belief that Milosevic would intervene to save the Krajina Serbs, but I was rooting for the Croatians. So was Helmut Kohl, who knew, as I did, that diplomacy could not succeed until the Serbs had sustained some serious losses on the ground.

Because we knew Bosnia's survival was at stake, we had not tightly enforced the arms embargo. As a result, both the Croatians and the Bosnians were able to get some arms, which helped them survive. We had also authorized a private company to use retired U.S. military personnel to improve and train the Croatian army.

As it turned out, Milosevic didn't come to the aid of the Krajina Serbs, and Croatian forces took Krajina with little resistance. It was the first defeat for the Serbs in four years, and it changed both the balance of power on the ground and the psychology of all the parties. One Western diplomat

in Croatia was quoted as saying, "There was almost a signal of support from Washington. The Americans have been
spoiling for a chance to hit the Serbs, and they are using
Croatia as their proxy to do the deed for them." On August
4, in a visit with veteran ABC News correspondent Sam
Donaldson at the National Institutes of Health, where he
was recovering from cancer surgery, I acknowledged that
the Croatian offensive could prove helpful in resolving the
conflict. Ever the good journalist, Donaldson filed a report
on my comments from his hospital bed.

In an effort to capitalize on the shift in momentum, I
sent Tony Lake and Undersecretary of State Peter Tarnoff to
Europe (including Russia) to present a framework for peace
that Lake had developed and to have Dick Holbrooke lead a
team to begin a last-ditch effort to negotiate an end to the
conflict with the Bosnians and Milosevic, who claimed not
to control the Bosnian Serbs, though everyone knew they
could not prevail without his support. Just before we
launched the diplomatic mission, the Senate followed the
House in voting to lift the arms embargo and I vetoed the
bill to give our effort a chance. Lake and Tarnoff immediately took off to make the case for our plan, then met with
Holbrooke on August 14 to report that the allies and Russians were supportive, and that Holbrooke could begin his
mission at once.

On August 15, after a briefing from Tony Lake on
Bosnia, Hillary, Chelsea, and I left for a vacation in Jackson
Hole, Wyoming, where we had been invited to spend a few
days at the home of Senator Jay and Sharon Rockefeller. We
all needed the time off, and I was really looking forward to
the prospect of hiking and horseback riding in the Grand
Tetons; rafting the Snake River; visiting Yellowstone
National Park to see Old Faithful, the buffalo and moose,
and the wolves we had brought back to the wild; and playing golf at the high altitude, where the ball goes a lot farther.
Hillary was working on a book about families and children,
and she was looking forward to making headway on it at
the Rockefellers' spacious, light-filled ranch house. We did

all those things and more, but the enduring memory of our vacation was about Bosnia, and heartbreak.

On the day my family went to Wyoming, Dick Holbrooke left for Bosnia with an impressive team, including Bob Frasure; Joe Kruzel; Air Force Colonel Nelson Drew; and Lieutenant General Wesley Clark, director of strategic policy for the Joint Chiefs and a fellow Arkansan I had first met at Georgetown in 1965.

Holbrooke and his team landed in the Croatian coastal city of Split, where they briefed the Bosnian foreign minister, Muhamed Sacirbey, on our plans. Sacirbey was the eloquent public face of Bosnia on American television, a handsome, fit man who, as a student in the United States, had been a starting football player at Tulane University. He had long sought greater American involvement in his beleaguered nation and was glad the hour had finally come.

After Split, the U.S. team went to Zagreb, Croatia's capital, to see President Tudjman, then flew to Belgrade to meet with Slobodan Milosevic. This inconclusive meeting was remarkable only for the fact that Milosevic refused to guarantee the safety of our team's plane from Bosnian Serb artillery if they flew from Belgrade into the airport at Sarajevo, their next stop. That meant they had to fly back to Split, from which they would helicopter to a landing spot, then take off for a two-hour drive to Sarajevo over the Mount Igman road, a narrow, unpaved route with no guardrails at the edges of its steep slopes and great vulnerability to nearby Serb machine gunners who regularly shot at UN vehicles. The EU negotiator, Carl Bildt, had been shot at when he traveled the road a few weeks earlier, and there were many wrecked vehicles in the ravines between Split and Sarajevo, some of which had simply slid off the road.

On August 19, my forty-ninth birthday, I started the day by playing golf with Vernon Jordan, Erskine Bowles, and Jim Wolfensohn, the president of the World Bank. It was a perfect morning until I heard about what had happened on the Mount Igman road. First from a news report, and later in an emotional phone call with Dick Holbrooke and Wes

Clark, I learned that our team had set out for Sarajevo with
Holbrooke and Clark riding in a U.S. Army Humvee, and
Frasure, Kruzel, and Drew following behind in a French
armored personnel carrier (APC) painted UN white. About
an hour into the trip, at the top of a steep incline, the road
gave way on the APC, and it somersaulted down the mountain and exploded into flames. Besides the three members of
our team, there were two other Americans and four French
soldiers in the vehicle. The APC had caught fire when the
live ammunition it was carrying exploded. In a brave
attempt to help, Wes Clark rappelled down the mountain
with a rope tied to a tree trunk and tried to get into the
burning vehicle to rescue the men still trapped inside, but it
was too damaged and scalding hot.

It was also too late. Bob Frasure and Nelson Drew had
been killed in the tumbling fall down the mountain. The
others all got out, but Joe Kruzel soon died of his injuries,
and one French soldier also perished. Frasure was fifty-
three, Kruzel fifty, Drew forty-seven; all were patriotic public servants and good family men who died too young trying
to save the lives of innocent people a long way from home.

The next week, after the Bosnian Serbs lobbed a mortar
shell into the heart of Sarajevo, killing thirty-eight people,
NATO began three days of air strikes on Serb positions. On
September 1, Holbrooke announced that all the parties
would meet in Geneva for talks. When the Bosnian Serbs
did not comply with all of NATO's conditions, the air
strikes resumed and continued until the fourteenth, when
Holbrooke succeeded in getting an agreement signed by
Karadzic and Mladic to end the siege of Sarajevo. Soon the
final peace talks would begin in Dayton, Ohio. Ultimately
they would bring an end to the bloody Bosnian war. When
they did, their success would be in no small measure a tribute to three quiet American heroes who did not live to see
the fruits of their labors.

While the August news was dominated by Bosnia, I continued to argue with the Republicans on the budget; noted that
a million Americans had lost their health insurance in the

year since the failure of health-care reform; and took executive action to limit the advertising, promotion, distribution, and marketing of cigarettes to teenagers. The Food and Drug Administration had just completed a fourteen-month study confirming that cigarettes were addictive, harmful, and aggressively marketed to teenagers, whose smoking rates were on the rise.

The teen smoking problem was a tough nut to crack. Tobacco is America's legal addictive drug; it kills people and adds untold billions to the cost of health care. But the tobacco companies are politically influential, and the farmers who raise the tobacco crop are an important part of the economic, political, and cultural life of Kentucky and North Carolina. The farmers were the sympathetic face of the tobacco companies' effort to increase their profits by hooking younger and younger people on cigarettes. I thought we had to do something to push them back. So did Al Gore, who had lost his beloved sister, Nancy, to lung cancer.

On August 8, we got a break in our efforts to eliminate the vestiges of Iraq's weapons of mass destruction program when two of Saddam Hussein's daughters and their husbands defected to Jordan and were given asylum by King Hussein. One of the men, Hussein Kamel Hassan al-Majid, had headed Saddam's secret effort to develop weapons of mass destruction and would supply valuable information on Iraq's remaining WMD stocks, the size and significance of which contradicted what the UN inspectors had been told by Iraqi officials. When confronted with the evidence, the Iraqis simply acknowledged that Saddam's son-in-law was telling the truth and took the inspectors to the sites he had identified. After six months in exile, Saddam's relatives were induced to return to Iraq. Within a couple of days, both sons-in-law were killed. Their brief journey to freedom had provided the UN inspectors with so much information that more chemical and biological stocks and laboratory equipment were destroyed during the inspections process than during the Gulf War.

August was also a big month in Whitewater World. Kenneth Starr indicted Jim and Susan McDougal and Governor

Jim Guy Tucker on charges unrelated to Whitewater, and the Senate and House Republicans held hearings all month. In the Senate, Al D'Amato was still trying to prove there was something more to Vince Foster's death than a depression-induced suicide. He hauled Hillary's staff and friends before the committee for bullying questioning and ad hominem attacks. D'Amato was especially unpleasant to Maggie Williams and his fellow New Yorker Susan Thomases. Senator Lauch Faircloth was even worse, scoffing at the notion that Williams and Thomases could have had so many phone conversations about Vince Foster just to share their grief. At the time, I thought that if Faircloth really didn't understand their feelings, his own life must have been lived in an emotional wilderness. The fact that Maggie had passed two lie detector tests about her actions in the aftermath of Vince's death didn't temper D'Amato's and Faircloth's accusatory questioning.

In the House Banking Committee, Chairman Jim Leach was behaving much like D'Amato. From the beginning, he trumpeted every bogus charge against Hillary and me, alleging that we had made, not lost, money on Whitewater, had used Madison Guaranty funds for personal and political expenses, and had engineered David Hale's SBA fraud. He kept promising "blockbuster" revelations, but they never materialized.

In August, Leach held a hearing starring L. Jean Lewis, the Resolution Trust Corporation investigator who had named Hillary and me as witnesses in a criminal referral shortly before the 1992 election. At the time, the Bush Justice Department inquired about Lewis's referral and the Republican U.S. attorney in Arkansas, Charles Banks, told them that there was no case against us, that it was an attempt to influence the election, and that to launch an investigation at that time would amount to "prosecutorial misconduct."

Nevertheless, Leach referred to Lewis as a "heroic" public servant whose investigation had been thwarted after my election. Before the hearings began, documents were released that supported our position, including Banks's letter refusing to pursue Lewis's allegations because of lack of evidence, and internal FBI cables and Justice Department evaluations saying that "no facts can be identified to support the designation" of Hillary and me as material witnesses. Although there was almost no press coverage of the documents refuting Lewis, the hearings fizzled.

By the time of the August hearings and Starr's latest round of indictments, I had settled into a routine of handling press questions about Whitewater with as little public comment as possible. I had learned from the press coverage over the gays-in-the-military issue that if I gave a meaty answer to a question on whatever the press was obsessing about, it would be on the evening news, blocking out whatever else I was doing in the public interest that day, and the American people would think I was spending all my time defending myself instead of working for them, when in fact Whitewater took up very little of my own time. On a scale of 1 to 10, a 7 answer on the economy was better than a 10 answer on Whitewater. So, with the help of constant reminders from my staff, I held my tongue on most days, but it was hard. I had always hated abuse of power, and as false charges flew, evidence of our innocence was ignored, and more blameless people were hounded by Starr, I was seething inside. No one can be as angry as I was without doing himself harm. It took me too long to figure that out.

September began with a memorable trip to Hawaii to commemorate the fiftieth anniversary of the end of World War II, followed by Hillary's trip to Beijing to address the United Nations Fourth World Conference on Women. Hillary gave one of the most important speeches delivered by anyone in our administration during our entire eight years, asserting that "human rights are women's rights" and condemning their all-too-frequent violation by those who sold women into prostitution, burned them when their marriage dowries were deemed too small, raped them in wartime, beat them in their homes, or subjected them to genital mutilation, forced abortions, or sterilization. Her speech got a standing ovation and struck a responsive chord with women all over the world, who knew now, beyond a doubt, that America was pulling for them. Once again, despite the abuse she had been taking on Whitewater, Hillary had come through for a cause she deeply believed in, and for our country. I was so proud of her; the unfair hard knocks she had endured had done nothing to dull the idealism that I had fallen in love with so long ago.

By the middle of the month, Dick Holbrooke had persuaded the foreign ministers of Bosnia, Croatia, and Yugoslavia to agree on a set of basic principles as a framework to settle the Bosnian conflict. Meanwhile, NATO air strikes and cruise missile attacks continued to pound Bosnian Serb positions, and Bosnian and Croatian military gains reduced the percentage of Bosnia controlled by the Serbs from 70 to 50 percent, close to what a negotiated settlement would likely require.

September 28 capped off a good month in foreign policy, as Yitzhak Rabin and Yasser Arafat came to the White House for the next big step in the peace process, the signing of the West Bank accord, which turned over a substantial portion of land to Palestinian control.

The most significant event occurred away from the cameras. The signing ceremony was scheduled to occur at noon, but first Rabin and Arafat met in the Cabinet Room to initial the annex to the agreement, three copies that included twenty-six different maps, each reflecting literally thousands of decisions the parties had reached on roads, crossings, settlements, and holy sites. I was also asked to initial the pages as the official witness. About midway through the process, when I had stepped outside to take a call, Rabin came out and said, "We have a problem." On one of the maps, Arafat had spotted a stretch of road that was marked as under Israeli control but that he was convinced the parties had agreed to turn over to the Palestinians. Rabin and Arafat wanted me to help resolve the dispute. I took them into my private dining room and they began to talk, with Rabin saying he wanted to be a good neighbor and Arafat replying that, as descendants of Abraham, they were really more like cousins. The interplay between the old adversaries was fascinating. Without saying a word, I turned and walked out of the room, leaving them alone together for the first time. Sooner or later, they had to develop a direct relationship, and today seemed the right moment to begin.

Within twenty minutes they had reached an agreement that the disputed crossing should go to the Palestinians. Because the world was waiting for the ceremony and we were already late, there was no time to change the map. Instead, Rabin and Arafat agreed to its modification with a handshake, then signed the maps before them, legally binding themselves to the incorrect designation of the disputed road.

It was an act of personal trust that would have been unthinkable not long before. And it was risky for Rabin. Several days later, with Israelis evenly divided on the West Bank accord, Rabin survived a no-confidence vote in the Knesset by only one vote. We were still walking a tightrope, but I was optimistic. I knew the handover would proceed according to the handshake, and it did. It was the handshake even more than the official signing that convinced me that Rabin and Arafat would find a way to finish the job of making peace.

The fiscal year ended on September 30, and we still didn't have a budget. When I wasn't working on Bosnia and the Middle East, I had spent the entire month traveling the country campaigning against the Republicans' proposed cuts in Medicare and Medicaid, food stamps, the direct student-loan program, AmeriCorps, environmental enforcement, and the initiative to put 100,000 new police officers on the street. They were even proposing to cut back the Earned Income Tax Credit, thus raising taxes on lower-income working families at the same time they were trying to cut taxes for the wealthiest Americans. At virtually every stop, I pointed out that our fight was not about whether to balance the budget and reduce the burden of unnecessary government, but how to do it. The big dispute involved what responsibilities the federal government should assume for the common good.

In response to my attacks, Newt Gingrich threatened to

refuse to raise the debt limit and thus put America in default if I vetoed their budget bills. Raising the debt limit was merely a technical act that recognized the inevitable: as long as America continued to run deficits, the annual debt would increase, and the government would be required to sell more bonds to finance it. Increasing the debt limit simply gave the Treasury Department authority to do that. As long as Democrats were in the majority, Republicans could cast symbolic votes against raising the debt limit and pretend that they hadn't contributed to the necessity to do it. Many Republicans in the House had never voted to raise the debt limit and didn't relish doing so now, so I had to take Gingrich's threat seriously.

If America defaulted on its debt, the consequences could be severe. In more than two hundred years, the United States had never failed to pay its debts. Default would shake investor confidence in our reliability. As we headed into the final showdown, I couldn't deny that Newt had a bargaining chip, but I was determined not to be blackmailed. If he followed through on his threat, he would be hurt, too. Default ran the risk of increasing interest rates, and even a small increase would add hundreds of billions of dollars to home mortgage payments. Ten million Americans had variable-rate mortgages tied to federal interest rates. If Congress didn't raise the debt limit, people could pay what Al Gore called a "Gingrich surcharge" on their monthly mortgage payments. The Republicans would have to think twice before letting America go into default.

In the first week of October, the pope came to America again, and Hillary and I went to meet him at Newark's magnificent Gothic cathedral. As we had in Denver and at the Vatican, His Holiness and I met alone and mostly talked about Bosnia. The pope encouraged our efforts for peace, with an observation that stuck with me: he said the twentieth century had begun with a war in Sarajevo, and I must not allow the century to end with a war in Sarajevo.

When our meeting concluded, the pope gave me a lesson in politics. First, he left the cathedral for a spot a couple of miles away so that he could drive back in his "popemobile," with its roof of clear, bulletproof glass, waving to the people who had crowded the streets. By the time he reached the church, the congregation was seated. Hillary and I were in the front pew with local and state officials and prominent New Jersey Catholics. The massive oak doors opened, revealing the pontiff in his resplendent white cassock and cape, and the crowd stood and began to clap. As the pope began to walk down the aisle with his arms spread out to touch hands with people on either side of the aisle, the applause turned into cheers and roars. I noticed a group of nuns standing on their pews and screaming like teenagers at a rock concert. When I asked a man near me about it, he explained that they were Carmelites, members of an order that lived a cloistered existence completely apart from society. The pope had given them a dispensation to come to the cathedral. He sure knew how to build a crowd. I just shook my head and said, "I'd hate to have to run against that man."

On the day after I met with the pope, we made progress on Bosnia, as I announced that all the parties had agreed to a cease-fire. A week later Bill Perry stated that a peace agreement would require NATO to send troops to Bosnia to enforce it. Moreover, since our responsibility to participate in NATO missions was clear, he did not believe we were required to seek advance approval from Congress. I thought Dole and Gingrich might be relieved not to have a vote on the Bosnia mission; they were both internationalists who knew what we had to do, but there were many Republicans in both chambers who strongly disagreed.

On October 15, I reinforced my determination to end the Bosnian war and hold those who had perpetrated war crimes accountable when I went to the University of Connecticut with my friend Senator Chris Dodd to inaugurate the research center named for his father. Before going to the Senate, Tom Dodd had been the executive trial counsel at the Nuremberg War Crimes Tribunal. In my remarks, I strongly endorsed the existing war crimes tribunals for the former Yugoslavia and Rwanda, to which we were contributing money and personnel, and supported the establishment of a permanent tribunal to deal with war crimes and other atrocities that violated human rights. Eventually, the idea would take root in the International Criminal Court.

While I was dealing with Bosnia at home, Hillary was off on another trip, this time to Latin America. In the post–Cold War world, with America the world's only military, economic, and political superpower, every nation wanted our attention, and it was usually in our interest to give it. But I couldn't go everywhere, especially during the budget struggles with Congress. As a result, both Al Gore and Hillary made an unusually large number of important foreign trips. Wherever they went, people knew they spoke for the United States, and for me, and on every trip, without fail, they strengthened America's standing in the world.

On October 22, I flew to New York to celebrate the fiftieth anniversary of the United Nations, using the occasion to call for greater international cooperation in the fight against terrorism, the spread of weapons of mass destruction, organized crime, and narco-trafficking. Earlier in the month, Sheikh Omar Abdel Rahman and nine others had been found guilty in the first World Trade Center bombing case, and not long before, Colombia had arrested several leaders of the infamous Cali drug cartel. In my address I outlined an agenda to build on those successes, including universal adherence to anti–money laundering practices; freezing the assets of terrorists and narco-traffickers, as I had just done with respect to Colombian cartels; a no-sanctuary pledge for members of terrorist or organized crime groups; shutting down the gray markets that provided arms and false identification papers to terrorists and narco-traffickers; intensified efforts to destroy drug crops and decrease demand for drugs; an international network to train police officers and provide them with the latest technology; ratification of the Chemical Weapons Convention; and strengthening of the Biological Weapons Convention.

The next day I returned to Hyde Park for my ninth meeting with Boris Yeltsin. Yeltsin had been ill and was under a lot of pressure at home from the ultra-nationalists over NATO expansion and the aggressive role the United States was playing in Bosnia at the expense of the Bosnian Serbs. He had given a tough speech the day before at the UN, which was mostly for domestic consumption, and I could tell he was stressed out.

To put him more at ease, I flew him to Hyde Park in my helicopter so that he could see the beautiful foliage along the Hudson River on an unseasonably warm fall day. When we arrived, I took him out to the front yard of the old house with its sweeping view of the river, and we talked awhile, sitting in the same chairs Roosevelt and Churchill had used when the prime minister visited there during World War II. Then I brought him into the house to show him a bust of Roosevelt sculpted by a Russian artist, a painting of the President's indomitable mother done by the sculptor's brother, and the handwritten note FDR had sent to Stalin informing him that the date for D-day had been set.

Boris and I spent the morning talking about his precarious political situation. I reminded him that I had done everything I could to support him, and though we disagreed on NATO expansion, I would try to help him work through it.

After lunch we returned to the house to talk about Bosnia. The parties were about to come to the United States to negotiate what we all hoped would be a final pact, the success of which depended on both a multinational NATO-led force and the participation of Russian troops, to reassure the Bosnian Serbs that they too would be treated fairly. Finally, Boris agreed to send troops, but said they could not serve under NATO commanders, though he would be glad to have them serve "under an American general." I assented, as long as it was understood that his troops would not in any way interfere with NATO's command and control.

I regretted that Yeltsin was in so much trouble back home. Yes, he had made his share of mistakes, but against enormous odds he had also kept Russia going in the right direction. I still thought he would come out ahead in the election.

At the press conference after our meeting, I said that we had made progress on Bosnia and that we would both push for the ratification of START II and work together to conclude a comprehensive nuclear test-ban treaty in 1996. It was a good announcement, but Yeltsin stole the show. He told the press that he was leaving our meeting with more optimism than he had brought to it, because of all the press reports saying that our summit "was going to be a disaster. Well, now, for the first time, I can tell you that you're a disaster." I almost fell over laughing, and the press laughed too. All I could say to them in response was "Be sure you get the right attribution there." Yeltsin could get away with saying the darnedest things. There's no telling how he would have answered all the Whitewater questions.

October was relatively quiet on the home front, as the budget pot slowly simmered toward a boil. Early in the month, Newt Gingrich decided not to bring the lobbying-reform legislation to a vote and I vetoed the legislative appropriations bill. The lobbying bill required lobbyists to disclose their activities and prohibited them from giving lawmakers gifts, travel, and meals beyond a modest limit. The Republicans were raising a lot of money from lobbyists by writing legislation that gave tax breaks, subsidies, and relief from environmental regulations to a wide array of interest groups. Gingrich saw no reason to disturb a beneficial situation. I vetoed the legislative appropriations bill because, apart from the appropriations act for military construction, it was the only budget bill Congress had passed as the new fiscal year started, and I didn't think Congress should be taking care of itself first. I didn't want to veto the bill and had asked the Republican leaders just to hold it until we had finished a few other budget bills, but they sent it to me anyway.

   While the budget battle continued, Energy Secretary Hazel O'Leary and I received a report from my Advisory Committee on Human Radiation Experiments detailing thousands of experiments done on humans at universities, hospitals, and military bases during the Cold War. Most of them were ethical, but a few were not: in one experiment scientists injected plutonium into eighteen patients without their knowledge; in another, doctors exposed indigent cancer patients to excessive radiation, knowing they would not benefit from it. I ordered a review of all current experimentation procedures and pledged to seek compensation in all appropriate cases. The release of this formerly classified information was part of a wider disclosure policy I followed throughout my tenure. We had already declassified thousands of documents from World War II, the Cold War, and President Kennedy's assassination.

At the end of the first week of October, Hillary and I took a weekend off to fly to Martha's Vineyard for the wedding of our good friend Mary Steenburgen to Ted Danson. We had been friends since 1980; our children had played together since they were young, and Mary had worked her heart out for me all over the country in 1992. I was thrilled when she and Ted met and fell in love, and their wedding was a welcome relief from the strains of Bosnia, Whitewater, and the budget battle.

At the end of the month, Hillary and I celebrated our twentieth wedding anniversary. I got her a pretty diamond ring to mark a milestone in our lives and to make up for the fact that when she agreed to marry me, I didn't have enough money to buy her an engagement ring. Hillary loved the little diamonds across the thin band, and wore the ring as a reminder that, through all our ups and downs, we were still very much engaged.

SIXTEEN

SATURDAY, NOVEMBER 4, started out to be a hopeful day. The Bosnian peace talks had begun three days earlier at Wright-Patterson Air Force Base in Dayton, Ohio, and we had just won a vote in Congress to beat back seventeen anti-environment riders to the EPA budget. I had prerecorded my usual Saturday-morning radio address, assailing the cuts that were still in the EPA budget, and was enjoying a rare, relaxing day, until 3:25 p.m., when Tony Lake called me in the residence to tell me that Yitzhak Rabin had been shot while leaving a huge peace rally in Tel Aviv. His assailant was not a Palestinian terrorist but a young Israeli law student, Yigal Amir, who was bitterly opposed to turning over the West Bank, including land occupied by Israeli settlements, to the Palestinians.

Yitzhak had been rushed to the hospital, and for a good while we didn't know how badly he'd been wounded. I called Hillary, who was upstairs working on her book, and told her what had happened. She came down and held me for a while as we talked about how Yitzhak and I had been together just ten days before when he had come to the United States to present me with the United Jewish Appeal's Isaiah Award. It was a happy night. Yitzhak, who hated to dress up, showed up for the black-tie event in a dark suit with a regular tie. He borrowed a bow tie from my presidential aide, Steve Goodin, and I straightened it for him just before we walked out. When Yitzhak presented the award to me, he insisted that, as the honoree, I stand on his right, even though protocol dictated that foreign leaders stand on the President's right. "Tonight we reverse the order," he said. I replied that he was probably right to do so before the United Jewish Appeal because, "after all, they may be more your crowd than mine." Now I hoped against hope that we would laugh together like that again.

About twenty-five minutes after his first call, Tony called again to say that Rabin's condition was grave, but he knew nothing else. I hung up the phone and told Hillary I wanted to go down to the Oval Office. After talking to my staff and pacing the floor for five minutes, I wanted to be alone, so I grabbed a putter and a couple of golf balls and headed for the putting green on the South Lawn, where I prayed to God to spare Yitzhak's life, hit the ball aimlessly, and waited.

After ten or fifteen minutes I saw the door to the Oval Office open and looked up to watch Tony Lake walking down the stone pathway toward me. I could tell by the look on his face that Yitzhak was dead. When Tony told me, I asked him to go back and prepare a statement for me to read.

In the two and a half years we had worked together, Rabin and I had developed an unusually close relationship, marked by candor, trust, and an extraordinary understanding of each other's political positions and thought processes. We had become friends in that unique way people do when they are in a struggle that they believe is great and good. With every encounter, I came to respect and care for him more. By the time he was killed, I had come to love him as I had rarely loved another man. In the back of my mind, I suppose I always knew he had put his life at risk, but I couldn't imagine him gone, and I didn't know what I would or could do in the Middle East without him. Overcome with grief, I went back upstairs to be with Hillary for a couple of hours.

The next day Hillary, Chelsea, and I went to Foundry Methodist Church with our guests from Little Rock, Vic and Susan Fleming and their daughter Elizabeth, one of Chelsea's closest friends from back home. It was All Saints' Day, and the service was full of evocations of Rabin. Chelsea and another young girl read a lesson from Exodus about Moses confronting God in the burning bush. Our pastor, Phil Wogaman, said that the site in Tel Aviv where Rabin "laid down his life has become a holy place."

After Hillary and I took communion, we left the church

and drove to the Israeli embassy to see Ambassador and Mrs. Rabinovich and sign the condolence book, which lay on a table in the embassy's Jerusalem Hall alongside a large photograph of Rabin. By the time we arrived, Tony Lake and Dennis Ross, our special envoy to the Middle East, were already there, sitting in silent respect. Hillary and I signed the book and then went home to get ready to fly to Jerusalem for the funeral.

We were accompanied by former Presidents Carter and Bush, the congressional leadership and three dozen other senators and representatives, General Shalikashvili, former secretary of state George Shultz, and several prominent business leaders. As soon as we landed, Hillary and I went to the Rabin home to see Leah. She was heartbroken, but trying to put on a brave front for her family and her country.

The funeral was attended by King Hussein and Queen Noor, President Mubarak, and other world leaders. Arafat wanted to come, but was persuaded not to because of the risk and the potentially divisive impact of his presence in Israel. It was also a risk for Mubarak, who had recently survived an assassination attempt himself, but he took it. Hussein and Noor were devastated by Rabin's death; they genuinely cared about him and thought he was essential to the peace process. For each of his Arab partners, Yitzhak's assassination was a painful reminder of the risks they, too, were running for peace.

Hussein gave a magnificent eulogy, and Rabin's granddaughter Noa Ben Artzi-Pelossof, then doing her service in the Israeli army, moved the audience by speaking to her grandfather: "Grandpa, you were the pillar of fire before the camp, and now we are just a camp left alone in the dark, and we're so cold." In my remarks, I tried to rally the people of Israel to keep following their fallen leader. That very week, Jews around the world were studying that portion of the Torah in which God commanded Abraham to sacrifice his beloved son Isaac, or Yitzhak; once Abraham demonstrated his willingness to obey, God spared the boy. "Now God tests our faith even more terribly, for he has taken our Yitzhak. But Israel's covenant with God, for freedom, for tolerance, for security, for peace—that covenant must hold. That covenant was Prime Minister Rabin's life's work. Now we must make it his lasting legacy." I closed with *"Shalom, chaver."*

Somehow those two words, *Shalom, chaver*—Good-bye, friend—had captured the feelings of Israelis about Rabin. I had a number of Jewish staff members who spoke Hebrew and knew how I felt about Rabin; I am still grateful that they gave me the phrase. Shimon Peres later told me that *chaver* means more than mere friendship; it evokes the comradeship of soul mates in common cause. Soon *Shalom, chaver* began to appear on billboards and bumper stickers all across Israel.

After the funeral I held a few meetings with other leaders at the King David Hotel, with its magnificent view of the Old City, then headed back to Washington. It was almost 4:30 a.m. when we touched down at Andrews Air Force Base, and all the weary travelers staggered off the plane to get whatever rest they could before the budget battle moved into its final phase.

Ever since the new fiscal year had begun on October 1, the government had been running on a continuing resolution (CR), which authorized funding for departments until their new budgets were enacted. It wasn't all that unusual for a new fiscal year to begin without Congress passing a couple of appropriations bills, but now we had the whole government on a CR, with no end in sight. By contrast, in my first two years, the Democratic Congress had approved the budgets on time.

I had offered a plan to balance the budget in ten years, and then one to balance it in nine, by 2004, but the Republicans and I were still far apart on our budgets. All my experts believed the GOP cuts in Medicare and Medicaid, education, the environment, and the EITC were larger than they needed to be to finance their tax cuts and reach balance, even in seven years. We had differences over the estimates of economic growth, medical inflation, and anticipated revenues. When they controlled the White House, the Republicans had consistently overestimated revenues and underestimated spending. I was determined not to make that mistake, and had always used conservative estimates that had enabled us to beat our deficit reduction targets.

Now that they controlled the Congress, the Republicans had gone too far in the other direction, underestimating economic growth and revenues and overestimating the rate of medical inflation, even as they promoted HMOs as a sure-fire way to slow it down. Their strategy appeared to be the logical extension of William Kristol's advice in his memo to Bob Dole, urging that he block all action on health care. If they could cut funding for Medicare, Medicaid, education, and the environment, middle-class Americans would see fewer benefits from their tax dollars, feel more resentful paying taxes, and become even more receptive to their appeals for tax cuts and their strategy of waging campaigns on divisive social and cultural issues like abortion, gay rights, and guns.

President Reagan's budget director, David Stockman, had acknowledged that his administration had intentionally run huge deficits to create a crisis that would "starve" the domestic budget. They succeeded partially, underfunding but not eliminating investments in our common future. Now the Gingrich Republicans were trying to use a balanced budget with unreasonable revenue and spending assumptions to finish the job. I was determined to stop them; the future direction of our nation hung in the balance.

On November 10, three days before the expiration of the continuing resolution, Congress sent me a new one that threw down the gauntlet: the price for keeping the government open was signing a new CR that increased Medicare premiums 25 percent, cut funding for education and the environment, and weakened environmental laws.

The following day, just a week after Rabin's assassination, I gave my radio address on the Republican attempts to pass their budget through the back door of the CR. It was Veterans Day, so I pointed out that eight million of the seniors whose Medicare premiums would be raised were veterans. There was no need for the GOP's draconian cuts: the combined rates of unemployment and inflation were at a twenty-five-year low; federal employment as a percentage of the overall workforce was the smallest since 1933; and the deficit was down. I still wanted to balance the budget, but in a way that was "consistent with our fundamental values" and "without threats and without partisan rancor."

On Monday night the Congress finally sent me an extension of the debt limit. It was worse than the CR, another backdoor effort to pass the budget cuts and weaken environmental laws. The legislation also stripped from the secretary of the Treasury the fund management flexibility he had had since the Reagan years to avoid defaults under extraordinary circumstances. Even worse, it lowered the debt limit again after thirty days, virtually ensuring a default.

Gingrich had been threatening since April to shut the government down and put America in default if I didn't accept his budget. I couldn't tell whether he really wanted to do it or whether he simply believed all the press coverage during my first two years that, in the face of ample evidence to the contrary, had portrayed me as too weak, too willing to abandon commitments, too eager to compromise. If so, he should have paid more attention to the evidence.

On November 13, with the existing CR scheduled to expire at midnight, the negotiators met one more time to try to resolve our differences before the government shutdown. Dole, Gingrich, Armey, Daschle, and Gephardt were there, as were Al Gore, Leon Panetta, Bob Rubin, Laura Tyson, and other members of our team. The atmosphere was already tense when Gingrich started the meeting by complaining about our TV ads. We had started running ads in targeted states in June to highlight administration achievements, beginning with the crime bill. When the budget debate heated up after Labor Day, we put up new ads targeting the proposed Republican cuts, especially in Medicare and Medicaid. After Newt carried on for a while, Leon Panetta tersely reminded him of all the terrible things he'd said about me before the 1994 election: "Mr. Speaker, you don't have clean hands."

Dole tried to calm things, saying that he didn't want the government to shut down. At that point, Dick Armey broke in to say Dole didn't speak for the House Republicans. Armey was a big man who always wore cowboy boots and seemed to be in a constant state of agitation. He launched into a tirade about how the House Republicans were determined to be true to their principles, and how angry he was that my TV ads on the Medicare cuts had frightened his elderly mother-in-law. I replied that I didn't know about his mother-in-law, but if the Republican budget cuts were to become law, large numbers of elderly people would be forced out of nursing homes or lose their home health care.

Armey replied gruffly that if I didn't give in to them, they would shut the government down and my presidency would be over. I shot back, saying I would never allow their budget to become law, "even if I drop to 5 percent in the polls. If you want your budget, you'll have to get someone else to sit in this chair!" Not surprisingly, we didn't make a deal.

After the meeting, Daschle, Gephardt, and my team were elated by my confrontation with Armey. Al Gore said he just wished everyone in America had heard my declaration, except I should have said I didn't care if I fell to zero in the polls. I looked back at him and said, "No, Al. If we drop to 4 percent, I'm caving." We all laughed, but our insides were still in knots.

I vetoed both the CR and the debt ceiling bill, and the next day at noon large portions of the federal government shut down. Almost 800,000 workers were sent home, disrupting the lives of millions of Americans who needed their applications for Social Security, veterans benefits, and business loans processed, their workplaces inspected for safety, their national parks open for visits, and much more. After the vetoes, Bob Rubin took the unusual step of borrowing $61 billion from retirement funds to pay our debt and avert default for a while longer.

Not surprisingly, the Republicans tried to blame me for the shutdown. I was afraid they'd get away with it, given their success at blaming me for the partisan divide in the '94 election. Then I got a break when, at a breakfast with reporters on the fifteenth, Gingrich implied that he had made the CR even harsher because I'd snubbed him during the flight back from Rabin's funeral by not talking to him about the budget and asking him to leave the plane by the back ramp instead of the front one with me. Gingrich said, "It's petty but I think it's human . . . nobody has talked to you and they ask you to get off the plane by the back ramp. . . . You just wonder, where is their sense of manners?" Perhaps I should have discussed the budget on the way home, but I couldn't bring myself to think about anything but the purpose of the sad trip and the future of the peace process. I did visit with the Speaker and the congressional delegation, as a photograph of Newt, Bob Dole, and me talking on the plane showed. As for getting off the back of the plane, my staff thought they were being courteous, because that was the exit closest to the cars that were picking up Gingrich and the others. And it was four-thirty in the morning; there were no cameras around. The White House released the photo of our conversation, and the press lampooned Gingrich's complaints.

On the sixteenth, at a news conference, I continued to ask the Republicans to send me a clean CR and to begin good-faith budget negotiations, even as they threatened to send me another one with all the same problems. The night before, I signed the Department of Transportation appropriations bill, only the fourth of the needed thirteen, and canceled my scheduled trip to the Asia Pacific leaders' meeting in Osaka, Japan.

On November 19, I made a move toward the Republicans, saying that, in principle, I would work for a seven-year balanced budget agreement but would not commit to the GOP tax and spending cuts. The economy had continued to grow, with the deficit dropping more than expected; Panetta, Alice Rivlin, and our economic team believed we could now get to balance in seven years without the harsh cuts the Republicans were pushing. I signed two more appropriations bills, for the legislative branch and for the Treasury Department, the Postal Service, and general government operations. With six of the thirteen bills signed, about 200,000 of the 800,000 federal employees were back at work.

On the morning of November 21, Warren Christopher called me from Dayton to say that the presidents of Bosnia, Croatia, and Serbia had reached a peace agreement to end the war in Bosnia. The agreement preserved Bosnia as a single state to be made up of two parts, the Bosnian Croat Federation and the Bosnian Serb Republic, with a resolution of the territorial disputes over which the war was begun. Sarajevo would remain the undivided capital city. The national government would have responsibility for foreign affairs, trade, immigration, citizenship, and monetary policy. Each of the federations would have its own police force. Refugees would be able to return home, and free movement throughout the country would be guaranteed. There would be international supervision of human rights and police training, and those charged with war crimes would be excluded from political life. A strong international force, commanded by NATO, would supervise the separation of forces and keep the peace as the agreement was being implemented.

The Bosnian peace plan was hard-won and its particulars contained bitter pills for both sides, but it would bring an end to four bloody years that claimed more than 250,000 lives and caused more than two million people to flee their homes. American leadership was decisive in pushing NATO to be more aggressive and in taking the final diplomatic initiative. Our efforts were immeasurably helped by the Croatian and Bosnian military gains on the ground, and the brave and stubborn refusal of Izetbegovic and his comrades to give up in the face of Bosnian Serb aggression.

The final agreement was a tribute to the skills of Dick Holbrooke and his negotiating team; to Warren Christopher, who at critical points was decisive in keeping the Bosnians on board and in closing the deal; to Tony Lake, who initially conceived and sold our peace initiative to our allies and who, with Holbrooke, pushed for the final talks to be held in the United States; to Sandy Berger, who chaired the deputies'

committee meetings, which kept people throughout the
national security operation informed of what was going on
without allowing too much interference; and to Madeleine
Albright, who strongly supported our aggressive posture in
the United Nations. The choice of Dayton and Wright-
Patterson Air Force Base was inspired, and carefully chosen
by the negotiating team; it was in the United States, but far
enough away from Washington to discourage leaks, and the
facilities permitted the kind of "proximity talks" that
allowed Holbrooke and his team to hammer out the tough
details.

On November 22, after twenty-one days of isolation in
Dayton, Holbrooke and his team came to the White House
to receive my congratulations and discuss our next steps. We
still had a big selling job on the Hill and with the American
people, who, according to the latest polls, were proud of the
peace agreement but were still overwhelmingly opposed to
sending U.S. troops to Bosnia. After Al Gore kicked off the
meeting by saying that the military testimony to date had
not been helpful, I told General Shalikashvili that I knew he
supported our involvement in Bosnia but that many of his
subordinates remained ambivalent. Al and I had orchestrated our comments to emphasize that it was time for everybody in the government, not just the military, to get with the
program. They had the desired effect.

We already had strong support from some important
members of Congress, especially Senators Lugar, Biden, and
Lieberman. Others offered a more qualified endorsement,
saying that they wanted a clear "exit strategy." To add to
their numbers, I began to invite members of Congress to the
White House, while sending Christopher, Perry, Shalikashvili, and Holbrooke to the Hill. Our challenge was
complicated by the ongoing debate over the budget; the government was open for the time being, but the Republicans
were threatening to shut it down again on December 15.

On November 27, I took my case for U.S. involvement
in Bosnia to the American people. Speaking from the Oval
Office, I said that our diplomacy had produced the Dayton
accords and that our troops had been requested not to fight,

but to help the parties implement the peace plan, which served our strategic interests and advanced our fundamental values.

Because twenty-five other nations had already agreed to participate in a force of sixty thousand, only a third of the troops would be Americans. I pledged that they would go in with a clear, limited, achievable mission and would be well trained and heavily armed to minimize the risk of casualties. After the address I felt that I had made the strongest case I could for our responsibility to lead the forces of peace and freedom, and hoped that I had moved public opinion enough so that Congress would at least not try to stop me from sending in the troops.

In addition to the arguments made in my speech, standing up for the Bosnians had another important benefit to the United States: it would demonstrate to Muslims the world over that the United States cared about them, respected Islam, and would support them if they rejected terror and embraced the possibilities of peace and reconciliation.

On November 28, after signing a bill to provide more than $5 billion for transportation projects that included my "zero tolerance" drinking standard for drivers under twenty-one, I left for a trip to the UK and Ireland to pursue another important peace initiative. Through all the activity in the Middle East and Bosnia and discussions over the budget, we had continued to work hard on Northern Ireland. On the eve of my trip, and with our urging, Prime Ministers Major and Bruton announced a breakthrough in the Irish peace process: a "twin tracks" initiative that provided for separate talks on arms decommissioning and the resolution of political issues; all parties, including Sinn Fein, would be invited to participate in talks overseen by an international panel, which George Mitchell had agreed to chair. It was nice to fly into good news.

On the twenty-ninth, I met with John Major and spoke to Parliament, where I thanked the British for their support of the Bosnian peace process and their willingness to play a major role in the NATO force. I commended Major for his pursuit of peace in Northern Ireland, quoting John Milton's lovely line, "Peace hath her victories, no less renowned than war." I also had my first meeting with the impressive young opposition leader, Tony Blair, who was in the process of reviving the Labour Party with an approach remarkably similar to what we had tried to do with the DLC. Meanwhile, back home, the Republicans had reversed their position on lobbying reform, and the House passed it without a dissenting vote, 421–0.

The next day I flew to Belfast as the first American President ever to visit Northern Ireland. It was the beginning of two of the best days of my presidency. On the road in from the airport, there were people waving American flags and thanking me for working for peace. When I got to Belfast, I made a stop on the Shankill Road, the center of Protestant Unionism, where ten people had been killed by an IRA bomb in 1993. The only thing most of the Protestants knew about me was the Adams visa. I wanted them to know I was working for a peace that was fair to them, too. As I bought some flowers, apples, and oranges from a local shop, I talked to people and shook a few hands.

In the morning I spoke to the employees and other attendees at Mackie International, a textile machine manufacturer that employed both Catholics and Protestants. After being introduced by two children who wanted peace, one Protestant, the other Catholic, I asked the audience to listen to the kids: "Only you can decide between division and unity, between hard lives and high hopes." The IRA's slogan was "Our day will come." I urged the Irish to say to those who still clung to violence, "You are the past, your day is over."

Afterward, I stopped on the Falls Road, the heart of Belfast's Catholic community. I visited a bakery and began to shake hands with a quickly growing crowd of citizens. One of them was Gerry Adams. I told him that I was reading *The Street*, his book of short stories about the Falls, and that it gave me a better feel for what the Catholics had been through. It was our first public appearance together, and it signaled the importance of his commitment to the peace process. The enthusiastic crowd that quickly gathered was obviously pleased at the way things were going.

In the afternoon Hillary and I helicoptered to Derry, the most Catholic city in Northern Ireland and John Hume's hometown. Twenty-five thousand cheering people filled the Guildhall Square and the streets leading to it. After Hume introduced me, I asked the crowd a simple question: "Are you going to be someone who defines yourself in terms of what you are against or what you are for? Will you be someone who defines yourself in terms of who you aren't or who you are? The time has come for the peacemakers to triumph in Northern Ireland, and the United States will support them as they do."

Hillary and I ended our day by returning to Belfast for the official lighting of the city's Christmas tree just outside city hall, before a crowd of about fifty thousand people, which was fired up by the singing of Northern Ireland's own Van Morrison: "Oh, my mama told me there'll be days like this." We both spoke; she talked about the thousands of letters we had received from schoolchildren expressing their hopes for peace, and I quoted from one written by a fourteen-year-old girl from County Armagh: "Both sides have been hurt. Both sides must forgive." Then I ended my remarks by saying that for Jesus, whose birth we celebrated, "no words were more important than these: 'Blessed are the peacemakers, for they shall inherit the earth.'"

After the tree lighting, we attended a reception, to which all the party leaders were invited. Even the Reverend Ian Paisley, the fiery leader of the Democratic Unionist Party, came. Though he wouldn't shake hands with the Catholic leaders, he was only too happy to lecture me on the error of my ways. After a few minutes of his hectoring, I decided the Catholic leaders had gotten the better end of the deal.

Hillary and I left the reception for our night at the Europa Hotel. On that first trip to Ireland, even our choice of lodging carried great symbolism. The Europa had been bombed on more than one occasion during the Troubles;

now it was safe for the President of the United States to stay there.

It was the end of a perfect day, which even included some progress back home, as I signed the Department of Defense Appropriations Act, in which the congressional leaders had provided funding for our troop deployments in Bosnia. Dole and Gingrich had come through, in exchange for a few billion dollars of extra spending that even the Pentagon said was unnecessary.

The next morning we flew into Dublin, where the streets were lined with even bigger and more enthusiastic crowds than we had seen in the north. Hillary and I met with President Mary Robinson and Prime Minister Bruton, then went to a site outside the Bank of Ireland on the Trinity College Green, where I spoke to 100,000 people waving Irish and American flags and cheering. By that time I had been joined by a large number of Irish-American congressmen; Secretary Dick Riley and Peace Corps director Mark Gearan; the Irish-American mayors of Chicago, Pittsburgh, and Los Angeles; my very Irish stepfather, Dick Kelley; and Secretary of Commerce Ron Brown, who, along with my special advisor Jim Lyons, had worked on our economic initiatives for Northern Ireland and kidded the rest of us about his being "black Irish." Once more, I urged the sea of people to set an example that would inspire the world.

When the event was over, Hillary and I walked back into the majestic Bank of Ireland to greet Bono, his wife, Ali, and other members of the Irish rock band U2. Bono was a big supporter of the peace process, and for my efforts he gave me a gift he knew I'd appreciate: a book of William Butler Yeats's plays inscribed by the author and by Bono, who wrote, irreverently, "Bill, Hillary, Chelsea—This guy wrote a few good lyrics—Bono and Ali." The Irish aren't known for understatement, but Bono pulled it off.

I left the College Green to address the Irish parliament, reminding them that all of us had to do more to bring the tangible benefits of peace to ordinary Irish citizens; as Yeats said: "Too long a sacrifice can make a stone of the heart."

Then I went to Cassidy's Pub, to which we had invited some of my distant relatives through my maternal grandfather, whose family had come from Fermanagh.

Feeling full of my Irishness, I went from the pub to the American ambassador's residence, where Jean Kennedy Smith had arranged a brief meeting with the opposition leader, Bertie Ahern, who would soon become prime minister and my newest partner for peace. I also met Seamus Heaney, the Nobel Prize–winning poet whom I'd quoted in Derry the day before.

The next morning, as I flew to see our troops in Germany, I had the feeling that my trip had shifted the psychological balance in Ireland. Until then, the advocates of peace had to argue their case to the skeptics, while their adversaries could just say no. After those two days, the burden had shifted to the opponents of peace to explain themselves.

In Baumholder, General George Joulwan, the NATO commander, briefed me on the military plan and assured me that the morale of the troops about to go to Bosnia was high. I met briefly with Helmut Kohl to thank him for his commitment to send four thousand German soldiers, then flew to Spain to thank Prime Minister Felipe González, the current EU president, for Europe's support. I also acknowledged the leadership of NATO's new secretary-general, the former Spanish foreign minister Javier Solana, an exceptionally able and delightful man who inspired the confidence of all his NATO leaders, no matter how large their egos.

Three days after I got home, I vetoed the Private Securities Litigation Reform Act, because it went too far in limiting access to our courts to innocent investors victimized by securities fraud. Congress overrode my veto, but in 2001, when all the problems with Enron and WorldCom arose, I knew I had done the right thing. I also vetoed another Republican budget. They had made a few changes and tried to make it harder to veto by including their welfare reform bill, but it still cut health and education, raised taxes on the working poor, and relaxed rules that kept pension funds from being depleted for nonpension purposes, less than a year after the Democratic Congress had stabilized America's pension system.

The next day I submitted my own seven-year balanced budget plan. The Republicans panned it because it didn't accept all their estimates for revenues and expenses. We were $300 billion apart over seven years, not an insurmountable difference in an annual budget of $1.6 trillion. I was confident we would eventually reach an agreement, though it might take another government shutdown to get us there.

In mid-month, Shimon Peres came to see me for the first time as prime minister, to reaffirm Israel's intention to turn over Gaza, Jericho, other major cities, and 450 villages in the West Bank to the Palestinians by Christmas, and to release at least another 1,000 Palestinian prisoners before the coming Israeli elections. We also discussed Syria, and I was encouraged enough by what Shimon said to call President Assad and ask him to see Warren Christopher about it.

On the fourteenth, I flew to Paris for a day, for the official signing of the agreement ending the Bosnian war. I met with the presidents of Bosnia, Croatia, and Serbia, and went to a lunch with them hosted by Jacques Chirac at the Elysée Palace. Slobodan Milosevic was sitting across from me, and we talked for a good while. He was intelligent, articulate, and cordial, but he had the coldest look in his eyes I had ever seen. He was also paranoid, telling me he was sure Rabin's assassination was the result of betrayal by someone in his security service. Then he said that everyone knew that's what had happened to President Kennedy, too, but that we Americans "have been successful in covering it up." After spending time with him, I was no longer surprised by his support of the murderous outrages of Bosnia, and I had the feeling that I would be at odds with him again before long.

When I came home to the budget war, the Republicans shut down the government again and it sure didn't feel as if Christmas was on the way, though seeing Chelsea dance in *The Nutcracker* brightened my mood considerably. This time the shutdown was somewhat less severe because about

500,000 federal employees deemed "essential" were allowed to work without pay until the government reopened. But benefits to veterans and poor kids still weren't being paid. It wasn't much of a Christmas present to the American people.

On the eighteenth, I vetoed two more appropriations bills, one for the Department of the Interior, the other for the Departments of Veterans Affairs and Housing and Urban Development. The next day I signed the Lobbying Disclosure Act, after the House Republicans reversed their opposition, and vetoed a third appropriations bill, for the Departments of Commerce, State, and Justice. This one was really something: it eliminated the COPS program in the face of clear evidence that more police on the beat reduced crime; it eliminated all the drug courts, like those that had been promoted by Janet Reno when she was a prosecuting attorney, which reduced crime and drug abuse; it eliminated the Commerce Department's Advanced Technology Program, which many Republican businesspeople supported because it helped them become more competitive; and it severely cut funding for legal services for the poor and for foreign operations.

By Christmas, I had felt for some time that if left to our own devices, Senator Dole and I could have resolved the budget impasse fairly easily, but Dole had to be careful. He was running for President, and Senator Phil Gramm was running against him with Gingrich-like rhetoric, in Republican primaries in which the electorate was well to the right of the country as a whole.

After breaking for Christmas, I vetoed one more budget bill, the National Defense Authorization Act. This one was tough because the legislation included a military pay increase and a larger military housing allowance, both of which I strongly supported. Nevertheless, I felt I had to do it because the bill also mandated the complete deployment of a national missile defense system by 2003, well before a workable system could be developed or would be needed; moreover, such action would violate our commitments under the ABM Treaty and jeopardize Russia's implementation of START I and its ratification of START II. The bill also restricted the President's ability to commit troops in emergencies and interfered too much with important management prerogatives of the Defense Department, including its actions to redress the threat of weapons of mass destruction under the Nunn-Lugar program. No responsible President, Republican or Democrat, could have allowed that defense bill to become law.

During the last three days of the year our forces deployed to Bosnia, and I worked with the congressional leaders on the budget, including one seven-hour session. We made some progress, but broke for New Year's without agreement on the budget or on ending the shutdown. In the first session of the 104th Congress, the new Republican majority had enacted only 67 bills, as compared with 210 in the first year of the previous Congress. And only 6 of the 13 appropriations bills were law, three full months after the beginning of the fiscal year. As our family headed down to Hilton Head for Renaissance Weekend, I wondered whether the American people's votes in the '94 elections had produced the results they wanted.

And I thought about the last two emotionally draining, exhausting, jam-packed months, and the fact that the enormity of the events—Rabin's death, the Bosnian peace and the deployment of our troops, the progress in Northern Ireland, the herculean budget fight—had done nothing to slow down the worker bees in Whitewater World.

On November 29, as I was making my way to Ireland, Senator D'Amato's committee called L. Jean Lewis to testify again about how her investigation of Madison Guaranty had been thwarted after I became President. During her appearance before Congressman Leach's committee the previous August, she had been so badly discredited by government documents and her own tape-recorded conversations with Resolution Trust Corporation attorney April Breslaw that I was amazed D'Amato would call her back. On the other hand, hardly anybody knew of the problems with Lewis's testimony, and D'Amato received a lot of publicity, as Leach had, by simply leveling charges that were unsupported and were actually disproved by subsequent testimony.

Lewis once again repeated her claim that her investigation was thwarted after I was elected. Richard Ben-Veniste, the committee's minority counsel, confronted her with evidence that, contrary to her sworn deposition, she had tried repeatedly to push federal authorities to act on her referral of Hillary and me as material witnesses in Whitewater before the election, not after I became President, and had told an FBI agent that she was "altering history" by her actions. When Senator Paul Sarbanes read to Lewis from the 1992 letter of U.S. Attorney Chuck Banks saying that acting on her referral would constitute "prosecutorial misconduct," then referred to a 1993 Justice Department appraisal of Lewis's inadequate knowledge of federal banking law, Lewis cried, slumped in her chair, and was led away, never to return.

Less than a month later, in mid-December, the complete Whitewater story finally came out, when the RTC inquiry from Pillsbury, Madison & Sutro was released. The report was written by Jay Stephens, who, like Chuck Banks, was a Republican former U.S. attorney whom I had replaced. It said, as had the preliminary report in June, that there were no grounds for a civil suit against us in Whitewater, much less any criminal action, and it recommended that the investigation be closed.

This was what the *New York Times* and the *Washington Post* had wanted to know when they called for an independent counsel. I eagerly awaited their coverage. Immediately after the RTC report was released, the *Post* mentioned it in passing, in the eleventh paragraph of a front-page story about an unrelated subpoena battle with Starr, and the *New York Times* didn't run a word. The *Los Angeles Times*, *Chicago Tribune*, and *Washington Times* ran an Associated Press story of about four hundred words on the inside pages of their papers. The TV networks didn't cover the RTC report, though. ABC's Ted Koppel mentioned it on *Nightline*, then dismissed its importance, because there were so many "new" questions. Whitewater wasn't about Whitewater anymore. It was about whatever Ken Starr could dig up on anybody in Arkansas or my administration. In the meantime, some Whitewater reporters were actually covering up evidence of our innocence. To be fair, a few journalists took note. *Washington Post,* writer Howard Kurtz wrote an article pointing out the way the RTC report had been buried, and Lars-Erik Nelson, a columnist for the New York *Daily News,* who had been a correspondent in the Soviet Union, wrote, "The secret verdict is in: There was nothing for the Clintons to hide . . . in a bizarre reversal of those Stalin-era trials in which innocent people were convicted in secret, the President and the First Lady have been publicly charged and secretly found innocent."

I was genuinely confused by the mainstream press coverage of Whitewater; it seemed inconsistent with the more careful and balanced approach the press had taken on other issues, at least since the Republicans won the Congress in 1994. One day, after one of our budget meetings in October, I asked Senator Alan Simpson of Wyoming to stay a moment to talk. Simpson was a conservative Republican, but we had a pretty good relationship because of the friendship we had in common with his governor, Mike Sullivan. I asked Alan if he thought Hillary and I had done anything wrong in Whitewater. "Of course not," he said. "That's not what this is about. This is about making the public think you did something wrong. Anybody who looked at the evidence would see that you didn't." Simpson laughed at how willing the "elitist" press was to swallow anything negative about small, rural places like Wyoming or Arkansas and made an interesting observation: "You know, before you were elected, we Republicans believed the press was liberal. Now we have a more sophisticated view. They are liberal in a way. Most of them voted for you, but they think more like your right-wing critics do, and that's much more important." When I asked him to explain, he said, "Democrats like you and Sullivan get into government to help people. The right-wing extremists don't think government can do much to improve on human nature, but they do like power.

So does the press. And since you're President, they both get
power the same way, by hurting you." I appreciated Simpson's candor and I thought about what he said for months.
For a long time, whenever I was angry about the Whitewater press coverage I would tell people about Simpson's
analysis. When I finally just accepted his insight as accurate,
it was liberating, and it cleared my head for the fight.

Despite my anger over Whitewater and my puzzlement
about what was behind the press coverage of it, I headed
into 1996 feeling fairly optimistic. In 1995, we had helped
save Mexico, gotten through Oklahoma City and increased
the focus on terrorism, preserved and reformed affirmative
action, ended the war in Bosnia, continued the Middle East
peace process, and helped make progress in Northern Ireland. The economy had continued to improve, and so far I
was winning the budget fight with the Republicans, a battle
that in the beginning seemed likely to doom my presidency.
It could still lead to that, but as we headed into 1996 I was
ready to see it through to the end. As I had told Dick Armey,
I didn't want to be President if the price of doing so was
meaner streets, weaker health care, fewer educational
opportunities, dirtier air, and more poverty. I was betting
that the American people didn't want those things either.

SEVENTEEN

BY JANUARY 2, we were back to the budget negotiations. Bob Dole wanted to make a deal to reopen the government, and after a couple of days so did Newt Gingrich. In one of our budget meetings, the Speaker admitted that in the beginning he had thought he could keep me from vetoing the GOP budget by threatening to shut the government down. In front of Dole, Armey, Daschle, Gephardt, Panetta, and Al Gore, he said frankly, "We made a mistake. We thought you would cave." Finally, on the sixth, with a severe blizzard covering Washington, the impasse was broken, as Congress sent me two more continuing resolutions that put all the federal employees back to work, though they still didn't restore all government services. I signed the CRs and sent the Congress my plan for a balanced budget in seven years.

The next week, I vetoed the Republican welfare reform bill, because it did too little to move people from welfare to work and too much to hurt poor people and their children. The first time I vetoed the Republican welfare reform proposal, it had been a part of their budget. Now a number of their budget cuts were simply put in a bill with the label "welfare reform" on it. Meanwhile, Donna Shalala and I had already gone far in reforming the welfare system on our own. We had given fifty separate waivers to thirty-seven states to pursue initiatives that were pro-work and pro-family. Seventy-three percent of America's welfare recipients were covered by these reforms, and the welfare rolls were dropping.

As we headed into the State of the Union speech on the twenty-third, we seemed to be making some progress on a budget agreement, so I used the address to reach out to the Republicans, rally the Democrats, and explain to the American people my position on both the budget debate, and on the larger question that the budget battle presented: What was the proper role of government in the global information age? The basic theme of the speech was "the era of big government is over. But we cannot go back to the time when our citizens were left to fend for themselves." This formulation reflected my philosophy of getting rid of yesterday's bureaucratic government while advocating a creative, future-oriented, "empowering government"; it also fairly described our economic and social policies and Al Gore's Rego initiative. By then my case was bolstered by the success of our economic policy: nearly eight million new jobs had been created since the inauguration and a record number of new businesses had been started for three years in a row. U.S. automakers were even outselling their Japanese competitors in America for the first time since the 1970s.

After offering again to work with the Congress to balance the budget in seven years and pass welfare reform, I outlined a legislative agenda concerning families and children, education and health care, and crime and drugs. It emphasized programs that reflected basic American values and the idea of citizen empowerment: the V-chip, charter schools, public school choice, and school uniforms. I also named General Barry McCaffrey to be America's new drug czar. At the time, McCaffrey was commander in chief of the Southern Command, where he had worked to stop cocaine from being sent to America from Colombia and elsewhere.

The most memorable moment of the evening came near the end of the speech, when, as usual, I introduced the people sitting in the First Lady's box with Hillary. The first person I mentioned was Richard Dean, a forty-nine-year-old Vietnam veteran who had worked for the Social Security Administration for twenty-two years. When I told Congress that he had been in the Murrah Building in Oklahoma City when it was bombed, risked his life to reenter the ruins four times, and saved the lives of three women, Dean got a huge standing ovation from the entire Congress, with the Republicans leading the cheers. Then came the zinger. As the applause died down, I said, "But Richard Dean's story doesn't end there. This last November, he was forced out of his office when the government shut down. And the second time the government shut down, he continued helping Social Security recipients, but he was working without pay. On behalf of Richard Dean . . . I challenge all of you in this chamber: let's never, ever shut the federal government down again."

This time the gleeful Democrats led the applause. The Republicans, knowing that they had been trapped, looked glum. I didn't think I had to worry about a third government shutdown; its consequences now had a human, heroic face.

Defining moments like that don't happen by accident. Every year we used the State of the Union as an organizing tool for the cabinet and staff to come up with new policy ideas, and then we worked hard on how best to present them. On the day of the speech, we held several rehearsals in the movie theater located between the residence and the East Wing. The White House Communications Agency, which also recorded all my public statements, set up a teleprompter and a podium, and various staff members moved in and out through the day in an informal process managed by my communications director, Don Baer. We all worked together, listening to each sentence, imagining how it would be received in the Congress and in the country, and improving the language.

We had defeated the philosophy behind the "Contract with America" by winning the government shutdown debate. Now the speech offered an alternative philosophy of government and, through Richard Dean, showed that federal employees were good people performing valuable services. It wasn't much different from what I had been saying all along, but in the aftermath of the shutdown, millions of Americans heard and understood it for the first time.

We began the year in foreign policy with Warren Christopher hosting talks between the Israelis and Syrians at Wye River Plantation in Maryland. Then, on January 12, I flew overnight to the U.S. Air Force base in Aviano, Italy, that had been the center of our NATO air operations over

Bosnia, where I boarded one of our new C-17 transport planes for the flight to Taszar Air Base in Hungary, from which our troops were deploying into Bosnia. I had fought in 1993 to keep the C-17 from being eliminated in the defense downsizing. It was an amazing plane with remarkable cargo capacity and the ability to operate in difficult conditions. The Bosnian mission was using twelve C-17s, and I had to fly one into Tuzla; the regular Air Force One, a Boeing 747, was too big.

After meeting with Hungarian President Arpad Goncz and seeing our troops in Taszar, I flew on to Tuzla in northeastern Bosnia, the area for which the United States was responsible. In less than a month and despite terrible weather, seven thousand of our troops and more than two thousand armored vehicles had crossed the flooded Sava River to reach their duty stations. They had turned an airfield with no lights or navigational equipment into one that was open for business around the clock. I thanked the troops and personally delivered a birthday present to a colonel whose wife had charged me with the duty when I stopped in Aviano. I met with President Izetbegovic, then flew on to Zagreb, Croatia, to see President Tudjman. Both of them were satisfied with the implementation of the peace agreement so far and very glad U.S. troops were part of it.

By the time I got back to Washington, it had been a long day, but an important one. Our troops were involved in NATO's first deployment beyond its members' borders. They were working with the soldiers of their Cold War adversaries Russia, Poland, the Czech Republic, Hungary, and the Baltic states. Their mission was pivotal to creating a united Europe, yet it was being criticized in Congress and in coffee shops across America. The troops were at least entitled to know why they were in Bosnia and how strongly I supported them.

Two weeks later the Cold War continued to fade into history as the Senate ratified the START II treaty, which President Bush had negotiated and submitted to the Senate three years earlier, just before he left office. Together with the START I treaty, which we had put into force in December

1994, START II would eliminate two-thirds of the nuclear arsenals the United States and the former Soviet Union had maintained at the height of the Cold War, including the most destabilizing nuclear weapons, the multiple-warhead intercontinental ballistic missiles.

Along with START I and II, we had signed an agreement to freeze North Korea's nuclear program, had led the effort to make the Nuclear Nonproliferation Treaty permanent, and were working to safeguard and ultimately dismantle nuclear weapons and materials under the Nunn-Lugar program. In congratulating the Senate on START II, I asked them to continue making America more secure by passing the Chemical Weapons Convention and my anti-terrorism legislation.

On January 30, Prime Minister Victor Chernomyrdin of Russia came to the White House for his sixth meeting with Al Gore. After they finished their commission business, Chernomyrdin came to see me to brief me on events in Russia and Yeltsin's prospects for reelection. Just before our meeting, I spoke to President Suleyman Demirel and Prime Minister Tansu Ciller of Turkey. They told me that Turkey and Greece were on the brink of military confrontation and implored me to intervene to stop it. They were about to go to war over two tiny Aegean islets called Imia by the Greeks and Kardak by the Turks. Both countries claimed the islets, but Greece apparently had acquired them in a treaty with Italy in 1947. Turkey denied the validity of the Greek claim. There were no people living there, though Turks often sailed to the larger islet for picnics. The crisis was triggered when some Turkish journalists had torn down a Greek flag and put up a Turkish one.

It was unthinkable that two great countries with a real dispute over Cyprus would actually go to war over ten acres of rock islets inhabited by only a couple of dozen sheep, but I could tell that Ciller was genuinely afraid it could happen. I interrupted the Chernomyrdin meeting to get briefed, then placed a series of calls, first to Greek prime minister Konstandinos Simitis, then to Demirel and Ciller again. After all the talk back and forth, the two sides agreed to hold their fire, and Dick Holbrooke, who was already working on Cyprus, stayed up all night to get the parties to agree to resolve the problem through diplomacy. I couldn't help laughing to myself at the thought that whether or not I succeeded in making peace in the Middle East, Bosnia, or Northern Ireland, at least I had saved some Aegean sheep.

Just when I thought things couldn't get any weirder in Whitewater World, they did. On January 4, Carolyn Huber found copies of Hillary's records for work the Rose firm had done for Madison Guaranty in 1985 and 1986. Carolyn had been our assistant at the Governor's Mansion and had come to Washington to help us with our personal papers and correspondence. She had already assisted David Kendall in turning over fifty thousand pages of documents to the independent counsel's office, but for some reason this copy of the billing records wasn't among them. Carolyn found it in a box she had moved to her office from the third-floor residence storage area the previous August. Apparently, the copy had been made in the 1992 campaign; it had Vince Foster's notes on it, because he was handling press questions for the Rose firm at the time.

On the surface, it must have looked suspicious. Why were the records turning up after all this time? If you had seen the disordered array of papers we brought up from Arkansas, you wouldn't have been surprised. I'm amazed that we found as much material as we did in a timely fashion. At any rate, Hillary was glad the records had been found; they proved her contention that she had done only a modest amount of work for Madison Guaranty. In a few weeks, the RTC would issue a report saying just that.

But that's not how the independent counsel, congressional Republicans, and the Whitewater reporters played it. In his *New York Times* column, William Safire called Hillary a "congenital liar." Carolyn Huber was called up to Congress to testify before Al D'Amato's committee on January 18. And on the twenty-sixth, Kenneth Starr hauled Hillary before the grand jury for four hours of questioning. Starr's summons was a cheap, sleazy publicity stunt. We had turned the records over voluntarily as soon as we found them, and they proved the truth of Hillary's account. If Starr had more questions, he could have come to the White House to ask them, as he had done three times before, rather than make her the first First Lady to appear before a grand jury. In 1992, President Bush's White House counsel, Boyden Gray, had withheld his boss's diary for more than a year, until after the election, in direct violation of a subpoena from the Iran-Contra prosecutor. No one put Gray or Bush before a grand jury, and the press uproar was nowhere near as great.

I was more troubled by the attacks on Hillary than on those directed at me. Because I was helpless to stop them, all I could do was stand by her, telling the press that America would be a better place "if everybody in this country had the character my wife has." Hillary and I explained to Chelsea what was going on; she didn't like it but seemed to take it in stride. She knew her mother a lot better than her assailants did.

Still, it was wearing on all of us. I had been struggling for months to keep my anger from interfering with my work, as I dealt with the budget fight, Bosnia, Northern Ireland, and Rabin's death. But it had been very hard; now I was anxious for Hillary and Chelsea as well. I was also concerned about all the other people being pulled into the congressional hearings and into Starr's net who were being hurt emotionally and financially.

Five days after the billing records were turned over, Hillary was scheduled to do an interview with Barbara Walters so that she could discuss her new book, *It Takes a Village*. Instead, the interview turned into a session on the billing records. *It Takes a Village* became a bestseller anyway, as Hillary bravely set out from Washington on a book tour across the country and found legions of friendly and supportive Americans who cared more about what she had to say about improving children's lives than about what Ken Starr, Al D'Amato, William Safire, and their friends had to say about her.

Those boys certainly seemed to get a big kick out of beating up on Hillary. My only consolation was the sure knowledge, rooted in twenty-five years of close observation, that she was a lot tougher than they would ever be. Some guys don't like that in a woman, but it was one of the reasons I loved her.

In early February, as the presidential campaign kicked into high gear, I returned to New Hampshire to highlight both the positive impact of my policies there and my commitment not to forget about the state after I took office. Although I had no primary opponent, I wanted to carry New Hampshire in November, and I needed to deal with the one issue I thought could keep me from doing it: guns.

One Saturday morning, I went to a diner in Manchester full of men who were deer hunters and NRA members. In impromptu remarks, I told them that I knew they had defeated their Democratic congressman, Dick Swett, in 1994 because he voted for the Brady bill and the assault weapons ban. Several of them nodded in agreement. Those hunters were good men who had been frightened by the NRA; I thought they could be stampeded again in 1996 only if no one presented them with the other side of the argument in language they could understand. So I gave it my best shot: "I know the NRA told you to defeat Congressman Swett. Now, if you missed a day, or even an hour, in the deer woods because of the Brady bill or the assault weapons ban, I want you to vote against me, too, because I asked him to support those bills. On the other hand, if you didn't, then they didn't tell you the truth, and you need to get even."

A few days later, at the Library of Congress, I signed the Telecommunications Act, a sweeping overhaul of the laws affecting an industry that was already one-sixth of our economy. The act increased competition, innovation, and access to what Al Gore had dubbed the "information superhighway." There had been months of sparring over complex economic issues, with the Republicans favoring greater concentration of ownership in media and telecommunications markets, and the White House and the Democrats supporting greater competition, especially in local and long-distance telephone service. With Al Gore taking the lead for the White House and Speaker Gingrich in his positive entrepreneurial mode, we reached what I thought was a fair compromise, and in the end the bill passed almost unanimously. It also contained a requirement that new television sets include the V-chip, which I had first endorsed at the Gores' annual family conference, to allow parents to control their children's access to programs; by the end of the month, executives from most of the television networks would agree to have a rating system for their programs in place by 1997. Even more important, the act mandated discounted Internet access rates for schools, libraries, and hospitals; the so-called E-rate would eventually save public entities about $2 billion a year.

The next day, the bloom came off the Irish rose, as Gerry Adams called to tell me the IRA had ended its cease-fire, allegedly because of foot-dragging by John Major and the Unionists, including their insistence on IRA arms decommissioning in return for Sinn Fein's participation in the political life of Northern Ireland. Later that day a bomb exploded at Canary Wharf in London.

The IRA would keep it up for more than a year, at great cost to themselves. While they killed two soldiers and two civilians and injured many others, they suffered the deaths of two IRA operatives, the breakup of their bombing team in Britain, and the arrest of numerous IRA operatives in Northern Ireland. By the end of the month, peace vigils were being held all over Northern Ireland to demonstrate the continuing support of ordinary citizens for peace. John Major and John Bruton said they would resume talks with Sinn Fein if the IRA reinstated its cease-fire. With John Hume's support, the White House decided to maintain contact with Adams, waiting for the moment when the march toward peace could resume.

The peace process in the Middle East was also threatened in late February, as two Hamas bombs killed twenty-six people. With elections coming up in Israel, I assumed Hamas was trying to defeat Prime Minister Peres and provoke the Israelis to elect a hard-line government that would not make peace with the PLO. We pushed Arafat to do more to prevent terrorist acts. As I had told him when we signed the original agreement back in 1993, he could never be the most militant Palestinian again, and if he tried to keep one foot in the peace camp and the other on the terrorist side he would eventually be undone.

We also had trouble closer to home when Cuba shot down two civilian planes flown by the anti-Castro group Brothers to the Rescue, killing four men. Castro hated the group and the leaflets critical of him that it had dropped over Havana in the past. Cuba claimed the planes were shot in its airspace. They weren't, but even if they had been, the downings still would have violated international law.

I suspended charter flights to Cuba, restricted travel by Cuban officials in the United States, expanded the reach of Radio Martí, which beamed pro-democracy messages into Cuba, and asked Congress to authorize compensation out of Cuba's blocked assets in the United States to the families of the men who were killed. Madeleine Albright asked the United Nations to impose sanctions, telling them that the shootdown reflected cowardice, "not *cojones*." She went to Miami to deliver a fiery speech to the Cuban-American community. Her macho remarks made her a heroine among South Florida's Cubans.

I also committed to signing a version of the Helms-Burton bill, which stiffened the embargo against Cuba and restricted the President's authority to lift it without congressional approval. Supporting the bill was good election-year politics in Florida, but it undermined whatever chance I might have if I won a second term to lift the embargo in return for positive changes within Cuba. It almost appeared that Castro was trying to force us to maintain the embargo as an excuse for the economic failures of his regime. If that wasn't the objective, then Cuba had made a colossal error. I later received word from Castro, indirectly of course, that the shootdown was a mistake. Apparently he had issued earlier orders to fire on any aircraft that violated Cuban airspace and had failed to withdraw them when the Cubans knew the Brothers to the Rescue planes were coming.

In the last week of the month, after visiting areas devastated by recent flooding in Washington, Oregon, Idaho, and Pennsylvania, I met with the new Japanese prime minister in Santa Monica, California. Ryutaro Hashimoto had been Mickey Kantor's counterpart before becoming the head of the Japanese government. An avid practitioner of kendo, a Japanese martial art, Hashimoto was a tough, intelligent man who enjoyed combat of all kinds. But he was also a leader with whom we could work; he and Kantor had concluded twenty trade agreements, our exports to Japan were up 80 percent, and our bilateral trade deficit had declined for three years in a row.

The month ended on a high note as Hillary and I celebrated Chelsea's sixteenth birthday by taking her to see *Les Misérables* at the National Theatre, then hosting a busload of her friends for a weekend at Camp David. We liked all Chelsea's friends, and we loved seeing them shooting at one another with paintball guns in the woods, bowling and playing other games, and generally being kids as their high school years were drawing to a close. The best part of the weekend for me was giving Chelsea a driving lesson around the Camp David compound. I missed driving and wanted Chelsea to enjoy it, and to do it safely and well.

The Middle East peace process was shaken again in the first weeks of March when, on successive days, a new round of Hamas bombs in Jerusalem and Tel Aviv killed more than thirty people and wounded many more. Among the dead were children, a Palestinian nurse who lived and worked among her Jewish friends, and two young American women. I met with their families in New Jersey and was deeply moved by their steadfast commitment to peace as the only way to prevent more children from being killed in the future. In a televised address to the people of Israel, I stated the obvious, that the terrorist acts were "aimed not just at killing innocent people but at killing the growing hope for peace in the Middle East."

On March 12, Jordan's King Hussein flew on Air Force One with me to a Summit of Peacemakers hosted by President Mubarak in Sharm el-Sheikh, a beautiful resort on the Red Sea favored by European scuba-diving enthusiasts. Hussein had come to see me at the White House a few days earlier to condemn the Hamas bombings and was determined to rally the Arab world to the cause of peace. I really enjoyed the long flight with him. We had always gotten along well, but we had become closer friends and allies in the aftermath of Rabin's assassination.

Leaders of twenty-nine nations from the Arab world, Europe, Asia, and North America, including Boris Yeltsin and UN Secretary-General Boutros Boutros-Ghali, joined Peres and Arafat at Sharm el-Sheikh. President Mubarak and I co-chaired the meeting. We and our staffs had worked day and night to ensure that we would come out of the conference with a clear and concrete commitment to fighting terror and preserving the peace process.

For the first time, the Arab world stood with Israel in condemning terror and promising to work against it. The united front was essential to give Peres the support necessary to keep the peace process going and to reopen Gaza, so that the thousands of Palestinians who lived there but had jobs in Israel could go back to work; it was also necessary to give Arafat the backing to make an all-out effort against the terrorists, without which Israeli support for peace would collapse.

On the thirteenth, I flew to Tel Aviv to discuss specific steps the United States could take to help the Israeli military and police. In a meeting with Prime Minister Peres and his cabinet, I pledged $100 million in support and asked Warren Christopher and CIA director John Deutch to stay in Israel to accelerate the implementation of our joint efforts. In the press conference with Peres after our meeting, I acknowledged the difficulty of providing complete protection from "young men who have bought some apocalyptic version of Islam and politics that causes them to strap their bodies with bombs" in order to commit suicide and kill innocent children. But I said we could improve our capacity to prevent such events and to break up the networks of money and national support that made them possible. I also used the occasion to urge congressional action on the anti-terrorism legislation that had been held up for more than a year.

After the press conference and a question-and-answer session with young Israeli students in Tel Aviv, I met with the Likud Party leader, Benjamin Netanyahu. The Hamas bombings had made a Likud victory in the election more likely. I wanted Netanyahu to know that if he won, I would be his partner in the fight against terror, but I also wanted him to stick with the peace process.

I couldn't go home without making the trip up Mount Herzl to visit Rabin's grave. I knelt, said a prayer, and, following Jewish custom, placed a small stone on Yitzhak's marble marker. I also took another small rock from the ground around the grave home with me as a reminder of my friend and the job he had left for me to do.

While I was preoccupied with trouble in the Middle East, China roiled the waters of the Taiwan Strait by "test"-firing three missiles close to Taiwan in an apparent attempt to discourage the Taiwanese politicians from pushing for independence in the election campaign then under way. Ever since President Carter normalized relations with mainland China, the United States had followed a consistent policy of recognizing "one China" while continuing to have good relations with Taiwan, and saying that the two sides should resolve their differences peacefully. We had never said whether we would or wouldn't come to the defense of Taiwan if it were attacked.

It seemed to me that the Middle East and Taiwan were polar opposite foreign policy problems. If nothing was done by political leaders in the Middle East, things would get worse. By contrast, I thought that if the politicians in China and Taiwan didn't do anything foolish, the problem would resolve itself over time. Taiwan was an economic power-house that had moved from dictatorship to democracy. It wanted no part of the mainland's bureaucratic communism. On the other hand, Taiwanese businesspeople were investing

BILL CLINTON

heavily in China, and there was travel back and forth. China liked the Taiwanese investment, but could not agree to give up its claim to sovereignty over the island; finding the right balance between economic pragmatism and aggressive nationalism was a constant challenge for China's leaders, especially during election season in Taiwan. I thought China had gone too far with the missile tests, and quickly, but without fanfare, I ordered a carrier group from the U.S. Navy's Pacific fleet to sail to the Taiwan Strait. The crisis passed.

After a rocky start in February, Bob Dole won all the Republican primaries in March, wrapping up his party's nomination with a late-month victory in California. Even though Senator Phil Gramm, who ran to the right of Dole, would have been easier to beat, I was pulling for Dole. No election is a sure thing, and if I lost, I believed the country would be in more solid and more moderate hands with him.

While Dole was moving toward the nomination, I campaigned in several states, including an event in Maryland with General McCaffrey and Jesse Jackson to highlight our efforts to stem teen drug use, and a stop at Harman International, a manufacturer of premier speakers in Northridge, California, to announce that the economy had produced 8.4 million jobs in just over three years since I took office; I had promised 8 million in four years. Middle-class incomes were also beginning to rise. In the last two years, two-thirds of the new jobs created were in industries that paid above the minimum wage.

During the course of the month, we didn't reach agreement on the appropriations bills still outstanding, so I signed three more CRs and sent my budget for the next fiscal year up to Capitol Hill. Meanwhile, the House continued to follow the NRA, voting to repeal the assault weapons ban and to delete from the anti-terrorism legislation sections the gun lobby opposed.

At the end of the month, I initiated an effort to accelerate the approval of anti-cancer drugs by the Food and Drug Administration. Al Gore, Donna Shalala, and FDA administrator

David Kessler had worked to cut the average approval process for new drugs from thirty-three months in 1987 to just under a year in 1994. The latest approval for an AIDS drug was issued in just forty-two days. It was important for the FDA to determine how drugs would affect the body before they were approved, but the process should be as speedy as safety permitted; lives were riding on it.

Finally, on March 29, eight months after Bob Rubin and I had first requested it, I signed a bill to increase the debt limit. The Damocles sword of default was no longer hanging over our budget negotiations.

On April 3, with springtime in full bloom in Washington, I was working in the Oval Office when I received word that the air force jet carrying Ron Brown and a U.S. trade and investment delegation he had organized to increase the economic benefits of peace to the Balkans had flown off course in bad weather and crashed into St. John's Mountain near Dubrovnik, Croatia. Everyone on board was killed. Barely a week earlier, on their trip to Europe, Hillary and Chelsea had been on the same plane with some of the same crew members.

I was devastated. Ron was my friend and my best political advisor in the cabinet. As chairman of the DNC, he had brought the Democratic Party back from our loss in 1988 and played a pivotal role in uniting the Democrats for the 1992 election. In the aftermath of the 1994 congressional election losses, Ron had remained upbeat, lifting everyone's spirits with his confident prediction that we were doing the right things on the economy and would win in 1996. He had revitalized the Commerce Department, modernizing the bureaucracy and using it to further not only our economic objectives but our larger interests in the Balkans and Northern Ireland. He had also worked hard to increase U.S. exports to ten "emerging markets" that were sure to loom large in the twenty-first century, including Poland, Turkey, Brazil, Argentina, South Africa, and Indonesia. After he died I received a letter from a business executive who had worked with him, saying he was "the finest Secretary of Commerce the United States ever had."

Hillary and I drove to Ron's house to see his wife, Alma, and his children, Tracey and Michael, and Michael's wife, Tammy. They were part of our extended family, and I was relieved to see them already surrounded by loving friends and dealing with their loss by telling Ron Brown stories; there were many worth repeating from the long journey he had traveled from his boyhood home at the old Hotel Teresa in Harlem to the pinnacle of American politics and public service.

When we left Alma, we went downtown to the Commerce Department to talk to the employees, who had lost both their leader and their friends. One of those who died was a young man Hillary and I knew well. Adam Darling was the idealistic and spunky son of a Methodist minister who had entered our lives in 1992 when he made news by riding his bicycle across America to support the Clinton-Gore ticket.

A few days later, just two weeks before the first anniversary of the Oklahoma City bombing, Hillary and I planted a dogwood on the back lawn of the White House in memory of Ron and the other Americans who had died in Croatia. Then we flew to Oklahoma City to dedicate a new day-care center to replace the one lost in the bombing and to visit with the victims' families who were there. At the University of Central Oklahoma, in nearby Edmond, I told the students that while we had apprehended more terrorists in the last three years than in any other previous time in our history, terror required us to do more: it was the threat of their generation just as nuclear war had been the threat for those of us who had grown up during the Cold War.

The next afternoon we made the sad trip to Dover Air Force Base in Delaware, where America brings home those who have died in service to the nation. After the caskets had been solemnly carried off the plane, I read the names of all who had perished on Ron Brown's plane and reminded those in attendance that tomorrow was Easter, which for Christians marks the passage from loss and despair to hope and redemption. The Bible says, "Though we weep through the night, joy will come in the morning." I took that verse as my theme for Ron's eulogy on April 10 at the National Cathedral, because for all of us who knew him, Ron was always our joy in the morning. I looked at his casket and said, "I want to say to my friend just one last time: Thank you; if it weren't for you, I wouldn't be here." We laid Ron to rest in Arlington National Cemetery; by then I was so exhausted and grief-stricken after the terrible ordeal that I could hardly stand. Chelsea, hiding her tears behind sunglasses, put her arm around me and I laid my head on her shoulder.

In the awful week between the crash and the funeral, I carried on with my duties as best I could. First, I signed the new farm bill. Just two weeks earlier, I had signed legislation that improved the farm credit system, to make more loans available to farmers at lower interest rates. Although I thought the new farm bill failed to provide an adequate safety net for family farms, I signed it anyway because if the current law expired without a replacement, farmers would have to plant their next crop under the completely inadequate support program put in place back in 1948. Also, the bill had many provisions I did support: greater flexibility for farmers in choosing what crops to plant without losing aid; money for economic development in rural communities; funds to help farmers prevent soil erosion, air and water pollution, and the loss of wetlands; and $200 million to begin work on one of my top environmental priorities, the restoration of Florida's Everglades, which had been damaged by extensive development and sugarcane growing.

On the ninth I signed legislation granting the President a line-item veto. Most governors had the authority and every President since Ulysses Grant in 1869 had sought it. The provision was also part of the Republican "Contract with America," and I had endorsed it in my 1992 campaign. I was pleased that it had finally passed, and I thought its main utility would be in the leverage it gave future Presidents to keep wasteful items out of budgets in the first place. Signing the bill had one significant downside: Senator Robert Byrd, the most respected authority in Congress on the Constitution, considered it an unconstitutional infringement on the legislative branch by the executive. Byrd hated the line-item veto with a passion most people reserve for more personal injuries, and I don't think he ever forgave me for signing the bill.

On the day of Ron Brown's memorial service, I vetoed a bill that banned a procedure its proponents called "partial-birth" abortion. The legislation as described by its anti-abortion advocates was highly popular; it prohibited a type of late-term abortion that seemed so heartless and cruel that many pro-choice citizens thought it should be banned. It was a bit more complicated than that. As far as I could determine, the procedure was rare, and it was predominantly performed on women whose doctors had told them it was necessary to preserve their own lives or health, often because they were carrying hydrocephalic babies who were certain to die before, during, or shortly after childbirth. The question was how badly damaged the mothers' bodies would be if they carried their doomed babies to term, and whether doing so could render them unable to bear other children. In such cases, it was far from clear that banning the operation was "pro-life."

I thought it should be a decision for the mother and her doctor. When I vetoed the bill, I stood with five women who had undergone partial-birth abortions. Three of them, a Catholic, an evangelical Christian, and an Orthodox Jew, were devoutly pro-life. One of them said she had prayed to God to take her life and spare her child, and all of them said they had consented to the late-term procedure only because their doctors had told them their babies could not have lived, and they wanted to be able to have other children.

If you consider how long it took me to explain why I vetoed the bill, you understand why it was terrible politics to do so. I vetoed it because no one had shown me evidence that the women's advocates had been untruthful in saying the procedure was necessary or that there was another alternative procedure that would have protected the mothers and their reproductive capacity. I had offered to sign a bill banning all late-term abortions except in cases where the life or health of the mother was at risk. Several states still permitted them, and such action could have prevented far more abortions than the partial-birth bill, but the anti-abortion forces in Congress killed it. They were looking for a way to erode *Roe* v. *Wade*; besides, there was no political advantage to a bill that even most pro-choice senators and representatives would support.

On April 12, I named Mickey Kantor secretary of commerce and his able deputy, Charlene Barshefsky, the new U.S. trade representative. I also named Frank Raines, vice chairman of Fannie Mae, the Federal National Mortgage Association, to be head of the Office of Management and Budget. Raines had the right combination of intellect, knowledge of the budget, and political skills to succeed at OMB, and was the first African-American ever to hold the job.

On April 14, Hillary and I boarded Air Force One for a busy one-week trip to Korea, Japan, and Russia. On South Korea's beautiful Cheju Island, President Kim Young-Sam and I proposed that we convene four-party talks with North Korea and China, the other signers of the forty-six-year-old armistice concluding the Korean War, in order to provide a framework within which North and South Korea could talk and, we hoped, make a final peace agreement. North Korea had been saying it wanted peace, and I believed we had to discover whether they were serious about it.

I flew from South Korea to Tokyo, where Prime Minister Hashimoto and I issued a declaration designed to reaffirm and modernize our security relationship, including greater cooperation in counterterrorism, which the Japanese were eager for after the sarin gas subway attack. The United States also pledged to maintain its troop presence of about 100,000 in Japan, Korea, and the rest of East Asia, while reducing our profile on the Japanese island of Okinawa, where criminal incidents involving U.S. military personnel had increased opposition to our presence there. America had a big economic stake in maintaining peace and stability in Asia. The Asians bought half our exports, and those purchases supported three million jobs.

Before leaving Japan, I visited U.S. forces from the Seventh Fleet aboard the USS *Independence*, attended an elegant state dinner hosted by the emperor and empress at the Imperial Palace, made a speech to the Japanese Diet, and enjoyed a lunch hosted by the prime minister that featured American-born sumo wrestlers and an outstanding Japanese jazz saxophonist.

To reinforce the importance of American-Japanese ties, I had named former vice president Walter Mondale as our ambassador. His prestige and skill at handling difficult problems sent an unmistakable message to the Japanese that they were important to the United States.

We flew on to St. Petersburg, Russia. On April 19, the first anniversary of the Oklahoma City bombing, Al Gore went to Oklahoma to speak for the administration, while I marked the occasion during a visit to the Russian military cemetery and prepared for a summit on nuclear safety with Boris Yeltsin and the G-7 leaders. Yeltsin had suggested the summit to highlight our commitment to the Comprehensive Test Ban Treaty, START I and START II, and our joint efforts to secure and destroy nuclear weapons and materials. We also agreed to improve safety at nuclear power plants, end the dumping of nuclear materials in the oceans, and help Ukrainian president Leonid Kuchma close the Chernobyl power plant within four years. Ten years after the tragic accident there, it was still running.

On the twenty-fourth, I was back home, but not out of foreign affairs. President Elias Hrawi of Lebanon was at the White House at a tense moment in the Middle East. In response to a barrage of Katyusha rockets fired into Israel from southern Lebanon by Hezbollah, Shimon Peres had ordered retaliatory attacks that killed many civilians. I had much sympathy for Lebanon; it was caught up in the conflict between Israel and Syria, and was full of terrorist operatives. I reaffirmed America's steadfast support for UN Security Council Resolution 425, which calls for a truly independent Lebanon.

The news from the Middle East was not all bad. While I was meeting with the Lebanese president, Yasser Arafat persuaded the PLO executive council to amend its charter to recognize Israel's right to exist, a policy shift very important to the Israelis. Two days later Warren Christopher and our Middle East envoy, Dennis Ross, secured an agreement among Israel, Lebanon, and Syria to end the Lebanese crisis and enable us to get back to the business of peace.

Shimon Peres came to see me at the end of the month to sign an anti-terrorism cooperative agreement that included $50 million for our joint efforts to reduce Israel's vulnerability to the kind of suicide bombings that had recently caused such havoc and heartbreak.

Just a week earlier, I had signed the anti-terrorism legislation that the Congress had finally passed, a full year after Oklahoma City. In the end, the bill had won strong bipartisan support after the deletion of the provisions requiring traceable markers in black and smokeless powder and giving federal authorities the ability to conduct the kind of roving wiretaps on suspected terrorists that already could be used against organized crime figures. The bill would give us more tools and resources to prevent terrorist attacks, disrupt terrorist organizations, and increase controls over chemical and biological weapons. The Congress also agreed to let us put chemical taggants in plastic explosives and left open the option requiring them in other types of explosives not clearly prohibited by the law.

April was another interesting month in Whitewater World. On the second, Kenneth Starr appeared in the Fifth Circuit Court of Appeals in New Orleans on behalf of four big tobacco companies that, at the same time, were engaged in a heated dispute with my administration over their marketing of cigarettes to teenagers and how much authority the FDA had to stop them. Starr didn't see any conflict of interest in keeping up a lucrative law practice in which he was paid large sums by my adversaries. *USA Today* had already revealed that in a court appearance defending the Wisconsin school voucher program, which I opposed, Starr had been paid not by the state but by the ultra-conservative Bradley Foundation. Starr was investigating the Resolution Trust

Corporation for its inquiry into the conduct of our accuser, L. Jean Lewis, while the RTC was negotiating with his law firm to settle a suit the agency had filed against the firm for its negligence in its representation of a failed Denver savings-and-loan institution. And, of course, Starr had offered to go on television to defend Paula Jones's lawsuit. Robert Fiske had been removed as the Whitewater independent counsel on the tenuous claim that his appointment by Janet Reno created the appearance of a conflict of interest. Now we had a prosecutor with real conflicts.

As I said, Starr and his allies in Congress and on the federal courts had created a new definition of "conflict of interest": anyone who might remotely be favorable or, as in Fiske's case, even fair to Hillary and me was by definition conflicted; Ken Starr's blatant political and economic conflicts of interest and the extreme bias against me they reflected presented no problem at all to his assumption of unlimited and unaccountable authority to go after us and many other innocent people.

Starr and his allies' curious view of what constituted a conflict of interest was never more apparent than in their treatment of Judge Henry Woods, a highly respected veteran jurist and former FBI agent who was assigned to preside over the trial of Governor Jim Guy Tucker and others whom Starr had indicted on federal charges completely unrelated to Whitewater. They involved the purchase of cable television stations. At first, neither Starr nor Tucker objected to Woods hearing the case; he was a Democrat but had never been close to the governor. Judge Woods dismissed the indictments after he determined that Starr had exceeded his authority under the independent counsel law because the charges had nothing to do with Whitewater.

Starr appealed Woods's decision to the Eighth Circuit Court and requested that the judge be thrown off the case for bias. The members of the appeals panel that heard the case were conservative Republicans appointed by Reagan and Bush. The lead judge, Pasco Bowman, rivaled David Sentelle in his right-wing politics. Without even giving Judge Woods an opportunity to defend himself, the court not only reversed his decision and reinstated the indictment but also kicked him off the case, citing not court records, but newspaper and magazine articles critical of him. One of the articles filled with false charges was written by Justice Jim Johnson in the right-wing *Washington Times*. After the ruling Woods pointed out that he was the only judge in American history to be removed from a case on the basis of press articles. When another enterprising defense lawyer appealed to the Eighth Circuit to get a trial judge removed and cited the Woods case as precedent, a different, less ideological panel refused the request and criticized the Woods decision, saying it was both unprecedented and unjustified. Of course it was, but there were different rules for Whitewater.

On April 17, even the *New York Times* couldn't take it any longer. Calling Starr "defiantly blind to his appearance problems and indifferent to the special obligation he owes to the American people" for his refusal "to divest himself of his own political and financial baggage," the *Times* said Starr should step down. I couldn't deny that the grand old paper still had a conscience; they didn't want Hillary and me handed over to a lynch mob. The rest of the Whitewater media was silent on the subject.

On April 28, I gave four and a half hours of videotaped testimony in another Whitewater trial. In this one, Starr had indicted Jim and Susan McDougal and Jim Guy Tucker for misappropriating funds from Madison Guaranty and from the Small Business Administration. The loans were not repaid, but the prosecutors didn't dispute that the defendants intended to repay them; instead, they were charged with crimes arising from the fact that the borrowed money was used for purposes other than those described on the loan application papers.

The trial had nothing to do with Whitewater, Hillary, or me. I mention it here because David Hale dragged me into it. He had swindled the SBA out of millions of dollars and was cooperating with Starr in hopes of getting a reduced prison sentence. In his testimony at the trial, Hale repeated his charge that I had pressured him to make a $300,000 loan to the McDougals.

I testified that Hale's account of his conversations with me was false and that I knew nothing of the dealings between the parties that had given rise to the charges. The defense attorneys believed that once the jury knew that Hale had lied about my role in his dealings with the McDougals and Tucker, his entire testimony would be compromised and the prosecutor's case would collapse, and therefore the defendants themselves did not need to testify. There were two difficulties with the strategy. First, against all advice, Jim McDougal insisted on testifying in his own defense. He had done so in a previous trial arising out of the collapse of Madison Guaranty in 1990, and he had been acquitted. But the manic depression from which he suffered had progressed since then, and according to many observers, his rambling, erratic testimony damaged not just himself but also Susan and Jim Guy Tucker, who did not testify in their own defense, even after McDougal had unwittingly imperiled them.

The other problem was that the jury didn't have all the facts about David Hale's connections to my political adversaries; some of them weren't yet known, and others were ruled inadmissible by the judge. The jury didn't know about the money and support Hale had been receiving from a clandestine effort known as the Arkansas Project.

The Arkansas Project was funded by the ultra-conservative billionaire Richard Mellon Scaife from Pittsburgh, who had also pumped money into the *American Spectator* to fund its negative stories on Hillary and me. For example, the project had paid one former state trooper $10,000 for the ridiculous yarn accusing me of drug smuggling. Scaife's people also worked closely with allies of Newt Gingrich. When David Brock was working on the *Spectator* article featuring the two Arkansas state troopers who claimed they had procured women for me, Brock had received not only his salary from the magazine but also secret payments from Chicago businessman Peter Smith, the finance chairman of Newt's political action committee.

Most of the Arkansas Project's efforts centered on David Hale. Working through Parker Dozhier, a former aide to

Justice Jim Johnson, the project set up a haven for Hale at Dozhier's bait shop outside Hot Springs, where Dozhier gave Hale cash and the use of his car and fishing cabin while Hale was cooperating with Starr. During this time Hale also received free legal advice from Ted Olson, a friend of Starr's and a lawyer for the Arkansas Project and the *American Spectator*. Olson later became the solicitor general in President George W. Bush's Justice Department after a Senate hearing in which he was less than candid about his work for the Arkansas Project.

For whatever reasons, the jury convicted all three defendants on several of the charges against them. In his closing, the lead OIC prosecutor went out of his way to state that I was not "on trial" and that there had "been no allegations of wrongdoing" directed at me. But Starr now had what he really wanted: three people he could pressure to give him something damaging on us in order to avoid a jail sentence. Since there was nothing to tell, I didn't worry about it, though I regretted the cost to the taxpayers of Starr's far-flung efforts, and the mounting casualties among people in Arkansas whose principal sin was that they had known Hillary and me before I became President.

I also had serious doubts about the jury verdict. Jim McDougal's mental illness had progressed to the point where he was probably not competent to stand trial, much less testify. And I felt that Susan McDougal and Jim Guy Tucker might have been convicted only because they were caught up in Jim McDougal's downward mental spiral and David Hale's desperate effort to save himself.

May was a relatively quiet month on the legislative front, which enabled me to do some campaigning in several states and to enjoy some of the ceremonial duties of the presidency, including the presentation of a Congressional Gold Medal to Billy Graham, the annual WETA-TV "In Performance" concert on the South Lawn, featuring Aaron Neville and Linda Ronstadt, and a state visit from the Greek president, Constantinos Stephanopoulos. When we were involved in high-stakes foreign and domestic problems, I often had a hard time relaxing enough to fully enjoy such things.

On May 15, I announced the latest round of community policing grants, which brought us to 43,000 of the 100,000 new police officers I'd promised. That same day Bob Dole announced that he was resigning from the Senate to pursue his presidential campaign full-time. He called to tell me of his decision and I wished him well. It was the only sensible course for him; he didn't have time to campaign against me and be majority leader, and the positions the Senate and House Republicans were taking on the budget and other matters were hurting him in his presidential race.

The next day I called for a global ban on anti-personnel land mines. There were about 100 million land mines, mostly relics of past wars, just beneath the surface of the earth in Europe, Asia, Africa, and Latin America. Many of them had been there for decades but were still lethal; twenty-five thousand people were killed or maimed by them every year. The damage they were doing, especially to children in places like Angola and Cambodia, was awful. There were a lot of them in Bosnia, too; the only casualty our troops had suffered came when an army sergeant was killed trying to pick up a land mine. I committed the United States to destroy four million of our own so-called dumb, or non-self-destructing, mines by 1999 and to help other nations with their demining efforts. Soon we would be financing more than half the cost of demining worldwide.

Unfortunately, what should have been a life-affirming event was marked by yet another tragedy, as I announced that our chief of naval operations, Admiral Mike Boorda, had died that afternoon of a self-inflicted gunshot wound. Boorda was the first enlisted man ever to rise through the ranks to the navy's highest position. His suicide was triggered by news stories alleging that he had worn two Vietnam battle ribbons on his uniform that he hadn't earned. The facts were in dispute and, in any case, should not have diminished his standing after a long career marked by devotion, stellar service, and evident courage. Like Vince Foster, he had never had his honor and integrity questioned before.

There's a big difference between being told that you are no good at your job and being told that you're just no good.

In mid-May, I signed the reauthorization of the Ryan White CARE Act, which funded medical and support services for people with HIV and AIDS, the leading cause of death for Americans between the ages of twenty-five and forty-four. Now we had doubled the money available for AIDS care since 1993, and one-third of the 900,000 people with HIV were receiving services under the act.

That same week I also signed a bill known as Megan's Law. Named after a little girl who had been killed by a sex offender, the legislation gave states the power to notify communities of the presence of violent sex offenders; several studies had shown they are rarely rehabilitated.

After the ceremony I flew to Missouri to campaign with Dick Gephardt. I really admired Gephardt, a hardworking, smart, kind man who looked twenty years younger than he was. Even though he was the Democratic leader in the House, he regularly came home on weekends to go into neighborhoods and knock on his constituents' doors to talk with them. Often, Dick would give me a list of things he wanted me to do for his district. While lots of congressmen asked for things from time to time, the only other member who regularly provided me a typed "to do" list was Senator Ted Kennedy.

At the end of the month, I announced that the Veterans Administration would provide compensation to Vietnam veterans for a series of severe illnesses, including cancers, liver disorders, and Hodgkin's disease, that were associated with exposure to Agent Orange, a cause long championed by Vietnam veterans, Senators John Kerry and John McCain, and by the late Admiral Bud Zumwalt.

On May 29, I stayed up until well past midnight watching the election returns in Israel. It was a real cliffhanger, as Bibi Netanyahu defeated Shimon Peres by less than 1 percent of the vote. Peres won the Arab vote by a large majority, but Netanyahu beat him badly enough among Jewish voters, who made up more than 90 percent of the electorate, to win. He did it by promising to be tougher on terrorism and slower with the peace process, and by using American-style television ads, including some attacking Peres that were made with the help of a Republican media advisor from New York. Peres resisted the pleas of his supporters to answer the ads until the very end of the campaign, and by then it was too late. I thought Shimon had done a good job as prime minister, and he had given his entire life to the state of Israel, but in 1996, by a narrow margin, Netanyahu proved to be a better politician. I was eager to determine whether and how he and I could work together to keep the peace process going.

In June, against the backdrop of the presidential campaign, I focused on two issues, education and the disturbing rash of black church burnings then sweeping the country. At the Princeton University commencement, I outlined a plan to open the doors of college to all Americans and to make at least two years of college as universally available as high school: a tax credit modeled on Georgia's Hope Scholarships of $1,500 (the average cost of community college tuition) for two years of higher education; a tax deduction of $10,000 a year for all higher education beyond the first two years; a $1,000 scholarship to students in the top 5 percent of every high school graduating class; funds to increase college work-study positions from 700,000 to 1 million; and annual increases in Pell Grants for lower-income students.

In mid-month I went to Grover Cleveland Middle School in Albuquerque, New Mexico, to support the community's curfew program, one of several such efforts across the country requiring young people to be in their homes after a certain hour on school nights; they had led to a decline in crime and an improvement in student learning. I also endorsed the policy of requiring school uniforms for elementary and middle school students. Almost without exception, school districts that required uniforms experienced higher student attendance, less violence, and increased student learning. The distinctions between poor and wealthier students diminished as well.

Some of my critics ridiculed my emphasis on what they

called "small bore" issues like curfews, uniforms, character education programs, and the V-chip, saying it was all politics, as well as a reflection of my inability to pass big programs in the Republican Congress. That was inaccurate. At the time, we were also implementing the large education and crime programs passed in my first two years, and I had another major education initiative before Congress. But I knew that federal money and laws could only give Americans the tools to make their lives better; the real changes still had to be effected by citizens at the grassroots level. Partly as a result of our promotion of school uniforms, more and more school districts embraced them, with positive results.

On June 12, I was in Greeleyville, South Carolina, to dedicate the new Mount Zion African Methodist Episcopal Church, after the congregation's old church had been burned. Less than a week earlier, a church in Charlotte, North Carolina, had become the thirtieth black church to be burned in the previous eighteen months. The whole black community in America was in an uproar and expected me to do something about it. I endorsed bipartisan legislation to make it easier for federal prosecutors to punish those who burn houses of worship, and pledged federal loan guarantees to support low-interest loans for the rebuilding efforts. The church burnings seemed to feed off one another, much as a rash of synagogue defacements had in 1992. They weren't connected by a conspiracy, but by a contagion of the heart, a hatred of those who are different.

During this time, I also had to acknowledge a problem in my White House operation so severe that I felt it was the first issue of my administration that merited an independent investigation.

In early June, news reports revealed that three years earlier, in 1993, my White House Office of Personnel Security had obtained from the FBI hundreds of FBI file summaries on people who had been cleared for entry into the Bush and Reagan White Houses. The files had been obtained when the office was attempting to replace security files on current White House employees, since those files had been taken away by the departing Bush administration for deposit in the Bush Library. The White House had no business possessing confidential FBI reports on Republicans. I was outraged when I heard about it.

On June 9, Leon Panetta and I apologized for the incident. Within a week, Louis Freeh announced that the FBI had wrongly turned over 408 files to the White House. A few days later, Janet Reno asked Ken Starr to investigate the files case. In 2000, the OIC found that the incident had been simply a mistake. The White House had not engaged in any kind of political espionage—the Secret Service had given the Personnel Security Office an outdated list of White House employees, which included Republicans' names, and this was the list that had been sent to the White House.

Late in June, at the annual Gore family conference in Nashville, I called for an expansion of the family leave law to allow people to take up to twenty-four hours a year, or three more workdays, to attend parent-teacher conferences at their children's school or to take their children, or a spouse, or their parents for routine medical care.

The problem of balancing work and family was weighing heavily on me because of the toll it was taking on the White House. Bill Galston, a brilliant member of the Domestic Policy Council staff whom I had first met through the DLC and who was a continuous source of good ideas, had recently resigned to spend more time with his ten-year-old son: "My boy keeps asking where I am. You can get somebody else to do this job; no one else can do that job. I have to go home."

My deputy chief of staff, Erskine Bowles, who had become a close friend and golfing partner and who was a superb manager and our best liaison to the business community, was going home, too. His wife, Crandall, a Wellesley classmate of Hillary's, ran a big textile company and had to travel a lot. Two of their kids were in college; their youngest was about to start his senior year in high school. Erskine told me he loved his job, "but my boy should not be at home alone in his last year in high school. I don't want him ever to wonder whether he was the most important thing in the world to his parents. I'm going home."

I respected and agreed with the decisions Bill and Erskine

had made, and I was thankful that Hillary and I lived and worked in the White House so we had no long commutes to and from work, and at least one of us was almost always with Chelsea for dinner at night and when she got up in the morning. But the experience of my staff members brought home the fact that all too many Americans, in all kinds of jobs earning widely different incomes, went to work every day worried sick that they were neglecting their kids for their jobs. The United States provided less support for balancing work and family than any other wealthy nation, and I wanted to change that.

Unfortunately, the Republican majority in Congress were opposed to imposing any new requirements on employers. A young boy had recently approached me and offered to tell me a joke; as he said, "Once you become President, it's hard to find a joke you can tell in public." Here it is: "Being President with this Congress is like standing in the middle of a cemetery. There are a lot of people under you, but nobody is listening." He was one smart kid.

At the end of the month, as I was preparing to leave for Lyon, France, for the annual G-7 conference, which would primarily be devoted to terrorism, nineteen air force personnel were killed and almost three hundred Americans and others were injured when terrorists drove a truck containing a powerful bomb to a security barrier just outside Khobar Towers, a military housing complex in Dhahran, Saudi Arabia. When an American patrol approached the truck, two of its occupants fled and the bomb exploded. I sent an FBI team of more than forty investigators and forensic experts to work with Saudi authorities. King Fahd called me to express his condolences and solidarity, and to pledge the commitment of his government to apprehend and punish the men who had killed our airmen. Eventually, Saudi Arabia would execute the people it determined to be responsible for the attack.

The Saudis had allowed us to establish the base after the Gulf War in the hope that having U.S. forces "prepositioned" in the Gulf would deter further aggression by

Saddam Hussein and allow us to respond quickly if deterrence was unsuccessful. It achieved that objective, but the base also made our forces more vulnerable to terrorists in the region. The security provisions at Khobar were plainly inadequate; the truck had been able to get too close to the building because our people and the Saudis had underestimated the ability of terrorists to build a bomb that powerful. I appointed General Wayne Downing, former commander in chief of the U.S. Special Operations Command, head of a commission to recommend what steps we should take to make our troops stationed overseas more secure.

As we prepared for the G-7 summit, I asked my staff to draw up recommended steps that the international community could take to work together more effectively against global terrorism. At Lyon, the leaders agreed to more than forty of them, including speeding up the extradition and prosecution of terrorists, doing more to seize the resources that funded their violence, improving our internal defenses, and limiting terrorists' access to high-tech communications equipment as much as possible.

By 1996, my administration had settled on a strategy for fighting terror that focused on preventing serious incidents, capturing and punishing terrorists through international cooperation, interrupting the flow of money and communications to terrorist organizations, cutting off access to weapons of mass destruction, and isolating and imposing sanctions on nations that support terrorism. As President Reagan's bombing raid on Libya in 1986 and the attack I ordered on Iraq's intelligence headquarters in 1993 demonstrated, American power could deter states that were directly involved in terrorist acts against us; neither nation attempted another one. However, it was more difficult to get at nonstate terrorist organizations; the military and economic pressures that were effective against nations were not as easily applied to them.

The strategy had brought many successes—we had prevented several planned terrorist attacks, including attempts to bomb the Holland and Lincoln tunnels in New York and to blow up several planes flying from the Philippines to the United States, and had brought terrorists back to the United States from all over the world to stand trial. On the other hand, terror is more than a form of international organized crime; because of their stated political objectives, terrorist groups often enjoy both state sponsorship and popular support. Moreover, getting to the bottom of the networks could raise difficult and dangerous questions, as the Khobar Towers investigation did when the possibility of Iran's support for the terrorists was raised. Even if we had a good defense against attacks, would law enforcement be a sufficient offensive strategy against terrorists? If not, would greater reliance on military options work? In the middle of 1996, it was clear that we didn't have all the answers on how to deal with attacks on Americans in this country and overseas, and that the problem would be with us for years to come.

The summer began with good news at home and abroad. Boris Yeltsin had been forced into a runoff on July 3 against the ultra-nationalist Gennady Zyuganov. The first election was close, but Boris won the runoff handily, after a vigorous campaign across all his country's eleven time zones that included American-style campaign events and TV ads. The election was a ratification of Yeltsin's leadership to secure democracy, modernize the economy, and reach out to the West. Russia still had a number of problems, but I believed it was moving in the right direction.

Things were moving in the right direction in America, too, as the unemployment rate dropped to 5.3 percent, with 10 million new jobs, economic growth at 4.2 percent for the quarter, and a deficit that had dropped to less than half what it was when I took office. Wages were also rising. After the Labor Department released the numbers, the stock market fell 115 points, prompting me to tease Bob Rubin again about how much Wall Street hated it when average Americans did well. Actually, it was more complicated than that. The market is about the future; when things are really good, investors tend to think they'll get worse. Soon they changed their minds, and the market resumed its upward movement.

On July 17, TWA Flight 800 exploded off Long Island, killing some 230 people. At the time everyone assumed—wrongly, as it turned out—that this was a terrorist act; there was even speculation that the plane had been downed by a rocket fired from a boat in Long Island Sound. While I cautioned against jumping to conclusions, it was clear that we had to do more to strengthen aviation safety.

Hillary and I went to Jamaica, New York, to meet with the victims' families, and I announced new measures to increase air travel security. We had been working on the problem since 1993, with a proposal to modernize the air traffic control system; add more than 450 safety inspectors and the issuance of uniform safety standards; and test new high-tech explosive detection machines. Now I said we would hand-search more luggage and screen more bags on domestic and international flights, and would require preflight inspections of every plane cargo hold and cabin before every flight. I also asked Al Gore to head a commission to review aviation safety and security and the air traffic control system, and report back in forty-five days.

Just ten days after the crash, we had an undisputed terrorist incident when a pipe bomb exploded at the Olympics in Atlanta, killing two people. Hillary and I had gone to the opening ceremonies, which featured Muhammad Ali lighting the Olympic flame. Hillary and Chelsea loved the Olympics and spent more time attending the events than I did, but I was able to visit with the American team, as well as with athletes from several other nations. Irish, Croatian, and Palestinian athletes thanked me for America's efforts to bring peace to their homelands. North and South Korean Olympians sat at adjoining tables in the dining room and talked to each other. The Olympics symbolized the world at its best, bringing people together across old divisions. The pipe bomb planted by a homegrown terrorist who had still not been apprehended was a reminder of how vulnerable the forces of openness and cooperation were to those who rejected the values and rules required to build an integrated global community.

On August 5, at George Washington University, I gave an extended analysis of how terrorism would affect our future, saying that it had become "an equal-opportunity destroyer, with no respect for borders." I outlined the steps we were taking to combat "the enemy of our generation" and said we would prevail if we maintained our confidence and our leadership as the world's "indispensable force for peace and freedom."

The rest of August was taken up with bill signings, the party conventions, and a positive development in Whitewater World. With the election approaching and the budget fight at least temporarily resolved, members of Congress in both parties were eager to give the American people evidence of bipartisan progress. As a result, they produced a raft of progressive legislation the White House had been fighting for. I signed the Food Quality Protection Act, to increase the safeguarding of vegetables, fruits, and grains from harmful pesticides; the Safe Drinking Water Act, to reduce pollution and provide $10 billion in loans to upgrade municipal water systems in the wake of deaths and illnesses caused by the contamination of drinking water by cryptosporidium; and the bill to increase the minimum wage by 90 cents an hour, give small businesses tax relief for new investments in equipment and for hiring new employees, make it easier for small businesses to offer their employees pension plans with a new 401(k) plan, and provide a new incentive that was very important to Hillary, a $5,000 tax credit for adopting a child, with $6,000 for a child with special needs.

In the last week of the month, I signed the Kennedy-Kassebaum bill, which helped millions of people by allowing them to take their health insurance from job to job while prohibiting insurance companies from denying anyone coverage because of a preexisting health problem. I also announced the Food and Drug Administration's final rule to protect young people from the dangers of tobacco. It required young people to prove their age with an ID card before buying cigarettes and significantly restricted advertising and vending machine placement by tobacco companies. We had made some enemies in the tobacco industry, but I thought the effort would save some lives.

On August 22, I signed a landmark welfare reform bill, which had passed with bipartisan majorities of more than 70 percent in both houses. Unlike the two bills I had vetoed, the new legislation retained the federal guarantee of medical care and food aid, increased federal child-care assistance by 40 percent to $14 billion, contained the measures I wanted for tougher child-support enforcement, and gave states the ability to convert monthly welfare payments into wage subsidies as an incentive for employers to hire welfare recipients.

Most advocates for the poor and for legal immigration, and several people in my cabinet, still opposed the bill and wanted me to veto it because it ended the federal guarantee of a fixed monthly benefit to welfare recipients, had a five-year lifetime limit on welfare benefits, cut overall spending on the food stamp program, and denied food stamps and medical care to low-income legal immigrants. I agreed with the last two objections; the hit on legal immigrants was particularly harsh and, I thought, unjustifiable. Shortly after I signed the bill, two high officials in the Department of Health and Human Services, Mary Jo Bane and Peter Edelman, resigned in protest. When they left, I praised them for their service and for following their convictions.

I decided to sign the legislation because I thought it was the best chance America would have for a long time to change the incentives in the welfare system from dependence to empowerment through work. In order to maximize the chances of success, I asked Eli Segal, who had done such a good job in setting up AmeriCorps, to organize a Welfare to Work Partnership to enlist employers who would commit to hiring welfare recipients. Eventually, twenty thousand companies in the partnership would hire more than one million people off welfare.

At the signing ceremony, several former welfare recipients spoke up for the bill. One of them was Lillie Hardin, the Arkansas woman who had so impressed my fellow governors ten years earlier when she said the best thing about leaving welfare for work was that "when my boy goes to school and they ask him, 'What does your mama do for a living?' he can give an answer." Over the next four years, the results of welfare reform would prove Lillie Hardin right. By the time I left office, the welfare rolls had been reduced from 14.1 million to 5.8 million, a 60 percent decrease; and child poverty was down 25 percent to its lowest point since 1979.

Signing the welfare reform bill was one of the most important decisions of my presidency. I had spent most of my career trying to move people from welfare to work, and ending welfare "as we know it" had been a central promise of my 1992 campaign. Though we had pursued welfare reforms through granting waivers from the existing system to most states, America needed legislation that changed the emphasis of assistance to the poor from dependence on welfare checks to independence through work.

The Republicans held their convention in San Diego in midmonth, nominating Bob Dole and his choice for vice president, former New York congressman, secretary of housing and urban development, and Buffalo Bills star quarterback Jack Kemp. Kemp was an interesting man, a free-market conservative with a genuine commitment to bringing economic opportunity to poor people and an openness to new ideas from all quarters, and I thought he would be an asset to Dole's campaign.

The Republicans didn't make the mistake of opening with harsh right-wing rhetoric as they had done at their convention in 1992. Featuring Colin Powell, Senator Kay Bailey Hutchison, Representative Susan Molinari, and Senator John McCain, they presented a more moderate, positive, and forward-looking image to the American people. Elizabeth Dole gave an impressive and effective nominating speech for her husband, leaving the podium to speak in a conversational way as she walked among the delegates. Dole gave a good speech, too, focusing on his lifetime of duty, his tax cuts, and his advocacy of traditional American values. He derided me for being part of a baby boomer "elite who never grew up, never did anything real, never sacrificed, never suffered, and never learned." He promised to build a bridge back to a better past of "tranquillity, faith, and confidence in action." Dole also took a swipe at Hillary for the theme of her book, that "it takes a village" to raise a child, saying that Republicans thought parents raised children while Democrats thought government should do the job. Dole's attack wasn't too harsh, and in a couple of weeks Hillary and I would have our chances to answer him.

While the Republicans were in San Diego, our family went to Jackson Hole, Wyoming, for the second time. This time I was finishing up a short book, *Between Hope and History*, which highlighted the policies of my first term through stories of individual Americans who had been positively affected by them, and articulated where I wanted to take our country in the next four years.

On August 12, we went back to Yellowstone National Park for the only public business of our vacation, as I signed an agreement that stopped a planned gold mine on property adjacent to the park. The agreement was the welcome result of cooperative efforts by the mining company, citizens' groups, and members of Congress and the White House environmental team, headed by Katie McGinty.

On the eighteenth, Hillary, Chelsea, and I were in New York City for a big party celebrating my fiftieth birthday at Radio City Music Hall. Afterward, I was saddened to learn that the plane carrying the equipment back to Washington from our Wyoming stay had crashed, killing all nine people on board.

The next day we joined Al and Tipper Gore in Tennessee, where we celebrated the birthday Tipper and I shared by helping to rebuild two rural churches, one white and one black, that had been burned in the recent rash of church burnings.

In the last week of the month, the nation's attention turned to the Democratic National Convention in Chicago. By then our campaign, chaired by Peter Knight, was well organized, and it was working closely with the White House through Doug Sosnik and Harold Ickes, who had overseen our convention organization. I was excited about going to Chicago because it was Hillary's hometown, had played a pivotal role in my 1992 victory, and had made good use of many of my most important initiatives in education, economic development, and crime control.

On August 25, in Huntington, West Virginia, Chelsea and I began a four-day train trip to Chicago. Hillary had gone ahead of us to be there when the convention opened. We had leased a wonderful old train we dubbed the "21st Century Express" for the trip through Kentucky, Ohio, Michigan, and Indiana to Chicago. We made fifteen stops along the way and slowed down as we passed through small towns so that I could wave to the people who had gathered by the tracks. I could feel from the excitement of the crowds that the train was connecting with the American people just as the bus tours had in 1992, and I could see from the expressions on people's faces that they felt much better about the condition of the country and about their own lives. When we stopped in Wyandotte, Michigan, for an education event, two children introduced me by reading *The Little Engine That Could*. The book and their enthusiastic reading captured the return of America's innate optimism and self-confidence.

On many stops we picked up friends, supporters, and local officials who wanted to be aboard for the next leg of the trip. I especially enjoyed sharing the leisurely travel with Chelsea, as we stood on the caboose, waved to the crowds, and talked about everything under the sun. Our relationship was as close as ever, but she was changing, growing into a mature young woman with her own opinions and interests. More and more, I found myself amazed at how she saw the world.

Our convention opened on the twenty-sixth, with appearances by Jim and Sarah Brady, who appreciated the support the Democrats had given to the Brady bill, and Christopher Reeve, the actor who, after being paralyzed in a fall from a horse, had inspired the nation with his courageous fight to recover and his advocacy for more research into spinal cord injuries.

On the day of my speech, our campaign was rocked by press reports that Dick Morris had frequently been with a prostitute in his hotel room when he was in Washington working for me. Dick resigned from the campaign, and I put out a statement saying that he was my friend and a superb political strategist who had done "invaluable work" over the past two years. I regretted his departure, but he was obviously under enormous stress and he needed time to work through his problems. I knew Dick was resilient and felt sure he would be back in the political arena before long.

My acceptance speech was easy to give because of the record: the lowest combined rate of unemployment and inflation in twenty-eight years; 10 million new jobs; 10 million people getting the minimum wage increase; 25 million Americans benefiting from the Kennedy-Kassebaum bill; 15 million working Americans with a tax cut; 12 million taking advantage of the family leave law; 10 million students saving money through the Direct Student Loan Program; 40 million workers with more pension security.

I stated that we were going in the right direction and, referring to Bob Dole's speech in San Diego, said, "with all respect, we do not need to build a bridge to the past; we need to build a bridge to the future. . . . Let us resolve to build that bridge to the twenty-first century." The "Bridge to the 21st Century" became the theme of the campaign and the next four years.

As good as the record was, I knew that all elections are about the future, so I outlined my agenda: higher school standards and universal access to college; a balanced budget that protected health care, education, and the environment; targeted tax cuts to support home ownership, long-term care, college education, and child-rearing; more jobs for people on welfare and more investment in poor urban and rural areas; and some new initiatives to fight crime and drugs and clean the environment.

I knew that if the American people saw the election as a choice between building a bridge to the past and building a bridge to the future, we would win. Bob Dole had unintentionally given me the central message of the 1996 campaign. On the day after the convention closed, Al, Tipper, Hillary, and I kicked off my last campaign with a bus tour, beginning in Cape Girardeau, Missouri, with Governor Mel Carnahan, who had been with me since early 1992, going through southern Illinois and western Kentucky, and winding up in Memphis, after several stops in Tennessee, with former governor Ned Ray McWherter, a huge bear of a man who was the only person I ever heard call the vice president "Albert." Ned Ray was worth so many votes that I didn't care what he called Al, or me for that matter.

In August, Kenneth Starr lost his first big case, one that reflected just how desperate he and his staff were to pin something on me. Starr had indicted the two owners of the Perry County Bank, lawyer Herby Branscum Jr. and accountant Rob Hill, on charges arising out of my 1990 gubernatorial campaign.

The indictment stated that Branscum and Hill had taken about $13,000 from their own bank for legal and accounting services they did not perform in order to reimburse themselves for political contributions they had made, and that they had instructed the man who ran the bank for them not to report two cash withdrawals of more than $10,000 each from my campaign account to the Internal Revenue Service as required by federal law.

The indictment also named Bruce Lindsey, who had served as my campaign treasurer, as an "unindicted co-conspirator," alleging that when Bruce withdrew the money to pay for our election day "get out the vote" activities, he had urged the bankers not to file the required report. Starr's people had threatened Bruce with an indictment, but he called their bluff; there was nothing wrong with our contributions or the way they had been spent, and Bruce had no motive for asking the bank not to make the required filing on it: we would be making all the information public in three weeks as required by Arkansas state election law. Since the contributions and their expenditure were legal and our public report was accurate, Starr's people knew Bruce hadn't committed a crime, so they settled for smearing him as an unindicted co-conspirator.

The charges against Branscum and Hill were absurd. First, they wholly owned the bank; if they did not impair the bank's liquidity, they could take money out of it as long as they paid income taxes on it, and there was no suggestion that they had not done so in this case. As to the second charge, the law that requires a bank to report cash deposits or withdrawals of $10,000 or more is a good one; it permits the government to follow large amounts of "dirty money" from criminal enterprises like money laundering or drug dealing. The reports filed with the government are checked every three to six months but are not open to the public. As of 1996, there had been two hundred prosecutions for failure to file the reports required by the act, but only twenty of them were for failures to report withdrawals. All of those involved money that was tainted by an illegal enterprise. Until Starr came along, no one had ever been indicted for a negligent failure to report deposits or withdrawals of legitimate funds.

Our campaign money was undisputably clean money that had been withdrawn at the end of the campaign to pay for our efforts to call voters and offer rides to the polls on election day. We had filed the required public report within three weeks after the election, detailing how much money we had spent and how we had spent it. Branscum, Hill, and Lindsey simply had no motive to hide from the government a legal cash withdrawal that would be a matter of public record in less than a month.

That didn't stop Hickman Ewing, Starr's deputy in Arkansas, who was just as obsessed as Starr with going after us and not nearly as good at disguising it. He threatened to send Neal Ainley, who ran the bank for Branscum and Hill and who had been responsible for filing the reports, to prison unless he testified that Branscum, Hill, and Lindsey had ordered him not to file it, even though Ainley had earlier denied any wrongdoing by them. The poor man was a little fish caught in a powerful net; he changed his story. Initially charged with five felonies, Ainley was now allowed to plead to two misdemeanors.

As in the earlier trial of the McDougals and Tucker, I testified on videotape at the request of the defendants. Though I had not been involved in the withdrawals, I was able to say I had not appointed Branscum and Hill to the two state boards on which they served in return for their contributions to my campaign.

After a vigorous defense, Branscum and Hill were acquitted on the reporting charges, and the jury deadlocked on the question of whether they had falsely reported the purposes for which they had withdrawn funds from their own bank. I was relieved that Herby, Rob, and Bruce Lindsey were cleared, but sickened by the abuse of prosecutorial power, the enormous legal costs my friends had been forced to bear, and the staggering costs to the taxpayers of a prosecution over the $13,000 of reimbursements the defendants got from their own bank and the failure to file federal reports on two legal and publicly reported withdrawals of campaign funds.

There were noneconomic costs as well: FBI agents working for Starr went to Rob Hill's teenage son's school and dragged him out of class for questioning. They could have talked to him after school or during lunch or on the weekend. Instead, they humiliated the young man in hopes of pressuring his father into telling them something that would damage me, whether it was true or not.

After the trial, several jurors burned the independent counsel's office with comments like "It's a waste of money. . . . I would hate to see the government waste more money on Whitewater"; "If they're going to spend my tax dollars, they need stronger evidence"; "If anyone is untouchable it is OIC [Office of Independent Counsel]." One juror who identified himself as an "anti-Clinton" person said, "I would have loved for them to have a little more evidence, but they didn't." Even conservative Republicans who lived in the real world, as opposed to Whitewater World, knew the independent counsel had gone too far.

As bad as Starr's treatment of Branscum and Hill was, it

was a tea party compared with what he was about to do to Susan McDougal. On August 20, Susan was sentenced to two years in prison. Starr's people had offered to keep her out of jail if she gave them information implicating Hillary or me in some illegal activity. On the day she was sentenced, when Susan repeated what she had said from the beginning—that she knew of nothing either of us had done wrong—she was served with a subpoena to appear before the grand jury. She appeared, but refused to answer the prosecutors' questions, fearing that they would charge her with perjury because she wouldn't lie and tell them what they wanted to hear. Judge Susan Webber Wright found her in contempt of court and sent her to jail for an indefinite period until she agreed to cooperate with the special prosecutor. She would remain confined for eighteen months, often under miserable conditions.

September opened with the campaign on a roll. Our convention had been a success, and Dole was tarred by his association with Gingrich and the government shutdown. Even more important, the country was in good shape, and the voters no longer saw issues like crime, welfare, fiscal responsibility, foreign policy, and defense as the exclusive province of the Republican Party. Polls showed that my job and personal approval ratings were around 60 percent, with the same percentage of people saying they felt comfortable with me in the White House.

On the other hand, I expected to be weaker in some parts of America because of my positions on the cultural issues—guns, gays, and abortion—and, at least in North Carolina and Kentucky, on tobacco. Also, it seemed certain that Ross Perot would receive far fewer votes than he had in 1992, making it harder for me to carry a couple of states where he had taken more votes from President Bush than from me. Still, on balance, I was in much better shape this time around. All through September the campaign drew large, enthusiastic crowds, or "October crowds," as I called them, beginning with nearly thirty thousand people at a Labor Day picnic in De Pere, Wisconsin, near Green Bay.

The inauguration and an inaugural ball,
January 20, 1993

Al Gore and I with the cabinet: (standing, from left) Madeleine Albright, Mack McLarty,
Mickey Kantor, Laura Tyson, Leon Panetta, Carol Browner, Lee Brown; (seated, from bottom
left) Lloyd Bentsen, Janet Reno, Mike Espy, Robert Reich, Henry Cisneros, Hazel O'Leary,
Richard Riley, Jesse Brown, Federico Peña, Donna Shalala, Ron Brown, Bruce Babbitt,
Les Aspin, and Warren Christopher

Al and I praying at our weekly lunch

With Mother, Dick Kelley, and Champ, in Hot Springs

Mack McLarty and I attending the Summit of the Americas, in Santiago, Chile

In the residence private study, with Presidents George Bush, Jimmy Carter, and Gerald Ford on the eve of the announcement of the campaign for NAFTA

With the White House residence butlers and staff

With Hillary in
Wyoming

Mother, Roger, and I celebrate our last
Christmas together.

Chelsea in *The Nut-cracker*

Ron Brown and I
playing an impromptu
basketball game in
South Central Los
Angeles

Al and I, on the South
Lawn, announcing the
elimination of forklifts
of government regula-
tions, part of our
Reinventing Govern-
ment initiative

Straightening Prime Minister Yitzhak Rabin's tie. It would be our last time together.

Right: Tony Lake informs me of Rabin's death.

Arriving on Marine One, with Bruce Lindsey and Erskine Bowles

Below: Bosnia briefing in the White House Situation Room

Above, left: With AmeriCorps volunteers at a tornado site in Arkansas

Above, right: Chelsea's graduation from Sidwell Friends

Rahm Emanuel and Leon Panetta brief me in the Oval Office dining room.

Below, left: Riding with Harold Ickes in Montana

With Hillary

Al and I on the edge of the Grand Canyon establishing the Grand Staircase–Escalante National Monument

On the golf course with Frank Raines, Erskine Bowles, Vernon Jordan, and Max Chapman

A strategy meeting in the Yellow Oval Room

With Republican leaders Representative Newt Gingrich and Senator Bob Dole in the Cabinet Room

With Democratic leaders Representative Richard Gephardt and Senator Tom Daschle in the Oval Office

Russian president Boris Yeltsin and I in Hyde Park, New York

With German chancellor Helmut Kohl at Wartburg Castle

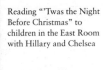

Reading "'Twas the Night Before Christmas" to children in the East Room with Hillary and Chelsea

Chelsea and I at Ron Brown's funeral

Our friends Queen Noor and King Hussein join Hillary and me on the Truman Balcony.

Above: Speaking about America's bridge to the twenty-first century at Arizona State University

Right: Promoting education at an event in California

Celebrating our 1996 victory aboard Air Force One

Signing an executive order with representatives of Native American Tribal Governments

Visiting with the troops in Kuwait

Briefing in Shepherdstown, West Virginia, with my Middle East team: Madeleine Albright, Dennis Ross, Martin Indyk, Rob Malley, Bruce Reidel, and Sandy Berger. Deputy Chief of Staff Maria Echaveste is at far right.

Below: With the economic team in the Oval Office

Playing cards with Bruce Lindsey, Doug Sosnik, and Joe Lockhart on Marine One

My legal team: Cheryl Mills, Bruce Lindsey, David Kendall, Chuck Ruff, and Nicole Seligman

With White House valets Fred Sanchez and Lito Bautista, my doctor Connie Mariano, valet Joe Fama, and Oval Office steward Bayani Nelvis

Oval Office steward Glen Maes shows Al and me the cake he made for my birthday.

Left: Playing with Buddy and my nephews Zachary and Tyler on the South Lawn

Below: Socks briefing the press

South African president Nelson Mandela and I in the cell on Robben Island, where he had spent the first eighteen of his twenty-seven years in captivity

With Japanese prime minister Keizo Obuchi in Tokyo

With Chinese president Jiang Zemin in the Oval Office

The Vallenato Children performing in Cartagena, with Chelsea and the president of Colombia, Andrés Pastrana

The G-8 meeting in Denver: (left to right) Jacques Santer, Tony Blair, Ryutaro Hashimoto, Helmut Kohl, Boris Yeltsin, me, Jacques Chirac, Jean Chrétien, Romano Prodi, and Wim Kok

With the cabinet: (first row) Bruce Babbitt, William Cohen, Madeleine Albright, me, Larry Summers, Janet Reno; (second row) George Tenet, Togo West, Bill Richardson, Andrew Cuomo, Alexis Herman, Dan Glickman, John Podesta, William Daley, Donna Shalala, Rodney Slater, Richard Riley, Carol Browner; (back row) Thurgood Marshall, Jr., Bruce Reed, James Lee Witt, Charlene Barshefsky, Martin Baily, Jack Lew, Barry McCaffrey, Aida Alvarez, Gene Sperling, and Sandy Berger

Above, left: With Tony Blair at Chequers

Above, right: Hillary and I touring a Kosovar refugee camp in Macedonia

Left: Hillary and I with a newborn child named Bill Clinton in Wanyange, Uganda

Below: Addressing a crowd of more than 500,000 in Independence Square, Ghana

Commemorating the thirty-fifth anniversary of the voting rights march in Selma, Alabama, by crossing the Edmund Pettus Bridge with Jesse Jackson, Coretta Scott King, John Lewis, and other veterans of the civil rights movement who had marched arm in arm with Martin Luther King, Jr.

Hillary, Chelsea, and I at an MIA excavation site in Vietnam, with the Evert family

Camp David Middle East peace summit, with Prime Minister Ehud Barak, Chairman Yasser Arafat, and my Arabic translator and Middle East advisor, Gemal Helal

Being showered with rose petals in a traditional ceremony in Naila, India

With Gerry Adams, John Hume, and David Trimble on St. Patrick's Day 2000

Addressing a crowd in Market Square, Dundalk, Ireland

Bringing the Internet into America's classrooms, with Dick Riley

Above: With my presidential aides Doug Band, Kris Engskov, Stephen Goodin, and Andrew Friendly

The special agents in charge, presidential protective division, United States Secret Service, with Nancy Hernreich, director of Oval Office Operations, and my secretary Betty Currie

Below: Celebrating with my staff after my final address to the nation

February 7, 2000: Hillary announces her campaign for the Senate

Chelsea and I wait for Hillary as she casts her first vote as a candidate, Chappaqua, New York.

My last moments in the Oval Office after placing the traditional letter to its next occupant on the *Resolute* desk

Since presidential elections are decided by electoral votes, I wanted to use our momentum to bring a couple of new states into our column and to force Senator Dole to spend time and money in states a Republican could normally take for granted. Dole wanted to do the same thing to me by contesting California, where I was opposing a popular ballot initiative to end affirmative action in college admissions and where he had helped himself by holding the GOP convention in San Diego.

My main target was Florida. If I could win there and hold most of the states I had won in '92, the election was over. I had worked hard in Florida for four years: helping the state recover from Hurricane Andrew; holding the Summit of the Americas there; announcing the relocation of the U.S. military's Southern Command from Panama to Miami; working to restore the Everglades; and even making inroads into the Cuban-American community, which normally had given Republicans more than 80 percent of its votes in presidential elections ever since the Bay of Pigs. I was also blessed with a good organization in Florida and the strong support of Governor Lawton Chiles, who had great rapport with voters in the more conservative areas of central and northern Florida. Those people liked Lawton in part because he hit back when attacked. As he said, "No redneck wants a dog that won't bite." In early September, Lawton went with me to north Florida to campaign and to honor retiring Congressman Pete Peterson, who had spent six and a half years as a prisoner of war in Vietnam and whom I had recently nominated to be our first ambassador there since the end of the war.

I spent most of the rest of the month in states I'd won in '92. On a western swing, I also campaigned in Arizona, a state that hadn't voted for a Democrat for President since 1948, but that I thought I could carry because of its growing Hispanic population and the discomfort of many of the state's moderate and traditional conservative voters with the more extreme politics of the Republican Congress.

On the sixteenth, I received the endorsement of the Fraternal Order of Police. The FOP usually endorsed Republicans for President, but our White House had worked with

them for four years to put more police on the streets, take
guns out of the hands of criminals, and ban cop-killer bullets;
they wanted four more years of that kind of cooperation.

Two days later, I announced one of the most important
environmental accomplishments of my entire eight years in
office, the establishment of the 1.7 million–acre Grand
Staircase–Escalante National Monument in the remote and
beautiful red rock area of southern Utah, which contains
fossils of dinosaurs and the remains of the ancient Anasazi
Indian civilization. I had the authority to do so under the
Antiquities Act of 1906, which allows the President to protect federal lands of extraordinary cultural, historic, and scientific value. I made the announcement with Al Gore on the
edge of the Grand Canyon, which Theodore Roosevelt had
first protected under the Antiquities Act. My action was
necessary to stop a large coal mine that would have fundamentally changed the character of the area. Most of the
Utah officials and many who wanted the mining operation's
economic boost were against it, but the land was priceless,
and I thought the monument designation would bring in
tourism income that over time would more than offset the
loss of the mine.

Apart from the size and exuberance of the crowds, the
September events offered anecdotal evidence that things
were going our way. After a rally in Longview, Texas, as I
was shaking hands in the crowd, I met a single mother of two
who had left welfare to serve in AmeriCorps and was using
its scholarship money to go to Kilgore Junior College;
another woman who had used the family leave law when her
husband became ill with cancer; and a Vietnam veteran who
was grateful for the health and disability benefits for children
born with spina bifida as a result of their fathers' exposure to
Agent Orange during the war. He had his twelve-year-old
daughter with him. The child had spina bifida and had
already endured a dozen operations in her short life.

The rest of the world didn't stop for our campaign. In the
first week of September, Saddam Hussein was making trouble again, assaulting and occupying the town of Irbil in the

Kurdish area of northern Iraq, in violation of restrictions imposed on him at the end of the Gulf War. Two Kurdish factions had been vying for control of the area; after one of them decided to support Saddam, he had attacked the other. I ordered bomb and missile attacks on the Iraqi forces and they withdrew.

On the twenty-fourth, I went to New York for the opening session of the United Nations, where I was the first of many world leaders to sign the Comprehensive Test Ban Treaty, using the pen with which President Kennedy had signed the Limited Test Ban Treaty thirty-three years earlier. In my remarks, I outlined a broader agenda to reduce the threat of weapons of mass destruction, urging the UN members to bring the Chemical Weapons Convention into force; strengthen the compliance provisions of the Biological Weapons Convention; freeze the production of fissile materials for use in nuclear weapons; and ban the use, production, stockpiling, and transfer of anti-personnel land mines.

While the UN was discussing nonproliferation, the Middle East exploded again. The Israelis had opened a tunnel that ran under the Temple Mount in Jerusalem's Old City. The ruins of the Temples of Solomon and Herod were under the mount, atop which stood the Dome of the Rock and the Al-Aqsa Mosque, two of the holiest sites to Muslims. Since the Israelis took East Jerusalem in the 1967 war, the Temple Mount, called Haram al-Sharif by the Arabs, had been under the control of Muslim officials; when the tunnel was opened, the Palestinians saw it as a threat to their religious and political interests, and riots and shooting broke out. After three days, more than sixty people had died, with many more wounded. I called on both sides to end the violence and get back to implementing the peace agreement, while Warren Christopher burned up the phone lines with Prime Minister Netanyahu and Chairman Arafat to stop the bloodshed. On Christopher's advice, I invited Netanyahu and Arafat to the White House to talk things over.

I ended the month by signing a health-care appropriations bill that ended so-called drive-by deliveries, by guaranteeing a minimum of forty-eight hours of coverage to mothers and newborns; provided medical assistance to children of Vietnam veterans who were born with spina bifida, as I mentioned earlier; and required the same annual and lifetime coverage limits in health insurance policies for mental and physical illness. The breakthrough in mental-health care was a tribute not only to the work of mental-health advocacy groups but also to the personal efforts of Senator Pete Domenici of New Mexico, Senator Paul Wellstone of Minnesota, and Tipper Gore, whom I had named my official advisor on mental-health policy.

I spent the first two days of October with Netanyahu, Arafat, and King Hussein, who had agreed to join us to try to get the peace process back on track. At the end of our talks, Arafat and Netanyahu asked me to field all the press questions. I said that while we had not yet resolved the tunnel issue, both sides had agreed to begin immediate talks in the region with a view toward ending the violence and returning to the peace process. In our meeting, Netanyahu had reaffirmed his commitment to implement the agreements made before he took office, including the withdrawal of Israeli troops from Hebron. Not long afterward, the tunnel was sealed again, consistent with the commitment both parties had made to do nothing to change the status quo in Jerusalem until it was negotiated.

On the third, I was back on the campaign trail again, stopping for a rally in Buffalo, New York, a city that had always been good to me, on the way to Chautauqua, to prepare for my first presidential debate with Bob Dole in Hartford, Connecticut, on October 6. Our whole team was there, including my media advisor, Michael Sheehan. George Mitchell came in to play Bob Dole in the mock debates. He cleaned my clock at first, but I got better with practice. In between sessions, Erskine Bowles and I got in a round of golf. My golf game was getting better. In June, I had finally scored below 80 for the first time, but I still couldn't beat Erskine when his game was on.

The debate itself turned out to be civilized, and educational for people who were interested in our different philosophies of government and positions on the issues.

There were a few fireworks when Dole hit me for scaring seniors with my ads criticizing the Medicare cuts in the Republican budget I had vetoed, and he repeated his claim from his convention speech that I had filled the administration with young elitists who "never grew up, never did anything real, never sacrificed, never suffered, and never learned" and who wanted "to fund with your earnings their dubious and self-serving schemes." I shot back that one of the young "elitists" who worked for me in the White House had grown up in a house trailer, and as for the charge that I was too liberal, "that's what their party always drags out when they get in a tight race. It's sort of their golden oldie . . . I just don't think that dog will hunt anymore."

The second debate was scheduled ten days later in San Diego. In the interim, Hillary, Al, Tipper, and I visited the massive AIDS quilt that covered the Mall in Washington, with separate squares in honor of people who had died; two of those commemorated were friends of Hillary's and mine. I was gratified that the death rate from AIDS was coming down, and I was determined to keep pushing for more research to develop lifesaving medicines.

Mickey Kantor had negotiated a town hall format for the San Diego debate. On the sixteenth, citizens at the University of San Diego asked good questions, and Dole and I answered them without hitting each other until the end. In his closing statement, Dole appealed to his base, reminding people that I opposed term limits as well as constitutional amendments to balance the budget and to protect the American flag, and forbid restrictions on voluntary school prayer. I closed with a summary of my proposals for the next four years. At least people knew what the choice was.

With two weeks to go until the election, the polls showed me with a twenty-point lead, and 55 percent of the vote. I wish the survey hadn't been released; it took some of the life out of our campaign when our supporters thought the election was over. I kept working hard, concentrating on our pickup targets, Arizona and Florida, and the states we'd won before, including three of those I was most worried about, Nevada, Colorado, and Georgia. On October 25, we had a great rally in Atlanta, where my longtime friend Max Cleland was in a tight race for the U.S. Senate. Sam Nunn gave a particularly effective argument for my reelection, and I left the state thinking we might have a chance.

On November 1, I headed into the homestretch of the campaign with a morning rally at Santa Barbara City College. On a warm, sunny day, a large crowd gathered on the campus hillside overlooking the Pacific Ocean. Santa Barbara was a good place to end the California campaign, a once solidly Republican area that had been trending our way.

From Santa Barbara, I flew on to Las Cruces, New Mexico, then to El Paso and the biggest crowd of the campaign, as more than forty thousand people came out to the airport to show their support, and finally to San Antonio and the traditional rally at the Alamo. I knew we couldn't win Texas, but I wanted to honor the loyalty of the state's Democrats, especially the Hispanics who had stuck with me.

As we headed into the last three days of the campaign, I had a choice to make. Senate candidates from several relatively small states were asking me to campaign for them. Mark Penn said that if I spent the last days of the campaign doing that, instead of going to the larger states, I might not get a majority of the vote, for several reasons. First, our campaign's momentum had been slowed in the last two weeks by allegations that the DNC had received several hundred thousand dollars in illegal campaign contributions from Asians, including people I had known when I was governor. When I heard about it, I was angry; my finance chair, Terry McAuliffe, had made sure the contributions to our campaign were reviewed scrupulously, and the DNC was also supposed to have a vetting operation to reject questionable contributions. There were clearly problems with the DNC clearance procedures. All I could say was that any unlawful contributions should be returned immediately. Regardless, the controversy seemed certain to hurt us on election day. Second, Ralph Nader was running on the Green Party ticket and would take some votes away from me on the left. Third, Ross Perot, who had entered the campaign in October, too late to get into the debates, wasn't doing nearly as well as he had in 1992, but he was ending this campaign as he had the previous one, with vicious attacks on me. He said that I would be "totally occupied for the next two years in staying out of jail," and called me a "draft dodger" who was tainted by "ethical lapses, corrupt campaign financing, and a lax attitude toward drug use." Finally, voter turnout was likely to be well below that of 1992, because the voters had been told for several weeks that the campaign was over.

Mark Penn advised me that if I wanted to win a majority of the votes, I needed to fly into the large media markets in the big states and ask people to go to the polls. Otherwise, he said, with the outcome not in doubt, lower-income Democrats were far less likely than more affluent or ideologically driven Republicans to vote. I was already scheduled to be in Florida and New Jersey, and on Mark's advice we added a stop in Cleveland. Beyond that, I scheduled appearances in the Senate race states: Louisiana, Massachusetts, Maine, New Hampshire, Kentucky, Iowa, and South Dakota. In the presidential race, only Kentucky was in doubt; I was well ahead in all the others except South Dakota, where I expected the Republicans to come home to Dole at the end. I decided to go to these states because I thought it was worth two or three points off my vote total to elect more Democrats to the Senate, and the candidates in six of the seven states had helped me in '92 or in the Congress.

On Sunday, November 3, after attending services at St. Paul's AME Church in Tampa, I flew to New Hampshire to support our Senate candidate, Dick Swett; to Cleveland, where Mayor Mike White and Senator John Glenn gave me a last-minute boost; and to Lexington, Kentucky, for a rally at the state university with Senator Wendell Ford, Governor Paul Patton, and our Senate candidate, Steve Beshear. I knew it was going to be tough to hold Kentucky because of the tobacco issue, and I was heartened by the presence on the stage of the University of Kentucky basketball coach, Rick Pitino. In a state where everyone loved the basketball team and nearly half of them disliked me, Pitino's presence was helpful and a gutsy move on his part.

By the time I got to Cedar Rapids, Iowa, it was 8 p.m. I really wanted to be there for Tom Harkin, who was in a tight race for reelection. Tom had strongly supported me in the Senate, and after the '92 primary he and his wife, Ruth, a lawyer who was serving with the administration, had become close friends of mine.

The last stop of the night was Sioux Falls, South Dakota, where Democratic congressman Tim Johnson had a real chance to unseat incumbent Republican Larry Pressler. Both Johnson and his chief supporter, Senator Tom Daschle, had been very good to me. As Senate minority leader, Daschle had been invaluable to the White House during the budget fights and the shutdown; when he asked me to come to South Dakota, I couldn't say no.

It was nearly midnight when I got up in the Sioux Falls Arena and Convention Center to speak "at the last rally of the last campaign I will ever run." Because it was my final speech, I gave them the whole load on the record, the budget fight, and what I wanted to do for the next four years. Since I was in a rural state like Arkansas, I told them a joke. I said the Republicans' budget reminded me of the story of a politician who wanted to ask a farmer to vote for him but was reluctant to come into his yard because a barking dog was there. The politician asked the farmer, "Does your dog bite?" "No," the farmer replied. When the politician walked through the yard toward the farmer, the dog bit him. "I thought you said your dog didn't bite!" he shouted. The farmer replied, "Son, that ain't my dog." The budget was their dog.

The election went as Mark Penn predicted: there was a record low turnout, and I won 49 to 41 percent. The electoral vote was 379 to 159, as I lost three states I had carried in 1992, Montana, Colorado, and Georgia, and won two new ones, Arizona and Florida, for a net gain of nine electoral votes.

Underneath the aggregate numbers, subtle differences in the state totals between 1992 and 1996 revealed the extent to which cultural factors influenced the election in some states, while more traditional economic and social matters dominated in others. All competitive elections are determined by such shifts, and in 1996 they told me a lot about what mattered to different groups of Americans. For example, in Pennsylvania, a state with many NRA members and pro-life voters, my winning percentage was the same as it had been in 1992, thanks to a bigger margin in Philadelphia and a strong vote in Pittsburgh, while my vote went down in the rest of the state because of guns and my veto of the partial-birth abortion bill. In Missouri, the same factors cut my victory margin almost in half, from 10 to 6 percent. I still got a majority in Arkansas, but my victory margin was slightly smaller than in 1992; in Tennessee, the margin was cut from 4.5 to 2.5 percent.

In Kentucky, tobacco and guns cut our margin from 3 to 1 percent. For the same reasons, though I was ahead in North Carolina all the way to the end, I lost by 3 percent. In Colorado, I went from a 4 percent victory in 1992 to a 1.5 percent loss because the '92 Perot voters in the West were more likely to vote Republican in '96 and because the Republicans had gained 100,000 registered voters on the Democrats since 1992, partly as a result of the large number of Christian Right organizations that had located their headquarters in the state. In Montana, I lost this time around largely because, as in Colorado, the lower vote for Perot meant more votes for Senator Dole than for me.

In Georgia, the last poll had me ahead by 4 percent; I lost by 1 percent. The Christian Coalition deserved a lot of credit for that; in 1992, they had cut my margin from 6 percent to under 1 percent with heavy distribution of their "voting guides" in conservative churches the Sunday before the election. Democrats had worked black churches like that for years, but the Christian Coalition, at least in Georgia, was particularly effective at it, changing the outcome by 5 percent in both 1992 and 1996. I was disappointed to lose Georgia, but glad that Max Cleland survived by getting a few more white votes than I did. The South was tough because of the cultural issues; the only southern state to give me a substantially larger victory margin in 1996 was Louisiana, which went from 4.5 to 12 percent.

By contrast, my winning percentage increased a good deal in less culturally conservative or more economically sensitive states. My margin over the Republicans was up 10 percent or more in 1996 over 1992 in Connecticut, Hawaii, Maine, Massachusetts, New Jersey, New York, and Rhode Island. We held on to our big '92 margins in Illinois, Minnesota, Maryland, and California, and substantially increased the edge in Michigan and Ohio. Despite the gun issue, I also gained 10 percent over my '92 margin in New Hampshire. And I held on for a 1 percent victory in Nevada, largely because of my opposition to dumping America's nuclear waste there without scientific evidence that it was safe to do so, and the constant publicity my position received thanks to my friend and Georgetown classmate Brian Greenspun, the president and editor of the *Las Vegas Sun*, who felt passionately about the issue.

On balance, I was happy with the results. I had won more electoral votes than in 1992, and four of the seven Senate candidates I had campaigned for won: Tom Harkin, Tim Johnson, John Kerry, and, in Louisiana, Mary Landrieu. But the fact that my share of the vote was considerably lower than my job rating, my personal approval rating, the percentage of people who said they felt comfortable with my presidency, was a sober reminder of the power of cultural issues like guns, gays, and abortion, especially among white married couples in the South, the inter-mountain West, and the rural Midwest, and among white men all across the country. All I could do was to keep searching for common ground, keep trying to temper the bitter partisanship in Washington, and keep doing my best as President.

The atmosphere at the victory rally at the Old State House in Little Rock was quite different this time around. The crowd was still large, but the celebration was marked not so much by shouting exuberance as by a genuine happiness that our nation was in better shape and that the American people had approved of the job I was doing.

Because the election had not been in doubt for several weeks, it was easy to miss its significance. After the 1994 elections, I had been ridiculed as an irrelevant figure, destined for defeat in 1996. In the early stages of the budget fight, with the government shutdown looming, it had been far from clear that I would prevail or that the American people would support my stance against the Republicans. Now I was the first Democratic President to be elected to a second term since FDR in 1936.

EIGHTEEN

ON THE DAY after the election, I was back at the White House for a celebration on the South Lawn with my staff, cabinet, other appointees, campaign workers, and Democratic Party officials. In my remarks, I mentioned that the night before, as I waited for the election results, I had held a reunion with people who had worked for me in Arkansas when I was attorney general and governor, and that "I told them something I want to tell you—that is, I have always been a very hardworking, kind of hard-driving person. I'm always focused on the matter before me. Sometimes I don't say 'Thank you' enough. And I've always been kind of hard on myself, and sometimes I think, just by omission, I'm too hard on the people who work here."

Our team had accomplished a lot in the last four years under extreme duress. This was the result of my own early mistakes, the first two years of intensely negative press coverage, the loss of Congress in '94, the financial and emotional toll of Whitewater, too much personal tragedy, and the constant demands inherent in trying to turn the country around. I had done my best to keep my own and everybody else's spirits up, and to keep us all from being too distracted by the tragedies, the trash, and the mishaps. Now that the American people had given us another term, I was hoping that in the next four years we would be freer to do the public's business without the turmoil and strife of the first term.

I had been inspired by a statement made in late October by the archbishop of Chicago, Joseph Cardinal Bernardin, a tireless advocate for social justice whom Hillary and I knew and admired very much. Bernardin was desperately ill and didn't have long to live when he said, "A dying person does not have time for the peripheral or the accidental. . . . It is wrong to waste the precious gift of time given to us on acrimony and division."

In the week after the election, several people central to the administration announced their intention to leave by the end of the year, including Leon Panetta and Warren Christopher. Chris had lived on an airplane for four years, and Leon had seen us through the budget battles, not to mention staying up on election night playing hearts with me. Both of them wanted to go home to California and to a more normal life. They had served me and the nation well, and I would miss them. On November 8, I announced that Erskine Bowles would become the new chief of staff. His youngest child was off to college now, and Erskine was free to serve again, though it would cost him an arm and a leg to do so, as he once again gave up his lucrative business ventures.

Thank goodness, Nancy Hernreich and Betty Currie were staying. By this time, Betty knew most of my friends around the country, could handle a lot of the phone traffic, and was a wonderful help to me in the office. Nancy understood the dynamics of our office and my need for both involvement in and distance from the details of the day-to-day work. She did everything she could to make it easier for me to do my job, and kept the Oval Office operations in great shape. My then presidential aide, Stephen Goodin, was leaving, but we had lined up a good replacement: Kris Engskov, who had been at the White House from the start and whom I first met in north Arkansas way back in 1974 during my first campaign. Since the President's aide sat just outside the Oval Office door, was with me all of the time, and was always by my side, it was good to have someone I'd known so long and who liked so much doing the job. I was also glad to have Janis Kearny, the White House diarist. Janis had been the editor of the *Arkansas State Press*, Little Rock's black newspaper, and she was keeping meticulous records of all our meetings. I don't know what I would have done without my Oval Office team.

A week later, after I announced an eighteen-month extension of our mission in Bosnia, Hillary and I were on our way to Australia, the Philippines, and Thailand for a combination of work and a vacation that we needed. We began with three days of pure fun in Hawaii, then flew on to

Sydney, Australia. After a meeting with Prime Minister John Howard, a speech to the Australian parliament in Canberra, and a day in Sydney, including an unforgettable game with one of the greatest golfers of our time, Greg Norman, we flew north to Port Douglas, a coastal resort on the Coral Sea near the Great Barrier Reef. While there, we walked through the Daintree Rainforest with an aboriginal guide, toured a wildlife preserve where I cuddled a koala named Chelsea, and snorkeled around the magnificent reef. Like coral reefs the world over, it was threatened by ocean pollution, global warming, and physical abuse. Just before we went out to see it, I announced America's support for the International Coral Reef Initiative, which was designed to prevent further destruction of reefs everywhere.

We flew from Australia to the Philippines for the fourth Asian Pacific leaders' meeting, hosted by President Fidel Ramos. The principal result of the conference was an agreement I had worked for that eliminated all tariffs on an array of computers, semiconductors, and telecommunications technology by 2000, a move that would result in more exports and more high-wage jobs for America.

We visited Thailand to honor the king's fiftieth year on the throne of one of America's oldest allies in Southeast Asia: the United States had signed a treaty of amity and commerce with the king of Siam in 1833. King Bhumibol Adulyadej was an accomplished pianist and a big jazz fan. I presented him with a golden anniversary gift any jazz aficionado would appreciate, a large portfolio of photographs of jazz musicians, autographed by the superb jazz photographer Herman Leonard.

We got home in time for our traditional Thanksgiving at Camp David. This year our group included our two delightful young nephews, Roger's son, Tyler, and Tony's son, Zach. Watching them play together made the spirit of the season come alive.

In December, I had to reconstitute a large part of my administration. Bill Perry, John Deutch, Mickey Kantor, Bob Reich, Hazel O'Leary, Laura Tyson, and Henry Cisneros were all leaving. We were losing valuable people in the White House, too. Harold Ickes was returning to his law practice and consulting business, and Deputy Chief of Staff Evelyn Lieberman was going to the State Department to head the Voice of America.

Early in the month I announced my new national security team: Madeleine Albright as secretary of state; Bill Cohen, former Republican senator from Maine, as secretary of defense; Tony Lake as CIA director; Bill Richardson as UN ambassador; and Sandy Berger as national security advisor. Albright had done an outstanding job at the United Nations and understood the challenges we faced, especially in the Balkans and the Middle East. I thought she had earned the chance to be the first female secretary of state. Bill Richardson had proved himself to be a skilled diplomat by his efforts in North Korea and Iraq, and I was pleased when he agreed to become America's first Hispanic ambassador to the United Nations.

Bill Cohen was an articulate, youthful-looking politician who had been an innovative thinker on defense issues for years. He had helped to craft the START I treaty and had played a key role in the legislation that reorganized and strengthened the military command structure in the 1980s. I wanted a Republican in the cabinet, liked and respected Cohen, and thought he could fill Bill Perry's very big shoes. When I pledged to him that I would never politicize defense decisions, he accepted the job. I hated to lose John Deutch at the CIA. He had done a fine job as deputy secretary of defense, then had stepped into the tough CIA job after Jim Woolsey's brief tenure. Tony Lake's work at the National Security Council had given him a unique understanding of the strengths and weaknesses of our intelligence operations, which were especially critical now with the threat of terrorism on the rise.

I didn't consider anyone other than Sandy Berger for the job of national security advisor. We had been friends for more than twenty years. He felt comfortable bringing me bad news and disagreeing with me at meetings, and he had done a superb job on a whole range of issues in the first term. Sandy's analytical powers were considerable. He thought through problems to the end, seeing potential pitfalls that others missed, without being paralyzed by them. He understood my strengths and weaknesses and how to make the most of the former and minimize the latter. He also never allowed his ego to get in the way of good decision making.

George Stephanopoulos was leaving, too. He had told me not long before the election that he was burned out and had to go. Until I read his memoir, I had no idea how difficult the pressure-packed years had been for him, or how hard he had been on himself, and me. George was going on to a career in teaching and television, where I hoped he would be happier.

Within two weeks I had filled the remaining vacancies in the cabinet. I named Bill Daley of Chicago to be secretary of commerce after Mickey Kantor, to my regret, told me he wanted to return to private life. Daley was a talented man who had led our campaign for NAFTA. Charlene Barshefsky had been acting trade representative in the eight months since Mickey Kantor had gone to Commerce. She was doing a terrific job, and it was time to take the word "acting" out of her title.

I also appointed Alexis Herman to succeed Bob Reich at the Labor Department; Assistant HUD Secretary Andrew Cuomo to follow Henry Cisneros at HUD; Federico Peña to replace Hazel O'Leary at Energy; Rodney Slater, the federal highway administrator, to succeed Peña as secretary of transportation; Aida Alvarez to become head of the Small Business Administration; Gene Sperling to head the National Economic Council on the departure of Laura Tyson; Dr. Janet Yellen, who had taught Larry Summers at Harvard, to be chair of the Council of Economic Advisers; Bruce Reed to be my domestic policy advisor, replacing Carol Rasco, who was going to the Department of Education to run our America Reads program; and Sylvia Matthews, a brilliant young woman who worked for Bob Rubin, to replace Harold Ickes as deputy chief of staff.

Bob Reich had done a good job at the Department of

Labor and as a member of the economic team, but it was becoming difficult for him; he disagreed with my economic and budget policies, believing I had put too much emphasis on deficit reduction and invested too little in education, training, and new technologies. Bob also wanted to go home to Massachusetts to his wife, Clare, and their sons.

I was heartsick about losing Henry Cisneros. We had been friends since before I ran for President, and he had done a brilliant job at HUD. For more than a year, Henry had been subject to an investigation by an independent counsel for making incorrect statements about his personal expenses in his FBI vetting interview for the HUD job. The law made it a crime for a nominee to make a "material" misstatement, one that would affect the confirmation process. Senator Al D'Amato, whose committee had recommended Cisneros's confirmation, wrote a letter saying that Henry's misstatement of the details of his expenses would not have affected his vote or that of any other senator on the committee. Prosecutors from the Justice Department's public integrity office argued against a special prosecutor.

Unfortunately, Janet Reno referred the Cisneros case to Judge Sentelle's panel anyway. True to form, they saddled him with a Republican special prosecutor: David Barrett, an active partisan who, though accused of no wrongdoing, reportedly had close ties with officials who were convicted in the HUD scandals of the Reagan administration. No one had accused Henry of any impropriety in his job, but he had been plunged into Whitewater World anyway. Henry's legal bills had left him deeply in debt and he had two kids in college. He had to earn more money to support his family and pay his lawyers. I was just thankful he had stayed for the full four years.

Though I had made a lot of changes, I thought we could maintain the spirit of camaraderie and teamwork that had marked the first term. Most of the new appointees were transferring from other positions in the administration, and many of my cabinet members were staying put.

There were several interesting developments in foreign policy in December. On the thirteenth, the UN Security Council, with the strong support of the United States, selected a new secretary-general, Kofi Annan of Ghana. Annan was the first person from sub-Saharan Africa to hold the post. As the UN undersecretary for peacekeeping during the previous four years, he had supported our efforts in Bosnia and Haiti. Madeleine Albright thought he was an exceptional leader and had urged me to support him, as had Warren Christopher, Tony Lake, and Dick Holbrooke. Kofi was an intelligent, impressive man with a quiet but commanding presence. He had given most of his professional life in service to the United Nations, but he was not blind to its shortcomings, nor wedded to its bad habits. Instead, he was committed to making the UN's operations more efficient and more accountable. That was important on the merits and vital to my ability to persuade the congressional Republicans to pay our UN dues. We were $1.5 billion in arrears, and since 1995, when the Republicans took over, the Congress had refused to pay until the UN reformed itself. I thought the refusal to pay our back dues was irresponsible and damaging to both the UN and the United States, but I agreed that reform was imperative.

In the Middle East, Prime Minister Netanyahu and Chairman Arafat were trying to resolve their differences, with Netanyahu going to Gaza for three hours of talks on Christmas Eve day. As the year ended, my envoy, Dennis Ross, was shuttling back and forth between them, trying to close a deal on the turnover of Hebron to the Palestinians. It wasn't done yet, but I began 1997 with more hope for the peace process than I'd had in months.

After spending the first days of the New Year on St. Thomas in the U.S. Virgin Islands, a part of our nation Presidents rarely visit, my family went home to get ready for the inauguration and my fifth year as President. In many ways, it would be the most normal year of my presidency so far. For most of the year, Whitewater World was just a low-grade fever that spiked up from time to time with the campaign finance investigations, and I was free to do my job.

In the run-up to the inauguration, we held a series of events to emphasize that things were going in the right direction, highlighting 11.2 million new jobs in the previous four years, the largest decline in the crime rate in twenty-five years, and a 40 percent drop in the student-loan default rate.

I corrected an old injustice by giving the Congressional Medal of Honor to seven African-American veterans of World War II. Amazingly, no Medals of Honor had ever been awarded to blacks who served in that war. The selections were made after an exhaustive study of battle records. Six of the medals were awarded posthumously, but one of the recipients, seventy-seven-year-old Vernon Baker, was at the White House for the ceremony. He was an impressive man of quiet dignity and clear intelligence: as a young lieutenant in Italy more than fifty years earlier, he had single-handedly wiped out three enemy machine-gun units, an observer post, and a dugout. When asked how he had dealt with discrimination and prejudice after having given so much to his country, Baker said he had lived his life by a simple creed: "Give respect before you expect it, treat people the way you want to be treated, remember the mission, set the example, keep going." It sounded good to me.

A day after the Medal of Honor ceremony, Prime Minister Netanyahu and Chairman Arafat called me to say they had finally reached an agreement on the Israeli deployment in Hebron, bringing to a successful conclusion the talks we had launched in September. The Hebron deal was a relatively small part of the peace process, but it was the first time Netanyahu and Arafat had accomplished something together. If it had not been achieved, the entire peace process would have been in grave peril. Dennis Ross had been working with them virtually around the clock for a couple of weeks, and both King Hussein and Warren Christopher had pressed the parties to agree in the closing days of the negotiations. President Mubarak weighed in, too, when I called him for help at one o'clock in the morning in Cairo at the end of Ramadan. The Middle East was like that; it often took all hands on board to get things done.

Three days before the inauguration I awarded the Presidential Medal of Freedom to Bob Dole, noting that from his service in World War II, in which he was badly wounded coming to the aid of a fallen comrade, through all the ups and downs of his political career, Dole had "turned adversity to advantage and pain to public service, embodying the motto of the state he loved and went on to serve so well: *Ad astra per aspera,* to the stars through difficulties." Though we had been opponents and disagreed on many issues, I liked Dole. He could be mean and tough in a fight, but he lacked the fanaticism and hunger for personal destruction that characterized so many of the hard-right Republicans who now dominated his party in Washington.

I had had a fascinating visit with Dole a month earlier. He came to see me with a little toy for our cat, Socks, which he said was from his dog. We discussed the election, foreign policy, and the budget negotiations. The press was still buzzing about campaign finance abuses. Besides the DNC, the Republican National Committee and the Dole campaign had committed some violations. I had been criticized for inviting supporters to spend the night at the White House and for hosting morning coffees with administration members, supporters, contributors, and others who had no political ties to us.

I asked Dole, based on his years of experience, whether politics and politicians in Washington were more or less honest than they had been thirty years earlier. "Oh, it's not close," he said. "Much more honest today." Then I asked, "Would you agree that people think things are less honest?" "Sure," he said, "but they're wrong about it."

I was strongly supporting the new campaign finance reform bill sponsored by Senator John McCain and Senator Russ Feingold, but I doubted that its passage would increase public confidence in the integrity of politicians. Fundamentally, the press objected to the influence of money on campaigns, though most of the money was spent on media advertising. Unless we were to legislate free or reduced-cost airtime, which the media generally opposed, or to adopt public financing of campaigns, an option with little public or congressional support, the media would continue to be the largest consumer of campaign dollars, even as they pilloried politicians for raising the funds to pay them.

In my inaugural address, I painted the most vivid picture I could of what America might be in the twenty-first century, and said that the American people had not "returned to office a President of one party and a Congress of another . . . to advance the politics of petty bickering and extreme partisanship they plainly deplored," but to work together on "America's mission."

The inaugural ceremonies, like our November victory celebration, were more serene, even relaxed, this time around, though the morning church service was enlivened by the fiery sermons of the Reverends Jesse Jackson and Tony Campolo, an Italian evangelical from Philadelphia who was perhaps the only white preacher in America who could keep up with Jesse. The atmosphere at the congressional luncheon was friendly, as I noted that the new Senate majority leader, Trent Lott of Mississippi, and I shared a profound debt to Thomas Jefferson: if he hadn't decided to buy the vast Louisiana Territory from France, neither of us would have been there. Ninety-four-year-old Senator Strom Thurmond was seated next to Chelsea and told her, "If I were seventy years younger, I'd court you!" No wonder he had lived so long. Hillary and I attended all fourteen inaugural balls; at one of them I got to dance with my beautiful daughter, now a senior in high school. She wouldn't be home much longer, and I savored the moment.

On the day after the inauguration, as a result of an investigation going back several years, the House of Representatives voted to reprimand Speaker Gingrich and fine him $300,000 for several violations of House ethics rules arising out of the use of tax-exempt funds for political purposes that had been given by his supporters to allegedly charitable organizations, and for several untruthful responses to congressional investigators about his activities. The counsel for the House Ethics Committee said that Gingrich and his political supporters had violated the tax laws and that there was evidence the Speaker had intentionally misled the committee about it.

In the late 1980s, Gingrich had led the charge to remove Jim Wright as Speaker of the House because his supporters had bought, in bulk, copies of a privately published book of Wright's speeches, in an alleged attempt to get around House rules prohibiting members from accepting speaking fees. Though the charges against Gingrich were much more serious, the Republican whip, Tom DeLay, complained that the fine and reprimand were out of proportion to the offense and an abuse of the ethics process. When I was asked about the affair, I could have urged the Justice Department or the U.S. attorney to investigate the charges of tax evasion and false statements to Congress; instead, I said the House should handle it "and then we should get back to the people's business." Two years later, when the shoe was on the other foot, Gingrich and DeLay would not be so charitable.

Shortly before the inauguration, in preparation for the second term and the State of the Union, I had gathered about eighty members of the White House staff and the departments for an all-day meeting at Blair House to focus on two things: the meaning of what we had done in the first four years and what we were going to do for the next four.

I believed the first term produced six important accomplishments: (1) restoring economic growth by replacing supply-side economics with our more disciplined "invest and grow" policy; (2) resolving the debate over the role of government in our lives by demonstrating that it is neither the enemy nor the solution, but the instrument to give our people the tools and conditions to make the most of their own lives; (3) reaffirming the primacy of community as the operative political model for America, and rejecting divisions by race, religion, gender, sexual orientation, or political philosophy; (4) replacing rhetoric with reality in our social policy, actually proving government action could make a difference in areas like welfare and crime if it reflected common sense and creative thinking, rather than just tough talk and hot rhetoric; (5) reestablishing the family as the primary unit of society, one that government could strengthen with policies like the family leave law, the Earned Income Tax Credit, the minimum wage increase, the V-chip, the anti–teen smoking initiative, efforts to increase adoption, and new reforms in health and education; and (6) reasserting America's leadership in the post–Cold War world as a force for democracy, shared prosperity, and peace, and against the new security threats of terror, weapons of mass destruction, organized crime, narco-trafficking, and racial and religious conflicts.

These accomplishments gave us a foundation from which we could launch America into the new century. Because the Republicans were in control of Congress and because it is more difficult to enact large reforms when times are good, I wasn't sure how much we could achieve in my second term, but I was determined to keep trying.

During the State of the Union on February 4, I first asked the Congress to conclude the unfinished business of our country: balancing the budget, passing the campaign finance reform bill, and completing the process of welfare reform by providing more incentives to employers and states to hire recipients and more training, transportation, and child-care support to help people go to work. I also asked for the restoration of health and disability benefits for legal immigrants, which the Republicans had cut off in 1996 to make room in the budget for their tax cuts.

Looking to the future, I asked Congress to join me in making education our number one priority because "every eight-year-old must be able to read; every twelve-year-old must be able to log on to the Internet; every eighteen-year-old must be able to go to college; and every adult American must be able to keep on learning for a lifetime." I offered a ten-point plan to achieve these goals, including the development of national standards and tests to measure progress in meeting them; certification of 100,000 "master teachers" by the National Board for Professional Teaching Standards, up from only 500 in 1995; the America Reads tutoring initiative for eight-year-olds, which sixty college presidents had already agreed to support; more children in preschool; public school choice in every state; character education in every school; a multi-billion-dollar school construction and repair program, the first since just after World War II, to repair run-down facilities and help build new ones in school districts so overcrowded that classes were being held in trailers; the $1,500 HOPE Scholarship tax credit for the first two years of college and a $10,000 tuition tax deduction for all higher education after high school; a "GI Bill" for America's workers to give a skill grant to adults who needed further training; and a plan to connect every classroom and library to the Internet by 2000.

I told the Congress and the American people that one of America's greatest strengths in the Cold War had been a bipartisan foreign policy. Now, with education critical to our security in the twenty-first century, I asked that we approach it in the same way: "Politics must stop at the schoolhouse door."

I also asked the Congress to support the other commitments I had made to the American people in my campaign: the expansion of the family leave law; a large increase in AIDS research to develop a vaccine; an extension of health insurance to the children of low-income working people who couldn't afford it on their own; a comprehensive assault on juvenile crime, violence, drugs, and gangs; a doubling of the number of empowerment zones and the number of toxic waste sites cleaned up; and the continued expansion of community service programs.

In foreign policy, I asked for support for the expansion of NATO; the North Korean nuclear agreement; the extension of our Bosnian mission; our increasing engagement with China; "fast track" authority in trade negotiations, which requires Congress to vote on trade agreements up or down without amendments; a weapons modernization program at the Pentagon to meet new security challenges; and ratification of the Chemical Weapons Convention, which I thought would go a long way toward protecting America from terrorist attacks with poison gas.

In the speech, I tried to reach out to Republicans as well

as Democrats, telling them that I would defend any member's vote on the right kind of balanced budget and quoting a scripture verse, Isaiah 58:12: "Thou shalt be called, The repairer of the breach, The restorer of paths to dwell in." In one way or another, that's what I had been trying to do for most of my life.

The media's limited appetite for policy, compared with breaking scandal, became humorously apparent near the end of my speech. I had what I thought was a fine closing: I pointed out that "a child born tonight will have almost no memory of the twentieth century. Everything that child will know about America will be because of what we do now to build a new century." I reminded all who were listening that there were just over a thousand days until that new century, "a thousand days to build a bridge to a land of new promise." While I was making my pitch, the networks split the television screen so that viewers could also watch the jury render its verdict in the civil suit against O. J. Simpson over the murder of his wife, a suit brought after the jury in the criminal case failed to convict him. The television audience heard the civil jury rule against Simpson and my exhortations about the future simultaneously. I felt fortunate that I wasn't cut off completely, and that the public response to the speech was still positive.

Two days later I presented my budget plan to Congress. The budget brought America into balance in five years; increased investment in education by 20 percent, including the largest increase in college aid in fifty years since the GI Bill; cut spending in hundreds of other programs; provided targeted middle-class tax relief, including a $500-per-child tax credit; secured the Medicare Trust Fund, which was about to go broke, for ten years; provided health insurance to five million uninsured children, respite care for families caring for a loved one with Alzheimer's, and, for the first time, mammograms for older women under Medicare; and reversed the downward spiral in international affairs spending so that we could do more to promote peace and freedom and to fight terrorism, weapons proliferation, and narco-trafficking.

Unlike two years earlier, when I had forced the Republicans to make their harsh budget proposals public before coming forward with my own, I went first. I thought it was the right thing to do, and also good politics. Now when the Republicans presented their budget, with its bigger tax cuts for upper-income people, they would have to cut back on my education and health-care proposals to pay for them. This wasn't 1994; the public had figured things out, and the Republicans wanted to get reelected. I felt sure that, within a few months, Congress would pass a balanced budget that would be pretty close to my plan.

A couple of weeks later, another attempt to pass the balanced budget amendment to the Constitution failed in the Senate as Senator Bob Torricelli of New Jersey decided to vote against it. It was a courageous vote. New Jersey was an anti-tax state, and Bob had voted for the amendment as a congressman. I hoped that his bravery would get us past the posturing and on to the business of actually balancing the budget.

In mid-month we got another economic boost when American-led negotiations in Geneva produced an agreement to liberalize world trade in telecommunications services, opening 90 percent of the markets to U.S. firms. The negotiations were launched by Al Gore and conducted by Charlene Barshefsky. Their work was certain to bring new jobs and services at lower prices to Americans, and to spread the benefits of new technologies across the world.

Around this time I was in Boston with Mayor Tom Menino. Crime, violence, and drug use were going down in America, but they were still on the rise among people under eighteen, though not in Boston, where no child had died from gun violence in eighteen months, a remarkable achievement for a large city. I proposed child trigger locks on guns to prevent accidental shootings, a massive anti-drug advertising campaign, required drug tests for young people seeking driver's licenses, and reforms in the juvenile justice system, including the kind of probation and after-school services that Boston had implemented so successfully.

There were some interesting developments in Whitewater World in February. On the seventeenth, Kenneth Starr announced he would leave his post on August 1 to become dean of the Pepperdine University Law School in southern California. He had obviously decided that Whitewater was a dry hole and this was a graceful way out, but he received heavy criticism for his decision. The press said it looked bad because his Pepperdine position had been funded by Richard Mellon Scaife, whose funding of the Arkansas Project was not yet public knowledge, but who was widely recognized as an extreme right-winger with an animus toward me. I thought their objection was flimsy; Starr was already earning lots of money representing political opponents of my administration while serving as independent counsel, and he would in fact reduce his conflicts of interest by going to Pepperdine.

What really rocked Starr was all the heat he got from the Republican right and the three or four reporters who were deeply vested in finding something we'd done wrong, or at least in continuing the torment. By then, Starr had already done a lot for them: he had saddled a lot of people with big legal bills and damaged reputations, and, at enormous cost to taxpayers, had managed to drag the investigation out for three years, even after the RTC report said there was no basis for any civil or criminal action against Hillary and me. But the right wing and the Whitewater press knew that if Starr quit, it was a tacit admission that there was "no there there." After they beat him up for four days he announced he would stay on. I didn't know whether to laugh or cry.

The press was also still writing about fund-raising in the 1996 campaign. Among other things, they were agitated that I had invited people who had contributed to my campaign in 1992 to spend the night at the White House, even though, as with all guests, I paid for the costs of meals and other refreshments. The implication was that I had been selling overnights in the White House to raise money for the DNC. It was ridiculous. I was an incumbent President who led in the polls from start to finish; raising money was no

problem, and even if it had been, I would never have used
the White House in that way. At the end of the month, I
released a list of all overnight guests in the first term. There
were hundreds of them, about 85 percent of whom were relatives, friends of Chelsea's, foreign visitors and other digni-
taries, or people whom Hillary and I had known before I
started running for President. As for my supporters from
'92 who were also my friends, I wanted as many of them as
possible to have the honor of spending the night in the
White House. Often, given the long hours I worked, the
only time I had to visit with people in an informal way was
late at night. There was never a single case when I raised
money because of this practice. My critics seemed to be saying that the only people who shouldn't be overnight guests
were friends and supporters. When I released the list, many
people on it were questioned by the press. One reporter
called Tony Campolo and asked if he'd given me a contribution. When he said he had, he was asked how much. "I
think $25," he said, "but it might have been $50." "Oh,"
the reporter replied, "we don't want to talk to you," and
hung up.

The month ended on a happy note, as Hillary and I took
Chelsea and eleven of her girlfriends to dinner at the Bom-
bay Club restaurant in Washington for her seventeenth
birthday, and later to New York to see some plays, and
Hillary won a Grammy Award for the audio version of *It
Takes a Village*. She has a great voice, and the book was full
of stories she loved to tell. The Grammy was another
reminder that at least beyond the Washington Beltway, a lot
of Americans were interested in the same things we were.

In mid-February, Prime Minister Netanyahu came to see me
to discuss the current state of the peace process, and Yasser
Arafat did the same in early March. Netanyahu was constrained politically in what he could do beyond the Hebron
deal. The Israelis had just begun to elect their prime minister
directly, so Netanyahu had a four-year term, but he still had
to put together a majority coalition in the Knesset. If he lost
his coalition on the right, he could form a national unity

government with Peres and the Labor Party, but he didn't want to do that. The hard-liners in his coalition knew this and were making it difficult for him to keep moving toward peace by opening the Gaza airport or even letting all the Palestinians from Gaza come back to work in Israel. Psychologically, Netanyahu faced the same challenge Rabin had: Israel had to give up something concrete—land, access, jobs, an airport—in return for something far less tangible: the best efforts of the PLO to prevent terrorist attacks.

I was convinced Netanyahu wanted to do more, and afraid that if he couldn't, Arafat would find it more difficult to keep the lid on violence. To further complicate matters, whenever the peace process slowed, or the Israelis retaliated for a terrorist attack or began another building program in a West Bank settlement, there was likely to be a UN Security Council resolution condemning Israel for its continued violation of UN resolutions, and doing so in a way that suggested what the negotiated settlement should be. The Israelis depended on the United States to veto such measures, which we normally did. That enabled us to maintain our influence with them, but weakened our claim to be an honest broker with the Palestinians. I had to keep reminding Arafat that I was committed to the peace process and that only the United States could help bring it about, because the Israelis trusted America, not the European Union or Russia, to protect its security.

When Arafat came to see me I tried to work through the next steps with him. Not surprisingly, he saw things differently from Netanyahu; he thought he was supposed to prevent all violence and wait around for Netanyahu's politics to permit Israel to honor its commitments under the peace agreement. I had developed a comfortable working relationship with both leaders by then and had decided the only realistic option was to keep the process from falling apart by staying in constant touch, putting things back on track when they *did* fall apart, and maintaining momentum, even if it came in baby steps.

On the night of March 13, after appearances in North Carolina and south Florida, I went to Greg Norman's house in Hobe Sound to visit with him and his wife, Laura. It was a very pleasant evening, and the time got away from us. Before I knew it, it was after one o'clock in the morning, and since we were supposed to play in a golf tournament a few hours later, I got up to leave. As we were walking down the steps, I didn't see the last one. My right foot came down on the step's edge and I began to fall. Had I fallen forward, the worst that could have happened was scratched palms. Instead, I jerked backward, heard a loud pop, and fell. The sound was so loud that Norman, who was a few feet in front of me, heard it, turned around, and caught me, or I would have been hurt far worse than I was.

An ambulance took me on the forty-minute drive to St. Mary's Hospital, a Catholic institution the White House medical team had chosen because it had an excellent emergency room. I was there for the rest of the night in agonizing pain. When an MRI revealed that I'd torn 90 percent of my right quadriceps, I was flown back to Washington. Hillary met Air Force One at Andrews Air Force Base and watched as they lowered me out of the belly of the plane in a wheelchair. She had been scheduled to leave for Africa, but delayed her trip to get me through the necessary surgery at Bethesda Naval Hospital.

About thirteen hours after my injury, a fine surgical team led by Dr. David Adkison gave me an epidural, put on some music by Jimmy Buffett and Lyle Lovett, and talked me through the surgery. I could see what they were doing in a glass panel above the operating table: the doctor drilled holes in my kneecap, pulled the torn muscle through them, sutured the ends to the solid part of the muscle, and put me back together. After it was over, Hillary and Chelsea helped me get through one horrible day of pain; then things began to get better.

The thing I dreaded most was the six months of rehabilitation, and not being able to jog and play golf. I would be on crutches for a couple of months and in a soft leg brace after that. And for a while I was still vulnerable to falling and reinjuring myself. The White House staff rigged my shower up with safety rails so that I could keep my balance. Soon I learned how to dress myself with the help of a little stick. I could do everything but put on my socks. The medical staff at the White House, headed by Dr. Connie Mariano, was available around the clock. The navy gave me two great physical therapists, Dr. Bob Kellogg and Nannette Paco, who worked with me every day. Even though I had been told I'd gain weight during my period of immobility, by the time the physical therapists were through with me, I had lost fifteen pounds.

When I got home from the hospital, I had less than a week to get ready to meet Boris Yeltsin in Helsinki, and a big issue to deal with before then. On the seventeenth, Tony Lake came to see me and asked me to withdraw his nomination for director of central intelligence. Senator Richard Shelby, the chairman of the Intelligence Committee, had delayed Lake's confirmation hearings largely on the grounds that the White House had not informed the committee of our decision to stop enforcing the arms embargo against Bosnia in 1994. I was not required by law to tell the committee and had decided that it was better not to do so in order to keep it from leaking. I knew a strong bipartisan majority of the Senate favored lifting the embargo; in fact, not long afterward, they voted for a resolution asking me to stop enforcing it.

Though I got along with Shelby well enough, I thought he was far off base in holding up Lake's confirmation and unnecessarily hampering the operations of the CIA. Tony had some strong Republican supporters, including Senator Lugar, and would have been voted out of committee and confirmed had it not been for Shelby, but he was worn down after working seventy- and eighty-hour weeks for four years. And he didn't want to risk hurting the CIA with further delays. If it had been up to me, I would have carried on the fight for a year if that's what it took to get a vote. But I could see Tony had had enough. Two days later I nominated George Tenet, the acting CIA director who had been John Deutch's deputy and before that had served as my senior aide for intelligence on the NSC, and staff director of the Senate Intelligence Committee. He was confirmed easily, but I still regret the raw deal handed to Lake, who had given thirty years to advancing America's security interests and had played a major role in so many of our foreign policy successes in my first term.

My doctors didn't want me to go to Helsinki, but staying home wasn't an option. Yeltsin had been reelected and NATO was about to vote to admit Poland, Hungary, and the Czech Republic; we had to have an agreement on how to proceed.

The flight was long and uncomfortable, but the time passed quickly as I discussed with Strobe Talbott and the rest of the team what we could do to help Yeltsin live with NATO expansion, including getting Russia into the G-7 and the World Trade Organization. At a dinner that night hosted by President Martti Ahtisaari of Finland, I was glad to see Yeltsin in good spirits and apparently recovering from open-heart surgery. He had lost a lot of weight and was still pale, but he was back to his old buoyant and aggressive self.

The next morning we got down to business. When I told Boris I wanted NATO both to expand and to sign an agreement with Russia, he asked me to commit secretly—in his words, "in a closet"—to limiting future NATO expansion to the Warsaw Pact nations, thus excluding the states of the former Soviet Union, like the Baltics and Ukraine. I said I couldn't do that because, first of all, it wouldn't remain secret, and doing so would undermine the credibility of the Partnership for Peace. Nor would it be in America's or Russia's interest. NATO's governing mission was no longer directed against Russia but against the new threats to peace and stability in Europe. I pointed out that a declaration that NATO would stop its expansion with the Warsaw Pact nations would be tantamount to announcing a new dividing line in Europe, with a smaller Russian empire. That would make Russia look weaker, not stronger, whereas a NATO-Russia agreement would boost Russia's standing. I also urged Yeltsin not to foreclose the possibility of future Russian membership.

Yeltsin was still afraid of the domestic reaction to expansion. At one point when we were alone, I asked, "Boris, do you really think I would allow NATO to attack Russia from bases in Poland?" "No," he replied, "I don't, but a lot of older people who live in the western part of Russia and listen to Zyuganov do." He reminded me that, unlike the United States, Russia had been invaded twice— by Napoleon and by Hitler—and the trauma of those events still colored the country's collective psychology and shaped its politics. I told Yeltsin that if he would agree to NATO expansion and the NATO-Russia partnership, I would make a commitment not to station troops or missiles in the new member countries prematurely, and to support Russian membership in the new G-8, the World Trade Organization, and other international organizations. We had a deal.

Yeltsin and I also faced two arms control problems at Helsinki: the reluctance of the Russian Duma to ratify START II, which would reduce both our nuclear arsenals by two-thirds from their Cold War peak; and the growing opposition in Russia to America's development of missile defense systems. When the Russian economy collapsed and the military budget was slashed, the START II treaty had turned into a bad deal for them. It required both countries to dismantle their multiple-warhead missiles, called MIRVs, and provided for parity in both sides' single-warhead arsenals. Since Russia relied more heavily than the United States on MIRVs, the Russians would have to build a considerable number of single-warhead missiles to regain parity, and they couldn't afford to do it. I told Yeltsin I didn't want START II to give us strategic superiority and suggested that our teams come up with a solution that included adopting targets for a START III treaty that would take both countries down to between 2,000 and 2,500 warheads, an 80 percent reduction from the Cold War high, and a number sufficiently small so that Russia wouldn't have to build new missiles to be at parity with us. There was some reluctance in the Pentagon to go that low, but General Shalikashvili believed it was safe to do so, and Bill Cohen backed him. Within a short time, we agreed to extend the deadline for START II from 2002 to 2007 and to have START III come into effect the same year, so that Russia would never be at a strategic disadvantage.

On the second issue, since the 1980s the United States had been exploring missile defense, beginning with President Reagan's idea of a sky-based system that would shoot down all hostile missiles and thus free the world from the specter of nuclear war. There were two problems with the idea: it wasn't yet technically feasible, and a national missile defense system (NMD) would violate the Anti-Ballistic Missile Treaty, which forbade such systems because if one country had an NMD and the other didn't, the latter's nuclear arsenal might no longer be a deterrent to an attack by the nation with the NMD.

Les Aspin, my first secretary of defense, had shifted the emphasis of our efforts away from developing defenses that could shoot down long-range Russian missiles to funding a theater missile defense (TMD) that could protect our soldiers and other people from shorter-range missiles like those being developed by Iran, Iraq, Libya, and North Korea. They were a real danger; in the Gulf War twenty-eight of our soldiers had been killed by an Iraqi Scud missile.

I strongly supported the TMD program, which was permitted by the ABM Treaty and which, as I told Yeltsin, might someday be used to defend both our nations on a common battlefield, in the Balkans or elsewhere. The problem Russia had with our position was that it was unclear what the dividing line was between theater missile defense and the larger ones prohibited by the treaty. The new technologies developed for TMD might later be adaptable for use against ABMs, in violation of the treaty. Eventually, both sides agreed to a technical definition of the dividing line between permissible programs and prohibited ones that allowed us to proceed with the TMD.

The Helsinki summit was an unexpected success, thanks in no small measure to Yeltsin's capacity to imagine a different future for Russia, in which it would affirm its greatness in terms other than territorial domination, and his willingness to stand against prevailing opinion in the Duma and sometimes even within his own government. Though our work never realized its full potential because the Duma still refused to ratify START II, the stage was set for a successful NATO summit in July in Madrid to move us further along the road to a united Europe.

When I got home, the reaction was generally favorable, though Henry Kissinger and some other Republicans criticized me for agreeing not to deploy nuclear weapons and foreign troops closer to Russia in the new member states. Yeltsin got hit hard by the old Communists, who said he had caved in to me on the important issues. Zyuganov said Yeltsin had let "his friend Bill kick him in the rear." Yeltsin had just kicked Zyuganov in the rear in the election by fighting for tomorrow's Russia instead of yesterday's. I thought he would weather this storm, too.

When Hillary and Chelsea got home from Africa, they regaled me with their adventures. Africa was important to America, and Hillary's trip, much like her earlier one to South Asia, emphasized our commitment to supporting leaders and ordinary citizens in their efforts to find peace, prosperity, and freedom and to roll back the tide of AIDS.

On the last day of the month, I announced the appointment of Wes Clark to succeed General George Joulwan as the commander in chief, U.S. European Command, and Supreme Allied Commander of the NATO forces in Europe. I admired both men. Joulwan had vigorously supported an aggressive NATO stance in Bosnia, and Clark had been an integral part of Dick Holbrooke's negotiating team. I felt he was the best person to continue our firm commitment to peace in the Balkans.

In April, I saw King Hussein and Prime Minister Netanyahu in an attempt to keep the peace process from falling apart. Violence had broken out again, in the wake of an Israeli decision to build new housing in Har Homa, an Israeli settlement on the outskirts of East Jerusalem. Every time Netanyahu took a step forward, as with the Hebron agreement, his governing coalition made him do something that drove a wedge between Israel and the Palestinians. During the same period, a Jordanian soldier had gone berserk and killed seven Israeli schoolchildren. King Hussein immediately went to Israel and apologized. That diffused the tensions between Israel and Jordan, but Arafat was left with the continuing demand of the United States and Israel that he suppress terror while living with the Har Homa project, which he felt contradicted Israel's commitment not to change areas on the ground that were supposed to be resolved in the negotiations.

When King Hussein came to see me, he was worried that the step-by-step peace process that had been working under Rabin couldn't succeed now because of the political constraints on Netanyahu. Netanyahu was concerned about that, too; he had expressed some interest in trying to accelerate the process by moving to the difficult final status issues quickly. Hussein thought that if this could be done, we should try. When Netanyahu came to the White House a few days later, I told him I would support this approach, but in order to get Arafat to agree, he would have to find a way to follow through on the interim steps the Palestinians had already been promised, including the opening of the Gaza airport, safe passage between Gaza and the Palestinian areas in the West Bank, and economic assistance.

I spent most of the month in an intense effort to convince the Senate to ratify the Chemical Weapons Convention: calling and meeting with members of Congress; agreeing with Jesse Helms to move the Arms Control and Disarmament Agency and the U.S. Information Agency into the State Department in return for his allowing a vote on the CWC, which he opposed; and holding an event on the South Lawn with distinguished Republicans and military supporters of the treaty, including Colin Powell and James Baker, to counter conservative Republican opposition from people like Helms, Caspar Weinberger, and Donald Rumsfeld.

I was surprised at the conservative opposition, since all our military leaders strongly supported the CWC, but it reflected the right's deep skepticism about international cooperation in general and its desire to maintain maximum freedom of action now that the United States was the world's only superpower. Near the end of the month, I reached an agreement with Senator Lott to add some language that he felt strengthened the treaty. Finally, with Lott's support, the CWC was ratified, 74–26. Interestingly, I watched the Senate vote on television with Japanese prime minister Ryutaro Hashimoto, who was in town to meet with me the next day, and I thought he would like to see the ratification after what Japan had suffered in the sarin gas attack.

On the home front, I named Sandy Thurman of Atlanta, one of America's foremost AIDS advocates, to head the Office of National AIDS Policy. Since 1993 our overall investment in combating HIV and AIDS had increased 60 percent, we had approved eight new AIDS drugs and nineteen others for AIDS-related conditions, and the death rate was going down in America. Still, we were a long way from a vaccine or a cure, and the problem had exploded in Africa, where we weren't doing enough. Thurman was bright, energetic, and forceful; I knew she would keep us all on our toes.

On the last day of April, Hillary and I made public Chelsea's decision to attend Stanford in the fall. In her typically methodical way, Chelsea had also visited Harvard, Yale, Princeton, Brown, and Wellesley, and had been to several of them twice to get a feel for the academic and social life of each institution. Given her excellent grades and test scores, she had been accepted by all of them, and Hillary had hoped she would stay closer to home. I always suspected Chelsea would like to get far away from Washington. I just wanted her to go to a school where she would learn a lot, make good friends, and enjoy herself. But her mother and I were going to miss her badly. Having Chelsea at home in our first four years in the White House, going to her school and ballet events, and getting to know her friends and their parents had been a joy, repeatedly reminding us, no matter what else was going on, of what a blessing our daughter was.

Economic growth in the first quarter of 1997 was reported to be 5.6 percent, which pushed the estimated deficit down to $75 billion, about a quarter of what it was when I took office. On May 2, I announced that, at long last, I had reached a balanced budget agreement with Speaker Gingrich and Senator Lott and the congressional negotiators for both parties. Senator Tom Daschle also announced his support for the agreement; Dick Gephardt did not, but I was hoping he would come around once he had a chance to review it. The deal was much easier to make this time because economic growth had brought unemployment below 5 percent for the first time since 1973, boosting payrolls, profits, and tax revenues.

In broad terms, the agreement extended the life of Medicare for a decade, while providing the annual mammogram and diabetes screening initiatives I wanted; extended health coverage to five million children, the largest expansion since the passage of Medicaid in the 1960s; contained the largest increase in education spending in thirty years; gave more incentives to businesses to hire welfare recipients; restored health benefits to disabled legal immigrants; funded the cleanup of five hundred more toxic waste sites; and provided tax relief close to the amount I had recommended.

I met the Republicans halfway on the amount of Medicare savings, which I now believed we could achieve with good policy changes that didn't hurt senior citizens, and the Republicans accepted a smaller tax cut, the child health insurance program, and the big education increase. We got about 95 percent of the new investments I had recommended in the State of the Union, and the Republicans took about two-thirds of the tax cut figure they had originally proposed. The tax cuts would now be far smaller than the Reagan tax reduction of 1981. I was elated that the countless hours of meetings, begun in late 1995 under the threat of a government shutdown, had produced the first balanced budget since 1969, and a good one to boot. Senator Lott and Speaker Gingrich had worked with us in good faith, and Erskine Bowles, with his negotiating skills and common sense, had kept things going with them and the principal congressional negotiators at critical moments.

Later in the month, when the budget agreement was brought to a vote in a resolution, 64 percent of the House Democrats joined 88 percent of the House Republicans in voting for it. In the Senate, where Tom Daschle was supporting the agreement, Democrats were in favor of the agreement even more strongly than Republicans, 82 to 74 percent.

I took some criticism from Democrats who objected to the tax cut or to the fact that we were making the agreement at all. They argued that if we did nothing, the budget would be balanced the next year or the year afterward anyway because of the 1993 plan only Democrats had voted for; now we were going to let Republicans share the credit. That was true, but we were also going to get the biggest increase in higher education aid in fifty years, health care for five million kids, and middle-class tax cuts I supported.

On the fifth, a day celebrating Mexican independence, I left for a trip to Mexico, Central America, and the Caribbean. Little over a decade earlier, our neighbors had been plagued with civil wars, coups, dictators, closed economies, and desperate poverty. Now every nation in the hemisphere except one was a democracy, and the region as a whole was our largest trading partner; we exported twice as much to the Americas as to Europe and almost 50 percent more than to Asia. Still, there was too much poverty in the region, and we had serious problems with drugs and illegal immigration.

I took a number of cabinet members and a bipartisan congressional delegation to Mexico with me as we announced new agreements designed to reduce illegal immigration and the influx of drugs across the Rio Grande. President Zedillo was an able, honest man with a strong supporting team, and I was sure he would try his best to deal with these problems. While I knew we could do better, I doubted there was a completely satisfactory solution to either of the two problems. There were a number of contributing factors to take into account. Mexico was poorer than the United States; the border was long; millions of Mexicans had relatives in our country;

and many illegal immigrants came to the United States looking
for work, often at low-paying, demanding jobs most Americans didn't want to do. As for drugs, our demand was a magnet
for them, and the drug cartels had a lot of money with which to
bribe Mexican officials and plenty of hired guns to intimidate
or kill those who didn't want to cooperate. Some Mexican border police were offered five times their annual salary to look the
other way on just one drug shipment. One honest prosecutor
in northern Mexico had been shot more than one hundred
times right in front of his house. These were tough problems,
but I thought the implementation of our agreements would
help.

In Costa Rica, a beautiful country with no permanent military organization and perhaps the most advanced environmental policy in the world, President José María Figueres
hosted the Central American leaders for a meeting that
focused on trade and the environment. NAFTA had inadver-
tently hurt Central America and the Caribbean nations by
putting them at a competitive disadvantage with Mexico in
trading with the United States. I wanted to do what I could to
rectify the inequity. The next day I made the same point in
Bridgetown, Barbados, where Prime Minister Owen Arthur
hosted the first meeting ever held between a U.S. President and
all the leaders of the Caribbean nations in their own territory.

Immigration was also a big issue at both meetings. Many
Central Americans and people from the Caribbean nations
were working in the United States and sending money back
home to their families, providing a major source of income
in the smaller nations. The leaders were worried about the
anti-immigration stance Republicans had taken and wanted
my assurances that there would be no mass deportations. I
gave it to them, but also said we had to enforce our immigration laws.

At the end of the month I flew to Paris for the signing of
the NATO-Russia Founding Act. Yeltsin had kept his
Helsinki commitment: NATO's Cold War adversary was
now its partner.

After a stop in the Netherlands to celebrate the fiftieth
anniversary of the Marshall Plan, I flew to London for my

first official meeting with the new British prime minister, Tony Blair. His Labour Party had won a big victory over the Tories in the recent election as a result of Blair's leadership, Labour's more modern and more moderate message, and the natural ebbing of support for the Conservatives after their many years in power. Blair was young, articulate, and force-ful, and we shared many of the same political views. I thought he had the potential to be an important leader for the UK and all of Europe, and was excited about the prospect of working with him.

Hillary and I went to dinner with Tony and Cherie Blair at a restaurant in a restored warehouse district on the Thames. We felt like old friends from the start. The British press was fascinated by the similarity in our philosophies and politics, and the questions they asked seemed to have an impact on the American press traveling with me. For the first time, I had the feeling that they were beginning to believe there was something more than rhetoric to my New Democrat approach.

On June 6, my mother's birthday, I gave the commence-ment address at Chelsea's graduation ceremony at Sidwell Friends School. Teddy Roosevelt had spoken to the Sidwell students almost a century earlier, but I was there in a differ-ent role, not as a President but as a father. When I asked Chelsea what she wanted me to say, she replied, "Dad, I want you to be wise, briefly," then added, "The girls want you to be wise; the boys just want you to be funny." I wanted the speech to be my gift to her, and I was up until three in the morning the night before the commencement writing it out, over and over again.

I told Chelsea and her classmates that on this day their parents' "pride and joy are tempered by our coming separa-tion from you. . . . We are remembering your first day in school and all the triumphs and travails between then and now. Though we have raised you for this moment of depar-ture and we are very proud of you, a part of us longs to hold you once more as we did when you could barely walk, to read to you just one more time *Goodnight Moon* or *Curious George* or *The Little Engine That Could*." I said that an exciting world beckoned and they had almost limitless choices, and I reminded them of Eleanor Roosevelt's adage that no one can make you feel inferior without your permission: "Do not give them permission."

When Chelsea walked up to get her diploma, I hugged her and told her I loved her. After the ceremony several parents thanked me for saying what they were thinking and feeling; then we went back to the White House for a graduation party. Chelsea was touched to see the entire residence staff gathered to congratulate her. She had come a long way from the young girl with braces we had brought to the White House four and a half years earlier, and she had only just begun.

Soon after Chelsea's graduation, I accepted the recommendation of the National Bioethics Advisory Commission that human cloning was "morally unacceptable" and proposed that Congress ban it. It had become an issue since the cloning of Dolly the sheep in Scotland. Cloning technology had been used for some time to increase agricultural production and to achieve biomedical advances in the treatment of cancer, diabetes, and other disorders. It held great promise for producing replacement skin, cartilage, and bone tissue for burn and accident victims, and nerve tissue to treat spinal cord injuries. I didn't want to interfere with all that, but thought we should draw the line at human cloning. Just a month earlier I had apologized for the unconscionable and racist syphilis experiments performed on hundreds of black men decades earlier by the federal government in Tuskegee, Alabama.

In mid-June, I went to the University of California at San Diego to speak about America's continuing struggle to rid itself of racial discrimination and make the most of our growing diversity. The United States still suffered from discrimination, bigotry, hate crimes, and great disparities in income, education, and health care. I appointed a seven-member commission chaired by the distinguished scholar John Hope Franklin to educate America about the state of race relations and to make recommendations to help build

"One America" in the twenty-first century. I would coordinate the efforts through a new White House office headed by Ben Johnson.

In late June, Denver served as the host city for the annual G-7 meeting. I had pledged to Yeltsin that Russia would be fully included, but the finance ministers opposed the move because of Russia's economic weaknesses. Since Russia depended on the financial support of the international community, they felt it shouldn't be in on the G-7's financial decision making. I could understand why the finance ministers needed to meet and make decisions without Russia, but the G-7 was also a political organization; being in it would symbolize Russia's importance to the future and strengthen Yeltsin at home. We had already called this meeting the Summit of Eight. In the end, we voted to take Russia in as a full member of the new G-8, but to allow the finance ministers of the other seven nations to continue to meet on appropriate matters. Now Yeltsin and I had both kept our Helsinki commitments.

At about this time, Mir Aimal Kansi, who was believed to be responsible for murdering two CIA employees and wounding three others at CIA headquarters in 1993, was brought back to the United States from Pakistan to stand trial after intense efforts to secure his extradition by the FBI, the CIA, and the Departments of State, Justice, and Defense. It was strong evidence of our determination to track down terrorists and bring them to justice.

A week later, after a heated debate, the House of Representatives voted to continue normal trade relations with China. Although the motion carried by eighty-six votes, it sparked strong opposition from conservatives and liberals who disapproved of China's human rights and trade policies. I also supported more political freedom in China, and had recently invited the Dalai Lama and Hong Kong human rights activist Martin Lee to the White House to highlight my support for the cultural and religious integrity of Tibet and for maintaining Hong Kong's democracy now that the UK had restored it to China. I thought the trade relationship could be improved only through negotiations leading to

China's entry into the World Trade Organization. Meanwhile, we needed to stay involved with, not isolate, China. Interestingly, Martin Lee agreed, and supported the continuation of our trade relationship.

Soon afterward, I flew home to Hope for the funeral of Oren Grisham, my ninety-two-year-old uncle Buddy, who had played such a large role in my life. When I got to the funeral home, his family and I immediately started swapping funny stories about him. As one of my relatives said, he was the salt of the earth and the spice of life. According to Wordsworth, the best portion of a good man's life is his little, unremembered acts of kindness and love. Buddy had showered them on me when I was young and fatherless. In December, Hillary gave me a beautiful chocolate Labrador retriever to keep me company with Chelsea gone. He was a good-natured, high-spirited, intelligent dog. I named him Buddy.

In early July, Hillary, Chelsea, and I, after a couple of relaxing days with King Juan Carlos and Queen Sofía on the island of Majorca, were in Madrid for the NATO meeting. I had a fruitful discussion with the Spanish president, José María Aznar, who had just decided to fully integrate Spain into NATO's command structure. Then NATO voted to admit Poland, Hungary, and the Czech Republic, and made clear to the two dozen other nations that had joined the Partnership for Peace that NATO's door remained open to new members. From the beginning of my presidency, I had pushed for the expansion of NATO and believed this historic step would help both to unify Europe and to maintain the transatlantic alliance.

The next day we signed a partnership agreement with Ukraine, and I left for stops in Poland, Romania, and Denmark to reinforce the meaning of NATO expansion. There were large, enthusiastic crowds in Warsaw, Bucharest, and Copenhagen. In Poland, they were celebrating their new NATO membership. In Bucharest, about 100,000 people chanted "U.S.A, U.S.A.!" to demonstrate their support for democracy and their desire to enter NATO as soon as possible. In Copenhagen, on a bright sunny day, the size and enthusiasm of the crowd reflected an affirmation of our alliance and an appreciation of the fact that I was the first sitting President ever to visit Denmark.

By mid-month, I was back at work in the White House, proposing legislation to ban discrimination based on genetic screening. Scientists were rapidly unlocking the mysteries of the human genome, and their discoveries were likely to save millions of lives and revolutionize health care. But genetic testing would also reveal an individual's propensity to develop various illnesses, like breast cancer or Parkinson's. We couldn't allow the results of genetic tests to be the basis for denying health insurance or access to a job, and we didn't want to discourage people from undergoing them out of fear that the results would be used against them rather than to lengthen their lives.

At about the same time, the IRA restored the cease-fire it had broken in February 1996. I had pushed hard for the cease-fire, and it would hold this time, making it possible at last for the Irish to find their way through the thicket of accumulated hurt and suspicion to a shared future.

As July was drawing to a close, we still hadn't been able to agree on a detailed budget consistent with the earlier, more general agreement with the Republicans. We remained at odds over the size and shape of the tax cuts and over the allocation of new funds. While our team continued to negotiate with Congress, I went on with the rest of my job, asserting that, contrary to the dominant opinion in Congress, global warming was a reality and that we had to cut our greenhouse gas emissions, and holding a forum with Al Gore and other federal and state officials at Incline Village, Nevada, on the condition of Lake Tahoe.

Tahoe was one of the deepest, purest, cleanest lakes in the world, but its quality was degrading as a result of development, air pollution from traffic, and direct pollution from fuel that was discharged into the water from inefficient motorboats and Jet Ski engines. There was broad bipartisan support in California and Nevada for restoring the lake, and Al and I were determined to do everything possible to help.

At the end of the month, after I spoke to the National Governors Association in Las Vegas, Governor Bob Miller took me and several of my former colleagues to play golf with Michael Jordan. I had started playing again only two weeks earlier and was still wearing a soft leg brace for protection. I didn't really think I needed it anymore, so I took it off for the golf match.

Jordan was a great golfer, a long if sometimes erratic driver who also had a great short game. I got some insight into why he had won so many NBA championships when our group played a short par-five hole. All five of us had a good chance to make a birdie four. Jordan looked at his forty-five-foot downhill breaking putt and said, "Well, I guess I have to make this to win the hole." I could tell by the look in his eyes that he actually expected to make the difficult putt. He did, and won the hole.

Jordan told me I'd play better if I put my leg brace back on: "Your body doesn't need it anymore, but your mind doesn't know it yet." One reason I wasn't playing better is that I was constantly on the phone to the White House for an update on the budget negotiations, as we made last-minute offers and compromises in an effort to conclude them.

A little more than halfway through the match, Rahm Emanuel called to say we had a deal. Then Erskine called to confirm it and tell me how good it was. We got all our education and health money, the tax cut was modest, about 10 percent of the Reagan cut in '81, the Medicare savings were manageable, the middle-class tax cuts were in, the capital gains tax rate would be reduced from 28 to 20 percent, and everyone agreed that the budget would be balanced by 2002, and probably before then if the economy kept growing. Erskine and our whole team, especially my legislative aide, John Hilley, had done a great job. I was so happy I parred the next three holes, with my leg brace back on.

The next day we had a big celebration on the South Lawn with all the members of Congress and the administration who had worked on the budget. The atmosphere was euphoric and the speeches were warm, generous, and bipartisan, although I did go out of my way to thank the Democrats, especially Ted Kennedy, Jay Rockefeller, and Hillary, for the children's health plan. Because the deficit had already been reduced by more than 80 percent from its $290 billion high in 1993, the agreement was basically a progressive budget, with middle-class tax cuts I supported and the Republican capital gains cut. In addition to the health, education, and tax cut provisions, it raised the cigarette tax fifteen cents a pack to help pay for the children's health insurance, restored $12 billion in disability and health benefits to legal immigrants, doubled the number of empowerment zones, and gave us the money to continue cleaning up the environment.

With all the sweetness and light at the White House that day, it was hard to remember that we'd been at each other's throats for more than two years. I didn't know how long the good feelings would last, but I'd worked hard to keep things more civil during the stressful negotiations. A few weeks earlier Trent Lott, who was miffed about having lost a minor legislative battle to the White House, had called me a "spoiled brat" on one of the Sunday-morning talk shows. A few days after Lott's remarks I called and told him I knew what had happened and not to give it a second thought. After a hard week he had awakened on Sunday morning feeling bad and wishing he had never agreed to do the TV interview. He was tired and irritable, and when the interviewer goaded him about me he took the bait. He laughed and said, "That's exactly what happened," and the matter was behind us.

Most people who work hard under a lot of pressure occasionally say things they wish they hadn't; I certainly had. Usually, I didn't even read what the Republicans were saying about me, and if a harsh comment came to my attention I tried to ignore it. People hire Presidents to act for them; getting agitated about personal slights interferes with that. I'm glad I called Trent Lott and wish I'd made more calls like it in similar situations.

I didn't feel the same sense of detachment toward Ken Starr's continuing efforts to coerce people into making false charges against Hillary and me, and to prosecute those who refused to lie for him. In April, Jim McDougal, having changed his story to suit Starr and his deputy in Arkansas, Hick Ewing, finally went to jail with a recommendation from Starr that his sentence be shortened. Starr had done the same thing for David Hale.

Starr's coddling of McDougal and Hale was in sharp contrast to his treatment of Susan McDougal, who was still being held in prison for contempt because of her refusal to answer Starr's questions before the grand jury. After a brief period in an Arkansas county jail, to which she was led in handcuffs, leg manacles, and a waist chain, Susan was transferred to a federal facility, where she was kept apart from the other prisoners in a medical unit for a few months. She was then taken to a Los Angeles jail to answer charges there that she had embezzled funds from a former employer. When newly discovered documentary evidence shredded the prosecution's case, she was acquitted. Meanwhile, she was forced to spend twenty-three hours a day in a windowless cell block usually inhabited by convicted murderers. She was also forced to wear a red dress, normally worn only by murderers and child molesters. After a few months of that, she was put in a Plexiglas cell in the middle of a jail pod; she couldn't talk to other inmates, watch television, or even hear outside sounds. On the prison bus to her court appearances, she was put in a separate cage otherwise reserved for dangerous criminals. Her Hannibal Lecter–like confinement finally came to an end on July 30, after the American Civil Liberties Union filed a suit alleging that McDougal was being held in "barbaric" conditions at Starr's request, in an attempt to coerce her to testify.

Years later, when I read McDougal's book, *The Woman Who Wouldn't Talk*, it sent chills up my spine. She could have ended her suffering at any time, and made a lot of money to boot, just by telling the lies Starr and Hick Ewing wanted her to tell. How she stood up to them I'll never know, but the sight of her in chains finally began to penetrate the shield the Whitewater reporters had erected around Starr and his staff.

Late in the spring, the Supreme Court ruled unanimously that the Paula Jones suit could go forward while I was still in the White House, dismissing my attorneys' arguments that the work of the presidency should not be interrupted by the suit, since it could be litigated at the end of my term. The Court's previous decisions had indicated that a sitting President could not be the subject of a civil suit arising out of his official actions while President because the defense would be too distracting and time-consuming. The Court said that adopting a principle of delay in involving a President's unofficial acts could cause harm to the other party in the suit, so Jones's suit should not be delayed. Besides, the Court said, defending the suit wouldn't be unduly burdensome or time-consuming for me. It was one of the most politically naïve decisions the Supreme Court had made in a long time.

On June 25 the *Washington Post* reported that Kenneth Starr was investigating rumors that twelve to fifteen women, including Jones, had been involved with me. He said he had no interest in my sex life; he just wanted to question anyone with whom I might have had a conversation about Whitewater. Eventually Starr would deploy scores of FBI agents, as well as taxpayer-funded private investigators, to look into the subject in which he professed no interest.

By the end of July, I was getting concerned about the FBI, for reasons far more important than the bureau's sex inquiries for Ken Starr. There had been a whole series of missteps on Louis Freeh's watch: botched reports from the FBI forensic laboratory that threatened several pending criminal cases; large cost overruns on two computer systems designed to upgrade the National Crime Information Center and to provide quick fingerprint checks to police officers all across the country; the release of FBI files on Republican officials to the White House; and the naming and apparent attempted entrapment of Richard Jewell, a suspect in the

Olympic bombing case who was subsequently cleared. There was also a criminal inquiry under way into the conduct of Freeh's deputy, Larry Potts, in the deadly standoff at Ruby Ridge in 1992, for which the FBI had been heavily criticized and Potts had been censured before Freeh appointed him.

Freeh had been criticized in the press and by Republicans in Congress, who cited the FBI missteps as the reason for their refusal to pass the provision in my anti-terrorism legislation that would have given the agency wiretap authority to track suspected terrorists as they moved from place to place.

There was one sure way for Freeh to please the Republicans in Congress and get the press off his back: he could assume an adversarial position toward the White House. Whether out of conviction or necessity, Freeh had begun to do just that. When the files case became public, his initial reaction was to blame the White House and decline to accept any responsibility for the FBI. When the campaign finance story broke, he wrote Janet Reno a memo that was leaked to the press, urging her to appoint an independent counsel. When reports surfaced of possible attempts by the Chinese government to funnel illegal contributions to members of Congress in 1996, lower-level agents briefed people well down the chain of command in the National Security Council about it and urged them not to tell their superiors. When Madeleine Albright was preparing to go to China, the White House counsel, Chuck Ruff, a respected former U.S. attorney and Justice Department official, asked the FBI for information about Beijing's plans to influence the government. This was clearly something the secretary of state needed to know about before meeting with the Chinese, but Freeh personally ordered the FBI not to send its prepared reply, despite the fact that it had been approved by the Justice Department and two of Freeh's top assistants.

I didn't believe Freeh was foolish enough to think the Democratic Party would knowingly accept illegal contributions from the Chinese government; he was just trying to avoid criticism from the press and the Republicans, even if it damaged our foreign policy operations. I thought back to the call I had received the day before I appointed Freeh from the retired FBI agent in Arkansas pleading with me not to name him and warning that he would sell me down the river the minute it would benefit him to do so.

Whatever Freeh's motives, the behavior of the FBI toward the White House was just one more example of how crazy Washington had become. The country was in good shape and getting better, and we were advancing peace and prosperity throughout the world, yet the mindless search for scandal continued. A few months earlier Tom Oliphant, the thoughtful and independent-minded *Boston Globe* columnist, summed up the situation well:

> The grand and vainglorious forces running The Great American Scandal Machine are very big on how things seem. The machine's lifeblood is appearances, which generate questions, creating more appearances, all in turn generating a righteous frenzy that demands intense inquiry by super-scrupulous inquisitors who must at all costs be independent. The frenzy, of course, can be resisted only by the complicit and the guilty.

August began with good and bad news. Unemployment was down to 4.8 percent, the lowest since 1973, and confidence in the future remained high in the aftermath of the bipartisan balanced budget agreement. On the other hand, the cooperation didn't extend to the appointments process: Jesse Helms was holding up my nomination of the Republican governor of Massachusetts, Bill Weld, to be ambassador to Mexico because he felt Weld had insulted him, and Janet Reno told the American Bar Association that there were 101 vacant federal judgeships because the Senate had confirmed only nine of my nominees in 1997, none for the court of appeals.

After a two-year hiatus, our family went back to Martha's Vineyard for our August vacation. We stayed at the home of our friend Dick Friedman near Oyster Pond. I celebrated my birthday by going for a jog with Chelsea, and I persuaded

Hillary to play her annual round of golf with me at the Mink Meadows public course. She had never liked golf, but once a year she humored me by strolling around a few holes. I also played a lot of golf with Vernon Jordan at the wonderful old Farm Neck course. He liked the game a lot more than Hillary did.

The month ended as it began, with both good and bad news. On the twenty-ninth, Tony Blair invited Sinn Fein to join the Irish peace talks, giving the party formal standing for the first time. On the thirty-first, Princess Diana was killed in an auto crash in Paris. Less than a week later, Mother Teresa died. Hillary was very saddened by their deaths. She had known and liked both of them very much, and she represented the United States at both funerals, flying first to London, then to Calcutta a few days later.

During August, I also had to announce a major disappointment: the United States would not be able to sign the international treaty banning land mines. The circumstances leading to our exclusion were almost bizarre. The United States had spent $153 million on demining all over the world since 1993; we had recently lost a plane with nine people on board after depositing a demining team in southwest Africa; we had trained more than 25 percent of the world's demining experts; and we had destroyed 1.5 million of our own mines, with another 1.5 million scheduled to be destroyed by 1999. No other nation had done as much as America to rid the world of dangerous land mines.

Near the end of negotiations on the treaty, I had asked for two amendments: an exception for the heavily marked UN-sanctioned minefield along the Korean border, which protected the people of South Korea and our troops there; and a rewording of the provision approving anti-tank missiles that covered those manufactured in Europe but not ours. Ours were just as safe and worked better to protect our troops. Both amendments were rejected, partly because the Landmine Conference was determined to pass the strongest possible treaty in the wake of the death of its most famous champion, Princess Diana, and partly because some people at the conference just wanted to embarrass the United States or bully us into signing the treaty as it was. I hated not to be part of the international agreement because it undermined our leverage in trying to stop the manufacture and use of more land mines, some of which could be bought for as little as three dollars each, but I couldn't put the safety of our troops or the people of South Korea at risk.

On September 18, Hillary and I took Chelsea to Stanford. We wanted her new life to be as normal as possible and had worked with the Secret Service to make sure she would be assigned young agents who would dress informally and be as unobtrusive as they could be. Stanford had agreed to bar media access to her on campus. We enjoyed the welcoming ceremonies and visits with the other parents, after which we took Chelsea to her dorm room and helped her move in. Chelsea was happy and excited; Hillary and I were a little sad and anxious. Hillary tried to deal with it by scurrying around and helping Chelsea organize things, even lining her drawers with Contac paper. I had carried her luggage up the stairs to her room, then fixed her bunk bed. After that, I just stared out the window, as her mother got on Chelsea's nerves with all the fixing up. When the student speaker at the convocation, Blake Harris, had said to all the parents that our children would miss us "in about a month and for about fifteen minutes," we all laughed. I hoped it was true, but we sure would miss her. When it was time to go, Hillary had pulled herself together and was ready. Not me; I wanted to stay for dinner.

On the last day of September, I attended the retirement ceremony of General John Shalikashvili and gave him the Presidential Medal of Freedom. He had been a superb chairman of the Joint Chiefs, supporting the expansion of NATO, the creation of the Partnership for Peace, and the deployment of our troops in more than forty operations, including Bosnia, Haiti, Iraq, Rwanda, and the Taiwan Strait. I had really enjoyed working with him. He was intelligent, straight-talking, and completely committed to the welfare of our men and women in uniform. As his replacement I named General Hugh Shelton, who had so impressed me with his handling of the Haiti operation.

The early fall was largely devoted to foreign affairs, as I took my first trip to South America. I traveled to Venezuela, Brazil, and Argentina to express the importance of Latin America to America's future and to keep pushing the idea of a free trade area covering all the Americas. Venezuela was our number one oil supplier and had always made more petroleum available to the United States when we needed it, from World War II to the Gulf War. My visit was brief and uncomplicated; its highlight was a speech to the people of Caracas at the tomb of Simón Bolívar.

Brazil was a different story. There had long been tensions between our two countries; many Brazilians had long resented the United States. Brazil was the leader of the Mercosur trading bloc, which also included Argentina, Paraguay, and Uruguay, and which had a larger volume of trade with Europe than with the United States. On the other hand, the Brazilian president, Fernando Henrique Cardoso, was a modern, effective leader who wanted a good relationship with the United States and who understood that a stronger partnership with us would help him to modernize his country's economy, reduce its chronic poverty, and increase its influence in the world.

I had been fascinated by Brazil since the great jazz saxophonist Stan Getz popularized its music in America in the 1960s, and ever since then I had wanted to see its cities and beautiful landscapes. I also respected and liked Cardoso. He had already been to Washington on a state visit, and I thought he was one of the most impressive leaders I had met. I wanted to affirm our mutual dedication to a closer economic partnership and to support his policies, especially those to sustain Brazil's vast rain forest, which had been severely reduced by overclearing, and to improve education. Cardoso had initiated an intriguing program called *bolsa escola*, which made monthly cash payments to poor Brazilians if their children attended school at least 85 percent of the time.

There was an interesting moment in our press conference, which, besides several questions on American-Brazilian relations and climate change, included four from the American press on the ongoing controversy back home over the financing of the '96 campaign. A reporter asked if it embarrassed me or the country to have such questions asked on a foreign trip. I replied, "That's a decision for you. You have to decide what questions you're going to ask. I can't be embarrassed about how you decide to do your job."

Before a visit to a school in a poor neighborhood in Rio de Janeiro with Brazil's soccer legend Pelé, Hillary and I went to Brasília for a state dinner at the presidential residence, where Fernando Henrique and Ruth Cardoso gave us a taste of the Brazilian music I had loved for more than thirty years, a women's percussion ensemble playing pulsating rhythms on different-sized metal plates tied to their bodies, and a fabulous singer from Bahia, Virginia Rodrigues.

Argentina's President Carlos Menem had been a strong ally of the United States, supporting America in the Gulf War and in Haiti and adopting a strong free-market economic policy. He hosted a barbeque at the Rural Center in Buenos Aires that included tango lessons for Hillary and me and a demonstration of Argentine horsemanship: a man riding around the rodeo arena standing atop two broad-shouldered stallions.

President Menem also took us to Bariloche, a beautiful resort town in Patagonia, to discuss global warming and what I hoped would be our common response to the problem. The international conference on climate change was coming up in December in Kyoto, Japan. I strongly favored setting aggressive targets for the reduction of greenhouse gas emissions for both developed and developing nations, but I wanted to achieve the targets not through regulations and taxes but through market incentives to promote energy conservation and the use of clean energy technology. Bariloche was a perfect site to highlight the importance of the environment. Just across the cold, clear lake from the Llao Llao Hotel where we stayed, Hillary and I walked through the magical Arrayanes forest, with its barkless myrtle trees.

The trees were stained orange by tannic acid and were cool to the touch. Their survival resulted from perfect soil, clean water, clean air, and a moderate climate. The right action against climate change would preserve the fragile, unique trees and the stability of much of the rest of our planet.

On October 26, back in Washington, Capricia Marshall, Kelly Craighead, and the rest of Hillary's staff put together a big fiftieth birthday celebration for her under a tent on the South Lawn. Chelsea came home to surprise her. There were tables with food and music from every decade of her life, with people standing by them who had known her in each period: from Illinois in the fifties, Wellesley in the sixties, Yale in the seventies, and Arkansas in the eighties.

The next day, Jiang Zemin came to Washington. I invited him to the residence for an informal meeting that night. After almost five years of working with him, I was impressed with Jiang's political skills, his desire to integrate China into the world community, and the economic growth that had accelerated under his leadership and that of his prime minister, Zhu Rongji, but I was still concerned about China's continued suppression of basic freedoms and its imprisonment of political dissidents. I asked Jiang to release some dissidents and told him that in order for the United States and China to have a long-term partnership, our relationship had to have room for fair, honest disagreement.

When Jiang said he agreed, we proceeded to debate how much change and freedom China could accommodate without risking internal chaos. We didn't resolve our differences, but our mutual understanding increased, and after Jiang went back to Blair House, I went to bed thinking that China would be forced by the imperatives of modern society to become more open, and that in the new century it was more likely that our nations would be partners than adversaries.

The next day at our press conference, Jiang and I announced that we would increase our cooperation to stop the spread of weapons of mass destruction; work together on the peaceful use of nuclear energy, and on fighting organized crime, drug trafficking, and alien smuggling; expand America's efforts to promote the rule of law in China by helping to train judges and lawyers; and cooperate to protect the environment. I also pledged to do all I could to bring China into the World Trade Organization. Jiang echoed my remarks and told the press we had also agreed to regular summit meetings and the opening of a direct telephone "hotline" to assure that we could maintain direct communication.

When we opened the floor to questions, the press asked the inevitable ones about human rights, Tiananmen Square, and Tibet. Jiang seemed a little taken aback but maintained his good humor, essentially repeating what he had said to me on the subjects the night before, and adding that he knew he was visiting a democracy where the people were free to voice their different opinions. I replied that while China was on the right side of history on so many issues, on the human rights issue "we believe the policy of the government is on the wrong side of history." A couple of days later, in a speech at Harvard, President Jiang acknowledged that mistakes had been made in dealing with the demonstrators at Tiananmen Square. China often moved at a pace that seemed maddeningly slow to Westerners, but it was not impervious to change.

October brought two developments on the legal front. After Judge Susan Webber Wright dismissed with prejudice (meaning they could not be refiled) two of the four counts in Paula Jones's lawsuit, I offered to settle it. I didn't want to, because it would take about half of everything Hillary and I had saved over twenty years, and because I knew, on the basis of the investigative work my legal team had done, that we would win the case if it ever went to trial. But I didn't want to waste any days in the three years I had left on it.

Jones refused to accept the settlement unless I also apologized for sexually harassing her. I couldn't do that because it wasn't true. Not long afterward, her lawyers petitioned the court to be released of their duties. Soon they were replaced by a Dallas firm closely associated with and funded by the Rutherford Institute, another right-wing legal foundation financed by my opponents. Now there was no longer even a pretense that Paula Jones was the real plaintiff in the case that bore her name.

Early in the month, the White House turned over videotapes of forty-four of the much-discussed White House coffees to the Justice Department and the Congress. They proved what I'd said all along, that the coffees were not fund-raisers, but wide-ranging and often interesting discussions with some people who were supporters and some who weren't. The only thing most of the critics could do was to complain that they weren't released sooner.

Soon after that, Newt Gingrich announced that he didn't have the votes to pass the fast-track trade legislation in the House. I had worked very hard for months to pass it. In an attempt to get more votes from my party, I had pledged to Democrats that I would negotiate trade agreements with labor and environmental provisions, and told them that I had secured Chile's agreement to put such requirements into the bilateral agreement we were working on. Unfortunately, I couldn't persuade very many of them, because the AFL-CIO, which was still angry about losing the NAFTA vote, had made the fast-track vote a test of whether Democrats were for or against labor. Even Democrats who agreed with me on the merits were reluctant to face a reelection campaign without the AFL-CIO's financial and organizational support. Several conservative Republicans conditioned their vote on whether or not I would impose further restrictions on U.S. policy for international family planning. When I wouldn't do it, I lost their votes. The Speaker had also worked to pass the bill, but at the end we were still six votes short at best. Now I would just have to continue making individual trade agreements and hope that Congress wouldn't kill them with amendments.

In mid-month we had a new crisis in Iraq, when Saddam expelled six American members of the UN weapons inspection teams. I ordered the USS *George Washington* carrier group to the region, and a few days later the inspectors returned.

The Kyoto global warming talks opened on December 1. Before they were over, Al Gore flew to Japan to help our chief negotiator, Undersecretary of State Stu Eizenstat, get an agreement we could sign, with firm targets but without undue restrictions on how to achieve them and with a call for developing countries like China and India to participate; within thirty years they would surpass the United States as emitters of greenhouse gases (the United States is now the world's leading emitter). Unless the changes were made, I couldn't submit the treaty to Congress; it would be difficult to pass in the best of circumstances. With the support of Prime Minister Hashimoto, who wanted Kyoto to be a success for Japan, and other friendly nations including Argentina, the negotiations produced an agreement I was happy to support, with targets I thought we could meet, if Congress would enact the tax incentives necessary to promote the production and purchase of more conservation technologies and clean energy products.

In the days before Christmas, Hillary, Chelsea, and I went to Bosnia to encourage the people in Sarajevo to stay on the path of peace and to meet with the troops in Tuzla. Bob and Elizabeth Dole joined our delegation, along with several military leaders and a dozen members of Congress of both parties. Elizabeth was the president of the American Red Cross, and Bob had just agreed to my request to head the International Commission on Missing Persons in the former Yugoslavia.

On the day before Christmas the United States agreed to put up $1.7 billion to provide financial support to the faltering South Korean economy. It marked the beginning of our commitment to solving the Asian financial crisis, which would grow much worse in the coming year. South Korea had just elected a new president, Kim Dae Jung, a longtime democracy activist who had been sentenced to execution in the 1970s until President Carter intervened on his behalf. I had first met Kim on the steps of Los Angeles City Hall in May 1992, when he proudly told me he represented the same new approach to politics that I did. He was both brave and visionary, and I wanted to support him.

As we headed to Renaissance Weekend and a new year, I looked back on 1997 with satisfaction, hoping the worst of the partisan wars had passed in the wake of all that had been accomplished: the balanced budget; the largest increase in college aid in fifty years; the biggest increase in children's health coverage since 1965; the expansion of NATO; the Chemical Weapons Convention; the Kyoto accord; sweeping reforms of our adoption laws and of our Food and Drug Administration to speed the introduction of lifesaving medicines and medical devices; and the One America initiative, which had already involved millions of people in conversations about the current state of race relations. It was an impressive list, but it would not be enough to bridge the ideological divide.

NINETEEN

WHEN 1998 BEGAN, I had no idea it would be the strangest year of my presidency, full of personal humiliation and disgrace, policy struggles at home and triumphs abroad, and, against all odds, a stunning demonstration of the common sense and fundamental decency of the American people. Because everything happened at once, I was compelled as never before to live parallel lives, except that this time the darkest part of my inner life was in full view.

January began on a positive note, with three major initiatives: (1) a 50 percent increase in the number of Peace Corps volunteers, primarily to support the new democracies that had emerged since the fall of communism; (2) a $22 billion child-care program to double the number of children in working families receiving child-care subsidies, provide tax credits to encourage employers to make child care available to their employees, and expand before- and after-school programs to serve 500,000 children; and (3) a proposal to allow people to "buy into" Medicare, which covered Americans sixty-five and older, at age sixty-two, or at age fifty-five if they had lost their jobs. The program was designed to be self-financing through modest premiums and other payments. It was needed because so many Americans were leaving the workforce early, through downsizing, layoffs, or choice, and couldn't find affordable insurance elsewhere after they lost their employer-based coverage.

In the second week of the month, I went to South Texas, one of my favorite places in America, to urge the largely Hispanic student body at Mission High School to help close the gap between the college-going rates of Hispanic young people and the rest of the student population by taking full advantage of the tremendous increase in college aid the Congress had authorized in 1997. While there, I was informed of the collapse of Indonesia's economy, and my economic team went to work on the next casualty of the Asian financial crisis; Deputy Treasury Secretary Larry Summers went to Indonesia to secure the government's agreement to implement the reforms necessary to receive assistance from the International Monetary Fund.

On the thirteenth, trouble broke out in Iraq again as Saddam's government blocked an American-led UN inspection team from doing its job, the beginning of a protracted effort by Saddam to coerce the United Nations into lifting sanctions in return for continuing the weapons inspections. The same day, the Middle East moved toward crisis as Prime Minister Netanyahu's government, which still had not completed the overdue opening of the Gaza airport or provided safe passage between Gaza and the West Bank, put the entire peace process in danger by voting to keep control of the West Bank indefinitely. The only bright spot on the world horizon in January was the White House signing of a NATO partnership with the Baltic nations, which was designed to formalize our security relationship and reassure them that the ultimate goal of all the NATO nations, including the United States, was the full integration of Estonia, Lithuania, and Latvia into NATO and other multilateral institutions.

On the fourteenth, I was in the East Room of the White House with Al Gore to announce our push for a Patients' Bill of Rights, to provide Americans in managed care plans with some basic treatment guarantees that were being denied all too frequently, and Hillary was being questioned by Ken Starr for the fifth time. The topic on this occasion was how the FBI files on Republicans got to the White House, something she knew nothing about.

My deposition in the Jones case came three days later. I had gone over a series of possible questions with my lawyers and thought I was reasonably well prepared, though I didn't feel well that day and certainly wasn't looking forward to my encounter with the Rutherford Institute lawyers. The presiding judge, Susan Webber Wright, had given Jones's lawyers broad permission to delve into my private life, allegedly to see if there was a pattern of sexual harassment involving any women who had held or sought state employment when I was governor or federal employment when I was President, during a time period from five years before Jones's alleged harassment to the present day. The judge had also given the Jones lawyers strict instructions not to leak the contents of any deposition or other aspects of their investigation.

The stated objective could have been achieved less intrusively by simply directing me to answer yes or no to questions about whether I had ever been alone with women working for the government; then the lawyers could have asked the women whether I had ever harassed them. However, that would have rendered the deposition useless. By this time, everyone involved in the case knew there was no evidence of sexual harassment. I was certain that the lawyers wanted to force me to acknowledge any kind of involvement with one or more women that they could then leak to the press, in violation of the judge's confidentiality order. As it turned out, I didn't know the half of it.

After I was sworn in, the deposition began with a request from the Rutherford Institute lawyers that the judge accept a definition of "sexual relations" that they had purportedly found in a legal document. Basically, the definition covered most intimate contact beyond kissing by the person being asked the question, if it was done for gratification or arousal. It seemed to require both a specific act and a certain state of mind on my part, and did not include any act by another person. The lawyers said they were trying to spare me embarrassing questions.

I was there for several hours, only ten or fifteen minutes of which were devoted to Paula Jones. The rest of the time was spent on a variety of topics with no connection to Jones, including a great many questions about Monica Lewinsky, who had worked in the White House in the summer of 1995 as an intern and then in a staff job from December through early April, when she was transferred to the Pentagon. The lawyers asked, among other things, how well I knew her, whether we had ever exchanged gifts, whether we had ever talked on the phone, and if I had had "sexual relations"

with her. I discussed our conversations, acknowledged that I
had given her gifts, and answered no to the "sexual relations" question.

The Rutherford Institute lawyers kept asking the same
questions with slight variations over and over again. When
we took a break, my legal team was perplexed, because
Lewinsky's name had shown up on the plaintiff's list of
potential witnesses only in early December, and she had been
given a subpoena to appear as a witness two weeks later. I
didn't tell them about my relationship with her, but I did say I
was unsure of exactly what the curious definition of sexual
relations meant. So were they. At the beginning of the deposition, my attorney, Bob Bennett, had invited the Rutherford
Institute lawyers to ask specific and unambiguous questions
about my contact with women. At the end of the discussion
of Lewinsky, I asked the lawyer who was questioning me if
there wasn't something more specific he wanted to ask me.
Once again he declined to do so. Instead he said, "Sir, I think
this will come to light shortly, and you'll understand."

I was relieved but somewhat concerned that the lawyer
seemed not to want to ask specific questions, nor to want to
get my answers to them. If he had asked such questions, I
would have answered them truthfully, but I would have
hated it. During the government shutdown in late 1995,
when very few people were allowed to come to work in the
White House and those who were there were working late,
I'd had an inappropriate encounter with Monica Lewinsky
and would do so again on other occasions between November and April, when she left the White House for the Pentagon. For the next ten months, I didn't see her, although we
talked on the phone from time to time.

In February 1997, Monica was among the guests at an
evening taping of my weekly radio address, after which I
met with her alone again for about fifteen minutes. I was disgusted with myself for doing it, and in the spring, when I
saw her again, I told her that it was wrong for me, wrong for
my family, and wrong for her, and I couldn't do it anymore.
I also told her that she was an intelligent, interesting person

who could have a good life, and that if she wanted me to, I would try to be her friend and help her.

Monica continued to visit the White House, and I saw her on some of those occasions, but nothing improper occurred. In October, she asked me to help her get a job in New York, and I did. She had received two offers and accepted one, and late in December, she came to the White House to say good-bye. By then, she had received her subpoena in the Jones case. She said she didn't want to be deposed, and I told her some women had avoided questioning by filing affidavits saying that I had not sexually harassed them.

What I had done with Monica Lewinsky was immoral and foolish. I was deeply ashamed of it and I didn't want it to come out. In the deposition, I was trying to protect my family and myself from my selfish stupidity. I believed that the contorted definition of "sexual relations" enabled me to do so, though I was worried enough about it to invite the lawyer interrogating me to ask specific questions. I didn't have to wait long to find out why he declined to do so.

On January 21, the *Washington Post* led with a story that I had had an affair with Monica Lewinsky, and that Kenneth Starr was investigating charges that I had encouraged her to lie about it under oath. The story first emerged publicly early on the eighteenth, on an Internet site. The deposition had been a setup; nearly four years after he first offered to help Paula Jones, Starr had finally gotten into her case.

In the summer of 1996, Monica Lewinsky had begun talking to a co-worker, Linda Tripp, about her relationship with me. A year later, Tripp had started taping their telephone conversations. In October 1997, Tripp offered to play the tapes for a *Newsweek* reporter and did play them for Lucianne Goldberg, a conservative Republican publicist. Tripp was subpoenaed in the Jones case, though she was never on any witness list provided to my attorneys.

Late on Monday, January 12, 1998, Tripp phoned Starr's office, described her secret taping of Lewinsky, and made arrangements to turn over those tapes. She was concerned about her own criminal liability, because the kind of taping she had done was a felony under Maryland law, but Starr's people promised to protect her. The next day Starr had FBI agents wire Tripp so that she could secretly record a conversation with Lewinsky over lunch at the Pentagon City Ritz-Carlton. A couple of days later, Starr asked the Justice Department for permission to expand his authority to encompass the investigation of Lewinsky, apparently being less than truthful about the basis for his request.

On the sixteenth, the day before my deposition, Tripp arranged to meet Lewinsky again at the hotel. This time Monica was greeted by FBI agents and attorneys who took her to a hotel room, questioned her for several hours, and discouraged her from calling a lawyer. One of Starr's lawyers told her she should cooperate if she wanted to avoid going to jail and offered her an immunity deal that expired at midnight. Lewinsky was also pressured to wear a wire to secretly tape conversations with people involved in the alleged cover-up. Finally, Monica was able to call her mother, who contacted her father, from whom she had long been divorced. He got in touch with a lawyer, William Ginsburg, who advised her not to accept the immunity deal until he learned more about the case, and who blasted Starr for holding his client "for eight or nine hours without an attorney" and for pressuring her to wear a wire to entrap others.

After the story broke, I called David Kendall and assured him that I had not suborned perjury or obstructed justice. It was clear to both of us that Starr was trying to create a firestorm to force me from office. He was off to a flying start, but I thought that if I could survive the public pounding for two weeks, the smoke would begin to clear, the press and the public would focus on Starr's tactics, and a more balanced view of the matter would emerge. I knew I had made a terrible mistake, and I was determined not to compound it by allowing Starr to drive me from office. For now, the hysteria was overwhelming.

I went on doing my job, and I stonewalled, denying what had happened to everyone: Hillary, Chelsea, my staff and cabinet, my friends in Congress, members of the press, and the American people. What I regret the most, other than my conduct, is having misled all of them. Since 1991 I had been called a liar about everything under the sun, when in fact I had been honest in my public life and financial affairs, as all the investigations would show. Now I was misleading everyone about my personal failings. I was embarrassed and wanted to keep it from my wife and daughter. I didn't want to help Ken Starr criminalize my personal life, and I didn't want the American people to know I'd let them down. It was like living in a nightmare. I was back to my parallel lives with a vengeance.

On the day the story broke, I did a previously scheduled interview with Jim Lehrer for the PBS *NewsHour.* I responded to his questions by saying that I had not asked anyone to lie, which was true, and that "there is no improper relationship." Although the impropriety was over well before Lehrer asked the question, my answer was misleading, and I was ashamed of telling Lehrer that; from then on, whenever I could, I just said I never asked anybody not to tell the truth.

While all this was going on, I had to keep doing my job. On the twentieth, I met with Prime Minister Netanyahu at the White House to discuss his plans for a phased withdrawal from the West Bank. Netanyahu had made a decision to move the peace process forward as long as he had "peace with security." It was a bold move because his governing coalition was shaky, but he could see that if he didn't act, the situation would quickly get out of hand.

The next day Arafat came to the White House. I gave him an encouraging report of my meeting with Netanyahu, assured him that I was pushing the prime minister to fulfill Israel's obligation under the peace process, reminded him of the Israeli leader's political problems, and stated, as I always did, that he had to keep fighting terror if he wanted Israel to move forward. The next day Mir Aimal Kansi was sentenced to death for the murder of the two CIA agents in January 1993, the first terrorist act to occur during my presidency.

By January 27, the day of the State of the Union address,

the American people had been deluged with a week of coverage of Starr's inquiry, and I had spent a week dealing with it. Starr had already issued subpoenas to a number of White House staff people and for our records. I had asked Harold Ickes and Mickey Kantor to help deal with the controversy. The day before the speech, at the urging of Harold and Harry Thomason, who felt I had been too tentative in my public comments, I reluctantly appeared once more before the press to say "I did not have sexual relations" with Lewinsky.

On the morning of the speech, on NBC's *Today* show, Hillary said that she didn't believe the charges against me and that a "vast right-wing conspiracy" had been trying to destroy us since the 1992 campaign. Starr issued an indignant statement complaining that Hillary had questioned his motives. Though she was right about the nature of our opposition, seeing Hillary defend me made me even more ashamed about what I had done.

Hillary's difficult interview and my mixed reaction to it clearly exemplified the bind I had put myself in: as a husband, I had done something wrong that I needed to apologize and atone for; as President, I was in a legal and political struggle with forces who had abused the criminal and civil laws and severely damaged innocent people in their attempt to destroy my presidency and cripple my ability to serve.

Finally, after years of dry holes, I had given them something to work with. I had hurt the presidency and the people by my misconduct. That was no one's fault but my own. I didn't want to compound the error by letting the reactionaries prevail.

By 9 p.m., when I walked into the packed House chamber, the tension was palpable both there and in living rooms across America, where more people were watching my State of the Union address than since I delivered my first one. The big question was whether I would mention the controversy. I began with what was not in dispute. The country was in good shape, with fourteen million new jobs, rising incomes, the highest rate of home ownership ever, the fewest people on the welfare rolls in twenty-seven years, and the smallest federal government in thirty-five years. The 1993 economic plan had cut the deficit, projected to be $357 billion in 1998, by 90 percent, and the previous year's balanced budget plan would get rid of it entirely.

Then I outlined my plan for the future. First, I proposed that before spending the coming surpluses on new programs or tax cuts, we should save Social Security for the baby boomers' retirement. In education, I recommended funding to hire 100,000 new teachers and to cut class size to eighteen in the first three grades; a plan to help communities modernize or build five thousand schools; and assistance to help schools end the practice of "social promotion," by providing funds for extra learning in after-school or summer-school programs. I reiterated my support for a Patients' Bill of Rights, opening Medicare to Americans between the ages of fifty-five and sixty-five, expanding the Family and Medical Leave Act, and called for a large enough expansion in federal child-care assistance to provide support for one million more children.

On the security front, I asked for congressional support in combating "an unholy axis of new threats from terrorists, international criminals, and drug traffickers"; Senate approval of the expansion of NATO; and continued funding for our mission in Bosnia and our efforts to confront the hazards of chemical and biological weapons and the outlaw states, terrorists, and organized criminals seeking to acquire them.

The last section of my speech dealt with appeals to bring America together and look to the future: tripling the number of empowerment zones in poor communities; launching a new clean water initiative for our rivers, lakes, and coastal waters; providing $6 billion in tax cuts and research funds for the development of fuel-efficient cars, clean-energy homes, and renewable energy; financing the "next generation" Internet to transmit information up to a thousand times faster; and funding the Equal Employment Opportunity Commission, which, because of congressional hostility, didn't have the resources to handle sixty thousand backlogged cases alleging discrimination in the workplace. I also

proposed the largest increase in history for the National
Institutes of Health, the National Cancer Institute, and the
National Science Foundation so that "ours will be the generation that finally wins the war against cancer and begins a
revolution in our fight against all deadly diseases."

I closed the speech thanking Hillary for leading our millennium campaign to preserve America's treasures, including the tattered old Star Spangled Banner, which inspired
Francis Scott Key to write our national anthem during the
War of 1812.

There wasn't a word in the address about the scandal,
and the biggest new idea had been to "save Social Security
first." I was afraid Congress would get into a bidding war
for the coming surpluses and squander them on tax cuts and
spending before we had dealt with the baby boomers' retirement. Most Democrats agreed with me, and most Republicans didn't, though over the coming years we would hold a
series of bipartisan forums around the country in which,
despite everything else that was going on, we searched for
common ground, arguing about how to provide for retirement security rather than whether to do so.

Two days after the speech, Judge Wright ordered that all
evidence related to Monica Lewinsky be excluded from the
Jones case because it was "not essential to the core issues,"
making Starr's inquiry into my deposition even more questionable, since perjury requires a false statement about a
"material" matter. On the last day of the month, ten days
after the firestorm began, the *Chicago Tribune* published a
poll showing that my job approval rating had risen to 72
percent. I was determined to show the American people that
I was on the job and getting results for them.

On February 5 and 6, Tony and Cherie Blair came to the
United States for a two-day state visit. They were a sight for
sore eyes for both Hillary and me. They made us laugh, and
Tony gave me strong support in public, emphasizing our
common approach to economic and social problems and to
foreign policy. We took them to Camp David for a dinner
with Al and Tipper Gore, and held a state dinner at the
White House with entertainment by Elton John and Stevie

Wonder. After the event Hillary told me that Newt Gingrich, who had been seated at her table with Tony Blair, had said the charges against me were "ludicrous" and "meaningless" even if true, and weren't "going anywhere."

At our press conference, after Tony said that I was not just his colleague but his friend, Mike Frisby, a reporter for the *Wall Street Journal*, finally asked the question I had been waiting for. He wanted to know, given the pain and all the issues about my personal life, "At what point do you consider that it's just not worth it, and do you consider resigning the office?" "Never," I answered. I said I had tried to take the personal venom out of politics, but the harder I tried, "the harder others have pulled in the other direction." Still, "I would never walk away from the people of this country and the trust they've placed in me," so "I'm just going to keep showing up for work."

In mid-month, as Tony Blair and I continued to build support around the world for launching air strikes on Iraq in response to the expulsion of the UN inspectors, Kofi Annan secured a last-minute agreement from Saddam Hussein to resume the inspections. It seemed that Saddam never moved except when forced to do so.

Besides plugging my new initiatives, I spent time working for the McCain-Feingold campaign finance reform bill, which the Senate Republicans killed at the end of the month; swearing in a new surgeon general, Dr. David Satcher, the director of the Centers for Disease Control; touring tornado damage in central Florida; announcing the first grants to help communities strengthen their efforts to prevent violence against women; and raising funds to help Democrats in the coming election.

In late January and in February, several White House staffers were called before the grand jury. I felt terrible that they had been caught up in all this, especially Betty Currie, who had tried to befriend Monica Lewinsky and was now being punished for it. I also felt bad that Vernon Jordan had been caught up in the maelstrom. We had been close friends for so long, and time and again I had seen him help people who needed it. Now he was being targeted because of me. I knew he hadn't done anything wrong and hoped someday he would be able to forgive me for the mess I had gotten him into.

Starr also subpoenaed Sidney Blumenthal, a journalist and old friend of Hillary's and mine who had come to work in the White House in July 1997. According to the *Washington Post*, Starr was exploring whether Sid's criticism of him amounted to an obstruction of justice. It was a chilling indication of how thin-skinned Starr was, and how willing to use the power of his office against anyone who criticized him. Starr also subpoenaed two private investigators who had been hired by the *National Enquirer* to run down a rumor that he had been having an affair with a woman in Little Rock. The rumor was false, apparently a case of mistaken identity, but again, it reflected a double standard. He was using FBI agents and private investigators to look into my life. When a tabloid looked at his, he went after them.

Starr's tactics were beginning to draw the attention of the press. *Newsweek* published a two-page chart, "Conspiracy or Coincidence," which traced the connections of more than twenty conservative activists and organizations that had promoted and financed the "scandals" Starr was investigating. The *Washington Post* ran a story in which a number of former federal prosecutors expressed discomfort not just with Starr's new focus on my private conduct, "but with the arsenal of weapons he has deployed to try to make his case against the president."

Starr was particularly criticized for forcing Monica Lewinsky's mother to testify against her will. Federal guidelines, which Starr was supposed to follow, said that family members should ordinarily not be forced to testify unless they were part of the criminal activity being investigated, or there were "overriding prosecutorial concerns." By early February, according to an NBC News poll, only 26 percent of the American people thought Starr was conducting an impartial inquiry.

The saga continued into March. My deposition in the Jones case was leaked, obviously by someone on the Jones side. Although the judge had repeatedly warned the Rutherford Institute lawyers not to leak it, no one was ever sanctioned. On the eighth, Jim McDougal died in a federal prison in Texas, a sad and ironic end to his long downward slide. According to Susan McDougal, Jim had changed his story to suit Starr and Hick Ewing because he desperately wanted to avoid dying in jail.

In mid-month, *60 Minutes* ran an interview with a woman named Kathleen Willey, who claimed I had made an unwanted advance toward her while she was working in the White House. It wasn't true. We had evidence that cast doubt on her story, including the affidavit of her friend Julie Hiatt Steele, who said Willey had asked her to lie by saying she had told Steele about the alleged episode shortly after it happened, when in fact she hadn't.

Willey's husband had killed himself, leaving her responsible for more than $200,000 of outstanding debt. Within a week, news stories reported that after I called her to offer my condolences on her husband's death, she had told people I was coming to his funeral; this was after the alleged incident. Eventually we released about a dozen letters Willey had written to me, again after the alleged encounter, saying things like she was my "number one fan" and that she wanted to help me "in any way that I can." After a report that she had sought $300,000 to tell her story to a tabloid or in a book, the story faded away.

I mention Willey's sad tale here because of what Starr did with it. First, in a highly unusual move, he gave her "transactional immunity"—complete protection against any kind of criminal prosecution—provided she told him the "truth." When she was caught being untruthful about some embarrassing details involving another man, Starr just gave her immunity again. By contrast, when Julie Hiatt Steele, a registered Republican, refused to change her story and lie for Starr, he indicted her. Even though she wasn't convicted, it ruined her financially. Starr's office even sought to challenge the legality of her adoption of a baby from Romania.

On St. Patrick's Day, I met with the leaders of all of the political parties in Northern Ireland that were participating in the political process, and had extended visits with Gerry Adams and David Trimble. Tony Blair and Bertie Ahern wanted to reach an agreement. My role was basically to keep reassuring and pushing all the parties into the framework George Mitchell was constructing. There were hard compromises still ahead, but I thought we were getting there.

A few days later, Hillary and I flew to Africa, far away from the clamor at home. Africa was a continent that America had too often ignored, and one that I believed would play a large role for good or ill in the twenty-first century. I was really glad Hillary was going with me; she had loved the trip she and Chelsea had made to Africa the previous year, and we needed the time away together.

The visit began in Ghana, where President Jerry Rawlings and his wife, Nana Konadu Agyemang, got us off to a rousing start with a ceremony in Independence Square; it was filled with more than half a million people. We were flanked on the stage by tribal kings draped in bright-colored native kente cloth and entertained by African rhythms played by several Ghanaians on by far the largest drum I had ever seen.

I liked Rawlings and respected the fact that after seizing power in a military coup, he was elected and reelected president, and was committed to relinquishing his office in 2000. Besides, we had an indirect family connection: when Chelsea was born, the doctor was assisted by a wonderful Ghanaian midwife who had come to Arkansas to continue her education. Hillary and I came to like Hagar Sam very much and were pleased to learn she had also helped to deliver the four Rawlings children.

On the twenty-fourth, we were in Uganda to meet with President Yoweri Museveni and his wife, Janet. Uganda had come a long way since the stifling dictatorship of Idi Amin. Just a few years earlier, it had had the highest AIDS rate in Africa. With a campaign called "the big noise," the death rate had been cut in half through a focus on abstinence, education, marriage, and condoms.

The four of us went to two small villages, Mukono and Wanyange, to highlight the importance of education and of American-financed micro-credit loans. Uganda had tripled education funding in the previous five years and had made a real effort to educate girls as well as boys. The schoolchildren we visited in Mukono wore nice pink uniforms. They were obviously bright and interested, but their learning materials were inadequate; the map on the classroom wall was so old it still included the Soviet Union. In Wanyange, the village cook had expanded her operation and another woman had diversified her chicken-raising business to include rabbits with micro-credit loans funded by U.S. aid. We met a woman with a two-day-old baby. She let me hold the infant boy as the White House photographer took a picture of two guys named Bill Clinton.

The Secret Service didn't want me to go to Rwanda because of ongoing security problems, but I felt that I had to. As a concession to the security issue, I met at the Kigali airport with the leaders of the country and with survivors of the genocide. President Pasteur Bizimungu, a Hutu, and Vice President Paul Kagame, a Tutsi, were trying to put the country back together. Kagame was the nation's most powerful political leader; he had decided that it would advance the reconciliation process to begin with a president from the majority Hutu tribe. I acknowledged that the United States and the international community had not acted quickly enough to stop the genocide or to prevent the refugee camps from becoming havens for the killers, and I offered to help the nation rebuild and to support the war crimes tribunal that would hold accountable the perpetrators of the genocide.

The survivors told me their stories. The last speaker was a dignified woman who said her family had been identified to the rampaging killers as Tutsis by Hutu neighbors whose children had played with hers for years. She was badly wounded by a machete and left for dead. She awoke in a pool of her own blood to find her husband and six children lying dead beside her. She told Hillary and me that she had cried out to God in despair that she had survived, then came to understand "that my life must have been spared for a reason, and it could not be something as mean as vengeance. So I do what I can to help us start again." I was overwhelmed; that magnificent woman had made my problems seem pathetically small. She had deepened my resolve to do whatever I could to help Rwanda.

I began the first visit by any American President to South Africa in Cape Town, with a speech to the parliament in which I said I had come "in part to help the American people see the new Africa with new eyes." It was fascinating to me to witness the supporters and victims of apartheid working together. They didn't deny the past or hide their current disagreements, but they seemed confident that they could build a common future. It was a tribute to the spirit of reconciliation that emanated from Mandela.

The next day Mandela took us to visit Robben Island, where he had spent the first eighteen years of his captivity. I saw the rock quarry where he had worked and the cramped cell where he was kept when he wasn't breaking rocks. In Johannesburg, I called on Deputy President Thabo Mbeki, who had been meeting with Al Gore twice a year on our common agenda and was almost certain to be Mandela's successor; dedicated a commercial center named after Ron Brown, who had loved South Africa; and visited a primary school. Hillary and I went to church with Jesse Jackson in Soweto, the teeming township that had produced so many of the anti-apartheid activists.

By this time I had developed a real friendship with Mandela. He was remarkable not only because of his astonishing journey from hatred to reconciliation during twenty-seven years in prison, but also because he was both a tough-minded politician and a caring person who, despite his long confinement, never lost his interest in the personal side of life or his ability to show love, friendship, and kindness.

We had one especially meaningful conversation. I said, "Madiba [Mandela's colloquial tribal name, which he asked me to use], I know you did a great thing in inviting your jailers to your inauguration, but didn't you really hate those who imprisoned you?" He replied, "Of course I did, for many years. They took the best years of my life. They abused me physically and mentally. I didn't get to see my children grow up. I hated them. Then one day when I was working in the quarry, hammering the rocks, I realized that they had already taken everything from me except my mind and my heart. Those they could not take without my permission. I decided not to give them away." Then he looked at me, smiled, and said, "And neither should you."

After I caught my breath, I asked him another question. "When you were walking out of prison for the last time, didn't you feel the hatred rise up in you again?" "Yes," he said, "for a moment I did. Then I thought to myself, 'They have had me for twenty-seven years. If I keep hating them, they will still have me.' I wanted to be free, and so I let it go." He smiled again. This time he didn't have to say, "And so should you."

The only vacation day on the trip came in Botswana, which had the highest per capita income in sub-Saharan Africa and the highest AIDS rate in the world. We went on a safari in Chobe National Park and saw lions, elephants, impalas, hippos, crocodiles, and more than twenty different species of birds. We got very close to a mother elephant and her child—apparently too close. She raised her trunk and sprayed us with water. It made me laugh to think how happy the Republicans would have been if they could have seen their party's mascot watering me. Late in the afternoon we took a leisurely boat ride down the Chobe River; Hillary and I held hands and counted our blessings as we watched the sun go down.

Our last stop was Senegal, where we visited the Door of No Return on Gorée Island, the point from which so many Africans were taken to slavery in North America. As I had in Uganda, I expressed my regret over America's responsibility for slavery and the long, hard struggle of African-Americans for freedom. I introduced the large delegation with me "representing over thirty million Americans that are Africa's great gift to America," and pledged to work with the Senegalese and all Africans for a better future. I also visited a mosque with President Abdou Diouf, out of respect for Senegal's overwhelmingly Muslim population; a

village that had recovered a section of desert with the help
of American aid; and Senegalese troops being trained by
American military personnel as part of the African Crisis
Response Initiative, which my administration had initiated,
our effort to better prepare Africans to stop wars and prevent other Rwandas.

The trip was the longest and most comprehensive ever
taken to Africa by an American President. The bipartisan
congressional delegation and the prominent citizens who
accompanied me, as well as the specific programs I was supporting, including the Africa Growth and Opportunity Act,
demonstrated to Africans that we were turning a new page
in our shared history. For all its problems, Africa was a
hopeful place. I had seen it in the faces of the massive
crowds in the cities, in those of the schoolchildren and villagers in the bush and on the edge of the desert. And Africa
had given me a great gift: in the wisdom of a Rwandan
widow and of Nelson Mandela, I had found more peace of
mind to face what lay ahead.

On April 1, while we were still in Senegal, Judge Wright
granted my lawyers' motion for a summary judgment in the
Jones case, dismissing it without a trial, because she found
that Jones had produced no credible evidence to support her
claim. The dismissal exposed the raw political nature of
Starr's investigation. Now he was pursuing me on the theory that I had given a false statement in a deposition the
judge had said was not relevant, and that I had obstructed
justice in a case that had no merit in the first place. No one
was even talking about Whitewater anymore. On April 2, to
no one's surprise, Starr said he would press on.

A few days later Bob Rubin and I announced that the
United States would block the importation of 1.6 million
assault weapons. Although we had banned the manufacture
of nineteen different assault weapons in the 1994 crime bill,
ingenious foreign gun makers were trying to evade the law
by making modifications on guns whose only purpose was
to kill people.

Good Friday, April 10, was one of the happiest days of

my presidency. Seventeen hours past the deadline for a decision, all the parties in Northern Ireland agreed to a plan to end thirty years of sectarian violence. I had been up most of the night before, trying to help George Mitchell close the deal. Besides George, I talked to Bertie Ahern, and to Tony Blair, David Trimble, and Gerry Adams twice, before going to bed at 2:30 a.m. At five, George woke me with a request to call Adams again to seal the deal.

The agreement was a fine piece of work, calling for majority rule and minority rights; shared political decision making and shared economic benefits; continued ties to the United Kingdom and new ties to Ireland. The process that produced the pact began with the determination of John Major and Albert Reynolds to seek peace, continued when John Bruton succeeded Reynolds, and was completed by Bertie Ahern, Tony Blair, David Trimble, John Hume, and Gerry Adams. My first visa to Adams and the subsequent intense engagement of the White House made a difference, and George Mitchell handled the negotiations brilliantly.

Of course, the main credit went to those who had to make the hard decisions, the Northern Irish leaders, Blair, and Ahern, and to the people of Northern Ireland who had chosen the promise of peace over a poisoned past. The agreement would have to be ratified in a referendum by the voters of Northern Ireland and the Irish Republic on May 22. With a touch of Irish eloquence, it became known as the Good Friday accord.

At around that time, I also flew to the Johnson Space Center in Houston to discuss our newest shuttle mission to conduct twenty-six experiments on the impact of space on the human body, including how the brain adapts and what happens to the inner ear and the human balance system. One of the crew was in the audience, seventy-seven-year-old senator John Glenn. After flying 149 combat missions in World War II and Korea, John had been one of America's first astronauts more than thirty-five years earlier. He was retiring from the Senate and was itching to go into space once more. NASA's director, Dan Goldin, and I were strongly in favor of Glenn's participation because our space agency wanted to study the effects of space on aging. I had always been a strong supporter of the space program, including the International Space Station and the upcoming mission to Mars; John Glenn's last hurrah gave us a chance to show the practical benefits of space exploration.

I then flew to Chile for a state visit and the second Summit of the Americas. After the long, harsh dictatorship of General Augusto Pinochet, Chile seemed firmly committed to democracy under the leadership of President Eduardo Frei, whose father had also been president of Chile in the 1960s. Shortly after the summit, Mack McLarty resigned as my special envoy to the Americas. By then my old friend had made more than forty trips to the region in the four years since he had taken the job and, in so doing, had sent an unmistakable message that the United States was committed to being a good neighbor.

The month ended on two high notes. I held a reception for members of Congress who had voted for the 1993 budget, including those who had lost their seats for doing so, to announce that the deficit had been completely eliminated for the first time since 1969. It was a development that would have been unthinkable when I took office, and impossible without the hard vote for the economic plan in 1993. On the last day of the month, the Senate voted, 80–19, to approve another of my major priorities—bringing Poland, Hungary, and the Czech Republic into NATO.

In mid-May our efforts to ban nuclear testing were shaken when India conducted five underground tests. Two weeks later, Pakistan responded with six tests of its own. India claimed its nuclear weapons were needed as a deterrent to China; Pakistan said it was responding to India. Public opinion in both nations strongly supported the possession of nuclear weapons, but it was a dangerous proposition. For one thing, our national security people were convinced that, unlike the United States and the Soviet Union in the Cold War, India and Pakistan knew little about each other's nuclear capabilities and policies for using them. After the Indian tests, I urged Pakistan's prime minister, Nawaz Sharif, not to follow suit, but he couldn't resist the political pressure.

I was deeply concerned about India's decision, not only because I considered it so dangerous, but also because it set back my policy of improving Indo-U.S. relations and made it harder for me to secure Senate ratification of the Comprehensive Test Ban Treaty. France and the UK had already done so, but there was a growing sense of isolation and unilateralism in Congress, as evidenced by the failure of the fast-track legislation and the refusal to pay our UN dues or our contribution to the International Monetary Fund. The IMF funding was especially important. With an Asian financial crisis threatening to spread to fragile economies in other parts of the world, the IMF needed to be able to organize an aggressive and well-funded response. The Congress was compromising the stability of the global economy.

While the nuclear testing controversy was unfolding, I had to leave on another trip, to the annual G-8 summit being held in Birmingham, England. On the way, I stopped in Germany for a meeting with Helmut Kohl at Sans Souci, the palace of Frederick the Great; for a celebration marking the fiftieth anniversary of the Berlin airlift; and for a public appearance with Kohl at a General Motors Opel plant in Eisenach, in the former East Germany.

Kohl was in a tough fight for reelection, and my appearances with him beyond the airlift ceremonies raised a few questions, especially since his Social Democratic Party opponent, Gerhard Schroeder, was running on a platform that was a lot like what Tony Blair and I were advocating. Helmut had already served longer than any German chancellor except Bismarck, and he was behind in the polls. But he had been America's friend, and mine, and no matter how the election came out, his legacy was secure: a reunited Germany, a strong European Union, a partnership with democratic Russia, and German support for ending the Bosnian war. Before I left Germany, I also had a good talk with Schroeder, who had risen from modest beginnings to the summit of German politics. He struck me as tough, smart, and clearheaded about what he wanted to do. I wished him well, and told him that if he won I would do whatever I could to help him succeed.

When I arrived in Birmingham, I saw that the city had undergone a remarkable revival and was much more beautiful than it had been when I first visited there almost thirty years earlier. The conference had a useful agenda, calling for international economic reforms; greater cooperation against drug trafficking, money laundering, and trafficking in women and children; and a specific alliance between the United States and the European Union against terrorism. However important, it was overshadowed by unfolding world events: the Indian nuclear tests; the political and economic collapse of Indonesia; the stalled peace process in the Middle East; the looming prospect of war in Kosovo; and the coming referendum on the Good Friday accord. We condemned the Indian nuclear tests, reaffirmed our support for the Nuclear Nonproliferation and Comprehensive Test Ban treaties, and said we wanted a global treaty to stop the production of fissile materials for nuclear weapons. On Indonesia, we urged both economic and political reforms, which seemed unlikely to occur because the country's finances were in such a terrible mess that the necessary reforms would make life even harder for ordinary Indonesians in the short run. Within a couple of days, President Suharto resigned, but Indonesia's problems did not leave with him. They would soon claim more of my time. Nothing could be done on the Middle East for the moment, until the Israeli political situation was sorted out.

In Kosovo, the southernmost province of Serbia, the majority of the people were Albanian Muslims who were chafing under Milosevic's rule. After Serbian attacks on the Kosovars earlier in the year, the United Nations had placed an arms embargo on the former Yugoslavia (Serbia and Montenegro) and several nations had imposed economic sanctions on Serbia. A Contact Group consisting of the United States, Russia, and several European nations was working to defuse the crisis. The G-8 supported the Contact Group's efforts, but soon we would have to do more.

Again, the only good news was in Northern Ireland. More than 90 percent of Sinn Fein party members had endorsed the Good Friday accord. With both John Hume and Gerry Adams working for it, a huge Catholic vote in favor of the agreement was certain. Protestant opinion was more closely divided. After consulting with the parties, I decided not to go from Birmingham to Belfast to speak in person for the agreement. I didn't want to give Ian Paisley any ammunition to attack me as an outsider telling the Northern Irish what to do. Instead, Tony Blair and I met with reporters and did two lengthy television interviews with the BBC and CNN supporting the referendum.

On May 20, two days before the vote, I also delivered a brief radio address to the people of Northern Ireland, pledging America's support if they voted for "a lasting peace for yourselves and your children." That's exactly what they did. The Good Friday accord was approved by 71 percent of the people in Northern Ireland, including a solid majority of Protestants. In the Irish Republic, more than 90 percent of the people voted for it. I was never more proud of my Irish heritage.

After a stop in Geneva to urge the World Trade Organization to adopt a more open decision-making process, take more account of labor and environmental conditions in trade negotiations, and listen to the representatives of ordinary citizens who felt left out of the global economy, I flew home to America, but not away from the world's problems.

That week, at the commencement ceremony of the U.S. Naval Academy, I outlined an aggressive approach to deal with sophisticated global terrorist networks, including a plan to detect, deter, and defend against attacks on our power systems, water supplies, police, fire and medical services, air traffic control, financial services, telephone systems, and computer networks, and a concerted effort to prevent the spread and use of biological weapons and protect our people from them. I proposed to strengthen the inspection system of the Biological Weapons Convention; vaccinate our armed forces against biological threats, especially anthrax; train more state and local officials and National Guard personnel to respond to biological attacks; upgrade our system of detection and warning; stockpile medicines and vaccines against the most likely biological attacks; and

increase research and development to create the next generation of vaccines, medicines, and diagnostic tools.

Over the previous several months I had become particularly worried about the prospect of a biological attack, perhaps with a weapon that had been genetically engineered to
resist existing vaccines and medicines. The previous December, at Renaissance Weekend, Hillary and I had arranged to
have dinner with Craig Venter, a molecular biologist whose
company was attempting to finish sequencing the human
genome. I asked Craig about the possibility that genetic
mapping would permit terrorists to develop synthetic genes,
reengineer existing viruses, or combine smallpox with
another deadly virus to make it even more harmful.

Craig said those things were possible and urged me to
read Richard Preston's new novel, *The Cobra Event*, a
thriller about a mad scientist's efforts to reduce the world's
population by infecting New York City with a "brainpox,"
a combination of smallpox and an insect virus that destroys
nerves. When I read the book I was surprised that Preston's
acknowledgments included more than one hundred scientists, military and intelligence experts, and officials in my
own administration. I urged several cabinet members and
Speaker Gingrich to read it.

We had begun working on the biological warfare issue
in 1993, after the World Trade Center bombing made it
clear that terrorism could strike at home, and a defector
from Russia had told us that his country had huge stocks of
anthrax, smallpox, Ebola, and other pathogens, and had
continued to produce them even after the demise of the
Soviet Union. In response, the mandate of the Nunn-Lugar
program was broadened to include cooperation with Russia
on biological as well as nuclear weapons.

After the sarin gas release in the Tokyo subway in 1995,
the Counterterrorism Security Group (CSG), headed by
National Security Council staffer Richard Clarke, began to
focus more on planning defenses against chemical and biological attacks. In June 1995, I signed Presidential Decision
Directive (PDD) 39 to allocate responsibilities among various government agencies for preventing and dealing with

such attacks, and for reducing terrorists' capabilities through covert action and aggressive efforts to capture terrorists abroad. In the Pentagon, a few military and civilian leaders were interested in the issue, including the commandant of the Marine Corps, Charles Krulak, and Richard Danzig, the undersecretary of the navy. In late 1996, the Joint Chiefs endorsed Danzig's recommendation to vaccinate the entire military force against anthrax, and Congress moved to tighten control over biological agents in American labs, after a fanatic, using false identification, was caught buying three vials of plague virus from a lab for about $300.

By late 1997, when it became clear that Russia had even larger stocks of germ warfare agents than we had believed, I authorized American cooperation with scientists who had worked at the institutes where a lot of the bioweapons had been built in the Soviet era, in the hope of finding out exactly what was going on and preventing them from providing their expertise or biological agents to Iran or other high bidders.

In March 1998, Dick Clarke gathered about forty members of the administration at Blair House for a "tabletop exercise" on handling terrorist attacks of smallpox, a chemical agent, and a nuclear weapon. The results were troubling. With smallpox, it took them too much time and the loss of too many lives to bring the epidemic under control. The stocks of antibiotics and vaccines were inadequate, the quarantine laws were antiquated, the public-health systems were in bad shape, and the state emergency plans were not well developed.

A few weeks later, at my request, Clarke assembled seven scientists and emergency response experts, including Craig Venter; Joshua Lederberg, a Nobel Prize–winning biologist who had spent decades crusading against biological weapons; and Jerry Hauer, director of Emergency Management in New York City. Along with Bill Cohen, Janet Reno, Donna Shalala, George Tenet, and Sandy Berger, I met with the group for several hours to discuss the threat and what to do about it. Although I had been up most of the previous night helping to close the Irish peace agreement, I listened carefully to their presentation and asked a lot of questions. Everything I heard confirmed that we were not prepared for bio-attacks, and that the coming ability to sequence and reconfigure genes had profound implications for our national security. As the meeting was breaking up, Dr. Lederberg gave me a copy of a recent issue of the *Journal of the American Medical Association* devoted to the threat of bioterrorism. After reading it, I was even more concerned.

Less than a month later, the group sent me a report containing its recommendations for spending almost $2 billion over the next four years to improve public-health capabilities, build a national stockpile of antibiotics and vaccines, especially against smallpox, and increase research into the development of better medicines and vaccines through genetic engineering.

On the day of the Annapolis speech, I signed two more presidential directives on terrorism. PDD-62 created a ten-point counterterrorism initiative, assigning responsibility to various government agencies for specific functions, including the apprehension, return, and prosecution of terrorists and the disruption of their networks; preventing terrorists from acquiring weapons of mass destruction; managing the aftermath of attacks; protecting critical infrastructure and cybersystems; and protecting Americans at home and overseas.

PDD-62 also established the position of National Coordinator for Counterterrorism and Infrastructure Protection; I appointed Dick Clarke, who had been our point person on anti-terrorism from the start. He was a career professional who had served under Presidents Reagan and Bush, and was appropriately aggressive in his efforts to organize the government to fight terror. PDD-63 established a National Infrastructure Protection Center to prepare for the first time a comprehensive plan to protect our critical infrastructure, such as transportation, telecommunications, and water systems.

At the end of the month, Starr tried and failed again to force Susan McDougal to testify before the grand jury; questioned Hillary for nearly five hours and for the sixth time; and indicted Webb Hubbell again on tax charges. Several former prosecutors questioned the propriety of Starr's highly unusual move; essentially Hubbell was being charged again for overcharging his clients because he hadn't paid taxes on the money. To make matters worse, Starr also indicted Hubbell's wife, Suzy, because she had signed their joint income tax returns, and Webb's friends, accountant Mike Schaufele and lawyer Charles Owen, because they had given Hubbell advice on his financial affairs, free of charge, when he was in trouble. Hubbell was blunt in his response: "They think by indicting my wife and my friends that I will lie about the President and the First Lady. I will not do so . . . I'm not gonna lie about the President. I'm not gonna lie about the First Lady, or anyone else."

In early May, Starr continued his strategy of intimidation by indicting Susan McDougal on charges of criminal contempt and obstruction of justice for her continuing refusal to talk to the grand jury, the same offense for which she had already served eighteen months for civil contempt. This one took the cake. Starr and Hick Ewing couldn't bully Susan McDougal into lying for them and it was driving them nuts. Although it would take Susan nearly another year to prove it, she was tougher than they were, and in the end she would be vindicated.

In June, Starr finally got into a little hot water. After Steven Brill published an article in *Brill's Content* on Starr's operation that highlighted the OIC's strategy of unlawful news leaks, and reported that Starr had admitted the leaks in a ninety-minute interview, Judge Norma Holloway Johnson ruled that there was "probable cause" to believe that Starr's office had engaged in "serious and repetitive" leaks to the news media and that David Kendall could subpoena Starr and his deputies to find the source of the leaks. Because the judge's decision involved grand jury proceedings, it was rendered in secret. Strangely, it was one aspect of Starr's operation that was not leaked to the press.

On May 29, Barry Goldwater died at the age of eighty-nine. I was saddened by his passing. Although we were of different parties and philosophies, Goldwater had been uncommonly kind to Hillary and me. I also respected him for being a genuine patriot and an old-fashioned libertarian who thought the government should stay out of citizens' private lives and who believed political combat should focus on ideas, not personal attacks.

I spent the rest of the spring lobbying for my legislative program and doing the business at hand: issuing an executive order to prohibit discrimination against gays in federal civilian employment; supporting Boris Yeltsin's new economic reform program; receiving the emir of Bahrain at the White House; addressing the UN General Assembly session on global drug trafficking; hosting a state visit for South Korean president Kim Dae Jung; holding a National Ocean Conference in Monterey, California, where I extended the ban on oil drilling off the California coast for fourteen years; signing a bill that provided funds to buy bulletproof vests for the 25 percent of our law-enforcement officers who didn't have them; speaking at three university commencements; and campaigning for Democrats in six states.

It was a busy but fairly normal month, except for an unhappy trip I took to Springfield, Oregon, where a troubled fifteen-year-old boy armed with a semiautomatic weapon had killed and wounded several of his classmates. It was the latest in a series of school shootings that included lethal incidents in Jonesboro, Arkansas; Pearl, Mississippi; Paducah, Kentucky; and Edinboro, Pennsylvania.

The killings were both heartbreaking and perplexing, because the overall juvenile crime rate was finally declining. It seemed to me that the violent outbursts were due, at least in part, to the excessive glorification of violence in our culture and the easy availability of deadly weapons to children. In all the school shooting cases, including several others in which no deaths had occurred, the young perpetrators seemed to be enraged, alienated, or in the grip of some dark philosophy of life. I asked Janet Reno and Dick Riley to put together a guide for teachers, parents, and students on the early warning signals troubled young people frequently exhibited, with suggested strategies on how to deal with them.

I went to the high school in Springfield to meet with the victims' families, listen to accounts of what had happened, and speak to the students, teachers, and citizens. They were traumatized, wondering how such a thing could have occurred in their community. Often at times like this, I felt all I could do was share people's grief, reassure them that they were good men and women, and encourage them to pick up the pieces and go on.

As spring turned to summer, it was time for my long-planned visit to China. Although the United States and China still had significant differences over human rights, religious and political freedom, and other matters, I was looking forward to the trip. I thought Jiang Zemin had done well on his trip to the United States in 1997 and he was eager to have me reciprocate.

The trip was not free of controversy in either country. I would be the first President to go to China since the suppression of pro-democracy forces in Tiananmen Square in 1989. The charges of Chinese attempts to influence the '96 election had not been resolved. Also, some Republicans were attacking me for allowing American companies to launch commercial satellites into space on Chinese missiles, though the satellite technology was not accessible to the Chinese, and the process had begun under the Reagan administration and continued during the Bush years in order to save money for U.S. companies. Finally, many Americans feared that China's trade policies and its tolerance of the illegal reproduction and sale of American books, movies, and music were causing job losses in the United States.

On the Chinese side, many officials resented our criticism of Chinese human rights policies as interference in their internal affairs, while others believed that, for all my positive talk, American policy was to contain, not cooperate, with China in the twenty-first century.

With a quarter of the world's population and a rapidly

growing economy, China was bound to have a profound economic and political impact on America and the world. If at all possible, we had to build a positive relationship. It would have been foolish not to go.

In the week before I left, I nominated UN Ambassador Bill Richardson to succeed Federico Peña as secretary of energy, and Dick Holbrooke to become the new UN ambassador. Richardson, a former congressman from New Mexico, where two of the Energy Department's important research labs were located, was a natural for the job. Holbrooke had the skills to solve our UN dues problem and the experience and intellect to make a major contribution to our foreign policy team. With trouble brewing in the Balkans again, we needed him.

Hillary, Chelsea, and I arrived in China on the night of June 25, along with Hillary's mother, Dorothy, and a delegation that included Secretary Albright, Secretary Rubin, Secretary Daley, and six members of Congress, including John Dingell of Michigan, the longest-serving member of the House. John's presence was important because Michigan's dependence on the automobile industry made it a center of protectionist sentiment. I was gratified that he wanted to see China firsthand, to make his own judgment about whether China should join the WTO.

We began the trip at the ancient capital of Xi'an, where the Chinese put on an elaborate and beautiful welcoming ceremony. The next day we had the opportunity to walk among the rows of the famous terra-cotta warriors, and to have a roundtable discussion with Chinese citizens in the small village of Xiahe.

We got down to business two days later, when President Jiang Zemin and I met and held a press conference that was televised live all over China. We frankly discussed our differences as well as our commitment to building a strategic partnership. It was the first time the Chinese people had ever seen their leader actually debate issues like human rights and religious liberty with a foreign head of state. Jiang had grown more confident in his ability to deal with such issues in public and he trusted me to disagree in a respectful way, as well as to stress our common interests in ending the Asian financial crisis, advancing nonproliferation, and promoting reconciliation on the Korean peninsula.

When I advocated more freedom and human rights in China, Jiang responded that America was highly developed, while China still had a per capita income of $700 a year. He emphasized our different histories, cultures, ideologies, and social systems. When I urged Jiang to meet with the Dalai Lama, he said the door was open if the Dalai Lama would first state that Tibet and Taiwan were part of China, and added that there were already "several channels of communication" with the leader of Tibetan Buddhism. I got a laugh from the Chinese audience when I said I thought that if Jiang and the Dalai Lama did meet, they would like each other very much. I also tried to make some practical suggestions to move forward on human rights. For example, there were still Chinese citizens in prison for offenses no longer on the books. I suggested they be released.

The main point of the press conference was the debate itself. I wanted Chinese citizens to see America supporting human rights that we believe are universal, and I wanted Chinese officials to see that greater openness wouldn't cause the social disintegration that, given China's history, they understandably feared.

After the state dinner hosted by Jiang Zemin and his wife, Wang Yeping, he and I took turns conducting the People's Liberation Army Band. The next day my family attended Sunday church services at Chongwenmen Church, Beijing's earliest Protestant church, one of the few houses of worship the government had sanctioned. Many Christians were meeting secretly in homes. Religious liberty was important to me, and I was pleased when Jiang agreed to let me send a delegation of American religious leaders, including a rabbi, a Catholic archbishop, and an evangelical minister, to pursue the matter further.

After we toured the Forbidden City and the Great Wall, I held a question-and-answer session with students at Beijing University. We discussed human rights in China, but they also asked me about human rights problems in the

United States and about what I could do to increase the American people's understanding of China. These were fair questions from young people who wanted their country to change but were still proud of it.

Premier Zhu Rongji hosted a lunch for the delegation in which we discussed the economic and social challenges facing China, as well as the remaining issues we still had to resolve in order to bring China into the World Trade Organization. I was strongly in favor of doing so, in order to continue China's integration into the global economy, and to increase both its acceptance of international rules of law and its willingness to cooperate with the United States and other nations on a whole range of other issues. That night President Jiang and Madame Wang invited us to dine alone with them at their official residence, which lay beside a placid lake inside the compound that housed China's most important leaders. The more time I spent with Jiang, the more I liked him. He was intriguing, funny, and fiercely proud, but always willing to listen to different points of view. Even though I didn't always agree with him, I became convinced that he believed he was changing China as fast as he could, and in the right direction.

From Beijing we went to Shanghai, which seemed to have more construction cranes than any other city in the world. Hillary and I had a fascinating discussion about China's problems and potential with a group of younger Chinese, including professors, businesspeople, a consumer advocate, and a novelist. One of the most enlightening experiences of the entire trip was a radio call-in show I did with the mayor. There were some good but predictable questions for me on economic and security matters, but the mayor got more questions than I did; his callers were interested in better education and more computers, and worried about the traffic congestion as a result of the city's growing prosperity and expansion. It struck me that if citizens were complaining to the mayor about traffic jams, Chinese politics was evolving in the right direction.

Before going home, we flew to Guilin for a meeting with environmentalists concerned about the destruction of forests and the loss of unique wildlife, and a leisurely boat trip down the Li River, which flows through a stunning landscape marked by large limestone formations that looked as if they had burst up through the landscape of the gentle countryside. After Guilin, we made a stop in Hong Kong to see Tung Chee-hwa, the chief executive chosen by the Chinese after the British left. An intelligent, sophisticated man who had lived in America for several years, Tung had his hands full balancing the boisterous Hong Kong political culture with the much more conformist Chinese central government. I also met again with democracy advocate Martin Lee. The Chinese had promised to let Hong Kong keep its much more democratic political system, but I had the clear impression that the details of their reunion were still being worked out, and that neither side was fully satisfied with the present state of affairs.

In mid-July, Al Gore and I held an event at the National Academy of Sciences to highlight our administration's efforts to avoid computer meltdowns at the dawn of the new millennium. There was widespread concern that many computer systems would not make the change to the year 2000, which would cause havoc in the economy and disrupt the affairs of millions of Americans. We organized an exhaustive effort led by John Koskinen to make sure all government systems were ready for the new millennium and to help the private sector make the adjustment. We wouldn't know for sure whether we had been successful until the date arrived.

On the sixteenth, I signed another of my priorities into law, the Child Support Performance and Incentive Act. We had already increased collections 68 percent since 1992; 1.4 million more families were now receiving child support. This bill penalized states that did not automate their child-support files and gave financial rewards to those that were successful in meeting performance goals.

Around this time I announced the purchase of eighty million bushels of wheat for distribution to poor nations with food shortages. Grain prices were down, and the purchase would both meet a humanitarian need and raise the price of wheat as much as thirteen cents a bushel for hard-pressed farmers. Because a severe heat wave was destroying crops in parts of the country, I also asked Congress to pass an emergency farm aid package.

Toward the end of the month, Mike McCurry announced that he would resign as White House press secretary in the fall, and I named his deputy, Joe Lockhart, who had served as press secretary for my reelection campaign, to succeed him. McCurry had done a fine job in a demanding position, answering tough questions, explaining the administration's policies with clarity and a quick wit, and working long hours with around-the-clock availability. He wanted to see his kids grow up. I liked Joe Lockhart a lot, and the press seemed to like him, too. Besides, he liked to play cards with me; we would have a smooth transition.

In July, as I continued to push my agenda at home, Dick Holbrooke flew to Belgrade to see Milosevic in an attempt to resolve the Kosovo crisis; Prime Minister Hashimoto resigned after election losses in Japan; Nelson Mandela got married to Graça Machel, the lovely widow of a former president of Mozambique and a leading figure in the struggle to stop the use of children in Africa's wars; and Ken Starr continued to build his case against me.

He insisted on taking the testimony of several of my Secret Service agents, including Larry Cockell, the head of my detail. The Secret Service had resisted this, and former President Bush had written two letters opposing it. Except when the President is on the residence floor of the White House, the Secret Service is always with him or just outside the door of whatever room he is in. Presidents depend on the Secret Service to protect them, and to protect their confidences. The agents overhear all kinds of conversations involving national security, domestic policy, political conflicts, and personal struggles. Their dedication, professionalism, and discretion had served Presidents of both parties and the nation well. Now Starr was willing to put all that at risk—to investigate not espionage, or Watergate-like abuses of the FBI, or Iran-Contra–like willful defiance of the law, but whether I had given false answers and encouraged Monica Lewinsky to do the same in response to questions asked in bad faith, in a case that had been thrown out of court because it had no merit in the first place.

By the end of the month, Starr had granted Monica Lewinsky immunity from prosecution in return for her testimony before the grand jury, and had subpoenaed me to testify as well. On the twenty-ninth, I agreed to testify voluntarily and the subpoena was withdrawn. I can't say I was looking forward to it.

Early in August, I met with ten Indian tribal leaders in Washington to announce a comprehensive effort to increase educational, health care, and economic opportunities for Native Americans. My assistant for intergovernmental affairs, Mickey Ibarra, and Lynn Cutler, my liaison to the tribes, had worked hard on the initiative and it was sorely needed. Although the United States was enjoying its lowest unemployment rate in twenty-eight years, the lowest crime rate in twenty-five years, and the smallest percentage of our citizens on welfare in twenty-nine years, Native American communities that had not grown wealthy from gambling operations were still in bad shape. Fewer than 10 percent of Native Americans went to college, they were three times more likely to suffer from diabetes as white Americans, and they still had the lowest per capita income of any American ethnic group. Some of the tribal communities had unemployment rates in excess of 50 percent. The leaders were encouraged by the new steps we were taking, and after the meeting I had some hope that we could help them.

The next day the American embassies in Tanzania and Kenya were hit by bombs that exploded within five minutes of each other, killing 257 people, including 12 Americans, and injuring 5,000 others. The initial evidence indicated that Osama bin Laden's network, which became known as al Qaeda, had launched the attacks. In late February, bin Laden had issued a fatwa calling for attacks on American military and civilian targets anywhere in the world. In May, he had said his supporters would hit U.S. targets in the Gulf and talked about "bringing the war home to America." In

June, in an interview with an American journalist, he had threatened to bring down U.S. military aircraft with anti-aircraft missiles.

By this time, we had been following bin Laden for years. Early in my first term, Tony Lake and Dick Clarke had pressed the CIA for more information about the wealthy Saudi, who had been expelled from his own country in 1991, had lost his citizenship in 1994, and had taken up residence in Sudan.

At first, bin Laden seemed to be a financier of terrorist operations, but over time we would learn that he was the head of a highly sophisticated terrorist organization, with access to large amounts of money beyond his own fortune, and with operatives in several countries, including Chechnya, Bosnia, and the Philippines. In 1995, after the war in Bosnia, we had thwarted mujahedin attempts to take over there and, in cooperation with local officials, had also stopped a plot to blow up a dozen planes flying out of the Philippines to the West Coast, but bin Laden's transnational network continued to grow.

In January 1996, the CIA had established a station focused exclusively on bin Laden and his network within its Counterterrorism Center, and shortly thereafter we began to urge Sudan to expel bin Laden. Sudan was then a virtual safe haven for terrorists, including the Egyptians who had tried to kill President Mubarak the previous June and who had succeeded in assassinating his predecessor, Anwar Sadat. The nation's leader, Hasan al-Turabi, shared bin Laden's radical views, and the two of them were involved in a whole host of business ventures, running the gamut from legitimate operations to weapons manufacturing and support for terrorists.

As we pressed Turabi to expel bin Laden, we asked Saudi Arabia to take him. The Saudis didn't want him back, but bin Laden finally left Sudan in mid-1996, apparently still on good terms with Turabi. He moved to Afghanistan, where he found a warm welcome from Mullah Omar, leader of the Taliban, a militant Sunni sect that was bent on establishing a radical Muslim theocracy in Afghanistan.

In September 1996, the Taliban captured Kabul and started seizing other areas of the country. By the end of the year, the CIA's bin Laden unit had developed significant information on him and his infrastructure. Almost a year later, Kenyan authorities arrested a man they believed was involved in a terrorist plot against the U.S. Embassy there.

In the week after the bombings, I kept up my regular schedule, traveling to Kentucky, Illinois, and California to promote the Patients' Bill of Rights and our clean water initiative, and to help Democrats up for election in those states. Beyond the public events, I spent most of my time with our national security team discussing how we were going to respond to the African attacks.

On August 13, there was a memorial service at Andrews Air Force Base for ten of the twelve American victims. The people bin Laden believed deserved to die just because they were Americans included a career diplomat I had met twice and his son; a woman who had just spent her vacation caring for her aged parents; an Indian-born foreign service officer who had traveled the world working for her adopted country; an epidemiologist working to save African children from disease and death; a mother of three small children; a proud new grandmother; an accomplished jazz musician with a day job in the foreign service; an embassy administrator who had married a Kenyan; and three sergeants, one each in the army, the air force, and the Marine Corps.

By all accounts, bin Laden was poisoned by the conviction that he was in possession of the absolute truth and therefore free to play God by killing innocent people. Since we had been going after his organization for several years, I had known for some time that he was a formidable adversary. After the African slaughter I became intently focused on capturing or killing him and with destroying al Qaeda.

One week after the embassy bombings, and after videotaping an address to the people of Kenya and Tanzania, whose losses were far greater than ours, I met with the national security principals. The CIA and FBI both confirmed that al Qaeda was responsible and reported that some of the perpetrators had already been arrested.

I had also received an intelligence report that al Qaeda had plans to attack yet another embassy, in Tirana, Albania, and that our enemies thought America was vulnerable because we would be distracted by the controversy over my personal behavior. We closed the Albanian embassy, sent in heavily armed marines to guard it, and began working with local authorities to break up the al Qaeda cell there. But we still had other embassies in countries with al Qaeda operations.

The CIA also had intelligence that bin Laden and his top staff were planning a meeting at one of his camps in Afghanistan on August 20 to assess the impact of their attacks and plan their next operations. The meeting would provide an opportunity to retaliate and perhaps wipe out much of the al Qaeda leadership. I asked Sandy Berger to manage the process leading up to a military response. We had to pick targets, move the necessary military assets into place, and figure out how to handle Pakistan. If we launched air strikes, our planes would pass over Pakistan's airspace.

Although we were trying to work with Pakistan to defuse tensions on the Indian subcontinent, and our two nations had been allies during the Cold War, Pakistan supported the Taliban and, by extension, al Qaeda. The Pakistani intelligence service used some of the same camps that bin Laden and al Qaeda did to train the Taliban and insurgents who fought in Kashmir. If Pakistan found out about our planned attacks in advance, it was likely that Pakistani intelligence would warn the Taliban or even al Qaeda. On the other hand, Deputy Secretary of State Strobe Talbott, who was working to minimize the chances of military conflict on the Indian subcontinent, was afraid that if we didn't tell the Pakistanis, they might assume the flying missiles had been launched at them by India and retaliate, conceivably even with nuclear weapons.

We decided to send the vice chairman of the Joint Chiefs of Staff, General Joe Ralston, to have dinner with the top Pakistani military commander at the time the attacks were scheduled. Ralston would tell him what was happening a few minutes before our missiles invaded Pakistan airspace, too late to alert the Taliban or al Qaeda, but in time to avoid having them shot down or sparking a counterattack on India.

My team was worried about one other thing: my testimony before the grand jury in three days, on August 17. They were afraid that it would make me reluctant to strike, or that if I did order the attack, I would be accused of doing it to divert public attention from my problems, especially if the attack didn't get bin Laden. I told them in no uncertain terms that their job was to give me advice on national security. If the recommendation was to strike on the twentieth, then that's what we would do. I said I would handle my personal problems. Time was running out on that, too.

TWENTY

ON SATURDAY MORNING, August 15, with the grand jury testimony looming and after a miserable, sleepless night, I woke up Hillary and told her the truth about what had happened between me and Monica Lewinsky. She looked at me as if I had punched her in the gut, almost as angry at me for lying to her in January as for what I had done. All I could do was tell her that I was sorry, and that I had felt I couldn't tell anyone, even her, what had happened. I told her that I loved her and I didn't want to hurt her or Chelsea, that I was ashamed of what I had done, and that I had kept everything to myself in an effort to avoid hurting my family and undermining the presidency. And after all the lies and abuse we had endured from the start of my presidency, I didn't want to be run out of office in the flood tide that followed my deposition in January. I still didn't fully understand why I had done something so wrong and stupid; that understanding would come slowly, in the months of working on our relationship that lay ahead.

I had to talk to Chelsea, too. In some ways, that was even harder. Sooner or later, every child learns that her parents aren't perfect, but this went far beyond the normal. I had always believed that I had been a good father. Chelsea's high school years and her freshman year in college had already been clouded by four years of intensely personal attacks on her parents. Now Chelsea had to learn that her father not only had done something terribly wrong, but had not told her or her mother the truth about it. I was afraid that I would lose not only my marriage, but my daughter's love and respect as well.

The rest of that awful day was dominated by another terrorist act. In Omagh, Northern Ireland, a breakaway faction of the IRA that did not support the Good Friday accord murdered twenty-eight people in a crowded shopping section of the city with a car bomb. All the parties to the peace process, including Sinn Fein, denounced the bombing. I issued a statement condemning the butchery, extending my sympathy to the victims' families, and urging the parties of peace to redouble their efforts. The outlaw group, which called itself the Real IRA, had about two hundred members and supporters, enough to cause real trouble, but not enough to disrupt the peace process: the Omagh bombing showed the utter insanity of going back to the old ways.

On Monday, after spending what time I could preparing, I went downstairs to the Map Room for four hours of testimony. Starr had agreed not to bring me down to the courthouse, probably because of the adverse reaction he got when he made Hillary do it. However, he insisted on videotaping my testimony, allegedly because one of the twenty-four grand jurors couldn't attend the session. David Kendall said the grand jury was welcome to come to the White House if Starr would not videotape my "secret" testimony. He refused; I suspected that he wanted to send the videotape to Congress, where it could be released without getting him into more hot water.

The grand jury was watching the proceedings on closed-circuit television back at the courthouse while Starr and his interrogators did their best to turn the videotape into a pornographic home movie, asking me questions designed to humiliate me and to so disgust the Congress and the American people that they would demand my resignation, after which he might be able to indict me. Samuel Johnson once said that nothing concentrates the mind as much as the prospect of one's own destruction. Moreover, I believed that a lot more was at stake than what might happen to me.

After the preliminaries, I asked to make a brief statement. I admitted that "on certain occasions in 1996 and once in 1997" I engaged in wrongful conduct that included inappropriate intimate contact with Monica Lewinsky; that the conduct, while morally wrong, did not constitute "sexual relations" as I understood the definition of the term that Judge Wright accepted at the request of the Jones lawyers; that I took full responsibility for my actions; and that I would answer to the best of my ability all the OIC's questions relating to the legality of my actions, but would not say more about the specifics of what had happened.

The principal OIC interrogator then took me through a long list of questions dealing with the definition of "sexual relations" that Judge Wright had imposed. I acknowledged that I had not been trying to be helpful to the Jones lawyers because they, like the OIC, had engaged in repeated unlawful leaks, and since they knew by then that their case had no merit, I believed that their objective in the deposition was to elicit damaging new information from me for the purpose of leaking it. I said that of course I didn't know that by the time I testified Starr's office had already become heavily involved.

Now Starr's lawyers were trying to capitalize on the setup by getting me on videotape discussing things in graphic detail that no one should ever have to talk about publicly.

When the OIC lawyer continued to complain about my deposition answers on the sex questions, I reminded him that both my lawyer and I had invited Jones's attorneys to ask specific follow-up questions, and that they declined to do so. I said it was now clear to me that they didn't do so because they were no longer trying to get a damaging admission that they could leak to the press. Instead, they were working for Starr. They wanted the deposition to lay the basis for forcing my resignation, or impeachment, or perhaps even an indictment. So they didn't ask follow-up questions "because they were afraid I would give them a truthful answer. . . . They were trying to set me up and trick me. And now you seem to be complaining that they didn't do a good enough job." I confessed that I "deplored" what the Rutherford Institute lawyers had done in Jones's name—the tormenting of innocent people, the illegal leaking, the pursuit of a bogus, politically motivated suit—"but I was determined to walk through the minefield of this deposition without violating the law, and I believe I did."

I did acknowledge that I had misled everyone who asked about the story after it broke. And I said over and over again that I never asked anyone to lie. When the agreed-upon four hours had expired, I had been asked many questions six or seven times, as the lawyers tried hard to turn my interrogation into admissions that were humiliating and incriminating. That's what the, to date, whole four-year $40 million investigation had come down to: parsing the definition of sex.

I finished the testimony at about six-thirty, three and a half hours before I was scheduled to address the nation. I was visibly upset when I went up to the solarium to see friends and staff who had gathered to discuss what had just happened, including White House counsel Chuck Ruff, David Kendall, Mickey Kantor, Rahm Emanuel, James Carville, Paul Begala, and Harry and Linda Thomason. Chelsea was there, too, and to my relief, at about eight, Hillary joined in.

We had a discussion about what I should say. Everyone knew I had to admit that I had made an awful mistake and had tried to hide it. The question was whether I should also take a shot at Starr's investigation and say it was time to end it. The virtually unanimous opinion was that I should not. Most people already knew that Starr was out of control; they needed to hear my admission of wrongdoing and witness my remorse. Some of my friends had given what they thought was strategic advice; others were genuinely appalled by what I had done. Only Hillary refused to express an opinion, instead encouraging everyone to leave me alone to write my statement.

At ten o'clock I told the American people about my testimony, said I was solely and completely responsible for my personal failure, and admitted misleading everyone, "even my wife." I said I was trying to protect myself and my family from intrusive questions in a politically inspired lawsuit that had been dismissed. I also said that Starr's investigation had gone on too long, cost too much, and hurt too many people, and that two years earlier, another investigation, a truly independent one, had found no wrongdoing by Hillary or me in Whitewater. Finally, I committed to doing my best to repair my family life, and I hoped we could repair the fabric of our nation's life by stopping the pursuit of personal destruction and prying into private lives, and moving on. I believed every word I said, but my anger hadn't worn off enough for me to be as contrite as I should have been.

The next day we left for Martha's Vineyard on our annual vacation. Usually I counted the days until we could get away for some family time; this year, though I knew we needed it, I wished that I was working around the clock instead. As we walked out to the South Lawn to get on the helicopter, with Chelsea between Hillary and me and Buddy walking beside me, photographers took pictures that revealed the pain I had caused. When there were no cameras around, my wife and daughter were barely speaking to me.

I spent the first couple of days alternating between begging for forgiveness and planning the strikes on al Qaeda. At night Hillary would go up to bed and I slept on the couch.

On my birthday General Don Kerrick, Sandy Berger's staffer, flew to Martha's Vineyard to go over the targets recommended by the CIA and the Joint Chiefs—the al Qaeda camps in Afghanistan and two targets in Sudan, a tannery in which bin Laden had a financial interest and a chemical plant the CIA believed was being used to produce or store a chemical used in the production of VX nerve gas. I took the tannery off the list because it had no military value to al Qaeda and I wanted to minimize civilian casualties. The hit on the camps would be timed to coincide with the meeting the intelligence indicated bin Laden and his top people would be having.

At 3 a.m. I gave Sandy Berger the final order to proceed, and U.S. Navy destroyers in the northern Arabian Sea launched cruise missiles at the targets in Afghanistan, while missiles were fired at the Sudanese chemical plant from ships in the Red Sea. Most of the missiles hit the targets, but bin Laden was not in the camp where the CIA thought he would be when the missiles hit it. Some reports said he had left the camp only a couple of hours earlier, but we never knew for sure. Several people associated with al Qaeda were killed, as were some Pakistani officers who were reported to be there to train Kashmiri terrorists. The Sudanese chemical plant was destroyed.

After announcing the attacks in Martha's Vineyard, I

flew back to Washington to speak to the American people for the second time in four days, telling them I had ordered the strikes because al Qaeda was responsible for the embassy bombings, and bin Laden was "perhaps the preeminent organizer and financier of international terrorism in the world today," a man who had vowed to wage a terrorist war on America with no distinction between military personnel and civilians. I said that our attacks were not aimed against Islam "but against fanatics and killers," and that we had been fighting against them on several fronts for years and would continue to do so, because "this will be a long, ongoing struggle."

Around the time I spoke of the long struggle, I signed the first of a series of orders to prepare for it by using all the tools available. Executive Order 13099 imposed economic sanctions on bin Laden and al Qaeda. Later the sanctions were extended to the Taliban as well. To date, we had not been effective in disrupting terrorists' financial networks. The executive order invoked the International Emergency Economic Powers Act, which we had earlier used successfully against the Cali drug cartel in Colombia.

I had also asked General Shelton and Dick Clarke to develop some options for dropping commando forces into Afghanistan. I thought that if we took out a couple of al Qaeda's training operations it would show them how serious we were, even if we didn't get bin Laden or his top lieutenants. It was clear to me that the senior military didn't want to do this, perhaps because of Somalia, perhaps because they would have to send in the Special Forces without knowing for certain where bin Laden was, or whether we could get our troops back out to safety. At any rate, I continued to keep the option alive.

I also signed several Memoranda of Notification (MONs) authorizing the CIA to use lethal force to apprehend bin Laden. The CIA had been authorized to conduct its own "snatch operation" against bin Laden the previous spring, months before the embassy bombings, but it lacked the paramilitary capability to do the job. Instead, it contracted with members of local Afghan tribes to get bin

Laden. When field agents or the Afghan tribals were apparently uncertain of whether they had to try to capture bin Laden before they used deadly force, I made it clear that they did not. Within a few months I had extended the lethal force authorization by expanding the list of targeted bin Laden associates and the circumstances under which they could be attacked.

By and large, the response of the congressional leaders of both parties to the missile strikes was positive, in large part because they had been well briefed and Secretary Cohen had assured his fellow Republicans that the attack and its timing were justified. Speaker Gingrich said, "The United States did exactly the right thing today." Senator Lott said the attacks were "appropriate and just." Tom Daschle, Dick Gephardt, and all the Democrats were supportive. Soon I was heartened by the arrest of Mohamed Rashed, an al Qaeda operative who was a suspect in the Kenyan embassy bombing.

Some people criticized me for hitting the chemical plant, which the Sudanese government insisted had nothing to do with the production or storage of dangerous chemicals. I still believe we did the right thing there. The CIA had soil samples taken at the plant site that contained the chemical used to produce VX. In a subsequent terrorist trial in New York City, one of the witnesses testified that bin Laden had a chemical weapons operation in Khartoum. Despite the plain evidence, some people in the media tried to push the possibility that the action was a real-life version of *Wag the Dog*, a movie in which a fictional President starts a made-for-TV war to distract public attention from his personal problems.

The American people had to absorb the news of the strike and my grand jury testimony at the same time. *Newsweek* ran an article reporting that the public's reaction to my testimony and television address about it was "calm and measured." My job rating was 62 percent, with 73 percent supporting the missile strikes. Most people thought I had been dishonest in my personal life but remained credible on public issues. By contrast, *Newsweek* said, "The first reaction of the pundit class was near hysteria." They were hitting me hard. I deserved a whipping, all right, but I was getting it at home, where it should have been administered.

For now, I just hoped that the Democrats wouldn't be pushed by the media pounding into calling for my resignation, and that I would be able to repair the breach I had caused with my family and with my staff, cabinet, and the people who had believed in me through all the years of constant attacks.

After the speech I went back to the Vineyard for ten days. There was not much thaw on the family front. I made my first public appearance since my grand jury testimony, traveling to Worcester, Massachusetts, at the invitation of Congressman Jim McGovern, to promote the Police Corps, an innovative program that provided college scholarships to people who committed to becoming law-enforcement officers. Worcester is an old-fashioned blue-collar city; I was somewhat apprehensive about the kind of reception I would get there, and was encouraged to find a large enthusiastic crowd at an event attended by the mayor, both senators, and four Massachusetts congressmen. Many people in the crowd urged me to keep doing my job; several said they had made mistakes in their lives, too, and were sorry that mine had been aired in public.

On August 28, the thirty-fifth anniversary of Martin Luther King Jr.'s famous "I have a dream" speech, I went to a commemorative service at Union Chapel in Oak Bluffs, which had been a vacation mecca for African-Americans for more than a century. I shared the platform with Congressman John Lewis, who had worked with Dr. King and was one of the most powerful moral forces in American politics. He and I had been friends for a long time, going back well before 1992. He was one of my earliest supporters and had every right to condemn me. Instead, when he rose to speak, John said that I was his friend and brother, that he had stood with me when I was up and would not leave me when I was down, that I had been a good President, and that if it were up to him, I would continue to be. John Lewis will never know how much he lifted my spirits that day.

We returned to Washington at the end of the month to face another tremendous problem. The Asian financial crisis had spread and was now threatening to destabilize the entire global economy. The crisis had begun in Thailand in 1997, then infected Indonesia and South Korea, and now it had spread to Russia. In mid-August, Russia had defaulted on its foreign debt, and by the end of the month the Russian collapse had caused large drops in stock markets across the world. On August 31, the Dow Jones industrial average dropped 512 points, following a drop of 357 just four days earlier; all the gains of 1998 were wiped out.

Bob Rubin and his international economics team had been working on the financial crisis since Thailand's trouble began. Although the details of each nation's problem were somewhat different, there were some common elements: flawed banking systems, bad loans, crony capitalism, and a general loss of confidence. The situation was aggravated by the lack of economic growth in Japan over the past five years. With no inflation and a 20 percent savings rate, the Japanese could stand it, but the absence of growth in Asia's largest economy increased the adverse consequences of bad policies elsewhere. Even the Japanese were getting restless; the stagnant economy had contributed to the election losses that had led to the recent resignation of my friend Ryutaro Hashimoto as prime minister. China, with the region's fastest-growing economy, had kept the crisis from growing even worse by refusing to devalue its currency.

The general formula for recovery in the 1990s was the extension of sizable loans from the International Monetary Fund and wealthy countries in return for necessary reforms in the affected nations. The reforms were invariably politically difficult. They always forced change on entrenched interests and often required fiscal austerity that made things harder on ordinary citizens in the short run, though it brought a quicker recovery and more stability in the long run.

The United States had supported the IMF efforts in Thailand, Indonesia, and South Korea, and had made contributions in the last two cases. The Treasury Department decided not to put money into Thailand because the $17 billion already available was sufficient and because the Exchange Stabilization Fund, which we had used to help Mexico, had some new, albeit temporary, restrictions imposed on it by Congress. The restrictions had expired by the time the other nations needed help, but I regretted not making at least a modest contribution to the Thai package. State, Defense, and the NSC all wanted to do it because Thailand was our oldest ally in Southeast Asia. So did I, but we let Treasury make the call. On the economics and in terms of domestic politics it was the correct decision, but it sent the wrong message to Thais and across Asia. Bob Rubin and I didn't make too many policy errors; I believe this was one of them.

We certainly didn't have the Thai problem with Russia. The United States had been supporting the Russian economy since my first year in office, and we had contributed almost a third of the $23 billion IMF package in July. Unfortunately, the first disbursement of about $5 billion from the package had virtually disappeared overnight, as the ruble was devalued and Russians began to move large sums of their own money out of the country. Russia's problems were aggravated by the irresponsible inflationary policies of its central bank and by the Duma's refusal to establish an effective system to collect taxes. The tax rates were high enough, maybe too high, but most taxpayers didn't pay them.

Right after we got back from Martha's Vineyard, Hillary and I took a quick trip to Russia and Northern Ireland with Madeleine Albright, Bill Daley, Bill Richardson, and a bipartisan congressional delegation. Ambassador Jim Collins invited a group of leaders of the Duma to his residence, Spaso House. I tried hard to convince them that no nation could escape the discipline of the global economy, and that if they wanted foreign loans and investment, Russia would have to collect taxes, stop printing money to pay bills and bail out troubled banks, avoid crony capitalism, and pay debts. I don't think I made many converts.

My fifteenth meeting with Boris Yeltsin went as well as it could, given his problems. The Communists and ultra-nationalists were blocking his reform proposals in the Duma. He had tried to create a more effective tax collection

system by executive action, but he still couldn't stop the
central bank from printing too much money, which only
encouraged greater capital flight from the ruble to more stable currencies and discouraged foreign credit and investment. For now, all I could do was encourage him and say
the rest of the IMF money would be available as soon as it
could make a difference. If we released it now, the funds
would disappear as quickly as the first installment had.

We did make one positive announcement, saying that
we would remove from each of our nuclear programs about
fifty tons of plutonium—enough to make thousands of
bombs—and render the material incapable of being used to
make weapons in the future. With terrorist groups as well as
hostile nations trying to get their hands on fissile material, it
was an important step that could save countless lives.

After a speech to the new Northern Ireland Assembly in
Belfast in which I encouraged the members to continue to
implement the Good Friday accord, Hillary and I went with
Tony and Cherie Blair, George Mitchell, and Mo Mowlan,
the UK secretary of state for Northern Ireland, to Omagh to
meet with victims of the bombing. Tony and I spoke as best
we could; then we all moved among the families, listening to
their stories, seeing the children who had been scarred, and
being struck by the victims' steady determination to stay on
the path of peace. During the Troubles someone had painted
a provocative question on a Belfast wall: "Is there life before
death?" Amidst the cruel carnage of Omagh, the Irish were
still saying yes.

Before leaving for Dublin, we and the Blairs attended a
Gathering for Peace in Armagh, the base from which St.
Patrick brought Christianity to Ireland and now the spiritual center in Northern Ireland for both Catholics and
Protestants. I was introduced by a lovely seventeen-year-old
girl, Sharon Haughey, who had written to me when she was
just fourteen, asking me to help end the fighting with a simple solution: "Both sides have been hurt. Both sides will
have to forgive."

In Dublin, Bertie Ahern and I spoke with the press after
our meeting. An Irish reporter said, "It usually seems to take

a visit from you to give the peace process a boost. Will we need to see you again?" I replied that for their sake I hoped not, but for my own sake I hoped so. Then Bertie said my quick response to the Omagh tragedy had galvanized the parties to make decisions quickly that "might have taken weeks and months." Just two days earlier, Martin McGuinness, the chief Sinn Fein negotiator, had announced that he would oversee the arms decommissioning process for Sinn Fein. Martin was Gerry Adams's top aide and a powerful force in his own right. The announcement sent a signal to David Trimble and the Unionists that for Sinn Fein and the IRA, violence, as Adams had said, "is a thing of the past, over, done with, and gone." In our private meeting, Bertie Ahern told me that after Omagh, the IRA had warned the Real IRA that if they ever did anything like that again, the British police would be the least of their worries.

The first question I got from an American reporter was a request to reply to the stinging rebuke I had received the day before on the floor of the Senate from my longtime friend Joe Lieberman. I replied, "I agree with what he said . . . I made a bad mistake, it was indefensible, and I'm sorry about it." Some of our staff were upset that Joe attacked me while I was overseas, but I wasn't. I knew he was a devoutly religious man who was angry about what I had done, and he had carefully avoided saying that I should be impeached.

Our last stop in Ireland was in Limerick, where fifty thousand supporters of peace filled the streets, including the relatives of one member of our delegation, Congressman Peter King of New York, who had brought his mother home for the event. I told the crowd that my friend Frank McCourt had memorialized the old Limerick in *Angela's Ashes*, but I liked the new one better.

On September 9, Ken Starr sent his 445-page report to Congress, alleging eleven impeachable offenses. Even with all the crimes of Watergate, Leon Jaworski hadn't done that. The independent counsel was supposed to report his findings to Congress if he found "substantial and credible" evidence to support an impeachment; Congress was supposed to decide whether there were grounds for impeachment. The report was made public on the eleventh; Jaworski's never was. In Starr's report, the word "sex" appeared more than five hundred times; Whitewater was mentioned twice. He and his allies thought they could wash away all their sins over the last four years in my dirty laundry.

On September 10, I called the cabinet to the White House and apologized to them. Many of them didn't know what to say. They believed in what we were doing and appreciated the opportunity I had given them to serve, but most of them felt I had been selfish and stupid and had left them hanging for eight months. Madeleine Albright led off, saying that I had done wrong and she was disappointed, but our only option was to go back to work. Donna Shalala was tougher, saying it was important for leaders to be good people as well as to have good policies. My longtime friends James Lee Witt and Rodney Slater talked about the power of redemption, and quoted scripture. Bruce Babbitt, a Catholic, talked about the power of confession. Carol Browner said she had been forced to talk with her son about subjects she never thought she'd have to discuss with him.

Listening to my cabinet, I really understood for the first time the extent to which the exposure of my misconduct and my dishonesty about it had opened a Pandora's box of emotions in the American people. It was easy enough to say that I had been through a lot in the past six years, and that Starr's inquisition had been awful and the Jones lawsuit was bogus and politically motivated; easy enough to say that even a President's personal life should remain private. But once what I had done was out there in all its stark ugliness, people's evaluations of it were inevitably a reflection of their own personal experiences, marked not only by their convictions but also by their own fears, disappointments, and heartbreak.

My cabinet's honest and very different reactions gave me a direct sense of what was going on in conversations all across America. As the impeachment hearings grew closer, I received many letters from friends and strangers alike. Some of the letter writers offered touching words of support and encouragement; some told their own stories of failure and recovery; some expressed outrage over the actions of Starr; some were full of condemnation and disappointment over what I had done; and still others reflected a combination of all these views. Reading the letters helped me to deal with my own emotions, and to remember that if I wanted to be forgiven, I had to forgive.

The atmosphere in the Yellow Oval Room remained awkward and tense until Bob Rubin spoke. Rubin was the one person in the room who best understood what my life had been like for the last four years. He had been through an exhaustive investigation of Goldman Sachs that featured one of his partners being hauled away in handcuffs before he was cleared. After several others had spoken, Rubin said, with characteristic bluntness, "There's no question you screwed up. But we all make mistakes, even big ones. In my opinion, the bigger issue is the disproportion of the media coverage and the hypocrisy of some of your critics." The atmosphere got better after that. I'm grateful that no one quit. We all went back to work.

On September 15, I hired Greg Craig, a fine lawyer and old friend of Hillary's and mine from law school, to work with Chuck Ruff, David Kendall, Bruce Lindsey, Cheryl Mills, Lanny Breuer, and Nicole Seligman on my defense team. On the eighteenth, just as I knew they would, the House Judiciary Committee voted on a straight party-line vote to release the video of my grand jury testimony to the public.

A few days later, Hillary and I hosted our annual break-fast for religious leaders at the White House. We usually discussed shared public concerns. This time I asked for their prayers during my personal travail:

> I have been on quite a journey these last few weeks to get to the end of this, to the rock-bottom truth of where I am and where we all are. I agree with those who have said that in my first statement after I testified, I was not contrite enough. I don't think there is a fancy way to say that I have sinned.

I said that I was sorry for all who had been hurt—my family, friends, staff, cabinet, and Monica Lewinsky and her family; that I had asked for their forgiveness; and that I would pursue counseling from pastors and others to find, with God's help, "a willingness to give the very forgiveness I seek, a renunciation of the pride and the anger which cloud judgment, lead people to excuse and compare and to blame and complain." I also said I would mount a vigorous defense in response to the charges against me and would intensify my efforts to do my job "in the hope that with a broken spirit and a still strong heart I can be used for greater good."

I had asked three pastors to counsel me at least once a month for an indefinite period: Phil Wogaman, our minister at Foundry Methodist Church; my friend Tony Campolo; and Gordon MacDonald, a minister and author of several books I had read on living one's faith. They would more than fulfill their commitment, usually coming to the White House together, sometimes separately. We would pray, read scripture, and discuss some things I had never really talked about before. The Reverend Bill Hybels from Chicago also continued to come to the White House regularly, to ask searching questions designed to check my "spiritual health." Even though they were often tough on me, the pastors took me past the politics into soul-searching and the power of God's love.

Hillary and I also began a serious counseling program, one day a week for about a year. For the first time in my life, I actually talked openly about feelings, experiences, and opinions about life, love, and the nature of relationships. I didn't like everything I learned about myself or my past, and it pained me to face the fact that my childhood and the life I'd led since growing up had made some things difficult for me that seemed to come more naturally to other people.

I also came to understand that when I was exhausted, angry, or feeling isolated and alone, I was more vulnerable to making selfish and self-destructive personal mistakes about which I would later be ashamed. The current controversy was the latest casualty of my lifelong effort to lead parallel lives, to wall off my anger and grief and get on with my outer life, which I loved and lived well. During the government shutdowns I was engaged in two titanic struggles: a public one with Congress over the future of our country, and a private one to hold the old demons at bay. I had won the public fight and lost the private one.

In so doing, I had hurt more than my family and my administration. It was also damaging to the presidency and the American people. No matter how much pressure I was under, I should have been stronger and behaved better.

There was no excuse for what I did, but trying to come to grips with why I did it gave me at least a chance to finally unify my parallel lives.

In the long counseling sessions and our conversations about them afterward, Hillary and I also got to know each other again, beyond the work and ideas we shared and the child we adored. I had always loved her very much, but not always very well. I was grateful that she was brave enough to participate in the counseling. We were still each other's best friend, and I hoped we could save our marriage.

Meanwhile, I was still sleeping on a couch, this one in the small living room that adjoined our bedroom. I slept on that old couch for two months or more. I got a lot of reading, thinking, and work done, and the couch was pretty comfortable, but I hoped I wouldn't be on it forever.

As the Republicans intensified their criticism of me, my supporters started to stand up. On September 11, eight hundred Irish-Americans gathered on the South Lawn as Brian O'Dwyer presented me with an award named after his late father, Paul, for my role in the Irish peace process. Brian's remarks and the crowd's response to them left no doubt about why they were really there.

A few days later, Václav Havel came to Washington for a state visit, telling the press I was his "great friend." As the press continued to ask questions about impeachment, resignation, and whether I had lost my moral authority to lead, Havel said America had many different faces: "I love most of these faces. There are some I don't understand. I don't like to speak about things which I don't understand."

Five days after that I went to New York for the opening
session of the UN General Assembly, to deliver a speech on
the world's shared obligations to fight terrorists: to give
them no support, sanctuary, or financial assistance; to bring
pressure on states that do; to step up extradition and prose-
cutions; to sign the global anti-terror conventions and
strengthen and enforce the ones designed to protect us
against biological and chemical weapons; to control the
manufacture and export of explosives; to raise international
standards for airport security; and to combat the conditions
that breed terror. It was an important speech, especially at
that time, but the delegates in the cavernous hall of the General Assembly were also thinking about events in Washington. When I stood up to speak, they responded with an
enthusiastic and prolonged standing ovation. It was unheard
of for the normally reserved UN, and I was profoundly
moved. I wasn't sure whether the unprecedented act was
more a gesture of support for me or opposition to what was
going on in Congress. While I was speaking to the UN about
terrorism, all the television networks were showing the
videotape of my grand jury testimony.

The next day, at the White House, I held a reception for
Nelson Mandela with African-American religious leaders. It
was his idea. The Congress had voted to give him the Congressional Gold Medal and he was to receive it the following day. Mandela called to say he suspected the timing of
the award was no accident: "As the President of South
Africa I cannot decline this award. But I would like to come
a day early and tell the American people what I think about
what the Congress is doing to you." And that's exactly what
he did, saying that he had never seen a reception at the UN
like the one I had received, that the world needed me, and
that my adversaries should leave me alone. The pastors
applauded their approval.

As good as Mandela was, the Reverend Bernice King,
Martin Luther King Jr.'s daughter, stole the show. She said
that even great leaders sometimes commit grievous sins;
that King David had done something far worse than I had
in arranging the death in battle of Bathsheba's husband,

who was David's loyal soldier, so that David could marry her; and that David had to atone for his sin and was punished for it. No one could tell where Bernice was going until she got to the closing: "Yes, David committed a terrible sin and God punished him. But David remained king."

Meanwhile, I kept working, pushing my proposal for school modernization and construction funds in Maryland, Florida, and Illinois; talking to the National Farmers Union about agriculture; giving an important address on modernizing the global financial system at the Council on Foreign Relations; meeting with the Joint Chiefs on the readiness of our armed forces; drumming up support for another minimum wage increase at the International Brotherhood of Electrical Workers union; receiving the final report of the President's Advisory Commission on Race from John Hope Franklin; holding a dialogue with Tony Blair, Italian prime minister Romano Prodi, and President Peter Stoyanov of Bulgaria on the applicability to other nations of the "Third Way" philosophy Tony and I had embraced; having my first meeting with the new Japanese prime minister, Keizo Obuchi; bringing Netanyahu and Arafat to the White House in an attempt to get the peace process going; and appearing at more than a dozen campaign events for Democrats in six states and Washington, D.C.

On September 30, the last day of the fiscal year, I announced that we had run a budget surplus of about $70 billion, the first one in twenty-nine years. Although the press was focused on little besides the Starr report, there were, as always, a lot of other things going on, and they had to be dealt with. I was determined not to let the public's business grind to a halt and was gratified that the White House staff and cabinet felt the same way. No matter what was in the daily news, they kept doing their job.

In October the House Republicans, led by Henry Hyde and his colleagues on the Judiciary Committee, continued to push for my impeachment. The committee Democrats, led by John Conyers of Michigan, fought them tooth and nail, arguing that even if the worst charges against me were true, they didn't amount to the "high crimes and misdemeanors" the Constitution required for impeachment. The Democrats were right on the law, but the Republicans had the votes; on October 8 the House voted to open an inquiry into whether I should be impeached. I wasn't surprised; we were just a month away from the midterm elections and the Republicans were running a single-issue campaign: get Clinton. After the election I believed the moderate Republicans would look at the facts and the law and decide against impeachment in favor of a resolution of censure or reprimand—which is what Newt Gingrich had received for false statements and apparent violations of the tax laws.

Many of the pundits were predicting disaster for the Democrats. The conventional wisdom was that we would lose twenty-five to thirty-five seats in the House and four to six seats in the Senate because of the controversy. It seemed a safe bet to most people in Washington. The Republicans had $100 million more than the Democrats to spend, and more Democrats than Republicans were up for reelection in the Senate. Among the contested Senate seats, the Democrats seemed sure to pick up the one in Indiana, where the candidate was Governor Evan Bayh, while Ohio governor George Voinovich seemed certain to win the seat being vacated by John Glenn for the Republicans. That left seven seats up in the air, five currently held by Democrats and only two by Republicans.

I disagreed with the conventional wisdom for several reasons. First, a majority of Americans disapproved of the way Starr was conducting himself, and resented the fact that the Republican Congress was more interested in hurting me than in helping them. Almost 80 percent disapproved of the release of my grand jury videotape, and overall approval of the Congress had dropped to 43 percent. Second, as Gingrich had shown with the "Contract with America" in 1994, if the public believed one party had a positive agenda and the other didn't, the party with the plan would win. The Democrats were united with a midterm program for the first time ever: save Social Security first before spending the surplus on new programs or tax cuts; put 100,000 teachers in our schools; modernize old schools and build new ones; raise the minimum wage; and pass the Patients' Bill of Rights. Finally, a sizable majority of Americans were opposed to impeachment; if Democrats ran on their plan and against impeachment, I thought they might actually be able to win the House.

I did some political events at the beginning and end of October, most of them near Washington, in settings designed to emphasize the issues our candidates were stressing. Otherwise, I spent most of the month on the job. There was plenty of work to do, by far the most important of which involved the Middle East. Madeleine Albright and Dennis Ross had been laboring for months to get the peace process back on track, and Madeleine had finally gotten Arafat and Netanyahu together when they were in New York for the UN General Assembly session. Neither of them was ready to take the next steps or to be seen by his own constituents as compromising too much, but both were concerned that the deteriorating situation could easily get out of hand, especially if Hamas launched a new round of attacks.

The next day, the leaders came down to Washington to see me, and I announced plans to bring them back to the United States within a month to hammer out an agreement. In the interim, Madeleine went to the region to see them. They met on the border between Israel and Gaza; then Arafat took them to his guest house for lunch, making the hard-liner Netanyahu the first Israeli prime minister to go into Palestinian Gaza.

Months of work had gone into preparation of the summit. Both parties wanted the United States to work with them on the hard decisions and believed that the high drama of the event would help them sell those decisions back home. Of course, in any summit there's always a risk that the two sides won't be able to reach an agreement, and that the high-profile effort will damage all involved. My national security team was worried about the possibility of failure and its consequences. Both Arafat and Netanyahu had staked out tough positions in public, and Bibi had bolstered his rhetoric by naming Ariel Sharon, the most hard-line of the prominent Likud leaders, foreign minister. Sharon had referred to the 1993 peace agreement as "national suicide" for Israel. It was impossible to know whether Netanyahu had given Sharon the portfolio to have someone to blame if the summit failed or to provide himself cover on the right if it succeeded.

I thought the summit was a good idea and was eager to hold it. It seemed to me that we didn't have much to lose, and I always preferred failure in a worthy effort to inaction for fear of failure.

On the fifteenth, we kicked things off at the White House; then the delegations moved to the Wye River Conference Center in Maryland. It was well suited to the task at hand; the public meeting and dining spaces were comfortable, and the living quarters were laid out in such a way that the delegations could each have all their people staying together and at a fair distance from the other side.

Originally, we had planned for the summit to last four days; it would end two days before Netanyahu had to be back in Israel to open the new session of the Knesset. We agreed on the usual rules: neither side was bound by interim agreements on specific issues until a complete accord was reached, and the United States would draft the final agreement. I told them I would be there as much as I could, but would helicopter back to the White House at night, no matter how late, so that I could work in the office the next morning to sign legislation and continue negotiating with Congress on the budget bills. We were in the new fiscal year, but less than a third of the thirteen appropriations bills had been passed and signed into law. The marines who ran HMX1, the presidential helicopter, did a great job for me over eight years, but during Wye River they were even more invaluable, staying on duty to fly me back to the White House at two and three o'clock in the morning after the late sessions.

At the first dinner I urged Arafat and Netanyahu to think about how they could help each other cope with their domestic opposition. They thought and talked for four days, but were exhausted from trying and were nowhere near an agreement. Netanyahu told me we couldn't reach agreement on all the issues and suggested a partial one: Israel would withdraw from 13 percent of the West Bank and the Palestinians would dramatically improve cooperation on security, following a plan developed with the help of CIA director George Tenet, who enjoyed the confidence of both sides.

Late that night I met alone with Ariel Sharon for the first time. The seventy-year-old former general had been part of Israel's creation and all its subsequent wars. He was unpopular among Arabs not only for his hostility to trading land for peace but also for his role in the Israeli invasion of Lebanon in 1982, in which a large number of unarmed Palestinian refugees were killed by the Lebanese militia that was allied with Israel. During our meeting, which ran more than two hours, I mostly asked questions and listened. Sharon was not without sympathy for the plight of the Palestinians. He wanted to help them economically, but did not believe giving up the West Bank was in Israel's security interest, nor did he trust Arafat to fight terror. He was the only member of the Israeli delegation who would not shake hands with Arafat. I enjoyed hearing Sharon talk about his life and his views, and when we finished, at nearly three in the morning, I had a better understanding of how he thought.

One thing that surprised me was how hard he pushed me to pardon Jonathan Pollard, a former U.S. Navy intelligence analyst who had been convicted in 1986 of spying for Israel. Rabin and Netanyahu had previously asked for Pollard's release, too. It was obvious that this was an issue in Israeli domestic politics and that the Israeli public didn't think the United States should have punished Pollard so severely since it was to an ally that he had sold highly sensitive information. The case would come up again before we finished. Meanwhile, I continued to work with the leaders and to talk with their team members, including the Israeli defense minister, Yitzhak Mordechai; Arafat's senior advisors Abu Ala and Abu Mazen, both of whom would later become Palestinian prime ministers; Saeb Erekat, Arafat's chief negotiator; and Mohammed Dahlan, the thirty-seven-year-old security chief in Gaza. Both the Israelis and the Palestinians were diverse, impressive groups. I tried to spend time with all of them; there was no telling who might make a decisive case for peace when they were alone in their separate delegations.

When we hadn't reached consensus by Sunday night, the parties agreed to extend the talks, and Al Gore joined me to add his powers of persuasion to our team, which included Sandy Berger, Rob Malley, and Bruce Reidel from the White House, and Secretary Albright, Dennis Ross, Martin Indyk, Aaron Miller, Wendy Sherman, and Toni Verstandig from the State Department. Every day they would take turns working on their Israeli and Palestinian counterparts on various issues, always looking for that streak of light that might break through the clouds.

The State Department translator, Gemal Helal, also played a unique role in these and other negotiations. The members of both delegations spoke English, but Arafat always conducted business in Arabic. Gemal was usually the only other person in the room during my one-on-one meetings with Arafat. He understood the Middle East and the role each member of the Palestinian delegation played in their deliberations, and Arafat liked him. He would become an advisor on my team. On more than one occasion, his insight and his personal connection with Arafat would prove invaluable.

On Monday I felt we were making headway again. I kept pushing Netanyahu to give Arafat the benefits of peace—the land, the airport, the safe passage between Gaza and the West Bank, a port in Gaza—so that he would be strong enough to fight terror, and I pressed Arafat not only to increase his efforts on security but to call the Palestinian National Council together to formally revise the Palestinian Covenant, excising the language calling for the destruction of Israel. The PLO Executive Council had already renounced the provisions, but Netanyahu thought Israeli citizens would never believe they had a partner for peace until the elected Palestinian Assembly voted to delete the offensive language from the charter. Arafat didn't want to call the council into session because he thought he might not be able to control the outcome. Palestinians the world over were eligible to vote for council members, and many of the expatriates were not as supportive of the compromises inherent in the peace process and of his leadership as were the Palestinians living in Gaza and the West Bank.

On the twentieth, King Hussein and Queen Noor joined us. Hussein was in the United States for cancer treatments at the Mayo Clinic. I had kept him briefed on our progress and problems. Although he was weakened by his illness and the chemotherapy treatments, he said he would come to Wye if I thought it would help. After talking to Noor, who assured me that he wanted to come, and that they would be fine in whatever guest quarters were available, I told Hussein we could use all the help we could get. It is difficult to describe or overstate the impact Hussein's presence had on the talks. He had lost a lot of weight, and the chemotherapy had taken all of his hair, even his eyebrows, but his mind and heart were still strong. He was very helpful, talking common sense to both sides, and the very sight of him diminished the posturing and pettiness that are a usual part of all such negotiations.

On the twenty-first, we had reached agreement only on the security issue, and it looked as if Netanyahu might celebrate his forty-ninth birthday by leaving the failed talks. The next day I came back to stay for the duration. After the two sides met alone for two hours, they came up with an ingenious way to get the Palestinian Council to vote on changing the charter: I would go to Gaza to address the group with Arafat, who would then ask for a show of support by raised hands or clapping or stamping of feet. Sandy Berger, although he was supportive of the plan, warned that it was a risky move for me. That was true, but we were asking the Israelis and Palestinians to take bigger risks; I agreed to do it.

That night we were still hung up on Arafat's demand for the release of one thousand Palestinian prisoners from

Israeli jails. Netanyahu said he couldn't release Hamas members or others "with blood on their hands," and he thought no more than five hundred could be let go. I knew we were at a breaking point and had asked Hussein to come to the large cabin where we were dining to talk to both delegations together. When he entered the room, his regal aura, luminous eyes, and simple eloquence seemed magnified by his physical decline. In his deep, sonorous voice, he said that history would judge us all, that the differences remaining between the parties were trivial compared with the benefits of peace, and that they had to achieve it for the sake of their children. His unspoken message was equally clear: I may not have long to live; it's up to you not to let the peace die.

After Hussein left, we kept going, with everyone staying in the dining room and collecting around different tables to keep working on various issues. I told my team we were out of time, and I wasn't going to bed. My strategy for success had now boiled down to endurance; I was determined to be the last man standing. Netanyahu and Arafat also knew it was now or never. They and their teams stayed with us through the long night.

Finally, at about 3 a.m., I worked out a deal on the prisoners with Netanyahu and Arafat, and we just kept plowing ahead until we finished. It was almost seven in the morning. There was one more obstacle: Netanyahu was threatening to scuttle the whole deal unless I released Pollard. He said I had promised him I would do so at an earlier meeting the night before, and that's why he had agreed on the other issues. In fact, I had told the prime minister that if that's what it took to make peace, I was inclined to do it, but I would have to check with our people.

For all the sympathy Pollard generated in Israel, he was a hard case to push in America; he had sold our country's secrets for money, not conviction, and for years had not shown any remorse. When I talked to Sandy Berger and George Tenet, they were adamantly opposed to letting Pollard go, as was Madeleine Albright. George said that after the severe damage the Aldrich Ames case had done to the CIA, he would have to resign if I commuted Pollard's sentence. I didn't want to do it, and Tenet's comments closed the door. Security and the commitments by the Israelis and Palestinians to work together against terror were at the heart of the agreement we had reached. Tenet had helped the sides to work out details and had agreed that the CIA would support their implementation. If he left, there was a real chance Arafat would not go forward. I also needed George in the fight against al Qaeda and terrorism. I told Netanyahu that I would review the case seriously and try to work through it with Tenet and the national security team, but that Netanyahu was better off with a security agreement that he could count on than he would have been with the release of Pollard.

Finally, after we talked again at length, Bibi agreed to stay with the agreement, but only on the condition that he could change the mix of prisoners to be released, so that he would free more ordinary criminals and fewer who had committed security offenses. That was a problem for Arafat, who wanted the release of people he considered freedom fighters. Dennis Ross and Madeleine Albright went to his cabin and convinced him that this was the best I could do. Then I went to see him to thank him; his last-minute concession had saved the day.

The agreement provided the Palestinians more land on the West Bank, the airport, a seaport, a prisoner release, safe passage between Gaza and the West Bank, and economic aid. In return, Israel would get unprecedented cooperation in the fight against violence and terror, the jailing of specific Palestinians whom Israelis had identified as the source of continuing violence and killing, the change in the Palestinian Covenant, and a quick start on the final status talks. The United States would provide aid to help Israel meet the security costs of redeployment and support for Palestinian economic development, and would play a central role in cementing the unprecedented security cooperation the two sides had agreed to embrace.

As soon as we finally shook hands on the deal, we had to rush back to the White House to announce it. Most of us had been up for almost forty hours straight and could have used a nap and shower, but it was Friday afternoon, and we had to finish the ceremony before sundown, the beginning of the Jewish Sabbath. The ceremony began at 4 p.m. in the East Room. After Madeleine Albright and Al Gore spoke, I outlined the particulars of the agreement and thanked the parties. Then Netanyahu and Arafat made gracious and upbeat remarks. Bibi was very statesman-like and Arafat renounced violence in unusually strong words. Hussein warned that the enemies of peace would try to undo the agreement with violence and urged the people on both sides to stand behind their leaders, and to replace destruction and death with a shared future for the children of Abraham "that is worthy of them under the sun."

In a gesture of friendship and an appreciation of what the Republicans in Congress were up to, Hussein said that he had been friends with nine Presidents, "But on the subject of peace . . . never—with all the affection I held for your predecessors—have I known someone with your dedication, clearheadedness, focus, and determination . . . and we hope you will be with us as we see greater success and as we help our brethren move ahead towards a better tomorrow."

Then Netanyahu and Arafat signed the agreement, just before the sun went down and Shabbat began. The Middle East peace was still alive.

While the talks were going on at Wye River, Erskine Bowles was managing intense negotiations with Congress over the budget. He had told me he was going to leave after the election, and he wanted to make the best agreement he could. We had a lot of leverage because the Republicans wouldn't dare shut the government down again, and they had wasted a lot of time in the previous months squabbling among themselves and attacking me instead of finishing their business.

Erskine and his team adroitly maneuvered through the details of the budget bills, giving a concession here and there in order to secure funding for our big priorities. We announced agreement on the afternoon of the fifteenth, and the next morning there was a celebration of it in the Rose Garden with Tom Daschle, Dick Gephardt, and our entire economic team. The final deal saved the surplus for Social Security reform and provided funding for the first installment of the 100,000 new teachers, a large increase in after-school and summer school programs, and our other education priorities. We secured a solid relief package for farmers and ranchers and scored impressive environmental gains: funding for the clean water initiative to restore 40 percent of our lakes and rivers that were still too polluted for fishing and swimming, as well as money to combat global warming and continue our efforts to protect precious lands from development and pollution. And after eight months of deadlock, we also won approval for America's contribution to the International Monetary Fund, enabling the United States to continue our efforts to end the financial crisis and stabilize the world economy.

Not all of our agenda passed, so we had plenty of ammunition for the last two and a half weeks of the campaign. The Republicans had blocked the Patients' Bill of Rights for the HMOs; killed the tobacco legislation, with its cigarette tax increase and anti–teen smoking measures for the big tobacco companies; filibustered campaign finance reform in the Senate, despite unanimous Senate Democratic support for it after it had passed the House; defeated the minimum wage increase; and, most surprising to me, refused to pass my proposal to build or repair five thousand schools. They also refused to pass the tax credit on the production and purchase of clean energy and energy conservation devices. I kidded Newt Gingrich that I had finally found a tax cut that he was against.

Still, it was a superb budget, given the political composition of Congress, and a real tribute to the negotiating skills of Erskine Bowles. After negotiating the balanced budget in 1997, he had come through again. As I said, he had "a great closing act."

Four days later, just before I left again for Wye River, I named John Podesta to succeed Erskine, who had strongly recommended him for the job. I had known John for nearly thirty years, since Joe Duffey's campaign for the Senate in 1970. He had already served as White House staff secretary and deputy chief of staff; he understood Congress and had helped guide our economic, foreign, and defense policies; he was an ardent environmentalist; and except for Al Gore, he knew more about information technology than anyone else in the White House. He had the right personal qualities, too: a fine mind, a tough hide, a dry wit, and he was a better hearts player than Erskine Bowles. John gave the White House an exceptionally able leadership team, with Deputy Chiefs of Staff Steve Ricchetti and Maria Echaveste and his aide, Karen Tramontano.

Through our trials and triumphs, our golf matches and card games, Erskine and I had become close friends. I would miss him, especially on the golf course. On many tough days Erskine and I would go out to Army-Navy golf course for a quick round. Until my friend Kevin O'Keefe left the counsel's office, he often joined us. We were always accompanied around the course by Mel Cook, a retired military man who worked there and knew the place like the back of his hand. Sometimes I would play four or five holes before hitting a decent shot, but eventually the beauty of the layout and my love for the game would drive away the pressures of the day. I kept up my trips to Army-Navy, but I always missed Erskine. At least he was leaving me in good hands with Podesta.

Rahm Emanuel had left, too. Since he had started with me as campaign finance director in 1991, he had married and started a family, and he wanted to provide for them. Rahm's great gift was putting ideas into action. He saw the potential in issues everyone else missed, and he stayed on top of the details that often determine success or failure. After our defeat in 1994, he had played a major role in bringing my image back into line with reality. Within a few years Rahm would be back in Washington, as a congressman from Chicago, the city he thought should be capital of the world. I replaced him with Doug Sosnik, the White House political director, who was almost as aggressive as Rahm, understood politics and the Congress, always told me the downside of every situation without wanting me to give in to it, and was a shrewd hearts player. Craig Smith took over the political director's job, the same position he had had in the 1992 campaign.

On the morning of the twenty-second, not long before I left for the last, never-ending day at Wye River, Congress adjourned after having sent me the administration's bill to establish three thousand charter schools in America by 2000. In the last week of the month, Prime Minister Netanyahu survived a no-confidence vote in the Knesset on the Wye River accord, and the presidents of Ecuador and Peru, with help from the United States, settled a contentious border dispute that had threatened to erupt into armed conflict. At the White House, I welcomed the new president of Colombia, Andrés Pastrana, and supported his courageous efforts to end the decades-old conflict with guerrilla groups. I also signed the International Religious Freedom Act of 1998 and appointed Robert Seiple, formerly head of World Vision U.S., a Christian charity, to be the secretary of state's special representative for international religious freedom.

As the campaign drew to a close, I made several stops in California, New York, Florida, and Maryland and went with Hillary to Cape Canaveral, Florida, to see John Glenn blast into space; the Republican National Committee began a series of television ads attacking me; Judge Norma Holloway Johnson ruled that there was probable cause to believe that Starr's office had violated the law against grand jury leaks twenty-four times; and news reports indicated that, according to DNA tests, Thomas Jefferson had fathered several children with his slave Sally Hemings.

On November 3, despite the huge Republican financial advantage, the attacks on me, and the pundits' predictions of the Democrats' demise, the elections went our way. Instead of the predicted loss of four to six Senate seats, there was no change. My friend John Breaux, who had helped me restore the New Democrat image of the administration after the '94 election and was a staunch foe of impeachment, was overwhelmingly reelected in Louisiana. In the House of Representatives, the Democrats actually won back five seats, the first time the President's party had done so in the sixth year of a presidency since 1822.

The election had presented a simple choice: the Democrats wanted to save Social Security first, hire 100,000 teachers, modernize schools, raise the minimum wage, and pass the Patients' Bill of Rights. The Republicans were against all that. By and large they ran a single-issue campaign, on impeachment, although in some states they also ran anti-gay ads, essentially saying that if the Democrats won Congress, we would force every state to recognize gay marriages. In states like Washington and Arkansas, the message was reinforced by pictures of a gay couple kissing or at a church altar. Not long before the election, Matthew Shepard, a young gay man, was beaten to death in Wyoming because of his sexual orientation. The whole country was moved, especially after his parents bravely talked about it in public. I couldn't believe the Far Right would run the gay-bashing ads in the wake of Shepard's death, but they always needed an enemy. The Republicans were also weakened because they were deeply divided over the late October budget agreement; the most conservative members thought they had given away the store and gotten nothing in return.

In the months before the elections, I had decided that the "sixth-year jinx" was way overrated, that citizens historically had voted against the President's party in the sixth year because they thought that the presidency was winding down, that the energy and new ideas were running out, and that they might as well give the other side a chance. In 1998, they saw me working on the Middle East and other foreign and domestic issues right up to the election, and they knew we had an agenda for the coming two years. The impeachment campaign galvanized the Democrats to vote in larger numbers than they had in 1994, and blocked any other message swing voters might have heard from the Republicans. By contrast, the incumbent Republican governors who essentially ran on my platform of fiscal responsibility, welfare reform, commonsense crime-control measures, and strong support for education did very well. In Texas, Governor George W. Bush, after handily defeating my old friend Garry Mauro, gave his victory speech in front of a banner that said "Opportunity, Responsibility," two-thirds of my 1992 campaign slogan.

Large turnouts of African-American voters helped a young lawyer named John Edwards defeat North Carolina senator Lauch Faircloth, Judge Sentelle's friend and one of my harshest critics, and in South Carolina, black voters propelled Senator Fritz Hollings to a come-from-behind victory. In New York, Congressman Chuck Schumer, an outspoken opponent of impeachment with a strong record on crime, easily defeated Senator Al D'Amato, who had spent much of the last several years attacking Hillary and her staff in his committee hearings. In California, Senator Barbara Boxer won reelection and Gray Davis was elected governor with far higher margins than their pre-election polls indicated, and the Democrats picked up two House seats on the anti-impeachment momentum and a large turnout of Hispanic and African-American voters.

In the House elections, we won back the seat that Marjorie Margolies-Mezvinsky had lost in 1994 when our candidate, Joe Hoeffel, who had lost in 1996, ran again and opposed impeachment. In Washington State, Jay Inslee, who had been defeated in 1994, won his seat back. In New Jersey, a physics professor named Rush Holt was behind by 20 percent ten days before the election. He pushed one TV ad highlighting his opposition to impeachment, and won a seat no Democrat had held in a century.

We all did our best to close the vast fund-raising gap and I taped telephone messages that were directed to the homes of Hispanics, blacks, and other likely Democratic voters. Al Gore campaigned vigorously all over the country, and Hillary probably made more appearances than anybody else. When her foot became badly swollen during a campaign stop in New York, a blood clot was discovered behind her right knee and she was put on blood thinners. Dr. Mariano wanted her to stay in bed for a week, but she kept going, giving confidence as well as support to our candidates. I was really concerned about her, but she was determined to push on. As angry as she was with me, she was even more upset about what Starr and the Republicans were trying to do.

Surveys by James Carville and Stan Greenberg and by Democratic pollster Mark Mellman had indicated that,

nationwide, voters were 20 percent more likely to vote for a
Democrat who said that I should be censured by the Congress and that we should get on with the public's business
than for a Republican who favored impeachment. After the
results came in, Carville and others implored all the challengers with a chance to win to adopt this strategy. Its
power was evident even in races we lost narrowly that the
Republicans should have won easily. For example, in New
Mexico, Democrat Phil Maloof, who had just lost a special
election in June by six points and was down by ten a week
before the November election, began anti-impeachment ads
the weekend before the election. He won on election day,
but lost the election by one percent because a third of the
voters had cast early ballots before they heard his message. I
believe the Democrats would have won the House if more
of our challengers had run on our positive program and
against impeachment. Many of them didn't do so because
they were afraid; they simply couldn't believe the plain evidence in the face of the massively negative coverage I had
received, and the near-universal view of the pundits that
what Starr and Henry Hyde were doing would be bad for
Democrats rather than Republicans.

On the day after the election I called Newt Gingrich to
talk about some business; when the conversation got around
to the election, he was very generous, saying that as a historian and "the quarterback for the other team," he wanted to
congratulate me. He hadn't believed we could do it, he said,
and it was a truly historic achievement. Later in November,
Erskine Bowles called to tell me about a very different
conversation he had had with Gingrich. Newt told Erskine
that they were going to go forward with the impeachment
despite the election results and the fact that many moderate
Republicans didn't want to vote for it. When Erskine asked
Newt why they would proceed with impeachment, instead
of other possible remedies such as censure or reprimand, the
Speaker replied, "Because we can."

The right-wing Republicans who controlled the House
believed that they had now paid for impeachment, so they
should just go on and do it before the new Congress came in.

They thought that by the next election there would be no more impeachment losses because the voters would have other things on their minds. Newt and Tom DeLay believed that they could bring most of the moderates into line through pressure—from right-wing talk shows and activists in their districts; with threats to cut off campaign funds, or to come up with opponents in the Republican primary, or to take leadership positions away; or with offers of new leadership positions or other benefits.

The right-wingers in the House caucus were seething over their defeat. Many actually believed they had lost because they had given in to too many White House demands in the last two budget negotiations. In fact, if they had run on the balanced budgets of 1997 and 1998, the Children's Health Insurance Program, and the 100,000 teachers, they would have done well, just as the Republican governors had. But they were too ideological and angry to do that. Now they were going to seize back control of the Republican agenda through impeachment.

I had already had four showdowns with the radical right: the '94 election, which they won, and the budget shutdown, the '96 election, and the '98 election, which went our way. In the interim I had tried to work in good faith with Congress to keep the country moving forward. Now, in the face of overwhelming public opinion against impeachment, and the clear evidence that nothing I was alleged to have done rose to the level of an impeachable offense, they were coming back for another bitter ideological fight. There was nothing to do but suit up and take the field.

TWENTY-ONE

WITHIN A WEEK of the election, two high-profile Washington politicians announced they wouldn't run again, and we were in the teeth of a new crisis with Saddam Hussein. Newt Gingrich stunned us all by announcing that he was resigning as Speaker and from the House. Apparently, he had a deeply divided caucus, was facing an assault on his leadership because of the election losses, and didn't want to fight anymore. After several moderate Republicans made clear that, based on the election results, impeachment was a dead issue, I had mixed feelings about the Speaker's decision. He had supported me on most foreign policy decisions, had been frank about what his caucus was really up to when the two of us talked alone, and, after the government shutdown battle, had shown flexibility in working out honorable compromises with the White House. Now he had the worst of both worlds: the moderate-to-conservative Republicans were upset because the party had offered no positive program in the '98 elections, and for a solid year had done nothing but attack me; his right-wing ideologues were upset because they thought he had worked with me too much and demonized me too little. The ingratitude of the right-wing cabal that now controlled the Republican caucus must have galled Gingrich; they were in power only because of his brilliant strategy in the 1994 election and his years of organizing and proselytizing before then.

Newt's announcement got more headlines, but the retirement of New York senator Pat Moynihan would have a bigger impact on my family. On the night Moynihan said he wouldn't seek reelection, Hillary got a call from our friend Charlie Rangel, the congressman from Harlem and ranking member of the House Ways and Means Committee, urging her to run for Moynihan's seat. Hillary told Charlie she was flattered but couldn't imagine doing such a thing.

She didn't completely close the door, and I was glad. It sounded like a pretty good idea to me. We had intended to move to New York after my term ended, with me spending a fair amount of time in Arkansas at my library. New Yorkers seemed to like having high-profile senators: Moynihan, Robert Kennedy, Jacob Javits, Robert Wagner, and many others had been seen as representatives of both the citizens of New York and the nation at large. I thought Hillary would do a great job in the Senate and that she would enjoy it. But that decision was months away.

On November eighth, I brought my national security team to Camp David to discuss Iraq. A week earlier Saddam Hussein had kicked the UN inspectors out again, and it seemed almost certain that we'd have to take military action. The UN Security Council had voted unanimously to condemn Iraq's "flagrant violations" of UN resolutions, Bill Cohen had gone to the Middle East to line up support for air strikes, and Tony Blair was ready to participate.

A few days later the international community took the next big step in our bid to stabilize the global financial situation with a $42 billion aid package to Brazil, $5 billion of it in U.S. taxpayers' money. Unlike the aid packages to Thailand, South Korea, Indonesia, and Russia, this one was coming before the country was on the brink of default, consistent with our new policy of trying to prevent failure and its spread to other nations. We were doing our best to convince international investors that Brazil was committed to reform and had the cash to fight off speculators. And this time, the IMF loan conditions would be less stringent, preserving programs to help the poor and encouraging Brazilian banks to keep making loans. I didn't know whether it would work, but I had a lot of confidence in President Fernando Henrique Cardoso, and as Brazil's major trading partner, the United States had a big stake in his success. It was another of those risks worth taking.

On the fourteenth, I asked Al Gore to represent the United States at the annual APEC meeting in Malaysia, the first leg of a long-scheduled trip to Asia. I couldn't go, because Saddam was still trying to impose unacceptable conditions on the return of the UN inspectors; in response, we were preparing to launch air strikes at sites our intelligence indicated were connected to his weapons program, as well as other military targets. Just before the attacks were launched, with the planes already on their way, we received the first of three letters from Iraq addressing our objections. Within hours, Saddam had backed down completely, and had committed to resolving all outstanding issues raised by the inspectors, to giving them unfettered access to all sites without any interference, to turning over all relevant documents, and to accepting all UN resolutions on weapons of mass destruction. I was skeptical, but I decided to give him one more chance.

On the eighteenth, I left for Tokyo and Seoul. I wanted to go to Japan to establish a working relationship with Keizo Obuchi, the new prime minister, and to try to influence Japanese public opinion to support the tough reforms necessary to end more than five years of economic stagnation. I liked Obuchi and thought he had a chance to tame the turbulent Japanese political scene and serve for several years. He was interested in American-style hands-on politics. As a young man in the 1960s, he had come to the United States and talked his way into meeting with then attorney general Robert Kennedy, who became his political hero. After our meeting Obuchi took me to the streets of Tokyo, where we shook hands with schoolchildren who were holding Japanese and American flags. I also did a televised town hall meeting in which the famously reticent Japanese surprised me with their open, blunt questions, not only about Japan's current challenges but also about whether I had ever visited victims of Hiroshima and Nagasaki; how Japan could get fathers to spend more time with their children, as I had with Chelsea; how many times a month I ate dinner with my family; how I was coping with all the pressures of the presidency; and how I had apologized to Hillary and Chelsea.

In Seoul, I supported both Kim Dae Jung's continuing efforts to move beyond the economic crisis and his outreach to North Korea, so long as it was clear that neither of us would allow the proliferation of missiles, nuclear weapons, or other weapons of mass destruction. We were both concerned about the recent North Korean test launch of a long-range missile. I had asked Bill Perry to head a small group to review our Korea policy, and to recommend a road map to the future that would maximize the chances of North Korea abandoning its weapons and missile programs and reconciling with South Korea, while minimizing the risks of its failure to do so.

At the end of the month Madeleine Albright and I hosted a conference at the State Department to support economic development for the Palestinians, with Yasser Arafat, Jim Wolfensohn of the World Bank, and representatives of the European Union, the Middle East, and Asia. The Israeli cabinet and the Knesset had supported the Wye River accord, and it was time to get some investment into Gaza and the West Bank to give the beleaguered Palestinians a taste of the benefits of peace.

While all this was going on, Henry Hyde and his colleagues kept pushing their agenda, sending me eighty-one questions that they demanded be answered with "admit or deny," and releasing twenty-two hours of the Tripp-Lewinsky tapes. Tripp's taping of those conversations without Lewinsky's permission, after her lawyer explicitly told her the taping was criminal and she should not do it again, was a felony under Maryland's criminal law. She was indicted for it, but the trial judge refused to allow the prosecutor to call Lewinsky as a witness to prove the conversations occurred, ruling that the immunity Starr had given Tripp to testify about her unlawful violation of Lewinsky's privacy prevented Lewinsky from testifying against her. Once more, Starr had succeeded in protecting lawbreakers who played ball with him even as he indicted innocent people who would not lie for him.

During this period Starr also indicted Webb Hubbell for a third time, claiming that he had misled federal regulators about work he and the Rose Law Firm had done for another failed financial institution. It was Starr's last, almost desperate attempt to break Hubbell and force him to say something damaging about Hillary or me.

On the nineteenth of November, Kenneth Starr appeared before the House Judiciary Committee, making comments that, like his report, went far beyond the scope of his responsibility to report the facts he had found to Congress. The Starr report had already been criticized for omitting one big piece of evidence helpful to me: Monica Lewinsky's adamant assertion that I never asked her to lie.

Three surprising things came out of Starr's testimony. The first was his announcement that he had found no wrongdoing on my part or Hillary's in the Travel Office and FBI file investigations. Congressman Barney Frank of Massachusetts asked him when he had reached those conclusions. "Some months ago," replied Starr. Frank then asked him why he waited until after the election to exonerate me on these charges, when he had submitted his report "with a lot of negative stuff about the President" before the election. Starr's brief response was confused and evasive.

Second, Starr admitted he had talked to the press, on background, a violation of the grand jury secrecy rules. Finally, he denied under oath that his office had tried to get Monica Lewinsky to wear a wire to record conversations with Vernon Jordan, me, or other people. When confronted with the FBI form proving that he had, he was evasive. The *Washington Post* reported that "Starr's denials . . . were shattered by his own FBI reports."

The fact that Starr had admitted violating the law on grand jury secrecy and had given false testimony under oath didn't slow him or the committee Republicans down a bit. They thought different rules applied to the home team.

The next day Sam Dash resigned as Starr's ethics advisor, saying that Starr had "unlawfully" injected himself into the impeachment process with his remarks at the congressional hearing. As my mother used to say, Dash was "a day late and a dollar short": Starr hadn't cared about the lawfulness of his behavior for a long time.

Shortly before Thanksgiving, the House Republicans returned to Washington to elect Bob Livingston of Louisiana, the chairman of the Appropriations Committee, as the new Speaker of the House. He would take office in January when the new session of Congress began. At the time, most people thought the movement to impeach me was stalled. Several moderate Republicans had said that they were opposed to it, and that the election had been a clear message that the American people wanted the Congress to reprimand or censure me and get on with the public's business.

In the middle of the month, I settled the Paula Jones case for a large amount of money and no apology. I hated to do it because I had won a clear victory on the law and the facts in a politically motivated case. Jones's lawyers had appealed her case to the Eighth Circuit Court of Appeals, but the governing case law was clear: if the Court of Appeals followed its own decisions, I would win the appeal. Unfortunately, the three-judge panel assigned to hear the case was headed by Pasco Bowman, the same ultra-conservative judge who had removed Judge Henry Woods from one of the Whitewater cases on the basis of spurious newspaper articles after Woods had rendered a decision Starr didn't like. Pasco Bowman, like Judge David Sentelle in Washington, had shown that he was willing to make exceptions to the normal rules of law in Whitewater-related cases.

Part of me almost wanted to lose the appeal so that I could go to court, get all the documents and depositions released, and show the public what my adversaries had been up to. But I had promised the American people I would spend the next two years working for them; I had no business spending five more minutes on the Jones case. The settlement took about half our life savings and we were already deeply in debt with legal bills, but I knew that if I stayed healthy, I could make enough money to take care of my family and pay those bills after I left office. So I settled a case I had already won and went back to work.

My promise to leave the Jones case behind would be tested once more, and severely. In April 1999, Judge Wright sanctioned me for violating her discovery orders and required me to pay her travel costs and the Jones lawyers' deposition expenses. I strongly disagreed with Wright's opinion but could not dispute it without getting into the very factual issues I was determined to avoid and taking more time away from my work. It really burned me up to pay the Jones lawyers' expenses; they had abused the deposition with questions asked in bad faith and in collusion with Starr, and they had repeatedly defied the judge's order not to leak. The judge never did anything to them.

On December 2, Mike Espy was acquitted on all charges brought against him by independent counsel Donald Smaltz. Smaltz had followed Starr's playbook in the Espy investigation, spending more than $17 million and indicting everybody he could in an effort to force them to say something damaging against Mike. The jury's stinging rebuke made Smaltz and Starr the only two independent counsels ever to lose jury trials.

A few days later, Hillary and I flew to Nashville for a memorial service for Al Gore's father, Senator Albert Gore Sr., who had died at ninety at his home in Carthage, Tennessee. The War Memorial Auditorium was full, with people from all walks of life who had come to pay their respects to a man whose Senate service included his role in building the interstate highway system, his refusal to sign the segregationist Southern Manifesto in 1956, and his courageous opposition to the Vietnam War. I had admired Senator Gore since I was a young man, and always enjoyed the chances my association with Al gave me to be with him. Senator and Mrs. Gore had campaigned hard for Al and me in 1992, and I got a big kick out of hearing the Senator give his old-fashioned stump speeches full of fire and brimstone.

The music at the memorial service was moving, especially when we heard an old tape of Senator Gore as a rising young politician playing the fiddle in Constitution Hall in 1938. Al delivered the eulogy, a loving and eloquent tribute to the father, the man, and the public servant. After the service I told Hillary I wished everyone in America could have heard it.

In mid-month, just as I was about to leave for Israel and Gaza to keep my commitments under the Wye River accord, the House Judiciary Committee voted, again along straight party lines, in favor of impeaching me for perjury in the deposition and the grand jury testimony, and for obstruction of justice. They also passed a fourth count accusing me of giving false answers to their questions. It was a truly bizarre proceeding. Chairman Hyde refused to set a standard for what constituted an impeachable offense, or to call any witnesses with direct knowledge of the matters in dispute. He took the position that a vote for impeachment was simply a vote to send the Starr report on to the Senate, which could determine whether the report was factually accurate and whether my removal from office was warranted.

A bipartisan group of prosecutors told the committee that no normal prosecutor would charge me with perjury on the evidence in this case, and a panel of distinguished historians, including Arthur Schlesinger of City University of New York, C. Vann Woodward of Yale, and Sean Wilentz of Princeton, said that what I was alleged to have done did not meet the framers' standard of impeachment—that is, a "high crime or misdemeanor" committed in the exercise of executive power. This had long been the accepted understanding, and their interpretation was backed up by an open letter to Congress signed by four hundred historians. For example, in the Watergate case, the House Judiciary Committee voted against impeaching President Nixon for alleged income tax evasion because it had nothing to do with his performance in office. But all this was entirely irrelevant to Hyde, to his equally hostile counsel, David Schippers, and to the right-wingers who controlled the House.

Ever since the election, Tom DeLay and his staff had been firing up the right-wing networks to demand my impeachment. The radio talk shows were pushing it hard, and moderates were beginning to hear from anti-Clinton activists in their home districts. They were convinced they could get enough moderate members of Congress to forget about the popular opposition to impeachment by making them fear the retaliation of disappointed Clinton haters.

In the context of this strategy, the Hyde committee's vote against a censure resolution was as important as its votes for the impeachment articles. Censure was the preferred option of 75 percent of the American people; if a censure motion were to be presented to the House, the moderate Republicans would vote for it and impeachment would be dead. Hyde claimed that Congress didn't have the authority to censure the President; it was impeachment or nothing. In fact, Presidents Andrew Jackson and James Polk had both been censured by Congress. The censure resolution was voted down by the committee, again on a partisan vote. The full House would not be able to vote on what most Americans wanted. Now it was just a question of how many moderate Republicans could be "persuaded."

After the committee vote, Hillary and I flew to the Middle East. We had a meeting and dinner with Prime Minister Netanyahu, lit candles on a menorah for Hanukkah, and visited Rabin's grave with his family. The next day Madeleine Albright, Sandy Berger, Dennis Ross, Hillary, and I helicoptered into densely populated Gaza to cut the ribbon on the new airport and have lunch with Arafat in a hotel overlooking Gaza's long, beautiful Mediterranean beach. And I gave the speech to the Palestinian National Council that I had pledged to deliver at Wye River. Just before I got up to speak, almost all the delegates raised their hands in support of removing the provision calling for the destruction of Israel from their charter. It was the moment that made the whole trip worthwhile. You could almost hear the sighs of relief in Israel; perhaps Israelis and Palestinians actually could share the land and the future after all. I thanked the delegates, told them I wanted their people to have concrete benefits from peace, and asked them to stay with the peace process.

It wasn't an idle plea. Less than two months after the triumph at Wye River, the negotiations were in trouble again. Even though Netanyahu's cabinet had narrowly approved the agreement, his coalition didn't really favor it, making it virtually impossible for him to proceed with troop redeployment and prisoner releases, or to move on to the even more difficult final status issues, including the question of Palestinian statehood and whether the eastern section of Jerusalem would become the capital of Palestine. The previous day's amendment of the Palestinian charter helped Netanyahu with the Israeli public, but his own coalition was a much harder crew to convince. It looked as if he would either have to form a more broad-based government of national unity or call elections.

On the morning after my speech to the Palestinians, Netanyahu, Arafat, and I met at the Erez border crossing to try to energize the implementation of Wye River and decide how to move to the final status issues. Afterward, Arafat took Hillary and me to Bethlehem. He was proud to have custody of a site so holy to Christians, and he knew it would mean a lot to us to visit it close to Christmas.

After we left Arafat, we joined Prime Minister Netanyahu for a visit to Masada. I was impressed that so much work had been done since Hillary and I had first been there in 1981 to recover the remains of the fortress where Jewish martyrs had fought to the death for their convictions. Bibi seemed somewhat pensive and subdued. He had gone beyond his political safety zone at Wye River, and his future was uncertain. There was no way to know whether the chances he had taken would bring Israel closer to lasting peace or bring an end to his government.

We bid the prime minister farewell and flew home to another conflict. Six days earlier, on just the second day of renewed UN inspections in Iraq, some inspectors had been denied access to Saddam's Ba'ath Party headquarters. On the day we returned to Washington, the chief UN weapons inspector, Richard Butler, reported to Kofi Annan that Iraq had not kept its commitments to cooperate with him and had even imposed new restrictions on the inspectors' work.

The next day the United States and the United Kingdom launched a series of attacks from airplanes and with cruise missiles on Iraq's suspected chemical, biological, and nuclear lab sites and its military capacity to threaten its neighbors. In my address to the American people that evening, I noted that Saddam had previously used chemical weapons on Iranians and Kurds in northern Iraq and had fired Scud missiles at other countries. I said I had called off an attack four weeks earlier because Saddam had promised full compliance. Instead, the inspectors had repeatedly been threatened, "so Iraq has abused its final chance."

At the time the strikes were launched, our intelligence indicated that substantial amounts of biological and chemical materials that had been in Iraq at the end of the Gulf War as well as some missile warheads were still unaccounted for, and that some elementary laboratory work toward acquiring a nuclear weapon was being done. Our military experts felt that unconventional weapons might have become even more important to Saddam because his conventional military forces were much weaker than they had been before the Gulf War.

My national security team was unanimous in the belief that we should hit Saddam as soon as the Butler report was issued, to minimize the chances that Iraq could disperse its forces and protect its biological and chemical stocks. Tony Blair and his advisors agreed. The Anglo-American assault lasted four days, with 650 air sorties and 400 cruise missiles, all carefully targeted to hit military and national security targets and to minimize civilian casualties. After the attack we had no way to know how much of the proscribed material had been destroyed, but Iraq's ability to produce and deploy dangerous weapons had plainly been reduced.

Although they talked about Saddam as if he were the devil himself, some of the Republicans were in a snit over the attacks. Several of them, including Senator Lott and Representative Dick Armey, criticized the timing of the attacks, saying I had ordered them in order to delay the House vote on impeachment. The next day, after several Republican senators had expressed support for the raid, Lott backed off his comments. Armey never did; he, DeLay, and their minions had worked hard to get their more moderate colleagues in line, and they were in a hurry to vote on impeachment before some of them started thinking again.

On December 19, not long before the House began to vote on impeachment, Speaker-designate Bob Livingston announced his retirement from the House in the wake of public disclosure of his own personal problems. I learned later that seventeen conservative Republicans had come to him and said he had to quit, not because of what he had done, but because he had become an obstacle to my impeachment.

Barely six weeks after the American people had plainly sent them a message against impeachment, the House passed two of the four articles of impeachment approved by the Hyde committee. The first, accusing me of lying to the grand jury, passed 228–206, with five Republicans voting against it. The second, alleging that I had obstructed justice by suborning perjury and hiding gifts, passed 221–212, with twelve Republicans voting no. The two charges were inconsistent. The first was based on the perceived differences between Monica Lewinsky's description of the details of our encounters in the Starr report and my grand jury testimony; the second ignored the fact that she also had testified that I never asked her to lie, a fact supported by all the other witnesses. The Republicans apparently believed her only when she disagreed with me.

Shortly after the election, Tom DeLay and company began roping in the moderate Republicans. They got some votes by depriving moderates of the chance to vote for censure, then telling them that since they wanted to reprimand me in some way, they should feel free to vote for impeachment, because I'd never be convicted and removed from office since the Republicans couldn't get the required two-thirds vote for removal in the Senate. A few days after the House vote, four moderate Republican House members—Mike Castle of Delaware, James Greenwood of Pennsylvania, and Ben Gilman and Sherwood Boehlert of New York—wrote to the *New York Times* saying that their votes for impeachment didn't mean they thought I should be removed.

I don't know all the individual carrots and sticks that were used on the moderates, but I did find out about some of them. One Republican committee chairman was plainly distraught when he told a White House aide that he didn't want to vote for impeachment but he would lose his chairmanship if he voted against it. Jay Dickey, an Arkansas Republican, told Mack McLarty he might lose his seat on the Appropriations Committee if he didn't vote to impeach me. I was disappointed when Jack Quinn, a Buffalo, New York, Republican who had been a frequent guest at the White House and who had told several people, including me, that he was opposed to impeachment, did an about-face and announced that he would vote for three articles. I had carried his district by a large majority in 1996, but a vocal minority of his constituents had apparently put a lot of heat on him. Mike Forbes, a Long Island Republican who had supported me in the impeachment battle, changed when he was offered a new leadership position on Livingston's team. When Livingston resigned, the offer evaporated.

Five Democrats also voted for impeachment. Four of them came from conservative districts. The fifth said he had wanted to vote for censure, then bought the argument that he was doing the next best thing. The Republicans who voted against impeachment included Amo Houghton of New York and Chris Shays of Connecticut, two of the most progressive and independent House Republicans; Connie Morella of Maryland, also a progressive whose district had voted overwhelmingly for me in 1996; and two conservatives, Mark Souder of Indiana and Peter King of New York, who simply refused to go along with their party's leadership in converting a constitutional question into a test of party loyalty.

Peter King, with whom I had worked on Northern Ireland, withstood weeks of enormous pressure, including threats to destroy him politically if he did not vote for impeachment. In several television interviews, King made a simple argument to his fellow Republicans: I'm against impeachment because if President Clinton were a Republican, you'd be against it, too. The pro-impeachment Republicans who appeared on the programs with him never had a good response to that. The right-wingers thought every person had a price or a breaking point, and more often than not they were right, but Peter King had an Irish soul: he loved the poetry of Yeats; he was not afraid to fight for a lost cause; and he was not for sale.

Although the pro-impeachment forces were said to have had prayer meetings in DeLay's office to seek God's support for their divine mission, the impeachment drive was fundamentally neither about morality nor the rule of law, but about power. Newt Gingrich had said it all in one phrase; they were doing it "because we can." My impeachment wasn't about my indefensible personal conduct; there was plenty of that on their side, too, and it was beginning to come out, even without a bogus lawsuit and a special prosecutor to do the digging. It wasn't about whether I had lied in a legal proceeding; when Newt Gingrich was found to have given false testimony several times during the House Ethics Committee investigation into the apparently unlawful practices of his political action committee, he got a reprimand and a fine from the same crowd that had just voted to impeach me. When Kathleen Willey, who had immunity from Starr as long as she told him what he wanted to hear, lied, Starr just gave her immunity again. When Susan McDougal wouldn't lie for him, he indicted her. When Herby Branscum and Rob Hill wouldn't lie for him, he indicted them. When Webb Hubbell wouldn't lie for him, he indicted him a second and a third time, and indicted his wife, his lawyer, and his accountant, only to drop the charges against the three of them later. When David Hale's first story about me was disproved, Starr let him change it until Hale finally came up with a version that was not disprovable. Jim McDougal's former partner and my old friend, Steve Smith, offered to take a lie-detector test regarding his assertion that Starr's people had prepared a typewritten statement for him to read to the grand jury and kept pressuring him to do so, even after he had told them repeatedly that it was a lie. Starr himself didn't tell the truth under oath about trying to get Monica Lewinsky to wear a wire.

And the House vote certainly wasn't about whether the House managers' accusations constituted impeachable offenses as historically understood: If the Watergate standard had been applied to my case, there would have been no impeachment.

This was about power, about something the House Republican leaders did because they could, and because they wanted to pursue an agenda I opposed and had blocked. I have no doubt that many of their supporters out in the country believed that the drive to remove me from office was rooted in morality or law, and that I was such a bad person it didn't matter whether or not my conduct fit the constitutional definition of impeachability. But their position didn't meet the first test of all morality and just law: The same rules apply to everyone. As Teddy Roosevelt once said, no man is above the law, but "no man is below the law either."

In the partisan wars that had raged since the mid-1960s, neither side had been completely blameless. I had thought the Democrats wrong to examine the movie tastes of Judge Bork and the drinking habits of Senator John Tower. But when it came to the politics of personal destruction, the New Right Republicans were in a class by themselves. My party sometimes didn't seem to understand power, but I was proud of the fact that there were some things Democrats wouldn't do just because they could.

Shortly before the House vote, Robert Healy wrote an article in the *Boston Globe* about a meeting that had occurred between Speaker Tip O'Neill and President Reagan in the White House in late 1986. The Iran-Contra story was out; White House aides John Poindexter and Oliver North had broken the law and lied about it to Congress. O'Neill did not ask the President if he had known about or authorized the lawbreaking. (Republican senator John Tower's bipartisan commission later found that Reagan did know about it.) According to Healy, O'Neill simply told the President that he would not permit an impeachment proceeding to go forward; he said he had lived through Watergate and wouldn't put the country through such an ordeal again.

Tip O'Neill may have been a better patriot than Gingrich and DeLay, but they and their allies were more effective in concentrating power and using it to whatever extent they could against their adversaries. They believed that, in the short run, might makes right, and they didn't care what they put the country through. It certainly didn't matter to them that the Senate wouldn't remove me. They thought if they trashed me long enough, the press and the public would eventually blame me for their bad behavior, as well as for my own. They badly wanted to brand me with a big "I," and believed that for the rest of my life and for some time thereafter, the fact of my impeachment would loom far larger than the circumstances of it, and that before long no one would even talk about what a hypocritical farce the whole process had been, and how it was the culmination of years of unconscionable conduct by Kenneth Starr and his cohorts.

Just after the vote, Dick Gephardt brought a large group of the House Democrats who had defended me to the White House so that I could thank them and we could show unity for the battle ahead. Al Gore gave a stirring defense of my record as President, and Dick made an impassioned plea to the Republicans to stop the politics of personal destruction and get on with the nation's business. Hillary commented to me afterward that the event almost had the feel of a victory rally. In a way it was. The Democrats had stood up not just for me but, far more importantly, for the Constitution.

I certainly hadn't wanted to be impeached, but I was consoled by the fact that the only other time it had happened, to Andrew Johnson in the late 1860s, there were also no "high crimes and misdemeanors"; just like this case, that was a politically motivated action by a majority party in Congress that couldn't restrain itself.

Hillary was more upset about the partisan political nature of the House proceedings than I was. As a young lawyer, she had served on John Doar's staff for the House Judiciary Committee during Watergate, when there was a serious, balanced, bipartisan effort to fulfill the constitutional mandate of defining and finding high crimes and misdemeanors in the official actions of the President.

From the beginning, I had believed that the best way to win the final showdown with the Far Right was for me to keep doing my job and let others handle the defense. During the proceedings in the House and Senate, that's what I tried to do, and many people told me they appreciated it.

The strategy worked better than it might have. The release of the Starr report and the determination of the Republicans to proceed with impeachment brought with them a marked shift in the media coverage. As I've said, the media was never a monolith; now even those who had previously been willing to give Starr a free ride began to point out the involvement of right-wing groups in the cabal, the abusive tactics of the OIC, and the unprecedented nature of what the Republicans were doing. And the TV talk shows began to show more balance, as commentators like Greta Van Susteren and Susan Estrich, and guests like lawyers Lanny Davis, Alan Dershowitz, Julian Epstein, and Vincent Bugliosi made sure that both sides of the case were heard. Members of Congress also made the case, including Senator Tom Harkin, House Judiciary Committee members Sheila Jackson Lee and Bill Delahunt, himself a former prosecutor. Professors Cass Sunstein of the University of Chicago and Susan Bloch of Georgetown released a letter on the unconstitutionality of the impeachment process signed by four hundred legal scholars.

As we headed into 1999, the unemployment rate was down to 4.3 percent and the stock market had rebounded to an all-time high. Hillary had hurt her back while making a Christmas visit to employees in the Old Executive Office Building, but it was getting better, after her doctor told her to stop wearing high heels on the hard marble floors. Chelsea and I decorated the tree and went on our annual Christmas shopping spree.

My best Christmas presents that year were the expressions of kindness and support from ordinary citizens. A thirteen-year-old girl from Kentucky wrote me to say that I'd made a mistake, but I couldn't quit, because my opponents were "mean." And an eighty-six-year-old white man from New Brunswick, New Jersey, after telling his family he was going to Atlantic City for the day, instead rode the train to Washington, where he took a cab to the Reverend Jesse Jackson's house. When he was greeted by Jesse's mother-in-law, he told her he was there because the Reverend Jackson was the only person he knew of who talked to the President, and he wanted to send me a message: "Tell the President not to quit. I was around when the Republicans tried to destroy Al Smith [our presidential nominee in 1928] for being a Catholic. He can't give in to them." The man got back in his cab, returned to Union Station, and took the next train home. I called that man to say thank you. Then my family and I went to Renaissance Weekend and into the new year.

TWENTY-TWO

ON JANUARY 7, Chief Justice William Rehnquist officially opened the impeachment trial in the Senate, and Ken Starr indicted Julie Hiatt Steele, the Republican woman who wouldn't lie to back up Kathleen Willey's story.

A week later, the House impeachment managers made a three-day presentation of their case. They now wanted to call witnesses, something they hadn't done in their own hearings, with the exception of Kenneth Starr. One of the managers, Asa Hutchinson from Arkansas, who had prosecuted my brother's drug case as U.S. attorney in the 1980s, said the Senate had to let them call witnesses, because if he were a prosecutor, he couldn't indict me for obstruction of justice, the issue he was charged with handling, based on the meager record the House had sent to the Senate! On the other hand, another of the House managers argued that the Senate had no right to judge whether my alleged offenses met the constitutional standard of impeachment; he said the House had done that for them and the Senate should be bound by their opinion, despite the fact that the Hyde committee had refused to articulate a standard for judging what conduct was impeachable.

In his closing argument to the Senate, Henry Hyde finally gave his interpretation of the constitutional meaning of impeachment when he said in essence that trying to spare oneself embarrassment over private misconduct was more of a justification for removal from office than misleading the nation about an important matter of state. My mother had raised me to look for the good in everybody. When I watched the vituperative Mr. Hyde, I was sure there must be a Dr. Jekyll in there somewhere, but I was having a hard time finding him.

On the nineteenth, my legal team began its three days of response. Chuck Ruff, the White House counsel and a former

U.S. attorney, led off, arguing for two and a half hours that the charges were untrue and that even if the senators thought they *were* true, the offenses did not come close to meeting the constitutional standard for impeachment, much less removal. Ruff was a mild-mannered man who had been wheelchairbound for most of his life. He was also a powerful advocate, who was offended by what the House managers had done. He shredded their evidentiary arguments and reminded the Senate that a bipartisan panel of prosecutors had already said that no responsible prosecutor would bring a perjury charge on the facts before them.

I thought Ruff's best moment was when he caught Asa Hutchinson red-handed in a telling misrepresentation of fact. Hutchinson had told the Senate that Vernon Jordan began helping Monica Lewinsky to get a job only after he learned she would be a witness in the Jones case. The evidence proved that Vernon had done so several weeks before he knew or could have known that, and that at the time Judge Wright made the decision to allow Lewinsky to be called as a witness (a decision that she later reversed), Vernon was on a plane to Europe. I didn't know whether Asa had misled the Senate because he thought that the senators wouldn't figure it out or because he thought that they, like the House managers, wouldn't care whether the presentation was accurate or not.

The next day Greg Craig and Cheryl Mills addressed the specific charges. Greg noted that the article charging me with perjury failed to cite a single specific example of it and instead tried to bring my deposition in the Jones case into play, even though the House had voted against the article of impeachment dealing with that. Craig also pointed out that some of the allegations of perjury now being made to the Senate were never made by Starr or any House member during the debates in the Judiciary Committee or on the floor of the House. They were making up their case as they moved along.

Cheryl Mills, a young African-American graduate of Stanford Law School, spoke on the sixth anniversary of the day she began her work in the White House. She dealt brilliantly with two of the obstruction of justice charges, presenting facts that the House managers couldn't dispute but had not told the Senate about and that proved their claims of obstruction of justice to be nonsense. Cheryl's finest moment was her closing. Responding to suggestions by Republican Lindsey Graham of South Carolina and others that my acquittal would send a message that our civil rights and sexual harassment laws are unimportant, she said, "I can't let their comments go unchallenged." Black people all over America knew that the drive to impeach me was being led by right-wing white southerners who had never lifted a finger for civil rights.

Cheryl pointed out that Paula Jones had had her day in court and a female judge had found that she didn't have a case. She said that we revered men like Jefferson, Kennedy, and King, all of whom were imperfect but "struggled to do humanity good," and that my record on civil rights and women's rights was "unimpeachable": "I stand here before you today because President Bill Clinton believed I could stand here for him. . . . It would be wrong to convict him on this record."

On the third and final day of our presentation, David Kendall led off with a cool, logical, and systematic dismantling of the charge that I had obstructed justice, citing Monica Lewinsky's repeated assertions that I never asked her to lie and once again detailing the House managers' misstatements or omissions of critical facts.

My defense was closed by Dale Bumpers. I had asked Dale to do it because he was a fine trial lawyer, a careful student of the Constitution, and one of the best orators in America. He had also known me a long time and had just left the Senate after serving twenty-four years. After loosening his former colleagues up with a few jokes, Dale said that he had been reluctant to appear because he and I had been close friends for twenty-five years and had worked together for the same causes. He said that while he knew the Senate might discount his defense as the words of a friend, he had come not to defend me but to defend the Constitution, "the most sacred document to me next to the Holy Bible."

Bumpers opened his argument by bashing Starr's investigation: "Javert's pursuit of Jean Valjean in *Les Misérables* pales by comparison." He said, "After all those years . . . the President was found guilty of nothing, official or personal. . . . We are here today because the President suffered a terrible moral lapse."

He chided the House managers for having no compassion. Then came the most dramatic moment of Dale's speech: "Put yourself in his position . . . we are, none of us, perfect . . . he should have thought of all that beforehand. And indeed he should have, just as Adam and Eve should have"—now he pointed at the senators—"just as *you* and *you* and *you* and *you* and millions of other people who have been caught in similar circumstances should have thought of it before. As I say, none of us is perfect."

Dale then said that I had already been punished severely for my mistake, that the people didn't want me removed, and that the Senate should listen to the world leaders who had stood up for me, including Havel, Mandela, and King Hussein.

He closed with an erudite and detailed history of the Constitutional Convention's deliberations on the impeachment provision, saying that our framers took it from English law, which plainly covered offenses "distinctly 'political' against the state." He pleaded with the Senate not to defile the Constitution, but instead to hear the American people "calling on you to rise above politics . . . and do your solemn duty."

Bumpers's speech was magnificent, by turns erudite and emotional, earthy and profound. If the Senate roll had been called at that moment, there wouldn't have been many votes for removal. Instead, the process would drag out for three more weeks, as the House managers and their allies tried to find a way to persuade more Republican senators to vote with them. After the two sides had made their presentations, it was clear that all the Democratic senators and several Republicans were going to vote no.

While the Senate was sitting in trial, I was doing what I always did at this time of the year—getting ready for the

State of the Union speech and promoting around the country the new initiatives that would be in it. The speech was
scheduled for the nineteenth, the same day my defense
opened in the Senate. Some Republican senators had urged
me to delay the speech, but I wasn't about to do that. The
impeachment had already cost the American people lots of
their hard-earned tax dollars, diverted the Congress from
pressing business, and weakened the fabric of the Constitution. If I had delayed my speech, it would have sent a message to the American people that their business had been
put on the back burner.

If possible, the atmosphere at this State of the Union was
even more surreal than it had been the previous year. As
always, I entered the Capitol and was taken to the Speaker's
quarters, which were now occupied by Dennis Hastert of Illinois, a stocky former wrestling coach who was quite conservative but less abrasive and confrontational than Gingrich,
Armey, and DeLay. Before long, a bipartisan delegation of
senators and representatives came to take me to the House
chamber. We shook hands and talked as if nothing else in the
world was going on. When I was introduced and began to
walk down the aisle, the Democrats cheered loudly as most
Republicans clapped politely. Since the aisle splits the
Republicans and Democrats, I expected to spend the trip
down to the podium shaking hands on the Democratic side
and was surprised that, for whatever reason, several Republican House members held out their hands, too.

I began with a salute to the new Speaker, who had said
he wanted to work with the Democrats in a spirit of civility
and bipartisanship. It sounded good and he might have
meant it, since the impeachment vote in the House had
occurred before he became Speaker. So I accepted his offer.

By 1999, our economic expansion was the longest in history, with eighteen million new jobs since I took office, real
wages going up, income inequality finally going down a little, and the lowest peacetime unemployment rate since
1957. The state of our union was stronger than ever, and I
outlined a program to make the most of it, beginning with a
series of initiatives to create a secure retirement for the baby

boom generation. I proposed to commit 60 percent of the surplus over the next fifteen years to extend the solvency of the Social Security Trust Fund until 2055, an increase of more than twenty years, a small portion of it to be invested in mutual funds; an end to the limit on what Social Security recipients could earn without penalty; and more generous payments to elderly women, who were twice as likely as men their age to live in poverty. I also proposed to use 16 percent of the surplus to add ten years to the life of the Medicare Trust Fund; a $1,000 long-term–care tax credit for the elderly and disabled; the option to let people between the ages of fifty-five and sixty-five buy into Medicare; and a new pension initiative, USA Accounts, which would take 11 percent of the surplus to provide tax credits to citizens who opened their own retirement accounts, and to match a portion of the savings of workers with more modest incomes. This was perhaps the largest proposal ever made to help modest-income families save and create wealth.

I also proposed a large package of education reforms, arguing that we should change the way we spent the more than $15 billion a year of education aid to "support what works and stop supporting what doesn't work," by requiring states to end social promotion, turn around failing schools or shut them down, improve the quality of the teaching force, issue report cards on every school, and adopt sensible discipline policies. I again asked Congress to provide funds to build or modernize five thousand schools and to approve a sixfold increase in the number of college scholarships for students who would commit to teaching in underserved areas.

To give more support to families, I recommended a minimum wage increase, expanded family leave, a child-care tax credit, and trigger locks on guns so that children could not fire them accidentally. I also asked Congress to pass the Equal Pay and Employment Non-Discrimination acts; to establish a new American Private Investment Corporation to help raise $15 billion to create new businesses and jobs in poor communities; to enact the Africa Trade and Development Act to open more of our markets to African products; and to fund a $1 billion Lands Legacy initiative to preserve natural treasures, and a package of tax cuts and research money to fight global warming.

On national security, I asked for funds to guard computer networks against terrorists, and to protect communities from chemical and biological attacks; to increase research into vaccines and treatments; to increase the Nunn-Lugar nuclear safety program by two-thirds; to support the Wye River accord; and to reverse the decline in military spending that had begun at the end of the Cold War.

Before closing, I honored Hillary for her leadership in the Millennium Project and in representing America so well all over the world. She was sitting in her box with the home run–hitting Chicago Cubs star Sammy Sosa, who had joined her on a recent trip to his native Dominican Republic. After all she had been through, Hillary got an even bigger round of applause than Sammy. I ended "the last State of the Union address of the twentieth century" by reminding the Congress that "perhaps, in the daily press of events, in the clash of controversy, we don't see our own time for what it truly is, a new dawn for America."

On the day after the speech, with the highest job approval ratings I had ever had, I flew to Buffalo, with Hillary and Al and Tipper Gore, to speak to an overflow crowd of more than twenty thousand at the Marine Midland Arena. Once again, in spite of all that was going on, the State of the Union address, with its full agenda for the year ahead, had struck a responsive chord with the American people.

I ended the month with a major speech at the National Academy of Sciences, outlining my proposals to protect America from terrorist attacks with biological and chemical weapons and from cyberterrorism; a trip home to Little Rock to view tornado damage in my old neighborhood, including the loss of several old trees on the grounds of the Governor's Mansion; a visit to St. Louis to welcome Pope John Paul II back to the United States; a meeting with a large bipartisan congressional delegation in the East Room to discuss the future of Social Security and Medicare; and a memorial service for my friend Governor Lawton Chiles of Florida, who had died suddenly not long before. Lawton had given me courage for the current fight with one of his favorite sayings: If you can't run with the big dogs, you ought to stay on the porch.

On February 7, King Hussein lost his fight against cancer. Hillary and I immediately left for Jordan with a delegation that included Presidents Ford, Carter, and Bush. I was very grateful for their willingness, on short notice, to honor a man we had all worked with and admired. The next day we walked in his funeral procession for almost a mile, attended the memorial service, and paid our respects to Queen Noor, who was heartbroken. So were Hillary and I. We had enjoyed some wonderful times with Hussein and Noor in Jordan and in the United States. I remembered with particular pleasure a meal the four of us had shared on the Truman Balcony of the White House not long before the king died. Now he was gone, and the world was a poorer place.

After meetings with the new monarch, Hussein's son Abdullah, as well as Prime Minister Netanyahu, President Assad, President Mubarak, Tony Blair, Jacques Chirac, Boris Yeltsin, and President Suleyman Demirel of Turkey, I flew home to await the Senate vote on my future. Though the outcome wasn't in doubt, the behind-the-scenes maneuvering had been interesting. Several Republican senators were upset with the House Republicans for putting them through the trial, but whenever the right wing turned the pressure up, most of them backed down and went along with dragging the whole thing out. When Senator Robert Byrd moved to have the charges dismissed as having no merit, David Kendall's partner, Nicole Seligman, made an argument on the law and the facts that most senators knew was undebatable. Nevertheless, Byrd's motion was defeated. When Senator Strom Thurmond told his Republican colleagues early on that the votes weren't there to remove me and the process should be stopped, he was overruled in the Republican caucus.

One Republican senator who was opposed to impeachment kept us informed of what was going on among his colleagues. Several days before the vote, he said there were
only thirty Republican votes for the perjury count and forty
to forty-five for the obstruction of justice count. They were
nowhere near the two-thirds majority the Constitution
requires for removal. A few days before the vote, the senator told us that the House Republicans had said they would
be humiliated if neither count got at least a token majority
of the votes, and their Senate colleagues had better not
humiliate them if they wanted the House to stay in Republican hands after the next election. The senator reported that
they would have to whittle the number of Republican "no"
votes down.

On February 12 the impeachment motions failed. The
vote on the perjury count failed by 22 votes, 45–55, and the
vote on the obstruction of justice count failed by 17 votes,
50–50, with all the Democrats and Republican senators
Olympia Snowe and Susan Collins of Maine, Jim Jeffords of
Vermont, Arlen Specter of Pennsylvania, and John Chafee
of Rhode Island voting no on both counts. Senators Richard
Shelby of Alabama, Slade Gorton of Washington, Ted
Stevens of Alaska, Fred Thompson of Tennessee, and John
Warner of Virginia voted no on the perjury count.

The vote itself was anticlimactic, coming three weeks
after the close of my defense. Only the margin of defeat was
in doubt. I was just glad the ordeal was over for my family
and my country. After the vote I said that I was profoundly
sorry for what I had done to trigger the events and the great
burden they imposed on the American people, and that I
was rededicating myself to "a time of reconciliation and
renewal for America." I took one question: "In your heart,
sir, can you forgive and forget?" I replied, "I believe any person who asks for forgiveness has to be prepared to give it."

After the impeachment ordeal, people often asked me
how I got through it without losing my mind, or at least the
ability to keep doing the job. I couldn't have done it if the
White House staff and cabinet, including those who were
angry and disappointed over my conduct, hadn't stayed

with me. It would have been much harder if the American people hadn't made an early judgment that I should remain President and stuck with it. If more congressional Democrats had bailed out when it looked like the safe thing to do in January, after the story broke, or in August, after I testified to the grand jury, it would have been tough; instead, they rose to the challenge. Having the support of world leaders like Mandela, Blair, King Hussein, Havel, Crown Prince Abdullah, Kim Dae Jung, Chirac, Cardoso, Zedillo, and others whom I admired helped to keep my spirits up. When I compared them with my enemies, as disgusted as I still was with myself, I figured I couldn't be all bad.

The love and support of friends and strangers made a big difference; those who wrote to me or said a kind word in a crowd meant more than they will ever know. The religious leaders who counseled me, visited me at the White House, or called to pray with me reminded me that, notwithstanding the condemnations I had received from some quarters, God is love.

But the biggest factors in my ability to survive and function were personal. Hillary's brothers and my brother were wonderfully supportive. Roger joked to me that it was nice to finally be the brother who wasn't in trouble. Hugh came up from Miami every week to play UpWords, talk sports, and make me laugh. Tony came over for our family pinochle matches. My mother-in-law and Dick Kelley were great to me.

Despite everything, our daughter still loved me and wanted me to stand my ground. And, most important, Hillary stood with me and loved me through it all. From the time we first met, I had loved her laugh. In the midst of all the absurdity, we were laughing again, brought back together by our weekly counseling and our shared determination to fight off the right-wing coup. I almost wound up being grateful to my tormentors: they were probably the only people who could have made me look good to Hillary again. I even got off the couch.

During the long year between the deposition in the Jones case and my acquittal in the Senate, on most of the nights when I was home in the White House I spent two to three hours alone in my office, reading the Bible and books on faith and forgiveness, and rereading *The Imitation of Christ* by Thomas à Kempis, the *Meditations* of Marcus Aurelius, and several of the most thoughtful letters I had received, including a series of mini-sermons from Rabbi Menachem Genack of Englewood, New Jersey. I was particularly affected by *Seventy Times Seven*, a book about forgiveness by Johann Christoph Arnold, the elder of Bruderhof, a Christian community with members in the northeastern United States and in England.

I still have poems, prayers, and quotations that people sent me or put into my hand at public events. And I have two stones with the New Testament verse John 8:7 inscribed on them. In what many people believe was Jesus' last encounter with his critics, the Pharisees, they brought to him a woman caught in the act of adultery and said the law of Moses commanded them to stone her to death. They taunted Jesus: "What sayest thou?" Instead of answering, Jesus leaned over and wrote on the ground with his finger, as if he had not heard them. When they continued to ask, he stood and said: "He that is without sin among you, let him first cast a stone at her." Those who heard him, "being convicted by their own conscience, went out one by one, beginning at the eldest, even unto the last." When Jesus was alone with the woman, he asked her, "Where are those thine accusers? Hath no man condemned thee?" She answered, "No man, Lord," and Jesus replied, "Neither do I condemn thee."

I had had a lot of stones cast at me, and through my own self-inflicted wounds I had been exposed to the whole world. In some ways it was liberating; I had nothing more to hide. And as I tried to understand why I had made my own mistakes, I also attempted to figure out why my adversaries were so consumed with hatred, and so willing to say and do things inconsistent with their professed moral convictions. I had always looked with a jaundiced eye at other people's attempts to psychoanalyze me, but it did seem to me that many of my bitterest critics among the Far Right political and religious groups and the most judgmental members of the press had sought safety and security in positions where they could judge and not be judged, hurt and not be hurt.

My sense of my own mortality and human frailty and the unconditional love I'd had as a child had spared me the compulsion to judge and condemn others. And I believed my personal flaws, no matter how deep, were far less threatening to our democratic government than the power lust of my accusers. In late January, I had received a moving letter from Bill Ziff of New York, a businessman I'd never met but whose son was a friend of mine. He said that he was sorry for the pain Hillary and I had endured but that much good had come of it, because the American people had shown maturity and judgment in seeing through "the demonizing mullahs in our midst. Though it was never your intention, you have done more to expose their underlying agenda than any President in history, including Roosevelt."

Whatever the motives of my adversaries, it became clear, on those solitary nights in my upstairs office, that if I wanted compassion from others, I needed to show it, even to those who didn't respond in kind. Besides, what did I have to complain about? I would never be a perfect person, but Hillary was laughing again, Chelsea was still doing well at Stanford, I was still doing a job I loved, and spring was on the way.

TWENTY-THREE

ON FEBRUARY 19, a week after the Senate vote, I gave the first posthumous pardon ever granted by a President, to Henry Flipper, the first black graduate of West Point, who, because of his race, had been wrongfully convicted of conduct unbecoming an officer 117 years earlier. Such actions by a President may seem unimportant compared with the power of current events, but correcting historical mistakes matters, not only to the descendants of those who were wronged but to us all.

In the last week of the month, Paul Begala announced his departure from the White House. I had relished having Paul there, because he had been with me since New Hampshire and he was smart, funny, combative, and effective. He also had small children who deserved more time with their father. Paul had stuck with me through the impeachment battle; now he needed to leave.

The only news out of Whitewater World was the lopsided vote of the American Bar Association, 384–49, on a resolution calling for the repeal of the independent counsel law, and a news report saying the Justice Department was investigating whether Kenneth Starr had deceived Janet Reno about his office's involvement with the Jones case and about the reasons he gave her for adding the Lewinsky matter to his jurisdiction.

March began with the announcement that after months of complex negotiations, the administration had succeeded in preserving the largest unprotected stand of old-growth redwoods in the world, the Headwaters Forest in northern California. The next week I took a four-day trip to Nicaragua, El Salvador, Honduras, and Guatemala to highlight a new era of democratic cooperation in a region in which, not long before, America had supported repressive regimes with horrible human rights records as long as they were anti-Communist. Viewing the aftermath of natural disasters that American troops were helping with, speaking to the parliament in El Salvador, where recent adversaries in a bloody civil war now sat together in peace, apologizing for America's past actions in Guatemala—all these seemed to me to be signs of a new era of democratic progress I was committed to support.

By the time I returned, we were moving toward another Balkan war, this time in Kosovo. The Serbs had launched an offensive against rebellious Kosovar Albanians a year earlier, killing many innocent people; some women and children were burned in their own homes. The last round of Serb aggression had sparked another exodus of refugees and had increased the desire of Kosovar Albanians for independence. The killings were all too reminiscent of the early days of Bosnia, which, like Kosovo, bridged the divide between European Muslims and Serb Orthodox Christians, a dividing line along which there had been conflict from time to time for six hundred years.

In 1974, Tito had given Kosovo autonomy, allowing it self-government and control over its schools. In 1989, Milosevic had taken autonomy away. The tensions had been rising ever since, and had exploded after the independence of Bosnia was secured in 1995. I was determined not to allow Kosovo to become another Bosnia. So was Madeleine Albright.

By April 1998, the United Nations had imposed an arms embargo, and the United States and its allies had imposed economic sanctions on Serbia for its failure to end the hostilities and begin a dialogue with the Kosovar Albanians. By the middle of June, NATO had begun to plan for a range of military options to end the violence. As summer came, Dick Holbrooke was back in the region to try to find a diplomatic solution for the standoff.

In mid-July, Serb forces again attacked armed and unarmed Kosovars, beginning a summer of aggression that would force 300,000 more Kosovar Albanians to leave their homes. In late September, the UN Security Council had passed another resolution demanding an end to hostilities, and at month's end we sent Holbrooke on yet another mission to Belgrade to try to reason with Milosevic.

On October 13, NATO had threatened to attack Serbia within four days unless the UN resolutions were observed. The air strikes were delayed when four thousand Yugoslav special police officers were withdrawn from Kosovo. Things got better for a while, but in January 1999 the Serbs were killing innocents in Kosovo again, and NATO air strikes seemed inevitable. We decided to try diplomacy one more time, but I wasn't optimistic. The parties' objectives were far apart. The United States and NATO wanted Kosovo to have the political autonomy it had enjoyed under the Yugoslav constitution between 1974 and 1989, until Milosevic took it away, and we wanted a NATO-led peacekeeping force to guarantee the peace and the safety of Kosovo's civilians, including the Serb minority. Milosevic wanted to keep control of Kosovo, and was opposed to any foreign troop deployments there. The Kosovar Albanians wanted independence. They were also divided among themselves. Ibrahim Rugova, the head of the shadow government, was a soft-spoken man with a penchant for wearing a scarf around his neck. I was convinced we could make a peace agreement with him, but not so sure about the other main Kosovar faction, the Kosovo Liberation Army (KLA), led by a young man named Hacim Thaci. The KLA wanted independence and believed it could actually go toe-to-toe with the Serbian army.

The parties met at Rambouillet, France, on February 6, to work out the details of an agreement that would restore autonomy, protect the Kosovars from oppression with a NATO-led operation, disarm the KLA, and allow the Serb army to continue to patrol the border. Madeleine Albright and her British counterpart, Robin Cook, pursued this policy aggressively. After a week of negotiations coordinated by U.S. Ambassador Chris Hill and his counterparts from the European Union and Russia, Madeleine found that our position was opposed by both sides: the Serbs didn't want to agree to a NATO peacekeeping force, and the Kosovars didn't want to agree to accept autonomy unless they were also guaranteed a referendum on independence. And the KLA weren't happy about having to disarm, partly because they weren't sure they could rely on the NATO forces to protect them. Our team decided to write the agreement in a way that would delay the referendum but not deny it forever.

On February 23, the Kosovar Albanians, including Thaci, accepted the agreement in principle, returned home to sell it to their people, and in mid-March traveled to Paris to sign the finished document. The Serbs boycotted the ceremony, as forty thousand Serbian troops massed in and around Kosovo and Milosevic said again that he would never agree to foreign troops on Yugoslavian soil. I sent Dick Holbrooke back to see him one last time, but even Dick couldn't budge him.

On March 23, after Holbrooke left Belgrade, NATO Secretary-General Javier Solana, with my full support, directed General Wes Clark to begin air strikes. On the same day, by a bipartisan majority of 58–41, the Senate voted to support the action. Earlier in the month, the House had voted 219–191 to support sending U.S. troops to Kosovo if there was a peace agreement. Among the prominent Republicans voting for the proposal were the new Speaker, Dennis Hastert, and Henry Hyde. When Congressman Hyde said America should stand up against Milosevic and ethnic cleansing, I smiled and thought to myself that maybe Dr. Jekyll was in there somewhere after all.

While a majority of Congress and all our NATO allies favored the air strikes, Russia did not. Prime Minister Yevgeny Primakov was on his way to the United States to meet with Al Gore. When Al notified him that a NATO attack on Yugoslavia was imminent, Primakov ordered his plane to turn around and take him back to Moscow.

On the twenty-fourth, I spoke to the American people about what I was doing and why. I explained that Milosevic had stripped the Kosovars of their autonomy, denying them their constitutionally guaranteed rights to speak their own language, run their own schools, and govern themselves. I described the Serb atrocities: killing civilians, burning villages, and driving people from their homes, sixty thousand in the last five weeks, a quarter million in all. Finally, I put the current events in the context of the wars Milosevic had already waged against Bosnia and Croatia, and the destructive impact of his killing on the future of Europe.

The bombing campaign had three objectives: to show Milosevic we were serious about stopping another round of ethnic cleansing, to deter an even bloodier offensive against innocent civilians in Kosovo, and, if Milosevic didn't throw in the towel soon, to seriously damage the Serbs' military capacity.

That night the NATO air strikes began. They would last for eleven weeks, as Milosevic continued to kill Kosovar Albanians and drive almost one million people from their homes. The bombs would inflict great damage on the military and economic infrastructure of Serbia. Alas, on a few occasions they would miss their intended targets and take the lives of people we were trying to protect.

Some people argued that our position would have been more defensible if we had sent in ground troops. There were two problems with that argument. First, by the time the soldiers were in position, in adequate numbers and with proper support, the Serbs would have done an enormous amount of damage. Second, the civilian casualties of a ground campaign would probably have been greater than the toll from errant bombs. I didn't find the argument that I should pursue a course that would cost more American lives without enhancing the prospects of victory very persuasive. Our strategy would often be second-guessed, but never abandoned.

At the end of the month, as the stock market closed above 10,000 for the first time ever, up from 3,200 when I took office, I sat down for an interview with CBS-TV's Dan Rather. After an extended discussion of Kosovo, Dan asked me whether I expected to be the husband of a United States senator. By then, many New York officials had joined Charlie Rangel in asking Hillary to consider the race. I told Rather that I had no idea what she would do, but that if she ran and won, "she would be magnificent."

In April, the Kosovo conflict intensified as we extended the bombing to downtown Belgrade, hitting the Interior Ministry, Serbia's state television headquarters, and Milosevic's party headquarters and his home. We also dramatically increased our financial support and troop presence in neighboring Albania and Macedonia to help them deal with the large number of refugees flooding in. By the end of the month, when Milosevic still hadn't folded, opposition to our policy was coming from both directions. Tony Blair and some members of Congress thought it was time to send in ground troops, while the House of Representatives voted to deny the use of troops without prior approval of Congress.

I still believed the air campaign would work, and hoped we could avoid sending ground troops until their mission was to keep the peace. On April 14, I called Boris Yeltsin to request Russian troop participation in a post-conflict peacekeeping force, as in Bosnia. I thought a Russian presence would help protect the Serb minority and might give Milosevic a face-saving way out of his opposition to foreign troops.

A lot of other things happened in April. On the fifth, Libya finally handed over two suspects in the bombing of Pan Am 103 over Lockerbie, Scotland, in 1988. They would be tried before Scottish judges in The Hague. The White House had been deeply involved in the issue for years. I had pressed the Libyans to do it, and the White House had reached out to the families of victims, keeping them informed and approving the construction of a memorial to their loved ones in Arlington National Cemetery. It was the beginning of a thaw in U.S.–Libyan relations.

In the second week of the month, Chinese premier Zhu Rongji made his first trip to the White House in the hope of resolving the remaining obstacles to China's entry into the World Trade Organization. We had made substantial progress in closing the gaps between us, but problems remained, including our desire for greater access to China's auto market, and China's insistence on a five-year limit for our "surge" agreement, under which the United States could limit a sudden large increase in Chinese imports when it occurred for other than normal economic reasons. It was an important issue in America because of the surge we had experienced in imported steel from Russia, Japan, and elsewhere.

Charlene Barshefsky told me that the Chinese had moved a long way and we should close the deal while Zhu was in the United States to avoid weakening him at home. Madeleine Albright and Sandy Berger agreed with her. The rest of the economic team—Rubin, Summers, Sperling, and Daley—along with John Podesta and my legislative aide Larry Stein, disagreed. They thought that without more progress, Congress would reject the deal and kill China's entry into the WTO.

I met with Zhu in the Yellow Oval Room the night before the start of his official visit. I told him frankly that my advisors were split but that we would work all night if it was important to have the deal done while he was in the United States. Zhu said if the timing was bad we could wait.

Unfortunately the false story that we had a deal leaked, so that when it didn't happen, Zhu was hurt for the concessions he had made and I was criticized as having turned away a good agreement under pressure from the opponents of China's entry into the WTO. The story was reinforced by a spate of anti-China stories circulating in the media. The allegations that the Chinese government had steered funds into the 1996 campaign had not been resolved, and Wen Ho Lee, a Chinese-American employee of our national energy lab in Los Alamos, New Mexico, had been accused of stealing sensitive technology for China. All of my team wanted China in the WTO this year; now it was going to be harder to achieve.

On April 12, a jury rendered its verdict in Kenneth Starr's case against Susan McDougal, who had been charged with obstruction of justice and criminal contempt for her continued refusal to testify before the grand jury. She was acquitted on the obstruction of justice charge and, according to press reports, the jury deadlocked 7–5 for acquittal on the contempt charges. It was an amazing verdict. McDougal admitted that she had refused a court order to testify because she didn't trust Starr and his chief deputy, Hick Ewing. She testified that, now, in open court, she would be glad to answer any questions that the OIC had wanted to ask in the secret grand jury proceedings. She said that even though she had been offered immunity, she had refused to cooperate with the OIC because Starr and his staff had repeatedly tried to get her to lie to incriminate Hillary or me, and she believed that if she testified truthfully before the grand jury he would indict her for her refusal to lie. To close her defense, she called Julie Hiatt Steele, who testified that Starr had done exactly that to her, indicting her after she twice refused to lie for him in a grand jury proceeding.

The victory couldn't give Susan McDougal her lost years back, but her vindication was a stunning setback for Starr, and a sweet triumph for all the other people whose lives and savings he had destroyed.

On the twentieth, America suffered another horrible school shooting. At Columbine High School in Littleton, Colorado, two heavily armed students opened fire on their classmates, killing twelve students and injuring more than twenty others before turning their guns on themselves. It could have been even worse. One teacher, who later died from his wounds, led many students to safety. Medics and police officers saved more lives. A week later, with a bipartisan group of members of Congress and mayors, I announced some measures to make it harder for guns to fall into the wrong hands: applying the Brady law's prohibition on gun ownership to violent juveniles; closing the "gun show loophole" to require background checks on people who bought guns at such events rather than at gun stores; cracking down on illegal gun trafficking; and prohibiting juveniles from owning assault rifles. I also proposed funds to help schools develop successful violence prevention and conflict-resolution programs like the one I had just observed at T. C. Williams High School in Alexandria, Virginia.

Senate majority leader Trent Lott called my initiative a "typical knee-jerk reaction," and Tom DeLay accused me of exploiting Columbine for political gain. But the legislation's principal sponsor, Congresswoman Carolyn McCarthy of New York, wasn't interested in politics; her husband had been killed and her son badly wounded on a commuter train by a deranged man with a handgun he should never have been able to possess. The NRA and its supporters blamed our violent culture. I agreed that children were exposed to too much violence; that's why I was supporting Al and Tipper Gore's drive to get V-chips into new TVs so that parents could limit children's exposure to excessive violence. But the violence in our culture only strengthened the argument for doing more to keep guns away from children, criminals, and mentally unstable people.

At the end of the month, Hillary and I hosted the largest gathering of heads of state ever to meet in Washington, as the leaders of NATO and the states in its Partnership for Peace gathered to celebrate the fiftieth anniversary of NATO, and to reaffirm our determination to prevail in Kosovo. Afterward, Al From of the DLC and Sidney Blumenthal put together another of our "Third Way" conferences to highlight the values, ideas, and strategies Tony Blair and I shared with Gerhard Schroeder of Germany, Wim Kok of the Netherlands, and the new Italian prime minister, Massimo D'Alema. By this time, I was focused on building a global consensus on economic, social, and security policies that I thought would serve America and the world well when my term was over by strengthening the forces of positive interdependence and weakening those of disintegration and destruction. The Third Way movement and the broadening of NATO's alliance and its mission had moved us a fair distance in the right direction, but as with so many of the best-laid plans, they would later be overtaken and redirected by events, principally the growing hostility to globalization and the rising tide of terror.

In early May, shortly after Jesse Jackson persuaded Milosevic to release three U.S. servicemen the Serbs had captured along their border with Macedonia, we lost two American soldiers when their Apache helicopter crashed in a training exercise; they would be the only U.S. casualties in the conflict. Boris Yeltsin sent Victor Chernomyrdin to see me to discuss Russia's interest in ending the war and its apparent willingness to participate in the peacekeeping force afterward. Meanwhile, we kept the pressure up, as I authorized 176 more aircraft for Wes Clark.

On May 7, we suffered the worst political setback of the conflict when NATO bombed the Chinese embassy in Belgrade, killing three Chinese citizens. I soon learned that the bombs had hit their intended target, which had been erroneously identified on the basis of old CIA maps as a Serbian government building used for military purposes. It was the kind of mistake we had worked hard to avoid. The military was mostly using aerial photography for targeting. I had begun meeting with Bill Cohen, Hugh Shelton, and Sandy Berger several times a week to go over the high-profile targets in an attempt to maximize damage to Milosevic's aggression while minimizing civilian casualties. I was dumbfounded and deeply upset by the mistake and immediately called Jiang Zemin to apologize. He wouldn't take the call, so I publicly and repeatedly apologized.

Over the next three days, protests escalated all over China. They were especially intense around the American embassy in Beijing, where Ambassador Sasser found himself besieged. The Chinese said they believed the attack was deliberate and declined to accept my apologies. When I finally talked with President Jiang on the fourteenth, I apologized again and told him I was sure he didn't believe I would knowingly attack his embassy. Jiang replied that he knew I wouldn't do that, but said he did believe that there were people in the Pentagon or the CIA who didn't favor my outreach to China and could have rigged the maps intentionally to cause a rift between us. Jiang had a hard time believing that a nation as technologically advanced as we were could make such a mistake.

I had a hard time believing it, too, but that's what happened. Eventually we got beyond it, but it was tough going for a while. I had just named Admiral Joe Prueher, who was retiring as commander in chief of our forces in the Pacific, to be the new U.S. ambassador to China. He was very respected by the Chinese military, and I believed he would be able to help repair the relationship.

By late May, NATO had approved a 48,000-troop peacekeeping force to go into Kosovo after the conflict was concluded, and we had begun quiet discussions about the possibility of sending in ground troops earlier if it became clear that the air campaign wasn't going to prevail before people were trapped in the mountains by winter. Sandy Berger was preparing a memo for me on options, and I was ready to send troops in if necessary, but I still believed the air war would succeed. On the twenty-seventh, Milosevic was indicted by the war crimes prosecutor in The Hague.

There was a great deal of activity in the rest of the world in May. In mid-month, Boris Yeltsin survived his own impeachment vote in the Duma. On the seventeenth, Prime Minister Netanyahu was defeated for reelection by the Labor Party leader, retired general Ehud Barak, the most decorated soldier in Israeli history. Barak was a brilliant Renaissance man: he had done graduate work in economic engineering systems at Stanford, was a concert-level classical pianist, and repaired clocks as a hobby. He had been in politics only a few years, and his close-cropped hair, intense stare, and blunt, staccato speaking style were more reflective of his military past than of the more murky political waters he now had to navigate. His victory was a clear signal that Israelis saw in him what they had seen in his role model, Yitzhak Rabin: the possibility of peace with security. Equally important, Barak's large victory margin had given him the chance to have a governing coalition in the Knesset that would support the hard steps to peace, something Prime Minister Netanyahu had never had.

The next day Jordan's King Abdullah came to see me, full of hope for peace and determination to be a worthy successor to his father. He clearly understood the challenges facing his nation and the peace process. I was also struck by his understanding of economics and the contribution that more growth could make to peace and reconciliation. After the meeting I was convinced that the king and his equally impressive wife, Queen Rania, would be positive forces in the region for a long time to come.

On May 26, Bill Perry delivered a letter from me to Kim Jong Il, North Korea's leader, proposing a road map to the future in which America would provide a broad range of assistance to him if, but only if, he gave up his attempts to develop nuclear weapons and long-range missiles. In 1998, North Korea had taken the constructive step of ending its tests of such missiles, and I thought Perry's mission had a fair chance to succeed.

Two days later, Hillary and I were at a DLC retreat at White Oak Plantation in northern Florida, which has the largest wild game preserve in the United States. I got up at four in the morning to watch the inaugural ceremonies for Nigeria's new president, former general Olusegun Obasanjo, on TV. Ever since gaining independence, Nigeria had been riddled by corruption, regional and religious strife, and deteriorating social conditions. Despite its large oil production, the country suffered periodic power outages and fuel shortages. Obasanjo had taken power briefly in a military coup in the 1970s, then had kept his promise to step aside as soon as new elections could be held. Later, he had been imprisoned for his political views and, while incarcerated, had become a devout Christian and had written books about his faith. It was hard to imagine a bright future for sub-Saharan Africa without a more successful Nigeria, by far its most populous nation. After listening to his compelling inaugural address, I hoped Obasanjo would be able to succeed where others had failed.

On the home front, I started the month with an important clean-air announcement. We had already reduced toxic air pollution from chemical plants by 90 percent, and had set tough standards to reduce smog and soot that would prevent millions of cases of childhood asthma. On May 1, I said that after extensive consultation with industry, environmental, and consumer groups, EPA administrator Carol Browner would promulgate a rule to require all passenger vehicles, including gas-guzzling SUVs, to meet the same pol-

lution standards, and that we would cut the sulfur content
of gasoline by 90 percent over five years.

I announced a new crime initiative, releasing the funds
to complete our efforts to put 100,000 police on the streets
(more than half of them were already in service); expanding
the COPS program to hire 50,000 more police officers in the
highest-crime areas; and making it a federal crime to possess
biological agents that could be turned into terrorist
weapons without a legitimate, peaceful purpose for having
them.

The twelfth was a day I had hoped would never come:
Bob Rubin was returning to private life. I believed he had
been the best and most important Treasury secretary since
Alexander Hamilton in the early days of our Republic. Bob
had also been the first head of the National Economic Council. In both positions he had played a decisive role in our
efforts to restore economic growth and spread its benefits to
more Americans, to prevent and contain financial crisis
abroad, and to modernize the international financial system
to deal with a global economy in which more than one trillion dollars crossed national borders every day. He had also
been a rock of stability during the impeachment ordeal, not
only speaking up at the meeting when I apologized to my
cabinet, but also constantly reminding our people that they
should be proud of what they were doing, and cautioning
them not to be too judgmental. One of our younger people
said that Bob had told him that if he lived long enough, he
would do something he'd be ashamed of, too.

When Bob came into the administration he was probably the wealthiest person on our team. After he supported
the 1993 economic plan, with its tax increase for the highest-
income Americans, I used to joke that "Bob Rubin came to
Washington to help me save the middle class, and when he
leaves, he'll be one of them." Now that Bob was moving
back into private life, I didn't think I'd have to worry about
that anymore.

I named Bob's able deputy secretary, Larry Summers, to
succeed him. Larry had been in the thick of all the major economic questions of the last six years, and he was ready. I also

named Stu Eizenstat, the undersecretary of state for economic affairs, to be deputy Treasury secretary. Stu had handled a lot of important assignments well, none more important than the so-called Nazi Gold matter. Edgar Bronfman Sr. had sparked our interest in it by contacting Hillary, who got things moving with an initial meeting. Eizenstat then spearheaded our attempt to secure justice and compensation for Holocaust survivors and their families whose assets had been looted as they were being packed off to concentration camps.

Soon afterward, Hillary and I flew to Colorado to meet with students and families from Columbine High School. A few days earlier the Senate had adopted my proposals to ban the import of large ammunition clips that were being used to evade the assault weapons ban, and to ban the possession of assault weapons by juveniles. And in the face of intense lobbying by the NRA, Al Gore had broken a 50–50 tie to pass the proposal to close the gun show loophole in the Brady law's requirement of background checks.

Although the community was still grieving, the students at Columbine were coming back, and they and their parents seemed determined to do something to reduce the chances of further Columbines. They knew that though there had been several school shootings before theirs, it was Columbine that had finally pierced the soul of America. I told them that they could help America build a safer future because of what they had endured. Although Congress would not close the gun show loophole, in the 2000 election, because of Columbine, the voters in conservative Colorado would pass a measure to do so in their state by an overwhelming margin.

Whitewater World was still alive and well in May, as Kenneth Starr, despite his defeat in the Susan McDougal trial, pursued his case against Julie Hiatt Steele. The case ended in a hung jury; in conservative northern Virginia, it was another setback for the independent counsel and his tactics. After all Starr's efforts to get into the Jones case, the only person who was indicted as a result was Steele, another innocent bystander who refused to lie. Starr's office had now conducted four trials and lost three.

In June, the punishing bombing raids on the Serbs

finally broke Milosevic's will to resist. On the second, Victor Chernomyrdin and Finnish president Martti Ahtisaari personally handed NATO's demands to Milosevic. The next day Milosevic and the Serbian parliament agreed to them. Predictably, the next few days were full of tension and disputes over the details, but on the ninth NATO and Serbian military officials agreed to a prompt withdrawal of Serb forces from Kosovo and the deployment of an international security force with a unified NATO chain of command. The next day Javier Solana instructed General Clark to suspend NATO's air operations, the UN Security Council passed a resolution welcoming the end of the war, and I announced to the American people that, after seventy-nine days, the bombing campaign was over, the Serb forces were withdrawing, and the one million men, women, and children driven from their land would be able to go home. In an Oval Office address to the nation, I thanked our armed forces for their superb performance and the American people for their stand against ethnic cleansing and their generous support of the refugees, many of whom had come to America.

Allied Commander Wes Clark had managed the campaign with skill and determination, and he and Javier Solana had done yeoman's work in holding the alliance together and in never wavering in our steadfast commitment to victory on the bad days as well as the good ones. So had my entire national security team. Even though when the bombing wasn't over in a week we were constantly second-guessed, Bill Cohen and Hugh Shelton had remained convinced that the air campaign would work if we could hold the coalition together for two months. Al Gore, Madeleine Albright, and Sandy Berger had all remained cool under fire in the nail-biting, roller-coaster weeks we had just been through together. Al had played a critical role in keeping our relationship with Russia intact by staying in contact with Victor Chernomyrdin and making sure that we and the Russians had a common position when Chernomyrdin and Ahtisaari went to Serbia to try to persuade Milosevic to give up his futile resistance.

On the eleventh, I took a congressional delegation to

Whiteman Air Force Base in Missouri to say a special word of thanks to the crews and support personnel on B-2 stealth bombers, which flew all the way from Missouri to Serbia and back, nonstop, to perform the nighttime bombing operations for which the B-2 was especially well suited. In all, 30,000 sorties were flown in the Kosovo campaign. Only two planes were lost, and their crews were recovered safely.

After the raids succeeded, John Keegan, perhaps the foremost living historian of warfare, wrote a fascinating article in the British press about the Kosovo campaign. He admitted frankly that he had not believed the bombing would work and that he had been wrong. He said the reason such campaigns had failed in the past is that most bombs had missed their targets. The weaponry used in Kosovo was more precise than that used in the first Gulf War; and though some bombs went astray in Kosovo and Serbia, far fewer civilians were killed than in Iraq. I'm also still convinced that fewer civilians died than would have perished if we had put in ground troops, a bridge I would nevertheless have crossed rather than let Milosevic prevail. The success of the air campaign in Kosovo marked a new chapter in military history.

There was one more tense moment before things settled down. Two days after hostilities officially ended, fifty vehicles carrying about two hundred Russian troops rushed into Kosovo from Bosnia and occupied the Pristina airport without advance agreement from NATO, four hours before the NATO troops authorized by the UN arrived. The Russians asserted their intention to keep control of the airport.

Wes Clark was livid. I didn't blame him, but I knew we weren't on the verge of World War III. Yeltsin was getting a lot of criticism at home for cooperating with us from ultra-nationalists whose sympathies lay with the Serbs. I thought he was just throwing them a temporary bone. Soon the British commander, Lieutenant General Michael Jackson, resolved the situation without incident, and on June 18, Secretary Cohen and the Russian defense minister reached an agreement under which Russian troops would join the UN-sanctioned NATO forces in Kosovo. On June 20, the

Yugoslav military completed its withdrawal, and just two weeks later the UN High Commissioner for Refugees estimated that more than 765,000 refugees had already returned to Kosovo.

As we had learned from our experience in Bosnia, even after the conflict there would still be a great deal of work ahead in Kosovo: getting the refugees home safely; clearing the minefields; rebuilding homes; providing food, medicine, and shelter to the homeless; demilitarizing the Kosovo Liberation Army; creating a secure environment for both Kosovar Albanians and the minority Serb population; organizing a civilian administration; and restoring a functioning economy. It was a big job, most of which would be performed by our European allies, even as America had borne the lion's share of responsibility for the air war.

Despite the challenges ahead, I felt an enormous sense of relief and satisfaction. Slobodan Milosevic's bloody ten-year campaign to exploit ethnic and religious differences in order to impose his will on the former Yugoslavia was on its last legs. The burning of villages and killing of innocents was history. I knew it was just a matter of time before Milosevic was history, too.

On the day we reached the agreement with Russia, Hillary and I were in Cologne, Germany, for the annual G-8 summit. It turned out to be one of the most important such meetings of my entire eight years. In addition to celebrating the successful end to the Kosovo conflict, we endorsed our finance ministers' recommendations to modernize the international financial institutions and our national policies to meet the challenges of the global economy, and we announced a proposal, which I strongly supported, for a massive millennium debt-relief initiative for poor countries if they agreed to put all the savings into education, health care, or economic development. The initiative was consistent with a chorus of calls for debt relief from all over the world, led by Pope John Paul II and my friend Bono.

After the summit we flew on to Slovenia to thank the Slovenians for supporting NATO in Kosovo and helping the refugees, then to Macedonia, where President Kiro Gligorov, despite his country's own economic hardships and ethnic tensions, had taken in 300,000 refugees. At the camp in Skopje, Hillary, Chelsea, and I got to visit with some of them and hear the horrible stories of what they had endured. We also met members of the international security force who were stationed there. It was my first chance to thank Wes Clark in person.

Politics began to heat up in June. Al Gore announced for President on the sixteenth. His likely opponent was Governor George W. Bush, the preferred candidate of both the Republican Party's right wing and its establishment. Bush had already raised more money than Al and his primary opponent, former New Jersey senator Bill Bradley, combined. Hillary was moving closer to getting into the Senate race in New York. By the time we left the White House she would have helped me in my political career for more than twenty-six years. I was more than happy to support her for the next twenty-six.

As we entered the political season, I was far more concerned about maintaining the momentum for action in Congress and in my own government. Traditionally, when presidential politics begin to heat up and the President isn't part of it, inertia sets in. Some of the Democrats thought they would be better off if little new legislation was passed; then they could run against a Republican "do nothing" Congress. Many Republicans just didn't want to give me any more victories. I was surprised at how bitter some of them still seemed to be four months after the impeachment battle, especially since I hadn't been hammering them in public or in private.

I tried to wake up every morning without bitterness and to keep working in a spirit of reconciliation. The Republicans seemed to have reverted to the theme they had trumpeted since 1992: I was a person without character who could not be trusted. During the Kosovo conflict some Republicans almost seemed to be rooting for us to fail. One Republican senator justified his colleagues' tepid support for what our troops were doing by saying I had lost their trust; they were blaming me for their own failure to oppose ethnic cleansing.

It seemed to me that the Republicans were trying to put me in a lose-lose situation. If I went around wearing a hair shirt, they would say I was too damaged to lead. If I was happy, they would say I was gloating and acting as if I'd gotten away with something. Six days after my acquittal in the Senate, I had gone to New Hampshire to celebrate the seventh anniversary of my New Hampshire primary. Some of my congressional critics said I shouldn't have been happy, but I was happy—and for good reasons: all my old friends came out to see me; I met a young man who said he'd cast his first vote for me, and I had done exactly what I said I would do; and I met a woman who said I had inspired her to get off welfare and go back to school to become a nurse. By 1999, she was a member of the New Hampshire Board of Nursing. Those were the people I got into politics for.

At first I couldn't for the life of me figure out how the Republicans and some commentators could say I'd gotten away with anything. The public humiliation, the pain to my family, the huge debts from legal bills and settling the Jones suit after I'd won it, the years of press and legal abuse Hillary had endured, and the helplessness I felt as countless innocent people in Washington and Arkansas were persecuted and ruined financially—these things took a terrible toll on me. I had apologized and tried to demonstrate my sincerity in the way I'd treated and worked with the Republicans. But none of it was enough. It would never be enough, for one simple reason: I had survived and continued to serve and fight for what I believed. First, last, and always, my struggle with the New Right Republicans was about power. I thought power came from the people and they should give it and take it away. They thought the people had made a mistake in electing me twice, and they were determined to use my personal mistakes to justify their continuing assault.

I was sure that my more positive strategy was the right thing for me as a person and for my ability to do my job. I wasn't as sure it was good politics. The more the Republicans pounded away at me, the more the memories of what Ken Starr had done or how they had behaved during impeachment faded. The press is naturally focused on today's story, not yesterday's, and conflict makes news. That tends to reward the aggressor, whether the underlying attack is fair or not. Soon, instead of asking me whether I could forgive and forget, the press was asking those earnest-sounding questions again about whether I had the moral authority to lead. The Republicans were barking away at Hillary, too, now that, instead of being a sympathetic figure standing by her flawed man, she was a strong woman finding her own way in politics. Yet, on balance, I still felt good about where things stood: the country was moving in the right direction, my job rating was high, and we still had plenty to do.

Although I would always regret what I had done wrong, I will go to my grave being proud of what I had fought for in the impeachment battle, my last great showdown with the forces I had opposed all of my life—those who had defended the old order of racial discrimination and segregation in the South and played on the insecurities and fears of the white working class in which I grew up; who had opposed the women's movement, the environmental movement, the gay-rights movement, and other efforts to expand our national community as assaults on the natural order; who believed government should be run for the benefit of powerful entrenched interests and favored tax cuts for the wealthy over health care and better education for children.

Ever since I was a boy I had been on the other side. At first, the forces of reaction, division, and the status quo were represented by anti–civil rights Democrats. When the national party under Truman, Kennedy, and Johnson began to embrace the cause of civil rights, the southern conservatives migrated to the Republican Party, which, beginning in the 1970s, formed an alliance with the rising religious right-wing movement.

When the New Right Republicans had taken power in Congress in 1995, I had blocked their most extreme designs and had made further progress in economic, social, and environmental justice the price of our cooperation. I understood why the people who equated political, economic, and social conservatism with God's will hated me. I wanted an America of shared benefits, shared responsibilities, and equal participation in a democratic community. The New Right Republicans wanted an America in which wealth and power were concentrated in the hands of the "right" people, who maintained majority support by demonizing a rolling succession of minorities whose demands for inclusion threatened their hold on power. They also hated me because I was an apostate, a white southern Protestant who could appeal to the very people they had always taken for granted.

Now that my private sins had been publicly aired, they would be able to throw stones until the day I died. I was letting go of my anger about it, but I was glad that, by accident of history, I had had the good fortune to stand against this latest incarnation of the forces of reaction and division, and in favor of a more perfect union.

TWENTY-FOUR

IN EARLY JUNE, I gave a radio address to increase awareness of mental-health issues with Tipper Gore, whom I had named my official advisor for mental health and who recently had courageously revealed her own treatment for depression. Two days later, Hillary and I joined Al and Tipper for a White House Conference on Mental Health, in which we dealt with the staggering personal, economic, and social costs of untreated mental illness.

For the rest of the month, I highlighted our gun safety proposals; our efforts to develop an AIDS vaccine; my efforts to include environmental and labor rights issues in trade talks; the report of the President's Foreign Intelligence Advisory Board on security at the Energy Department's weapons labs; a plan to restore health and disability benefits to legal immigrants; a proposal to allow Medicaid to cover disabled Americans who couldn't meet the costs of treatments if they lost their health-care coverage because they entered the workforce; legislation to help older children who leave foster care to make the adjustment to independent living; and a plan to modernize Medicare and extend the life of its trust fund.

I had been looking forward to July. I thought it would be a predictable, positive month. I would announce that we were taking the bald eagle off the endangered species list, and Al Gore would outline our plan to complete the restoration of the Florida Everglades. Hillary would begin her "listening tour" at Senator Moynihan's farm at Pindars Corners in upstate New York, and I would take a tour of poor communities across the country to promote my "New Markets" initiative to attract more investment to areas that were still not part of our recovery. All those things happened, but so did events that were unplanned, troublesome, or tragic.

Prime Minister Nawaz Sharif of Pakistan called and

asked if he could come to Washington on July 4 to discuss the dangerous standoff with India that had begun several weeks earlier when Pakistani forces under the command of General Pervez Musharraf crossed the Line of Control, which had been the recognized and generally observed boundary between India and Pakistan in Kashmir since 1972. Sharif was concerned that the situation Pakistan had created was getting out of control, and he hoped to use my good offices not only to resolve the crisis but also to help mediate with the Indians on the question of Kashmir itself. Even before the crisis, Sharif had asked me to help in Kashmir, saying it was as worthy of my attention as the Middle East and Northern Ireland. I had explained to him then that the United States was involved in those peace processes because both sides wanted us. In this case, India had strongly refused the involvement of any outside party.

Sharif's moves were perplexing because that February, Indian prime minister Atal Behari Vajpayee had traveled to Lahore, Pakistan, to promote bilateral talks aimed at resolving the Kashmir problem and other differences. By crossing the Line of Control, Pakistan had wrecked the talks. I didn't know whether Sharif had authorized the invasion to create a crisis he hoped would get America involved or had simply allowed it in order to avoid a confrontation with Pakistan's powerful military. Regardless, he had gotten himself into a bind with no easy way out.

I told Sharif that he was always welcome in Washington, even on July 4, but if he wanted me to spend America's Independence Day with him, he had to come to the United States knowing two things: first, he had to agree to withdraw his troops back across the Line of Control; and second, I would not agree to intervene in the Kashmir dispute, especially under circumstances that appeared to reward Pakistan's wrongful incursion.

Sharif said he wanted to come anyway. On July 4, we met at Blair House. It was a hot day, but the Pakistani delegation was used to the heat and, in their traditional white pants and long tunics, seemed more comfortable than my team. Once more, Sharif urged me to intervene in Kashmir, and again I explained that without India's consent it would be counter-productive, but that I would urge Vajpayee to resume the bilateral dialogue if the Pakistani troops withdrew. He agreed, and we released a joint statement saying that steps would be taken to restore the Line of Control and that I would support and encourage the resumption and intensification of bilateral talks once the violence had stopped.

After the meeting, I thought perhaps Sharif had come in order to use pressure from the United States to provide himself cover for ordering his military to defuse the conflict. I knew he was on shaky ground at home, and I hoped he would survive, because I needed his cooperation in the fight against terrorism.

Pakistan was one of the few countries with close ties to the Taliban in Afghanistan. Before our July 4 meeting, I had asked Sharif on three occasions for help in apprehending Osama bin Laden: in our meeting the previous December, at King Hussein's funeral, and in a June phone conversation and follow-up letter. We had intelligence reports that al Qaeda was planning attacks on U.S. officials and facilities in various places around the world and perhaps in the United States as well. We had been successful in breaking up cells and arresting a number of al Qaeda members, but unless bin Laden and his top lieutenants were apprehended or killed, the threat would remain. On July 4, I told Sharif that unless he did more to help, I would have to announce that Pakistan was in effect supporting terrorism in Afghanistan.

On the day I met with Sharif, I also signed an executive order placing economic sanctions on the Taliban, freezing its assets and prohibiting commercial exchanges. Around this time, with Sharif's support, U.S. officials also began to train sixty Pakistani troops as commandos to go into Afghanistan to get bin Laden. I was skeptical about the project; even if Sharif wanted to help, the Pakistani military was full of Taliban and al Qaeda sympathizers. But I thought we had nothing to lose by exploring every option.

The day after the Sharif meeting, I started the New Markets tour, beginning in Hazard, Kentucky, with a large delegation including several business executives, congressmen, cabinet members, the Reverend Jesse Jackson, and Al From.

I was glad that Jackson was making the tour and that we were starting in Appalachia, America's poorest all-white area. Jesse had long worked to bring more private-sector investment to poor areas, and we had grown even closer during the impeachment year, when he had strongly supported my whole family and made a special effort to reach out to Chelsea. From Kentucky we traveled to Clarksdale, Mississippi; East St. Louis, Illinois; the Pine Ridge Reservation in South Dakota; a Hispanic neighborhood in Phoenix, Arizona; and the Watts neighborhood in Los Angeles.

Even though America had had two years of unemployment rates just above 4 percent, all the communities I visited and many like them suffered from unemployment that was far higher than that and per capita incomes well below the national average. The unemployment rate at Pine Ridge was over 70 percent. Yet everywhere we went, I met intelligent, hardworking people who were capable of contributing much more to the economy.

I thought doing more to get investment into these areas was both the right thing to do and economically smart. We were already enjoying the largest economic expansion in history, with a rapidly growing rate of productivity. It seemed to me there were three ways to continue to increase growth without inflation: sell more products and services overseas; increase the workforce participation of particular populations, like welfare recipients; and bring growth to new markets in America where investment was too low and unemployment too high.

We were doing well in the first two areas, with more than 250 trade agreements and welfare reform. And we had made a good start on the third, with more than 130 empowerment zones and enterprise communities, community development banks, and aggressive enforcement of the Community Reinvestment Act. But too many communities had been left behind. I was putting together a legislative proposal to increase available capital to inner cities, rural towns, and Indian reservations by $15 billion. Since it would promote free enterprise, I hoped to get strong bipartisan support and was encouraged by the fact that Speaker Hastert seemed especially interested in the effort.

On July 15, Ehud and Nava Barak accepted an invitation to spend the night at Camp David with Hillary and me. We had an enjoyable dinner, and Ehud and I stayed up talking until nearly three in the morning. It was clear that he wanted to complete the peace process and believed that his big election victory gave him a mandate to do so. He was interested in doing something substantive at Camp David, especially after I showed him the building where most of the negotiations President Carter mediated between Anwar Sadat and Menachem Begin had taken place in 1978.

At the same time I was also occupied with trying to get the Northern Ireland peace process back on track. There was a deadlock caused by a disagreement between Sinn Fein and the Unionists over whether the IRA's decommissioning could occur after the new government was formed or had to come before it. I explained the situation to Barak, who was intrigued by the differences and similarities between the Irish problems and his own.

The next day John Kennedy Jr., his wife, Carolyn, and her sister Lauren were killed when the small plane John was flying crashed off the coast of Massachusetts. I had liked John ever since I had met him in the 1980s when he was a law student working as an intern in Mickey Kantor's firm in Los Angeles. He had come to one of my first New York campaign events in 1991, and not long before they perished I had enjoyed showing Carolyn and John the residence floors of the White House. Ted Kennedy gave another magnificent eulogy for a fallen family member: "Like his father, he had every gift."

On July 23, King Hassan II of Morocco died at the age of seventy. He had been an ally of the United States, and a supporter of the Middle East peace process, and I had enjoyed a good personal relationship with him. Again on short notice, President Bush agreed to fly to Morocco for the funeral with Hillary, Chelsea, and me. I walked behind the king's horse-drawn casket with President Mubarak,

Yasser Arafat, Jacques Chirac, and other leaders on a three-mile route through downtown Rabat. Well over one million people lined the streets, ululating and shouting in grief and respect to their fallen monarch. The deafening din of the huge, emotional throng made the march one of the most incredible events I had ever participated in. I think Hassan would have approved.

After a brief meeting with Hassan's son and heir, King Mohammed VI, I flew home for a couple of days of work, then left again for Sarajevo, where I joined several European leaders as we committed to a stability pact for the Balkans, an agreement to support the region's short-term needs and long-term growth by providing greater access to our markets for Balkan products; working for the inclusion of southeastern European countries into the WTO; and providing investment funds and credit guarantees to encourage private investment.

The rest of the summer flew by as I continued to disagree with the Republicans over the budget and the size and distribution of their proposed tax cut; Dick Holbrooke was finally confirmed as UN ambassador after an unconscionable delay of fourteen months; and Hillary moved closer to declaring her Senate candidacy.

In August, we took two trips to New York to look for a home. On the twenty-eighth, we visited a late-nineteenth-century farmhouse with a large addition from 1989 in Chappaqua, about forty miles from Manhattan. The old part of the house was charming, the new part spacious and full of light. The instant I walked upstairs into the master bedroom I told Hillary we had to buy the house. It was part of the 1989 addition; it had extra-high ceilings with a row of glass doors facing the backyard, and had two huge windows on the other walls. When Hillary asked me why I was so sure, I replied, "Because you're about to start a hard campaign. There'll be some bad days. This beautiful room is bathed in light. You'll wake up every morning in a good humor."

Later in August, I traveled to Atlanta to give the Medal of

Freedom to President and Mrs. Carter for the extraordinary work they had done as private citizens since leaving the White House. A couple of days later, in a White House ceremony, I gave the award to several other distinguished Americans, including President Ford and Lloyd Bentsen. The other recipients were civil rights, labor, democracy, and environmental activists. All were less famous than Ford and Bentsen, but each had made unique and enduring contributions to America.

I did a little campaigning, going to Arkansas with Al Gore for meetings with local farmers and black leaders from across the South and a large fund-raiser full of people from my old campaigns. I also spoke and played saxophone at an event for Hillary on Martha's Vineyard, and appeared with her at events in New York, including a stop at the state fair in Syracuse, where I was right at home with the farmers. I enjoyed campaigning for both Hillary and Al, and I was beginning to look forward to a time when, after a lifetime of being helped by others, I could end my life in politics the way I'd started it, campaigning for other people I believed in.

In early September, Henry Cisneros finally resolved his case with independent counsel David Barrett, who had indicted him, unbelieveably, on eighteen felony counts for understating personal expenses to the FBI during his 1993 interview. On the day before his trial began, Barrett, who knew he had an unwinnable case, offered Cisneros a deal: a guilty plea to one misdemeanor, a $10,000 fine, and no jail time. Henry took it to avoid the crushing legal expense of a long trial. Barrett had spent more than $9 million of the taxpayers' money to torment a good man for four years. Just a few weeks earlier, the independent counsel law had expired.

Most of September was devoted to foreign policy. Early in the month Madeleine Albright and Dennis Ross were in Gaza to support Ehud Barak and Yasser Arafat as they agreed on the next steps to implement the Wye River accord, approving a port for the Palestinians, a road connecting the West Bank and Gaza, the handover of 11 percent of the West Bank, and the release of 350 prisoners. Albright and

Ross then went to Damascus to urge President Assad to respond to Barak's desire for peace talks with him soon.

On the ninth, I made my first trip to New Zealand for the APEC summit. Chelsea went with me, while Hillary stayed home to campaign. The big news at the summit involved Indonesia and the support its military had given to the violent suppression of the pro-independence movement in East Timor, a long-troubled Roman Catholic enclave in the world's most populous Muslim country. Most of the APEC leaders favored an international peacekeeping mission for East Timor, and Australian prime minister John Howard was willing to take the lead. At first the Indonesians were opposed to it, but soon they would be forced to relent. An international coalition was formed to send troops to East Timor under the leadership of Australia, and I pledged to Prime Minister Howard that I would send a couple of hundred American troops to provide the logistical support our allies needed.

I also met with President Jiang to discuss WTO issues, held joint discussions with Kim Dae Jung and Keizo Obuchi to reaffirm our common position on North Korea, and had my first meeting with Boris Yeltsin's new prime minister and chosen successor, Vladimir Putin. Putin presented a stark contrast to Yeltsin. Yeltsin was large and stocky; Putin was compact and extremely fit from years of martial arts practice. Yeltsin was voluble; the former KGB agent was measured and precise. I came away from the meeting believing Yeltsin had picked a successor who had the skills and capacity for hard work necessary to manage Russia's turbulent political and economic life better than Yeltsin now could, given his health problems; Putin also had the toughness to defend Russia's interests and protect Yeltsin's legacy.

Before we left New Zealand, Chelsea and I and my staff took some time to enjoy the beautiful country. Prime Minister Jenny Shipley and her husband, Burton, hosted us in Queenstown, where I played golf with Burton, Chelsea explored caves with the Shipley kids, and several of my staff went bungee jumping off a high bridge. Gene Sperling tried to goad me into trying it, but I told him I'd had about all the free falls I could stand.

Our last stop was the International Antarctic Center in Christchurch, America's launching station for our operations in Antarctica. The center contained a large training module in which the frigid conditions of Antarctica were replicated. I went there to highlight the problem of global warming. Antarctica is a great cooling tower for our planet, with ice more than two miles thick. A huge chunk of Antarctic ice, about the size of Rhode Island, had recently broken free as a result of thawing. I released previously classified satellite photos of the continent to aid in studying the changes that were occurring. The biggest thrill of the event for Chelsea and me was the presence of Sir Edmund Hillary, who had explored the South Pole in the 1950s, was the first man to reach the top of Mount Everest, and was a reminder of another Hillary whom Chelsea and I so loved and who was working on her campaign at home.

Soon after I returned to America, I went to New York to open the last UN General Assembly of the twentieth century, urging the delegates to adopt three resolutions: to do more to fight poverty and put a human face on the global economy; to increase our efforts to prevent or quickly stop the killing of innocents in ethnic, religious, racial, or tribal conflicts; and to intensify our efforts to prevent the use of nuclear, chemical, or biological weapons by irresponsible nations or terrorist groups.

At the end of the month I got back to domestic affairs, vetoing the latest Republican tax cut because it was "too big, too bloated," and put too great a burden on America's economy. Under the budget rules, the bill would have forced large cuts in education, health care, and environmental protection. It would have prevented us from extending the life of the Social Security and Medicare trust funds, and from adding a much-needed prescription drug benefit to Medicare.

We were going to have a surplus that year of about $100 billion, but the proposed GOP tax cut would cost nearly $1 trillion over a decade. Republicans' justification for it was based on projected surpluses. On this issue I was far more conservative than they were. If the projections were wrong, the deficits would return, and, with them, higher interest rates and slower growth. Over the previous five years, Congressional Budget Office estimates had been off by an average of 13 percent a year, though our administration's had been closer to the mark. It was an irresponsible risk. I asked the Republicans to work with the White House and the Democrats in the same spirit that had produced the bipartisan welfare reform bill in 1996 and the Balanced Budget Act in 1997.

On September 24, Hillary and I hosted an event in the Old Executive Office Building to celebrate the success of bipartisan efforts to increase the adoption of children out of the foster-care system. They had increased almost 30 percent in the two years since our legislation had passed. I paid tribute to Hillary, who had been working on the issue for more than twenty years, and to perhaps the most ardent supporter of the reforms in the House, Tom DeLay, himself an adoptive parent.

I would have liked a few more moments like that, but with this one exception, DeLay didn't believe in consorting with the enemy.

Partisanship returned in early October, when the Senate rejected, on a party-line vote, my nomination of Judge Ronnie White to a federal district judgeship. White was the first African-American man to serve on the Missouri Supreme Court and was a highly regarded judge. He was defeated after Missouri's conservative senator John Ashcroft, who was in a tough fight for reelection against Governor Mel Carnahan, grossly distorted White's record on the death penalty. White had voted to uphold 70 percent of the death penalty cases that had come before him. On more than half of those he had voted to reverse, he was part of a unanimous state supreme court ruling. Ashcroft got his Republican colleagues to go along with the smear because he thought it would help him and hurt White's supporter Governor Carnahan with pro–death penalty voters in Missouri.

Ashcroft wasn't alone in completely politicizing the confirmation process. By this time, Senator Jesse Helms had refused for years to allow the Senate to vote on a black judge for the Fourth Circuit Court of Appeals, even though there had never been an African-American on the court. And the Republicans wondered why African-Americans wouldn't vote for them.

Our partisan differences extended even to the nuclear test ban treaty, which had been supported by every Republican and Democratic President since Eisenhower. The Joint Chiefs were for it, and our nuclear experts said tests weren't necessary to check the reliability of our weapons. But we didn't have the votes of two-thirds of the senators necessary to ratify the treaty, and Trent Lott tried to get me to promise not to raise it for the rest of my term. I couldn't figure out whether the Senate Republicans had really moved that far to the right of their own party's traditional position or just didn't want to give me another victory. Regardless, their refusal to ratify the test ban treaty weakened America's ability to argue that other nations shouldn't develop or test nuclear weapons.

I continued doing political events for Al Gore and the Democrats, including two with gay activists who were strongly supportive of both Al and me because of the substantial number of openly gay and lesbian citizens serving in the administration, and because of our strong support of the Employment Nondiscrimination Act and the hate crimes bill, which made crimes committed against people because of their race, disability, or sexual orientation a federal offense. I also went to New York whenever I could to support Hillary. Her likely opponent was New York mayor Rudy Giuliani, who was a combative, controversial figure but was much less conservative than the national Republicans. I had had a cordial relationship with him, largely because of our shared support for the COPS program and gun safety measures.

George W. Bush seemed well on his way to winning the Republican nomination, as several of his challengers dropped out, leaving only Senator John McCain with any chance of stopping him. I had been impressed with Bush's campaign since I first saw him articulate his "compassionate conservative" theme in a farm setting in Iowa. I thought it was a brilliant formulation, virtually the only argument he could make to swing voters against an administration with approval ratings in the 65 percent range. He couldn't dispute the fact that we had 19 million new jobs, the economy was still growing, and crime was down for the seventh year in a row. Instead, his compassionate conservative message to the swing voters was this: "I'll give you the same good conditions you have now, with a smaller government and a bigger tax cut. Wouldn't you like that?" On most issues, Bush was in line with the conservative congressional Republicans, though he had criticized their budget for being harsh to the poor because it raised taxes for low-income Americans by cutting back on the Earned Income Tax Credit, while reducing taxes on the wealthiest Americans.

Although Bush was a formidable politician, I still thought Al Gore would win, despite the fact that only two previous vice presidents, Martin Van Buren and George H. W. Bush, had been elected directly from the vice presidency, because the country was in good shape and our administration had strong support. All vice presidents who run for President have two problems: most people don't know what they've done and don't give them credit for the accomplishments of the administration, and they tend to get typecast as number two men. I had done everything I could to help Al avoid those problems by giving him many high-profile assignments and making sure he received public recognition for his invaluable contribution to our successes. Yet even though he was indisputably the most active and influential vice president in history, there was still a gap between perception and reality.

The biggest challenge Al faced was how to show independence while still getting the benefit of our record. He had already said he disagreed with my personal misconduct but was proud of what we had accomplished for the American people. Now I thought he should say that no matter who became the next President, change was inevitable; the question for the voters was whether we would keep changing in the right way or make a U-turn to the failed policies of the past. Governor Bush was clearly advocating a return to trickle-down economics. We had tried it that way for twelve years and our way for seven. Our way worked better, and we had the evidence to prove it.

The campaign gave Al the chance to remind voters that I was leaving, but that the Republicans who had pursued impeachment and supported Starr were staying. America needed a President to stand up to them so that they couldn't abuse their power like that again, or succeed in implementing the harsh policies I had stopped in the budget battles, beginning with the government shutdown. There was ample evidence, less than a year old, that if the voters saw the election as a choice for the future and were reminded of what the Republicans had done, the advantage would shift markedly to the Democrats.

When a few people in the press began pushing the theory that I could cost Al the election, I had a funny telephone conversation with him about it. I said I was interested only in his winning, and if I thought it would help I would stand on the doorstep of the *Washington Post*'s headquarters and let him lash me with a bullwhip. He deadpanned, "Maybe we ought to poll that." I laughed and said, "Let's see whether it works better with my shirt on or off."

On October 12, Pakistan's prime minister Nawaz Sharif was overthrown in a military coup headed by General Musharraf, who had led the Pakistani armed forces over the Line of Control in Kashmir. I was concerned about the loss of democracy, and urged the restoration of civilian rule as soon as possible. Musharraf's ascendancy had one immediate consequence: the program to send Pakistani commandos into Afghanistan to catch or kill Osama bin Laden was canceled.

In mid-month, Ken Starr announced he was stepping down. Judge Sentelle's panel replaced him with Robert Ray, who was on Starr's staff and before that had been on the staff of Donald Smaltz during the failed attempt to convict Mike Espy. Near the end of my term, Ray wanted his pound of flesh, too: a written statement admitting that I had given false testimony in my deposition, and an agreement to accept a temporary suspension of my law license in return for Ray's shutting down the independent counsel's investigation. I doubted that he would actually indict me, given the fact that a bipartisan panel of prosecutors had testified at the impeachment proceedings that no responsible prosecutor would do so. But I was ready to get on with my life and didn't want to complicate Hillary's new life in politics. However, I couldn't agree to intentionally giving false testimony because I didn't believe I had. After carefully rereading my deposition and finding a couple of instances in which I gave answers that were not accurate, I gave Ray a statement that said that though I had tried to testify lawfully, some of my responses were false. He accepted the statement. After almost six years and $70 million in tax money, Whitewater was over.

Not everyone wanted a pound of flesh. In the middle of the month, I invited my high school classmates to the White House for our thirty-fifth high school reunion—as I had done five years earlier, for our thirtieth. I had loved my high school years and always enjoyed seeing my classmates. On this occasion several of them told me that their lives had gotten better over the last seven years. The son of one of them said that he thought I had been a good president, but "the most proud I ever was of you was when you stood up to that impeachment thing." I heard that often from people who'd felt helpless in the face of their own mistakes and misfortunes; somehow the fact that I had just kept going struck a chord with them, because that's what they had had to do.

At the end of the month, a Senate filibuster killed campaign finance reform again; we marked the fifth anniversary of AmeriCorps, in which 150,000 Americans had now served; Hillary and I held a White House Conference on Philanthropy in the hope of increasing the amount and impact of charitable giving; and we celebrated her birthday with a "Broadway for Hillary" event reminiscent of what Broadway stars had done for me back in 1992.

I began November by going to Oslo, where the negotiations between the Israelis and Palestinians had begun, to observe the fourth anniversary of Yitzhak Rabin's assassination, honor his memory, and join with the parties in rededicating ourselves to the peace process. Norwegian prime minister Kjell Bondevik had decided that an Oslo event might move the process forward. Our ambassador, David Hermelin, an irrepressible man of Norwegian-Jewish descent, tried to do his part by serving kosher hot dogs to both Barak and Arafat. Shimon Peres and Leah Rabin were there, too. The event had the desired effect, though I was convinced that both Barak and Arafat already wanted to complete the peace process and would do so in 2000.

Around this time several members of the press began to ask me about my legacy. Would I be known for bringing prosperity? For being a peacemaker? I tried to formulate an answer that captured not only concrete achievements but also the sense of possibility and community I wanted America to embody. The truth is, though, I didn't have time to think about such things. I wanted to press ahead until the last day. The legacy would take care of itself, probably long after I was dead.

On November 4, I began another New Markets tour, this time to Newark, Hartford, and Hermitage, Arkansas, the little town I had helped get living facilities for its migrant tomato workers in the late seventies. The tour ended in Chicago with Jesse Jackson and Speaker Hastert, who had decided to support the initiative. Jesse was looking resplendent in a fine pin-striped suit, and I kidded him about dressing up "like a Republican today" for the Speaker. I was encouraged by Hastert's support and confident we would pass legislation in the coming year.

In the second week of the month, I joined Al From for the first online presidential town hall meeting. Since I had been President, the number of Web sites had grown from 50 sites to 9 million, and new pages were being added at a rate of 100,000 per hour. The voice recognition software that converted my responses to type is routine today but was novel then. Two people asked me what I was going to do after I left the White House. I hadn't figured it all out yet, but I had begun to make plans for my presidential library.

I had thought a lot about the library and its exhibits on my years as President. Each President has to raise all the funds to build his library, plus an endowment to maintain the facility. The National Archives then provides the staff to organize and care for its contents. I had pored over the work of several architects and had visited many of the presidential libraries. The overwhelming majority of people who visit them come to see the exhibits, but the building has to be built in a way that preserves the records. I wanted the exhibit space to be open, beautiful, and full of light, and I wanted the material presented in a way that demonstrated America's movement into the twenty-first century.

I chose Jim Polshek and his firm as my architects, largely because of his design for the Rose Center for Earth and Space in New York, a huge glass-and-steel structure with a massive globe inside. I asked Ralph Applebaum to do the exhibits, because I thought his work on the Holocaust Museum in Washington was the best I had ever seen. I had already begun working with both of them. Before it was over, Polshek would say I was the worst client he had ever had: if he came to see me after a six-month hiatus with only a minor change in the drawings, I would notice and ask him about it.

I wanted to situate the library in Little Rock because I felt I owed it to my native state and because I thought the library should be in the heartland of America, where people who didn't travel to Washington or New York would have direct access to it. The city of Little Rock, on the initiative of Mayor Jim Dailey and city board member Dr. Dean Kumpuris, had offered twenty-seven acres of land along the Arkansas River in the old section of town, which was being revitalized and was not far from the Old State Capitol, the scene of so many important events in my life.

Beyond the library, I knew that I wanted to write a book about my life and the presidency and that I would have to work hard for three or four years to pay my legal bills, buy our home—two homes, if Hillary won the Senate race—and put aside some money for her and Chelsea. Then I wanted to devote the rest of my life to public service. Jimmy Carter had made a real difference in his post-presidential years, and I thought I could, too.

In mid-month, on the day I left for a ten-day trip to Turkey, Greece, Italy, Bulgaria, and Kosovo, I hailed Kofi Annan's announcement that President Glafcos Clerides of Cyprus and Turkish Cypriot leader Rauf Denktash would begin "proximity talks" in New York in early December. Cyprus had received its independence from the UK in 1960. In 1974, the president of Cyprus, Archbishop Makarios, was deposed in a coup orchestrated by the Greek military regime. In response, the Turkish military sent troops to the island to protect the Turkish Cypriots, dividing the country and creating a de facto Turkish enclave of independence in the north. Many Greeks in the north of Cyprus left their homes and moved south. The island had been divided ever since, and tensions had remained high between Turkey and Greece. Greece wanted to end the Turkish military presence in Cyprus and find a resolution that would at least allow the Greeks the possibility of returning to the north. I had tried for years to solve the problem and hoped the secretary-general's effort would succeed. It did not, and I would leave office disappointed that Cyprus remained an obstacle to Greek-Turkish reconciliation and to Turkey's being fully embraced by Europe.

We also finally reached agreement with the Republican leadership on three of my important budget priorities: funding the 100,000 new teachers, doubling the number of children in after-school programs, and, at long last, paying our back dues to the United Nations. Somehow, Madeleine Albright and Dick Holbrooke had worked it out with Jesse Helms and the other UN skeptics. It took Dick longer than making peace in Bosnia, but I'm not sure anyone else could have done it.

Hillary, Chelsea, and I arrived in Turkey for a five-day visit, an unusually long stay. I wanted to support the Turks in the aftermath of two devastating earthquakes, and to encourage them to continue to work with the United States and Europe. Turkey was a NATO ally and was hoping to be admitted to the European Union, a development I had been strongly supporting for years. It was one of a handful of countries whose future course would have a large impact on the twenty-first–century world. If it could resolve the Cyprus problem with Greece, reach an accommodation with its restive and sometimes repressed Kurdish minority, and maintain its identity as a secular Muslim democracy, Turkey could be the West's gateway to a new Middle East. If peace in the Middle East fell victim to a rising tide of Islamic extremism, a stable, democratic Turkey could be a bulwark against its spread into Europe.

I was glad to see President Demirel again. He was a large-minded man who wanted Turkey to be a bridge between East and West. I made my pitch for that vision to Prime Minister Bülent Ecevit and to the Turkish Grand National Assembly, urging them to reject isolationism and nationalism by resolving their problems with the Kurds and Greece and moving toward EU membership.

The next day I made the same arguments to American and Turkish business leaders in Istanbul, after a stop at a tent city near Izmit to meet with earthquake victims. We visited with some of the families who had lost everything, and I thanked all the nations that had helped the victims, including Greece. Not long after the Turkish quakes, Greece had an earthquake of its own, and the Turks had returned the favor. If earthquakes could bring them together, they should be able to work together when the ground stopped moving.

My whole trip became defined for the Turks by the visit to the quake victims. When I held a young child in my arms, he reached up and grabbed my nose, just as Chelsea used to do when she was a toddler. A photographer got a shot of it, and the picture was in all the Turkish papers the next day. One of them carried it with the headline, "He's a Turk!"

After my family visited the ruins of Ephesus, including one of the largest libraries in the Roman world and an open amphitheater where St. Paul had preached, I participated in a meeting of the fifty-four–nation Organization for Security and Cooperation in Europe, which had been organized in 1973 to advance democracy, human rights, and the rule of law. We were there to support the Stability Pact for the Balkans and a resolution of the continuing crisis in Chechnya that would end the terrorism against Russia and the excessive use of force against noncombatant Chechens. I also signed an agreement with the leaders of Kazakhstan, Turkmenistan, Azerbaijan, and Georgia committing the United States to support the development of two pipelines that would carry oil from the Caspian Sea to the West without going through Iran. Depending on what kind of future Iran chose to pursue, the pipeline agreement could prove to be of enormous consequence to the future stability of both the producing and consuming countries.

I was fascinated by Istanbul and its rich history as the capital of both the Ottoman Empire and the Roman Empire in the East. In another attempt to promote reconciliation, I visited the ecumenical patriarch of all the Orthodox churches, Bartholomew of Constantinople, and asked the Turks to reopen the Orthodox monastery in Istanbul. The patriarch gave me a beautiful scroll inscribed with what he knew was one of my favorite scriptural passages, from the eleventh chapter of Hebrews. It begins, "Faith is the assurance of things hoped for, the conviction of things not seen."

While I was in Turkey, the White House and Congress reached a budget agreement that, in addition to my education initiatives, provided funding for more police, the Lands Legacy initiative, our commitments under the Wye River accord, and the new debt-relief initiative for the poorest countries. The Republicans also agreed to give up their most damaging anti-environmental riders to the appropriation bills.

There was also good news in Northern Ireland, where George Mitchell had reached an agreement with the parties to proceed simultaneously with a new government and decommissioning with the support of Tony Blair and Bertie Ahern. Bertie was with me in Turkey when we heard the news.

In Athens, after a thrilling early-morning tour of the Acropolis with Chelsea, and a public expression of regret over America's support of the repressive anti-democratic regime that took control of Greece in 1967, I reaffirmed my commitment to a fair resolution to the Cyprus problem as a condition of Turkey's EU membership and thanked Prime Minister Kostas Simitis for staying with the allies in Kosovo. Because the Greeks and Serbs shared the Orthodox faith, it had been difficult for him. I left the meeting encouraged by the prime minister's openness to reconciliation with Turkey and its entry into the EU if the Cyprus problem could be resolved, in part because the two countries' foreign ministers, George Papandreou and Ismael Cem, were young, forward-looking leaders who were working together for a common future—the only course that made sense.

From Greece, I flew to Florence, where Prime Minister D'Alema hosted another of our Third Way conferences. This one had a distinctly Italian flavor, as Andrea Bocelli sang at the dinner and Academy Award–winning actor Roberto Benigni kept us in stitches. He and D'Alema were a well-matched pair—two lean, intense, passionate men who were always finding something to laugh about. When I met Benigni, he said, "I love you!" and jumped into my arms. I was thinking that maybe I should run for office in Italy; I had always loved it there.

This was by far our most substantive Third Way meeting. Tony Blair, EU president Romano Prodi, Gerhard Schroeder, Fernando Henrique Cardoso, and French prime minister Lionel Jospin were all there as we worked to articulate a progressive consensus for domestic and foreign policies in the twenty-first century, and for reforms in the international financial system to minimize financial crises and intensify our efforts to spread the benefits and reduce the burdens of globalization.

On the twenty-second, Chelsea and I flew to Bulgaria, which I was the first American President to visit. In a speech to more than thirty thousand people in the shadow of the brightly lit Alexander Nevsky Cathedral, I pledged America's support for their hard-won freedom, their economic aspirations, and their partnership with NATO.

My last stop before going home for Thanksgiving was in

Kosovo, where Madeleine Albright, Wes Clark, and I got a roaring welcome. I spoke to a group of citizens who kept interrupting my speech by shouting my name. I hated to break the mood, but I tried to get them to listen to my plea not to take out resentment over past wrongs by retaliating against the Serb minority, a point I made privately to the leaders of various factions in Kosovar politics. Later that day I went to Camp Bondsteel to thank the troops and share an early Thanksgiving dinner with them. They were clearly proud of what they had done, but Chelsea was a bigger hit with the young soldiers than I was.

While we were on the trip, I sent Charlene Barshefsky and Gene Sperling to China to try to close the deal for China's entry into the WTO. The agreement had to be good enough to enable us to pass legislation establishing permanent normal trade relations with China. Gene's presence would ensure that the Chinese knew that I was supporting the negotiations. The negotiations were difficult until the very end, when we got the protections against dumping and import surges and access to the automobile market that earned the support of Michigan Democratic congressman Sandy Levin. His support ensured congressional approval of permanent normal trade relations and thus China's entry into the WTO. Gene and Charlene had done a great job.

Shortly after Thanksgiving, David Trimble's Ulster Unionist Party approved the new peace agreement, and the new Northern Ireland government was formed with David Trimble as first minister and Seamus Mallon from John Hume's SDLP as deputy first minister. Sinn Fein's Martin McGuinness was named education minister. It would have been unthinkable not long before.

In December, when the members of the World Trade Organization met in Seattle, violent protests from anti-globalization forces rocked the downtown area. Most of the demonstrators were peaceful, however, and had legitimate grievances, as I told the convention delegates. The process of interdependence probably could not be reversed, but the WTO would have to be more open, and more sensitive to trade and environmental issues, and the wealthy countries that benefited from globalization would have to do more to bring its benefits to the other half of the world that was still living on less than two dollars a day. After Seattle, there would be more demonstrations at international financial meetings. I was convinced they would continue until we addressed the concerns of those who felt left out and left behind.

Early in December, I was able to announce that after seven years our economy had now created more than twenty million new jobs, 80 percent of them in job categories paying above our median wage, with the lowest African-American and Hispanic unemployment rates ever recorded and the lowest female unemployment rate since 1953, when a far smaller percentage of women were in the workforce.

On December 6, I had a special visitor: eleven-year-old Fred Sanger, from St. Louis. Fred and his parents came to see me with representatives of the Make-a-Wish foundation, which helps seriously ill children fulfill their wishes. Fred had heart problems that required him to stay indoors a lot. He watched the news and knew a surprising amount about my work. We had a good conversation and stayed in touch for some time afterward. During my eight years in office, the Make-a-Wish people brought forty-seven children to see me. They always brightened my day and reminded me why I had wanted to be President.

In the second week of the month, after a telephone conversation with President Assad, I announced that, within a week, Israel and Syria would resume their negotiations in Washington at a site to be determined, with the goal of reaching an agreement as soon as possible.

On the ninth, I went back to Worcester, Massachusetts, the city that had welcomed me in the dark days of August 1998, for the funeral of six firefighters who had been killed in action. The heartbreaking tragedy had galvanized the community and all of America's firefighters; hundreds of them from across the country and several from overseas filled the city's convention center, a poignant reminder that the mortality rate of firemen is even higher than that of police officers.

A week later at the FDR Memorial, I signed the legislation that extended Medicare and Medicaid benefits to disabled people in the workforce. It was the most important piece of legislation for the disabled community since the passage of the Americans with Disabilities Act, allowing otherwise uninsurable people with AIDS, muscular dystrophy, Parkinson's, diabetes, or crippling injuries to "buy into" the Medicare program. The law would change the quality of life for countless people who would now be able to earn an income and enhance the quality of their lives. It was a tribute to the hard work of disability activists, especially my friend Justin Dart, a wheelchair-bound Wyoming Republican who was never without his cowboy hat and boots.

All during the Christmas season we were looking forward to New Year's Eve and the new millennium. For the first time in many years, our family would miss Renaissance Weekend to stay in Washington for the millennium celebration. It was all privately funded; my friend Terry McAuliffe raised several million dollars so that we could offer citizens a chance to enjoy the festivities, which included two days of public family activities at the Smithsonian Institution, and on the thirty-first a children's celebration in the afternoon and a concert on the Mall produced by Quincy Jones and George Stevens, with a big fireworks display. We also had a large dinner at the White House, filled with fascinating people from literary, artistic, musical, academic, military, and civic circles, and a long dance after the fireworks on the Mall.

It was a wonderful evening, but I was nervous the entire time. Our security team had been on high alert for weeks due to numerous intelligence reports that the United States would be hit with several terrorist attacks. Particularly since the embassy bombings in 1998, I had been focused intently on bin Laden and his al Qaeda supporters. We had rolled up a score of al Qaeda cells, captured terrorist operatives, broken up plots against us, and continued to urge Pakistan and Saudi Arabia to press Afghanistan to give bin Laden up. Now, with this new warning, Sandy Berger convened all of my top national security staff in the White House virtually every day for a month.

One man with bomb-making materials was arrested crossing the Canadian border in Washington State; he had planned to bomb the Los Angeles airport. Two terrorist cells in the Northeast and one in Canada were discovered and broken up. Planned attacks in Jordan were thwarted. The millennium came to America with lots of celebration and no terror, a tribute to the hard work of thousands of people, and perhaps to a bit of luck as well. Regardless, as the new year, the new century, and the new millennium began, I was filled with joy and gratitude. Our country was in excellent shape, and we were moving into the new era in good condition.

TWENTY-FIVE

HILLARY AND I began the first day of the new century and the last year of my presidency with a joint radio address to the American people, which was also televised live. We had stayed up with the revelers at the White House until about two-thirty in the morning, and we were tired but eager to mark this day. A remarkable worldwide celebration had taken place the night before: billions of people had watched on television as midnight broke first in Asia, then in Europe, then in Africa, South America, and finally North America. The United States was entering the new century of global interdependence with a unique combination of economic success, social solidarity, and national self-confidence, and with our openness, dynamism, and democratic values being celebrated the world over. Hillary and I said that we Americans had to make the most of this opportunity to keep making our own country better and to spread the benefits and share the burdens of the twenty-first–century world. That's what I intended to spend my last year doing.

Defying historical trends, the seventh year of my presidency had been full of achievement because we had continued to work on the public's business through the impeachment process and afterward, following the agenda laid out in the State of the Union address and dealing with problems and opportunities as they arose. The traditional winding down in the last half of a President's second term had not occurred. I was determined not to let it happen this year, either.

The new year brought the loss of one of my old partners, as Boris Yeltsin resigned and was succeeded by Vladimir Putin. Yeltsin had never fully recovered his strength and stamina after his heart surgery, and he believed Putin was ready to succeed him and able to put in the long hours the job required. Boris also knew that giving the Russian people the chance to see Putin perform would increase the chances that he would win the next election. It was both a wise and a shrewd move, but I was going to miss Yeltsin. For all his physical problems and occasional unpredictability, he had been a courageous and visionary leader. We trusted each other and had accomplished a lot together. On the day he resigned we talked on the phone for about twenty minutes, and I could tell he was comfortable with his decision. He left office as he had lived and governed, in his own unique way.

On January 3, I went to Shepherdstown, West Virginia, to open peace talks between Syria and Israel. Ehud Barak had pressed me hard to hold the talks early in the year. He was growing impatient over the peace process with Arafat, and was unsure whether their differences over Jerusalem could be resolved. By contrast, he had told me months before that he was prepared to give the Golan Heights back to Syria as long as Israel's concerns could be satisfied about its early-warning station on the Golan and its dependence on Lake Tiberias, otherwise known as the Sea of Galilee, for one-third of its water supply.

The Sea of Galilee is a unique body of water: the bottom part is salt water fed by underground springs, while the top layer is fresh water. Because fresh water is lighter, care had to be taken not to draw down the lake too much in any given year lest the covering layer of fresh water becomes too light to hold the salt water down. If the fresh water were to fall below a certain point, the salt water could rush upward and mix with it, taking out a water supply that is essential for Israel.

Before he was killed, Yitzhak Rabin had given me a commitment to withdraw from the Golan to the June 4, 1967, borders as long as Israel's concerns were satisfied. The commitment was given on the condition that I keep it "in my pocket" until it could be formally presented to Syria in the context of a complete solution. After Yitzhak's death, Shimon Peres reaffirmed the pocket commitment, and on this basis we had sponsored talks between the Syrians and the Israelis in 1996 at Wye River. Peres wanted me to sign a security treaty with Israel if it gave up the Golan, an idea that was suggested to me later by Netanyahu and would be advanced again by Barak. I had told them I was willing to do it.

Dennis Ross and our team had been making progress until Bibi Netanyahu defeated Peres in the election amid a rash of terrorist activity. Then the Syrian negotiations faltered. Now Barak wanted to start them up again, though as yet he was unwilling to reaffirm the precise words of the Rabin pocket commitment.

Barak had to contend with a very different Israeli electorate from the one Rabin had led. There were many more immigrants, and the Russians in particular were opposed to giving up the Golan. Natan Sharansky, who had become a hero in the West during his long imprisonment in the Soviet Union and had accompanied Netanyahu to Wye in 1998, explained the Russian Jews' attitude to me. He said they had come from the world's largest country to one of its smallest ones, and didn't believe in making Israel even smaller by giving up the Golan or the West Bank. They also considered Syria to be no threat to Israel. They weren't at peace but were not at war either. If Syria attacked Israel, the Israelis could win easily. Why give up the Golan?

While Barak didn't agree with this view, he had to contend with it. Nevertheless, he wanted to make peace with Syria, was confident the issues could be resolved, and wanted me to convene negotiations as soon as possible. By January, I had been working for more than three months with the Syrian foreign minister, Farouk al-Shara, and by telephone with President Assad to set the stage for the talks. Assad was not in good health and wanted to regain the Golan before he died, but he had to be careful. He wanted his son Bashar to succeed him, and apart from his own conviction that Syria should get back all the land it had occupied before June 4, 1967, he had to make an agreement that would not be subject to attack from forces within Syria whose support his son would need.

Assad's frailty and a stroke suffered by Foreign Minister Shara in the fall of 1999 heightened Barak's sense of urgency. At his request, I sent Assad a letter saying I thought Barak was willing to make a deal if we could resolve the definition of the border, the control of water, and the early-warning post, and that if they did reach agreement, the United States would be prepared to establish bilateral relations with Syria, a move Barak had urged. That was a big step for us, given Syria's past support of terrorism. Of course, Assad would have to stop supporting terrorism in order to achieve normal relations with the U.S., but if he had the Golan back, the incentive to support the Hezbollah terrorists who attacked Israel from Lebanon would evaporate.

Barak wanted peace with Lebanon, too, because he had committed to withdrawing Israeli forces from the country by the end of the year, and a peace agreement would make Israel safer from Hezbollah attacks along the border, and would not make it appear that Israel had withdrawn because of the attacks. As he well knew, no agreement with Lebanon would come without Syria's consent and involvement.

Assad replied a month later in a letter that appeared to back away from his previous position, perhaps because of the uncertainties in Syria that his and Shara's health problems had caused. However, a few weeks after that, when Madeleine Albright and Dennis Ross went to see Assad and Shara, who seemed completely recovered, Assad told them that he wanted to resume negotiations and was ready to make peace because he believed Barak was serious. He even agreed to have Shara negotiate, something he had not done before, as long as Barak would personally handle the Israeli side.

Barak accepted eagerly and wanted to begin immediately. I explained that we could not do it during the Christmas holidays, and he agreed to our timetable: preliminary talks in Washington in mid-December, to be resumed early in the New Year with my participation and to continue uninterrupted until agreement was reached. The Washington talks got off to a bit of a rocky start with an aggressive public statement by Shara. Nevertheless, in the private talks, when Shara suggested that we should start where the talks had left off in 1996, with Rabin's pocket commitment of the June 4 line provided Israel's needs were met, Barak responded that while he had made no commitment on territory, "we do not erase history." The two men then agreed that I could decide the order in which the issues—including borders, security, water, and peace—would be discussed. Barak wanted the negotiations to continue uninterrupted; that would require the Syrians to work through the end of Ramadan on January 7 and not go home to celebrate the traditional feast of Eid Al Fitr at the end of the fasting period. Shara agreed, and the two sides went home to prepare.

Although Barak had pushed hard for the early negotiations, he soon began to worry about the political consequences of giving up the Golan without having prepared the Israeli public for it. He wanted some cover: the resumption of the Lebanon track to be conducted by the Syrians in consultation with the Lebanese; the announcement by at least one Arab state of an upgrade of relations with Israel; clear security benefits from the United States; and a free-trade zone on the Golan. I agreed to support all these requests and took things a step further, calling Assad on December 19 and asking him to resume the Lebanese track at the same time as the Syrian talks and to help retrieve the remains of three Israelis still listed as missing in action from the Lebanon war almost twenty years earlier. Assad agreed to the second request and we sent a forensics team to Syria, but unfortunately the remains weren't where the Israelis thought they would be. On the first issue, Assad hedged, saying the Lebanese talks should resume once some headway had been made on the Syrian track.

Shepherdstown is a rural community a little more than an hour's drive from Washington; Barak had insisted on an isolated setting to minimize leaks, and the Syrians didn't want to go to Camp David or Wye River because other high-profile Middle East negotiations had occurred there. That was fine with me; the conference facilities in Shepherdstown were comfortable, and I could get there from the White House in about twenty minutes by helicopter.

It quickly became apparent that the two sides were not that far apart on the issues. Syria wanted all of the Golan back but was willing to leave the Israelis a small strip of land, 10 meters (33 feet) wide, along the border of the lake;

Israel wanted a wider strip of land. Syria wanted Israel to withdraw within eighteen months; Barak wanted three years. Israel wanted to stay in the early-warning station; Syria wanted it manned by personnel from the UN or perhaps from the U.S. Israel wanted guarantees on the quality and quantity of water flowing from the Golan into the lake; Syria agreed as long as it got the same guarantees on its water flow from Turkey. Israel wanted full diplomatic relations as soon as withdrawal began; Syria wanted something less until the withdrawal was complete.

The Syrians came to Shepherdstown in a positive and flexible frame of mind, eager to make an agreement. By contrast, Barak, who had pushed hard for the talks, decided, apparently on the basis of polling data, that he needed to slow-walk the process for a few days in order to convince the Israeli public that he was being a tough negotiator. He wanted me to use my good relationship with Shara and Assad to keep the Syrians happy while he said as little as possible during his self-imposed waiting period.

I was, to put it mildly, disappointed. If Barak had dealt with the Syrians before or if he had given us some advance notice, it might have been manageable. Perhaps, as a democratically elected leader, he had to pay more attention to public opinion than Assad did, but Assad had his own political problems, and had overcome his notorious aversion to high-level involvement with the Israelis because he trusted me and had believed Barak's assurances.

Barak had not been in politics long, and I thought he had gotten some very bad advice. In foreign affairs, polls are often useless; people hire leaders to win for them, and it's the results that matter. Many of my most important foreign policy decisions had not been popular at first. If Barak made real peace with Syria, it would lift his standing in Israel and across the world, and increase the chances of success with the Palestinians. If he failed, a few days of good poll numbers would vanish in the wind. As hard as I tried, I couldn't change Barak's mind. He wanted me to help keep Shara on board while he waited, and to do it in the isolated setting of

Shepherdstown, where there were few distractions from the business at hand.

Madeleine Albright and Dennis Ross tried to think of creative ways to at least clarify Barak's commitment to the Rabin pocket commitment, including opening a back channel between Madeleine and Butheina Shaban, the only woman in the Syrian delegation. Butheina was an articulate, impressive woman who had always served as Assad's interpreter when we met. She had been with Assad for years, and I was sure she was in Shepherdstown to guarantee the president an unvarnished version of what was happening.

On Friday, the fifth day, we presented a draft peace agreement with the two sides' differences in brackets. The Syrians responded positively on Saturday night, and we began meetings on border and security issues. Again, the Syrians showed flexibility on both matters, saying they would accept an adjustment of the strip of land bordering Galilee to as much as 50 meters (164 feet), provided that Israel accepted the June 4 line as the basis of discussion. There was some practical validity to this; apparently the lake had shrunk in size in the last thirty years. I was encouraged, but it quickly became apparent that Barak still had not authorized anyone on his team to accept June 4, no matter what the Syrians offered.

On Sunday, at a lunch for Ehud and Nava Barak at Madeleine Albright's farm, Madeleine and Dennis made a last pitch to Barak. Syria had shown flexibility on what Israel wanted, providing its needs were met; Israel had not responded in kind. What would it take? Barak said he wanted to resume the Lebanese negotiations. And if not, he wanted to break for several days and come back.

Shara was in no mood to hear this. He said that Shepherdstown was a failure, that Barak was not sincere, and that he would have to say as much to President Assad. At the last dinner, I tried again to get Barak to say something positive that Shara could take back to Syria. He declined, instead telling me privately that I could call Assad after we left Shepherdstown and say he would accept the June 4 line once the Lebanese negotiations resumed or were about to start. That meant Shara would go home empty-handed from negotiations he had been led to believe would be decisive, so much so that the Syrians had been willing to stay through the end of Ramadan and the Eid.

To make matters worse, the latest bracketed text of our treaty leaked in the Israeli press, showing the concessions that Syria had offered without getting anything in return. Shara was subjected to intense criticism at home. It was understandably embarrassing to him, and to Assad. Even authoritarian governments are not immune to popular opinion and powerful interest groups.

When I called Assad with Barak's offer to affirm the Rabin commitment and demarcate the border on the basis of it as long as the Lebanese negotiations also started, he listened without comment. A few days later, Shara called Madeleine Albright and rejected Barak's offer, saying the Syrians would open negotiations on Lebanon only after the border demarcation was agreed upon. They had been burned once by being flexible and forthcoming, and they weren't about to make the same mistake again.

For the time being we were stumped, but I thought we should keep trying. Barak still seemed to want the Syrian peace, and it was true that the Israeli public had not been prepared for the compromises that peace required. It was also still in Syria's interest to make peace, and soon. Assad was in ill health and had to pave the way for his son's succession. Meanwhile, there was more than enough still to do on the Palestinian track. I asked Sandy, Madeleine, and Dennis to figure out what we should do next, and turned my attention to other things.

On January 10, after a White House celebration with Muslims marking the end of Ramadan, Hillary and I went to the U.S. Naval Academy Chapel in Annapolis, Maryland, for the funeral of former chief of naval operations Bud Zumwalt, who had become our friend through Renaissance Weekend. After I took office, Bud had worked with us to provide aid to the families of servicemen who, like his late son, had become ill as a result of their exposure to Agent

Orange during the Vietnam War. He had also lobbied the Senate to ratify the Chemical Weapons Convention. His personal support to our family during and after the House impeachment proceedings was a gift of kindness we would never forget. As I was dressing for the funeral, one of my valets, Lito Bautista, a Filipino-American who had been in the navy for thirty years, said he was glad I was going to the service because Bud Zumwalt "was the best we ever had. He was for us."

That night I flew to the Grand Canyon, staying at the El Tovar Hotel in a room with a balcony right on the canyon's edge. Nearly thirty years earlier, I had seen the sun set over the Grand Canyon; now I wanted to watch it rise, lighting the layers of differently colored rocks from the top down. The next morning, after a sunrise just as beautiful as I had hoped it would be, Secretary of the Interior Bruce Babbitt and I designated three new national monuments and expanded a fourth in Arizona and California, including one million acres around the Grand Canyon and a stretch of thousands of small islands and exposed reefs along the California coast.

It was ninety-two years to the day since President Theodore Roosevelt had set aside the Grand Canyon itself as a national monument. Bruce Babbitt, Al Gore, and I had done our best to be faithful to Roosevelt's conservation ethic and to his admonition that we should always be taking what he called "the long look ahead."

On the fifteenth I commemorated Martin Luther King Jr.'s birthday in my Saturday morning radio address by marking the economic and social progress of African-Americans and Hispanics in the last seven years and pointing out how far we had to go: Though minority unemployment and poverty rates were at historically low levels, they were still far above the national average. We had also suffered a recent spate of hate crimes against victims because of their race or ethnicity—James Byrd, a black man dragged from the back of a pickup truck and killed by white racists in Texas; bullets fired at a Jewish school in Los Angeles; a Korean-American student, an African-American basketball coach, and a Filipino postal worker all killed because of their race.

A few months earlier, at one of Hillary's millennium evenings at the White House, Dr. Eric Lander, director of the Whitehead Institute Center for Genome Research at MIT, and high-tech executive Vinton Cerf, who is known as the "Father of the Internet," discussed how digital chip technology had enabled the human genome project to succeed. The thing I remembered most clearly about the evening was Lander's statement that all human beings are more than 99.9 percent alike genetically. Ever since he said that, I had thought of all the blood that had been shed, all the energy wasted, by people obsessed with keeping us divided over that one-tenth of a percent.

In the radio address, I again asked the Congress to pass the hate-crimes bill, and asked the Senate to confirm a distinguished Chinese-American lawyer, Bill Lann Lee, as the new assistant attorney general for civil rights. The Republican majority had been holding him up; they seemed to have an aversion to many of my non-Caucasian nominees. My main guest that morning was Charlotte Fillmore, a one hundred–year-old former White House employee who decades earlier had had to enter the White House through a special door because of her race. This time we brought Charlotte through the front door to the Oval Office.

In the week leading up to the State of the Union address, I followed my usual custom of highlighting important initiatives that would be in the speech. This time I was incorporating two proposals Hillary and Al Gore were advocating on the campaign trail. I recommended allowing parents of children eligible for health insurance under the CHIP program to purchase insurance for themselves, a plan Al was promoting, and I supported making the first $10,000 of college tuition tax-deductible, an idea that Senator Chuck Schumer was pushing in Congress and Hillary was advocating in her campaign.

If all the parents and children who were income-eligible—about fourteen million—bought into the CHIP program, it would take care of about a third of our uninsured population. If people fifty-five and over were allowed to buy into Medicare as I had recommended, the two programs together would cut the number of uninsured Americans in half. If the tuition tax credit was adopted, along with the college aid expansions I had already signed into law, we could rightly claim to have opened the doors of college to all Americans. The college-enrollment rate had already risen to 67 percent, almost 10 percent higher than when I took office.

In a speech to scientists at the California Institute of Technology, I unveiled a proposed increase of nearly $3 billion in research, which included $1 billion for AIDS and other biomedical purposes and $500 million for nanotechnology, and major increases for basic science, space, and clean energy. On the twenty-fourth, Alexis Herman, Donna Shalala, and I asked Congress to help close the 25 percent pay gap between men and women by passing the Paycheck Fairness Act, giving us the funds to clear up the large backlog of employment discrimination cases at the Equal Employment Opportunity Commission, and supporting the Labor Department's efforts to increase female employment in high-wage jobs in which women were underrepresented. For example, in most high-tech occupations, men outnumbered women by more than two to one.

On the day before the speech, I sat down with Jim Lehrer of PBS's *NewsHour* for the first time since our interview two years earlier, right after the storm over my deposition broke. After we went through the achievements of the administration over the previous seven years, Lehrer asked me if I was worried about what historians were going to write about me. The *New York Times* had just published an editorial saying historians were beginning to say I was a politician with great natural talent and some significant accomplishments who had "missed the greatness that once seemed within his grasp."

He asked me about my reaction to the "what might have been" assessment. I said that it seemed to me that the time most like our own was at the turn of the last century, when we were also moving into a new era of economic and social change, and were being drawn into the world beyond our shores more than ever before. Based on what had happened then, I thought the tests of my service would be: Did we manage the transition of America into the new economy and an era of globalization well or not? Did we make social progress and change the way we approached our problems to fit the times? Were we good stewards of the environment? And what were the forces we stood against? I told him I felt comfortable with the answers to those questions.

Moreover, I had read enough history to know that it is constantly being rewritten. While I was in office, two major biographies of Grant had been published that dramatically revised the conventional assessment of his presidency upward. That sort of thing was going on all the time. Besides, as I told Lehrer, I was more focused on what I could accomplish in my last year than on what the future might think of me.

Beyond the domestic agenda, I told Lehrer that I wanted to prepare our nation to deal with the biggest security challenges of the twenty-first century. The congressional Republicans' first priority was building a national missile defense system, but I said the main threat was "the likelihood that you'll have terrorists and narco-traffickers and organized criminals cooperating with each other, with smaller and smaller and more difficult to detect weapons of mass destruction and powerful traditional weapons. So we've tried to lay in a framework for dealing with cyberterrorism, bioterrorism, chemical terrorism. . . . Now, this is not in the headlines, but . . . I think the enemies of the nation-state in this interconnected world are likely to be the biggest security threat."

I was thinking about terrorism a great deal then because of the nail-biting two months we'd had leading up to the millennium celebration. The CIA, National Security Agency, FBI, and our entire counterterrorism group had worked hard to thwart several planned attacks in the United States and the Middle East. Now two submarines were in the northern Arabian Sea, ready to fire missiles at any point the CIA determined to be bin Laden's whereabouts. Dick

Clarke's counterterrorism group and George Tenet were working hard to find him. I felt we were on top of the situation but still did not have either the offensive or defensive capabilities we needed to combat an enemy adept at finding the opportunities to attack innocent people that an increasingly open world offered.

Before the interview was over, Lehrer asked the question I knew was coming: if, two years ago, I had answered his question and other questions about my conduct differently right at the beginning, did I think that there might have been a different result and that I might not have been impeached? I told him that I didn't know, but that I deeply regretted having misled him and the American people. I still don't have the answer to his question, given the hysterical atmosphere that had engulfed Washington at the time. As I told Lehrer, I had apologized and tried to make amends for my mistakes. That was all I could do.

Then Lehrer asked if I took satisfaction in knowing that if there was a conspiracy to run me out of office, it hadn't worked. I believe that was as close as any journalist ever came in my presence to admitting the existence of the conspiracy they all knew existed but could not bring themselves to acknowledge. I told Jim I had learned the hard way that life always humbles you if you give in to anger or take too much satisfaction in having defeated someone, or think that no matter how bad your own sins are, those of your adversaries are worse. I had a year to go; there was no time to be angry or satisfied.

My last State of the Union address was a joy to deliver. We had more than twenty million new jobs, the lowest unemployment rate and smallest welfare rolls in thirty years, the lowest crime rate in twenty-five years, the lowest poverty rate in twenty years, the smallest federal workforce in forty years, the first back-to-back surpluses in forty-two years, seven years of declining teen pregnancies and a 30 percent increase in adoptions, and 150,000 young people who had served in AmeriCorps. Within a month we would have the longest economic expansion in American history, and by the end of the year we would have three consecutive surpluses for the first time in more than fifty years.

I was concerned that America would become complacent in our prosperity, so I asked our people not to take it for granted, but to take that "long look ahead" to the nation we could build in the twenty-first century. I offered more than sixty initiatives to meet an ambitious set of goals: every child would start school ready to learn and graduate ready to succeed; every family would be able to succeed at home and at work, and no child would be raised in poverty; the challenge of the baby boomers' retirement would be met; all Americans would have access to quality, affordable health care; America would be the safest big country on earth and debt-free for the first time since 1835; prosperity would come to every community; climate change would be reversed; America would lead the world toward shared prosperity and security and to the far frontiers of science and technology; and we would at last become one nation, united in all our diversity.

I did my best to reach out to Republicans and Democrats, recommending a mix of both tax cuts and spending programs to move toward the goals; greater support for faith-based efforts to fight poverty and drug abuse and help teen mothers; a tax break for charitable contributions by low- and moderate-income citizens who couldn't claim one now because they didn't itemize their deductions; tax relief from the so-called marriage penalty and another expansion of the EITC; greater incentives to teach English and civics to new immigrants; and passage of the hate crimes bill and the Employment Non-Discrimination Act. I also thanked the Speaker for his support of the New Markets initiative.

For the last time, I introduced the people sitting with Hillary who represented what we were trying to accomplish: the father of one of the students killed at Columbine, who wanted Congress to close the gun show loophole; a Hispanic father who proudly paid child support and who would benefit from the tax-relief package for working families I had proposed; an air force captain who had rescued a downed pilot in Kosovo, to illustrate the importance of finishing our work in the Balkans; and my friend Hank Aaron, who had spent his years after baseball working to help poor children and bridge the racial divide.

I closed with an appeal for unity, getting a laugh when I reminded Congress that even Republicans and Democrats were genetically 99.9 percent the same. I said, "Modern science has confirmed what ancient faiths have always taught: the most important fact of life is our common humanity."

The speech was criticized by one congressman who said I sounded like Calvin Coolidge in wanting to make America debt-free, and by some conservatives who said I was spending too much money on education, health care, and the environment. Most citizens seemed to be reassured that I was going to work hard in my last year, interested in the new ideas I was advancing, and supportive of my efforts to keep them focused on the future.

The last time America seemed to be sailing on such smooth seas was in the early sixties, with the economy booming, civil rights laws promising a more just future, and Vietnam a distant blip on the screen. Within six years the economy was sagging, there were race riots in the streets, John and Robert Kennedy and Martin Luther King Jr. had been killed, and Vietnam had consumed America, driven President Johnson from office, and ushered in a new era of division in our politics. Good times are to be seized and built upon, not coasted through.

After a stop in Quincy, Illinois, to hit the high points of my agenda, I flew to Davos, Switzerland, to address the World Economic Forum, an increasingly important annual gathering of international political and business leaders. I brought five cabinet members with me to discuss the popular uprising against globalization that we had witnessed in the streets of Seattle during the recent WTO meeting. The multinational corporations and their political supporters had largely been content to create a global economy that served their needs, believing that the growth resulting from trade would create wealth and jobs everywhere.

Trade in well-governed countries had helped lift many

people out of poverty, but too many people in poor countries were left out: half the world still lived on less than $2 a day, a billion people lived on less than a dollar a day, and more than a billion people went to bed hungry every night. One in four people had no access to clean water. Some 130 million children never went to school at all, and 10 million children died every year of preventable diseases.

Even in wealthy countries, the constant churning of the economy was always dislocating some people, and the United States wasn't doing enough to get them back in the workforce at the same or higher pay. Finally, the global financial institutions had not been able to head off or mitigate crises in developing countries in a way that minimized damage to working people, and the WTO was perceived as being too captive to wealthy countries and multinational corporations.

In my first two years, when the Democrats were in the majority, I had gotten more money for training displaced workers and signed the NAFTA side agreements on the environment and labor standards. Afterward, the Republican Congress was less sympathetic to such efforts, especially those designed to reduce poverty and create new jobs in poor nations. Now it seemed to me that we had a chance to build a bipartisan consensus on at least three initiatives: the New Markets program, the trade bill for Africa and the Caribbean, and the Millennium Debt Relief effort.

The larger question was whether we could have a global economy without global social and environmental policies and more open governance by the economic decision makers, especially the WTO. I thought the anti-trade, anti-globalization forces were wrong in believing that trade had increased poverty. In fact, trade had lifted more people out of poverty and pulled more nations out of isolation. On the other hand, those who thought all we needed were unregulated flows of more than $1 trillion a day of capital and ever increasing trade were wrong, too.

I said globalization imposed on its beneficiaries the responsibility of sharing its gains and its burdens and empowering more people to participate in it. Essentially, I advocated a Third Way approach to globalization: trade plus a concerted effort to give people and nations the tools and conditions to make the most of it. Finally, I argued that giving people hope through economic growth and social justice was essential to our ability to persuade the twenty-first–century world to walk away from the modern horrors of terrorism and weapons of mass destruction and the old conflicts rooted in racial, religious, and tribal hatreds.

When the speech was over, I couldn't know if I'd succeeded in getting the thousand business leaders there to agree with me, but I felt that they had listened and at least were wrestling with the problems of our global interdependence and their own obligations to create a more unified world. What the movers and shakers of the world needed was a shared vision. When good people with energy act on a shared vision, most of the problems get worked out.

Back home, it was time for my last National Prayer Breakfast. Joe Lieberman, the event's first Jewish speaker, gave a fine talk on the values common to all faiths. I discussed the practical implications of his remarks: if we are admonished not to turn away strangers, to treat others as we would like to be treated, and to love our neighbors as ourselves, "who are our neighbors, and what does it mean to love them?" If we were virtually the same genetically, and our world was so interdependent that I had a cousin in Arkansas who played chess twice a week on the Internet with a man from Australia, we obviously had to broaden our horizons in the years ahead.

The direction of those years, of course, would be shaped by the outcome of this year's election. Al Gore and George W. Bush had both won handily in Iowa, as expected. Then the campaign moved on to New Hampshire, where voters in both parties' primaries delight in upsetting expectations. Al's campaign had gotten off to a rocky start, but when he moved his campaign headquarters to Nashville and began doing informal town hall meetings in New Hampshire, he really started connecting with voters, got better press coverage, and pulled ahead of Senator Bradley. After the State of the Union, in which I featured some of his important accomplishments, he picked up a few more points in the "bounce" we always received from the speech. Then Bradley began to attack him harshly. When Al didn't respond, Bradley cut into his lead, but Al held on to win 52–47 percent. After that, I knew he was home free for the nomination. He was going to carry the South and California big, and I thought he would do well in the large industrial states, too, especially after the AFL-CIO endorsed him.

John McCain defeated George W. Bush in New Hampshire 49–31 percent. It was a state tailor-made for McCain. They liked his independent streak and his support for campaign finance reform. The next big contest was in South Carolina, where McCain would be helped by his military background and the endorsements of two congressmen, but Bush had the backing of both the party establishment and the religious right.

On Sunday afternoon, February 6, Hillary, Chelsea, Dorothy, and I drove from Chappaqua to the State University of New York's campus in nearby Purchase for Hillary's formal announcement of her Senate candidacy. Senator Moynihan introduced her. He said that he had known Eleanor Roosevelt and that she "would love you." It was a sincere compliment and a funny one, since Hillary had taken a lot of good-natured ribbing for saying she had had imaginary conversations with Mrs. Roosevelt.

Hillary gave a terrific speech, one she had written carefully and practiced hard; it displayed how much she had learned about the concerns of the different regions of the state and how clearly she understood the choices voters were facing. She also had to explain why she was running; show that she understood why New Yorkers might be wary of voting for a candidate, even one they liked, who had never lived in the state until a few months before; and say what she would do as a senator. There was some discussion about whether I should speak. New York was one of my best states; at the time my job approval was over 70 percent there and my personal approval was at 60 percent. But we decided I shouldn't talk. It was Hillary's day, and the voters wanted to hear from her.

For the rest of the month, while politics dominated the news, I was dealing with a wide variety of domestic and foreign policy issues. On the home front, I endorsed a bipartisan bill to provide Medicaid coverage to lower-income women for breast and cervical cancer treatment; made a deal with Senator Lott to bring five of my judicial nominees to the Senate floor for a vote in return for appointing the person he wanted, a rabid foe of campaign finance reform, to the Federal Election Commission; argued with the Republicans over the Patients' Bill of Rights—they said they'd pass it as long as no one could bring a lawsuit to enforce it, and I argued that that would make it a bill of "suggestions"; dedicated the White House press room to James Brady, President Reagan's courageous press secretary; announced a record increase in funds for Native American education and health care; supported a change in food stamp regulations to allow welfare recipients who went to work to own a used car without losing their food aid; received an award from the League of United Latin American Citizens (LULAC) for my economic and social policies and for my major Hispanic appointments; and hosted the National Governors Association for the last time.

In foreign affairs, we dealt with a lot of headaches. On the seventh, Yasser Arafat suspended his peace talks with Israel. He was convinced that Israel was putting Palestinian issues on the back burner in favor of pursuing peace with Syria. There was some truth in it, and at the time, the Israeli public was more willing to make peace with the Palestinians, with all the difficulties that entailed, than to give up the Golan Heights and put the Palestinian talks at risk. We spent the rest of the month trying to get things going again.

On the eleventh, the UK suspended home rule in Northern Ireland, despite the IRA's last-minute assurance of an act of arms decommissioning to General John de Chastelain, the Canadian who was overseeing the process. I had gotten George Mitchell involved again, and we had done our best to help Bertie Ahern and Tony Blair avoid this day. The fundamental problem, according to Gerry Adams, was that the IRA wanted to disarm because their people had voted for it, not because David Trimble and the Unionists had made decommissioning the price of their continued participation in the government. Of course, without decommissioning, the Protestants would lose faith in the process, and eventually Trimble would be replaced, a result Adams and Sinn Fein did not want. Trimble could be dour and pessimistic, but beneath his stern Scots-Irish front was a brave idealist who was also taking risks for peace. At any rate, the sequencing issue had delayed establishment of the government for more than a year; now we were back to no government. It was frustrating, but I thought the impasse would be resolved because no one wanted to return to the bad old days.

On March 5, I commemorated the thirty-fifth anniversary of the voting rights march in Selma, Alabama, by walking across the Edmund Pettus Bridge as the civil rights demonstrators had on that "Bloody Sunday," risking their lives to gain the right to vote for all Americans. Many of the veterans of the civil rights movement who had marched with or supported Martin Luther King Jr. marched arm in arm again that day, including Coretta Scott King, Jesse Jackson, John Lewis, Andrew Young, Joe Lowery, Julian Bond, Ethel Kennedy, and Harris Wofford.

In 1965, the Selma march galvanized the conscience of the nation. Five months later, President Johnson signed the Voting Rights Act into law. Before the Voting Rights Act, there were only 300 black elected officials at any level, and just three African-American congressmen. In 2000, there were nearly 9,000 black elected officials and 39 members of the Congressional Black Caucus.

In my remarks, I noted that Martin Luther King Jr. was right when he said that when black Americans "win their struggle to become free, those who have held them down will themselves be free for the first time." After Selma, white and black southerners crossed the bridge to the New South, leaving hatred and isolation behind for new opportunities and prosperity and political influence: without Selma, Jimmy Carter and Bill Clinton would never have become President of the United States.

Now, as we crossed the bridge into the twenty-first century with the lowest unemployment and poverty rates and the highest home and business ownership rates among African-Americans ever recorded, I asked the audience to remember what was yet to be accomplished. As long as there were wide racial disparities in income, education, health, vulnerability to violence, and perceptions of fairness in the criminal justice system, as long as discrimination and hate crimes persisted, "we have another bridge to cross."

I loved that day in Selma. Once again, I was swept back across the years to my boyhood longing for and belief in an America without a racial divide. Once again, I returned to the emotional core of my political life in saying farewell to the people who had done so much to nourish it: "As long as Americans are willing to hold hands, we can walk with any wind, we can cross any bridge. Deep in my heart, I do believe, we shall overcome."

I spent most of the first half of the month campaigning for my gun safety measures: closing the gun show loophole, putting child trigger locks on guns, and requiring gun owners to have a photo-ID license showing that they had passed the Brady background check and had taken a gun safety course. America had been rocked by a series of tragic shooting deaths, one of them caused by a very young child firing a gun he had found in his apartment. The accidental gun death rate for children under fifteen in America was nine times higher than that of the twenty-five next largest economies combined.

Despite the crying need and rising public support for gun control, the NRA so far had kept anything from happening in Congress, though most gun manufacturers, to their credit, were now providing child trigger locks. On the gun show loophole, the NRA said, as it had in opposing the Brady bill, that it didn't object to instant background checks, but it didn't want anyone inconvenienced for the public's safety by having to endure a three-day waiting period. Already, 70 percent of the checks were completed in an hour, 90 percent in a day. A few took longer. If we didn't have a waiting period, people with bad records could buy their guns at closing time on Friday afternoon. The NRA was also adamantly against licensing gun owners, seeing it as the first step toward depriving them of the right to own weapons. It was a spurious argument; we had required driver's licenses for a long time, and no one had ever suggested banning automobile possession.

Still, I knew the NRA could scare a lot of people. I had grown up in the hunting culture in which its influence was greatest and had seen the devastating impact the NRA had had on the '94 congressional elections. But I had always felt most hunters and sports shooters were good citizens and would listen to a reasonable argument plainly stated. I knew I had to try, because I believed in what I was doing and because Al Gore had put himself squarely within the NRA's gunsights by endorsing the licensing idea even before I did.

On the twelfth, Wayne LaPierre, the executive vice president of the NRA, said that I needed a "certain level of violence" and was "willing to accept a certain level of killing" to further my political objectives, "and his vice president's, too." LaPierre's position was that we should prosecute gun crimes more severely and punish adults who recklessly allow children access to guns. The next day, in Cleveland, I answered him, saying that I agreed with his proposals for punishment but that I thought his position that no preventive measures were needed was nonsense. The NRA was even against banning cop-killer bullets. It was they who were willing to accept a certain level of violence and killing to keep their membership up and their ideology pure. I said I'd like to see LaPierre look into the eyes of the parents who had lost their children at Columbine, or in Springfield, Oregon, or Jonesboro, Arkansas, and say those things.

I didn't think I could beat the NRA in the House, but I was having a good time trying. I asked people how they would feel if the NRA's "no prevention, all punishment" strategy were applied to every aspect of our lives: getting rid of seat belts, air bags, and speed limits and adding five years to the sentences of reckless drivers who kill people; and getting rid of airport metal detectors and adding ten years to the sentence of anyone who blows up a plane.

On my previous trip to Cleveland, I had visited an elementary school where AmeriCorps volunteers were tutoring young children in reading. A six-year-old boy looked up at me and asked, "Are you really the President?" When I said that I was, he replied, "But you're not dead yet!" He knew only about George Washington and Abraham Lincoln. I was running out of time, but with a high-class fight like this one on my hands, I knew the boy was right. I wasn't dead yet.

On March 17, I announced a breakthrough agreement between Smith & Wesson, one of the largest gun manufacturers, and federal, state, and local governments. The company agreed to include locking devices with its guns, to develop a "smart gun" that could be fired only by the adult who owned it, to cut off gun dealers who sold a disproportionate number of guns used in crimes, to require its dealers not to sell at gun shows unless background checks were conducted, and to design new guns that did not accept large-capacity magazines. It was a brave thing for the company to do. I knew Smith & Wesson would be subject to withering attacks from the NRA and from its competitors.

The presidential nominating process was over by the second week of March, as John McCain and Bill Bradley withdrew after Al Gore and George W. Bush won big victories in the sixteen Super Tuesday primaries and caucuses. Bill Bradley had run a serious campaign, and in pressing Al early he had made him a better candidate, as Al scrapped his endorsement-laden approach for a grassroots effort in which he looked more like a relaxed but aggressive challenger. Bush had righted his campaign after losing in New Hampshire by winning in South Carolina, aided by a telephone campaign into conservative white households reminding them that Senator McCain had a "black baby." McCain had adopted a child from Bangladesh, one of the many reasons I admired him.

Before the primaries were over, an ad hoc veterans' group supporting Bush accused McCain of betraying his country in the five and a half years he was a POW in North Vietnam. In New York, the Bush people attacked McCain for opposing breast cancer research. Actually, he had voted against a defense bill with some breast cancer money in it to protest all the pork-barrel spending included in the bill; the senator had a sister with breast cancer and had always voted for the appropriations that contained well over 90 percent of the cancer research funds. Senator McCain didn't hit back hard at the Bush campaign or the right-wing extremists for smearing him until it was too late.

The developments on the international front in March were largely positive. Barak and Arafat agreed to restart their talks. On my last St. Patrick's Day as President, Seamus Heaney read his poetry, we all sang "Danny Boy," and it was clear that, although the government was still down in Northern Ireland, no one was prepared to let the peace process die. I spoke with King Fahd of Saudi Arabia about the possibility of OPEC increasing its production. A year earlier, the price of oil had dropped to $12 a barrel, too low to meet the basic needs of producing countries. Now it was jumping to between $31 and $34, too high to avoid adverse effects in the consuming nations. I wanted to see the price stabilize at between $20 and $22 a barrel and hoped OPEC could increase production enough to do that; otherwise, the United States could have significant economic problems.

On the eighteenth, I left for a week-long trip to India, Pakistan, and Bangladesh. I was going to India to lay the foundation for what I had hoped would be a positive long-term relationship. We had wasted too much time since the end of the Cold War, when India had aligned itself with the Soviet Union principally as a counterweight to China. Bangladesh was the poorest country in South Asia, but a large one with some innovative economic programs and a friendly attitude toward the United States. Unlike Pakistan and India, Bangladesh was a non-nuclear nation that had ratified the Comprehensive Test Ban Treaty, which was more than could be said for the United States. My stop in Pakistan was the most controversial because of the recent military coup there, but I decided I had to go for several reasons: to encourage an early return to civilian rule and a lessening of tensions over Kashmir; to urge General Musharraf not to execute the deposed prime minister, Nawaz Sharif, who was on trial for his life; and to press Musharraf to cooperate with us on bin Laden and al Qaeda.

The Secret Service was strongly opposed to my going to Pakistan or Bangladesh because the CIA had intelligence that indicated al Qaeda wanted to attack me on one of those stops, either on the ground or during takeoffs or landings. I felt I had to go because of the adverse consequences to American interests of going only to India and because I didn't want to give in to a terrorist threat. So we took sensible precautions and proceeded. I believe it was the only request the Secret Service ever made that I refused.

Hillary's mother, Dorothy, and Chelsea were going with me to India. We flew there first, where I left them in the good hands of our ambassador, my old friend Dick Celeste, the former Ohio governor, and his wife, Jacqueline. Then I took a reduced group on two small planes into Bangladesh, where I met with the prime minister, Sheikh Hasina. Later, I was forced to make another concession to security. I had been scheduled to visit the village of Joypura with my friend Muhammad Yunus to observe some of Grameen Bank's micro-credit projects. The Secret Service had determined that our party would be defenseless on the narrow roads or flying in a helicopter to the village, so we brought the villagers, including some schoolchildren, to the American embassy in Dacca, where they set up a classroom and some displays in the inner courtyard.

While I was in Bangladesh, thirty-five Sikhs were murdered in Kashmir by unknown killers intent on getting publicity tied to my visit. When I got back to Delhi, in my meeting with Prime Minister Vajpayee I expressed outrage and deep regret that terrorists had used my trip as an excuse to kill. I got on well with Vajpayee and hoped he would have an opportunity to reengage Pakistan before he left office. We didn't agree on the test ban treaty, but I already knew that, because Strobe Talbott had been working with Foreign Minister Jaswant Singh and others for months on nonproliferation issues. However, Vajpayee did join me in pledging to forgo future tests, and we agreed upon a set of positive principles that would govern our bilateral relationship, which had been cool for so long.

I also had a good visit with the leader of the opposition Congress Party, Sonia Gandhi. Her husband and mother-in-law, the grandson and daughter of Nehru, were both victims of political assassination. Sonia, an Italian by birth, had bravely remained in public life.

On the fourth day of my trip, I had the opportunity to address the Indian parliament. The Parliament Building is a large circular structure in which the several hundred parliamentarians sit tightly bunched at row after row of narrow tables. I spoke of my respect for India's democracy, diversity, and impressive strides in building a modern economy, frankly discussed our differences over nuclear issues, and urged them to reach a peaceful solution to the Kashmir problem. Somewhat to my surprise, I got a grand reception. They applauded by slapping the table, demonstrating that the Indians were as eager as I was for our long estrangement to end.

Chelsea, Dorothy, and I visited the Gandhi Memorial, where we were given copies of his autobiography and other writings, and we traveled to Agra, where the Taj Mahal, perhaps the world's most beautiful structure, was threatened by severe air pollution. India was working hard to establish a pollution-free zone around the Taj, and Foreign Minister Singh and Madeleine Albright signed an agreement for Indo-U.S. cooperation on energy and the environment, with the United States providing $45 million in USAID funds and $200 million from the Export-Import Bank to develop clean energy in India. The Taj was breathtaking, and I hated to leave.

On the twenty-third, I visited Naila, a small village near

Jaipur. After the village women in their brightly colored saris greeted me by surrounding me and showering me with thousands of flower petals, I met with the elected officials who were working together across caste and gender lines that had traditionally divided Indians, and discussed the importance of micro-credit loans with the women of the local dairy cooperative.

The next day I went to the thriving high-tech city of Hyderabad as the guest of the state's chief minister, Chandrababu Naidu, an articulate and very modern political leader. We visited the HITECH Center, where I was amazed to see the variety of companies that were growing like wildfire, and a hospital where, along with USAID administrator Brady Anderson, I announced a grant of $5 million to help it deal with AIDS and tuberculosis. At the time, AIDS was just beginning to be recognized in India, and there was still a lot of denial. I hoped our modest grant would help increase public awareness and willingness to act before the AIDS problem in India reached Africa's epidemic proportions. My last stop was in Mumbai (Bombay), where I met with business leaders, then had an interesting conversation with young leaders at a local restaurant. I left India feeling that our nations had begun a solid relationship, but wishing I had another week to absorb the country's beauty and mystery.

On the twenty-fifth, I flew to Islamabad, the leg of the trip the Secret Service thought was most dangerous. I took as few people as possible, leaving most of our party behind, to fly on the larger plane to our refueling stop in Oman. Sandy Berger joked that he was a little older than I, and since we had been through so much in almost thirty years of friendship he might as well go along to Pakistan for the ride. Again we went in on two small planes, one with U.S. Air Force markings, the other, in which I was riding, painted plain white. The Pakistanis had cleared an area a mile wide around the runway to make certain that we couldn't be hit by a shoulder-fired missile. Nevertheless, landing was a bracing experience.

Our motorcade traveled an empty highway to the Presidential Palace for a meeting with General Musharraf and his cabinet and a televised address to the people of Pakistan. In the speech, I noted our long friendship through the Cold War and asked the Pakistani people to turn away from terror and nuclear weapons toward a dialogue with India on Kashmir, to embrace the test ban treaty, and to invest in education, health, and development rather than arms. I said I had come as a friend of Pakistan and the Muslim world who had stood against the slaughter of Muslims in Bosnia and Kosovo, spoken to the Palestinian National Council in Gaza, marched with the mourners at the funerals of King Hussein and King Hassan, and celebrated the end of Ramadan at the White House with American Muslims. The point I tried to make is that our world was not divided by religious differences, but between those who chose to live with the pain of the past and those who chose the promise of the future.

In my meetings with Musharraf, I saw why he had emerged from the complex, often violent culture of Pakistani politics. He was clearly intelligent, strong, and sophisticated. If he chose to pursue a peaceful, progressive path, I thought he had a fair chance to succeed, but I told him I thought terrorism would eventually destroy Pakistan from within if he didn't move against it.

Musharraf said he didn't believe Sharif would be executed, but he was noncommittal on the other issues. I knew he was still trying to solidify his position and was in a tough spot. Sharif subsequently was released into exile in Jedda, Saudi Arabia. When Musharraf began serious cooperation with the United States in the war against terror after September 11, 2001, it remained a risky course for him. In 2003, he survived two assassination attempts within days of each other.

On the way home, after the stop in Oman to see Sultan Qaboos and get our delegation back on Air Force One, I flew to Geneva to meet with President Assad. Our team had been working to get Barak to make a specific proposal on Syria for me to present. I knew it wouldn't be a final offer, and the Syrians would know it, too, but I thought that if Israel finally responded with the same flexibility the Syrians had shown at Shepherdstown, we might still be able to make a deal. It was not to be.

When I met Assad, he was friendly as I gave him a blue tie with a red-line profile of a lion, the English meaning of his name. It was a small meeting: Assad was joined by Foreign Minister Shara and Butheina Shaban; Madeleine Albright and Dennis Ross accompanied me, with the National Security Council's Rob Malley serving as notetaker. After some pleasant small talk, I asked Dennis to spread out the maps I had studied carefully in preparing for our talks. Compared with his stated position at Shepherdstown, Barak was now willing to accept less land around the lake, though he still wanted a lot, 400 meters (1,312 feet); fewer people at the listening station; and a quicker withdrawal period. Assad didn't want me even to finish the presentation. He became agitated and, contradicting the Syrian position at Shepherdstown, said that he would never cede any of the land, that he wanted to be able to sit on the shore of the lake and put his feet in the water. We tried for two hours to get some traction with the Syrians, all to no avail. The Israeli rebuff in Shepherdstown and the leak of the working document in the Israeli press had embarrassed Assad and destroyed his fragile trust. And his health had deteriorated even more than I knew. Barak had made a respectable offer. If it had come at Shepherdstown, an agreement might have emerged. Now Assad's first priority was his son's succession, and he had obviously decided that a new round of negotiations, no matter how it came out, could put that at risk. In less than four years, I had seen the prospects of peace between Israel and Syria dashed three times: by terror in Israel and Peres's defeat in 1996, by the Israeli rebuff of Syrian overtures at Shepherdstown, and by Assad's preoccupation with his own mortality. After we parted in Geneva, I never saw Assad again.

That same day Vladimir Putin was elected president of Russia in the first round, with 52.5 percent of the vote. I called to congratulate him and hung up the phone thinking he was tough enough to hold Russia together and hoping he was wise enough to find an honorable way out of the

Chechnya problem and committed enough to democracy to preserve it. He was soon off to a strong start, as the Duma ratified both START II and the Comprehensive Nuclear Test Ban Treaty. Now even the Russian Duma was more progressive on arms control than the U.S. Senate.

In April, I continued to travel the country pushing my education, gun safety, and technology access issues from the State of the Union address; established another national monument, Grand Sequoia, in California; vetoed the bill to put all America's low-level nuclear waste in Nevada because I didn't think all the legitimate questions had been answered; signed the bill ending the earnings limitations for retirees who were collecting Social Security; visited the people of the Navajo Nation in Shiprock in northern New Mexico to highlight our efforts to use the Internet to bring educational, health, and economic opportunities to remote communities; and dedicated the simple but powerful memorial to the victims of the Oklahoma City bombing, 168 empty chairs in rows on a small knoll flanked by two large entryways and overlooking a large reflecting pool.

April also brought the final act in the long saga of little Elián González. Several months earlier his mother had fled Cuba with him for the United States in a rickety boat. The boat capsized and she drowned after putting Elián in an inner tube to save his life. The boy was taken to Miami and put in the temporary custody of a great-uncle, who was willing to keep him. His father in Cuba wanted him back. The Cuban-American community made Elián's case a crusade, saying that his mother had died trying to bring her son to freedom and it would be wrong to send him back to Castro's dictatorship.

The governing law seemed clear. The Immigration and Naturalization Service was supposed to determine whether the boy's father was a fit parent; if he was, Elián had to be returned to him. An INS team went to Cuba and discovered that though Elián's parents were divorced, they had maintained a good relationship and had shared child-rearing duties. In fact, Elián had spent about half his time with his father, who lived closer to the boy's school. The INS found that Juan Miguel González was a fit parent.

Advocates for the American relatives took the case to court in an attempt to question the validity of the process in Cuba, thinking it might have been compromised by the presence of Castro's people at the hearing. Some sought to apply the normal state-law standard in child custody cases: what is in the best interest of the child? The Congress got in on the act, with various bills being proposed to keep Elián in the United States. Meanwhile, the Cuban-American community was whipped into a frenzy by permanent demonstrations outside the house of Elián's relatives and regular TV interviews with one of them, a highly emotional young woman.

Janet Reno, who had served as prosecuting attorney in Miami and had been a popular figure among Cuban-Americans, enraged them by stating that federal law should control the situation and Elián should be returned to his father. It wasn't easy for Janet. She told me that one of her former secretaries would hardly speak to her; the woman's husband had been jailed for fifteen years by Castro, and she had waited all that time for him to be released and reunited with her. Many Cuban-Americans and other immigrants believed the boy would be better off staying here.

I backed Reno, believing that the fact that Elián's father loved him and had been a good parent should count for more than the poverty or the closed and repressive politics of Cuba. Moreover, the United States had frequently tried to get children returned to our country who had been taken away, usually by parents who had lost child custody cases here. If we kept Elián, our arguments for the return of those children to their American parents would be weakened.

Eventually, the case became an election issue. Al Gore publicly disagreed with us, saying that he had problems with the INS process and that even if Elián's father was a fit parent, the boy might still be better off in America. It was a defensible position on the merits, and understandable, given the importance of Florida in the election. I had worked for eight years to strengthen our position in the state and among Cuban-Americans; at least in that community, the Elián case had wiped out most of our gains. Hillary saw the case as a child advocate and a parent: she backed our decision to reunite the boy and his father.

Early in the month Juan Miguel González came to America hoping to take custody of his son, in accordance with a federal court order. A couple of weeks later, after Janet Reno had tried for several days to secure the voluntary surrender of the boy, a group of four leading citizens—the president of the University of Miami, a highly regarded lawyer, and two respected Cuban-Americans—suggested that the Miami family hand over custody to the father in a secluded place where they could all be together for a few days to ease the transition. On Good Friday evening, I talked to Reno at midnight and they were still negotiating, but she was running out of patience. At two o'clock Saturday morning, John Podesta called to say the talks were still going on. At quarter to five, Podesta called again and said the Miami family was now refusing even to recognize the father's custody rights. Thirty minutes later, at five-fifteen, I got another call from John saying it was over. Reno had authorized a predawn raid on the great-uncle's house by federal officials. It lasted three minutes, no one was hurt, and Elián was returned to his father. A small boy had become a pawn in the never-ending struggle against Castro.

Photographs of an obviously happy Elián with his father were published, and sentiment shifted markedly in favor of the reunification. I was confident we had followed the only course open to us, but I was still concerned that it could cost Al Gore Florida in November. Juan Miguel and Elián González remained in the United States a few more weeks, until the Supreme Court finally upheld the lower court's custody order. Mr. González could have stayed in the United States, but he wanted to take his son home to Cuba.

In May, I toured schools in Kentucky, Iowa, Minnesota, and Ohio to push our education package; hosted a state visit for Thabo Mbeki, who had just been elected president of South Africa; and promoted the China trade bill, which was necessary for China's admission into the WTO. Presidents Ford and Carter, along with James Baker and Henry Kissinger, came to the White House to promote it. This turned out to be a very difficult legislative fight—an especially tough vote for Democrats who depended on labor support—and I brought groups of a dozen or so members down to the residence for several weeks in an intensive effort to explain the importance of integrating China into the global economy.

On May 17, I gave my last service academy speech to the U.S. Coast Guard Academy in New London, Connecticut. In eight years I had now spoken to each of the service academies twice. Every class filled me with pride in the quality of young men and women who wanted to serve our country in uniform. I was also proud of the young people who came to our service academies from all over the world. This class included graduates from our Cold War adversaries Russia and Bulgaria.

I spoke to the new officers about the fateful struggle in which they would be engaged between the forces of integration and harmony and those of disintegration and chaos, a struggle in which globalization and information technology had magnified both the creative and destructive potential of humankind. I discussed the attacks that Osama bin Laden and al Qaeda had planned for the millennium, which were thwarted through hard work and domestic and international cooperation. To build on that work, I said that I was allocating another $300 million to our anti-terrorism budget; on top of the $9 billion request I had already sent to Congress, it amounted to an increase of more than 40 percent in three years.

After discussing other security challenges, I made the best case I could for an activist foreign policy, cooperating with others in a world in which no nation was protected any longer by geography or conventional military strength.

In late May, just before I left on a trip to Portugal, Germany, Russia, and Ukraine, I went to Assateague Island, Maryland, to announce a new initiative to protect our coral

reefs and other marine treasures. We had already quadrupled funding for national marine sanctuaries. I signed an
executive order to create a national protective network for
our coasts, reefs, underwater forests, and other important
structures, and I said we were going to permanently protect
the coral reefs of the northwest Hawaiian Islands, more
than 60 percent of America's total, stretching over 1,200
miles. It was the biggest conservation step I had taken since
preserving 43 million roadless acres in our national forests,
and a needed one, since ocean pollution was threatening
reefs the world over, including the Great Barrier Reef in
Australia.

I went to Portugal for the annual meeting between the
United States and the European Union. Portuguese prime
minister Antonio Guterres was serving as president of the
European Council. He was a bright young progressive who
was a member of our Third Way group, as was EU president
Romano Prodi. We saw eye to eye on most things, and I
enjoyed the meeting, as well as my first visit to Portugal. It
was beautiful and warm, with friendly people and a fascinating history.

On June 2, I went with Gerhard Schroeder to the ancient
city of Aachen to receive the Charlemagne Prize. In a sunny
outdoor ceremony in a public space near the medieval city
hall and the old cathedral holding Charlemagne's remains, I
thanked Chancellor Schroeder and the German people for
giving me an honor shared by Václav Havel and King Juan
Carlos and rarely awarded to an American. I had done
everything I could to help Europe become united, democratic, and secure, to expand and strengthen the transatlantic alliance, to reach out to Russia, and to end ethnic
cleansing in the Balkans. It was gratifying to be recognized
for it.

The next day Gerhard Schroeder hosted another of our
Third Way conferences in Berlin. This time Gerhard, Jean
Chrétien, and I were joined by three Latin Americans—Fernando Henrique Cardoso of Brazil, President Ricardo Lagos
of Chile, and President Fernando de la Rúa of Argentina—
as we outlined the kinds of progressive partnerships leaders

of developed and developing countries should form. Tony Blair wasn't there because he and Cherie, already the parents of three children, had recently brought a fourth into the world, a boy they named Leo.

I flew into Moscow for my first meeting with Vladimir Putin since his election. We agreed to destroy another thirty-four metric tons each of weapons-grade plutonium, but could not reach accord on amending the ABM Treaty to enable the United States to deploy a national missile defense system. I wasn't too concerned about that; Putin probably wanted to wait to see how the U.S. election turned out. The Republicans had been enamored of missile defense since the Reagan era, and many of them wouldn't hesitate to abrogate the ABM Treaty in order to deploy it. Al Gore basically agreed with me. Putin didn't want to have to deal with this twice.

At the time, we didn't have a missile defense system reliable enough to deploy. As Hugh Shelton had said, shooting down an incoming missile was like "a bullet hitting a bullet." If we ever did develop a workable system, I thought that we should offer the technology to other nations and that, in so doing, we could probably persuade the Russians to amend the ABM Treaty. I wasn't at all sure that, even if it worked, erecting a missile defense system was the best way to spend the staggering sums it would cost. We were far more likely to face attacks from terrorists having smaller nuclear, chemical, or biological weapons.

Moreover, putting up a missile defense could actually expose the world to greater danger. For the foreseeable future, the system would knock out only a few missiles even if it worked. If the United States and Russia were to erect such a system, China would probably build more missiles to overcome it in order to maintain its deterrent capability. Then India would follow suit, as would Pakistan. The Europeans were convinced it was a terrible idea. But we didn't have to deal with all those issues until we had a system that worked, and so far, we didn't.

Before I left Moscow, Putin hosted a small dinner in the Kremlin with a jazz concert afterward, featuring Russian musicians from teenagers to an octogenarian. The finale began on a dark stage, a haunting series of tunes by my favorite living tenor saxophonist, Igor Butman. John Podesta, who loved jazz as much as I did, agreed with me that we had never heard a finer live performance.

I went to Ukraine to announce America's financial support for President Leonid Kuchma's decision to close the final reactor at the Chernobyl nuclear power plant by December 15. It had taken a long time, and I was glad to know that at least the problem would be resolved before I left. My last stop was an outdoor speech to a huge crowd of Ukrainians whom I urged to stay on the course of freedom and economic reform. Kiev was beautiful in the late spring sunshine, and I hoped its people could keep up the high spirits I had observed in the crowd. They still had many hurdles to clear.

On June 8, I flew to Tokyo for the day to pay my respects at the memorial service of my friend Prime Minister Keizo Obuchi, who had died of a stroke a few days before. The service was held in the indoor section of a soccer stadium, with a few thousand seats on the floor divided by an aisle in the middle, and several hundred more people sitting in balconies above. A stage had been constructed with a large ramp up the front and smaller ones on the side. Behind the stage was a wall covered in flowers twenty-five or thirty feet high. The flowers were beautifully arranged to show the Japanese rising sun against a pale blue sky. At the very top there was an indented space where at the beginning of the ceremony a military aide solemnly placed a box containing Obuchi's ashes. After his colleagues and friends had paid tribute to him, several young Japanese women appeared holding trays full of white flowers. Beginning with Obuchi's wife and children, members of the imperial family, and leaders of the government, the mourners all walked up the center ramp, bowed in respect before his ashes, and placed our flowers on a waist-high strip of wood that ran the entire length of the flowered wall.

After I bowed to my friend and placed my flower, I returned to the U.S. Embassy to see our ambassador, former

House Speaker Tom Foley. I turned on the television to see the ceremony still in progress. Thousands of Obuchi's fellow citizens were creating a cloud of sacred flowers against the rising sun. It was one of the most moving tributes I had ever witnessed. I stopped briefly at the reception to pay my respects to Mrs. Obuchi and Keizo's children, one of whom was in politics herself. Mrs. Obuchi thanked me for coming and gave me a beautiful enamel letter box that had belonged to her husband. Obuchi had been a friend to me, and to America. Our alliance was important, and he had valued it even as a young man. I wished he had had longer to serve.

Several days later, while I was participating in the Carleton College commencement exercises in Minnesota, an aide passed me a note informing me that President Hafez al-Assad had just died in Damascus, only ten weeks after our last meeting in Geneva. Although we had our disagreements, he had always been straightforward with me, and I had believed him when he said he had made a strategic choice for peace. Circumstances, miscommunication, and psychological barriers had kept it from happening, but at least we now knew what it would take for Israel and Syria to get there once both sides were ready.

As spring turned to summer, I hosted our largest state dinner ever, as more than four hundred people gathered under a tent on the South Lawn to honor King Mohammed VI of Morocco, one of whose ancestors was the first sovereign to recognize the United States shortly after our original thirteen states joined together.

The next day I corrected an old injustice, awarding the Congressional Medal of Honor to twenty-two Japanese-Americans who had volunteered to serve in Europe during World War II after their families were interned in camps. One of them was my friend and ally Senator Daniel Inouye of Hawaii, who had lost an arm and very nearly his life in the war. A week later I nominated the first Asian-American to the cabinet: former congressman Norm Mineta of California agreed to serve for the remainder of my term as commerce secretary, replacing Bill Daley, who was leaving to become the chairman of Al Gore's campaign.

In the last week of the month, I held a gathering in the East Room of the White House, where almost two hundred years earlier Thomas Jefferson had spread out the path-breaking map of the western United States that his aide Meriwether Lewis had made on his courageous expedition from the Mississippi River to the Pacific Ocean in 1803. The crowd of scientists and diplomats had gathered to celebrate a twenty-first–century map: more than a thousand researchers in the United States, the UK, Germany, France, Japan, and China had decoded the human genome, identifying nearly all of the three billion sequences of our genetic code. After battling each other for years, Francis Collins, head of the government-funded international human genome project, and Celera president Craig Venter had agreed to publish their genetic data together later in the year. Craig was an old friend, and I had done my best to bring them together. Tony Blair joined us on a satellite hookup, giving me a chance to joke that his infant son's life expectancy had just gone up by about twenty-five years.

As the month drew to a close, I announced that our budget surplus would exceed $200 billion, with a ten-year projected surplus of over $4 trillion. Once again, I recommended that we lock away the Social Security surplus, about $2.3 trillion, and that we save about $550 billion for Medicare. It was beginning to look as if we could handle the baby boomers' retirement after all.

I also did a number of political events to support Democrats in Arizona and California and to help Terry McAuliffe raise the rest of the money we needed to put on our convention in Los Angeles in August. We were working closely with him and the Gore campaign through my political director Minyon Moore.

Most polls had Gore trailing Bush, and at my press conference on June 28, I was asked by an NBC News reporter whether Al was being held accountable for the "scandals" of the administration. I said there was no evidence that he was being punished for my mistakes; that the only wrongdoing he had been accused of involved campaign fund-raising, and he wasn't guilty; and that the other so-called scandals were bogus: "The word 'scandal' has been thrown around here like a clanging teapot for seven years." I also said I knew three things about Al Gore: he had had a more positive impact on our country as vice president than any of his predecessors; he had the right positions on the issues and would keep the prosperity going; and he understood the future, both its possibilities and its dangers. I believed if all the voters understood that, Al would win.

In the first week of July, I announced that our economy had now produced twenty-two million jobs since I took office, and went out to the Old Soldiers' Home a few miles north of the White House to protect the old cottage Abraham Lincoln and his family had used for a summer home when the Potomac generated hordes of mosquitoes and there was no air conditioning. Several other Presidents had used it, too. It was one of Hillary's Save America's Treasures projects, and we wanted to know the old place would be cared for when we left the White House.

On July 11, I opened a summit with Ehud Barak and Yasser Arafat at Camp David in an attempt to resolve the remaining obstacles to peace, or at least to narrow their differences so that we could finish before I left office, a result both leaders said they wanted.

They came to the summit with very different attitudes. Barak had pushed hard for the summit because the piecemeal approach of the 1993 agreement and the Wye River accord didn't work for him. The 180,000 Israeli settlers in the West Bank and Gaza were a formidable force. Every Israeli concession that failed to bring an end to terror and a formal Palestinian recognition that the conflict was over was a death by a thousand cuts. Barak had just survived a no-confidence vote in the Knesset by only two votes. He was also eager for a deal before September, when Arafat had threatened to unilaterally declare a state. Barak believed that if he could present a comprehensive peace plan to Israeli citizens, they would vote for it as long as Israel's fundamental interests were achieved: security, the protection of its religious and cultural sites on the Temple Mount, an end to the Palestinian claim to an unlimited right of return to Israel, and a declaration that the conflict was over.

Arafat, on the other hand, didn't want to come to Camp David, at least not yet. He had felt abandoned by the Israelis when they turned to the Syrian track, and was angry that Barak had not kept previous commitments to turn over more of the West Bank, including villages near Jerusalem. In Arafat's eyes, Barak's unilateral withdrawal from Lebanon and his offer to withdraw from the Golan had weakened him. While Arafat had patiently continued the peace process, Lebanon and Syria had benefited by taking a hard line. Arafat also said he needed two more weeks to develop his proposals. He wanted as close to a hundred percent of the West Bank and Gaza as he could get; complete sovereignty over the Temple Mount and East Jerusalem, except for the Jewish neighborhoods there; and a solution to the refugee problem that did not require him to give up the principle of the right of return.

As usual, each leader saw his own position more clearly than he saw the other side. There was not a high probability of success for the summit. I called it because I believed that the collapse of the peace process would be a near certainty if I didn't.

On the first day, I tried to get Arafat past his grievances to focus on the work ahead and to get Barak to agree on how to move through the issues, especially the most contentious ones: territory, settlements, refugees, security, and Jerusalem. As he had at Shepherdstown, Barak wanted to slow-walk things for a couple of days. It didn't matter that much this time—Arafat hadn't come with a set of negotiating points; this was all strange territory to him. In previous negotiations he would just hold out for the best offer he could get from Israel on issues such as land, an airport, connecting roads, and prisoner releases, then pledge his best efforts on the security front. Now if we were going to get this done, Arafat had some compromising of his own to do on concrete matters: He couldn't get a hundred percent of the West Bank or an unlimited right of return to a much smaller·Israel. He also would have to meet some of Israel's security concerns about potential enemies east of the Jordan River.

I spent the first couple of days trying to get Arafat and Barak in the right frame of mind, while Madeleine, Sandy, Dennis, Gemal Helal, John Podesta, and the rest of our team began working with their Israeli and Palestinian counterparts. I was immensely impressed with the quality of both delegations. They were all patriotic, intelligent, and hardworking, and they genuinely seemed to want an agreement. Most of them had known each other and their counterparts on the other side for years, and the chemistry between the two groups was quite good.

We tried to create a comfortable, informal atmosphere for the Israelis and Palestinians. In addition to our regular Middle East team, I asked Hillary's aide, Huma Abedin, to join us. An Arabic-speaking Muslim American raised in Saudi Arabia, Huma was an impressive young woman who understood the Middle East and was especially effective at making the Israeli and Palestinian delegates feel at home and at ease. Capricia Marshall, the White House social secretary, arranged for the White House butlers, chefs, and valets to come help the Camp David staff in making sure the meals were enjoyable. And Chelsea stayed with me the whole time, entertaining our guests and helping me deal with the endless hours of tension.

Most nights we all had dinner together at Laurel, the large gathering cabin at Camp David, which had dining facilities, a large den, a meeting room, and my private office. Breakfast and lunch were more informal, and the Israelis and Palestinians could often be seen talking among themselves in small groups. Sometimes it was business; often they were telling stories and jokes or relating family histories. Abu Ala and Abu Mazen were Arafat's oldest and longest-serving advisors. Abu Ala took a lot of kidding from the Israelis and the Americans for his family. His father was so prolific that the sixty-three-year-old Palestinian had an eight-year-old brother; the boy was younger than some of Abu's own grandchildren. Eli Rubinstein, the Israeli attorney general, knew more jokes than I did and told them better.

While the chemistry between the teams was good, the same could not be said of Arafat and Barak. I had put them in cabins close to mine and visited at length with both of them every day, but they didn't visit each other. Arafat continued to feel aggrieved. Barak didn't want to meet alone with Arafat; he was afraid that they would fall into the old patterns where Barak did all the giving and Arafat made no response in kind. Ehud spent most of the day in his cabin, much of it on the phone to Israel trying to hold his coalition together.

By this time, I had gotten to understand Barak better. He was brilliant and brave, and he was willing to go a long way on Jerusalem and on territory. But he had a hard time listening to people who didn't see things the way he did, and his way of doing things was diametrically opposed to honored customs among the Arabs with whom I'd dealt. Barak wanted others to wait until he decided the time was right; then, when he made his best offer, he expected it to be accepted as self-evidently a good deal. His negotiating partners wanted trust-building courtesies and conversations and lots of bargaining.

The culture clash made my team's job harder. They came up with a variety of strategies to break the impasse, and some progress was made after the delegations broke up into different groups to work on specific issues, but neither side had permission to go beyond a certain point.

On the sixth day, Shlomo Ben-Ami and Gilead Sher, with Barak's blessing, went well beyond previously stated Israeli positions in the hope of getting some movement from Saeb Erekat and Mohammed Dahlan, younger members of Arafat's team who we all believed wanted a deal. When the Palestinians didn't offer Barak anything in return for his moves on Jerusalem and territory, I went to see Arafat, taking Helal with me to interpret and Malley to take notes. It was a tough meeting, and it ended with my telling Arafat that I would end the talks and say he had refused to negotiate unless he gave me something to take back to Barak, who was off the wall because Ben-Ami and Sher had gone as far as they had and gotten nothing in return. After a while Arafat gave me a letter that seemed to say that if he was satisfied with the Jerusalem question, I could make the final call on how much land the Israelis kept for settlements and what constituted a fair land swap. I took the letter to Barak and spent a lot of time talking to him, often alone or with the NSC notetaker for Israel, Bruce Reidel. Eventually Barak agreed that Arafat's letter might mean something.

On the seventh day, July 17, we almost lost Barak. He was eating and working when he choked on a peanut and stopped breathing for about forty seconds, until Gid Gernstein, the youngest member of his delegation, administered the Heimlich maneuver. Barak was a tough customer; when he got his breath back, he went back to work as if nothing had happened. For the rest of us, nothing *was* happening. Barak had kept his entire delegation working with him all day long and into the night.

In any process like this, there are always periods of downtime, when some people are working and others aren't. You have to do something to break the tension. I spent several hours of my downtime playing cards with Joe Lockhart, John Podesta, and Doug Band. Doug had worked at the White House for five years while putting himself through graduate and law school at night, and in the spring had become my last presidential aide. He had an interest in the Middle East and was very helpful to me. Chelsea played cards, too. She made the highest Oh Hell! score in the entire two weeks at Camp David.

It was after midnight when Barak finally came to me with proposals. They were less than what Ben-Ami and Sher had already presented to the Palestinians. Ehud wanted me to present them to Arafat as U.S. proposals. I understood his frustration with Arafat, but I couldn't do that; it would have been a disaster, and I told him so. We talked until two-thirty. At three-fifteen he came back, and we talked another hour alone on the back porch of my cabin. Essentially he gave me the go-ahead to see if I could work out a deal on Jerusalem and the West Bank that he could live with and that was consistent with what Ben-Ami and Sher had discussed with their counterparts. That was worth staying up for.

On the morning of the eighth day, I was feeling both anxious and hopeful, anxious because I had been scheduled to leave for the G-8 summit in Okinawa, which I had to attend for a variety of reasons, and hopeful because Barak's sense of timing and his enormous courage had kicked in. I delayed my departure for Okinawa by a day and met with Arafat. I told him that I thought he could get 91 percent of the West Bank, plus at least a symbolic swap of land near Gaza and the West Bank; a capital in East Jerusalem; sovereignty over the Muslim and Christian quarters of the Old City and the outer neighborhoods of East Jerusalem; planning, zoning, and law-enforcement authority over the rest of the eastern part of the city; and custodianship but not sovereignty over the Temple Mount, which was known as Haram al-Sharif to the Arabs. Arafat balked at not having sovereignty over all of East Jerusalem, including the Temple Mount. He turned the offer down. I asked him to think about it. While he fretted and Barak fumed, I called Arab leaders for support. Most wouldn't say much, for fear of undercutting Arafat.

On the ninth day, I gave Arafat my best shot again. Again he said no. Israel had gone much further than he had, and he wouldn't even embrace their moves as the basis for future negotiations. Again I called several Arab leaders for help. King Abdullah and President Ben Ali of Tunisia tried to encourage Arafat. They told me he was afraid to make compromises. It looked as if the talks were dead, and on disastrous terms. Both sides clearly wanted a deal, so I asked them to stay and work while I was in Okinawa. They agreed, though after I left, the Palestinians still refused to negotiate on the basis of the ideas I had advanced, saying they had already rejected them. Then the Israelis balked. That was in part my fault. Apparently I had not been as clear with Arafat as I thought I had been about what the terms of staying on should be.

I had left Madeleine and the rest of our team with a real

mess. She took Arafat to her farm and Barak to the famous Civil War battlefield at nearby Gettysburg. It lightened them up, but nothing happened between them. Shlomo Ben-Ami and Amnon Shahak, himself a former general, had good talks with Mohammed Dahlan and Mohamed Rashid, but they were the most forward leaning of their respective groups; even if they agreed on everything, they probably couldn't get their leaders on board.

I returned on the thirteenth day of discussions, and we worked all night again, mostly on security issues. Then we did it again on the fourteenth day, going well past 3 a.m. before giving up when effective control over the Temple Mount and all East Jerusalem was not enough for Arafat without the word "sovereignty." In a last-ditch effort I offered to try to sell Barak on full sovereignty for East Jerusalem's outer neighborhoods, limited sovereignty over the inner ones, and "custodial" sovereignty over the Haram. Again Arafat said no. I shut down the talks. It was frustrating and profoundly sad. There was little difference between the two sides on how the affairs of Jerusalem would actually be handled; it was all about who got to claim sovereignty.

I issued a statement saying I had concluded that the parties could not reach agreement at this time given the historical, religious, political, and emotional dimensions of the conflict. To give Barak some cover back home and indicate what had occurred, I said that while Arafat had made clear that he wanted to stay on the path of peace, Barak had shown "particular courage, vision, and an understanding of the historical importance of this moment."

I said that the two delegations had shown each other a genuine respect and understanding unique in my eight years of peacemaking around the world, and for the first time had openly discussed the most sensitive matters in dispute. We now had a better idea of each side's bottom line and I still believed we had a chance to reach an agreement before the year was out.

Arafat had wanted to continue the negotiations, and on more than one occasion had acknowledged that he was unlikely to get a future Israeli government or American team so committed to peace. It was hard to know why he had moved so little. Perhaps his team really hadn't worked through the hard compromises; perhaps they wanted one session to see how much they could squeeze out of Israel before showing their hand. For whatever reasons, they had left Barak exposed in a precarious political situation. It was not for nothing that he was the most decorated soldier in the history of Israel. For all his brusque bullheadedness, he had taken great risks to win a more secure future for Israel. In my remarks to the press, I assured the people of Israel that he had done nothing to compromise their security and said they should be very proud of him.

Arafat was famous for waiting until the very last minute to make a decision, or "five minutes to midnight" as we used to say. I had only six months to go as President. I certainly hoped Arafat's watch kept good time.

TWENTY-SIX

WHILE THE CAMP DAVID talks were going on, positive things happened elsewhere. Charlene Barshefsky completed a sweeping trade agreement with Vietnam, and the House adopted an amendment by my longtime supporter Maxine Waters that funded a down payment on our share of the Millennium Debt Relief effort. By this time debt relief had an amazing array of supporters, led by Bono.

By then Bono had become a fixture in Washington political life. He turned out to be a first-class politician, partly through the element of surprise. Larry Summers, who knew everything about economics but little about popular culture, came into the Oval Office one day and remarked that he'd just had a meeting on debt relief with "some guy named Bono—just one name—dressed in jeans, a T-shirt, and big sunglasses. He came to see me about debt relief, and he knows what he's talking about."

The trip to Okinawa was a big success, as the G-8 put some teeth into our commitment to have all the world's children in primary school by 2015. I led off with a $300 million program to provide one good meal a day to nine million children, provided they came to school to get the meal. The initiative had been brought to me by our ambassador to the UN food programs in Rome, George McGovern; McGovern's old partner in pioneering food stamps, Bob Dole; and Congressman Jim McGovern of Massachusetts. I also visited the U.S. forces in Okinawa, thanked Prime Minister Yoshiro Mori for letting them be stationed there, and pledged to reduce the tensions our presence had caused. It was my last G-8 summit, and I was sorry to rush through it to get back to Camp David. The other leaders had been very supportive of my initiatives over eight years, and we had accomplished a lot together.

Chelsea traveled to Okinawa with me. One of the best

things about the year for both Hillary and me was that Chelsea was home for the last half of it. She had amassed far more credits in her first three years at Stanford than she needed to graduate so that she could spend the last six months in the White House with us. Now she would be dividing her time between campaigning for her mother and helping me with events in the White House and going with me on foreign trips. She did a great job on both counts, and her presence made life much better for her parents.

At the end of the month I resumed my battle with the Republicans over tax cuts. They still wanted to spend a decade's worth of projected surpluses on them, claiming that the money belonged to the taxpayers and we should give it back to them. It was a persuasive argument except for one thing: the surpluses were projected and the tax cuts would take effect whether the surpluses materialized or not. I attempted to illustrate the point by asking people to imagine that they had gotten one of those heavily advertised letters from well-known TV personality Ed McMahon that started with, "You may have already won $10 million." I said that the people who would spend $10 million upon receiving that letter should support the Republican plan; everyone else should "stick with us and keep the prosperity going."

August was a busy month. It began with the nomination of George W. Bush and Dick Cheney in Philadelphia. Hillary and I went to Martha's Vineyard for a couple of fund-raisers for her; then I flew to Idaho to visit firefighters who were fighting a large and dangerous forest fire. On the ninth, I awarded the Medal of Freedom to fifteen Americans, including the late senator John Chafee, Senator Pat Moynihan, Children's Defense Fund founder Marian Wright Edelman, AIDS activist Dr. Mathilde Krim, Jesse Jackson, civil rights lawyer Judge Cruz Reynoso, and General Wes Clark, who had ended his brilliant military career by commanding our arduous campaign against Milosevic and his ethnic cleansing in Kosovo.

Amid a blizzard of political events, I did one completely nonpolitical one: I went to my friend Bill Hybels's Willow

Creek Community Church in South Barrington, Illinois, near Chicago, for a conversation before several hundred people at Bill's ministers' leadership conference. We talked about when I decided to go into politics, where my family went to church and what it meant to me, why so many people still believed I had never apologized for my misconduct, how I used polls, what the most important elements of leadership were, and how I wanted to be remembered. Hybels had an uncanny way of stripping things down to basics and getting me to discuss things I normally would not talk about. I enjoyed taking a few hours away from politics and work to think about the inner life that politics often crowds out.

On August 14, opening night of the Democratic convention, Hillary gave a moving expression of thanks to the Democrats for their support and a mighty declaration of what was at stake in this year's election. Then, after my third convention film produced by Harry and Linda Thomason, which outlined the accomplishments of our eight years, I was brought onstage to thunderous applause and inspirational music. When the noise died down, I said that the election was about one simple question: "Are we going to keep this progress and prosperity going?"

I asked the Democrats to make sure we applied President Reagan's 1980 standard for whether a party should continue in office: "Are we better off today than we were eight years ago?" The answer proved that Harry Truman was right when he said, "If you want to live like a Republican, you better vote for the Democrats." The crowd roared. We were better off, and not just economically. Jobs were up, but so were adoptions. The debt was down, but so was teen pregnancy. We were becoming both more diverse and more united. We had built and crossed our bridge to the twenty-first century, "and we're not going back."

I made the case for a Democratic Congress, saying that what we did with our prosperity was just as sure a test of America's character, values, and judgment as how we had dealt with adversity in the past. If we had a Democratic Congress, America would already have the Patients' Bill of Rights, a minimum wage increase, stronger equal-pay laws for women, and middle-class tax cuts for college tuition and long-term care.

I praised Hillary for thirty years of public service and especially her work in the White House for children and families, and said that just as she had always been there for our family, she would always be there for the families of New York and America.

Then I argued for Al Gore, emphasizing his strong convictions, good ideas, understanding of the future, and fundamental decency. I thanked Tipper for her mental-health advocacy and applauded Al's selection of Joe Lieberman, and spoke of our thirty-year friendship and Joe's work for civil rights in the South in the sixties. As the first Jewish-American ever to be on a major party's national ticket, Joe provided clear evidence of Al Gore's commitment to building One America.

I ended the speech with personal thanks and a personal plea:

> My friends, fifty-four years ago this week I was born in a summer storm to a young widow in a small southern town. America gave me the chance to live my dreams. And I have tried as hard as I knew how to give you a better chance to live yours. Now, my hair is a little grayer, my wrinkles are a little deeper, but with the same optimism and hope I brought to the work I loved so eight years ago, I want you to know my heart is filled with gratitude.
>
> My fellow Americans, the future of our country is now in your hands. You must think hard, feel deeply, and choose wisely. And remember . . . keep putting people first. Keep building those bridges. And don't stop thinking about tomorrow.

The next day Hillary, Chelsea, and I flew to Monroe, Michigan, for a "passing the torch" rally with Al and Tipper Gore. A good crowd in a battleground state sent Al off to Los Angeles to claim the nomination and become the leader of our party, and me to the local McDonald's, a stop I hadn't made in years.

The Bush-Cheney ticket had settled on a two-pronged campaign message. The positive argument was "compassionate conservatism," giving America the same good conditions we had provided, but with a smaller government and a bigger tax cut. The negative one was that they would elevate the moral tone and end bitter partisanship in Washington. That was, to say the least, disingenuous. I had done everything I knew to reach out to the Republicans in Washington; they had tried to demonize me from day one. Now they were saying, "We'll stop misbehaving if you give us the White House back."

The morality argument should have had no resonance, unless people believed Gore had done something wrong, especially with the super-straight Lieberman on the ticket. I wasn't on the ballot; it was both unfair and self-defeating for voters to blame them for my personal mistakes. I knew their strategy wouldn't work unless the Democrats accepted the legitimacy of the Republican argument and failed to remind voters of the impeachment fiasco and how much more damage the right wing could inflict if they controlled both the White House and the Congress. An NRA vice president had already boasted that if Bush were elected, the NRA would have an office in the White House.

After our convention, the polls showed Al Gore had come from behind to hold a narrow lead, and I accompanied Hillary to the Finger Lakes area of upstate New York for a couple of days of vacation and campaigning. She was running a different race from the one she had begun. Mayor Giuliani had withdrawn, and her new opponent, Long Island congressman Rick Lazio, presented a new challenge: he was attractive and smart, a less polarizing figure who was nevertheless more conservative than Giuliani.

I ended the month with two short trips. After meeting in Washington with Vicente Fox, the president-elect of Mexico, I flew to Nigeria to see President Olusegun Obasanjo. I wanted to support his efforts to curb AIDS before Nigeria's infection rates reached the levels of southern African nations, and to highlight the recent passage of the African trade bill, which I hoped would help Nigeria's struggling economy. Obasanjo and I attended a gathering on AIDS at which a young girl spoke of her efforts to educate her schoolmates about the disease, and a man named John Ibekwe told the gripping story of his marriage to a woman who was HIV-positive, his becoming infected, and his frantic search to get the medicine for his wife that would enable their child to be born without the virus. Eventually John succeeded, and little Maria was born HIV-free. President Obasanjo asked Mrs. Ibekwe to come up onstage, where he embraced her. It was a touching gesture and sent a clear signal that Nigeria would not fall into the trap of denial that had contributed so much to the spread of AIDS in other countries.

From Nigeria, I flew to Arusha, Tanzania, to the Burundi peace talks, which Nelson Mandela had been chairing. Mandela wanted me to join him and several other African leaders for the closing session to exhort the leaders of Burundi's numerous factions to sign the agreement and avoid another Rwanda. Mandela gave me clear instructions: We were doing a good cop/bad cop routine. I would give a positive speech urging them to do the right thing, then Mandela would demand that the parties sign on to his proposal. It worked: President Pierre Buyoya and thirteen of the nineteen warring parties signed the agreement. Soon all but two of them would sign. Although it was a burdensome trip, going to the Burundi peace conference was an important way to demonstrate to Africa and the world that the United States was a peacemaker. As I said to myself before we began our Camp David talks, "We're either going to succeed or get caught trying."

On August 30, I flew to Cartagena, Colombia, with Speaker Dennis Hastert and six other House members, Senator Joe Biden and three other senators, and several cabinet members. We all wanted to reinforce America's commitment to President Andrés Pastrana's Plan Colombia, which was intended to free his country of the narco-traffickers and terrorists who controlled about one-third of its territory. Pastrana had risked his life in an attempt to make peace, going alone to meet with the guerrillas in their lair. When he failed, he had asked the United States to help him defeat them with Plan Colombia. With Hastert's strong support, I had gotten more than $1 billion from Congress to do our part.

Cartagena is a beautiful old walled city. Pastrana took us out into the streets to meet officials who were fighting the narco-traffickers and some of the people who had been affected by the violence, including the widow of a police officer slain in the line of duty, one of hundreds killed for their honesty and bravery. Andrés also introduced Chelsea and me to an adorable group of young musicians who called themselves the Children of Vallenato, their home village in an area often ruled by violence. They sang and danced for peace in traditional native dress, and that evening in the streets of Cartagena, Pastrana, Chelsea, and I danced with them.

At the end of the first week of September, after vetoing a bill repealing the estate tax, announcing that I would defer a decision on deploying a missile defense system to my successor, and campaigning with Hillary at the New York State Fair, I went to the United Nations for its Millennium Summit. It was the largest assembly of world leaders ever gathered. My last UN speech was a brief but impassioned appeal for international cooperation on the issues of security, peace, and shared prosperity, in order to build a world that operated according to simple rules: "Everyone counts; everyone has a role to play; and we all do better when we help each other."

After the speech I walked out into the hall to sit with Madeleine Albright and Dick Holbrooke to listen to the next speaker: President Mohammed Khatami of Iran. Iran had held several elections in recent years, for the presidency, for parliament, and for municipal offices. In every case the reformers had won between two-thirds and 70 percent of the vote. The problem was that under the Iranian constitution, a council of Islamic fundamentalists led by Ayatollah Sayyed Ali Khamenei held enormous power; they could nullify certain legislation and prohibit candidates from running for office. And they controlled Iran's foreign intelligence operations and funded its support for terrorism. We had tried to reach out to Khatami and to promote more people-to-people contacts. I had also said that the United States was wrong to support the overthrow of an elected government in Iran in the 1950s. I hoped my gesture of respect would make more progress possible under the next President.

Kofi Annan and I hosted the traditional luncheon, and when it was over I followed my usual custom of standing by my table to shake hands with the leaders who stopped by on the way out. I thought I was at the end when I shook hands with a giant Namibian official, who towered over me. He then moved on, revealing a last greeter who had been invisible behind him: Fidel Castro. Castro stuck out his hand and I shook it, the first President to do so in more than forty years. He said he didn't wish to cause me any trouble but wanted to pay his respects before I left office. I replied that I hoped that someday our nations would be reconciled.

After the UN meetings, OPEC announced an increase in oil production of 800,000 barrels a day, Prime Minister Vajpayee of India came to Washington for a state visit, and on September 19, the Senate followed the House in approving the bill granting normal trade relations with China, thus clearing the way for its entry into the WTO. I was convinced that in time it would prove to be one of the most important foreign policy developments of my eight years.

Hillary had a good September. She won the primary on the twelfth and handily defeated Lazio in their debate moderated by Tim Russert in Buffalo. Lazio had three problems: he claimed that the still distressed economy of upstate New York had turned the corner; ran a misleading ad (for which he was called to account) that implied that Senator Moynihan was supporting him, not Hillary; and got in Hillary's face and tried to bully her into signing a pledge on campaign finance that was not credible. All Hillary had to do was keep her composure and answer the questions, which she did very well. A week later, a new poll showed her leading Lazio 48–39 percent, with new strength among suburban women.

On September 16, I bid an emotional farewell to a large, predominantly African-American crowd at the Congressional Black Caucus dinner, reviewing the record, making my case for Gore and Lieberman, and asking their support for well-qualified but still unconfirmed black judges. Then I threw away the script and closed with these words:

> I thank you from the bottom of my heart. Toni Morrison once said I was the first black President this country ever had. And I would rather have that than a Nobel Prize, and I'll tell you why. Because somewhere, in the deep and lost threads of my own memory, are the roots of understanding of what you have known. Somewhere, there was a deep longing to share the fate of the people who had been left out and left behind, sometimes brutalized, and too often ignored or forgotten.
>
> I don't exactly know who all I have to thank for that. But I'm quite sure I don't deserve any credit for it, because whatever I did, I really felt I had no other choice.

I made the same points a few days later, on September 20, to the Congressional Hispanic Caucus dinner, and to the Bishops Conference of the Church of God in Christ, where I noted that there were only 120 days left in my presidency and that I would give them "120 hard days" working with Congress and trying to make peace in the Middle East. I knew I'd have an opportunity to win some more victories as Congress wound down, but I wasn't so sure about the Middle East.

Several days later my economic team was with me as I announced that median income had risen by more than $1,000 in the last year, taking it above $40,000 for the first time in our history, and that the number of Americans without health insurance had dropped by 1.7 million the previous year, the first major decline in twelve years.

On September 25, after weeks of efforts by our team to get peace talks back on track, Barak invited Arafat to his home for dinner. Near the end of the meal, I called and had a good talk with both of them. The next day both sides sent negotiators to Washington to take up where they had left off at Camp David. On the twenty-eighth, everything changed, as Ariel Sharon became the first leading Israeli politician to walk on the Temple Mount since Israel captured it in the 1967 war. At the time, Moshe Dayan had said that Muslim religious sites would be respected, and thereafter the mount was overseen by Muslims.

Arafat said he had asked Barak to prevent Sharon's stroll, which was clearly intended to affirm Israel's sovereignty over the site and to strengthen his hand against a challenge to his leadership of the Likud Party from former prime minister Netanyahu, who was now sounding more hawkish than Sharon. I had also hoped Barak would prevent Sharon's inflammatory escapade, but Barak told me he couldn't. Instead, Sharon was forbidden to enter the Dome of the Rock, or the Al-Aqsa Mosque, and was escorted to the Mount by a large number of heavily armed police officers.

I and others on our team had urged Arafat to prevent violence. It was a great opportunity for the Palestinians, for once, to refuse to be provoked. I thought Sharon should have been greeted with flowers by Palestinian children and told that when the Temple Mount was under Palestinian control, he would be welcome anytime. But as Abba Eban had said long ago, the Palestinians never miss an opportunity to miss an opportunity. The next day there were large Palestinian demonstrations near the Western Wall, during which Israeli police opened fire with rubber bullets on stone throwers and others. At least five people were killed and hundreds were wounded. As the violence persisted, two vivid images of its pain and futility emerged: a twelve-year-old Palestinian boy shot in the crossfire and dying in his father's arms, and two Israeli soldiers pulled from a building and beaten to death, with their lifeless bodies dragged through the streets and one of their assailants proudly showing his bloodstained hands to the world on television.

While the Middle East was exploding, the Balkans were getting better. In the last week of September, Slobodan Milosevic was defeated for the presidency of Serbia by Vojislav Kostunica in a campaign in which we had helped ensure that the election could not be stolen and Kostunica could get his message out. Milosevic tried to steal the election anyway, but massive demonstrations convinced him he couldn't get away with it, and on October 6, the prime mover behind the Balkan slaughters admitted defeat.

In early October, I hosted a meeting in the Cabinet Room for supporters of the debt-relief initiative. Reverend Pat Robertson was there. His strong support and that of the evangelical Christian community showed how broad and deep support for debt relief had become. In the House, the effort was being pushed by Maxine Waters, one of our most liberal members, and conservative Budget Committee chairman John Kasich. Even Jesse Helms was supporting it, thanks in no small measure to Bono's personal outreach to him. The early results were encouraging: Bolivia had spent $77 million on health and education; Uganda had doubled primary school enrollment; and Honduras was to go from six to nine years of mandatory schooling. I was aiming to get the rest of our contribution in the final budget agreement.

In the second week of the month, Hillary did well in her second, more civilized debate with Rick Lazio. I signed the China trade bill and thanked Charlene Barshefsky and Gene Sperling for their arduous trek to China to hammer out our agreement at the eleventh hour; signed into law my Lands Legacy Initiative and the new investments for Native American communities; and on October 11, in Chappaqua, met Hillary to celebrate our twenty-fifth wedding anniversary. It seemed like only yesterday when we were young and just beginning. Now our daughter was almost out of college and the White House years were almost over. I was confident Hillary would win the Senate race, and optimistic about what the future held for all of us.

My brief reverie was shattered the next day, when a small boat laden with explosives blew up beside the USS *Cole*, in port in Aden, Yemen. Seventeen sailors were killed in what was obviously a terrorist attack. We all thought it was the work of bin Laden and al Qaeda, but we couldn't be sure. The CIA went to work on it, and I sent officials from Defense, State, and the FBI to Yemen, where President Ali

Saleh had promised to cooperate fully in the investigation and in bringing the murderers to justice.

Meanwhile, I continued to push the Pentagon and the national security team for more options to get bin Laden. We came close to launching another missile strike at him in October, but the CIA recommended that we call it off at the last minute, believing that the evidence of his presence was insufficiently reliable. The Pentagon recommended against putting Special Forces into Afghanistan, with all the attendant logistical difficulties, unless we had more reliable intelligence on bin Laden's whereabouts. That left bigger military options: a large-scale bombing campaign of all suspected campsites or a sizable invasion. I thought neither was feasible without a finding of al Qaeda responsibility for the *Cole*. I was very frustrated, and I hoped that before I left office we would locate bin Laden for a missile strike.

After campaign stops in Colorado and Washington, I flew to Sharm el-Sheikh, Egypt, for a summit on the Middle East violence with President Mubarak, King Abdullah, Kofi Annan, and Javier Solana, now secretary-general of the European Union. All of them wanted to end the violence, as did Crown Prince Abdullah of Saudi Arabia, who was not there but had already weighed in on the subject. Barak and Arafat were present, but might as well have been on opposite sides of the world from each other. Barak wanted the violence stopped; Arafat wanted an inquiry into the alleged excessive use of force by the Israeli military and police. George Tenet worked out a security plan with both sides, and I had to sell it to Barak and Arafat, as well as a statement to be read at the end of the summit.

I told Arafat that I had intended to present a proposal to resolve the outstanding issues in the peace talks but couldn't do so until he agreed to the security plan. There could be no peace without shutting down the violence. Arafat agreed to the plan. We then worked until early in the morning on a statement for me to issue on behalf of all the parties. It contained three parts: a commitment to end the violence; the establishment of a fact-finding committee to look into what had caused the uprising and the conduct of both sides, appointed by the United States with the Israelis and Palestinians and in consultation with Kofi Annan; and a commitment to move forward with the peace talks. It sounds simple, but it wasn't. Arafat wanted a UN committee and immediate resumption of the talks. Barak wanted a U.S. committee and enough delay to see whether the violence would subside. Mubarak and I finally met alone with Arafat and persuaded him to accept the statement. I couldn't have done it without Hosni. I had thought he was often too resistant to getting deeply involved in the peace process, but that night he was strong, clear, and effective.

When I returned to the United States, Hillary, Chelsea, and I went to Norfolk, Virginia, for a memorial service for victims of the USS *Cole* bombing and private meetings with their grieving families. Like the airmen at Khobar Towers, our sailors had been killed in a very different conflict from the kind they had been trained to fight. In this one, the enemy was elusive, everyone was a potential target, our enormous arsenal was not a deterrent, and the openness and information technology of the modern world were being used against us. I knew that eventually we would prevail in the struggle against bin Laden, but I didn't know how many innocent people would lose their lives before we figured out how to do it.

Two days later Hillary, Al and Tipper Gore, and I went to Jefferson City, Missouri, for a memorial service for Governor Mel Carnahan, his son, and a young aide who had been killed when their small plane crashed. Carnahan and I had been close since he endorsed me early in the 1992 campaign. He had been a fine governor and a leader in welfare reform, and at the time of his death he was in a tight race with the incumbent, John Ashcroft, in the U.S. Senate race. It was too late to put someone else on the ballot. A few days later, Jean Carnahan said that if the people of Missouri voted for her husband, she would serve. They did, and Jean served with distinction.

In the last days of October, as the presidential election came down to the wire, I signed a trade agreement with Jordan's King Abdullah, continued to sign and veto bills, and campaigned in Indiana, Kentucky, Massachusetts, and New York, where I did several events for Hillary. The most fun was a birthday celebration in which Robert De Niro gave me instructions on how to talk like a real New Yorker.

Ever since the convention Al Gore had framed the election as a contest of "the people versus the powerful." That it was; every conceivable conservative interest group—the health insurance industry, the tobacco companies, the heavily polluting industries, the NRA, and many more—was for Governor Bush. The problem with the slogan was that it didn't give Al the full benefit of our record of economic and social progress or put into sharp relief Bush's explicit commitment to undo that progress. Also, the populist edge sounded to some swing voters as if Al, too, might change the economic direction of the country. Along toward the end of the month, Al started saying, "Don't put the prosperity at risk." By the first of November, he was moving up in the polls, though still down by about four points.

In the last week of the campaign, at Governor Gray Davis's request, I flew to California for two days of campaigning for the ticket and our congressional candidates, did a big event in Harlem for Hillary, then on Sunday went home to Arkansas to campaign for Mike Ross, who had served as my driver in the 1982 governor's campaign and was running against Republican congressman Jay Dickey.

I spent the day before the election and election day doing more than sixty radio interviews across the country urging people to vote for Al and Joe and our local Democrats. I had already recorded more than 170 radio ads and telephone messages to be dialed into homes of hard-core Democrats and minorities, asking them to vote for our candidates.

On election day, Hillary, Chelsea, and I voted at Douglas Grafflin Elementary School, our local polling station in Chappaqua. It was a strange and wonderful experience: strange because the school was the only place I'd ever voted outside Arkansas, and after twenty-six years in political life, my name wasn't on the ballot; wonderful because I got to vote for Hillary. Chelsea and I voted first, then hugged each other as we watched Hillary close the curtain and cast a ballot for herself.

Election night was a roller coaster. Hillary won her election, 55–43 percent, a much larger margin than she had in all the pre-election polls but one. I was so proud of her. New York had put her through the wringer, just as it had done to me in 1992. She had been up, down, and up again, but she kept her bearings and pressed ahead.

As we celebrated her victory at the Grand Hyatt Hotel in New York City, Bush and Gore were neck and neck. For weeks everyone had known the election would be close, with many commentators saying that Gore might lose the popular vote but still win the electoral college. Two days before the election, as I looked at the map and the latest polls, I told Steve Ricchetti that I was afraid the reverse could occur. Our base voters had been activated and would turn out as eagerly as the Republicans who wanted the White House back. Al was going to win big states by large margins, but Bush was going to win more small rural states, and they had an advantage in the electoral college because every state got one electoral vote for each House member plus two extra ones for its senators. Going into election day, I still thought Al would win because he had the momentum and he was right on the issues.

Gore did win, by more than 500,000 votes, but the electoral college was in doubt. The race came down to Florida, after Gore won a narrow victory of 366 votes in New Mexico, one of several states that were closer than they would have been had Ralph Nader not been on the ballot. I had asked Bill Richardson to spend the last week in his home state, and he may well have made the difference.

Of the states I had won in 1996, Bush picked up Nevada, Arizona, Missouri, Arkansas, Tennessee, Kentucky, Ohio, West Virginia, and New Hampshire. Tennessee had been growing increasingly Republican. In 1992, 1996, and 2000, the Democratic vote had held steady at between 47 and 48 percent. The NRA also hurt Al badly there and in several other states, including Arkansas. For example, Yell County, where the Clintons had settled a century earlier, is a populist, culturally conservative county a Democrat has to win to carry the state in a tight race. Gore lost it to Bush 50–47 percent. The NRA did that. I might have been able to turn it around, but it would have taken two or three days of rural work to do it, and I didn't know how big the problem was until I went home right before the election.

The gun lobby tried to beat Al in Michigan and Pennsylvania, and might have done so had it not been for a heroic effort by the local labor unions, which had a lot of NRA members themselves. They fought back by saying, "Gore won't take your gun away, but Bush will take your union away!" Unfortunately, in the rural areas of Arkansas, Tennessee, Kentucky, West Virginia, Missouri, and Ohio, there weren't enough union members to win the war on the ground.

In Kentucky, our stand against the big tobacco companies marketing cigarettes to kids hurt Al in the tobacco-growing areas. In West Virginia, he was damaged by the failure of Weirton Steel, an employee-owned company; the employees and their families were convinced the collapse was caused by my failure to limit cheap imported steel from Russia and Asia during the Asian financial crisis. The evidence indicated that the company had failed for other reasons, but the Weirton workers thought otherwise and Al paid the price.

New Hampshire went for Bush by a margin of just over 7,000 because Nader got 22,198 votes. Even worse, Nader received more than 90,000 votes in Florida, where Bush was hanging on by a thread in an election contest that would drag on for more than a month.

As the Florida vote battle began, it was clear that we had picked up four seats in the Senate and one in the House. Three incumbent House Republicans were defeated, including Jay Dickey, who lost to Mike Ross in Arkansas, and the Democrats picked up four seats in California, prevailing in all but one of the contested races. Al was at a disadvantage going into the election recount in Florida because the chief election official, Secretary of State Katherine Harris, was a conservative Republican who was close to Governor Jeb

Bush, and the state legislature that would certify the electors was dominated by conservative Republicans. On the other hand, the state supreme court, which presumably would have the final say on the counting of ballots, had more judges appointed by Democratic governors and was thought to be less partisan.

Two days later, still not knowing who my successor would be, I saw Arafat in the Oval Office. The violence was subsiding and I thought he might be serious about peace. I told him that I had only ten weeks left to make an agreement. In a private moment I held his arm, stared straight at him, and told him I also had a chance to make an agreement with North Korea to end its long-range missile production, but I would have to go there to do it. The whole trip would take a week or longer by the time I made the obligatory stops in South Korea, Japan, and China.

If we were going to make peace in the Middle East, I knew I would have to close the deal. I told Arafat I had done everything I could to get the Palestinians a state on the West Bank and Gaza while protecting the security of Israel. After all my efforts, if Arafat wasn't going to make peace, he owed it to me to tell me, so that I could go to North Korea to end another serious security threat. He pleaded with me to stay, saying that I had to finish the peace and that if we didn't do it before I left office, it would be at least five years before we'd be this close to peace again.

That night, we had a dinner to celebrate the two hundredth anniversary of the White House. Lady Bird Johnson, President and Mrs. Ford, President and Mrs. Carter, and President and Mrs. Bush were all there to mark the birthday of the people's house, which every President since John Adams had inhabited. It was a wonderful moment in American history, but a tense one for President and Mrs. Bush, who had to be on edge with their son's election hanging fire. I was glad they had come.

A few days later Chelsea and I went to Brunei for the annual APEC summit. Sultan Hassanal Bolkiah hosted our meeting in a beautiful new hotel and convention center. We made some headway on the reforms necessary to avoid another Asian financial crisis, and Singapore prime minister Goh Chok Tong and I agreed to start negotiations on a bilateral free-trade agreement. I also enjoyed a round of golf with Prime Minister Goh on a night golf course designed to help golfers manage the intense heat. I had instituted the APEC leaders' meeting back in 1993, and I was pleased with the expansion of the group and the work done since then. At my last APEC meeting I thought the effort had borne fruit, not simply in specific agreements, but also in building an institution that tied the United States to Asia in the new century.

After Brunei, Chelsea and I went to Vietnam for a historic visit to Hanoi, Ho Chi Minh City (the old Saigon), and a site where Vietnamese were working with Americans to unearth the remains of our men still listed as missing in action. Hillary flew in to join us from Israel, where she had gone to attend the funeral of Leah Rabin.

I met with the Communist Party leader, the president, the prime minister, and the mayor of Ho Chi Minh City. The higher the position, the more likely the leader was to sound like an old-style Communist. The party leader, Le Kha Phieu, tried to use my opposition to the Vietnam War to condemn what the United States had done as an imperialist act. I was angry about it, especially since he said it in the presence of our ambassador, Pete Peterson, who had been a prisoner of war. I told the leader in no uncertain terms that while I had disagreed with our Vietnam policy, those who had pursued it were not imperialists or colonialists, but good people who believed they were fighting communism. I pointed at Pete and said he hadn't spent six and a half years in the prison known as the Hanoi Hilton because he wanted to colonize Vietnam. We had turned a new page with normalized relations, the trade agreement, and two-way cooperation on MIA issues; now was not the time to reopen old wounds. The president, Tran Duc Luong, was only a little less dogmatic.

Prime Minister Phan Van Khai and I had established a good relationship at the APEC meetings; a year earlier he had told me he appreciated my opposition to the war. When

I said that the Americans who disagreed with me and supported the war were good people who wanted freedom for the Vietnamese, he replied, "I know." Khai was interested in the future and hoped the United States would give Vietnam assistance in caring for the victims of Agent Orange and developing its economy. The mayor of Ho Chi Minh City, Vo Viet Thanh, sounded like every good aggressive American mayor I knew. He bragged about balancing his budget, reducing his payroll, and working for more foreign investment. Besides the officials, I shook hands with a large crowd of friendly people who gathered spontaneously to greet us after an informal lunch at a local restaurant. They wanted to build a common future.

The trip to the MIA site was an experience none of us would ever forget. I thought back over the years to my high school classmates who had died in Vietnam and to the man I'd helped when I was in Moscow in 1970, who was searching for information about his missing son. The Americans working with the Vietnamese crew believed, based on information from local residents, that a missing pilot, Lieutenant Colonel Lawrence Evert, had crashed there more than thirty years earlier. His now grown children accompanied us to the site. Working knee-deep in mud with the Vietnamese, our soldiers cut the mud into large chunks, took it to a nearby shed, and sifted through it. They had already recovered parts of the plane and a uniform, and were close to having enough for an identification. The work was supervised by an American archaeologist who was himself a Vietnam veteran. He said this was the most rewarding dig in the world. The care and detail of their work was amazing, as were the efforts of the Vietnamese to help. Soon, the Everts found their father.

On the way home from Vietnam, I found out that Chuck Ruff, my White House counsel during the impeachment proceeding, had died suddenly. When I landed, I went to see his wife, Sue; Chuck was an extraordinary man who had led our defense team in the Senate with skill and courage.

The rest of November was consumed by the Middle East and the Florida recount, which was cut off with thousands of votes still uncounted in three big counties, a result unfair to Gore since it was obvious from the votes that had been thrown out for errors resulting from confusing ballots and flawed punch-card devices that thousands more Floridians had intended to vote for Gore than for Bush. Gore contested the election in court. At the same time, Barak and Arafat were meeting again in the Middle East. It wasn't clear to me whether we were going to win or lose either the battle for Florida or the struggle for peace.

On December 5, Hillary went to Capitol Hill for her initiation as a freshman senator. The night before, I kidded her about going to her first day of "Senator School," telling her she had to get a good night's sleep and wear a nice outfit. She was excited about it, and I was really happy for her.

Three days later, I traveled to Nebraska, the only state I had not yet visited as President, for a speech at the University of Nebraska at Kearney. It was in effect a valedictory address in the heartland urging continued American leadership in the world beyond our borders. Meanwhile, the Florida Supreme Court ordered the inclusion of more recounted votes in Palm Beach and Dade counties, and the recount of 45,000 more votes according to the standard of Florida law: a ballot was to be counted only if the intent of the voter was clear. Bush's margin was now down to 154 votes.

Governor Bush immediately appealed to the U.S. Supreme Court to stop the recount. Several lawyers told me the Supreme Court wouldn't take the case; the mechanics of elections were a question of state law unless they were used to discriminate against a group of citizens, like racial minorities. Also, it is difficult to get a court-ordered injunction against an otherwise legal action, like an election recount or razing a building when the owner agrees. To do so, a party must show that irreparable harm would result unless the activity is stopped. In a 5–4 decision, Justice Scalia wrote an astonishingly honest opinion granting the injunction. What was the irreparable harm? Scalia said. That counting the ballots might "cast a cloud upon what [Bush] claims to be the legitimacy of his election." Well, he was right about that. If Gore got more votes than Bush in Florida, it would be harder for the Supreme Court to give Bush the presidency anyway.

We were having a Christmas reception at the White House that night, and I asked every lawyer who came through the receiving line if he or she had ever heard of such a ruling. No one had. The Court was to hand down another opinion shortly, on the underlying issue of whether the recount itself was constitutional. Now we knew they would kill it 5–4. I told Hillary that Scalia would never be allowed to write the second opinion; he had been too candid in this one.

On December 11, Hillary, Chelsea, and I flew to Ireland, to the land of my ancestors and the scene of so much of the peacemaking I had done. We stopped in Dublin to see Bertie Ahern, then went to Dundalk near the border for a massive rally in a city that was once a hotbed of IRA activity and was now a force for peace. The streets were bright with Christmas lights as the large crowd cheered wildly and sang "Danny Boy" to me. Seamus Heaney once said of Yeats: "His interest was to clear a space in the mind and in the world for the miraculous." I thanked the Irish for filling that space with the miracle of peace.

We went to Belfast, where I met with the Northern Irish leaders, including David Trimble, Seamus Mallon, John Hume, and Gerry Adams. Then we went with Tony and Cherie Blair, Bertie Ahern, and George Mitchell to a large meeting of both Catholics and Protestants in the Odyssey Arena. It was still somewhat unusual for them to gather together in Belfast. Some sharp disputes remained involving the new police force and the schedule and method of putting arms beyond use. I asked them to keep working on the problems and remember that the enemies of peace didn't need their approval: "All they need is your apathy." I reminded the audience that the Good Friday accord had given heart to peacemakers the world over, and cited the just announced agreement ending the bloody conflict between Eritrea and Ethiopia that the United States had helped broker. I closed by saying how much I had loved working with them for peace, "but the issue is not how I feel; it's how your kids are going to live."

After the event, my family flew to England to stay with the Blairs at Chequers and listen to Al Gore give his concession speech. The night before, at 10 p.m., the Supreme Court had ruled, 7–2, that the Florida recount was unconstitutional because there were no uniform standards for defining the clear intent of the voter for purposes of a recount, and therefore different vote counters might count or interpret the same ballots differently. Therefore, the Court said, allowing any of the disputed votes to be counted, no matter how clear the voters' intent, would deny equal protection of the law to those whose ballots weren't counted. I disagreed strongly with the decision, but I was heartened that Justices Souter and Breyer wanted to send the case back to the Florida Supreme Court to set a standard and proceed with the recount in a hurry. The electoral college was meeting soon. The other five justices in the majority disagreed. By 5–4, the same five justices who had stopped the vote count three days earlier now said it had to give the election to Bush because under Florida law the recount had to be finished by midnight on that day anyway.

It was an appalling decision. A narrow conservative majority that had made a virtual fetish of states' rights had now stripped Florida of a clear state function: the right to recount votes the way it always had. The five justices who didn't want the votes counted by any standard claimed to advance equal protection by depriving thousands of people of their constitutional right to have their votes counted even if their intent was crystal clear. They said Bush should be awarded the election because the votes couldn't be counted in the next two hours, when, after already killing three days of recounting, they had delayed issuing the opinion until 10 p.m., to make absolutely sure the recount could not be completed on time. The five-vote majority didn't make any bones about what it was up to: the opinion clearly stated that the ruling could not be used as precedent in future election law cases; its reasoning was "limited to the present circumstances, for the problem of equal protection in election processes generally presents many complexities." If Gore had been ahead in the vote count and Bush behind, there's not a doubt in my mind that the same Supreme Court would have voted 9–0 to count the votes. And I would have supported the decision.

Bush v. *Gore* will go down in history as one of the worst decisions the Supreme Court ever made, along with the *Dred Scott* case, which said that a slave who escaped to freedom was still a piece of property to be returned to its owner; *Plessy* v. *Ferguson*, upholding the legality of racial segregation; the cases in the twenties and thirties invalidating legislative protections for workers, like minimum wage and maximum workweek laws, as violations of the property rights of employers; and the *Korematsu* case, in which the Supreme Court approved the blanket internment of Japanese-Americans in camps after Pearl Harbor. We had lived through and rejected the premises of all those previous reactionary decisions. I knew America would also get beyond this dark day when five Republican justices stripped thousands of their fellow Americans of their votes, just because they could.

Al Gore gave a marvelous concession speech. It was genuine, gracious, and patriotic. When I called to congratulate him, he told me that a friend who was a professional comedian had joked to him that he had gotten the best of both worlds: he had won the popular vote and didn't have to do the job.

The next morning, after Tony Blair and I talked a bit, I walked outside, complimented Al, and pledged to work with President-elect Bush. Then Tony and Cherie accompanied Hillary, Chelsea, and me to the University of Warwick, where I gave another of my farewell speeches, this one on the approach to globalization our Third Way group had embraced: trade plus a global contract for economic empowerment, education, health care, and democratic governance. The speech also gave me a chance to publicly thank Tony Blair for his friendship and our partnership. I had treasured our times together and would miss them.

Before we left England, we went to Buckingham Palace, accepting Queen Elizabeth's kind invitation to tea. We had a pleasant visit, discussing the election and world affairs. Then Her Majesty took the unusual step of accompanying us down to the ground floor of the palace and walking us out to our car to say good-bye. She, too, had been gracious and kind to me over the past eight years.

On December 15, I reached an omnibus budget agreement with Congress, the last major legislative victory of my eight years. The education budget was especially good. Finally, I secured more than $1 billion to repair schools; the largest increase ever in Head Start; enough money to put 1.3 million students in after-school programs; a 25 percent increase in the fund to hire 100,000 teachers; and more funding for Pell Grants, for our Gear Up mentoring program, and for our efforts to turn around failing schools. The bill also included the New Markets initiative, a large increase in biomedical research, health-care coverage for welfare recipients and disabled people moving into the workforce, and the Millennium Debt Relief initiative.

John Podesta, Steve Ricchetti, my legislative aide Larry Stein, and our whole team had done a great job. My last year, when I was supposed to be a lame duck, had resulted in the passage of a surprising number of the State of the Union recommendations. Besides those mentioned above, Congress had passed the Africa-Caribbean trade bill, the China trade bill, the Lands Legacy initiative, and a large increase in child-care assistance to working families.

I was still deeply disappointed in the election outcome and concerned about the Middle East, but after the visit to Ireland and England and the budget victories, I was finally getting into the Christmas spirit.

On the eighteenth, Jacques Chirac and Romano Prodi came to the White House for my last meeting with European Union leaders. By then we were old friends, and I was glad to receive them one last time. Jacques thanked me for supporting the growth of the EU and transatlantic relations. I responded that we had managed three great questions well: the growth and expansion of the EU; the expansion of

NATO and the new relationship with Russia; and the problems of the Balkans.

While I was meeting with Chirac and Prodi, the Middle East teams began talks at Bolling Air Force Base in Washington, Hillary received Laura Bush at the White House, and our family went house shopping in Washington. The people of New York had decided she wasn't leaving town after all. Eventually we found a lovely house that bordered Rock Creek Park in the embassy area off Massachusetts Avenue.

The next day President-elect Bush came to the White House for the same meeting I had had with his father eight years earlier. We talked about the campaign, White House operations, and national security. He was putting together an experienced team from past Republican administrations who believed that the biggest security issues were the need for national missile defense and Iraq. I told him that based on the last eight years, I thought his biggest security problems, in order, would be Osama bin Laden and al Qaeda; the absence of peace in the Middle East; the standoff between nuclear powers India and Pakistan, and the ties of the Pakistanis to the Taliban and al Qaeda; North Korea; and then Iraq. I said that my biggest disappointment was not getting bin Laden, that we still might achieve an agreement in the Middle East, and that we had almost tied up a deal with North Korea to end its missile program, but that he probably would have to go there to close the deal.

He listened to what I had to say without much comment, then changed the subject to how I did the job. My only advice was that he should put together a good team and try to do what he thought was right for the country. Then we talked a little more politics.

Bush had been a very adept politician in 2000, building a coalition with moderate rhetoric and quite conservative-specific proposals. The first time I had seen him give his "compassionate conservative" speech in Iowa, I knew he had a chance to win. After the primaries he was badly positioned way out on the right and behind in the polls, but he had walked back to the center by moderating his rhetoric,

urging the Republican Congress not to balance the budget
on the backs of the poor, and even supporting my position
on a couple of foreign policy issues. When he was governor,
his conservatism had been leavened by the need to work
with a Democratic state legislature and by the support he
had received from Democratic lieutenant governor Bob Bul-
lock, who wielded a lot of the day-to-day power under the
Texas system. Now he would govern with a conservative
Republican Congress. He had to choose his own way. After
our meeting I knew he was fully capable of getting his way,
but I couldn't tell whether it would be the path he had followed as governor or the one he had taken to defeat John
McCain in the South Carolina primary.

December 23 was a fateful day for the Middle East
peace process. After the two sides had been negotiating
again for several days at Bolling Air Force Base, my team
and I became convinced that unless we narrowed the range
of debate, in effect forcing the big compromises up front,
there would never be an agreement. Arafat was afraid of
being criticized by other Arab leaders; Barak was losing
ground to Sharon at home. So I brought the Palestinian and
Israeli teams into the Cabinet Room and read them my
"parameters" for proceeding. These were developed after
extensive private talks with the parties separately since
Camp David. If they accepted the parameters within four
days, we would go forward. If not, we were through.

I read them slowly so that both sides could take careful
notes. On territory, I recommended 94 to 96 percent of the
West Bank for the Palestinians with a land swap from Israel
of 1 to 3 percent, and an understanding that the land kept by
Israel would include 80 percent of the settlers in blocs. On
security, I said Israeli forces should withdraw over a three-
year period while an international force would be gradually
introduced, with the understanding that a small Israeli presence in the Jordan Valley could remain for another three
years under the authority of the international forces. The
Israelis would also be able to maintain their early-warning
station in the West Bank with a Palestinian liaison presence.
In the event of an "imminent and demonstrable threat to

Israel's security," there would be provision for emergency deployments in the West Bank.

The new state of Palestine would be "nonmilitarized," but would have a strong security force; sovereignty over its airspace, with special arrangements to meet Israeli training and operational needs; and an international force for border security and deterrence.

On Jerusalem, I recommended that the Arab neighborhoods be in Palestine and the Jewish neighborhoods in Israel, and that the Palestinians should have sovereignty over the Temple Mount/Haram and the Israelis sovereignty over the Western Wall and the "holy space" of which it is a part, with no excavation around the wall or under the Mount, at least without mutual consent.

On refugees, I said that the new state of Palestine should be the homeland for refugees displaced in the 1948 war and afterward, without ruling out the possibility that Israel would accept some of the refugees according to its own laws and sovereign decisions, giving priority to the refugee populations in Lebanon. I recommended an international effort to compensate refugees and assist them in finding houses in the new state of Palestine, in the land-swap areas to be transferred to Palestine, in their current host countries, in other willing nations, or in Israel. Both parties should agree that this solution would satisfy United Nations Resolution 194.

Finally, the agreement had to clearly mark the end of the conflict and put an end to all violence. I suggested a new UN resolution saying that this agreement, along with the final release of Palestinian prisoners, would fulfill the requirements of resolutions 242 and 338.

I said these parameters were nonnegotiable and were the best I could do, and I wanted the parties to negotiate a final status agreement within them. After I left, Dennis Ross and other members of our team stayed behind to clarify any misunderstanding, but they refused to hear complaints. I knew the plan was tough for both parties, but it was time—past time—to put up or shut up. The Palestinians would give up the absolute right of return; they had always known they would have to, but they never wanted to admit it. The

Israelis would give up East Jerusalem and parts of the Old City, but their religious and cultural sites would be preserved; it had been evident for some time that for peace to come, they would have to do that. The Israelis would also give up a little more of the West Bank and probably a larger land swap than Barak's last best offer, but they would keep enough to hold at least 80 percent of the settlers. And they would get a formal end to the conflict. It was a hard deal, but if they wanted peace, I thought it was fair to both sides.

Arafat immediately began to equivocate, asking for "clarifications." But the parameters were clear; either he would negotiate within them or not. As always, he was playing for more time. I called Mubarak and read him the points. He said they were historic and he could encourage Arafat to accept them.

On the twenty-seventh, Barak's cabinet endorsed the parameters with reservations, but all their reservations were within the parameters, and therefore subject to negotiations anyway. It was historic: an Israeli government had said that to get peace, there would be a Palestinian state in roughly 97 percent of the West Bank, counting the swap, and all of Gaza, where Israel also had settlements. The ball was in Arafat's court.

I was calling other Arab leaders daily to urge them to pressure Arafat to say yes. They were all impressed with Israel's acceptance and told me they believed Arafat should take the deal. I have no way of knowing what they told him, though the Saudi ambassador, Prince Bandar, later told me he and Crown Prince Abdullah had the distinct impression Arafat was going to accept the parameters.

On the twenty-ninth, Dennis Ross met with Abu Ala, whom we all respected, to make sure Arafat understood the consequences of rejection. I would be gone. Ross would be gone. Barak would lose the upcoming election to Sharon. Bush wouldn't want to jump in after I had invested so much and failed.

I still didn't believe Arafat would make such a colossal mistake. The previous day I had announced that I would not travel to North Korea to close the agreement banning its production of long-range missiles, saying I was confident the next administration would consummate the deal based on the good work that had been done. I hated to give up on ending the North Korean missile program. We had stopped their plutonium and missile testing programs, and had refused to deal with them on other issues without involving South Korea, setting the stage for Kim Dae Jung's "sunshine policy." Kim's brave outreach offered more hope for reconciliation than at any time since the end of the Korean War, and he had just been awarded the Nobel Peace Prize for it. Madeleine Albright had made a trip to North Korea and was convinced that if I went, we could make the missile agreement. Although I wanted to take the next step, I simply couldn't risk being halfway around the world when we were so close to peace in the Middle East, especially after Arafat had assured me that he was eager for an agreement and had implored me not to go.

Besides the Middle East and the budget, a surprising number of other things had happened in the last thirty days. I marked the seventh anniversary of the Brady bill with the announcement that it had now prevented 611,000 felons, fugitives, and stalkers from buying handguns; observed World AIDS Day at Howard University with representatives from twenty-four African countries, saying that we had cut the death rate by more than 70 percent in the United States and now had to do much more in Africa and other places where the disease was raging; unveiled the design of my presidential library, a long, narrow glass-and-steel "bridge to the twenty-first century" jutting out above the Arkansas River; announced an effort to increase immunizations among inner-city children, whose vaccination rates remained far below the national average; signed my last veto, of a bankruptcy reform bill that was much harsher to lower-income debtors than to wealthy ones; issued strong regulations to protect the privacy of medical records; hailed India's decision to maintain its cease-fire in Kashmir and Pakistan's upcoming withdrawal of troops along the Line of Control; and announced new regulations to reduce unhealthy diesel fuel emissions from trucks and buses. Together with the year-old emissions standards on cars and SUVs, the new rules ensured that by the end of the decade, new vehicles would be up to 95 percent cleaner than those now on the road, preventing many thousands of cases of respiratory illness and premature death.

Three days before Christmas, I granted executive clemency or commutations of sentences to 62 people. I hadn't given many pardons in my first term and was anxious to deal with the backlog. President Carter had granted 566 clemencies in four years. President Ford had granted 409 in two and a half years. President Reagan's total was 406 in his eight years. President Bush had granted only 77, and they included the controversial pardons of the Iran-Contra figures, and the release of Orlando Bosch, an anti-Castro Cuban the FBI believed to be guilty of multiple murders.

My philosophy on pardons and commutations of sentences, developed while I was attorney general and governor of Arkansas, was conservative when it came to shortening sentences and liberal in granting pardons for nonviolent offenses once people had served their sentences and spent a reasonable amount of time afterward as law-abiding citizens, if for no other reason than to give them their voting rights back. There was a pardon office in the Justice Department that reviewed applications and made recommendations. I had been receiving them for eight years and had learned two things: the people over at Justice took too long to review the applications, and they recommended denial in almost all the cases.

I understood how it had happened. In Washington everything was political and almost every pardon was potentially controversial. If you were a civil servant, the only surefire way to stay out of trouble was to say no. The Justice Department's pardon office knew that they couldn't get heat for delaying cases or for recommending denials; a constitutional function vested in the President was slowly being transferred into the bowels of the Justice Department.

For the last several months, we had been pushing Justice hard to send us more files, and they were doing better. Of the fifty-nine people I pardoned and the three whose sentences I commuted, most were people who'd made a mistake, served their time, and become good citizens. I also issued pardons in the so-called girlfriend cases. They involved women who had been arrested because their husbands or boyfriends had committed an offense, usually drug-related. The women were threatened with long sentences, even if they hadn't themselves been directly involved in the crime, unless they provided testimony against their men. Those who refused or didn't know enough to be helpful got long jail terms. In several cases, the men in question later cooperated with prosecutors and received shorter sentences than the women had. We had been working on these cases for months. I had already pardoned four of them the previous summer.

I also pardoned former House Ways and Means Committee chairman Dan Rostenkowski. Rostenkowski had done a lot for his country and had more than paid for his mistakes. And I pardoned Archie Schaffer, an executive of Tyson Foods who was caught in the Espy investigation and was facing a mandatory jail sentence for violating an old law Schaffer knew nothing about, because he had made travel arrangements, as instructed, so that Espy could come to a Tyson retreat.

After the Christmas clemencies, we were flooded with requests, many from people upset at the delay in the regular process. Over the next five weeks we worked through hundreds of requests, rejecting hundreds more and granting 140, bringing my eight-year total to 456, out of more than 7,000 petitions for clemency. My White House counsel Beth Nolan, Bruce Lindsey, and my pardon attorney, Meredith Cabe, worked through as many as they could, getting information and clearance from the Justice Department. Some of the decisions were easy, like the cases of Susan McDougal and Henry Cisneros, who had been horribly mistreated by independent counsels; more girlfriend cases; and a large number of routine requests that probably should have been granted years earlier. One of them was a mistake based on inadequate information because the Justice Department didn't know that the man in question was under investigation in a different state.

Most of the pardons were for people of modest means who had no way to break through the system.

The most controversial pardons went to Marc Rich and his partner, Pincus Green. Rich, a wealthy businessman, had left the United States for Switzerland shortly before he was indicted on tax and other charges for allegedly falsely reporting the price of certain oil transactions to minimize his tax liability. There were several such cases in the 1980s, when some oil was under price controls and some was not, inviting the dishonest to underestimate their income or to overcharge their customers. During that time, several people and companies were charged with violating the law, but the individuals were usually charged with a civil offense. It was extremely rare for tax charges to be prosecuted under the racketeering statutes, as Rich and Green were, and after they were charged, the Justice Department ordered U.S. attorneys to stop doing it. After he was indicted, Rich stayed overseas, mostly in Israel and Switzerland.

The government had allowed Rich's business to continue to operate after he agreed to pay $200 million in fines, more than four times the $48 million in taxes the government claimed he had evaded. Professor Marty Ginsburg, a tax expert and husband of Justice Ruth Bader Ginsburg, and Harvard Law professor Bernard Wolfman had reviewed the transactions in question and concluded that Rich's companies were right in their tax computations, which meant that Rich himself had not owed any taxes on these transactions. Rich agreed to waive the statute of limitations so that he could still be sued by the government in a civil action as all other offenders had been. Ehud Barak asked me three times to pardon Rich because of Rich's services to Israel and his help with the Palestinians, and several other Israeli figures in both major parties urged his release. Finally, the Justice Department said it had no objections and would lean toward granting the pardon if it advanced our foreign policy interests.

Most everyone thought I was wrong to pardon a wealthy fugitive whose ex-wife was a supporter of mine and who had retained one of my former White House counsels on his legal team, along with two prominent Republican lawyers. Rich had also been recently represented by Lewis "Scooter" Libby, Vice President–elect Dick Cheney's chief of staff. I may have made a mistake, at least in the way I allowed the case to come to my attention, but I made the decision based on the merits. As of May 2004, Rich still had not been sued by the Justice Department, a surprising development, since the burden of proof is much easier for the government to make in a civil case than in a criminal one.

Although I would later be criticized for some of the pardons I granted, I was more concerned by a few I didn't grant. For example, I thought Michael Milken had a persuasive case, because of the good work he had done on prostate cancer after his release from prison, but Treasury and the Securities and Exchange Commission were adamantly against my pardoning him, saying it would send the wrong signal at a time when they were trying to enforce high standards in the financial industry. The two cases I most regretted turning down were Webb Hubbell and Jim Guy Tucker. Tucker's case was on appeal and Hubbell had actually broken the law and had not been out of jail for the usual period before being considered for a pardon. But they both had been abused by Ken Starr's office for their refusal to lie. Neither of them would have endured a fraction of what they did had I not been elected President and fallen into Starr's clutches. David Kendall and Hillary strongly urged me to pardon them. Everyone else was adamantly against it. Finally, I gave in to my staff's hard-nosed judgment. I've regretted it ever since. I later apologized to Jim Guy Tucker when I saw him and will do the same to Webb one day.

Our Christmas was like all the others, but more savored because we knew it was our last at the White House. I would enjoy these last receptions more and the chance to see so many people who shared our time in Washington. I was looking more carefully now at all the ornaments Chelsea, Hillary, and I put on our tree, and at the bells, books, Christmas plates, stockings, pictures, and standing Santa Clauses with which we filled the Yellow Oval Room. I found myself taking time to walk into all the rooms on the second and third floors to look more closely at all the paintings and old furniture. And I finally got around to getting the White House ushers to provide me with a history of all the White House grandfather clocks, which I used as I studied them. The portraits of my predecessors and their wives took on a new meaning as Hillary and I realized we'd be among them before long. Both of us had chosen Simmie Knox to paint our portraits: we liked Knox's lifelike style, and he would be the first African-American portraitist to have his work hang in the White House.

In the week after Christmas I signed a few more bills and appointed Roger Gregory to be the first African-American judge on the Fourth Circuit Court of Appeals. Gregory was well qualified, and Jesse Helms had blocked a black judge there long enough. It was a "recess" appointment, one a President can make for a year, when Congress is not in session. I was betting the new President wouldn't want an all-white court of appeals in the Southeast.

I also announced that with the budget just enacted, there would be enough money to pay $600 billion of the debt down over four years, and if we stayed on the present course, we would be debt-free by 2010, freeing up twelve cents of every tax dollar for tax cuts or new investments. Because of our fiscal responsibility, long-term interest rates were now, after all the growth, 2 percent lower than when I took office, reducing the costs of mortgages, car payments, business loans, and student loans. The low interest rates had put more money in people's pockets than tax cuts would have.

Finally, on the last day of the year, I signed the treaty by which America joined the International Criminal Court. Senator Lott and most Republican senators were strongly opposed to it, fearing that U.S. soldiers sent to foreign lands would be hauled before the court for political purposes. I had been concerned about that, too, but the treaty was now drafted in a manner that I was convinced would prevent that from happening. I had been among the first world leaders to call for an International War Crimes Tribunal, and I thought the United States should support it.

We passed up Renaissance Weekend again that year so that our family could spend the last New Year's at Camp David. I still hadn't heard from Arafat. On New Year's Day, I invited him to the White House the next day. Before he came, he received Prince Bandar and the Egyptian ambassador at his hotel. One of Arafat's younger aides told us that they had pushed him hard to say yes. When Arafat came to see me, he asked a lot of questions about my proposal. He wanted Israel to have the Wailing Wall, because of its religious significance, but asserted that the remaining fifty feet of the Western Wall should go to the Palestinians. I told him he was wrong, that Israel should have the entire wall to protect itself from someone using one entrance of the tunnel that ran beneath the wall from damaging the remains of the temples beneath the Haram. The Old City has four quarters: Jewish, Muslim, Christian, and Armenian. It was assumed that Palestine would get the Muslim and Christian quarters, with Israel getting the other two. Arafat argued that he should have a few blocks of the Armenian quarter because of the Christian churches there. I couldn't believe he was talking to me about this.

Arafat was also trying to wiggle out of giving up the right of return. He knew he had to but was afraid of the criticism he would get. I reminded him that Israel had promised to take some of the refugees from Lebanon whose families had lived in what was now northern Israel for hundreds of years, but that no Israeli leader would ever let in so many Palestinians that the Jewish character of the state could be threatened in a few decades by the higher Palestinian birthrate. There were not going to be two majority-Arab states in the Holy Land; Arafat had acknowledged that by signing the 1993 peace agreement with its implicit two-state solution. Besides, the agreement had to be approved by Israeli citizens in a referendum. The right of return was a deal breaker. I wouldn't think of asking the Israelis to vote for it. On the other hand, I thought the Israelis would vote for a final settlement within the parameters I had laid out. If there was an agreement, I even thought Barak might be able to come back and win the election, though he was running well behind Sharon in the polls, in an electorate frightened by the intifada and angered by Arafat's refusal to make peace.

At times Arafat seemed confused, not wholly in command of the facts. I had felt for some time that he might not be at the top of his game any longer, after all the years of spending the night in different places to dodge assassins' bullets, all the countless hours on airplanes, all the endless hours of tension-filled talks. Perhaps he simply couldn't make the final jump from revolutionary to statesman. He had grown used to flying from place to place, giving mother-of-pearl gifts made by Palestinian craftsmen to world leaders and appearing on television with them. It would be different if the end of violence took Palestine out of the headlines and instead he had to worry about providing jobs, schools, and basic services. Most of the young people on Arafat's team wanted him to take the deal. I believe Abu Ala and Abu Mazen also would have agreed but didn't want to be at odds with Arafat.

When he left, I still had no idea what Arafat was going to do. His body language said no, but the deal was so good I couldn't believe anyone would be foolish enough to let it go. Barak wanted me to come to the region, but I wanted Arafat to say yes to the Israelis on the big issues embodied in my parameters first. In December the parties had met at Bolling Air Force Base for talks that didn't succeed because Arafat wouldn't accept the parameters that were hard for him.

Finally, Arafat agreed to see Shimon Peres on the thirteenth after Peres had first met with Saeb Erekat. Nothing came of it. As a backstop, the Israelis tried to produce a letter with as much agreement on the parameters as possible, on the assumption that Barak would lose the election and at least both sides would be bound to a course that could lead to an agreement. Arafat wouldn't even do that, because he didn't want to be seen conceding anything. The parties continued their talks in Taba, Egypt. They got close, but did not succeed. Arafat never said no; he just couldn't bring himself to say yes. Pride goeth before the fall.

Right before I left office, Arafat, in one of our last conversations, thanked me for all my efforts and told me what a great man I was. "Mr. Chairman," I replied, "I am not a great man. I am a failure, and you have made me one." I warned Arafat that he was single-handedly electing Sharon and that he would reap the whirlwind.

In February 2001, Ariel Sharon would be elected prime minister in a landslide. The Israelis had decided that if Arafat wouldn't take my offer he wouldn't take anything, and that if they had no partner for peace, it was better to be led by the most aggressive, intransigent leader available. Sharon would take a hard line toward Arafat and would be supported in doing so by Ehud Barak and the United States. Nearly a year after I left office, Arafat said he was ready to negotiate on the basis of the parameters I had presented. Apparently, Arafat had thought the time to decide, five minutes to midnight, had finally come. His watch had been broken a long time.

Arafat's rejection of my proposal after Barak accepted it was an error of historic proportions. However, many Palestinians and Israelis are still committed to peace. Someday peace will come, and when it does, the final agreement will look a lot like the proposals that came out of Camp David and the six long months that followed.

On January 3, I sat in the Senate with Chelsea and the rest of Hillary's family as Al Gore administered the oath of office to New York's new senator. I was so excited I almost jumped over the railing. For seventeen more days we would both be in office, the first couple to serve in the White House and the Senate in American history. But Hillary was on her own now. About all I could do was ask Trent Lott not to be too hard on her and offer to be Hillary's caseworker for Westchester County.

The next day we held a White House event that for me was about Mother: a celebration of the Breast and Cervical Cancer Protection and Treatment Act of 2000, which allowed women without health insurance who were diagnosed with these cancers to have full Medicaid benefits.

On the fifth, I announced that we would protect sixty million acres of pristine national forest in thirty-nine states from road building and logging, including the Tongass National Forest in Alaska, the last great temperate rain forest in America. The timber interests were against the move and I thought the Bush administration might try to undo it on economic grounds, but only 5 percent of the nation's timber came from national forests, and only 5 percent of that amount came from roadless areas. We could do without that tiny amount of logging to preserve another priceless national treasure.

After the announcement I drove out to Fort Myer to receive the traditional farewell tribute from the armed forces, a fine military ceremony that included the presentation of an American flag, a flag with the presidential seal, and medals from each of the service branches. They gave Hillary a medal, too. Bill Cohen noted that in appointing him I became the only President ever to ask an elected official of the opposite party to become secretary of defense.

Being President carries no greater honor than being Commander in Chief of men and women of every race and religion who trace their ancestry to every region on earth. They are the living embodiment of our national creed, *E pluribus unum.* I had seen them cheered in refugee camps in the Balkans, helping the victims of disasters in Central America, working against narco-traffickers in Colombia and the Caribbean, welcomed with open arms in the former Communist nations of Central Europe, manning distant outposts in Alaska, standing guard in the deserts of the Middle East, and patrolling the Pacific.

Americans know about our forces when they go into battle. There will never be a full account of the wars never fought, the losses never suffered, the tears never shed because American men and women stood guard for peace. I may have gotten off to a rocky start with the military, but I worked hard at being Commander in Chief, and I was confident that I was leaving our military in even better shape than I found it.

On Saturday, January 6, after a visit to the National Zoo to see the pandas, Hillary and I held a farewell party on the South Lawn with Al and Tipper for all the people who had worked or volunteered in the White House over the past eight years. Hundreds of people came, many from long distances. We talked and reminisced for several hours. Al got a rousing welcome when I introduced him as the people's choice in the recent election. When he asked for a show of hands of all the people who had married or had children during our time in the White House, I was amazed at the number of hands that shot up. No matter what the Republicans said, we were a pro-family party.

The White House social secretary, Capricia Marshall, who had supported me since 1991 and had been with Hillary since early in our first campaign, had arranged a special surprise for me. The curtain behind us rose to reveal Fleetwood Mac singing "Don't Stop Thinkin' About Tomorrow" one more time.

On Sunday, Hillary, Chelsea, and I went to Foundry United Methodist Church, where the Reverend Phil Wogaman invited Hillary and me to make farewell remarks to the congregation that had embraced us for eight years. Chelsea had made good friends there and had learned a lot working in a distant hollow of rural Kentucky on the church's Appalachian Service Project. The church members came from many races and nations, and were rich and poor, straight and gay, old and young. Foundry had supported Washington's homeless population and refugees in parts of the world where I tried to make peace.

I didn't know what I was going to say, but Wogaman had told the congregation that I would tell them what I anticipated my new life would be like. So I said that my faith would be tested by a return to commercial air travel and that I would be disoriented by walking into large rooms because no band would be playing "Hail to the Chief." And I said I would do whatever I could to be a good citizen, to lift the hopes and fortunes of those who deserve a better hand than they have been dealt, and to keep working for peace and reconciliation. Despite my best efforts for the last eight years, that kind of work still seemed to be in strong demand.

Later that night in New York City, I spoke to the pro-peace Israel Policy Forum. At the time we still had some hope of making peace. Arafat had said he accepted the parameters with reservations. The problem was that his reservations, unlike Israel's, were outside the parameters, at least on refugees and the Western Wall, but I treated the acceptance as if it were real, based on his pledge to make peace before I left office. The American-Jewish community had been very good to me. Some, like my friend Haim Saban and Danny Abraham, were deeply involved with Israel and had given me helpful advice over the years. Many others simply supported my work for peace. Regardless of what happened, I thought I owed it to them to explain my proposal.

The next day, after presenting the Citizens Medal to twenty-eight deserving Americans, including Muhammad Ali, I went over to the Democratic Party headquarters to thank the chairmen, Mayor Ed Rendell of Philadelphia and Joe Andrew, and to give a plug to Terry McAuliffe, who had done so much for Al Gore and for me, and who now was campaigning to be the new party chair. After all the work he'd done, I couldn't believe Terry wanted the job, but if he did, I was for him. I told the people who'd slaved away at the party work without glory or recognition how much I appreciated them.

On the ninth, I began a farewell tour to places that had been especially good to me, Michigan and Illinois, where victories in the primaries on St. Patrick's Day 1992 had virtually assured me of the nomination. Two days later, I went to Massachusetts, which gave me the highest percentage of any state in '96, and to New Hampshire, where they had made me the Comeback Kid in early 1992. In between, I dedicated a statue of Franklin Roosevelt in his wheelchair at the FDR Memorial on the Mall. The disability community had lobbied hard for it, and most of the Roosevelt family had supported it. Of the more than 10,000 photos of FDR in his archives, only four depict him in his wheelchair. Disabled Americans had come a long way since then.

I said farewell to New Hampshire in Dover, where almost nine years earlier I had promised to be with them "'til the last dog dies." Many of my old supporters were in the audience. I called several by name, thanked them all, then gave them a full account of the record their hard work in that long-ago winter had made possible. And I asked them never to forget that, "even though I won't be President, I'll always be with you until the last dog dies."

On the eleventh through the fourteenth, I had parties for the cabinet, the White House staff, and friends at Camp David. On the night of the fourteenth, Don Henley gave us a wonderful solo concert after dinner in the Camp David Chapel. The next morning was our family's last Sunday in the beautiful chapel, where we had shared many services with the fine young sailors and marines who staffed the camp and their families. They had even let me sing with the choir, always leaving the sheet music in Aspen, our family cabin, on Friday or Saturday so that I could review it in advance.

On Monday, I spoke at the Martin Luther King Jr. holiday celebration at the University of the District of Columbia. Usually I marked the day by doing some community service work, but I wanted to take this opportunity to thank the District of Columbia for being my home for eight years. The D.C. representative in Congress, Eleanor Holmes Norton, and Mayor Tony Williams were good friends of mine, as were several city council members. I had worked to help them get needed legislation through Congress and to prevent unduly meddlesome laws from being enacted. The District still had a lot of problems, but it was in much better condition than it had been eight years earlier when I took my pre-inaugural walk down Georgia Avenue.

I also sent my last message to Congress: "The Unfinished Work of Building One America." It was based in large part on the final report of the Commission on Race and included a wide array of recommendations: further steps to close the racial divide in education, health care, employment, and the criminal justice system; special efforts to help low-income absent fathers succeed at parenting; new investments for Native American communities; improved immigration policies; passage of the hate crimes bill; reform of the voting laws; and the continuation of AmeriCorps and the White House Office on One America. We had made a lot of headway in eight years, but America was growing more diverse, and there was still much to be done.

On the seventeenth, I held my last ceremony in the East Room, as Bruce Babbitt and I announced eight more national monuments, two of them along the trail Lewis and Clark blazed in 1803 with their Indian guide Sacagawea and a slave named York. We had now protected more land in the lower forty-eight states than any administration since that of Theodore Roosevelt.

After the announcement, I left the White House on the last trip of my presidency, going home to Little Rock to address the Arkansas legislature. Some of my old pals were still in the state House or Senate, as were people who had gotten their start in politics working with me and a few who began by working against me. More than twenty Arkansans who were then serving or had served with me in Washington joined me that day, as did three of my high school classmates who lived in the Washington area, and several Arkansans who had served as my liaisons to the legislature when I was governor. Chelsea came with me, too. We passed two of her schools on the way in from the airport, and I thought of how much she had grown up since Hillary and I had attended her school programs at Booker Arts Magnet School.

I tried to thank all the Arkansans who had helped me reach this day, beginning with two men who were no longer living, Judge Frank Holt and Senator Fulbright. I urged the legislators to keep pushing the federal government to support the states on education, economic development, health care, and welfare reform. Finally, I told my old friends that I would leave office in three days grateful that "somehow the mystery of this great democracy gave me the chance to go from a little boy on South Hervey Street in Hope, Arkansas, to the White House. . . . I may be the only person ever elected President who owed his election purely to his personal friends, without whom I could never have won." I left my friends and flew home to finish the job.

The next night, after a day working on last-minute business, I gave a brief farewell address to the nation from the Oval Office. After thanking the American people for giving me the chance to serve and briefly summarizing my philosophy and record, I offered three observations about the future, saying that we should stay on the path to fiscal responsibility; that our security and prosperity required us to lead in the fight for prosperity and freedom and against terrorism, organized crime, narco-trafficking, the spread of deadly weapons, environmental degradation, disease, and global poverty; and finally, that we must continue to "weave the threads of our coat of many colors into the fabric of one America."

I wished President-elect Bush and his family well and said I would "leave the presidency more idealistic, more full of hope than the day I arrived, and more confident than ever that America's best days lie ahead."

On the nineteenth, my last full day as President, I issued a statement on land mines, saying that since 1993 the United States had destroyed more than 3.3 million of our own land mines, spent $500 million to remove land mines in thirty-five countries, and was making a vigorous effort to find a sensible alternative to mines that would protect our troops as well. I asked the new administration to continue our global demining effort for ten more years.

When I got back to the residence it was late and we still weren't completely packed. There were boxes everywhere, and I still had to decide which clothes were going where—to New York, Washington, or Arkansas. Hillary and I didn't want to sleep; we just wanted to keep strolling from room to room. We felt as honored to be living in the White House on our last night as we had when we came home after our first inaugural balls. I never ceased to be thrilled by it all. It seemed almost unbelievable that it had been our home for eight years; now it was almost over.

I went back into the Lincoln Bedroom, read Lincoln's handwritten copy of the Gettysburg Address one last time, and stared at the lithograph of him signing the Emancipation

Proclamation, on the very spot where I was standing. I went into the Queen's Room and thought of Winston Churchill spending three weeks there in the difficult days of World War II. I sat behind the Treaty Table in my office looking at the empty bookshelves and bare walls, thinking of all the meetings and calls I'd had in that room on Northern Ireland, the Middle East, Russia, Korea, and domestic struggles. And it was in this room where I read my Bible and books and letters, and prayed for strength and guidance all through 1998.

Earlier in the day I had prerecorded my final radio address, to be aired not long before I was to leave the White House for the inaugural ceremony. In it I thanked the White House staff, the residence staff, the Secret Service, the cabinet, and Al Gore for all they had done to make my service possible. And I kept my promise to work until the last hour of the last day, releasing another $100 million to fund more police officers; those new police had helped give America the lowest crime rate in a quarter century.

Well past midnight, I went back to the Oval Office again to clean up, pack, and answer a few letters. As I sat alone at the desk, I thought about all that had happened during the last eight years, and how quickly it would be over. Soon I would observe the transfer of power and take my leave. Hillary, Chelsea, and I would board Air Force One for a last flight with the fine crew that had taken us to the far corners of the world; our closest staff members; my new Secret Service detail; some of the career military staff such as Glen Maes, the navy steward who baked all my specially decorated birthday cakes, and Glenn Powell, the air force sergeant who made sure our luggage never got lost; and a few of the folks who "brought me to the dance"—the Jordans, the McAuliffes, the McLartys, and Harry Thomason.

Several members of the press corps were also scheduled to make the last trip. One of them, Mark Knoller of CBS Radio, had covered me all eight years and had conducted one of the many wrap-up interviews I had done in the past several weeks. Mark had asked me if I was afraid that "the best part of your life is over." I said I had enjoyed every part of my life and that in each stage I had been "absorbed, interested, and found something useful to do."

I was looking forward to my new life, to building my library, doing public service work through my foundation, supporting Hillary, and having more time for reading, golf, music, and unhurried travel. I knew I would enjoy myself and believed that if I stayed healthy I could still do a lot of good. But Mark Knoller had hit a soft spot with his question. I was going to miss my old job. I had loved being President, even on the bad days.

I thought about the note to President Bush I would write and leave behind in the Oval Office, just as his father had done for me eight years earlier. I wanted to be gracious and encouraging, as George Bush had been to me. Soon George W. Bush would be President of all the people, and I wished him well. I had paid close attention to what Bush and Cheney had said in the campaign. I knew they saw the world very differently from the way I did and would want to undo much of what I had done, especially on economic policy and the environment. I thought that they would pass their big tax cut and that before long we would be back to the big deficits of the 1980s, and in spite of Bush's encouraging comments on education and AmeriCorps, he would feel pressure to cut back on all domestic spending, including education, child care, after-school programs, police on the streets, innovative research, and the environment. But those were not my calls to make anymore.

I thought that the international partnerships that we had developed in the aftermath of the Cold War could be strained by the more unilateral approach of the Republicans—they were opposed to the test ban treaty, the climate change treaty, the ABM Treaty, and the International Criminal Court.

I had watched the Washington Republicans for eight years and imagined that President Bush would, from the outset of his term, be under pressure to abandon compassionate conservatism by the more right-wing leaders and interest groups now in control of his party. They believed in their way as deeply as I believed in mine, but I thought the evidence, and the weight of history, favored our side.

I couldn't control what happened to my policies and programs; few things are permanent in politics. Nor could I affect the early judgments on my so-called legacy. The history of America's move from the end of the Cold War to the millennium would be written and rewritten over and over. The only thing that mattered to me about my presidency was whether I had done a good job for the American people in a new and very different era of global interdependence.

Had I helped to form a "more perfect union" by widening the circle of opportunity, deepening the meaning of freedom, and strengthening the bonds of community? I had certainly tried to make America the twenty-first century's leading force for peace and prosperity, freedom and security. I had tried to put a more human face on globalization by urging other nations to join us in building a more integrated world of shared responsibilities, shared benefits, and shared values; and I had tried to lead America through its transition into this new era with a sense of hope and optimism about what we could do, and a sober sense of what the new forces of destruction could do to us. Finally, I had tried to build a new progressive politics rooted in new ideas and old values, and to support like-minded movements around the world. No matter how many of my specific initiatives the new administration and its congressional majority might undo, I believed that if we were on the right side of history, the direction I had taken into the new millennium would eventually prevail.

On my last night in the now barren Oval Office, I thought of the glass case I had kept on the coffee table between the two couches, just a few feet away. It contained a rock Neil Armstrong had taken off the moon in 1969. Whenever arguments in the Oval Office heated up beyond reason, I would interrupt and say, "You see that rock? It's 3.6 billion years old. We're all just passing through. Let's calm down and go back to work."

That moon rock gave me a whole different perspective on history and the proverbial "long run." Our job is to live as well and as long as we can, and to help others to do the same. What happens after that and how we are viewed by others is beyond our control. The river of time carries us all away. All we have is the moment. Whether I had made the most of mine was for others to judge. It was almost dawn when I returned to the residence to do some more packing and share some private moments with Hillary and Chelsea.

The next morning, I returned to the Oval Office to write my note to President Bush. Hillary came down, too. We gazed out the windows to take a long, admiring look at the beautiful grounds where we had shared so many memorable times and I had thrown countless tennis balls to Buddy. Then she left me to write my letter. As I placed the letter on the desk, I called my staff in to say good-bye. We hugged, smiled, shed a few tears, and took a few pictures. Then I walked out of the Oval Office for the last time.

As I stepped out the door with my arms opened wide, I was greeted by members of the press there to capture the moment. John Podesta walked with me down the colonnade to join Hillary, Chelsea, and the Gores on the state floor, where we would soon greet our successors. The entire residence staff had gathered to say good-bye—the housekeeping staff, the kitchen staff, the florist, the grounds crew, the ushers, the butlers, my valets. Many of them had become like family. I looked into their faces and stored the memories, not knowing when I would see them again, and knowing that when I did, it would never be quite the same. They would soon have a new family who would need them as much as we had.

A small combo from the marine band was playing in the grand foyer. I sat down at the piano with Master Sergeant Charlie Corrado, who had played for Presidents for forty years. Charlie was always there for us, and his music had brightened a lot of days. Hillary and I had a last dance, and at about ten-thirty the Bushes and the Cheneys arrived. We drank coffee and chatted for a few minutes; then the eight of us got in the limousines, and I rode with George W. Bush for the drive down Pennsylvania Avenue to the Capitol.

Within an hour, the peaceful transfer of power that has

kept our country free for more than two hundred years had taken place again. My family said good-bye to the new First Family and drove to Andrews Air Force Base for our last flight on the presidential plane that was no longer Air Force One for me. After eight years as President, and half a lifetime in politics, I was a private citizen again, but a very grateful one, still pulling for my country, still thinking about tomorrow.

EPILOGUE

I WROTE THIS BOOK to tell my story, and to tell the story of America in the last half of the twentieth century; to describe as fairly as I could the forces competing for the country's heart and mind; to explain the challenges of the new world in which we live and how I believe our government and our citizens should respond to them; and to give people who have never been involved in public life a sense of what it is like to hold office, and especially what it is like to be President.

While writing, I found myself falling back in time, reliving events as I recounted them, feeling as I did then and writing as I felt. During my second term, as the partisan battles I tried to defuse continued unabated, I also tried to understand how my time in office fit into the stream of American history.

That history is largely the story of our efforts to honor our founders' charge to form a "more perfect union." In calmer times, our country has been well served by our two-party system, with progressives and conservatives debating what to change and what to preserve. But when change is forced upon us by events, we are all tested, and thrown back to our fundamental mission to widen the circle of opportunity, deepen the meaning of freedom, and strengthen the bonds of our community. To me, that is what it means to make our union more perfect.

At every turning point, we have chosen union over division: in the early days of the Republic, by building a national economic and legal system; during the Civil War, by preserving the Union and ending slavery; in the early twentieth century, as we moved from an agricultural to an industrial society, by making our government stronger to preserve competition, promote basic safeguards for labor, provide for the poor, the elderly, and the infirm, and protect our natural resources from plunder; and in the sixties and seventies, by advancing civil rights and women's rights. In each instance, while we were engaged in the struggle to define, defend, and expand our union, powerful conservative forces resisted, and as long as the outcome was in doubt, the political and personal conflicts were intense.

In 1993, when I took office, we were facing another historic challenge to the Union, as we moved from the industrial age into the global information age. The American people were faced with big changes in the way they lived and worked, and with big questions to be answered: Would we choose global economic engagement or economic nationalism? Would we use our unrivaled military, political, and economic power to spread the benefits and confront the emerging threats of the interdependent world or become Fortress America? Would we abandon our industrial-age government, with its commitments to equal opportunity and social justice, or reform it so as to retain its achievements while giving people the tools to succeed in the new era? Would our increasing racial and religious diversity fracture or strengthen our national community?

As President, I tried to answer these questions in a way that kept moving us toward a more perfect union, lifting people's vision, and bringing them together to build a new vital center for American politics in the twenty-first century. Two-thirds of our citizens supported my general approach, but on the controversial cultural questions and on the always appealing tax cuts, the electorate was more closely divided. With the outcome in doubt, bitter partisan and personal attacks raged, bearing a striking resemblance to those of the early Republic.

Whether my historical analysis is right or not, I judge my presidency primarily in terms of its impact on people's lives. That is how I kept score: all the millions of people with new jobs, new homes, and college aid; the kids with health insurance and after-school programs; the people who left welfare for work; the families helped by the family leave law; the people living in safer neighborhoods—all those people have stories, and they're better ones now. Life got better for all Americans because the air and water were cleaner and more of our natural heritage was preserved. And we brought more hope for peace, freedom, security, and prosperity to people all over the world. They have their stories, too.

When I became President, America was sailing into uncharted waters, into a world full of apparently disconnected positive and negative forces. Because I had spent a lifetime trying to bring together my own parallel lives and had been raised to value all people, and, as governor, had seen both the bright and dark sides of globalization, I felt I understood where my country was and how we needed to move into the new century. I knew how to put things together, and how hard it would be to do.

On September 11, things seemed to fall apart again as al Qaeda used the forces of interdependence—open borders, easy immigration and travel, easy access to information and technology—to murder close to 3,000 people, from more than seventy nations, in New York, Washington, D.C., and Pennsylvania. The world rallied around our loss and the American people in our determination to fight terrorism. In the years since, the battle has intensified, with understandable and honestly held differences at home and around the world about how best to pursue the war on terror.

The interdependent world we live in is inherently unstable, full of both opportunity and forces of destruction. It will remain so until we find our way from interdependence to a more integrated global community of shared responsibilities, shared benefits, and shared values. Building that kind of world, and defeating terror, cannot be done quickly; it will be the great challenge of the first half of the twenty-first century. I believe there are five things the United States should be doing to lead the way: fight terror and the spread of weapons of mass destruction and improve our defenses against them; make more friends and fewer terrorists by helping the 50 percent of the world not reaping the benefits of globalization to overcome poverty, ignorance, disease, and bad government; strengthen the institutions of global cooperation and work through them to promote security and prosperity and combat our shared problems, from terror to AIDS to global warming; continue to make America a better model of how we want the world to work; and work to end the age-old compulsion to believe that our differences are more important than our common humanity.

I believe the world will continue its forward march from isolation to interdependence to cooperation because there is no other choice. We have come a long way since our ancestors first stood up on the African savannah more than a hundred thousand years ago. In just the fifteen years since the end of the Cold War, the West has been largely reconciled to its old adversaries, Russia and China; more than half of the world's people are living under governments of their own choosing for the first time in history; there has been an unprecedented degree of global cooperation against terror and a recognition that we must do more to fight poverty, disease, and global warming and to get all the world's children in school; and America and many other free societies have shown that people of all races and religions can live together in mutual respect and harmony.

Our nation will not be undone by terror. We will defeat it, but we must take care that in so doing we do not compromise the character of our country or the future of our children. Our mission to form a more perfect union is now a global one.

As for myself, I'm still working on that list of life goals I made as a young man. Becoming a good person is a lifelong effort that requires letting go of anger at others and holding on to responsibility for the mistakes I've made. And it requires forgiveness. After all the forgiveness I've been given from Hillary, Chelsea, my friends, and millions of people in America and across the world, it's the least I can do. As a young politician, when I started going to black churches, for the first time I heard people refer to funerals as "homegoings." We're all going home, and I want to be ready.

In the meantime, I take great joy in the life Chelsea is building, the superb job Hillary is doing in the Senate, and my foundation's efforts to bring economic, educational, and service opportunities to poor communities in America and across the world; to fight AIDS and bring low-cost medicine to those who need it; and to continue my lifelong commitment to racial and religious reconciliation.

Do I have regrets? Sure, both private and public ones, as I've discussed in this book. I leave it to others to judge how to balance the scales.

I've simply tried to tell the story of my joys and sorrows, dreams and fears, triumphs and failures. And I've tried to explain the difference between my view of the world and that held by those on the Far Right with whom I did battle. In essence they honestly believe they know the whole truth. I see things differently. I think Saint Paul had it right when he said that in this life we "see through a glass darkly" and "know in part." That's why he extolled the virtues of "faith, hope, and love."

I've had an improbable life, and a wonderful one full of faith, hope, and love, as well as more than my share of grace and good fortune. As improbable as my life has been, it would have been impossible anywhere but America. Unlike so many people, I have been privileged to spend every day working for things I've believed in since I was a little boy hanging around my grandfather's store. I grew up with a fascinating mother who adored me, have learned at the feet of great teachers, have made a legion of loyal friends, have built a loving life with the finest woman I've ever known, and have a child who continues to be the light of my life.

As I said, I think it's a good story, and I've had a good time telling it.

AFTERWORD TO THE
VINTAGE EDITION

AS THE PAPERBACK edition of *My Life* goes to press, President Bush has just begun his second term in office and I have begun the "second term" of my post Presidency. Over the last four years, I have found a good life after the White House. As was true of my eight years as President, it has been full of well-laid plans—building my library in Arkansas and my Foundation in Harlem—and unexpected events, from 9/11 to my recent encounter with heart disease.

By the time I left the White House, I had given a lot of thought to what I wanted to do. There is no job description for a former President, but some of my predecessors have made a real difference. John Quincy Adams served eight terms in the House of Representatives, where he led the fight against slavery. Theodore Roosevelt became disillusioned with the conservative drift of the Republican Party and started a new political movement, which he called "The New Nationalism." He ran for President on the Bull Moose ticket in 1912 and finished second, the only third-party candidate to do so since the advent of the modern two-party system. His successor, William Howard Taft, became Chief Justice of the Supreme Court. Herbert Hoover led a commission to reform the federal civil service under President Truman. Richard Nixon wrote several informative books on foreign policy. And Jimmy Carter set up a foundation from which he has monitored elections, promoted human rights, worked for peace, and reduced the scourge of river blindness in Africa.

Carter's experience seemed the most relevant to me. He has made a bigger difference than any other of my predecessors, with the possible exception of John Quincy Adams, and won a well-deserved Nobel Peace Prize for a lifetime of good works. I wanted to work in areas that I cared about, where I could still make a difference, both in America and around the world. Finally I settled on four areas that roughly parallel the Millennium Development Goals adopted by the UN: bringing economic opportunity to poor areas in America and throughout the world; promoting education and citizen service for young people at home and abroad; fighting HIV/AIDS; and advancing religious, racial, and ethnic reconciliation.

Soon after leaving office, I set up my Foundation's headquarters in Harlem in New York City, an area that has fascinated me for more than thirty years. Harlem was also designated as one of our first "enterprise zones" established under the budget bill of 1993. By 2001, the unemployment rate in Harlem had been cut by two-thirds.

At the same time, I embarked on an ambitious campaign to fund my library and presidential center in Little Rock, which I wanted to be America's first museum of the twenty-first century: to illuminate America's transformation after the Cold War in how we live, work, and relate to the rest of the world; to describe the philosophy and policies we embraced to deal with the new challenges and opportunities of this "Age of Interdependence"; and to demonstrate the results of our efforts.

In early 2001 a devastating earthquake struck Gujarat, in western India. At the request of then Prime Minister Vajpayee, I worked with Indian Americans to establish the American India Foundation, through which we raised several million dollars to help rebuild homes, schools, hospitals, and local village economies.

After the attacks on the United States on 9/11, I did what I could to support President Bush in building a global alliance to topple the Taliban and go after Osama bin Laden and his top lieutenants, and to support Hillary in her work to help New Yorkers cope with the tragedy and rebuild. I teamed up with Senator Bob Dole to raise $100 million for the Families of Freedom fund, which guarantees a college education to the children and spouses of all those killed or disabled on 9/11; the benefits will continue to flow for more than two decades. And for more than a year, I traveled around our country and the world to reassure people in open societies that the terrorists would not prevail but that we must defeat them in a way that does not compromise the character of our country or the future of our children. The ideas I advanced are summarized in the epilogue of this book.

2001 was also a happy time for my family. Chelsea graduated from Stanford in the spring in a wonderful ceremony marked by the seniors doing all kinds of stunts on the football field as the faculty and administrators solemnly marched in. In the fall she began a two-year masters program in international relations at Oxford. She enrolled in my old college, University. As I wrote, I loved helping her move into her first-year digs, which were on the same little courtyard I had lived in thirty-three years earlier. When Chelsea completed her thesis on the Global Fund to Fight AIDS, TB, and Malaria, she invited Hillary and me to return to Oxford to see her oral presentation on it. We were bursting with pride as she answered questions with a clarity and eloquence we could not have matched at her age.

In 2002, the work of my Foundation really began to get off the ground. In Harlem, we began a Small Business Initiative to give top financial and management advice to new and established businesses under the leadership of Reggie Van Lee, a managing partner of Booz Allen Hamilton. The program has now been adopted by the Stern School of Business at New York University, and we are working to extend it into Brooklyn and the Bronx. I also began an annual effort to increase the number of New Yorkers applying for tax relief under the Earned Income Tax Credit, which lifted millions of working poor and their children out of poverty after we doubled it in 1993. Unfortunately, millions of eligible people still don't know about it or apply for it.

In July 2002, Nelson Mandela and I, as co-chairs of the International AIDS Trust, were invited to close the International AIDS Conference in Barcelona, Spain. After our speeches, Prime Minister Denzel Douglas of St. Kitts and

Nevis asked me if I would be willing to help the Caribbean nations establish health care systems for the prevention, care, and treatment of HIV/AIDS. I instantly agreed, though I had no idea how to begin. At the time, I had fewer than twenty people working in Harlem and Little Rock and still had to raise more than $100 million to complete my presidential library. I called my old friend Ira Magaziner, who had spearheaded our efforts in health care and e-commerce in the White House, and asked if he would organize and lead the project.

He, too, instantly agreed and soon had a plan. We would assemble volunteers to work with governments that asked our help in developing comprehensive care and treatment plans, then send teams to help implement the plans. Meanwhile, I would try to get wealthier nations to agree to finance the necessary health infrastructure and the purchase of generic AIDS medicines and the testing necessary to assure that they were working. At the time, there were more than forty million people in the world with HIV and more than six million with full-blown AIDS desperately in need of treatment.

Despite the availability of generic drugs at $500 per person, per year, only 300,000 people in developing countries were receiving them, 130,000 in Brazil, where drug companies manufacture the medicine and the government provides it to those who can't pay for it. Seventy percent of those in need were in Africa, but the epidemic was growing fastest in the nations of the former Soviet Union, the Caribbean, India, and China.

What began as a modest effort in the Caribbean has spread rapidly. After just two years, my Foundation is working in thirteen Caribbean nations, with over 95 percent of the region's HIV cases; in India and China, with over 80 percent of Asia's cases; and in the African nations of Rwanda, Mozambique, Tanzania, Lesotho, and South Africa, with over 35 percent of that continent's affected people. Ireland, Canada, Norway, Sweden, and France have made generous commitments to fund the programs, with other nations offering lesser amounts. Money flows directly from governments to fund the clinics and medicine. The only money my Foundation collects is from generous private citizens in the United States and the United Kingdom who have given millions of dollars to fund our part of the operations. We now have more than forty full-time people on staff and more than one hundred Foundation volunteers working in twenty countries.

In 2003, we made a breakthrough in the availability of generic drugs when Indian and South African manufacturers negotiated a drastic price reduction with my Foundation from $500 to $139 per person, per year. Soon, we had also achieved an 80 percent reduction in the cost of diagnostic testing and equipment in agreements with the major U.S. and European companies providing them. Meanwhile, we have made agreements that enable thirty more countries to buy medicine and tests based on our low-cost contracts, a number that I expect will grow to sixty over the next few years.

At the beginning of 2005, the countries we were working with were providing medicine to 80,000 more people, with other nations using our low-cost contract to cover another 30,000. One hundred ten thousand people is a small dent in the 6 million who should be getting the medicine, but it is a huge addition to the 170,000 outside Brazil who were getting it when we started two years ago. By 2008, we hope the nations we work with and those who purchase drugs through our contract will be providing care and treatment to 2 million people. As the impact of the larger funding increases obtained by President Bush, the contributions of other nations to the Global Fund to Fight AIDS, TB, and Malaria, and the efforts of the Gates Foundation and other NGOs kick in, the number of people with HIV and AIDS receiving lifesaving care and treatment should increase dramatically.

In early 2005, I went back to the Bahamas, where we had started our work, and where, with our help, the government has quadrupled the number of people receiving treatment. The death rates have been cut in half, and in 2004, there were no transmissions of the HIV virus from infected mothers who had taken preventative medicine to their newborn children. I met with three children who were frail and sick when I first saw them in 2003; today they are much stronger and healthier, a testament to what can be done all over the world. We are all acting later than we should have, but still soon enough to save millions of lives.

In my first three years out of office, I traveled all over America and to fifty-four other nations, many more than once, to pursue the work of my Foundation and promote my ideas for building a global community of shared responsibilities, benefits, and values.

My Foundation has done some good work on education and citizen service, helping to establish City Year service projects in South Africa and Little Rock, and a scholarship program to bring American students to study at American University in Dubai, the nation with perhaps the fastest growing and most diverse economy in the Middle East, proof that Islam is not incompatible with the modern world and religious and ethnic diversity. Each year, my Foundation also holds a one-day seminar at New York University on a different topic important to all our futures. So far we have brought together people from all around the globe to discuss Islam and the West; how to bring the benefits of globalization to the billions of people who remain poor; and how to develop a clean-energy future and combat global warming.

This fall we are sponsoring the Clinton Global Initiative, a conference on major global problems for business and NGO leaders coinciding with the opening of the United Nations General Assembly. It will be unique in only one respect: at the end of the two-day session, every participant must commit to undertake some specific action to make a positive difference in one of the problem areas.

The Clinton School of Public Service also opens this fall under the leadership of my old friend Senator David Pryor, offering graduate degrees to young people who are committed to careers in public life. I look forward to doing a little teaching there and to bringing in people from all over the world to inspire a new generation of public servants.

In my first three years out of office, I traveled to many nations to push for peace and reconciliation: to Israel, Saudi

Arabia, Jordan, Dubai, and Qatar in the Middle East; to Rwanda, to support the completion of the national monument to the victims of the genocide and to visit one of the "reconciliation villages" where former enemies are living as neighbors; to Nigeria, where I urged the parliament not to let the nation be torn apart by legal and political conflicts between Muslims and Christians; to Kosovo and Bosnia, where I spoke at the dedication of the memorial to the victims of the slaughter at Srebrenica and listened as widows said the West came to save Bosnia too late, "but if it hadn't been for you, no one would have come at all"; to Colombia, to urge the business community to stay in Latin America's oldest democracy and support the government's stand against the narco-traffickers and their terrorist supporters who control nearly one-third of the nation's territory; to East Timor, to represent the United States at the launching of the first new nation of the twenty-first century, made possible by a multinational military intervention in which United States forces took part; and to Northern Ireland, where Irish-Americans endowed a peace center in my name at Enniskillen, which brings together citizens from troubled places to talk through their differences.

I have also done what I could to support efforts to increase the capacity of fragile democratic governments to solve big problems, through the Club of Madrid, a group of former heads of government, and on my own in Latin America and Africa. In the coming years, I hope to do more of this work. Americans sometimes forget that many democracies don't have the kind of effective institutions and legions of dedicated public servants we too often take for granted.

For the first three months of 2004, I stayed in Chappaqua most days, working feverishly to finish my book in order to meet our June deadline. Hillary's book, *Living History*, was published a year earlier and quickly became a record-breaking bestseller. It was a fine book, and I was so proud of her, but it sure added to the pressure as I raced to finish my own account. *My Life* came out on June 22, and I embarked on a book tour that took me across America and to several foreign countries. As Americans bought the book, there were some good reviews and some bad ones. Most people thought it was too long—a fair criticism. Thomas Jefferson once said that if he had had more time he could have written shorter letters. The reviewers who were interested in people, politics, and government policy seemed to like it better than those who weren't. Perhaps the most favorable review came from the great American novelist Larry McMurtry, who was obviously interested in all three. I was gratified that so many of the book buyers I met were people who said they had been personally helped by my policies in the White House.

Of course, my book tour took place against the backdrop of the presidential campaign in which Senator John Kerry quickly emerged from a crowded field as our nominee. In July, Hillary and I, along with former President Carter, spoke on the opening night of the Democratic convention in Boston in support of Senator Kerry and his running mate, Senator John Edwards. I like Senator Kerry and was glad to praise his Senate record and his proposals for dealing with terrorism; to draw a clear picture of the very different ideas Democrats and Republicans have on economics, health care, education, crime, and the environment; and to point out that, based on the evidence, our policies work better.

I strongly disagreed with returning America to big budget deficits through huge permanent tax cuts that mostly benefit the wealthiest Americans, impose a burden on future generations, and require massive borrowing from the Social Security taxes paid by middle-class Americans and from other countries, led by China and Japan.

In 2004, the financing of our deficits consumed about 80 percent of the world's net new savings; foreign interests now hold over 40 percent of America's debt. We are repeating the 1980s, raising spending, cutting taxes, and exploding the debt. In 1993, when my administration and the congressional Democrats reversed the trend, it sparked the longest economic expansion in our history, produced four budget surpluses in a row, and enabled us to reduce the national debt by hundreds of billions of dollars. I still believe that's the right policy.

Late Wednesday night, September 1, 2004, I flew home from New Orleans, the latest stop on my book tour. As I was getting off the plane, I felt a tightness in my chest. I had felt the same sensation a few times before during the previous few months, but only when I was exercising. The pain was not severe and always went away quickly, so I had just dismissed it as evidence that I was exhausted after finishing the book. Now I was hurting with no exercise.

Not long after I got home, the tightness eased, but I called my doctor about it the next morning. On her advice, I drove to Northern Westchester Hospital, where tests revealed no signs of a heart attack. Still, the doctors there recommended that I go to Westchester Medical Center early Friday morning for an angiogram, an invasive procedure in which a dye is injected into the blood vessels around the heart to show if there is blockage in the arteries.

I called Hillary, who was in Syracuse at the New York State Fair. I was looking forward to joining her the next day in what had become an enjoyable annual event for us. I told her that I would be fine and that she should continue with her schedule. Early the next morning, I drove to the hospital for the angiogram. It was worse than anyone had anticipated. I had severe blockage in four arteries, over 90 percent in two of them. I was a heart attack waiting to happen.

The doctors at Westchester Medical Center quickly informed me that in their view the only responsible option was immediate bypass surgery—the blockage was too severe simply to put in stents to open the arteries, a procedure known as angioplasty. I was told not only that I couldn't join Hillary at the State Fair, I couldn't even go back home. Instead, I was taken directly to New York–Presbyterian Hospital in northwest Manhattan.

Hillary left the State Fair early and Chelsea came home from a business trip abroad to spend the weekend with me. When we announced to the press what had happened, I was touched by the thousands of calls, letters, and e-mails that came in, and grateful for the educational content of the media coverage. My illness gave the general public a lot of information about how to prevent, detect, and beat heart disease.

Facing the operation was tougher for my family than for me. After all, I had already dodged a heart attack, and the procedure, while severe, is now almost routine, performed several hundred thousand times a year in the United States alone. Also, I had been living with my own mortality for a long time, because my father died before I was born and other men in my family had died relatively young. I never expected to live forever and was grateful for the years I'd had. Still, I was hoping God wasn't through with me yet.

The surgery began early Monday morning, September 6. About the only thing I remember is a strange set of images that flew through my mind as the anesthesia took hold. At first I saw a series of dark faces, like death masks, flying toward me and being crushed. Then I saw circles of light with the faces of Hillary, Chelsea, and others I cared about flying toward me, then away into a bright, sun-like source. Hillary later told me that as I came out of the anesthesia toward consciousness, I waved to people, said I was all right, and laughed, but I have no memory of it.

After a few days of recovery at the hospital under the watchful eye of my medical team, led by Doctors Craig Smith and Allan Schwartz, I was allowed to go home and begin the recovery process.

The first three weeks were rough because I was sore, and, having lost all the muscle tone in my upper chest and back, I often had uncomfortable back spasms. As soon as I started serious daily walking and could stretch a little, my condition got better. Many people say they suffered from brief periods of depression during the first couple of months after bypass surgery, but I'm thankful I never did. After decades of hard work, I enjoyed the time off to read, listen to music, and watch movies and sports, especially the baseball playoffs and the World Series.

I had to abandon my low-carbohydrate, high-fat diet for a low-fat diet, but I enjoyed the challenge and eventually lost about twenty pounds, leaving me close to what I weighed when I graduated from high school. My hometown bar-beque restaurant, McClard's, even introduced lean, low-fat meat in my honor. With childhood obesity at an all-time high in the United States, I hope more eating establishments, especially the fast-food chains, will follow McClard's example.

By late October I felt strong enough to make a few appearances in the presidential campaign, though my stamina had still not completely returned. After a slow start, Senator Kerry made a real race of it with outstanding performances in the debates, but it was not enough to convince a majority of voters, impressed by President Bush's strong leadership after 9/11, to replace an incumbent president during an ongoing conflict for the first time in our history. With the race a virtual dead heat, a substantial majority of the voters who made up their minds in the last few days of the campaign broke for the President on the security issue.

The 2004 election was remarkable for the high voter turnout and for the staggering number of small contributions given to both parties, often over the Internet. Predictably, the election results produced the usual round of dire predictions that the Democratic Party is in long-term decline. It's more complicated than that.

At the presidential level our party remains in much better shape than it was in the '70s and '80s. In each of the three elections of the 1980s, we didn't win more than ten states. We won more than thirty in 1992 and 1996. Al Gore won the popular vote in 2000, and in 2004 Americans gave President Bush the closest victory margin of any reelected president since Woodrow Wilson in 1916. The Democratic Party, thanks to Terry McAuliffe, is on solid financial footing and technologically as advanced as the Republicans. Progressive think tanks and grassroots organizations are beginning to balance their right-wing counterparts. Air America is at last offering progressives an alternative to the right-wing radio talk shows. Also, the changing demographics of America continue to favor our communitarian approach over the Republicans' more divisive policies and tactics.

On the other hand, the Republicans are in much better shape at the congressional level, especially in the Senate, than they were in the 1980s, largely because more and more culturally conservative voters, heavily concentrated in small towns, rural areas, and less populous states, are voting not just for President but for senators and congressmen based on their belief that Republicans better reflect their values on abortion, gay rights, guns, and other cultural issues.

Since the Republicans have moved further to the right and continue to win, many analysts say that the obvious course for the Democrats is to move further to the left. I think that view reflects a misunderstanding of what has happened. First, the election was as close as it was because the administration had moved so far to the right. Indeed, if it had not been for the 9/11 attacks and the ongoing power of security issues, Senator Kerry probably would have won. Second, President Bush has never presented himself as a hard-core right-winger. The hard-core attacks on Senator Kerry were mostly leveled by others supporting the President's candidacy. In 2000, he said he was a "compassionate conservative." In 2004, with pro-life voters seizing on his election as a way to repeal *Roe* v. *Wade*, he said he was for a "culture of life" but pointedly refused to promise new Supreme Court appointments that would repeal *Roe*. He made several minority appointments to important positions in his administration, and when environmental groups said he had perhaps the worst environmental record in history, Bush claimed he had made real advances in environmental protection. In other words, he did what successful politicians must do: consolidate and excite his base vote *and* win enough moderate voters to make a majority.

The Democrats can come back, not by moving hard to the left, but by looking forward, with a clear vision for the future and good ideas to realize it, a strong security posture, and better tactics. A candidate simply cannot let personal and political attacks go unanswered.

Beyond that, if we want to be competitive in the so-called red states, we have to engage in a serious debate on the cultural issues. The number of abortions dropped by almost 20 percent during my eight years, but almost no one knew about it in 2004, much less about the policies we pursued to achieve that result. We also had an office of religious outreach in the White House that worked on issues of common concern with all kinds of religious groups, including those I knew would never support us at election time. Hillary recently called for a renewed dialogue on abortion, and I think she was right to do so. As Senator Barak Obama said in his eloquent speech at the Democratic convention, "red" and "blue" Americans have a lot more in common than they know, but they'll never find out if they don't talk and listen to each other. I think such an effort would help the Democrats, and I know it would be good for the country.

Two weeks after the election, we held the opening of my library, museum, and presidential center in Little Rock. Twenty-five thousand people braved a heavy rain to hear President Bush as well as former Presidents Bush and Carter speak. Six Americans talked about the impact of my policies on their lives and work. A group of children from Colombia, whose efforts against narco-trafficking and terrorism I had supported, sang and danced. So did Bono and the Edge of U2, marking my work for peace in Northern Ireland.

Bono got a good laugh when he sang, "When the rains came, we got four Presidents out of bed." Coming so soon after an intensely fought election, the bipartisan spirit seemed to lift the country. President Carter spoke warmly of our long association, going back to his 1976 campaign. The first President Bush stole the show with an often hilarious account of our 1992 battle and a touching affirmation of our personal friendship. And the President was extremely warm and generous to me and my family, as he had been a few months earlier at the White House ceremony to unveil the official portraits of Hillary and me.

The museum was especially important to me, because I wanted to show visitors from across the country and around the world that political ideas, policies, and decisions have real consequences to their lives and therefore that public service and well-informed citizens are as essential to

America in the twenty-first century as they were at the time of our founding.

Only a few weeks after the library opening, I found myself involved in another bipartisan endeavor as President Bush asked his father and me to lead an effort to increase private contributions in the United States to aid the victims of the tsunami that struck eleven nations in the Indian Ocean on December 26, leaving 300,000 dead and missing and more than 1 million homeless. I was honored to be asked and eager to work with former President Bush. We joined the President in visiting the embassies of Thailand, Indonesia, Sri Lanka, and India, the hardest hit countries, then did media interviews, public-service announcements, and other events designed to encourage people to help and to provide information on reliable organizations and the work they were doing. At my request, UNICEF established a special fund for water and sanitation to minimize the spread of sickness and disease in areas in which all the normal sources of clean water had been destroyed.

In mid-February, former President Bush and I traveled to Thailand, Aceh in Indonesia, Sri Lanka, and the Maldives to see the destruction firsthand and to witness the impressive rebuilding efforts already under way. Though the media had done a terrific job in covering the tragedy, the full impact of it didn't hit me until I actually saw it and met so many people who had lost their families, all their worldly possessions, and their livelihoods. We were grateful that people at every stop expressed their thanks to our military for the outstanding job they did in distributing humanitarian supplies to remote areas and in helping people in the initial efforts to clean up the destruction and begin again. And we were deeply moved by the children who had been orphaned and the fine people who were helping them to express their feelings, deal with their grief, and find the strength to carry on.

As of this writing, American citizens have contributed more than $700 million to help the victims of the tsunami; about one-third of American households have participated, more than half of them through contributions made over the Internet. Generous contributions have been made by citizens in other parts of the world, especially in northern European nations that lost so many of their citizens who were vacationing in the affected areas, and in other Asian nations. Even tiny East Timor, with a per capita income of about a dollar a day, made a contribution to its old foe Indonesia.

All told, governments and citizens have pledged more than $6 billion to tsunami relief, including $950 million from the Bush administration. Secretary General Kofi Annan has asked me to coordinate UN efforts to see that pledges are honored, that any additional money needed is raised, and that the ongoing reconstruction is done with maximum coordination and effectiveness by all the governments, local citizens, international organizations, and hundreds of nongovernmental organizations working on it. We also want to make sure the area has an early warning system, disaster mitigation projects, and good emergency management systems. As the tsunami fades from the headlines, it will be easy to move on to other things. But an enormous amount has already been done, and the good people who are determined to rebuild their lives deserve our support until the job is finished.

In the opening chapter of my book, I said that because my father died before I was born, I "was always in a hurry." After I left the White House, my financial obligations, building my library, and getting my Foundation work going kept me as busy as ever.

My brush with mortality a few months ago forced me to slow down. My long daily walks in the beautiful area where I live have given me the chance to think about life, count my blessings, and enjoy the time I have instead of trying so hard to fill it up.

I hope I can spend the rest of my life in public service largely beyond partisan politics, while urging those in politics to appreciate each other as people, even as they do battle over their honest differences. Of course, I will do whatever I can to help Hillary, whose success in the Senate—both on the Armed Services Committee and in her work for all parts of New York—has made me very proud.

Everything that has happened in the last four years has confirmed my belief in the basic values that have guided my work: every person counts, deserves a chance, and has a responsible role to play; competition is good, but we all do better when we work together; the role of government is to give people the tools to make the most of their lives and to strengthen the community we share; our differences are important and make life more interesting, but our common humanity matters more. My heart disease reminded me that we're all on borrowed time; we just don't know for sure how much. I want to do my best with whatever I have left.

ACKNOWLEDGMENTS

I AM PARTICULARLY indebted to the many people without whom this book could not have been written. Justin Cooper gave up more than two years of his young life to work with me every day and, on many occasions in the last six months, all night. He organized and retrieved mountains of materials, did further research, corrected many errors, and typed the manuscript over and over from my illegible scrawling in more than twenty large notebooks. Many of the sections were rewritten a half dozen times or more. He never lost his patience, his energy never flagged, and by the time we got to the last lap, he sometimes seemed to know me and what I wanted to say better than I did. Though he is not responsible for its errors, this book is a testament to his gifts and efforts.

Before we began to work together, I was told that my editor, Robert Gottlieb, was the best there was at his craft. He turned out to be that and more. I only wish I'd met him thirty years earlier. Bob taught me about magic moments and hard cuts. Without his judgment and feel, this book might have been twice as long and half as good. He read my story as a person who was interested in but not obsessed with politics. He kept pulling me back to the human side of my life. And he convinced me to take out countless names of people who helped me along the way, because the general reader couldn't keep up with them all. If you're one of them, I hope you'll forgive him, and me.

A book this long and full requires a mammoth amount of fact checking. This lion's share of work was done by Meg Thompson, a brilliant young woman who carefully waded through the minutiae of my life for a year or so; then for the last few months she was assisted by Caitlin Klevorick and other young volunteers. They now have many examples of the fact that my memory is far from perfect. If any factual errors remain, it is not for lack of effort to correct them on their part.

I can't thank the people at Knopf enough, beginning with Sonny Mehta, the president and editor-in-chief. He believed in the project from the beginning and did his part to keep it going, including giving me an amazed look wherever and whenever I ran into him over the last two years, a look that said something like, "Are you really going to finish on time?", and "Why are you here instead of at home writing?" Sonny's look always had the desired effect.

I also owe thanks to the many people at Knopf who helped. I am grateful that the editorial/production team at Knopf is as obsessed with accuracy and detail as I am (even with a book on a slightly accelerated pace, as mine was) and especially appreciate the tireless efforts and meticulous work of managing editor Katherine Hourigan; noble director of manufacturing Andy Hughes; indefatigable production editor Maria Massey; copy chief Lydia Buechler, copy editor Charlotte Gross, and proofreaders Steve Messina, Jenna Dolan, Ellen Feldman, Rita Madrigal, and Liz Polizzi; design director Peter Andersen; jacket art director Carol Carson; the ever-helpful Diana Tejerina and Eric Bliss; and Lee Pentea.

In addition, I want to thank the many other people at Knopf who have helped me: Tony Chirico, for his valued guidance; Jim Johnston, Justine LeCates, and Anne Diaz; Carol Janeway and Suzanne Smith; Jon Fine; and the promotion/marketing talents of Pat Johnson, Paul Bogaards, Nina Bourne, Nicholas Latimer, Joy Dallanegra-Sanger, Amanda Kauff, Anne-Lise Spitzer, and Sarah Robinson. And thanks to the staffs at North Market Street Graphics, Coral Graphics, and Offset Paperback Manufacturers.

And my thanks to the folks at Vintage: Anne Messitte, Russell Perreault, Roz Parr, Stephen McNabb, Barbara Richard, Nicole Pedersen, Marla Jea, Daniel Gillespie, John Gall, Chris Zucker, and Quinn O'Neill.

Robert Barnett, a fine lawyer and longtime friend, negotiated the contract with Knopf; he and his partner Michael O'Connor worked throughout the project as foreign publishers joined in. I am very grateful to them. I appreciate the careful technical and legal review that David Kendall and Beth Nolan gave the manuscript.

When I was in the White House, beginning in late 1993, I met with my old friend Taylor Branch about once a month to do an oral history. Those contemporaneous conversations helped in recalling particular moments of the presidency. After I left the White House, Ted Widmer, a fine historian who worked in the White House as a speechwriter, did an oral history of my life before the presidency that helped me bring back and organize old memories. Janis Kearney, the White House diarist, left me with voluminous notes that enabled me to reconstruct day-to-day events.

The photographs were selected with the help of Vincent Virga, who found many that captured special moments discussed in the book, and Carolyn Huber, who was with our family throughout our years in the Governor's Mansion and the White House. While I was President, Carolyn also organized all my private papers and letters from the time I was a little boy to 1974, an arduous task without which much of the first part of the book could not have been written.

I am deeply indebted to those who read all or part of the book and made helpful suggestions for additions, subtractions, reorganization, context, and interpretation, including Hillary, Chelsea, Dorothy Rodham, Doug Band, Sandy Berger, Tommy Caplan, Mary DeRosa, Nancy Hernreich, Dick Holbrooke, David Kendall, Jim Kennedy, Ian Klaus, Bruce Lindsey, Ira Magaziner, Cheryl Mills, Beth Nolan, John Podesta, Bruce Reed, Steve Ricchetti, Bob Rubin, Ruby Shamir, Brooke Shearer, Gene Sperling, Strobe Talbott, Mark Weiner, Maggie Williams, and my friends Brian and Myra Greenspun, who were with me when the first page was written.

Many of my friends and colleagues took time to do impromptu oral histories with me including Huma Abedin, Madeleine Albright, Dave Barram, Woody Bassett, Paul Begala, Paul Berry, Jim Blair, Sidney Blumenthal, Erskine Bowles, Ron Burkle, Tom Campbell, James Carville, Roger Clinton, Patty Criner, Denise Dangremond, Lynda Dixon, Rahm Emanuel, Al From, Mark Gearan, Ann Henry, Denise Hyland, Harold Ickes, Roger Johnson, Vernon Jordan, Mickey Kantor, Dick Kelley, Tony Lake, David Leopoulos, Capricia Marshall, Mack McLarty, Rudy Moore, Bob Nash, Kevin O'Keefe, Leon Panetta, Betsey Reader, Dick Riley, Bobby Roberts, Hugh Rodham, Tony Rodham, Dennis Ross, Martha Saxton, Eli Segal, Terry Schumaker, Marsha Scott, Michael Sheehan, Nancy Soderberg, Doug Sosnik, Rodney Slater, Craig Smith, Gayle Smith, Steve Smith, Carolyn Staley, Stephanie Street, Larry Summers, Martha Whetstone, Delta Willis, Carol Willis, and several of my readers. I'm sure there are others I've forgotten; if so, I'm sorry and I appreciate their help as well.

My research was also helped greatly by many books written by members of the administration and others, and of course by the memoirs of Hillary and my mother.

David Alsobrook and the staff of the Clinton Presidential Materials Project were patient and persistent in recovering materials. I want to thank them all: Deborah Bush, Susan Collins, Gary Foulk, John Keller, Jimmie Purvis, Emily Robison, Rob Seibert, Dana Simmons, Richard Stalcup, Rhonda Wilson. And Arkansas historian David Ware. The archivists and historians at Georgetown and Oxford were also helpful.

While I was absorbed in writing for much of the last two and a half years, especially the last six months, the work of my foundation continued as we built the library and pursued our missions: fighting AIDS in Africa and the Caribbean and providing low-cost drugs and testing around the world; increasing economic opportunity in poor communities in the United States, India, and Africa; promoting education and citizen service among young people at home and abroad; and advocating religious, racial, and ethnic reconciliation across the world. I want to thank those whose donations have made possible my foundation work, and the construction of the Presidential Library and the Clinton School of Public Service at the University of Arkansas. I am deeply indebted to Maggie Williams, my chief of staff, for all she did to keep things moving and for her help on the book. I want to thank members of my foundation and office staff for all they did to continue the work of the foundation and its programs while I was writing the book. A special word of thanks goes to Doug Band, my counselor, who helped me from the day I left the White House to build my new life and who struggled to protect my book-writing time on our travels across America and the world.

I also owe a debt to Oscar Flores, who keeps things going at my home in Chappaqua. On the many nights when Justin Cooper and I worked into the wee hours, Oscar went out of his way to make sure we remembered to have dinner and that we were well supplied with coffee.

Finally, I cannot list all the people who made the life chronicled in these pages possible—all the teachers and mentors of my youth; the people who worked on and contributed to all my campaigns; those who worked with me in the Democratic Leadership Council, National Governors Association, and all the other organizations that contributed to my education in public policy; those who worked with me for peace, security, and reconciliation around the world; those who made the White House run and my trips work; the thousands of gifted people who worked in my adminstrations as attorney general, governor, and President without whose dedicated service I would have little to say about my years in public life; those who provided security to me and my family; and my friends of a lifetime. None of them are responsible for the failures of my life, but for whatever good has come out of it they deserve much of the credit.

INDEX

The names of people who appear in the photograph insert are followed by *.